THE WESTMINSTER HANDBOOKS
TO CHRISTIAN THEOLOGY

The Westminster Handbook to Evangelical Theology

Roger E. Olson

Westminster John Knox Press
LOUISVILLE • LONDON

Book design by Sharon Adams
Cover design by Cynthia Dunne
Cover art: Monks Copying Manuscripts
(Corbis/© Archivo Iconografico)

First edition

Published by Westminster John Knox Press
Louisville, Kentucky

This book is printed on acid-free paper that meets the American National Standards Institute Z39.48 standard. ∞

PRINTED IN THE UNITED STATES OF AMERICA

04 05 06 07 08 09 10 11 12 13 — 10 9 8 7 6 5 4 3 2 1

Library of Congress Cataloging-in-Publication Data

Olson, Roger E.
    The Westminster handbook to evangelical theology / Roger E. Olson.
       p. cm. — (The Westminster handbooks to Christian theology)
    Includes bibliographical references.
    ISBN 0-664-22464-4 (alk. paper)
    1. Evangelicalism. I. Title. II. Series.

BR1640.O46   2004
230'.04624—dc22   2003064512

*Dedicated with gratitude and affection to
Donald G. Bloesch, who has served as
a model of irenic evangelical theology
and generous orthodoxy.*

Contents

Series Introduction

The Westminster Handbooks to Christian Theology series provides a set of resources for the study of historic and contemporary theological movements and Christian theologians. These books are intended to assist scholars and students find concise and accurate treatments of important theological terms. The entries for the handbooks are arranged in alphabetical format to provide easy access to each term. The works are written by scholars with special expertise in these fields.

We hope this series will be of great help as readers explore the riches of Christian theology as it has been expressed in the past and as it will be formulated in the future.

The Publisher

Preface

The *Westminster Handbook to Evangelical Theology* is different from some other volumes in the series *The Westminster Handbooks to Christian Theology* in significant ways. First, it is a single-author work rather than an edited work. Second, it contains a historical essay on the topic and articles on people, organizations, and controversial subjects related to evangelical theology, in addition to the articles on doctrines. My hope is that this volume will serve not only as a reference work but also as a helpful introduction to evangelical theology for students, pastors, teachers, and all other interested persons. I have attempted to keep my own theological biases to a minimum in my expositions of evangelical theology in this book. Many parties of evangelical theology exist, and I have tried to give attention and fair treatment to as many of them as possible. The evangelical theology treated here is pri-

marily North American; the publisher and I hope that people around the world will find that the articles contained here reflect Evangelicalism's reality in their contexts as well.

I would like to thank my editor at Westminster John Knox Press, Donald K. McKim, for his help and support throughout this writing endeavor. I also thank my students in "Studies in Twentieth-Century Theology" during the fall semester 2001 at George W. Truett Theological Seminary of Baylor University for their research, which—with their permission—aided me in writing some of the articles here. I would also like to thank Baylor University for granting me two summer sabbaticals to work on this project. Finally, thanks to my wife Becky and daughter Sonja for putting up with my hours of solitude as I wrote. Their love and support have sustained me.

Roger E. Olson

Introduction

Evangelical is an essentially contested concept; at least seven distinct definitions exist and lie behind its frequent uses in the secular media, in the academy, and in religious contexts. This volume contains a fairly lengthy essay that attempts to explain Evangelicalism, its various meanings, and the history of the contemporary North American evangelical movement with special attention to its theological development. "The Story of Evangelical Theology" may be read by itself and the rest of the volume used as a reference work, or the entire volume may be used as a textbook plus reference work. In any case, the intention of the volume is to give readers a fairly thorough acquaintance with the theological side of the evangelical movement, with special focus on the post–World War II postfundamentalist evangelical movement in North America.

Some readers may wonder about the selections of topics of articles here. There are hundreds of influential organizations and individuals in the history and contemporary reality of Evangelicalism; as a result many that are near and dear to some readers' hearts will inevitably be left out. The primary criterion of selection is contemporary influence on the evangelical movement and its theology, especially as it faces toward the larger Christian world and worlds of culture. Only theologians and writers who are

either dead or retired were selected for the section on influential persons in evangelical theology. Living theologians who are still actively teaching or working before retirement were left out of that section, even if their influence is significant. They may be included in future editions as they reach retirement or die. Many of them are discussed in the articles on traditional doctrines and on issues in evangelical theology. Our apologies to those who may think they or their favorite thinkers should be given more treatment here; it is simply not possible to include everyone who is important.

Some readers and reviewers may wonder about the inclusion of persons who are not professional theologians and of some nontheological organizations. For example, why include Billy Graham and his organization in a handbook about theology? The simple explanation is that no single individual has been as crucial in the development and relative cohesion of the evangelical movement as Billy Graham, and his organization has spawned, supported, and controlled many other organizations that have directly or indirectly influenced evangelical thought. The shadow of Billy Graham is long and heavy on the evangelical landscape. The same may be said of C. S. Lewis, who may not have been an evangelical in the subcultural sense; that is, he did not

1

belong to the evangelical movement as such. Nevertheless, his influence on it has been profound. Theology and sociology cannot be separated neatly and precisely. Some persons and organizations are included here because they have impacted evangelical theology without being precisely theologians or theological organizations themselves.

The first use in each article of a term that appears as an article elsewhere in the handbook will be highlighted in bold italic type. Derivatives of terms (other than plurals and possessives) will not be so highlighted. For example, the first appearance of "theology" in each article will be highlighted (even as "theology's" or "theologies," but not "theological"), because an article on *theology* appears in the section on traditional doctrines.

We trust that a future edition of this volume will be able to give greater attention to the contributions of women and persons of color. So far, much to many evangelicals' chagrin and to the movement's discredit, they have not profoundly impacted its theological side. Like many, if not most, religious movements (other than the contemporary religious feminist movement), evangelicalism has been male-dominated. It has also been dominated by persons of Caucasian ancestry. That is gradually changing as more women, African Americans, Asians, and persons of Hispanic descent enter the evangelical academy. To include some now in this handbook would be a disservice; it would reflect political correctness rather than reality. We hope that the predominance of white males here will challenge the movers and shakers of Evangelicalism and of evangelical theology to go the extra mile to include and nurture the scholarship of women and persons of color within their communities.

The Story of
Evangelical Theology

TOWARD A DEFINITION OF EVANGELICALISM

Defining *evangelical, Evangelicalism,* and *evangelical theology* has become something of a cottage industry in the waning years of the twentieth century and early years of the twenty-first century. At least since a national news magazine in the United States declared 1977 "The Year of the Evangelical," numerous religious scholars have attempted to provide a definitive portrait, if not concrete definition, of the term *evangelical* and the religious movement it describes. Entire scholarly conferences and symposia have devoted great effort and energy to the cause of investigating and finally comprehensively describing Evangelicalism. Even some self-identified evangelical scholars have declared *evangelical* an essentially contested concept—an idea and category with no precise or agreed-on meaning.[1] In fact, so it seems, there are several justifiable uses of the term *evangelical.* They are all legitimized by either broad historical usage or common contemporary usage. Here we will delineate seven distinct though occasionally overlapping meanings of *evangelical* and then identify which one of them is intended by the title of this handbook and will be its subject.

Etymologically *evangelical* simply means "of the good news" or "related to the gospel." The Greek root, a word for "good message" or "good news," was used by the apostles of Christianity and the early Greek-speaking church fathers for the gospel they proclaimed. In this broadest sense of *evangelical,* then, *Evangelicalism* is simply synonymous with authentic Christianity as it is founded on and remains faithful to the "evangel"—the good news of Jesus Christ. It is not unusual to see the term *evangelical* used in documents of the Roman Catholic Church and almost all so-called mainline Protestant denominations to denote the message of the incarnation of God in Jesus Christ, God's love for humanity demonstrated in Christ's death and resurrection, and especially salvation by God's grace alone apart from human achievements. In this sense, then, evangelical is contrasted with moralistic or legalistic religion; Evangelicalism is the Christian movement proclaiming the good news that human persons can be saved by receiving a free gift won for them by Jesus Christ in his death and resurrection.

---

1. See Donald W. Dayton, "Some Doubts about the Usefulness of the Category 'Evangelical'" in *The Variety of American Evangelicalism,* ed. Donald W. Dayton and Robert K. Johnston (Downers Grove, IL: InterVarsity Press, 1991), 245–51.

The second historical use of *evangelical* derives from the Protestant Reformation of the sixteenth century. In parts of Europe dominated by Protestant state churches rooted in the reforming works of Martin Luther, Ulrich Zwingli, and John Calvin in the sixteenth century, *evangelical* is simply synonymous with *Protestant*. While traveling around Germany, Switzerland, and portions of eastern France, for example, one may see many churches labeled simply "evangelical" and know they are Protestant without knowing precisely which Protestant traditions they represent. Lutherans especially like to use the term *evangelical* in the names of their churches and denominations; some Reformed (Calvinist) churches also use it. In the United States this use of the term appears in the name of the largest Lutheran denomination—the Evangelical Lutheran Church in America—which is a union of two previously existing Lutheran synods or denominations in the U.S. The architects of the union consciously chose to incorporate the word *evangelical* into the name of the new denomination in order to state publicly that it would be gospel-centered in the Lutheran sense of proclaiming the doctrine of salvation by grace through faith alone.

The third definition of *evangelical* is tied to the British context of the Church of England, which is sometimes called Anglican. In the United States it is known as the Episcopal Church. The Church of England, though doctrinally Protestant since the time of Elizabeth I in the sixteenth century, has also always contained different and sometimes conflicting parties. The evangelical party within the Church of England is not organized, but it is composed of those priests and bishops and lay members who seek to "Protestantize" Anglicanism and who resist the party that would retrieve and strengthen Roman Catholic elements within the church's history and liturgy. The evangelicals tend to be "low church" in that they reduce the liturgical aspects of worship to a minimum, stress the priesthood of all believers (without discarding the ministerial office), and emphasize the necessity of personal faith in Jesus Christ for salvation (as opposed to baptismal regeneration). The evangelicals within the worldwide Anglican/Church of England/Episcopal communion look back to the first-generation reformers of the English church under Henry VIII in the mid-sixteenth century, most of whom were martyred by his Catholic daughter Mary Tudor ("Bloody Mary") for their enthusiastic Protestant zeal.

The fourth distinct use of *evangelical* arises out of the Pietist and revivalist attempts to reform and revive Protestant Christianity in Germany, Great Britain, and North America in the early eighteenth century. At a time when the state churches and even most of the so-called sects (dissenting denominations) had fallen into a state of spiritual lethargy described as "dead orthodoxy" by the "enthusiasts" (spiritual reformers), the latter broke on the scene to enliven Protestant Christianity with a greater sense of spiritual fervor and vitality. In Germany this movement of "heart Christianity" that came to be known as Pietism emphasized the necessity of personal conversion to Jesus Christ through repentance and faith, a life of devotion through Bible reading and study, prayer and worship, and holiness of life. The Pietists often met in conventicles or small groups outside the formal structure of the state churches and were sometimes persecuted as a result. Lutheran leaders such as Philip Spener and August Francke firmly established a spiritual renewal movement within the state church; Count von Zinzendorf turned a small band of wandering spiritual Christians known as the Moravian Brethren into an influential renewal movement within Protestant Christianity.

In Great Britain and the American colonies a revival known as the Great Awakening broke out under the leadership of John and Charles Wesley, their friend George Whitefield, and Puritan preacher Jonathan Edwards. Those who embraced these "new measures" of Christianity that tended toward emotion and appeal for personal decision for Christ called themselves evangelicals. Thus, in the second half of the eighteenth century and into the nineteenth century in Great Britain and North America, evangelical was virtually synonymous with Great Awakening-inspired revivalism. Evangelicals rejected sacramental salvation and covenant salvation as inadequate views of true conversion to Christ and urged all people—baptized and born "in the covenant" (i.e., into Christian homes and churches), as well as those entirely outside the church's embrace—to repent and believe in Jesus Christ for the remission (forgiveness) of sins and for transformation of life (regeneration).

The fifth definition of *evangelical* comes from the conservative Protestant reaction to the rise of liberal Protestantism in the nineteenth and early twentieth centuries. It is nearly synonymous with fundamentalism—at least as that term was originally used and understood. Conservative Protestants who wished to reaffirm what they considered the "fundamentals of the faith"—such as a supernatural worldview (including the miracles of the Bible), the transcendence of God, the reality of the Trinity, the deity of Jesus Christ, the virgin birth and bodily resurrection of Jesus, and the inspiration and authority of the Bible—called themselves both fundamentalists and evangelicals. Many of their leading thinkers, speakers, and writers stood in the Reformed Protestant tradition and looked back to the great Protestant orthodox thinkers such as Francis Turretin, Archibald Alexander, and Charles Hodge for guidance and inspiration. The paradigm of such a fundamentalist evangelical was Presbyterian scholar J. Gresham Machen, who taught at Princeton Seminary and then helped found Westminster Theological Seminary in Philadelphia to rival Princeton as it allegedly declined into modernistic Bible scholarship and theology around the beginning of the twentieth century. The early twentieth-century fundamentalists (especially before 1925) were by and large simply defenders of Protestant orthodoxy with a somewhat militant attitude toward fighting the encroachments of revisionist Protestantism. *Evangelical* was one of the terms used to identify them. After 1925, the year of the infamous Scopes evolution trial in Tennessee, fundamentalism gradually began to withdraw from the mainstream of denominational Protestantism into its own subculture, with a plethora of newly founded Bible schools, publishing houses, denominations, conventions, and missionary agencies.

The sixth use of *evangelical* is the one that provides at least the beginning point and center of this handbook and its subject matter. In the 1940s and 1950s postfundamentalist Evangelicalism began to break away from the increasingly militant and separatistic fundamentalism of the 1920s and 1930s. There is no absolute line dividing the older fundamentalism from the newer Evangelicalism, and matters are especially confused by the fact that nearly all fundamentalists—no matter how militant and separatistic—have continued to call themselves evangelicals. Most postfundamentalist evangelicals do not wish to be called fundamentalists, even though their basic theological orientation is not very different (in most cases, at least) from that of the early fundamentalists such as J. Gresham Machen. The new, postfundamentalist evangelicals were derisively labeled "neo-evangelicals" by their more militant and separatistic cousins, who accused them of accommodating to the secular spirit of the age and to liberal-modernistic Protestantism. Postfundamentalist evangelicals wanted to be known simply as evangelicals and asserted that there was an evangelical heritage that was greater than fundamentalism. They appealed to prefundamentalist evangelicals such as the Pietist-revivalist leaders and thinkers of the Great Awakening and to the great theologians of Protestant orthodoxy, and they sought to engage evangelical belief and experience with contemporary society and issues in a less negative way than militant fundamentalists. During the crucial decades of the 1940s and 1950s postfundamentalist evangelicals formed a strong multidenominational coalition in Britain and America and created a large and broad network of cooperating organizations to renew conservative, revivalist Christianity and spread its influence in Western society.

In the United States the National Association of Evangelicals (NAE) was formed to provide an alternative to the liberal-dominated Federal Council of Churches; eventually over fifty conservative Protestant denominations with at least some sympathy with revivalism (e.g., Billy Graham's evangelistic ministry) joined. One motto of the NAE became the old Pietist saying "In essentials unity, in nonessentials liberty, in all things charity."

The seventh definition of *evangelical* and *Evangelicalism* is popular rather than scholarly or historical. One often hears or reads the adjective *evangelical* used by journalists to describe anyone or any group that seems particularly (by the journalist's standards) enthusiastic, aggressive, fanatical, or even simply missionary-minded. True fundamentalists (militant, separatistic, ultraconservative Protestants) are often described in the media as evangelical; sometimes Roman Catholic missionaries and even Muslim groups that engage in missionary endeavors are labeled evangelical by journalists. This seventh use cannot simply be rejected; it has caught on in contemporary language. Jehovah's Witnesses, considered a cult by many conservative Protestants, are often called evangelical simply because of their door-to-door witnessing techniques. However, for the purpose of this handbook, this journalistic and popular use of *evangelical* will be ignored.

Like many good terms and categories, then, *evangelical* and *Evangelicalism* have a broad semantic range, one that is so variegated that the terms seem to lose all shape. It is tempting even for evangelicals at times to give up the label. However, it should be remembered that many other religious labels for movements and categories for theological orientations suffer the same vagueness and contested nature as *Evangelicalism*. Exactly what is Reformed Christianity and Reformed theology? Beyond the fact that it is a tradition rooted in the theological contributions of sixteenth-century reformers Martin Bucer, Ulrich Zwingli, and John Calvin, there is little consensus even among those who call themselves Reformed. Can anyone precisely define the charismatic movement? Who is a charismatic; what makes a person truly charismatic? What is liberal Protestant Christianity? These and many other good and useful and even necessary labels and categories are notoriously difficult to pin down, and yet they continue to be used by scholars and lay people alike. Each one does refer to some phenomenon—a tradition-community that may be bewilderingly diverse and yet at the same time somewhat united in contrast to other tradition-communities.

Our approach to describing Evangelicalism—which is the context within which evangelical theology functions—will be historical; here we will attempt to define by telling a story. It is the story of the rise of postfundamentalist Evangelicalism—its roots, crucible, birth, and contemporary existence. The focus of our story will be theology—the distinctive ideas about authority for religious belief, revelation and Scripture, God and Jesus Christ, salvation, and so forth. However, the story of theology is never the narrative of pure ideas falling out of the sky. Evangelicalism is a tradition-community, and evangelical theology is its peculiar recipe of religious commitments, values, and beliefs. Before delving into the background history of Evangelicalism, it will be helpful to set forth at least a tentative definition of the category and of evangelical theology. The perceptive reader will recognize immediately that the definitions set forth here draw together several of the seven definitions of *evangelical* outlined above.

Evangelicalism is a loose affiliation (coalition, network, mosaic, patchwork, family) of mostly Protestant Christians of many orthodox (Trinitarian) denominations and independent churches and parachurch organizations that affirm a supernatural worldview; the unsurpassable authority of the Bible for all matters of faith and religious practice; Jesus Christ as unique Lord, God, and Savior; the fallenness of humanity and salvation provided by Jesus Christ through his suffering, death, and resurrection; the necessity of personal repentance and faith (conversion) for full salvation; the importance of a devotional life and growth in holiness and discipleship; the urgency of gospel evangelism and social transformation; and the return of Jesus Christ to judge the world and establish the final, full rule and reign of God. Many evangelicals affirm more; none affirm less or deny any of these basic belief commitments. The genius of Evangelicalism is its combination of orthodox Protestantism, conservative revivalism, and transdenominational ecumenism. Within it coexist and cooperate peacefully (most of the time) Protestants committed to competing secondary doctrines: predestination, free will, premillennialism, amillennialism, infant baptism, believer baptism, pouring, immersion, literal creationism, theistic evolution. Occasionally, of course, and perhaps increasingly, evangelicals of differing doctrinal persuasions with regard to secondary doctrines (denominational distinctives) fight with each other. The old Calvinist versus Arminian (predestination versus free will) argument erupts from time to time and threatens to disrupt the uneasy unity of Evangelicalism. The powerfully unifying figure of evangelist Billy Graham has helped keep the evangelical community together in cooperation in spite of such differences. What will happen when the "Graham glue" dissolves with his passing (or passing the torch) is a favorite subject of speculation among evangelical-watchers.

Another way of describing Evangelicalism is by saying that it is a movement for the renewal of Protestant Christianity. It shares with the Protestant Reformers and classical Protestantism in general basic Christian beliefs about the Scriptures, God, Jesus Christ, and salvation, but it regards classic, historic Protestant Christianity as needing reform. Thus, Evangelicalism represents a reform of the Reformation. Evangelical reform has a program that centers around *retrieval, restoration, revival*, and *relevance*. Evangelicals have always wanted to retrieve the original impulses of Christianity as they are revealed in the New Testament and early church documents as well as the ideals of the Protestant Reformers. This retrieval is necessary because of the occasional declensions of Protestantism from these original impulses. Evangelicals have often decried a condition they call "dead orthodoxy" in the churches, a condition in which church leaders and members confess correct doctrine but show little or no evidence of personal experience of the transforming presence and power of God. They have also criticized the modern deviations from historic Christianity known as "neo-Protestantism" or liberal modernism. In order to challenge and correct these diseases in Protestantism, evangelicals have sought to recover both basic Christian doctrine and the New Testament and original Protestant experiences of God's transforming power in people's lives.

Not only have evangelicals sought to renew Protestant Christianity through retrieval, they have also sought to restore the spirit of early Christianity within the churches. While they may differ about the details of this restoration, all evangelicals firmly believe that contemporary Christianity is authentic to the extent that it reflects the heart of the apostolic Christian movement as that appears in the New Testament. The missionary journeys of Paul, for example, form a favorite theme of evangelical preaching and teaching, and evangelicals believe that missionary and evangelistic endeavor is just as important for authentic Christianity today as it was in the first century. Most evangelicals would not go so far as to declare the entire church between the New Testament and the rise of Evangelicalism apostate, but many would consider it seriously defective and in dire need of renewal and revival. Many evangelicals, then, view evangelical revivalism and conservative Christian theology and proclamation at least a partial restoration of the "true Christianity" that declined into partial obscurity for centuries after the deaths of the apostles.

Thus, crucial to the renewal of Christianity that evangelicals envision is revival. Revival does not necessarily connote emotional responses to emotional preaching. That has, of course, been a feature of some of Evangelicalism. But more important to true revival for most evangelicals is heartfelt, passionate appeals for personal appropriation of God's grace in Jesus Christ and his cross through repentance and faith and a "daily, personal relationship with Jesus Christ" through prayer and Bible reading. Evangelicals have always suspected that authentic Christianity involves the affections and will as much as, if not more than, the intellect. Evangelical revival appeals to religious affections and calls for people to make personal decisions for and lifelong commitments to Jesus Christ. Many evangelical churches have institutionalized revival by holding special "protracted meetings" over several days or even weeks. These were called "Holy Fairs" in seventeenth-century Scotland; in twentieth-century North America they were sometimes referred to as Jesus festivals. Everyone is familiar with the Billy Graham crusades. But whatever they are called, evangelicals of all kinds initiate spiritual renewal events that seek to breathe new life into individuals and churches.

Finally, Evangelicalism seeks renewal of Christianity through relevance. Evangelicals have in varying degrees emphasized the importance of contextualizing the Christian message and relating it to contemporary problems and issues. They criticize and seek to avoid real accommodation to culture, while at the same time translating the gospel into cultural idioms, using contemporary means of communication in order to facilitate retrieval, restoration, and revival. The "new measures" used by the revival preachers of the first and second Great Awakenings of the eighteenth and nineteenth centuries give examples of this evangelical interest in renewal through relevance. During the Great Awakenings those churches that cooperated with itinerant, circuit-riding preachers and produced sermons and used illustrations that related to the everyday lives of people in the colonies and along the frontiers grew, while those that resisted such new measures and insisted on sticking to old language and methods tended to lose members. Evangelicalism has not usually been noted for its relevance, but that is no doubt because of its reaction against liberal Christianity's (neo-Protestantism's) attempts to accommodate the biblical and historic Christian message to the ever-changing climates of contemporary cultures. Evangelicals seek to retain the original biblical message, as they understand it, while communicating it in contemporary ways using modern means. Above all, they seek to appeal to the personal spiritual needs of individuals in their everyday lives—needs for release from anxiety of guilt, acceptance within a community of true believers, and hope for a better future, even if only after this life.

Evangelical theology is, most simply, that theological scholarship done within the context of the evangelical movement for renewal of historic Protestant Christianity. The postfundamentalist evangelical coalition contains several publishing houses and publications as well as professional theological societies, and there is a sense in which any theological reflection published, read, or widely discussed within these is evangelical theology. That is, of course, a descriptive approach to defining evangelical theology. What about a prescriptive approach? Are there boundaries of evangelical theology? How might one determine whether a particular book or article or scholarly paper that is published or read within Evangelicalism by a self-identified evangelical theologian truly is evangelical? If *evangelical* is compatible with anything and everything, it is literally meaningless. Identifying either a controlling center or limiting boundaries of authentically evangelical theology is notoriously dangerous; others are bound to disagree most strongly.

Our approach is to use history as the guide. Rather than setting boundaries and examining every theological contribution by a predetermined set of rigid criteria, we prefer to look at each contribution through the lens of the history of evangelical Christianity, which has always contained a strong reforming and reshaping impulse within itself. In other words, Evangelicalism is dynamic rather than static. Just because something is new does not automatically mean it is not evangelical. However, Evangelicalism's history does have a unifying ethos as described above—a strong, gravitational center that holds it together. This can take many new shapes, and it can be expressed and interpreted in different ways. Evangelical theology, then, is that form of mostly Protestant Christian reflection on God and salvation (etc.) that is guided by the ultimate authority of Scripture, acknowledges that God is supremely revealed in Jesus Christ, and includes a strong focus on personal salvation by repentance and faith. More could be included, of course, but this brief definition is sufficient to give some shape to evangelical theology. It is not any and all Protestant theological reflection and formulation. Liberal theology that is characterized by "maximal acknowledgment of the claims of modernity" is not compatible with evangelical theology. Nor is all Protestant orthodoxy; in order to count as evangelical, it would have to include affirmation of and reflection on "conversional piety"—the dimension of salvation dear to the hearts of all evangelicals in which persons come to know God as Savior only through a personal relationship with Jesus Christ that begins with, or at least comes to full fruition in, conscious repentance and trust.

Evangelicalism and evangelical theology cross denominational and confessional boundaries; one can find evangelicals and evangelical theologians in many Protestant traditions and communities. One of the most influential evangelical theologians of the later decades of the twentieth century and early years of the twenty-first century is Donald G. Bloesch, who taught theology for many years at a mainline Presbyterian seminary (University of Dubuque Theological Seminary) and maintained membership and ministerial ordination in the mainline Protestant United Church of Christ. Bloesch's definitions and descriptions of evangelical express the category's unity and diversity and continuity and discontinuity with fundamentalism:

> "Evangelical" can therefore be said to indicate a particular thrust or emphasis within the church, namely, that which upholds the gospel of free grace as we see this in Jesus Christ. An evangelical will consequently be Christocentric and not merely theocentric (as are the deists and a great many mystics). Yet it is not the teachings of Jesus Christ that are considered of paramount importance but his sacrificial life and death on the cross of Calvary. The evangel is none other than the meaning of the cross.[2]

> Evangelicalism unashamedly stands for the fundamentals of the historic faith, but as a movement it transcends and corrects the defensive, sectarian mentality commonly associated with Fundamentalism. Though many, perhaps most, fundamentalists are evangelicals, evangelical Christianity is wider and deeper than Fundamentalism, which is basically a movement of reaction in the churches in this period of history. Evangelicalism in the classical sense fulfills the basic goals and aspirations of Fundamentalism but rejects the ways in which these goals are realized.[3]

According to Bloesch and many other commentators on evangelical history and theology, then, Evangelicalism is a broad and diverse movement that includes within itself many (but not all) Lutherans, Reformed Protestants (i.e., "Calvinists"), Wesleyans, Baptists, Pentecostals, and adherents of other Protestant traditions. It also includes many fundamentalists, although Bloesch is reluctant to identify Evangelicalism with fundamentalism because of their different mind-sets and approaches to culture, other Christians, higher education, and a variety of other subjects. Some evangelical spokespersons define and describe Evangelicalism and evangelical theology more restrictively than Bloesch. Those who value Evangelicalism's fundamentalist roots tend to limit it to people and organizations that affirm biblical inerrancy. Others

---

2. Donald G. Bloesch, *The Future of Evangelical Christianity* (Garden City, NY: Doubleday, 1983), 15.

3. Ibid., 22.

who especially value Evangelicalism's Pietist and revivalist roots tend to limit it to people and organizations that affirm radical conversion as the only true initiation into Christian existence and who reject infant baptism as a sacrament. A few evangelicals would argue that authentic Evangelicalism is limited to those who believe in the classical Calvinist doctrines of unconditional election and irresistible grace. However, the majority of evangelicals and scholarly commentators on Evangelicalism emphasize its diversity as well as its unity; the genius of postfundamentalist Evangelicalism and evangelical theology is its ability to embrace a variety of confessional and liturgical differences within a unifying framework of belief and experience.

THE ROOTS OF EVANGELICAL THEOLOGY IN PIETISM

Was there a first evangelical theologian or first volume of evangelical theology? Probably not. Instead of identifying a definite beginning of Evangelicalism or evangelical theology, we should explore the distant roots of postfundamentalist Evangelicalism in several movements to reform Protestantism in Europe, Great Britain, and North America. In other words, the story of post–World War II postfundamentalist Evangelicalism and its theology begins three hundred years earlier with a general rise of spiritual fervor and a renaissance of biblical theology among Protestants that has come to be known vaguely as Pietism. The Pietist movement began among German Lutherans in the late seventeenth cenutury and quickly spread to Scandinavia. It influenced Great Britain through Puritans who were influenced by Pietism and through John and Charles Wesley, the founders of the Methodist movement. It was brought to the American colonies by leading Pietists such as Count Nikolaus von Zinzendorf and his Moravian followers, as well as by other groups of "heart Christians" who often called themselves Brethren. The ethos of Pietism is well described by F. Ernest Stoeffler: "Wherever it is found its ethos is manifested in a religious self-understanding which the author has characterized elsewhere as experiential, biblical, perfectionistic, and oppositive."[4] In other words, Pietists are always concerned that Christianity be something more than historical knowledge and mental assent to doctrines; they want to distinguish authentic Christianity from false or merely nominal Christianity by identifying the "real thing" by life-transforming experience of God in conversion and devotion to God in the "inner man" and by discipleship that is shaped by the Bible, aims towards perfection, and seeks to be "in the world but not of the world."

The Pietist movement is usually thought to have begun with the publication of a book entitled *Pia Desideria* (Pious desires) by German Lutheran minister Philip Spener (1635–1705) in 1675. Spener, a highly regarded and influential minister of the Lutheran state church of Prussia, was concerned that true Christianity was being replaced by dead orthodoxy, ritualism, and legalism. His understanding of "true Christianity" was greatly influenced by his godly mother and by her favorite devotional book, *True Christianity*, by Protestant mystic and spiritual writer Johann Arndt (1555–1621). Spener, following Arndt, defined true Christianity in contrast with the conventional orthodoxy of the state church with reference to the "inner man." That is, according to Spener and later Pietists, each person has within himself or herself a spiritual organ sometimes loosely called "the heart" that is the core of personality and seat of governing affections. This inner man is the locus of God's work in conversion and regeneration, and each person who becomes a true Christian experiences a transformation there. Such a transformation, which later evangelicals commonly came to call being

---

4. F. Ernest Stoeffler, ed., *Continental Pietism and Early American Christianity* (Grand Rapids: Wm. B. Eerdmans, 1976), 9.

"born again," transcends intellect and will; through it the person who repents and trusts in Christ for salvation receives "the expulsive power of a new affection" that inclines him or her to have a taste for the things of God and turn away from desires of the "world, flesh and devil." Spener returned repeatedly to this basic theme of the inner man, and it became, in various permutations, the constant leitmotif of Pietism and later Evangelicalism:

> One should therefore emphasize that the divine means of Word and sacrament are concerned with the inner man. Hence it is not enough that we hear the Word with our outward ear, but we must let it penetrate to our heart, so that we may hear the Holy Spirit speak there, that is, with vibrant emotion and comfort feel the sealing of the Spirit and the power of the Word. Nor is it enough to be baptized, but the inner man, where we have put on Christ in Baptism, must also keep Christ on and bear witness to him in our outward life. Nor is it enough to have received the Lord's Supper externally, but the inner man must truly be fed with that blessed food. Nor is it enough to pray outwardly with our mouth, but true prayer, and the best prayer, occurs in the inner man, and it either breaks forth in words or remains in the soul, yet God will find and hit upon it. Nor, again, is it enough to worship God in an external temple, but the inner man worships God best in his own temple, whether or not he is in an external temple at the time.[5]

Spener organized conventicles (small groups) of "heart Christians" in his parish in Frankfurt, and from there the "conventicle movement" (original Pietism) spread throughout Lutheran and Reformed churches in Europe. The conventicles were to be spiritual renewal groups under the auspices of trained, Pietist clergymen, but they quickly evolved into home meetings of "Bible readers" outside the authority of church and state. In many parts of Europe these groups were persecuted, and some of them emigrated to North America to find religious freedom. There they organized new denominations of "free churches" composed of "true Christians." Some became Baptists under the influence of Baptist missionaries. Some remained independent of any particular tradition. Denominations in the United States such as the Church of the Brethren, the Baptist General Conference (formerly the Swedish Baptist Conference), the Evangelical Free Church of America, and the Evangelical Covenant Church of America all evolved out of the European Pietist movement begun by Spener. While these and other Pietist-evangelical groups disagree about specific practices such as baptism and church government, they agree that authentic Christian existence begins with conversion to Jesus Christ by the Spirit of God within the inner man (heart, soul, inward being) and that it always involves heartfelt repentance and faith (trust) in Jesus Christ. Furthermore, they emphasize a semimystical "daily relationship with Christ" that flows out of that initial conversion experience. Some commentators on Pietism-Evangelicalism have labeled this distinctive evangelical spirituality "conversional piety." In traditional theological terms this distinctive Pietist and evangelical ethos may be described as an elevation of regeneration and sanctification over or alongside justification. Critics have labeled it "decisionism" and decried its perceived subjective emphasis.

In spite of his emphasis on the inner man and inward spiritual transformation, Spener was not a true mystic or subjectivist. He was most certainly not a religious fanatic (except to some of his harshest critics). Throughout *Pia Desideria* and other writings he strove to balance biblical authority, confessional fidelity, and theological scholarship with experience of God in the inner man. He did not reject either side of this

---

5. Philip Jacob Spener, *Pia Desideria*, trans. Theodore G. Tappert (Philadelphia: Fortress Press, 1964), 117.

equation and insisted that "head" and "heart" be held in complementary relationship. Clearly, however, he perceived the greater danger as that of rejecting or neglecting heart Christianity, which led later Pietists to coin the motto "Better a live heresy than a dead orthodoxy!" This was clearly intended as hyperbole. Spener advocated spiritual training for ministerial students and argued against merely educating them in orthodoxy and theological polemics. He railed against corruption in government, society, and church and laid out a program for reforming Protestantism through rigorous examination of the character and spiritual lives of ministerial candidates. He preached boldly against princes and magistrates who neglected church attendance and called for renewal, revival, and reform in all areas of public and private life. Typical of his advice to ministers and students is this exhortation in *Pia Desideria*:

> Let us remember that in the last judgment we shall not be asked how learned we were and whether we displayed our learning before the world; to what extent we enjoyed the favor of men and knew how to keep it; with what honors we were exalted and how great a reputation in the world we left behind us; or how many treasures of earthly goods we amassed for our children and thereby drew a curse upon ourselves. Instead, we shall be asked how faithfully and with how childlike a heart we sought to further the kingdom of God; with how pure and godly a teaching and how worthy an example we tried to edify our hearers amid the scorn of the world, denial of self, taking up of the cross, and imitation of our Savior; with what zeal we opposed not only error but also wickedness of life; or with what constancy and cheerfulness we endured the persecution or adversity thrust upon us by the manifestly godless world or by false brethren, and amid such suffering praised our God.[6]

Contrary to what one might think, Spener and other early Pietist leaders were not at all fanatical, overly emotional, or anti-intellectual. Nor did they depart from basic Protestant doctrinal orthodoxy. In fact, they expressed nothing but the highest praise for Luther and quoted him often; those who were of the Reformed heritage revered Calvin and affirmed the classical Reformed confessions of faith. Spener and those who followed him simply believed that the Reformation was unfinished and that the heirs of Luther and Calvin had fallen into a stale, overly intellectualized and polemical religion that lacked life and power. Of course, the Pietists were accused of heresy by their critics within the state churches of Europe. They were labeled "enthusiasts," which was at that time virtually a synonym for "religious fanatics." As noted earlier, some of them were hounded and persecuted by civil authorities at the behest of religious leaders. In many places it was illegal to meet for Bible study and discussion and for prayer without benefit of clergy. Nevertheless, the Pietist movement grew very quickly, and its influence spread into all corners of Protestant Europe in the early eighteenth century. Some church historians have labeled it "the second Reformation" and many have come to regard it as the beginning of what is now known as Evangelicalism.

Two other early leaders of Pietism deserve mention in this brief account of the history and theology of Evangelicalism. They are August Hermann Francke (1663–1727) and Count Nikolas Ludwig von Zinzendorf (1700–1760). Francke was raised in a home and church deeply imbued with Spener's Pietist influence. Spener eventually became his teacher and mentor in Leipzig, where Spener was court preacher to the prince of Saxony and Francke was a student. Francke was studying to be a minister and yet doubted his own salvation because he had not experienced the regenerating power of God in the inner man. One night before he was to preach, the young student minister fell on his knees and asked God for such a heart-changing and assuring experience. According to his own testimony he endured a protracted *Busskampf* or "struggle of

---

6. Spener, 36–37.

repentance" with tears and crying out to God before receiving the sought-after assurance. This became a model for true initiation into authentic Christianity for many Pietists and later evangelicals. Francke helped found the first Pietist university at Halle in Germany, and in the same city he established and led a variety of charitable institutions including free schools, an orphanage, a hospital, and a publishing house. From Halle, Francke also sent out missionaries to India and other countries that had previously been virtually ignored by Protestants. Like Spener before him, Francke was a devout Lutheran (within a united Lutheran and Reformed state church) who never questioned the classical Protestant doctrines of biblical authority and justification by grace through faith alone. Also like Spener, however, Francke believed that one could participate in the sacraments and learn the catechism and even assent to correct doctrine and not be saved. That was his own story. What made the difference between the two conditions? For Francke and Pietism in general, it was the experience of *Busskampf*—struggle of repentance and the life of Christ dwelling in the inner man that flowed from it. Francke added to the stream of Pietism and early Evangelicalism a passion for missions and world evangelism, as well as concern for the poor and disadvantaged. Under his leadership the city of Halle became a great center of Christian education, social work, publishing, and missionary endeavor.

Zinzendorf has been described somewhat tongue in cheek as the "noble Jesus freak." He was a member of the German nobility and quite eccentric, as well as passionate about Jesus. Spener was his godfather; Francke was his mentor. As a child and adolescent he seemed to have an inordinate obsession with matters spiritual. The young count became disillusioned with the spiritual aridity of the state church of Saxony and allowed a roving band of Moravian Christian pilgrims to settle on his estate at Berthelsdorf that he renamed Herrnhut—"the Lord's Watch." The Moravians were spiritual descendents of Jan Hus, the forerunner of the Protestant Reformation in Prague (Bohemia), who was burned at the stake by the Catholic Council of Constance about a century before Luther's Reformation divided the church. They had existed as a separate Protestant body within a predominantly Catholic country for two centuries before some left it and found refuge on Zinzendorf's land. The count joined their church and became their bishop; they became a semi-autonomous branch of the Lutheran church of Germany. Although small in number, the Moravians exercised tremendous influence within the burgeoning Pietist movement in Europe. They sent missionaries to many places including South Africa, Labrador, and the Caribbean as well as the North American colonies. They founded a chapel in London where John Wesley's heart was "strangely warmed," and afterwards Wesley lived among them in Germany for a time. They began traditions such as New Year's Eve prayer vigils ("watchnight services") and Easter morning sunrise services that entered into the stream of evangelical Christianity. Their worship was intense, although not particularly loud or overly emotional, and Zinzendorf and the Moravians emphasized inward experience of Jesus Christ as crucified and risen Savior ("personal Savior and Lord") over precise doctrinal knowledge and assent. As with Spener and Francke, however, this did not mean they discarded doctrine. Rather, they heartily affirmed the basic confessional statements of Lutheranism. Nevertheless, Zinzendorf and the Moravians held in highest esteem a semimystical experience that is devoid of concepts and ushers one into authentic Christian existence. In a lecture entitled "On the Essential Character and Circumstance of the Life of a Christian" delivered at the Moravian Brethren chapel in London, Zinzendorf attempted to explain the nature of this experience and the life with Christ into which it leads. The beginning of Christianity is when the crucified Savior Jesus "appears and looks into the heart" of a person, which can happen at any moment but most often happens when a sermon is preached or a hymn is sung:

He who in this moment, in this instant, when the Saviour appears to him and when He says to him, as to Peter, "Do you love me in this figure?"—he who can say, "You know all things; you know that I love you"; he who in this minute, in this instant, goes over to Him with his heart, passes into Him, and loses himself in His tormented form and suffering figure—he remains in Him eternally, without interruption, through all eons; he can no longer be estranged from Him. . . . Then our perdition is at an end; then flesh and blood have lost. Satan, who had already lost his case in court, really lays no more claim on such a soul; and it is just as if a man, who had sold himself to Satan, gets back his promissory note, as if the slip of paper came flying into the meeting, torn to pieces. The signature, the note, says the apostle, is torn up and fastened to the cross, pounded through with nails, and forever cancelled; and this is registered at the same time, that is, we are set free; we are legally acquitted. When the books are opened, so it will be found.[7]

This statement of conversion nicely illustrates, in admittedly flowery and somewhat eccentric language, the Pietistic and evangelical doctrine of salvation: it is an experience of Jesus Christ in which Christ encounters a person, calls him or her to respond in love (which necessarily includes repentance and trust), whereupon Christ enters the person's heart (Spener's inner man) and unites with him or her. This is at once justification (forgiveness and imputed righteousness) and regeneration (cleansing from corruption of sin and impartation of the Holy Spirit). Of course, Spener, Francke, and Zinzendorf all believed, like many evangelicals past and present, that this transforming experience, which happens in a moment, may be preceded by a process of preparation that begins with infant baptism and continues through Christian nurture; but they rejected any idea that persons can be truly saved and enter into authentic Christian life without this kind of conversion experience.

Pietism was the original Protestant renewal movement, and it did manage to revive large portions of European, British, and North American Protestantism in the eighteenth century. It assumed the truth and authority of the Bible and the major Christian creeds, such as the Nicene Creed and the basic Protestant confessional statements like the Augsburg Confession (Lutheran) and Heidelberg Confession and Catechism (Reformed), but it sought to add to objective truth the dimension of subjective, inward experience. It moved the standard for authentic Christianity beyond baptism and doctrinal belief to include genuine conversion to Christ through repentance and faith and a life of visible Christianity. For this it was widely denounced by defenders of confessional orthodoxy and the status quo in the state churches as divisive, sectarian, superspiritual, spiritually proud, and fanatical. The basic ethos of Pietism set the mood and course for all Evangelicalism; post–World War II postfundamentalist Evangelicalism is Pietism's heir, even though it also often looks back to Pietism's enemies among the Protestant scholastic theologians with great respect and reverence. This is the pathos of modern Evangelicalism: its dual heritage. It was born in Pietism, but it has always flirted with rationalistic, scholastic Protestant orthodoxy. From Pietism evangelical theology inherits its fascination with soteriology—the doctrine of salvation. If Evangelicalism and evangelical theology are about anything, they are about the meaning of true salvation and authentic Christianity, defined in terms of the experience of salvation. At the same time, clearly modern Evangelicalism and evangelical theology are also heirs of Protestant orthodoxy, with its precise definitions of doctrinal correctness and polemical arguments over the fine points of dogma. While these are not necessarily conflictual, they do often fall into some tension with each other.

---

7. Nicholaus Ludwig Count von Zinzendorf, *Nine Public Lectures on Important Subjects in Religion*, trans. George W. Forell (Eugene, OR: Wipf & Stock Publishers, 1998), 83–84.

THE REVIVALIST ROOTS OF EVANGELICAL THEOLOGY

Following closely upon the heels of Pietism was the revivalist movement, which also profoundly impacted Evangelicalism and evangelical theology. Revivalism was the phenomenon in Great Britain and North America that saw emotional preaching calling masses of mostly already baptized people, often outdoors, to make decisions to repent and follow Jesus Christ. It began with three ministers of traditional Protestant denominations and swept through the English-speaking world and from there to the whole world. The three eighteenth-century founders of revivalism were John Wesley, George Whitefield, and Jonathan Edwards. Their numerous followers and imitators include Charles G. Finney, Dwight L. Moody, Billy Sunday, Aimee Semple McPherson, and Billy Graham. Unlike some of their spiritual descendants, Wesley, Whitefield, and Edwards were highly educated clergy and scholars in biblical and theological studies. They were not merely religious entrepreneurs seeking a following. They were faithful sons of their Protestant traditions who happened to be deeply influenced by versions of Pietism. Edwards, of course, was also a Puritan, and through him and his influence the Puritan tradition entered into the stream of evangelical life and thought.

None of these early revivalist leaders of the so-called Great Awakening (1730s and 1740s) envisioned a departure from or split within their respective Protestant churches. That became inevitable when the leaders of those denominations (Anglican/ Episcopalian and Congregational/Presbyterian) refused to support the revival fires that burned where the revivalists preached. Wesley, Whitefield, and Edwards, however, unanimously and sincerely affirmed the basic doctrines of historic Christian orthodoxy (as expressed for example in the Nicene Creed) and of Protestant orthodoxy (as expressed in their denominational statements of faith such as the Westminster Confession and Catechism and the Church of England's Thirty-Nine Articles of Religion). Like the Pietists of Europe, they believed that "head knowledge" and "historical faith" must be distinguished from "heart knowledge" and "inward faith" and that the latter are what distinguishes true Christianity from nominal Christianity. The revivalists simply went a step beyond the Pietists and proclaimed the need for each person publicly to repent and receive Jesus Christ by an act of inward faith as well as outward profession. They firmly believed that the gospel they proclaimed and the "new measures" they used to proclaim it could facilitate radical spiritual transformations in individuals and societies.

Nothing quite like the Great Awakening of 1739–42 had ever happened in Christianity—at least not since the days of the apostles. Church of England minister John Wesley (1703–91) and his brother Charles (1707–88) had founded something called "the Holy Club" by its detractors at Oxford University when they were students. Their friend George Whitefield (1714–70), who also later became a minister of the Church of England, was a member of the club. Much later these three friends all had experiences that led them beyond the striving for holiness through strict spiritual disciplines that brought on them the appellation Holy Club and caused them to accept and proclaim the Pietist doctrine of salvation. John Wesley struggled with doubts about his salvation even as a priest of the state church and was not freed from doubt until his heart was "strangely warmed" during a service at the Moravian Brethren chapel in Aldersgate Street in London. Eventually, the three friends began and cooperated together in an evangelistic venture that included open-air preaching throughout England. Whitefield traveled to the American colonies and preached to large numbers of people in cities such as Philadelphia, where he was "puffed" by journalist Benjamin Franklin. Among the "new measures" used by these revivalists and those who joined with them was vivid description of the consequences of neglecting repentance and conversion. Whitefield especially was both criticized and applauded for his rhetorical flourishes that resulted in thousands of emotional responses. He loudly described to his mass of eager listeners the feelings of a person who has died without repenting and accepting Christ:

> O wretched Man that I am, who shall deliver me from the Body of Death! Are all the Grand Deceiver's inviting Promises come to this? O Damned Apostate! Oh that I had never hearkened to his beguiling Insinuations! Oh that I had rejected his very first Suggestions with the utmost Detestation and Abhorrence! Oh that I had taken up my cross and followed Christ! But alas! These reflections come now too late. But must I live for ever tormented in these Flames? Oh, Eternity! That thought fills me with Despair. I cannot, will not, yet I must be miserable for ever.[8]

In New England Whitefield met Puritan minister Jonathan Edwards (1703–58), whose preaching in Northampton, Massachusetts, had sparked revival there with sermons such as "Sinners in the Hands of an Angry God." Like Whitefield and unlike the Wesley brothers, Edwards was an ardent Calvinist, but unlike many Calvinists of that time he believed that God uses extraordinary means to win the elect to himself. Among those means was powerful preaching about the torments of hell and the absolute necessity of sincere, heartfelt repentance and faith in Jesus Christ. John and Charles Wesley, who remained in England while their friend and colleague Whitefield preached up and down the American coast, preferred to dwell on God's love more than the punishments that await the unconverted in hell. Eventually differences between their Arminianism (belief in genuine free will) and Whitefield's and Edwards's Calvinism (belief in unconditional election and irresistible grace) led to a schism between them. This difference over the background belief about God's agency and human agency in salvation has remained a rift within Evangelicalism and evangelical theology since the falling out between the Wesleys and Whitefield.

John Wesley and Jonathan Edwards may fairly be seen as the two great founders of Evangelicalism in the English-speaking world. Wesley was profoundly influenced by Zinzendorf, although he rejected the German count's seeming cult-personality status among the Moravians. Edwards was influenced by a Pietist streak within Puritanism. His grandfather Solomon Stoddard, whose pulpit in Northampton he inherited, had preached salvation through conversion and the absolute necessity of a life of devotion and holiness (even as he became the architect of the so-called Half-Way Covenant, which allowed unconverted children of church members to participate in the sacraments and life of the church). What makes Edwards and Wesley the founders of the evangelical movement is their tremendous influence on church and culture through their persuasive insistence on the necessity of radical conversion experience for salvation and authentic Christian existence. While both men affirmed the absolute authority of Scripture and insisted on the classical doctrines of Christian orthodoxy, they also elevated experience over doctrine as the true centerpiece of Christian existence. Each in his own way inserted "conversional piety" firmly into the mainstream of British and American religious life. Through them the message and belief that "you must be born again" became more than the peculiar distinctive of a fringe group of enthusiastic fanatics and became instead the hallmark of a major movement that inserted itself firmly and permanently within Protestant life in the English-speaking world.

THE PURITAN ROOTS OF EVANGELICAL THEOLOGY

Jonathan Edwards's contribution to Evangelicalism and evangelical theology is rooted in his Puritan heritage combined with his Pietist-like and revivalistic passion

---

8. Quoted in Frank Lambert, *Inventing the "Great Awakening"* (Princeton, NJ: Princeton University Press, 1999), 98.

for conversion as a change of religious affections. Before expounding Edwards's distinctive evangelical theology and its role in shaping Evangelicalism, it will be helpful to examine Puritanism and Puritan theology. The Puritan movement began in Elizabethan England in the late sixteenth century. Scholars debate the identity of the first Puritan; that is largely a matter of definition. Puritanism broadly defined began as the English movement to purify the Church of England under Queen Elizabeth I and her appointed archbishops of Canterbury of all vestiges of "Romish" doctrine and practice. The Puritans objected to the imposition of a uniform liturgy on all churches in the English realm. They wanted to abolish the office of bishop or reduce it to an administrative role. They regarded some of the trappings of Anglican worship as more Catholic than Protestant and thus "un-Reformed." Many of them were strongly influenced by the continental Reformed tradition of Protestantism generally associated with the name of John Calvin and the city of Geneva in Switzerland. This influence was also mediated to the English Puritans by the reformer of Scotland (at that time a separate kingdom from England), John Knox (1514–72), who referred to Calvin's Geneva as the most perfect school of Christ since the days of the apostles. Knox transformed the kingdom of Scotland into a constitutional monarchy with republican aspects, with his Presbyterian Church as the national church. The Puritans in England wanted a similar thorough reform of England, but they were opposed in their efforts by Queen Elizabeth, her archbishops, and the leading theologians of Anglicanism, such as Richard Hooker (1554–1600), who wrote a multivolume defense of Anglicanism entitled *The Laws of Ecclesiastical Polity*.

The so-called Elizabethan Settlement was carefully constructed in England throughout Elizabeth's reign (1558–1603) and brought together Protestant theology (Scripture as the ultimate authority for faith and practice and justification by grace through faith alone) and some elements of Catholic polity and worship. The Puritans perceived this as unjustified compromise and argued strenuously for a thoroughly Protestant national church. They lost that part of their cause but became so powerful in England that they managed to lead a civil war in the 1640s that led to King Charles's beheading at the hands of Puritan-dominated Parliament and a brief period of Puritan rule during which Great Britain (which had included Scotland beginning in 1603) was a commonwealth (similar to a republic) under radical separatist Puritan military leader Oliver Cromwell (1599–1658). Eventually the Puritan cause was lost and both the monarchy (with the sovereign as the governor of the Church of England) and Anglican church were reestablished. Throughout the turmoil of the first half of the seventeenth century, thousands of Puritans left England to settle in New England, where they hoped to establish a Puritan commonwealth to the glory of God, and where many of them dropped their Presbyterianism and became Congregationalists.

One of the Puritan theologians of the seventeenth century who greatly influenced the beginning and course of Evangelicalism was John Owen (1616–83), who was for a while dean of Christ Church, Oxford and served as vice-chancellor of England under Cromwell. Owen wrote numerous volumes of Puritan theology, some of which are still in print and widely read by Reformed Christians three and a half centuries later. He was a strong defender of the Congregational form of Puritanism that insisted on a "gathered church" model, in which the true, visible church consists of believers only, and the autonomy of individual congregations. He wrote against the high church Arminianism of the Church of England in the seventeenth century and argued for a strict form of Calvinist theology. He also wrote on the substitutionary atonement of Christ and the person and work of the Holy Spirit. His theological and devotional works stressed the importance of personal repentance and faith as well as of a life of holiness. Owen combined in his life and writings the distinctively Puritan blend of rigorous Reformed-Calvinistic doctrine (unconditional election and irresistible grace) and strict spirituality revolving around repentance, prayer and devotional exercises, Bible reading and study, and other Protestant spiritual disciplines. Owen and other seventeenth-century Puritan divines (minister-theologians) displayed a decidedly pietistic attitude toward Christian life before the Pietist movement began in Europe, but they did not highlight the emotional and decisionistic aspects of authentic Christian experience as much as later Pietists. For them, salvation was a process that began at the moment Christ died on the cross for the sins of all the elect (thus the title of Owens's best-known book, *The Death of Death in the Death of Christ*); continued through infant baptism (children are born into the "covenant people of God") and childhood Christian nurture within the home and church; and included repentance, faith, confession of doctrinal belief, and a daily life of devotion and discipleship. Revivalism was not envisaged by the Puritans before Jonathan Edwards, but they did emphasize the absolute necessity of true Christianity as *visible Christianity* showing forth in "signs of grace," including ability to express one's struggle from preparation for personal faith through repentance and conversion into assurance of salvation and solid church membership and good citizenship. Of course, they stressed that all of this is completely dependent upon the supernatural grace of God and is for the glory of God and not the exaltation of the individual.

The Puritan vision of authentic Christianity was brought to the New England colonies of Massachusetts and Connecticut by ministers such as Thomas Hooker (1586–1647), who converted from Anglicanism to Puritanism of the Congregational variety while a student at Cambridge University. Under persecution by the crown and state church for his noncomformity (e.g., refusing to use the *Book of Common Prayer* in worship), to find religious freedom Hooker fled first to Holland and then to Cambridge, Massachusetts, where he pastored a Puritan congregation. In 1636 he led his entire congregation into the wilderness to found the city of Hartford and establish the commonwealth of Connecticut. Hooker wrote an influential volume on Congregational polity and social theory entitled *Survey of the Summe of Church Discipline* (1648) and taught his own unique form of "federal theology," which was the distinctively Puritan form of Reformed covenant theology. According to Hooker's federal theology God deals with humanity through covenants (social-spiritual contracts), and so long as human persons keep their side of the bargain God is obligated (by his promise) to bless them with spiritual and material blessings. One can know that one is part of God's elect (predestined) people and destined for heaven by examining one's own covenant-keeping in inward attitudes and outward disciplines. This is also how the gathered church discerns which of all the inhabitants of a city or colony are fit for full church membership including participation in the sacrament of the Lord's Supper.

Throughout the seventeenth century the original zeal of Puritanism in both England and the New England colonies cooled considerably. By the turn of the new century (1701) in most Puritan churches it was difficult to tell which church attenders were true believers and which were mere "professors" of Christian religion. The gathered churches of New England were becoming mixed assemblies as children and grandchildren of the Puritan diaspora of the 1630s and 1640s grew up within the congregations and simply learned how to play their roles without ever experiencing the stages of conversion or giving testimony of radical repentance or showing signs of grace in their lives. Arminian theology—once the sworn enemy of the Calvinist Puritans—was bleeding out of the congregations of the Church of England and into the Presbyterian and Congregational churches of the Puritans as well as into their colleges for ministerial training. The elders of Puritanism in New England, such as Jonathan Edwards's grandfather Solomon Stoddard (1643–1729), created compromises in order to keep the unconverted children of Puritans active within the Puritan congregations. The so-called Half-Way Covenant, of which Stoddard was a main architect, allowed unconverted but baptized children of Puritan church members to partake of the Lord's Supper with the hope that it would serve as a "converting influence" in their lives and the lives of their children. Eventually their children were baptized and allowed to grow up within the church without ever being required to recount their experiences of repentance and coming to know Christ as redeemer and Lord.

By 1730 New England was ripe for spiritual and theological renewal. The majority of its inhabitants participated in church worship and sacraments merely because they had been born "in the covenant" and had never chosen to opt out of it. (Church attendance was required in most places, but passionate participation in the life of the church was not.) The line of demarcation between nominal Christianity and authentic Christianity that had been so fiercely identified and defended by the first Puritans was blurred at best. Jonathan Edwards came from a long line of Puritans and was by all accounts a child prodigy with a strong interest in the life of the mind well before he entered Yale College in 1716. He became his grandfather's associate pastor at the Congregational church in Northampton, Massachusetts, in 1724 and then succeeded him as pastor in 1729. He was intensely interested in the new philosophy emanating from Europe and Great Britain that later came to be known as Enlightenment science and philosophy, and he was especially influenced by some of the ideas of the philosopher John Locke. His greatest passion, however, was biblical study and exposition. While he is best known for his sermon "Sinners in the Hands of an Angry God," Edwards also wrote calm, well-reasoned treatises on philosophy, biblical themes, science, theology, and religious experience. His sermons tended to be strongly doctrinal, with emphasis upon the necessity of repentance to avoid the wrath of God. His theological underpinnings were strongly Calvinistic with the flavoring of federal theology. His two overriding themes were the glory of God and human dependence upon God and God's grace for everything. He attributed all that happens to the sovereign providence of God and affirmed God's justice in condemning some portion of humanity to hell by his own free, sovereign good pleasure.

Throughout the 1730s Edwards was quietly, persistently preparing his Northampton congregation and his entire network of like-minded Puritan ministers for a spiritual renewal. There had been something like revivals before, but by and large they had been local and with little lasting effect. Many Puritans were wary of emotional appeals for individual decision for Christ, preferring instead a quiet preparation of souls for repentance and faith within the normal structures of Word and sacrament within the local churches. During the 1730s New England Puritans, including Edwards and his congregation, heard of a new phenomenon taking place primarily within the Church of England in London and other English cities. George Whitefield's fame as a stirring preacher, who held crowds spellbound out of doors and to whose sermons hundreds and even thousands responded becoming "born again," preceded his arrival in Philadelphia in 1739. When Whitefield arrived in New England, he and Edwards almost immediately bonded in friendship and ministry. Edwards's own congregation had begun to experience an "awakening" in 1734 with people crying out during the minister's sermons and sometimes falling to the ground speechless in sorrow for their sins and fear of hell. Many were profoundly converted and, according to Edwards, the spiritual atmosphere of the entire town was uplifted.

In 1737 he wrote a defense of the Northampton revival entitled *A Faithful Narrative of the Surprising Work of God in the Conversion of Many Hundred Souls in Northampton, and the Neighboring Towns and Villages.* Leading Presbyterian and Congregational ministers and theologians were harshly critical of the revivals that preceded Whitefield's arrival, and they ridiculed him and those who swarmed to his "imported Divinity" once he arrived. Nevertheless, the ground was prepared for the Great Awakening, and for about fifteen years wave after wave of highly emotional responses to preaching by itinerant ministers swept the New England and middle colonies. The centerpiece of all the commotion was the experience of the "new birth." The revivalists—led primarily by Edwards and Whitefield—proclaimed an immediate change of heart, soul, and mind brought about by the Spirit of God whenever a person truly repented and trusted in Jesus Christ alone for salvation. Edwards brought his mind to bear on the controversy over the revivals, which were being labeled "enthusiasm" (which meant roughly what "fanaticism" means today) in several essays and treatises. Most notably he examined the criteria by which false religious affections could be distinguished from true religious affections in *A Treatise concerning Religious Affections* (1746).

What did Edwards contribute to the evangelical movement and its theology? Without any doubt his main contribution was and remains his incisive examination of the nature of human persons and how they are ruled by *affections* more than by reason or free will. The affections are roughly what is meant by "heart" in popular evangelical preaching and teaching. According to Edwards, the reason and will are both governed by an inner core of personality that he labeled affections. One is what one loves, and salvation is an act of God upon the affections. Without reducing authentic religion (Christianity) to affections, Edwards more closely identified them than almost anyone before him: "From hence it clearly and certainly appears, that great part of true religion consists in the affections. For love is not only one of the affections, but it is the first and chief of the affections, and the fountain of all the affections."[9] Most theologians of Edwards's day emphasized either the will or the mind as the chief "seat" of human actions and thus appealed to one or both for religious renewal. Either persons were urged to study, understand, and confess true doctrine, or they were exhorted to exercise their wills toward higher moral endeavor. Many distrusted emotions and affections. Jonathan Edwards did not necessarily trust emotions and affections, but he did regard them as the seat of true religion, including authentic Christianity. A person who is truly converted to Christ will have "benevolence for being" placed in him or her by the grace and mercy of God and will display that in acts of loving-kindness. Edwards had little use for excessive displays of emotion, although he did not think they were always necessarily evil or contrary to true Christian faith; he simply preferred the manifestation of love. Both he and Whitefield believed that this inward change of affections could take place only by the power of God's Spirit through a new birth and that such an experience would always be a work of sovereign grace (God's free choice, predestination) that appeared to be freely chosen by the repentant sinner in response to God's Word proclaimed.

The Great Awakening transformed the culture of the New World, which was imbued with a profound religious sensitivity. Churches throughout the colonies took sides either for or against Whitefield and the revivals. New churches sprang up wherever the established churches opposed the revivals; even though the revival fires eventually burned lower, revivalism remained a permanent feature of life in the North American colonies and the United States of America. Evangelicalism as a movement was born in the 1730s and 1740s Great Awakening.

THE WESLEYAN ROOTS OF EVANGELICAL THEOLOGY

John Wesley picked up in England where Whitefield left off when he boarded a ship for the colonies in 1739. Whitefield and John and Charles Wesley had become close friends while students at Oxford University where they formed the core of the Holy

---

9. Jonathan Edwards, "Religious Affections," in *Jonathan Edwards: Representative Selections*, ed. Clarence H. Faust and Thomas H. Johnson, rev. ed. (New York: Hill & Wang, 1962), 220.

Club—a student conventicle for practicing spiritual disciplines. John Wesley became a priest of the Church of England as did Whitefield, but while Whitefield became an itinerant preacher to coal miners and Londoners in the parks, Wesley became a parish priest and short-term missionary to the colony of Georgia. Eventually Wesley experienced a much-needed spiritual awakening in a Moravian meeting, where someone was reading Luther's Introduction to his *Commentary on Paul's Epistle to the Romans*. He felt his heart "strangely warmed" and received assurance of his salvation. Some Wesley scholars have argued that this was Wesley's new birth experience while others have argued that he was already born again and this was simply an assurance of that. In any case, Wesley considered this a turning point in his spiritual life, and afterwards he was more willing to take Whitefield's open-air preaching style to those who would not or could not enter church buildings to hear the gospel. With his brother Charles writing the songs and leading the singing, John traveled around England preaching the love of God for all people and everyone's need of repentance in order to receive the grace and mercy of God unto salvation. While Wesley never repudiated infant baptism as a sacrament, he definitely believed and preached that every person—baptized or not—needs a conversion and new birth by repentance and faith. This is expressed in numerous of Wesley's sermons, such as "Scriptural Christianity" and "Justification by Faith." For Wesley, true "scriptural Christianity" begins in a person with the experience of being "born anew" by the Spirit of God. Of course, he did not deny the efficacy of the sacrament of infant baptism, but he did deny that it alone establishes a person's right relationship with God. For Wesley, authentic Christianity is *experiential Christianity* and must be freely chosen; it can never be inherited or the product of an effort to "turn over a new leaf." Nor can it be caused by a sacrament of the church alone.

By experiential (or "experimental") Christianity Wesley did not mean salvation by emotions or willpower ("enthusiasm"). He believed that only God can save a person and that if a person is saved it is entirely due to God's grace, but people must respond to God's grace and to the gospel with a free decision of repentance and faith. He was theologically Arminian rather than Calvinist. This led to a falling out with his friend Whitefield, who agreed that people must decide for Christ in order to be saved, but also believed that such decisions are always foreordained by God. Wesley did not agree; he believed that free decisions are foreknown but not foreordained. Wesley and Whitefield agreed entirely, however, on the crucial dimension of revivalism: appeal to persons to make decisions for Christ through repenting of their sins and trusting in Christ alone for forgiveness and inward renewal. Wesley wrote of his response to those who trusted in their baptism for full salvation:

> I tell a sinner, "You must be born again." "No," say you, "He was born again in baptism. Therefore he cannot be born again now." Alas! What trifling is this? What if he was then a child of God? He is now manifestly a "child of the devil"? . . . Therefore do not play upon words. He must go through an entire change of heart [without which] if either he or you die . . . your baptism will be so far from profiting you that it will greatly increase your damnation.[10]

Wesley recognized two conditions for receiving this "entire change of heart"—true repentance and true belief in Jesus Christ as God's Son and one's own only Savior. *True* is meant to distinguish these conditions from mere mental sorrow and intellectual belief. For Wesley, as for Whitefield, genuine repentance and genuine faith in Jesus Christ necessarily involve the whole person and must be reflected in a change of life

---

10. Quoted in Thomas C. Oden, *John Wesley's Scriptural Christianity* (Grand Rapids: Zondervan, 1994), 302.

that is visible to others. Wesley made absolutely clear in his theological writings that this change from the old life to a new life is a work of God and that apart from God's prevenient (calling and assisting) grace no person could ever exercise true repentance or true faith and be saved.

One aspect of Wesley's theology that gained partial acceptance among evangelicals but was rejected by others is "Christian perfection"—his distinctive idea of sanctification. In spite of its rejection by more Reformed evangelicals including Whitefield and even the Pietist leader Zinzendorf, Wesley's teaching that Christians could attain eradication of the sinful impulses and all presumptuous sinning entered into the evangelical movement and left a profound impression there. Even evangelical persons and groups that believe sanctification will always remain a process until death (the traditional Reformed view) have often absorbed some degree of Wesley's perfectionism, and it has appeared in revivalists, theologians, and submovements of Evangelicalism that are not specifically Wesleyan (e.g., Charles Finney and later the Keswick movement). In a little book entitled *A Plain Account of Christian Perfection* Wesley spelled out his notion of entire sanctification. According to him, it is possible for Christians, by the power of the Holy Spirit appropriated by faith, to reach a state of inner transformation where the struggle against the "world, flesh, and devil" cease and conscious, willful, presumptuous sinning never again disrupts the Christian's relationship with God or others. Wesley made abundantly clear in the little book that he did not mean such entirely sanctified persons would rise above all flaw or fault, and he affirmed that they would continue to commit sins of omission out of ignorance or even goodwill (e.g., trusting people too much). While Wesley did not claim to have reached such a stage in his Christian life, he did offer accounts of others who had reached it. He did not consider entire sanctification abnormal or a mark of particular saintliness. Rather, he treated it as the normal Christian experience for all who seek and receive it by faith. Later Wesleyans sometimes added to Wesley's doctrine of sanctification an initiation experience often called the "second blessing," which they believed would catapult persons wholly submissive to God's will and power into a sin-free existence. Many nineteenth-century revivals inspired by Wesley's followers featured "mourners' benches" at the front of the sanctuary or revival tent, where seekers after entire sanctification could "tarry" in prayer for the experience. Often such "tarrying meetings" after revival sermons lasted for hours and were marked by great emotion. What Wesley would have thought about this Holiness movement that erupted a few decades after his death along the margins of his Methodist movement is unknown and a favorite subject of speculation among Wesley scholars.

THE CRUCIBLE OF MODERN EVANGELICAL THEOLOGY IN THE GREAT AWAKENINGS

Evangelicalism and evangelical theology were born in the eighteenth-century Great Awakening in England and North America. They had a gestation period if not a preexistence in continental Pietism. Jonathan Edwards and John Wesley are the two fathers of evangelical Christianity, which had numerous ancestors (e.g., the Anabaptists and Puritans) and aunts and uncles (e.g., Quakers, Separatists, Baptists, Scottish Holy Fairs, the Jansenists). Something quite new appeared out of the Great Awakening and Edwards's and Wesley's sermons and essays—a mass movement, a subculture of experiential Christianity solidly rooted in Protestant orthodoxy.

Edwards and Wesley also bequeathed to Evangelicalism and evangelical theology a legacy of tension between two competing paradigms of Protestant orthodoxy—Reformed (Calvinist) theology and free-will theism (Arminianism). Edwards, together with his Puritan forebears and followers, believed that God's sovereignty is absolute and unconditioned by humans' decisions and actions except insofar as they are foreordained by God himself. Furthermore, Edwards taught that human beings are born totally depraved and utterly dependent on God's sovereign grace, mercy, and regenerating power for their salvation (should they be so fortunate as to be among the elect). When Edwards preached his famous revival sermon "Sinners in the Hands of an Angry God," he did not intend his listeners to conclude that their salvation from God's wrath against sin depended on their own free choices and actions. Instead, he inculcated in his listeners the belief that, though they must repent and believe in order to be saved from God's wrath and eternal torment in hell, their eternal destinies really depended entirely upon God's free decision of election and regeneration; their decisions to repent and believe would be sovereign works of God in them. God would create the new affections and cause them to be "born again," and only then would they experience affection for God and benevolence for all beings.

Wesley, on the other hand, preached and wrote about the free will of human beings without denying total depravity (or what he preferred to call "deprivation") and divine sovereignty. He believed that God gives to each person some measure of "prevenient grace" that enables him or her to make a free decision in response to the gospel call to repent and believe. Whereas Edwards emphasized the glory and majesty of God and the inability and dependence of humanity, Wesley emphasized the love of God and human persons' ability to respond to God on the basis of God's gift of assisting grace. These two streams of thought about salvation entered into Evangelicalism and have been present ever since. They have made evangelical theology an unstable compound always about to explode into internecine rivalry, if not warfare.

The revivalist impulse that gave birth to modern Evangelicalism during the Great Awakening became part of the fabric of American society and especially of its religious life. Unfortunately, many, if not most, of the revivals and revivalists after that did not live up to the high standards set by Edwards, Whitefield, and John and Charles Wesley. Evangelicals have always looked back upon them and their Great Awakening as the "Golden Age" of evangelical life. And yet there have been numerous effective revivals since then that have given great impetus to evangelical growth and stimulated evangelical thought about the gospel, salvation, the church, and Christian living.

The so-called Second Great Awakening was a diffuse collection of revivals in New England and along the North American frontier during the last decade of the eighteenth century and first three decades of the nineteenth century. Like the original Great Awakening, the Second Great Awakening is much debated by historians: When did it begin? What was it exactly? When did it end?[11] Whatever its exact nature and parameters may have been, the Second Great Awakening profoundly affected the religious landscape of the new United States of America and through missionary endeavors sparked by it influenced much of the world. By some accounts it began in 1795 at Yale College in Connecticut under the leadership of its president, Timothy Dwight, Jonathan Edwards's grandson. Dwight preached passionately against what he perceived to be increasing infidelity among Yale's students and engaged in vigorous classroom defenses of the authority of the Bible and supernatural work of God in salvation. A revival of Christianity broke out among the students with numerous remarkable conversions; soon the awakening was spreading to other campuses and cities in New England. One of Dwight's best students, Lyman Beecher, carried the revival to cities in New England and then to the frontier towns and cities.

---

11. For an example of scholarly debate about the nature of the first, original Great Awakening, see Frank Lambert, *Inventing the "Great Awakening"* (Princeton, NJ: Princeton University Press, 1999).

At about the same time, in Kentucky a revival began that was marked by protracted camp meetings attended by thousands of men and women and their families living on the frontier. The largest, at Cane Ridge in 1801, was led by Barton Stone, who went on later to found one of the first American-born Christian denominations, the Christian Churches. The Cane Ridge camp meeting revival and others like it witnessed amazing displays of fervent preaching and emotional responses. Hundreds and perhaps thousands of churches were started out of the camp meetings, and several denominations were born. Both the New England and frontier revivals focused on the necessity of personal, free decisions of repentance and acceptance of Christ for the salvation experience of being "born again."

Perhaps the single most influential person associated with the Second Great Awakening was the evangelist Charles G. Finney (1792–1875), who left an indelible mark upon nineteenth-century Christianity in North America. Some historians have called him the first true American evangelist. He certainly established a pattern for most later independent evangelists and revivalists. He organized highly efficient and productive mass evangelistic campaigns on the assumption that revivals of religion are humanly contrived and are not sovereign works of God's grace. Finney was an attorney by profession, but he experienced a radical conversion on October 10, 1821, in Adams, New York, after which he left his law practice and entered the Presbyterian ministry. He eventually switched to Congregationalism, as it allowed greater freedom for his own style of entrepreneurial evangelism. Finney met with great success and public acclaim as he preached revivals from town to town and city to city throughout New York and New England and Great Britain. His methods were based on business; he did not believe in waiting for God's Spirit to "move," but instead manipulated revivals with prerevival publicity and citywide ministerial cooperation and preparation. His preaching focused on God's moral government of humanity and humanity's rebelliousness against God's moral government and need and ability to repent and return to obedience to God's moral demands. His *Lectures on Revivals of Religion* (1835) laid out a program for initiating revivals and argued that revivals automatically occur when churches plan for them in the right ways, including prayer and social justice. Finney believed and taught that one of the greatest hindrances to revivals is social injustice, including slavery and denial of equality to women.

Finney's theology was strongly Arminian, if not semi-Pelagian. That is, unlike Edwards and Whitefield before him, he believed that humans have a natural ability from God to decide to repent, trust in Christ, and obey God's moral law. He denied unconditional election and irresistible grace and radically reinterpreted divine sovereignty and providence. His was a gospel message and program for Christian renewal that fit with the individualistic and activist temper of the times. Thousands of people "accepted Christ," often with great emotion, in Finney's revival meetings, which often lasted for weeks in the same city. Eventually Finney settled in Oberlin, Ohio, and became professor of theology and then president of Oberlin College, where he led the students and faculty in acts of civil disobedience against slavery and admitted women students to ministerial courses of study.

The Second Great Awakening, including Finney's revivalism, left an impact on evangelical Christianity that lasts into the twenty-first century. Without denying the "unpredictable sovereignty of God's grace," these revivalists, ministers, and theologians elevated human means of bringing about individual and mass conversions and tended to regard Christian endeavors from evangelism to church planting to social reform as activities of humans inspired and empowered by God's Spirit. The older Puritan ideas of total depravity and human dependence upon God's initiative were demoted and often even ignored. Pragmatic criteria of success replaced more traditional and stringent tests of works of God and manifestations of God's kingdom. Many of these revivals—including Finney's—were transdenominational, leading to a lessening of denominational identities and loyalties. By and large, basic Protestant orthodoxy was assumed and, when necessary, defended by the Second Great Awakening revivalists; those on the margins of the renewal were pushed out when they espoused heterodox or heretical views. The so-called Burnt-Over District of western New York witnessed the rise of numerous homegrown sects and cults toward the end of the Second Great Awakening. Nevertheless, the Evangelicalism of the early nineteenth-century revivals was a form of experiential Christianity that placed premium value on human cooperation with divine grace and the Holy Spirit in initiating and establishing works of God. One example was Finney's innovation called the "anxious bench," where people who felt first stirrings of God's work in their lives calling them to Christ sat during his preaching. Finney and later imitators would direct arguments toward them, enticing them with reason as well as with traditional exhortation from the Bible to believe the gospel, repent, and embrace Christ as Savior and Lord.

Later evangelical revivalists and evangelists who influenced the course of Evangelicalism and its theology included Dwight Lyman Moody (1837–99), Billy Sunday (1862–1935), Aimee Semple McPherson (1890–1944), and Billy Graham (b. 1918). All followed in the footsteps of Charles Finney, and each, in his or her own way, appealed to emotion and will in order to bring listeners to "personal decisions for Christ" so that they were converted. All assumed that people in their multidenominational audiences were not already authentic Christians merely because they were born in the United States or baptized as infants into a Christian church. All believed in and preached a basic Protestant orthodoxy that included the supreme authority of the Bible, a supernatural life and worldview, a personal and transcendent God who is in charge of nature and history, and Jesus Christ as God, Lord, and Savior. Each one led a new Great Awakening during his or her own time, and out of their revivalist campaigns arose new churches and denominations determined to restore authentic, primitive Christianity as it was in the New Testament in the days of the apostles. Each of them assumed an "evangelical synergism" in which God initiates the event of salvation through the proclaimed Word and human hearers complete it through making the appropriate response freely, often with tears and confessions of sin.

Through the revivalist tradition Evangelicalism became what some historians have called "America's folk religion."[12] That is, it became a transdenominational, grassroots movement including millions of ordinary people with differing lifestyles and class identities who embraced a common stock of beliefs that were held together by two basic themes: the Bible as God's infallible, authoritative Word and salvation through a personal experience of conversion to Christ followed by a personal relationship with Jesus Christ in everyday life. The preaching of evangelical revivalists was and is always based on biblical passages, and appeal is to the authority of the Bible as God's written Word. Evangelicals have acknowledged the Bible as a unique book supernaturally inspired by God, and they have loved to read and study it. They have also believed that authentic Christianity begins with a personal "crisis experience" that involves a decision to repent and trust in Christ alone for salvation (conversion). This "folk religion" has developed its own common stock of stories, songs, customs, habits, and forms of life that cross many denominational boundaries. For many evangelicals, being evangelical is as important as or more important than being Methodist, Baptist, Presbyterian, or any other denomination.

---

12. See Randall Balmer, *Mine Eyes Have Seen the Glory: A Journey through America's Evangelical Subculture* (New York: Oxford University Press, 1989).

Revivalists were primarily concerned about the prevalence of what some of them called "dead orthodoxy" among church members. They were also concerned, of course, about the masses of people who had no knowledge of the gospel or had left the churches and had no particular connection with organized Christianity. Their evangelical response to nominal Christianity and modern paganism was, "Repent and be born again." Their vision of authentic Christianity and fulfilled humanity was and is "conversional piety"—a personal relationship with God through Jesus Christ that begins with and is maintained by repentance of sin and personal, heartfelt trust in Jesus Christ and his death on the cross for sins. Revivalists usually felt no special calling to defend Protestant orthodoxy; they assumed it and added the dimension of experiential Christianity. Another group of nineteenth-century evangelicals, however, who came to be called fundamentalists, believed that the greatest threat to authentic Christianity and fulfilled humanity ("man fully alive") was not dead orthodoxy but paganism (i.e., life lived apart from Christian commitment) or modern secularism manifested in philosophical and theological skepticism. These evangelicals often sympathized and cooperated with some revivalists, but their special "calling" was to be apostles to those adversely affected by the Enlightenment's acids of modernity and especially to Christian denominations and churches that were falling under secularism's influence and creating a new brand of Christian theology called "liberal theology." Whereas revivalists and their followers elevated *orthopathy*—right affections—as the most important test of authentic Christianity, fundamentalists elevated *orthodoxy*—right beliefs—as the most important test of authentic Christianity. To be sure, both groups of evangelicals valued *orthopraxy*—right behavior—as a test of authentic Christianity, but neither of them considered it ultimate in guiding and determining authentic Christianity. Liberal theology tended to specialize in orthopraxy—especially in matters of social reform.

OLD PRINCETON THEOLOGY AND EVANGELICAL THEOLOGY

The Enlightenment of the eighteenth century was a cultural revolution in Europe, Great Britain, and North America that was summed up, according to German philosopher Immanuel Kant, in the phrase *sapere aude!*—"think for yourself." It was a revolt against the stifling authorities of tradition and dogmatic religion and a search for truth through autonomous human reason without any appeal to special revelation, faith, or tradition. It had its philosophical and scientific manifestations, and in religion it gave rise to three main movements: deism, unitarianism, and liberal Protestantism. All three sought to reform Protestant Christianity along Enlightenment lines by appealing to common reason, public evidence, natural religion and theology, and universal human spiritual experience. Enlightenment thinkers sought to undermine the absolute authority of theological tradition and the Bible by demonstrating inconsistencies, errors, discrepancies between texts and translations, and other flaws. Not all Enlightenment thinkers were anti-Christian, but most tended to believe it good and necessary to question traditional Christian beliefs. Pietists and revivalists thought that the best response to dead orthodoxy and modern paganism was also the best response to Enlightenment secularism and skepticism: proclamation of the gospel of Jesus Christ and appeal to people to repent and trust in Christ alone for salvation. Had not John Calvin himself argued that belief in the Bible as God's Word is by the "internal testimony of the Holy Spirit" and not by arguments and evidences? Fundamentalists, however, believed that the best response to the "acids of modernity" was tearing down "proud arguments" and militantly exposing them as errors, as well as strong reaffirmation of traditional, orthodox beliefs.

The prehistory of fundamentalism as an antimodernist and antiliberal evangelical movement begins with the so-called Princeton School of theology, best exemplified by five great Presbyterian theologians who taught at Princeton Theological Seminary in the nineteenth and early twentieth centuries: Archibald Alexander (1772–1851), Charles Hodge (1797–1878), Archibald Alexander Hodge (1823–86), Benjamin Breckenridge Warfield (1851–1921), and John Gresham Machen (1881–1937). Many evangelical Christians, especially evangelical theologians, look back to these Reformed exponents of Protestant orthodoxy as the true movers and shakers of evangelical theology, while admitting that Evangelicalism's folk religion is shaped more by revivalism.[13] J. Gresham Machen is often treated as the first and perhaps the greatest "true fundamentalist theologian" by historians of American Christianity, but he stood in a direct line of theological influence from Alexander through the Hodges (father and son) and Warfield (Machen's mentor). The Princeton School of theology and early fundamentalism (at its best) believed that authentic Christianity's enduring essence is orthodox doctrine—theological correctness—and attempted to systematize and defend it against the rising tides of Enlightenment skepticism and liberal Protestantism. In the process they sometimes forged uneasy alliances with revivalists, but by and large they did not consider Second Great Awakening revivalism and the Evangelicalism that stemmed from it very helpful. Nevertheless, they had a common enemy—skepticism about the truth claims of the gospel—and so they sometimes cooperated in spite of profound differences of style and substance.

Charles Hodge taught theology to more than two thousand students at Princeton Theological Seminary during his fifty-six-year tenure (1822–78). Without any doubt he was the most influential conservative Protestant theologian of nineteenth-century America. Although Hodge and Finney were very different, the comparison between them is irresistible. Hodge placed his stamp upon conservative evangelical theology just as Finney placed his stamp upon revivalistic Evangelicalism and the evangelical theology that has arisen within evangelical folk religion. They are probably the two most influential nineteenth-century evangelicals, and yet they were in many ways as different as night and day. Hodge was an ardent Calvinist steeped in Protestant scholasticism—the post-Reformation tendency to use rigorous logical methods to systematize the truths of divine revelation in Scripture. He was a powerful polemicist who argued vehemently against any and all deviations from traditional, orthodox Protestant belief among Christians. He was a social conservative who defended slavery and traditional gender roles in family and church. Just as Finney's *Lectures on Revivals of Religion* and *Lectures on Systematic Theology* influenced evangelicals inclined toward revivalism, Hodge's three-volume *Systematic Theology* (1872–73) profoundly influenced evangelicals inclined toward fundamentalism.

Hodge believed that the best way to confront and counter the deleterious effects of the Enlightenment upon Christianty was to use its own methods in defense of the truth of Christianity. This he sought to do without capitulation or compromise by defining Christian theology as a science. Of course, he was not the first to regard theology as a "science" in the sense of "wisdom" or "disciplined study," but Hodge opened his systematic theology by describing it as an inductive science of facts similar to the natural sciences: "We find in nature the facts which the chemist or the mechanical philosopher has to examine, and from them to ascertain the laws by which they are determined. So the Bible contains the truths which the theologian has to collect, authenticate, arrange,

---

13. See for example David Wells, *No Place for Truth: Whatever Happened to Evangelical Theology?* (Grand Rapids: Wm. B. Eerdmans, 1993) and "The Stout and Persistent 'Theology' of Charles Hodge," *Christianity Today* 18, no. 23 (August 30, 1974): 10–15.

and exhibit in their internal relation to each other."[14] Throughout his systematic theology Hodge attempted to demonstrate that theology is scientific in the modern sense and not at all superstitious or obscurantist. Just as the natural scientist observes natural phenomena and organizes its data and deduces principles from it, so the theological scientist observes divine revelation in Scripture and organizes its truths into a coherent whole that, as a whole, provides a better explanation of the universe and human life than any competing philosophy or theology.

Thus, Hodge tended to treat the Bible as a presystematized systematic theology and systematic theology as a comprehensive, rationally coherent worldview. Some critics have labeled this approach to theology the "evangelical Enlightenment" because it so closely parallels the general attitude of the Enlightenment toward knowledge. The particular branch of the Enlightenment being used to understand Hodge in this case is Scottish common sense realism, which argued against David Hume's skepticism that reasonable people are allowed to make certain assumptions about the objective reality of nature outside the mind and about our human mind and senses and their ability to grasp that reality. Hodge seemed to believe that if he could present conservative Reformed Protestant theology as a rationally coherent system of divinely revealed facts, a system that explains human existence better than any competing account, the tide of modern skepticism could be resisted. This approach to theology was taken up by later evangelical theologians and made the basis of many truth claims about its superiority to secular and liberal systems of thought.

Another area of Hodge's theology that profoundly influenced later fundamentalism and conservative evangelical theology is his doctrine of Scripture. Hodge stood in a tradition that highly valued Scripture as God's Word written and as authoritative above traditions. He noticed a trend toward redefining Scripture's authority within the churches being affected by Enlightenment modernism, and he wanted to guard and protect the Bible from its critics both inside and outside the church. He developed a doctrine of Scripture that he believed would do that—the doctrine of the Bible's verbal, plenary inspiration and infallibility. While denying that Scripture (the canon of sixty-six books that compose the Protestant Bible) was written under any mechanical compulsion, Hodge argued that the supernatural process of communication known as "inspiration" extended from God through the human authors to the very words, with the result that what they wrote were the very words of God and thus infallible:

> On this subject the common doctrine of the Church is, and ever has been, that inspiration was an influence of the Holy Spirit on the minds of certain select men, which rendered them the organs of God for the infallible communication of his mind and will. They were in such a sense the organs of God, that what they said God said.[15]

Hodge argued that since God controls human beings in salvation without robbing them of their personalities, God can and did control the human authors of Scripture, so that they wrote what he wanted them to write, without in any way detracting from their personal involvement in the process. The Bible, then, is God's oracle to humanity. Even if there are minor inconsistencies and discrepancies in it, Hodge averred, they are not sufficient to detract from its supernatural origin and authority. For the Princeton theologian, only this account of Scripture upholds its authority; any other one (mystical, intuitionist, naturalistic) undermines its authority and thereby undermines Christian truth.

A later Princeton theologian, even closer to fundamentalism than Hodge, attempted to nail down even more firmly this high doctrine of Scripture in the face of

---

14. Charles Hodge, *Systematic Theology*, vol. 1 (Grand Rapids: Wm. B. Eerdmans, 1973), 1.
15. Ibid., 154.

mounting skepticism about the Bible's reliability and compatibility with modern knowledge. Benjamin Breckenridge Warfield taught systematic theology at Princeton beginning in 1887. During his tenure at the Presbyterian seminary, so-called modernism or theological liberalism began to be felt on its faculty, and Warfield fought against it with all his might. Like Hodge, whom he greatly admired, he was an ardent Calvinist and had little sympathy for the revivalist movement among evangelicals. Also like Hodge, he considered true evangelical Christianity to be synonymous with confessional-Protestant orthodoxy, which he thought was entirely dependent upon a view of Scripture as verbally inspired and inerrant. Warfield's legacy to fundamentalism and conservative evangelical theology is largely in his volume *Revelation and Inspiration*, which contains several essays on subjects related to the Bible and in which the Princeton theologian argued that strict inerrancy of Scripture is necessary to its authority. Warfield never tired of arguing that any demonstrable error in the Bible would necessarily mean that it is not trustworthy as God's authoritative Word and that Christianity would in that case rest on very shaky ground.

The Princeton theologian was locked in debate with the beginnings of influential higher criticism of the Bible in his own denomination and the wider Protestant world. Some liberal theologians such as Washington Gladden and biblical scholars such as Charles Briggs were calling for fairly radical revisions of Christian doctrines, including the doctrine of Scripture, in the light of modern knowledge. Among other things, the reconstructionists claimed that belief in the Bible's supernatural, plenary, verbal inspiration and infallibility or inerrancy was no longer possible due to inconsistencies within Scripture itself and between scriptural texts and known facts of history and cosmology. Warfield was incensed by such claims and argued that they were based on shaky evidence and conflicted not only with secondary Christian beliefs but with Christianity's very foundations. Unlike certain later fundamentalist theologians, he did not claim that Christianity itself, let alone the gospel of Jesus Christ, rests necessarily on the doctrine of plenary, verbal inspiration; but he did claim that denial of it inevitably undermines other, if not all, fundamental Christian beliefs. He extended this reasoning to Scripture's inerrancy, which he saw as a logical deduction from its supernatural inspiration as "God's oracles." If Scripture contains errors in any subject, he asked, how is it to be trusted even in matters pertaining to salvation?

Because of this conflict with the skeptics, Warfield defined the Christian doctrine of Scripture more precisely than most Protestant theologians before him:

> The Church, then, has held from the beginning that the Bible is the Word of God in such a sense that its words, though written by men and bearing indelibly impressed upon them the marks of their human origin, were written, nevertheless, under such an influence of the Holy Ghost as to be also the words of God, the adequate expression of His mind and will. It has always recognized that this conception of co-authorship implies that the Spirit's superintendence extends to the choice of the words by the human authors (verbal inspiration), and preserves its product from everything inconsistent with a divine authorship—thus securing, among other things, that entire truthfulness which is everywhere presupposed in and asserted for Scripture by the Biblical writers (inerrancy).[16]

Warfield argued that this definition of the doctrine of Scripture by no means implies divine dictation, although some critics have had great difficulty distinguishing the two. The Princeton theologian also argued that this is the Christian doctrine of Scripture because it is the doctrine held by the biblical writers themselves, and that to question it is to question the credibility of the Bible itself.[17]

---

16. Benjamin Breckinridge Warfield, *The Inspiration and Authority of the Bible* (Philadelphia: Presbyterian & Reformed Publishing Co., 1948), 173.

17. Ibid., 175.

Thus, Warfield sought to stave off the attacks on traditional Christianity by skeptics and revisionists by affirming and defending the Bible's absoluteness—including detailed, technical inerrancy—as God's oracles. The Bible contains "difficulties" and these may appear to be minor errors, he admitted, but these were becoming fewer as historical studies and archeology confirmed more and more of the biblical record; those difficulties (e.g., discrepancies, apparent contradictions) that remain are so minor as to represent no real problem for believing in Scripture's trustworthiness. He compared them to the specks of sandstone detected here and there in the marble of the Parthenon: "They do not for the most part require explaining away, but only to be fairly understood in order to avoid them. They constitute no real strain upon faith, but when approached in a candid spirit one is left continually marveling at the excessive fewness of those which do not, like ghosts, melt away from vision as soon as faced."[18] In Warfield's hands, then, the Bible became an impregnable fortress of faith providing absolute certainty beyond reasonable doubt about all matters crucial to salvation. For if it is God's infallible oracle, as it claims to be and as it proves itself to be, it serves as a proper foundation for the edifice of Christian belief in an often hostile, increasingly secular and skeptical world, as well as in an increasingly apostate church.

Hodge's and Warfield's theological method and doctrine of Scripture had significant influence beyond Princeton and Presbyterianism. Baptist students earned doctoral degrees under them and returned to teach in Baptist seminaries, bringing Princeton Theology with them. James Petrigu Boyce (1827–88), for example, studied theology under Charles Hodge at Princeton and went on to found Southern Baptist Theological Seminary in 1859. The influence of Princeton Theology is indelibly stamped on that seminary through the "Abstract of Principles" that Boyce wrote and all professors are required to sign. Methodists were relatively untouched by Princeton Theology as were many, if not most, turn-of-the-century revivalists in the Pentecostal-Holiness movement. Many evangelicals knew little or nothing of Princeton, its theology, and its theologians, but eventually the evangelical movement as a whole was touched by it through the last of the great Princeton School theologians, J. Gresham Machen.

Machen was one of Warfield's brightest students at Princeton during the first decade of the twentieth century. After completing graduate degrees at both Princeton University and Princeton Seminary, the Baltimore scholar studied New Testament and theology at two of Germany's leading universities—Marburg and Göttingen. He then served as instructor and professor of New Testament at his alma mater from 1906 until his departure to help found Westminster Theological Seminary in Philadelphia in 1929. Machen and some of his conservative colleagues believed that Princeton Seminary was departing from its true, historical heritage and succumbing to liberal influences. Westminster was to be the new home of "old school Princeton theology." In 1935 Machen was suspended from ministry by the Presbyterian Church because he helped found a conservative mission board rivaling the official board of the church, and in 1936 he helped found a new conservative denomination that eventually came to be called the Orthodox Presbyterian Church. Both Westminster Seminary and the Orthodox Presbyterian Church have exercised influence within Evangelicalism far beyond their sizes through conservative, Reformed theologians such as Machen, Cornelius Van Til, Gordon Clark, Harold John Ockenga, and Francis Schaeffer. Over the years both the seminary and denomination (which are not officially related to each other) suffered severe controversies and divisions as professors and ministers sought to preserve strict doctrinal orthodoxy against any and all deviations, real or imagined. One of militant, separatistic fundamentalism's most outspoken leaders, Carl McIntire

---

18. Ibid., 221.

(1906–2002), left both Westminster and the Orthodox Presbyterian Church rather noisily to found even more conservative Faith Theological Seminary and the Bible Presbyterian Church.

Machen's influence on Evangelicalism and evangelical theology is manifold. Without doubt he was a great scholar of the New Testament who knew his liberal opponents well. He studied under them and understood them before publishing his disagreements. Whereas Hodge and Warfield had been loyal opponents of the increasingly influential liberal mood of theology and biblical studies within the Presbyterian Church, Machen advocated division rather than compromise or coexistence. His little book *Christianity and Liberalism* (1923), a major splash on the theological scene, represented a manifesto of conservative Protestant Christianity against liberal theology, which the author described as a different religion from Christianity. The book pitted Machen's version of historic, orthodox Protestant Christianity (which was colored by Princeton Theology) against the mainline, liberal Protestant Christianity represented by influential ministers such as Harry Emerson Fosdick and left little room for a mediating, middle ground. Influential secular columnist and cultural commentator Walter Lippmann read Machen's manifesto and sided with it (without becoming a conservative himself, of course!). Machen's little volume appeared at the height of the great liberal-fundamentalist controversy that consumed several mainline denominations for several decades and eventually led to schisms within their ranks. Without doubt the book contributed to that situation by convincing many conservative evangelicals within the historic, mainline Protestant denominations—especially the Northern Baptist Convention and the Presbyterian Church in the U.S.A. ("Northern Presbyterian")—that they must leave those "apostate" churches.

The 1920s and 1930s probably saw the foundings of more new conservative denominations and new, independent, conservative Bible colleges than any other period of time in American history. Machen was hailed as a hero and embraced by fundamentalists everywhere, but he hardly fit the stereotypical image of fundamentalists promoted by writer H. L. Mencken, who portrayed them as ignorant, legalistic, and mean-spirited. Machen was a refined and reserved man of letters who saw nothing wrong with strong drink or smoking in moderation and was extremely uncomfortable at revival meetings. He believed that some combination of the theory of biological evolution with the Christian doctrine of creation was possible and had little use for the anti-evolution crusades launched and led by many fundamentalist leaders.

The Princeton School of theology from Alexander through Machen formed a kind of second pole to revivalism within Evangelicalism and evangelical theology. Revivalism, based on Pietism but going beyond it, created Evangelicalism in its awakenings, frontier revivals, mass evangelistic campaigns, and numerous spiritual retreats, conferences, and evangelistic networks. Its emphasis on *conversional* piety led evangelical theology to focus a great deal on salvation, including especially the experience of the new birth, the regenerating power of God through faith, and the progress of sanctification toward sinless perfection or "victorious Christian living." Princeton Theology, based on Puritanism but going beyond it, stamped Evangelicalism and evangelical theology with an emphasis on theological correctness and especially the foundations of orthodoxy in the doctrine of Scripture as supernaturally, verbally inspired and inerrant.

These two poles or impulses rest uneasily alongside each other within Evangelicalism and evangelical theology. One is passionate, relatively subjective (personal, inward, experience-oriented) and the other is cognitive, relatively objective (propositional, rational, intellectually oriented). During the last two decades of the nineteenth century and the first two decades of the twentieth century, many, if not most, North American Protestant Christians were coming increasingly under the influence of this dipolar Evangelicalism. Among Protestants, only Episcopalians and Lutherans were relatively untouched by either pole. Increasingly by the 1920s most Protestants of most denominations were finding the combination of the two poles irresistible. Wheaton College, perhaps the stackpole of evangelical higher education, begun under the influence of Finney-style revivalism in the middle of the nineteenth century, during the 1930s came increasingly under the influence of Princeton theology. Many churches and institutions dominated by Princeton-style conservative theology came to be influenced by revivalism.

HOLINESS-PENTECOSTALISM AND EVANGELICAL THEOLOGY

Two movements that especially influenced Evangelicalism and evangelical theology in the twentieth century are the Holiness-Pentecostal movement and fundamentalism. Many people tend to equate them or subsume the former under the latter as an especially emotional form of fundamentalism. However, this is not correct. In spite of certain similarities, the Holiness-Pentecostal movement and fundamentalism moved on separate tracks. When the postfundamentalist "neo-evangelical" coalition was forged in the 1940s and 1950s, it left separatistic fundamentalism behind while retaining many fundamentalist concerns and habits. It embraced most of the Holiness-Pentecostal movement while shunning its most extreme forms and manifestations.

The Holiness-Pentecostal movement is older than fundamentalism, so it will be described and discussed first. It grew out of revivalism in North America in the middle of the nineteenth century and may have been founded by a woman—Phoebe Palmer (1807–74). Palmer was a New York Methodist married to a medical doctor. In her thirties she became involved in a small group called the "Tuesday Meeting for the Promotion of Holiness" modeled after John and Charles Wesley's "Holy Club" at Oxford University. She studied Wesley's writings on sanctification and especially his *A Plain Account of Christian Perfection* and developed her own version of Methodist "entire sanctification," which she popularized through books such as *The Way of Holiness* and through a magazine entitled *Guide to Holiness*. Palmer led or preached in more than three hundred camp meetings and revivals throughout North America and Great Britain and without doubt was the single most influential personality in the rise of the Holiness movement, which stressed conversion, a "second blessing" subsequent to conversion called Spirit baptism or baptism of the Holy Spirit, and "holiness unto the Lord" through personal consecration to Jesus Christ and cleansing from the corruption of sin through the indwelling presence and power of the Holy Spirit. The New York Holiness revivalist developed a three-step process for acquiring entire sanctification known as "altar theology": entire consecration of oneself to God, trust in God to keep his promise to sanctify that which is laid on the altar in consecration (the self), and witnessing to what God has done. This simple, straightforward method of sanctification caught on among many of the Methodist renewal offshoots and became a standard formula holding the Holiness churches and organizations together.

The Holiness movement emerged out of various independent organizations for renewal within the Methodist Episcopal Church and other Protestant denominations and some that had no denominational roots or affiliation. In 1867 these groups came together in a loose coalition known as the National Camp Meeting Association for the Promotion of Holiness or National Holiness Association. In 1971 the name of this umbrella organization was changed to the Christian Holiness Association. Although the association was mostly lay led and loosely organized, it helped give impetus to a growing movement that involved many small, new denominations, including the Church of the Nazarene, the Free Methodist Church, the Wesleyan Holiness Church, the Fire-Baptized Holiness Church, and the Church of God in Christ. Holiness people believed in the second blessing taught by Phoebe Palmer—the Spirit baptism for entire sanctification. They believed that the fallen, sinful nature could be cleansed and sinful urges and impulses eradicated in a moment so that from that time on the sanctified Christian would no longer struggle daily against temptation ("the flesh") or sin presumptuously. Such a person would, so Holiness preachers and teachers proclaimed, experience "Christian perfection," even though he or she would still commit sins of omission out of ignorance.

Camp meetings, conferences, and new churches centered around this experience sprang up all over North America and spread to other parts of the world through Holiness missions organizations. Perhaps the best-known Holiness denomination in the world is the Salvation Army, founded by Methodist Holiness social reformer William Booth in England in 1865. Many nineteenth-century Holiness Christians were social reformers in the forefronts of movements for equal rights for African Americans and women. Holiness denominations were among the first Christian churches to ordain women. When the new evangelical coalition emerged out of fundamentalism in the 1940s and 1950s, Holiness groups and leaders were involved; Free Methodists were among the founders of the National Association of Evangelicals.

Pentecostalism grew out of the wider Holiness movement in the first decade of the twentieth century.[19] "Wider" here indicates an influence of Holiness revivalism far beyond the specific boundaries of the National Holiness Association. Many North American and British revivalists of the later nineteenth century were proclaiming a "higher life" message that included a second-blessing experience subsequent to conversion that propels Christians into a more profound relationship with God through Jesus Christ and results in peace from the struggle between the spiritual side of the person and the world, the flesh, and the devil. This higher dimension of spiritual life, the revivalists taught, is initiated by a Spirit infilling or Spirit baptism, such as Jesus' disciples experienced on the day of Pentecost (Acts 2), and results in extraordinary power to live a consecrated life set apart unto God and to exercise the special, supernatural gifts of the Holy Spirit ("charismata") such as divine healing.

The Keswick movement, begun in Great Britain in 1876, emphasized higher Christian life through cessation of effort to live a life pleasing to God and replacement of that effort with complete emptiness of self and fullness of the Holy Spirit. Leaders of the Keswick movement, Great Britain's equivalent to the North American Holiness movement, included F. B. Meyer, Andrew Murray, and G. Campbell Morgan. Keswick teaching tended to be less emotional and somewhat more mystical than Holiness revivalism, but the basic impulse was the same—Christian perfectionism through Spirit baptism. In New York and New England two American revivalists of the later nineteenth and early twentieth centuries especially laid the groundwork for Pentecostalism: A. J. Gordon (1836–95) and A. B. Simpson (1843–1919). Through their devotional writings, preaching, conference teaching, and hymns, these men promoted a popular version of Keswick higher-life theology that focused on the infilling of the Holy Spirit for power over sin and power for Christian service. A. B. Simpson, who founded a new denomination known as the Christian and Missionary Alliance, taught that divine healing was provided for by Christ's atoning death on the cross and that faith-filled prayer for healing should be a normal aspect of higher life Christianity.

By the dawn of the new century in 1901, the North American Holiness movement was at its peak of popularity and fervor and Holiness ideas about the second blessing,

---

19. For an account of the rise of Pentecostalism see Harvey Cox, *Fire from Heaven: The Rise of Pentecostal Spirituality and the Reshaping of Religion in the Twenty-first Century* (Reading, MA: Addison-Wesley Publishing Co., 1995).

entire sanctification, higher life, divine healing, and the infilling of the Holy Spirit as an enduement with power for all Christians were permeating evangelical Christianity in many denominations and among nondenominational Christians. Holiness camp meetings, protracted revivals, higher-life conferences, and Bible training institutes were cropping up all over North America. Out of this milieu emerged the Pentecostal movement. The precise date of its birth is debated by scholars. Some argue that it was born at the moment of the birth of the twentieth century—midnight, January 1, 1901. At that moment (or near it) a woman student at a Holiness Bible institute in Topeka, Kansas, spoke in tongues as she received the second-blessing experience of Spirit baptism. The founder of Topeka's Bethel Bible School, Charles Parham, interpreted speaking in tongues as the "initial, physical evidence" of the baptism of the Holy Spirit and spread the message of this special sign of the "latter rain" (of God's Spirit upon all flesh) throughout North America. Other Holiness revivalists took up that message and speaking in tongues became for many Holiness Christians the sine qua non of higher Christian life. Some scholars date the birth of Pentecostalism to the Azusa Street Revival in Los Angeles, California, in 1906 led by African American Holiness evangelist William Seymour. The revival lasted for months, and thousands of Holiness Christians flocked to it from everywhere to witness what was happening as people prophesied, spoke in tongues, claimed divine healing. Many of them went back to their home churches with the new sign of Spirit baptism.

Some Holiness Christians accepted the Pentecostal message—sometimes called the "Full Gospel"—and some did not. Several Holiness denominations split over it; others converted completely to it. The predominantly African American Church of God in Christ became Pentecostal. White Pentecostal leaders founded the Assemblies of God denomination in 1914. They disagreed with the Holiness distinctive of entire sanctification but agreed with A. B. Simpson about Spirit baptism and divine healing. They expected Simpson to join the new movement, but instead he published his policy toward speaking in tongues as "Seek not; forbid not," and his Christian and Missionary Alliance denomination split. Many of the white founders of Pentecostalism in North America were former followers of Simpson.

Pentecostalism represented an intense form of revivalism. Its theological underpinnings were the same as those of other orthodox Arminian Protestant Christian groups, although the movement divided over the doctrine of the Trinity early in its history. Some Pentecostals rejected orthodox Trinitarianism in favor of a "Oneness" message that reduced the persons of the Trinity to manifestations of one person. This branch of Pentecostalism, sometimes known as Jesus Only or Oneness Pentecostalism, was rejected by the majority and never played any significant role in Evangelicalism. Above and beyond basic Protestant orthodoxy, however, Pentecostals embraced the higher-life message of A. B. Simpson and/or the Holiness message of Phoebe Palmer and the National Holiness Association. Some Pentecostals believe in entire sanctification and some do not; all believe in the experience of second blessing of Spirit baptism or Spirit infilling for all Christians with the accompanying, verifying sign of speaking in tongues. They base this doctrine on a perceived pattern in the New Testament book of Acts in which early converts to Christianity spoke in tongues and prophesied when they were filled with the Holy Spirit. Nearly all Pentecostals adopted a theology borrowed from A. B. Simpson: the so-called "foursquare gospel" of Jesus Christ as Savior (including his deity, lordship and blood atonement for remission of sins); Baptizer with the Holy Spirit (including his special indwelling presence for power for holy living and Christian service); Healer (including his provision for physical healing in his atoning death on the cross and by his bodily resurrection from the dead); and Coming King (including his imminent, visible return to establish his kingdom on earth). Like the Holiness movement from which it emerged, Pentecostalism is thoroughly

Arminian in its theology of salvation, emphasizing not divine sovereignty in predestination but instead proclaiming unlimited atonement and every person's ability to respond freely to the gospel unto salvation.

The Holiness-Pentecostal movement that flourished between the mid-nineteenth century and the mid-twentieth century (and still exists and grows) was intensely experiential and emotional. It tended to downplay theological correctness and doctrinal precision, as well as intellectual inquiry in general. Some scholars have argued that it was and remains severely anti-intellectual and otherworldly in ethos, even though in the later part of the twentieth century some genuine biblical and theological scholarship has arisen from within its ranks. Its emphasis on emotional experiences, miracles, rejection of "worldliness" in appearance and amusement, and imminent return of Christ gained it the pejorative descriptor "Holy Rollers" and caused even many evangelical Christians to reject it as fanatical. B. B. Warfield published a scholarly volume against the movement entitled *Counterfeit Miracles,* and many conservative Protestants argued that the so-called "sign gifts" of the Holy Spirit such as divine healing, prophecy, and speaking in tongues ceased when the canon of inspired Scripture was completed (cessationism).

Throughout the first half of the twentieth century, Pentecostalism especially languished in a limbo state in relation to the rest of conservative, evangelical Protestant Christianity. It was harshly condemned by nearly everyone, including its own Holiness and higher-life cousins. When the National Association of Evangelicals was formed in 1942, however, the decision was made to include both Holiness and Pentecostal denominations. The Free Methodist Church and the Assemblies of God were both among its charter members, and leaders of those two groups served on the NAE's board in later years. By the 1970s and 1980s Holiness and Pentecostal Christians were in the thick of Evangelicalism in North America, and their influence on evangelical worship, spirituality, and doctrine has been noticeable. They have always remained, however, a distinct subset of Evangelicalism. The vast majority of evangelicals have never embraced either entire sanctification or speaking in tongues. The legacy of the Holiness-Pentecostal movement to evangelical theology is an emphasis on higher spiritual life—especially second-blessing-type experiences subsequent to conversion—and interest in the gifts of the Holy Spirit. While many evangelical Christians have little or no use for emotional displays of spirituality, almost all have been affected by the renewal of the doctrine of the Holy Spirit and the Spirit's work in the Christian life introduced by Holiness-Pentecostal revivalists. So-called "contemporary worship" (chorus singing with arms raised, hand clapping to energetic "praise and worship" choruses, informal worship) is an obvious extension of certain worship styles that were born in the Holiness-Pentecostal meetings of the turn of the century. Another possible legacy of Holiness-Pentecostalism to the wider evangelical community is an active disinterest in rigorous biblical and theological study, doctrine, and evangelical intellectual creativity and participation in the wider culture.[20]

FUNDAMENTALISM AND EVANGELICAL THEOLOGY

In the immediate background of Evangelicalism and evangelical theology lies fundamentalism or the fundamentalist movement. Some untutored religious journalists and commentators tend to equate fundamentalism with Evangelicalism in an overly simplistic way. The connection is correct, but a distinction is important. Some people tend to equate fundamentalism with revivalism in general. Again, there is a connection, but

---

20. See Mark A. Noll, *The Scandal of the Evangelical Mind* (Grand Rapids: Wm. B. Eerdmans, 1994).

there is also an important distinction. *Fundamentalism* is a term used correctly to describe three distinct but interrelated religious phenomena. During the 1970s many journalists and scholars began to use the term *fundamentalism* to describe any and all militant religious reactions to modernity.[21] By modernity they mean the secularizing impulses that began with the scientific revolution of the seventeenth and eighteenth centuries and with its philosophical counterpart in the cultural revolution known as the Enlightenment. In this sense, fundamentalism includes militantly antimodern conservatives within all world religions. This fairly recent, generally secular journalistic definition of *fundamentalism* is not used here.

An older and more historically correct meaning of fundamentalism is the conservative Protestant reaction to the rise of liberal Protestantism in the later decades of the nineteenth century and early decades of the twentieth century. All such fundamentalists also called themselves evangelicals and regarded themselves as guardians and defenders of evangelical truth in an increasingly secularized and liberal theological world. In this sense, B. B. Warfield and his student J. Gresham Machen were fundamentalists. So were many, if not nearly all, conservative evangelicals of the first few decades of the twentieth century. A few evangelical groups sat out the so-called liberal-fundamentalist conflict that raged within mainline Protestantism at that time. They tended to be immigrant Pietist churches and Holiness-Pentecostals.

A third, more historically legitimate, definition of *fundamentalism* is the narrower, more militant and separatistic movement of conservative Protestants that emerged out of disappointment and despair in the 1920s and 1930s, as the major Protestant denominations of North America were lost for conservative theology and became increasingly liberal and pluralistic. The difference between early fundamentalism and later fundamentalism is not so much one of doctrine as of mood. The single most important distinction between them has to do with later fundamentalism's adoption of a militant stance toward exposing the "heresies" of other Christians and of a policy of separation not only from liberal Christians but also from fellow evangelicals who do not separate from liberal Christian denominations and organizations.[22]

Scholars do not agree on the precise beginnings of early Christian fundamentalism. The term itself arose in stages. Some conservative Protestants were talking about the need to reaffirm the "fundamentals of the faith" in the 1890s as they became aware of the influence of higher criticism of the Bible (i.e., literary criticism) in their denomination's seminaries. In direct response to perceived destructive biblical scholarship within those seminaries, conservative Protestants began to organize Bible conferences around the country where speakers explored biblical themes and exhorted listeners to take the Bible literally as God's Word. One such influential Bible conference, the Niagara Bible Conference, began in the 1860s (before moving to Niagara-on-the-Lake, Ontario) and lasted until 1897. Each year thousands of pastors and lay Christians flocked to the summer conference at Niagara-on-the-Lake in Ontario, Canada, to hear prominent conservative biblical teachers and expositors teach about subjects such as the second coming of Jesus Christ and the importance of biblical inerrancy. In 1878 the conference produced a list of essentials of authentic Christian belief—the "Niagara Creed"—which may have been the first list of "fundamentals" other than the historic creeds and confessions of Christianity and the Reformation. It included biblical inerrancy and the "personal and premillennial advent" of Jesus Christ. After that,

---

21. See *The Fundamentalism Project*, 7 vols., ed. Scott Appleby and Martin Marty (Chicago: University of Chicago Press, 1991–95).

22. See Alan P. F. Sell, *Theology in Turmoil: The Roots, Course, and Significance of the Conservative-Liberal Debate in Modern Theology* (Grand Rapids: Baker Book House, 1986).

many such lists of fundamentals were proposed by conservative Protestants in reaction to the rise of liberalism within their denominations. Most such lists included biblical inspiration and inerrancy, the virgin birth of Christ (because it was increasingly under attack by liberals of the "new theology"), Christ's resurrection, salvation by the blood atonement of Christ on the cross, and Christ's second coming.

The term *fundamentalism* may derive from a set of booklets entitled *The Fundamentals*, published between 1910 and 1915 and sent free of charge to all Protestant ministers, church workers, and YMCA directors by two California businessmen. The booklets contained articles on the Bible, doctrine, and controversial issues by leading conservative theological scholars such as B. B. Warfield, Southern Baptist seminary president and theologian E. Y. Mullins, Scottish theologian James Orr. The first use of the labels *fundamentalist* and *fundamentalism*, however, appeared in 1920 in the magazine *Baptist Watchman-Examiner*, whose editor, Curtis Lee Laws, coined them to designate conservative Protestant orthodoxy in contrast to liberal, modernist theology that was skeptical toward traditional doctrines and miracles. Around the same time, a leading conservative Baptist minister, William Bell Riley (1861–1947) of Minneapolis, Minnesota, founded the World's Christian Fundamentals Association to counter liberalism's influence. By the mid-1920s *fundamentalism* was a widely used term for relatively aggressive conservatism in Protestant theology in North America.

The early fundamentalists may have been very conservative in almost every sense, but they were not militant or separatistic. They remained within their mainline Protestant denominations, hoping to reform them away from debilitating modernism (i.e., overaccommodation to the skeptical spirit of the modern age) toward what they regarded as historic Protestant orthodoxy. This would be true especially of the great Scottish Presbyterian theologian James Orr (1844–1913), who made several trips to the United States to give lectures and aid in the conservative effort to stem the tide of liberal theology. His books *The Christian View of God and the World* (1893) and *The Ritschlian Theology and the Evangelical Faith* (1897) represented scholarly critiques of liberal theology without harsh polemics or narrow, sectarian presentations of Protestant orthodoxy. Orr never did advocate belief in the inerrancy of the Bible; yet he was embraced by American fundamentalists as an ally in the cause. Later fundamentalists would reject fellowship with anyone who, like Orr and other early conservative Protestant scholars, did not wholeheartedly affirm biblical inerrancy and other peculiar beliefs such as a pretribulational rapture of the church (dispensationalism). J. Gresham Machen was another early fundamentalist who, although quite conservative and a true believer in biblical inerrancy, tried to keep the antiliberal crusade among conservatives focused on true essentials of Christian belief. However, his *Christianity and Liberalism*, along with his own departure from Princeton Seminary and the Presbyterian Church, gave impetus to the development of later "second-stage" fundamentalism with its militancy of rhetoric and separatistic behavior.

Several developments in the battle between conservatives and liberals for control of America's major Protestant institutions in the 1920s resulted in the rise of later, second-stage fundamentalism. The famous Scopes "monkey trial" in Dayton, Tennessee, in 1925 convinced many fundamentalists that American culture—including the media and church institutions—was set against them. The Northern Baptist Convention and the Presbyterian Church in the U.S.A. took firm stands against exclusion of moderates and liberals from their ministerial ranks. Leading Protestant seminaries such as the University of Chicago's Divinity School and Union Theological Seminary in New York fell decisively into the liberal camp. Liberal preacher Harry Emerson Fosdick Jr. appeared on the cover of *Time* magazine and was widely applauded for his stand against fundamentalism. To many fundamentalists, all this was sure evidence of the apostasy of the American mainline Protestant denominations.

Like many disillusioned Puritans in seventeenth-century England, the fundamentalists began to harden their own categories and exit mainline Protestantism to found smaller, archconservative, rival denominations and institutions. William Bell Riley (1861–1947), a leading warhorse of fundamentalism, led the transition between the movement's early and later manifestations. He added belief in the premillennial return of Christ (i.e., belief in a literal one-thousand-year kingdom of God on earth after Christ's return) to his organization's list of fundamentals of Christianity and began to urge separation of true conservative Christians from all doctrinally reduced or polluted denominations and organizations. His own Northern Baptist Convention divided many times as fundamentalists of different types and degrees broke away to found new Baptist groups. The same happened in the Presbyterian Church and, to a lesser extent, in the Methodist Episcopal Church and the American Congregational Church. Almost overnight numerous new fundamentalist denominations, organizations, and institutions sprang up. Fundamentalist leaders such as John R. Rice, Bob Jones, and Carl McIntire criticized fellow conservatives who would not leave the mainline churches or who remained in any kind of Christian cooperation or fellowship with them.

Second-stage fundamentalists by and large condemned not only belief in evolution (including theistic evolution) but also "compromise" with "Godless evolution," which is how they regarded any attempt to accommodate Christian belief about origins with modern science. They adopted in whole or in part the relatively new approach to biblical interpretation and the end times known as dispensationalism and insisted that faithfulness to Scripture required belief in a literal millennium, if not a "secret rapture" of the church before a seven-year "tribulation period" at the end of history as we know it. They developed belief in and practice of "secondary separation," which means rejecting cooperation and fellowship with even fellow evangelicals who did not remain separated from "apostate" liberals in the mainline churches. Their formal or informal lists of fundamentals (essentials) of Christian belief and practice grew until little remained to private interpretation or opinion. Many of the leading fundamentalists were willing, if not eager, to support segregation of the races, anti-Catholicism in public speech and policy, and extreme right-wing politics. With regard to the doctrine of Scripture, at least some of them reverted past Princeton orthodoxy to blatant advocacy of a dictation theory of the Bible's origins. John R. Rice, for example, wrote that "God raised up men, prepared the men and prepared their vocabularies, and God dictated the very words which they would put down in the Scriptures." The spirit of second-stage fundamentalism is conveyed clearly in Rice's harsh criticism of anyone who disagreed with him: "Shame! So you want big prophets and a little God, do you? You do not want a man simply hearing what God says and writing it down, do you? Well, then, your attitude is simply the carnal attitude of the unbelieving world that always wants to give man credit instead of God, whether for salvation or inspiration."[23]

Many evangelical Protestant Christians who were not of the same militant, separatistic spirit as men like Riley, Jones, Rice, and McIntire continued to call themselves fundamentalists throughout the 1930s and 1940s. But the label became more and more problematic for anyone who wished to be taken seriously as thoughtful, reflective, and even relatively gentle and open-minded. By the beginning of the 1940s many conservative, evangelical Protestants in North America and Great Britain were disillusioned with the course and cause of second-stage fundamentalism and wanted to reform it. Such reform of fundamentalism began with the founding of a new organization by a

---

23. Quoted in Donald K. McKim, *What Christians Believe about the Bible* (Nashville: Thomas Nelson Publishers, 1985), 57.

leading moderately fundamentalist Protestant minister named Harold John Ockenga (1904–85), who pastored influential Park Street Congregational Church in Boston, Massachusetts. Together with several other prominent conservatives who were disillusioned with separatistic fundamentalism, Ockenga formed the New England Fellowship to be a panevangelical alliance transcending narrow, sectarian boundaries. In 1942 the National Association of Evangelicals emerged out of the New England Fellowship and postfundamentalist, new Evangelicalism was born.

POSTFUNDAMENTALIST EVANGELICAL THEOLOGY

The Evangelicalism that forms the context for this resource on evangelical theology is the postfundamentalist, new evangelical coalition that came into existence as a result of the efforts of Ockenga and his colleagues in the 1940s. Of course, they did not create an entire new religious movement. Instead, they managed to reform the fundamentalist movement by giving it a new face, so to speak. They reorganized and refurbished it and pushed out to its periphery those militant, separatistic leaders who had captivated it throughout the 1930s.[24] The latter continued to exist, of course, and so the two movements—later fundamentalism (militant, separatistic) and the new Evangelicalism (irenic, cooperative)—have existed alongside each other since then as the two wings of conservative Protestant Christianity. Eventually Jerry Falwell of Lynchburg, Virginia, emerged as the new spokesman for fundamentalism, even as Billy Graham emerged as the spokesman for Evangelicalism. They believe most of the same doctrines, but their approaches to culture and the churches are very different.

When Ockenga and his colleagues were organizing the National Association of Evangelicals (NAE) in 1942, Carl McIntire and some of his fundamentalist colleagues were organizing a rival, more separatistic umbrella organization called the American Council of Churches (later the International Council of Christian Churches). Talks were held between the two groups to see if they could merge as one evangelical-fundamentalist alliance of churches, but the NAE's inclusion of the Holiness-Pentecostal groups was a stumbling block for McIntire, who considered Pentecostals deluded. More importantly, however, Ockenga's group had visions of a "broad tent Evangelicalism" that would include as many conversionist, conservative Protestants as possible—not so much to fight liberalism in the mainline churches (which had their own Federal Council of Churches), but to coordinate activities among evangelicals and provide a greater evangelical witness to culture at large. The NAE charter and vision were too broad for McIntire and most other fundamentalists, so the merger never occurred.

The NAE produced a minimal statement of faith and adopted as its motto "In essentials unity, in non-essentials liberty, in all things charity [love]." While belief in Scripture's inspiration and authority are required, NAE does not require belief in inerrancy of the Bible or in premillennialism. Membership has been very diverse, including Reformed (Calvinist) churches, Arminian and Wesleyan denominations, Adventist groups, and many Holiness and Pentecostal denominations. One holdover from its fundamentalist beginnings is the exclusion of organizations already affiliated with the Federal Council of Churches/National Council of Churches—the mostly liberal, mainline ecumenical organization.

The new Evangelicalism desperately needed a figurehead and a leading theological spokesman. It also needed a seminary and a publication. By the early 1950s a young evangelist named Billy Graham was emerging as the movement's figurehead, and by

---

24. Joel Carpenter, *Revive Us Again: The Reawakening of American Fundamentalism* (New York and Oxford: Oxford University Press, 1997).

the mid-1950s its leading theologian was Carl F. H. Henry. Fuller Theological Seminary became its seminary and *Christianity Today* its publication. These forces, funded largely by contributions from wealthy evangelical businessman Howard Pew, held the fledgling postfundamentalist movement together in spite of tremendous inner tensions and conflicts.

Some new evangelicals were and are strong believers in biblical inerrancy; others are not. All believe in supernatural inspiration of Scripture, but some prefer to leave the nature of that process mysterious, while others believe it is important to describe it in terms of Warfield's "plenary, verbal inspiration." Some new evangelicals were and are five-point Calvinists (total depravity, unconditional election, limited atonement, irresistible grace, perseverance of the saints); others are Arminians and even open theists (God's limited foreknowledge). Some are passionate premillennialists and even dispensationalists; others are amillennialists, and a few are postmillennialists. Some are Pentecostals and charismatics; others are cessationists. Some believe in church hierarchy and high liturgy; others insist on the autonomy of the local congregation and prefer worship that is extremely informal.

Ockenga and his colleagues in the forging of the new evangelical coalition wanted all these diverse types of evangelicals to coexist and cooperate with each other in a loose network of evangelical fellowship. Due to the diversity within Evangelicalism, Ockenga's vision seemed doomed to fail until a single powerful leader with a strong organization emerged to hold it together around a common, unifying mission. That person was Billy Graham (William Frank Graham, b. 1918). The organization was the Billy Graham Evangelistic Association, and the mission was Christian world evangelism, interpreted not only as individual spiritual salvation but also as permeation of the whole world, including social structures, with the gospel of Jesus Christ. Billy Graham's influence on Evangelicalism and evangelical theology is beyond calculation. It is doubtful whether either one would exist without him and his ministry. Graham's twin themes have provided the dual focus of Evangelicalism and evangelical theology in their postfundamentalist manifestation: conversion to Christ through personal repentance and faith in his cross, and the Bible as God's specially revealed Word, wholly inspired and completely trustworthy in all matters related to faith and practice. Of course evangelical theologians have gone far beyond merely exploring those two themes, but they have together provided the unifying foci of evangelical thought, witness, and work.

Fuller Theological Seminary was founded in 1947 by Ockenga with the inspiration and provision of California evangelist Charles E. Fuller. It was to become the premier, transdenominational evangelical seminary. *Christianity Today* was started in 1956 by Billy Graham and his father-in-law L. Nelson Bell, with financial support from Howard Pew. It was to become the evangelical counterpart and rival to the more liberal *Christian Century* magazine and provide a conservative alternative to such fundamentalist publications as John R. Rice's *Sword of the Lord*. Carl F. H. Henry (1913–2003) was a conservative Baptist doctoral student at Boston University who became a founding faculty member at Fuller Theological Seminary and then founding editor of *Christianity Today*. He went on to publish numerous articles and books expounding the new evangelical theology. An article in *Time* February 4, 1977, declared him "the leading theologian of the nation's growing Evangelical flank." Henry has often also been called the "dean of evangelical theologians."

Evangelicalism came to include many more publications, institutions, theologians, organizations, and ministries, but its path was determined by these early pioneers and symbols. Other leading movers and shakers of postfundamentalist evangelical theology—the theology of the postfundamentalist evangelical coalition—have included Henry's colleague and Ockenga's successor as president of Fuller Theological Seminary Edward John (E. J.) Carnell, Baptist theologian Bernard Ramm, Congregationalist-

Presbyterian thinker Donald G. Bloesch, and postconservative evangelical theologian Clark Pinnock. While there have been and are many other evangelical thinkers who have contributed to the postfundamentalist evangelical movement's theology, these five theologians represent the best and are the most influential of all.

CARL F. H. HENRY:
DEAN OF EVANGELICAL THEOLOGIANS

Carl Henry's overriding concern throughout his theological career was to expound and defend what he saw as a distinctly evangelical view of theological method, including especially a view of divine revelation as the sole, supreme authority for Christian faith and practice. He argued, of course, that this evangelical approach to method and authority is the same as that of the classical Protestant Reformation. The only difference is that it is updated for twentieth-century (and now twenty-first century) Christians using modern tools of logical analysis and comparing and contrasting it with modern philosophical and theological alternatives. The *Time* article about Henry in 1977 was entitled "Theology for the Tent Meeting." The title writer apparently knew little of the evangelical theologian's thought. While Henry did not eschew the right kind of revivalism, he was never particularly friendly to attitudes toward belief often inspired by revivalists and embraced by those who attend tent revivals. His theological thinking was the antithesis of emotionalism, subjectivism, fideism, and obscurantism. To Henry, these are the bane of evangelical existence and need correction, if not rejection, by modern evangelical theologians. Henry's pattern of evangelical thinking escapes simple labeling, but one appropriate term for it may be "rational, evangelical, theistic presuppositionalism."

Behind Henry's thinking stands the shaping influence of a highly rationalistic philosopher, Gordon Clark (1902–86). Clark was Henry's philosophy instructor at Wheaton College in the 1930s. Henry later called him "one of the profoundest evangelical Protestant philosophers of our time." Clark was an ardent Calvinist who believed that logic provided the God-given key to thinking God's thoughts after him and arriving at *A Christian View of Men and Things*—the title of one of his most influential books (1951). Henry took up Clark's philosophy, which centered around the critical uses of presuppositions and logical deduction in eliminating all but conservative, evangelical Protestant belief from the realm of possibility. He attempted to show that without belief in a personal God who "speaks and shows" in propositional, inerrant divine revelation, any and every human belief system (set of answers to life's ultimate questions) will inevitably end up in nihilism (belief in the ultimate absurdity of existence), which is itself contradictory. Like his mentor Clark, Henry wielded the law of noncontradiction to dissect and reduce to absurdity every non-Christian worldview and theology—including especially liberal Protestantism.

Henry's theology, then, was not exactly what one expects from a "theology for the tent meeting," and it has been criticized by some of Henry's evangelical colleagues as too rationalistic. Nevertheless, it has influenced a large number of evangelical theologians, pastors, and lay leaders, especially through Henry's columns in *Christianity Today*, which he edited for over a decade and served as contributing editor for almost a decade after his retirement in 1968. Henry's books tend to be weighty theological tomes—even when they are relatively brief. His *Towards a Recovery of Christian Belief* (Wheaton, IL: Crossway Books, 1990) comprises only 120 pages but, like most of Henry's writings, is a challenge to the mind of the reader. His magnum opus is a seven-volume work on theological method and divine revelation entitled *God, Revelation, and Authority* (Waco, TX: Word, 1976–84). Few persons, if any, could claim to have read all of it. And yet the wide use of individual volumes of the set as textbooks in evangelical colleges, universities, and seminaries has influenced thousands of evangelical students who went on to become ministers and denominational and parachurch leaders and teachers.

Carl Ferdinand Howard Henry was born to German immigrant parents in New York City on January 22, 1913, and experienced a "great awakening" or conversion to Jesus Christ at the age of twenty. After his Christian conversion he attended Wheaton College, the mecca of progressive fundamentalist higher education in the 1930s. Billy Graham would attend it soon after Henry. Numerous other evangelicals who helped form the postfundamentalist evangelical coalition went through Wheaton College, where they were shaped by a rigorously intellectual faculty and a theology of "generous orthodoxy." There Henry fell under the influence of Gordon Clark and drank deeply of what has been called by some critics "the evangelical enlightenment." That is, Clark's philosophy focused on the need for rational certainty about God that left little room for faith other than as a personal trust in what reason could prove. Some critics have found in it—and in other, similar evangelical approaches to philosophy and theology—an echo, if not an influence, of René Descartes's Enlightenment rationalism. Clark had little use for any epistemological role for the Holy Spirit, such as the traditional Calvinist "internal testimony of the Holy Spirit." He believed and taught that the classical Protestant Christian belief system (without the epistemological role of the Holy Spirit as authenticating power of the truth of divine revelation) could be demonstrated to be rationally superior to all competing, alternative belief systems including naturalism, absolute idealism, pantheism, and humanism.

After graduating from Wheaton College, Henry attended Northern Baptist Theological Seminary in Chicago and was ordained a Baptist minister. After seminary he pursued a Ph.D. in theology from the University of Boston, where he studied with philosopher of religion Edgar Sheffield Brightman, one of the founders of the liberal Personalist school of theology. His doctoral dissertation, entitled "Personal Idealism and Strong's Theology," was a critical study of turn-of-the-century mediating Baptist theologian Augustus Hopkins Strong's theology. Henry attempted to show the influence of early Personalist philosophy on Strong's thought. Strong had been and remained for many years after Henry's dissertation the single most influential theologian among conservative Protestants after Charles Hodge. Strong's three-volume 1907 *Systematic Theology* was widely used in free-church colleges and seminaries as the basic textbook of evangelical thought. It was generally considered conservative and Calvinistic, although not as congenial to fundamentalism as Hodge's three-volume *Systematic Theology*. Strong was more open to theistic evolution than Hodge or his most faithful followers, and he promoted a "dynamical theory" of inspiration of Scripture that differed significantly from Hodge's plenary, verbal theory. Also, Strong believed that errors in "secular matters" in Scripture would not undermine its inspiration and infallibility, which he regarded as having to do with Scripture as "a textbook of religion." While an irenic treatment of Strong's theology, Henry's dissertation served to undermine its influence among progressive fundamentalists (it had little or no influence among separatistic fundamentalists), who would eventually become postfundamentalist evangelicals, by purporting to show alien philosophical elements in it.

While he was working on his doctorate, Henry taught part-time at evangelical Gordon College in suburban Boston and helped found Fuller Theological Seminary with Ockenga and a group of progressive fundamentalists from the United States and Great Britain. This group became the nucleus of the postfundamentalist evangelical movement. Originally, their main concern was to establish conservative, conversionist Protestant thought on a less separatistic, less anti-intellectual foundation than fundamentalism. They were disillusioned with their own fundamentalist coalition and its theology, which they thought had degenerated into militancy, sectarianism, and fideism. In 1949 Henry helped found the Evangelical Theological Society, whose only confessional requirement for membership was biblical inerrancy. The stated purpose of the society was to combat liberal theology without embracing fundamentalism.

Many commentators on postfundamentalist Evangelicalism regard Henry's *The Uneasy Conscience of Modern Fundamentalism* (1947) the first neo-evangelical (i.e., post-fundamentalist evangelical) book. In it the young evangelical theologian criticized fundamentalism for neglecting the social world outside the confines of the separated church. Fundamentalism—including almost all evangelicals—had been in sharp reaction against the social gospel movement that arose with liberal theology in the late nineteenth and early twentieth centuries. As Donald W. Dayton and other evangelical historians have shown, evangelicals in the nineteenth century—especially prior to the Civil War—had been social reformers.[25] Some had been quite radical abolitionists and practiced civil disobedience. Evangelicals were once in the forefront of progressive social change, but all that changed with the revivalism of D. L. Moody and later Billy Sunday. They and other evangelical revivalists were strongly premillennial and pessimistic about changing the structures of society. Early fundamentalism was wary of the social gospel movement of men like Washington Gladden and Walter Rauschenbusch because it was closely associated with and greatly influenced by the liberal Protestant thinking of German theologian Albrecht Ritschl and his followers.

Henry's book, then, fell like a bombshell on conservative Protestantism in North America as he called fundamentalism (by which he still at that time meant conservative Protestantism in general) to repent of its indifference to social sin and become involved once again in helping to ameliorate the effects of sin in the social order. Because separatistic fundamentalists reacted negatively to the book, while it was hailed by many moderate evangelicals, *The Uneasy Conscience of Modern Fundamentalism* came to be viewed as a neo-evangelical manifesto decisively breaking the new evangelical movement away from its older fundamentalist roots.

Overall and in general, however, Henry's career in theology was conservative. He sought to warn fellow evangelicals (and anyone else who would listen) of the poison of subjectivism in philosophy and theology, and his focus returned again and again to fighting that poison as he believed it appeared in and corrupted Christianity. The two main examples of subjectivism's deleterious affects are, in Henry's analysis, liberal Protestantism and neo-orthodoxy. The former, Henry claimed, represents near-capitulation to the modern secular spirit of the age that elevates the autonomous reasoning of sinful humanity to godlike status and removes religion, including Christianity, from its rational foundation onto the shifting sands of "common human religious experience"—whether intuitional (as in Schleiermacher) or ethical (as in Ritschl). The liberals came to view the Bible, Henry claimed, as little more than representation of universal human sentiments about God and humanity. In their hands it lost its authority as the governing norm of Christian faith and practice, precisely because liberals gave up belief in its supernatural divine origin in verbal inspiration and denied its inerrancy.

Neo-orthodoxy came in for special criticism from Henry because in his view it is such a seductive alternative to Protestant orthodoxy; many evangelicals, once loosed from the iron grip of militant, separatistic fundamentalism, turned to major neo-orthodox thinkers such as Karl Barth and Emil Brunner for guidance in rethinking theological method and the nature of divine revelation and Scripture.[26] According

25. Donald W. Dayton, *Rediscovering an Evangelical Heritage* (Peabody, MA: Hendrickson Publishers, 1988).

26. For an examination of the influence of Karl Barth, the leading neo-orthodox theologian, on evangelicals and evangelical theology, see Gregory G. Bolich, *Karl Barth and Evangelicalism* (Downers Grove, IL: InterVarsity Press, 1980).

to neo-orthodoxy or, as many of its proponents prefer to call it, dialectical theology, divine revelation is supernatural (contrary to liberal theology) but nonpropositional. That is, according to Barth and Brunner and their colleagues and disciples, when God reveals he reveals only *himself* and never *information about himself.* Revelation, so neo-orthodoxy seems to say, is personal, historical, and dialogical, not rational, propositional, or cognitive. At least this is how Henry interpreted neo-orthodoxy.

The upshot is that Henry surveyed the theological scene in the 1950s through the 1990s and thought he noticed *one, single, main disease* infecting and corrupting Christian theology: *anti-intellectualism*—a "flight from reason." Fundamentalism's brand of anti-intellectualism was obvious to Henry, and he felt little need to expose it at great length or in great detail. The fundamentalism of the 1920s and since had fallen into obscurantist isolation from the world of thought and cared little about the life of the mind outside of its own esoteric biblical studies, such as detailed examination of the biblical apocalyptic prophecies of the end times and reading the "signs of the times" to detect when Christ might return.

Liberal theology's brand of anti-intellectualism was more subtle, and Henry endeavored to expose it in many of his writings. According to his critical analysis, liberal Protestant theology had begun rejecting rigorous rational and intellectual activity in theology with Schleiermacher's emphasis on universal religious feeling as the basis for even Christian theology and had continued its anti-intellectual project with Ritschl's divorce between "facts" and "values"—relegating religious and theological judgments to the latter realm. As a result, Christian theology became little more than an extension of mystical intuition, with no objective truth content, or else an extension of universal human moral intuition, in which case it still has no objective truth content.

Neo-orthodoxy, Henry complained, is guilty of its own anti-intellectualism because it denies objective divine revelation of information, revels in paradoxes if not contradictions, and rejects the Bible as supernaturally verbally inspired and inerrant. For neo-orthodoxy, the Bible "becomes the Word of God" in the mysterious, unpredictable encounter between God and the human person. Henry regarded that as undermining the Bible as an objective authority for critically examining teaching and constructing sound doctrine. The upshot of all these forms of twentieth-century theology, Henry argued, is a noncognitive, anti-intellectual, subjective Christian faith that cannot sustain its public prophetic role of teaching truth about God.

Henry's proposed cure for all of modern theology's ills is a theological "back to the Bible movement" in which Scripture is once again understood as a propositional, verbally inspired and inerrant revelation of God that communicates a life and worldview logically and experientially superior to all alternatives. Henry's theology has a decidedly apologetic thrust. He was interested in demonstrating the rational superiority of Protestant orthodoxy over all competing theologies and worldviews, but he believed the key to such a project and to putting Christian theology on a sound foundation is proper presuppositions ("axioms") and correct logical deduction.

Every comprehensive system of belief, Henry averred, rests on unprovable axioms. In order for reasonable discourse (dialogue, debate, proclamation) to take place, there must be certain universally agreed-on axioms that transcend particular belief systems. For example, if a person does not agree that "[t]here can be but one comprehensive system of truth,"[27] that person either does not understand the meaning of "comprehensive system of truth" or is wrongheaded. It is impossible to communicate reasonably with such a person about matters of ultimate meaning—that is, truth claims about ulti-

---

27. Carl F. H. Henry, *Towards a Recovery of Christian Belief* (Wheaton, IL: Crossway Books, 1990), 88.

mate reality. Henry was interested only in universal, absolute truth; he considered all forms of relativism self-contradictory and therefore anti-intellectual. It is strictly impossible to discuss truth without agreement about its nature as unified correspondence with reality. Postmodern cognitive nihilism was of little or no interest to Henry because it makes adjudication of competing truth claims and systems of truth impossible. A second universal axiom of all rational discourse about ultimate matters is that axioms (presuppositions, first principles), though unprovable, can be tested by the criteria of logical consistency and explanatory power. That is, those axioms are true that give rise to a coherent system of thought and explain reality comprehensively. Finally, according to Henry, "Propositional expressibility is, of course, a precondition for evaluating any system. A system that is not propositionally expressible involves no shareable truth claims and can in no way be tested."[28] Once one accepts these basic rational, epistemological, and metaphysical axioms, Henry argued, the real fun can begin. That is, which of the several or many competing systems of belief about ultimate reality and the meaning of the whole of reality is true? Like his mentor Clark, of course, Henry believed that only Protestant Christian orthodoxy provides a universally, publicly true account of reality; all competing belief systems are so seriously flawed in terms of coherence and explanatory power that they cannot make serious claim to belief.

What are Christianity's distinctive axioms? This was an all important question for Henry. If one begins with flawed presuppositions, the entire system of belief is bound to fail. This is why Christianity is waning in public acceptance, Henry maintained. Its proper starting points have been replaced with faulty ones. According to Henry, the dean of evangelical theologians, there are two and only two necessary basic axioms of Christian theology, and any departure from them gives rise to something other than a truly Christian belief system and form of life: (1) the basic Christian ontological axiom of *the living God*, and (2) the basic Christian epistemological axiom of *divine revelation*. Thus, proper Christian theology—"biblical theism"—must start with *the God who speaks and shows*. Because his theology's first principles are so crucial to its entire outcome, Henry spent most of his time and energy as a theologian exploring and defending them. He became convinced early in his career as the new Evangelicalism's premier theologian that it would fail as a force for reform of both church and culture if it did not adhere strictly to these two axioms; it would inevitably fall into incoherence, subjectivism, irrelevance. The first axiom must be understood as presupposing that the God of Christianity actually exists as a transcendent-immanent person who actually communicates in a reasonable way with human beings. The second axiom must be understood as presupposing that God's revelation is "a mental activity." That is, it aims to communicate univocal (not equivocal or even analogical) truths—literal facts in propositional form—to human minds. And, of course, these divinely communicated propositions must be coherent with each other and must illumine reality and human experience of reality better than any other system of belief. Henry believed that they do and that this fact justifies embrace of Christian theology's basic presuppositions.

Besides expounding proper theological methodology (in the style of Gordon Clark), Henry expended a great deal of time and energy defending what he regarded as the classical Protestant Christian view of the Bible that has largely been abandoned by the modern churches: its nature as propositional revelation of truth; its verbal, plenary inspiration; and its inerrancy. Henry did not argue that revelation itself must necessarily be propositional or that the Bible must always be interpreted literally. He recognized and acknowledged that revelation may be personal and historical, but he argued that without propositional revelation we could not know what the "mighty acts of

---

28. Ibid., 71.

God" in history mean and we could not test personal revelation for accuracy. Also, the Bible contains more than direct, rational propositional communication, but without that the other literary forms of the Bible (poetry, apocalyptic imagery, etc.) would be opaque as to their meaning. *For theology*, then, according to Henry, the propositional content of the Bible is all-important. Furthermore, if the propositional content of the Bible is divine revelation and trustworthy, it must be factually reliable, supernatural communication from God and not merely the inspiring human ideas about God. Henry was careful to distinguish verbal inspiration from mechanical dictation and inerrancy from modern, technical accuracy. The point of all this, for Henry, is that Christianity is a religion of truth, not myth, and contains an irreducible doctrinal element that defines it. While Christianity is not reducible to doctrine, and faith is not reducible to rationalism, Christianity cannot live without doctrine, and faith cannot justify its beliefs without reason. Without an objective source and norm of doctrinal authority, such as only an inerrant, rational, propositional communication from God can supply, Christianity would ultimately reduce to a folk religion of subjective feelings.

Some of Henry's fellow evangelical theologians have expressed sharp disagreement with aspects of his theological method and view of divine revelation and Scripture. He has been accused of overrationalizing Christianity and of inflating the importance of propositional revelation and inerrancy. Evangelicals who have been influenced more by Pietism than by Princeton Theology, for example, find Henry's theology one-sided in its emphasis on objectivity and fear of subjectivism. It can appear overly rational and cognitive at times, and Henry's view of divine revelation may seem to imply that all the nonpropositional forms of revelation are unimportant compared with propositional revelation. Some critics believe that Henry has overreacted to neo-orthodoxy and failed to move far enough from fundamentalism. However, Henry's impact on postfundamentalist, conservative evangelical theology has been both deep and broad. His theological approach (as distinct from every specific conclusion he has reached) is the "gold standard" by which other evangelical approaches to theology tend to be judged.

E. J. CARNELL: APOLOGIST FOR EVANGELICAL THEOLOGY

Less well known than Henry, but also influential in postfundamentalist evangelical theology is Henry's Fuller Theological Seminary colleague E. J. Carnell (1919–67). Carnell's theological career and his theological methodology both parallel Henry's rather closely. Like Henry, Carnell attended Wheaton College and came under the influence of Gordon Clark, whose rigorously rationalist methodology stamped Carnell's work as much as it did Henry's. Carnell attended Westminster Theological Seminary, founded by J. Gresham Machen, and was strongly influenced toward Calvinism there. He followed Henry at Boston University, where he pursued a doctorate in philosophy of religion and wrote a dissertation on the Danish existentialist philosopher Søren Kierkegaard under E. S. Brightman. Carnell also completed a doctorate in theology at Harvard Divinity School, where he wrote a dissertation on theologian and ethicist Reinhold Niebuhr. He taught part-time at Gordon College and helped Ockenga and Henry found Fuller Theological Seminary in Pasadena, California. Carnell moved to Fuller Theological Seminary after completing his doctoral program at Boston University. His first book, *An Introduction to Christian Apologetics*, published in 1948, won an award from its publisher, which helped propel the author into the spotlight of evangelical theology.

In 1954, at age thirty-five, much to the chagrin of some of his colleagues, Carnell succeeded Ockenga as president of Fuller Theological Seminary. Throughout the 1950s and into the 1960s the evangelical theologian and president of Evangelicalism's flagship seminary pursued an ambitious schedule of publishing, administration, teaching, and speaking. He resigned the presidency of the seminary in 1959 and suffered an emotional collapse shortly afterwards. He died of an overdose of sleeping medicine in 1968; whether his death was accidental or a suicide is unknown.

Carnell's greatest influence as an evangelical theologian came through his teaching of hundreds, if not thousands, of evangelical students at Fuller Theological Seminary during his twenty-year tenure there and through his books, which included *A Philosophy of the Christian Religion* (1952), *Christian Commitment* (1957), and *The Case for Orthodoxy* (1959). Like Henry's, Carnell's theology carried forward the rationalist philosophy of Gordon Clark by arguing in a variety of ways that sharp use of the law of noncontradiction shows that Christianity is the only truly coherent and comprehensive, systematic and rational account of the world and human life in it. He was less interested than Henry in developing a sustained polemical defense of the supernatural nature of Scripture or the propositional nature of divine revelation, although he agreed with both points. Instead, Carnell's main interests and contributions lay in demonstrating the superiority of orthodox Christianity (as defined, for example, by Augustine in the early church and Calvin in the Reformation) over naturalism and idealist humanism and showing that liberal theology—including American neo-orthodoxy—falls short of internal consistency and explanatory power.

Much to his own chagrin and his colleagues', however, Carnell's most significant splash in the water of mid-twentieth-century theology came with the publication of *The Case for Orthodox Theology*, which was one of three volumes dedicated to the three main types of mid-century Protestant theology—liberal, neo-orthodox, and conservative. Carnell preferred "orthodox" to "conservative," just as another author, William Hordern, preferred "new Reformation theology" to "neo-orthodox theology." In his *Case* book Carnell attacked fundamentalism, much to the surprise and dismay of some of his friends and colleagues. It seemed like a waste of his scholarly energies, and his criticism seemed at times too polemical, as when he referred to fundamentalism as "orthodoxy gone cultic."[29] Overall and in general, however, Carnell's *Case* book did Evangelicalism a service by driving a second nail in the coffin of its connection with the old militant, separatistic fundamentalism. In hindsight it seems this was necessary, as many postfundamentalist evangelicals had not yet shaken off their fundamentalist past and most nonevangelicals still equated Evangelicalism with fundamentalism. In *The Case for Orthodox Theology* Carnell made clear that, at least in his view, evangelical theology is nothing more or less than contemporary historic, classical Protestant theology and not at all tied to a narrow, sectarian, dogmatic, or anti-intellectual mind-set. In the book Carnell explained the difference between Evangelicalism and fundamentalism in a way that is still used by many evangelicals:

> The mentality of Fundamentalism [in contrast to Evangelicalism] is dominated by ideological thinking. Ideological thinking is rigid, intolerant, and doctrinaire; it sees principles everywhere, and all principles come in clear tones of black and white; it exempts itself from the limits that original sin places on history; it wages holy wars without acknowledging the elements of pride and personal interest that prompt the call to battle; it creates new evils while trying to correct old ones.[30]

Orthodox theology—evangelical theology—is different. According to Carnell it rises above ideology and militancy, while holding fast to original Christianity against the

29. Edward John Carnell, *The Case for Orthodox Theology* (Philadelphia: Westminster Press, 1959), 113.

30. Ibid., 114.

acids of modernity and liberalism. He defined it as "that branch of Christendom which limits the ground of religious authority to the Bible"[31] without falling into literalism, separatism, inellectual stagnation, and a negative ethic. Carnell called orthodox Christianity, by which he meant Evangelicalism, away from fundamentalist habits and into the light of a better day by calling it to return to early Christianity's creeds, Reformation confessions, recognition that "all truth is God's truth," and fearless pursuit of truth using universal canons of rationality (viz., logic). Above all, he called for evangelical engagement with modern knowledge, which he sharply distinguished from intellectual trends, theories, and fashions.

BERNARD RAMM:
MODERATE EVANGELICAL THEOLOGIAN

A third significant and influential postfundamentalist evangelical theologian was Bernard Ramm, born the same year as Carnell. His career and theology went in a somewhat different direction from either Henry's or Carnell's. Ramm was born and raised in Montana and, after a conversion experience and graduation from university, pursued seminary studies at Eastern Baptist Theological Seminary in Philadelphia and then graduate studies in philosophy at the University of Southern California, where he earned the Ph.D. in 1950. He began his teaching career at fundamentalist Los Angeles Baptist Theological Seminary and Bible Institute of Los Angeles (now Biola University). During his career as a professor of theology Ramm taught at a number of institutions, including Baylor University, Bethel College and Seminary, Eastern Baptist Theological Seminary, and American Baptist Seminary of the West. Among his most influential books are *The Christian View of Science and Scripture* (1954), *Special Revelation and the Word of God* (1961), and *The Evangelical Heritage* (1973). He also wrote books on Christian apologetics (including philosophy of religion), biblical interpretation, the doctrine of sin, and Christology. Ramm was also a frequent contributor to two evangelical periodicals—*Christianity Today* and *Eternity*—and a regular speaker at Young Life summer retreats.

Like Henry and Carnell, Ramm was intent on distancing the new evangelical theology from fundamentalism, while at the same time preserving and strengthening Evangelicalism's conservative Protestant integrity over against liberal theology. His *The Evangelical Heritage* strove to demonstrate that evangelical theology and spirituality are not sectarian or modernist but instead rooted in the Protestant Reformation. Throughout his career as an evangelical theologian Ramm's primary nemesis was obscurantism—the tendency of many conservative Protestants and especially of fundamentalists to bury their heads in the sands of traditional responses to difficult questions and issues and ignore the modern world. At the same time, he did not want to throw the baby of orthodox theology out with the bathwater of obscurantism. It seems that all of the first-generation postfundamentalist evangelical theologians had to publish at least one book critical of fundamentalism to prove that they had departed decisively from it. Henry's was *The Uneasy Concience*. Carnell's was *The Case for Orthodox Theology*. Ramm's was *The Christian View of Science and Scripture*, in which he argued against those conservative Christian responses to modern science that simply ignore mountains of evidence and plain facts in favor of traditional readings of Genesis. In the book Ramm urged his evangelical readers to come to terms with modern science without capitulating to naturalistic philosophies disguised as science, and he chided fundamentalists for their attitude of "maximal conservatism." Ramm explicated a

---

31. Ibid., 139.

number of possible orthodox interpretations of the biblical creation narratives and promoted one, called "progressive creationism," that attempts to combine some elements of evolution with intelligent design of the universe. What had not been particularly controversial nearly a century earlier, when proposed (in rough form) by Warfield and other conservative evangelicals who wanted to correlate Scripture with the new scientific knowledge about the age of the earth, was very controversial in Ramm's time. Fundamentalists reacted angrily to Ramm's "compromise" with "godless evolution," while many younger evangelicals gladly embraced his integrative vision.

In *Special Revelation and the Word of God* Ramm tackled the difficult problem of authority for Christian belief, especially the natures of special revelation and the Bible. Rather than rooting Christian authority in the Bible per se, the author elevated the category of divine revelation above inspiration and especially above the propositions of Scripture. Divine revelation is God's self-communication in a variety of "modalities" such as historical event, incarnation, prophetic speech, and divine condescension. Scripture is one of revelation's primary "products" and takes the form of divinely inspired literature that is also, of course, accommodated to human culture, as is every modality of divine revelation. Ramm expressed caution toward extremes of "biblicism" and "criticism" within modern theology with regard to the Bible:

> The literary character of special revelation suggests another very important matter for the proper understanding of Scripture. If the Scriptures are fundamentally in the form of literature (and also of history), then they must be judged and assessed by the standards and judgments of literature, not by rules or principles foreign to them. At this point *biblicism* and *criticism* can fail to come into proper focus. Biblicism may fail to see the literary character of Scripture and treat Scripture like a code book of theological ordinances. Criticism may be so preoccupied with the literary aspects of Scripture that it fails to see the substance of which literature happens to be the vehicle.[32]

Ramm's criticism of biblicism may be taken as a subtle correction to Henry's and Carnell's treatments of Scripture, which place rational propositions to the fore and treat Scripture like a set of yet-to-be-systematized metaphysical and doctrinal facts. On the other hand, Ramm was critical of liberal theology and neo-orthodoxy insofar as they failed to do justice to the propositional content of the Bible as a deposit or product of divine speech. Ramm sought a balanced view of the Bible:

> The disjunction presented so frequently in modern theology between revelation as either "information" or "encounter" is false. The historic version of revelation is frequently misrepresented as if it were merely a revelation of information. Such a view is not difficult to run through with a sword. But on the other hand to represent revelation as only encounter or as only event is also defective. A professed knowledge of God which is not rooted in historical event at the critical junctures is but powerless abstraction; and historical events without a powerful interpreting word of God are opaque occurrences. The structure of special revelation calls for a hard event and a hard word of interpretation. There cannot be a hard event with a soft interpretation.[33]

Without ever denying a propositional side to divine revelation and without ever denying supernatural inspiration and infallibility of Scripture (in fact Ramm affirmed all of that!), Ramm called for evangelicals to avoid a view of revelation, inspiration, and Scripture that conflicted with the plain facts of the Bible and indulged in over-rationalization for the sake of some elusive Enlightenment-like certainty. Ramm

32. Bernard Ramm, *Special Revelation and the Word of God* (Grand Rapids: Wm. B. Eerdmans, 1961), 68.
33. Ibid., 158.

distinguished between "certitude" (assurance, confidence) and "certainty" and argued that the Holy Spirit provides the "full spiritual certitude" necessary for robust proclamation of the gospel. Rational certainty, however, is a chimera wrongly promoted by the Enlightenment and too often chased by conservative apologists. Much to the dismay of many more conservative evangelicals, Ramm rejected rational presuppositionalism and the test of coherence as the supreme test of all truth and affirmed a pattern of authority for evangelical theology that included both Word and Spirit. The ultimate guarantee of truth is not some a priori foundation, whether logic or the Bible or both; it is God himself in Jesus Christ and the Holy Spirit. The Bible is the book of Jesus Christ, and the Holy Spirit is the one who inspires and illumines the book, pointing to Jesus Christ more than to some coherent worldview. Ramm insisted on placing revelation as God's speech over inspiration, and he viewed inspiration as a dynamic process that involved the personalities of the human authors. He also relegated inerrancy to a lower place in the hierarchy of evangelical doctrines, arguing that in order to make the concept fit the plain facts of the biblical text ("phenomena of Scripture") it had to be qualified and relativized. He eschewed heated debates about inerrancy within Evangelicalism, as these, he believed, detract from the more important quality of Scripture, which is to bring humans into encounter with God through Jesus Christ.

Toward the end of his life (Ramm died in 1992), the progressive evangelical theologian began to recommend the theological method of Karl Barth—not "neo-orthodoxy"—to evangelicals. In a poorly titled book, *After Fundamentalism* (1983), Ramm dispelled many common fundamentalist and conservative evangelical myths about the great Swiss theologian—with whom Ramm studied briefly in the 1950s—and argued that Barth's theological methodology of "Christocentrism" could help evangelicals out of their obsessive love-hate relationship with the Enlightenment. According to Ramm, Barth's theology was constructed in full view of the Enlightenment without accommodating to its secularist impulses. Evangelicals could learn from Barth to be fearless with regard to all genuine questions raised by the worlds of science and philosophy—including biblical criticism—because Christianity is based on the gospel of Jesus Christ and not on some rigidly defined system of doctrines about the nature of Scripture or the way the world works. By no means did Ramm sacrifice his evangelical commitment to the authority of the Bible as God's Word, but he relativized the defensive doctrines about it—such as verbal inspiration and factual inerrancy—making them secondary to commitment to Jesus Christ and more flexible.

What is interesting is that by near the end of his life and career as a leading evangelical theologian Ramm was coming to quite the opposite conclusion regarding Barth from Henry's. Whereas Henry never gave up accusing Barth of anti-intellectualism, Ramm came to recommend Barth as the liberator of Evangelicalism from its anti-intellectual, fundamentalist roots. Ramm saw that such doctrines as biblical inerrancy, defined factually rather than functionally and separated from the gospel and the Holy Spirit, were obstacles to evangelical reform. They served only to keep evangelical theology in its fundamentalist intellectual ghetto. For Ramm, only Barth could help evangelical theology break out of that ghetto by fearlessly coming to terms with the undeniable facts of the new knowledge brought about by the Enlightenment without compromising its commitment to the gospel of free grace through Jesus Christ.

Some critics charged Ramm with capitulation to neo-orthodoxy, but the charge misses the mark. The increasingly postconservative evangelical theologian never did deny propositional revelation or affirm that the Bible "becomes God's Word." (Whether Barth really embraced these stereotypes of neo-orthodox theology is another question worth considering!) He never rejected supernatural inspiration or every definition of inerrancy. He did, however, breathe new life into these concepts by tying them inextricably to the Holy Spirit's witness and to their main purpose of testifying to Jesus Christ and bringing people into saving encounter with him. Ramm came to see evangelical theology less as a defensive fortress against the acids of modernity and more as a second-order, flexible witness and therefore servant to divine revelation.

A nonevangelical commentator on evangelical theology, Gary Dorrien, captured the essence of Ramm's revolution in evangelical theology, which was carried on after Ramm's death by a diverse collection of postconservative evangelical thinkers. Writing with irony, Dorrien expressed Ramm's complaint and that of his postconservative disciples:

> Evangelicals are prone to fret that everything will be lost if they have no ground of absolute certainty or no proof that Christianity is superior to Islam or Buddhism. This fear drives them to impose impossible tests on Christian belief. Inerrancy or the abyss! It also drives them to invest religious authority in a posited epistemological capacity that exists outside the circle of Christian faith. The truth of Christianity is then judged by rational tests that are not only external to Christian revelation but given authority over revelation.[34]

Naturally, evangelical theologians sprung from the mold of Gordon Clark and Carl Henry (to say nothing of fundamentalists!) are critical of Ramm's and the postconservative evangelicals' turn away from rational presuppositionalism, deductive propositionalism, verbal plenary inspiration, and strict, technical inerrancy of Scripture. To them this can only mean a reduction of the evangelical witness toward subjectivism. To postconservative evangelicals inspired by the later Ramm, however, the discovery of the epistemological role of the Holy Spirit, embrace of paradoxes, abandonment of a defensive, often hostile attitude toward the Enlightenment and culture, and willingness to reconsider traditional evangelical notions of inspiration and inerrancy have the same exhilarating feel experienced by the postfundamentalist evangelicals in the 1940s and 1950s as they took the risk of stepping outside the stifling abode of fundamentalism. The harsh criticisms of their conservative evangelical colleagues remind them of the hardening of the categories among the fundamentalists who condemned the neoevangelicals for opening their minds and methods to the larger world of ideas and of education.

DONALD BLOESCH:
PROGRESSIVE EVANGELICAL THEOLOGIAN

A fourth influential evangelical theologian closely associated with the postfundamentalist evangelical coalition is Donald G. Bloesch (b. 1928). Bloesch represents something of an anomaly, as he has never taught at a college, university, or seminary that is part of the evangelical coalition, nor was any of his theological education completed in an evangelical institution. In other words, unlike the other theologians under consideration here, Bloesch has never operated within the evangelical subculture except by publishing book reviews and articles in *Christianity Today* and *Eternity*. Some of his books have been published by evangelical publishers. Bloesch was raised in and has always remained a part of the Protestant mainstream; he was untouched by the fundamentalist movement and its militancy and separatism. Revivalism is not part of his heritage. Because of all this, he is sometimes dismissed as a "mediating theologian" rather than a true postfundamentalist evangelical thinker. Nevertheless, he has produced a large body of theological literature that is closely identified with postfundamentalist

---

34. Gary Dorrien, *The Remaking of Evangelical Theology* (Louisville, KY: Westminster John Knox Press, 1998), 201.

Evangelicalism, and he has stood as an influential theological voice on the boundary between mainline Protestantism and the evangelical coalition.

Bloesch's evangelical theology attempts to combine several seemingly disparate strands of Protestant thought: magisterial Protestantism with its catholicity (emphasis on the church universal throughout the ages) and confessionalism (emphasis on formal, written statements of belief), Reformed theology within a free-church framework, Pietism, and neo-orthodoxy (especially the theologies of Karl Barth and Emil Brunner). Bloesch pursued his doctoral studies in theology at the University of Chicago, where he studied with leading liberal Protestant thinkers and wrote his dissertation on the apologetics of American neo-orthodox theologian and ethicist Reinhold Niebuhr. While at the University of Chicago's Divinity School he became involved with the university's chapter of InterVarsity Christian Fellowship—a moderate evangelical student group. Bloesch's strongly Pietist early spiritual formation inclined him toward Evangelicalism more than toward the liberalism he was encountering at the Divinity School. Nevertheless, he studied liberal theology—including process theology—in order to understand it on its own terms and has remained in close dialogue with liberal Protestant thought throughout his life. After receiving his doctorate in theology, the Indiana-born young theologian went to Europe to study at Oxford and at Basel, where he met and was impressed with Barth. Upon returning to the United States, he embarked on a teaching career at the Presbyterian-related University of Dubuque Theological Seminary in Iowa, from which he retired in 1993 after thirty-five years.

Bloesch has authored between thirty-five and forty books (some are moving toward publication as this is being written), including two sets of systematic theology. Many of his books have promoted spiritual and theological renewal in the American church; some have especially focused on Evangelicalism and its renewal through rediscovering its roots in the early church and Reformation and through overcoming sectarianism and strife over secondary matters of the Christian faith. Among his most notable and influential volumes are *The Evangelical Renaissance* (1973), *The Future of Evangelical Christianity: A Call for Unity amid Diversity* (1983), *Essentials of Evangelical Theology* (2 volumes, 1978 and 1979), and a projected seven-volume system of theology—undoubtedly his magnum opus—with the general title *Christian Foundations*. Bloesch's primary contribution to evangelical thought has been to call it out of its captivity to the old liberal-fundamentalist controversy and out of narrow sectarianism and into a greater appreciation for the historic Reformation tradition with an emphasis on spirituality.

In this project, spanning more than thirty years, the Iowa theologian has stood on the shoulders of previous Protestant thinkers such as John Calvin, the Pietists Spener and Zinzendorf, John Wesley, Jonathan Edwards, the "melancholy Dane" Søren Kierkegaard, English Christian theologians P. T. Forsyth and John Stott, and twentieth-century neo-orthodox thinkers Karl Barth and Emil Brunner. Notably missing from the list are fundamentalists, including very conservative postfundamentalist evangelicals. Bloesch has never sympathized with or wished to promote rationalism, including evangelical presuppositionalism and propositionalism (Henry, Carnell, et al.). Also notably missing, however, are liberals. While engaging in constructive dialogue with liberal Protestant theologians, Bloesch has never viewed himself or his theology as a version of liberal thought or sympathetic with it. He prefers to describe himself as a "progressive evangelical" and a "catholic evangelical theologian." These two labels point up twin concerns of Bloesch's theology: to retrieve the great tradition of Christian theology, especially as that was reformed and renewed by the sixteenth-century Protestant reformers, and to keep evangelical theology both faithful to its roots and reforming itself in light of new knowledge and "new light" breaking forth from God's Word. In *Essentials of Evangelical Theology* Bloesch clearly set forth his centrist evangelical theological intention: "The theological options today are liberalism or modernism . . . , a reactionary Evangelicalism or Fundamentalism, and a catholic Evangelicalism, which alone is truly evangelical and biblical."[35]

Bloesch labels his theological method "fideistic revelationism," which requires a bit of explaining. This approach to constructive Christian theology avoids the extremes of both rationalism and sheer fideism (blind faith) while combining faith and reason in the service of God's Word, which stands over them:

> While rationalism holds to *credo quia intelligo* (I believe because I understand) and fideism to *credo quia absurdum est* (I believe because it is absurd), evangelical theology in the classical tradition subscribes to *credo ut intelligam* (I believe in order to understand). In this last view faith is neither a blind leap into the unknown (Kierkegaard) nor an assent of the will to what reason has already shown to be true (Carl Henry), but a venture of trust based on evidence that faith itself provides. We do not believe without our reason, but we also do not believe on the basis of reason. Faith entails thinking and examining. In order to come to a mature faith we need to search and examine the Scriptures as well as the tradition of the church.[36]

Bloesch seeks to guide theological reflection and construction between two dangerous rocks: the Scylla of experientialism and the Charybdis of philosophism. Experientialism allows the individual's subjective feelings to guide and control Christian belief and confession. In a more sophisticated form it appears in the theology of Schleiermacher, according to Bloesch, as the religious a priori of universal human God-consciousness. In either case, it shipwrecks Christianity and theology on the rock of subjectivism. Just as great a danger, however, is philosophism, which in the form of rationalism shipwrecks theology by giving control to autonomous (unregenerate) human intellect and, inevitably, some particular philosophical school of thought. According to Bloesch this danger appears whenever Christian theologians begin their reflections with some presupposed system of philosophical thought or a priori rules of reason, rather than with God's Word—special divine revelation. Instead, he avers, authentic Christian theology must always use reason in the service of revelation and must remain suspicious of philosophical systems that threaten to predetermine what God's Word can say and what it can mean.

For Bloesch, the renewal of Evangelicalism requires rejection of rationalistic, apologetic approaches to theology and retrieval of the Reformation method of Word and Spirit, in which all authority—even authenticating authority—rests in the Holy Spirit-attested Word of God, which creates faith rather than being authenticated by human faith:

> Against [rationalism] I contend that the claims of Christianity are true because they rest on events that really happened, events that cannot possibly be synchronized or harmonized with ordinary human experience and reason; and because their credibility and veracity is confirmed in our hearts by the Spirit of God himself as he authenticates the message of faith in the church through the ages where the Bible is read and

---

35. Donald G. Bloesch, *Essentials of Evangelical Theology,* vol. 2: *Life, Ministry, and Hope* (San Francisco: Harper & Row, 1979), 283.

36. Donald G. Bloesch, *A Theology of Word and Spirit: Authority and Method in Theology* (*Christian Foundations,* vol. 1) (Downers Grove, IL: InterVarsity Press, 1992), 58. For a critical analysis of Bloesch's theological method, see Stanley J. Grenz, "'Fideistic Revelationism': Donald Bloesch's Antirationalist Theological Method," in *Evangelical Theology in Transition: Theologians in Dialogue with Donald Bloesch,* ed. Elmer M. Colyer (Downers Grove, IL: InterVarsity Press, 1999), 35–60.

believed and where the faith is proclaimed in fidelity and love. Because human reason is in the service of sin apart from faith (Rom. 8:7, 14:23), it needs to be shattered and transformed before it can lay hold of the mystery of the truth of the gospel, which is hidden from natural sight and understanding but becomes the glorious possession of those who break with the arrogance and pretension that presently cloud their reasoning and cry out for salvation that God alone can and does provide in the person of his Son, Jesus Christ.[37]

Thus, Bloesch's theology is intended to be a "kerygmatic theology" rather than an "apologetic theology," and it is self-consciously set against the rationalistic approaches to evangelical theology that dominated the early postfundamentalist evangelical coalition's beginnings (Clark, Henry, Carnell). It is most closely comparable with the neo-orthodox or dialectical theologies of Barth and Emil Brunner. However, Bloesch is not satisfied with neo-orthodoxy's doctrine of Scripture and with some of Barth's or Brunner's specific ideas. While expressing genuine regard for Barth's theology, Bloesch criticizes the Swiss theologian's doctrine of salvation in *Jesus Is Victor!: Karl Barth's Doctrine of Salvation* (1976). Sprinkled throughout his books are numerous positive references to both Barth and Brunner. He shares enthusiastically their rejections of natural knowledge of God and literalistic biblicism (Brunner's accusation that some conservative Protestants have exchanged a pope in Rome for a "paper pope"). On the other hand, he is always careful to distance himself from their criticisms of belief in the inspiration and infallibility of Scripture. Bloesch's preferred term for his own view of the relationship between divine revelation (God's Word) and Scripture is "sacramental." Once again, this is intended to mediate between distorted and extreme views. Against liberal Protestant theology Bloesch argues for a close relationship between the Bible and supernatural divine revelation; against Fundamentalism he argues for a distinction between them. "The Bible is not in and of itself the revelation of God but the divinely appointed means and channel of this revelation. . . . The Word of God transcends the human witness, and yet it comes to us only in the servant form of the human words."[38]

Bloesch breaks decisively with fundamentalism and the rationalist-propositionalist view of revelation when he illustrates his sacramental view:

> One might say that the Bible is the Word of God in a formal sense—as a light bulb is related to light. The light bulb is not itself the light but its medium. The light of God's truth is ordinarily shining in the Bible, but it is discerned only by the eyes of faith. Even Christians, however, do not see the light in its full splendor. It is refracted and obscured by the form of the Bible, but it nonetheless reaches us if we have faith.[39]

Bloesch makes clear that he holds a high view of Scripture as God's inspired witness to Jesus Christ, who is God's Word in person. The Holy Spirit communicates Jesus Christ and spiritual truth and life through the Bible as through no other earthly medium (aside from Jesus' humanity). And yet, Bloesch avers, even the Bible has its "highs" and "lows," in that "the message of revelation is explicit in some parts of the Bible and implicit in others" and the Bible contains flaws and blemishes that remind us of its "participation in the real world of decay and death."[40] Bloesch drives the nail in the coffin of a fundamentalist view of Scripture (so far as he is concerned) when he affirms that "our final authority [for Christian faith and practice] is not what the Bible

---

37. Ibid., 272.

38. Donald G. Bloesch, *Holy Scripture: Revelation, Inspiration, and Interpretation* (*Christian Foundations*, vol. 2) (Downers Grove, IL: InterVarsity Press, 1994), 57.

39. Ibid., 59.

40. Ibid.

says but what God says in the Bible."[41] Ultimately, it is the task of the Spirit-guided exegete of Scripture to discern the difference.

Bloesch holds to a high view of Scripture—even if some conservative evangelicals do not think so. "I hold to an ontic difference between the Bible and other books, for the Bible has both a divine origin and a divine goal."[42] He makes abundantly clear that he regards the Bible as unique in its authority for Christian faith and practice in that it stands in judgment over all traditions and thoughts of human beings. He affirms the classical Protestant *sola scriptura* and argues that the Bible is supernaturally inspired by the Holy Spirit of God and is the indispensable witness to Jesus Christ. On the other hand, he questions traditional evangelical interpretations of both inspiration of Scripture and of Scripture's inerrancy. With Baptist theologian Strong a century earlier, Bloesch affirms a dynamic rather than a verbal view of inspiration: "In my view inspiration is the divine election and superintendence of particular writers and writings in order to ensure a trustworthy and potent witness to the truth."[43] As for verbal inspiration, "It means that the words of human beings [the authors of Scripture] are adopted [by the Holy Spirit] to serve the purposes of God."[44] Without denying a propositional aspect to revelation in Scripture, Bloesch states that the "purpose of inspiration is not the production of an errorless book but the regeneration of the seeker after truth."[45] As for inerrancy, "[a] distinction should always be made between what Scripture reports and includes and what it teaches or intends."[46] In other words, the Bible is without error in matters crucial to the encounter with God and salvation but not in every detail: "Scriptural inerrancy can be affirmed if it means the conformity of what is written to the dictates of the Spirit regarding the will and purpose of God. But it cannot be held if it is taken to mean the conformity of everything that is written in Scripture to the facts of world history and science."[47] Bloesch prefers the term "infallible" to "inerrant" for describing Scripture's trustworthiness.

Bloesch's theology creates a hybrid between the strict propositionalism and rationalism of the first generation of postfundamentalist evangelical theologians (Henry, Carnell, et al.) and neo-orthodoxy (Barth, Brunner). However, it is much closer to the classical evangelical synthesis of Protestant orthodoxy and Pietism than to either fundamentalism or neo-orthodoxy, and there is nothing liberal about it (except its liberality as displayed in its generous orthodoxy). Bloesch's influence within Evangelicalism has been a moderating one that helps postfundamentalists discover on a number of crucial theological matters a centrist view that is not mediocre or lukewarm. His is a strongly confessional Protestant theology that affirms all the classical doctrines of Christian orthodoxy stripped of their sectarian imbalance introduced by fundamentalism and often maintained by conservative evangelicals. Conservative evangelicals often find Bloesch frustrating; he is notoriously difficult to categorize. He is certainly not modernist or liberal. His critiques of liberal and radical theologies are devastating, and yet he finds something of value in almost every theologian. His treatment of the controversial issues of feminism, patriarchy, and inclusive language for God is a good example of his nonliberal, mediating approach. While affirming equality of women with men in every area of life, Bloesch condemns radical revisioning of

---

41. Ibid., 60.
42. Ibid., 128.
43. Ibid., 119.
44. Ibid., 120.
45. Ibid., 118.
46. Ibid., 127–28.
47. Ibid., 107.

God (e.g., as "divine Mother") and calls instead for retrieval of biblical feminine metaphors for God. He is certainly not fundamentalist or even traditionally conservative as an evangelical. He consistently criticizes Carl Henry and that type of evangelical rationalism and propositionalism as wooden and sterile. And yet he affirms the supernatural reality of God and God's activity, efficacy of prayer, miracles and classical orthodox doctrines.

What Bloesch brings to Evangelicalism is a balanced perspective that is free from the distorting effects of fundamentalism and the internecine battles that have racked Evangelicalism because of its fundamentalist roots. Yet his influence within Evangelicalism is somewhat muted because he is widely regarded as a "mainliner"—a theologian who may be relatively conservative theologically (in the overall scheme of things) but stands outside the evangelical subculture ("Evangelicalism") and speaks more *to* it than *from within* it. To the extent this is true, however, it may just be the reason he is able to speak such a moderating, balanced message that many, if not most, evangelical theologians need to hear and heed.

POSTCONSERVATIVE EVANGELICAL THEOLOGY

At the turn of the century and millennium, evangelical theology is undergoing special stress and strain. Up until this time, most evangelical theologians have been *postfundamentalist* and yet *conservative*. Postfundamentalist evangelical theology during the first half century of its existence has been marked by a profound anxiety of wanting to distance itself from fundamentalism without being anything other than conservative or traditional. Fear of theological liberalism and fundamentalism has been its obsession. As soon as someone moves too far from fundamentalism—even in terms of harsh rhetoric against its narrowness and dogmatism—he or she falls under "concern" by fellow evangelicals for possibly moving too close to liberalism. The same thing happens whenever an evangelical calls for dialogue with liberals in theology. Anyone who talks of separation from heretical or apostate denominations falls under suspicion from some quarters of having a fundamentalist spirit.

In this milieu of evangelical obsessiveness over its own identity vis-à-vis liberalism and fundamentalism, a few courageous evangelical thinkers have begun to step out and develop what can best be described as a *postconservative* evangelical theology.[48] Postconservative does not indicate "anti-conservative" (contrary to what some critics have suggested) but only a desire to move beyond the category of conservatism insofar as it biases Evangelicalism and evangelical theology in favor of the status quo and keeps it bound to its fundamentalist heritage and habits. Postconservative evangelicals are extremely diverse and can hardly be called a movement. They represent a mood that is dissatisfied with old forms of old debates and with traditionalism for its own sake and especially with maximal conservatism. They believe that "the received evangelical tradition" (whatever that is, exactly) is often a form of bondage that hinders creativity, innovation, and renewal. There is no organization of postconservative evangelicals; they prefer to network with each other and with nonevangelicals. By and large they consider the Evangelical Theological Society too narrow and restrictive; they do not like its requirement of belief in and confession of inerrancy for

---

48. For description and critique of this new movement (or mood) among evangelical theologians, see Roger E. Olson, "Postconservative Evangelicals Greet the Postmodern Age," *Christian Century*, 112, no. 15 (May 3, 1995): 480–83; Dorrien, *The Remaking of Evangelical Theology*; and Millard Erickson, *The Evangelical Left: Encountering Postconservative Evangelical Theology* (Grand Rapids: Baker Books, 1997).

membership. Postconservatives tend to think "outside the box" and are willing to take risks in reforming traditional evangelical formulas. They think of theology as a journey or pilgrimage and of theologians as pioneers rather than guardians or gate-keepers. They desire a "generous orthodoxy" that eschews both narrow dogmatism and liberal relativism. They see value in constructive evangelical engagement and dialogue with postmodern culture and philosophy and are saddened by the harsh polemics that evangelicals often hurl at nonevangelicals and secular culture. Above all, postconservative evangelicals want to rise above the traditional spectrum of "left" (liberal) and "right" (conservative) in modern theology by leaving behind obsessions with issues of the Enlightenment and liberal or fundamentalist habits of the mind.[49] They are willing to reconsider traditional evangelical doctrinal formulations insofar as they are held only because they are traditional and defensive against liberal theology.

The acknowledged leader of postconservative evangelical theology is maverick Canadian evangelical theologian Clark Pinnock (b. 1937). While he is certainly not formally the leader of postconservative evangelical theologians and has not identified himself that way, he is the best known and most widely discussed and influential theologian of this new evangelical theological mood.[50] By his own confession, Pinnock's early evangelical journey was quite typical. He was raised in a fairly liberal Baptist church in Ontario, Canada, but his grandparents were deeply pious, evangelical missionaries to Africa. Their influence on his life was more profound than he realized as a child and young person. In 1950 he experienced conversion to Christ and, by his own confession, became a fundamentalist. His spiritual and theological life was being nurtured and shaped by radio preachers such as Charles Fuller, Billy Graham, and Donald Grey Barnhouse. He became involved with the Youth for Christ movement in Toronto and there also fell under the influence of famous fundamentalist pastor Oswald J. Smith, pastor of the Peoples Church. Later he was influenced by the Keswick movement, InterVarsity Christian Fellowship, Francis Schaeffer's L'Abri retreat and movement, and by Christian authors such as C. S. Lewis and John R. Stott. After graduating from university in Canada, Pinnock began doctoral studies in New Testament with British evangelical scholar F. F. Bruce at the University of Manchester in England.

After completing his doctoral work, the young evangelical scholar returned to North America and taught at a succession of seminaries: New Orleans Baptist Theological Seminary, Trinity Evangelical Divinity School, Regent College, and McMaster Divinity College. His major works include *A Defense of Biblical Infallibility* (1967), *Reason Enough: A Case for the Christian Faith* (1980), *The Scripture Principle* (1985), *A Wideness in God's Mercy* (1992), *Flame of Love: A Theology of the Holy Spirit* (1996), and *Most Moved Mover: A Theology of the Openness of God* (2001). Pinnock also edited several volumes, contributed to many more, and published numerous articles. His early writings reveal his early conservative, rationalistic, and Reformed orientation. Under the influence of Carl Henry and Francis Schaeffer the young Pinnock followed the traditional postfundamentalist evangelical line very closely and was aggressive in his defenses of biblical inerrancy and rationalist apologetics. He was brought from England to New Orleans by the seminary president to "hold the line" against neo-orthodoxy there. (Whether there really was an influence of neo-orthodoxy at that seminary or that was a false perception is debatable.)

---

49. See Nancey Murphy, *Beyond Liberalism and Fundamentalism: How Modern and Postmodern Philosophy Set the Theological Agenda* (Valley Forge, PA: Trinity Press International, 1996).

50. See the intellectual biography of Pinnock by Barry L. Callen, *Clark Pinnock: Journey Toward Renewal* (Nappanee, IN: Evangel Publishing House, 2000).

In midcareer, while teaching theology at Trinity Evangelical Divinity School in suburban Chicago, Pinnock began to undergo a change in theological orientation that he described in a chapter entitled "From Augustine to Arminius: A Pilgrimage in Theology." There he stated that "I guess it is time for evangelicals to grow up and recognize that evangelical theology is not an uncontested body of timeless truth. There are various accounts of it. . . . Like it or not, we are embarked on a pilgrimage in theology and cannot determine exactly where will it [sic] lead and how it will end."[51] As part of his theological turn he came to understand doctrine as changeable and theology as a pilgrimage toward truth. To his critics this seemed relativistic, but to Pinnock it was merely appreciation for the theologian's own finitude and fallenness. As part of his change Pinnock turned away from the Augustinian-Calvinist model of God and God's relationship with the world (God as the all-determining reality) toward the Arminian model of God's self-limiting relationship with humanity for the sake of human freedom and participation in their own salvation. Even as he began to throw off Reformed theology, he realized that it might mean a radical revisioning of God's attributes toward a more relational understanding. Eventually he did develop and promote the idea of God's "openness"—that God freely chooses to learn what the future holds as humans use their free will to make morally responsible decisions. He has consistently argued that he came to this view independently of the liberal school of thought known as process theology and that he has little sympathy with it, but his critics have often charged him with compromising with that perceived enemy of evangelical thought.

Another change came about in Pinnock's understanding of Scripture. In *The Scripture Principle* he affirmed a high view of Scripture stripped of fundamentalist and conservative evangelical biblicism. While paying lip service to inerrancy (minimized and highly qualified), the pilgrim theologian argued for evangelical acknowledgment of diversity within the Bible:

> I suggest that we think of inspiration in broader terms than is customary—less as a punctilinear enlightenment of a few elect persons and more as a long-term divine activity operating within the whole history of revelation. Inspiration means that God gave us the Scriptures, but it does not dictate how we must think of the individual units being produced. Scripture exists because of the will of God and is a result of his ultimate causality, but it comes into existence through many gifts of prophecy, insight, imagination, and wisdom that the Spirit gives as he wills. The all-important point is that everything taught in the Scriptures is meant to be heard and heeded, because it is divinely intended. Every segment is inspired by God, though not in the same way, and the result is a richly variegated teacher, richer for all its diversity. The very differences are what enables the Bible to speak with power and relevance to so many different people in so many different settings, and to address the many-sidedness of the human condition.[52]

As Pinnock continued on his journey in theology he reconsidered the issue of salvation and discovered a "wideness in God's mercy" that stops short of universal salvation but requires embrace of "inclusivism." In *A Wideness in God's Mercy: The Finality of Jesus Christ in a World of Religions*, the maverick evangelical theologian threw out the traditional evangelical pessimism about the possibility of salvation for the unevangelized and argued in favor of an "optimism of salvation" in Christ for those who never had a chance to hear about the Savior of the world. "God sent Jesus to be the Savior of the world, not the Savior of a select few."[53] Pinnock argued from the logic of God's

51. In *The Grace of God, The Will of Man: A Case for Arminianism*, ed. Clark H. Pinnock (Grand Rapids: Zondervan, 1989), 28.

52. Clark H. Pinnock, *The Scripture Principle* (San Francisco: Harper & Row, 1984), 64.

53. Clark H. Pinnock, *A Wideness in God's Mercy: The Finality of Jesus Christ in a World of Religions* (Grand Rapids: Zondervan, 1992), 47.

love and provision of redemption that any sincere truth-seeker may be encountered by God on the journey toward truth and be reconciled to God by God's grace and mercy. Contrary to critics, nowhere does Pinnock affirm unconditional universal salvation; instead he affirms that God does not automatically reject all who do not hear and explicitly respond to the gospel message as preached by a Christian missionary. In several publications he has suggested a postmortem opportunity for acceptance of Jesus Christ for the unevangelized. In *A Wideness In God's Mercy*, however, he suggests that people may be saved by Jesus Christ (never apart from his life and death) through the universal light of God that is present in human conscience and cultures.

Another part of Pinnock's postconservative theological pilgrimage is his experience with the charismatic movement and the so-called Third Wave of the Holy Spirit in the "signs and wonders movement." He became involved in a charismatic Bible study and prayer meeting in the 1970s and then in the Vineyard movement in Toronto. While retaining his Baptist identity and church membership, Pinnock began to consider himself part of the Third Wave of the Holy Spirit (the first being Pentecostalism, the second the charismatic movement) associated with the ministry of John Wimber and his followers. In *Flame of Love: A Theology of the Holy Spirit* the Canadian evangelical theologian sought to bring the person and work of the Holy Spirit back into the foreground of evangelical theological reflection without in any way diminishing the roles of the Father and the Son. There he affirmed the present supernatural activity of the Spirit in all of the gifts mentioned in the New Testament (contra traditional evangelical cessationism) while admonishing Pentecostals. With regard to speaking in tongues, he proposed the principle that while it is normal, it is not the norm. In other words, unlike conventional evangelicals who resist tongues and other supernatural gifts of utterance, Pinnock believes these are contemporary gifts of the Spirit to the churches and should be practiced by believers; but unlike classical Pentecostals and many charismatics, he does not think they are required signs of spiritual life.

Finally, Pinnock broke the patience of many conservative evangelicals by rejecting conventional theism or classical theism and embracing what he calls the "openness of God," or "open theism." Although he had strongly hinted at it earlier, Pinnock first laid out his program for a new evangelical understanding of God's relationship with the world in *The Openness of God*, which he coauthored with four other evangelical theologians and philosophers in 1994. In his chapter, entitled simply "Systematic Theology," he argued that so-called classical theism is problematic from a biblical perspective and also inconsistent with many essential aspects of evangelical Christian spirituality. For example, Scripture reveals God as interactive with humans, such that prayer can change God's mind. And yet classical theism and much of the received evangelical tradition claims that God is strictly immutable. Also, if prayer cannot change God's mind because God is strictly immutable, why pray petitionary prayers at all? If God already foreknows the future exhaustively and infallibly, there does not seem to be any urgency in petitionary prayers such as evangelicals traditionally pray. In *The Openness of God* and in his later volume, *Most Moved Mover* (2001), Pinnock laid out an entire program for the renewal of evangelical theism through an infusion of "biblical theism." God, he argues, voluntarily limits himself such that he can be affected by the freewill decisions and prayers of his human creatures. Futhermore, God does not know the future exhaustively and infallibly, because much of the future is determined by genuinely free decisions of human beings, and God will not abrogate that freedom by determining all decisions and actions—which would be the only way God could foreknow them. For Pinnock and other open theists (Gregory Boyd, John Sanders, et al.) this is the only view that does justice to God's personal interaction with human beings in history. To their critics it is heresy, if not idolatry. The controversy surrounding open theism led to a resolution by the Evangelical Theological

Society (of which Pinnock is a member) in 2001 affirming God's absolute knowledge of all events past, present, and future.

Pinnock has been and remains both a catalyst for reform and renewal and a lightning rod for controversy within Evangelicalism and among evangelical theologians. He has been called a pioneer, a moving target, and a false prophet. Few who know his theology are indifferent to it. His overall impact on evangelical theology remains to be seen; his career is not completed and his magnum opus remains unwritten. He may never write a theological system or anything approaching it, because he prefers the journey model, which centers around ad hoc contributions to theology, to the closed system model, which seeks to summarize all theological truth in a coherent system. Although Pinnock has not explicitly embraced postmodernism, it seems that he is influenced by postmodernity, whether he is aware of that or not. He has expressed strong sympathy for narrative theology that views divine revelation more as story (epic, not fiction) than as a set of propositions and called for a "postmodern orthodoxy."[54] For him, then, the "essence of Christianity" is the "epic story of salvation," rather than law, dogma, theory, or experience. Doctrine is second-order speech that seeks to interpret the metanarrative delivered in Scripture. Systematic theology, Pinnock fears, tends to replace the narrative structure of revelation with all its wonder and mystery. However, Pinnock's sympathizers hope that he will eventually write a summary of Christian doctrine from his own postconservative evangelical perspective. They find his approach refreshing and liberating as well as consistent both with the gospel of Jesus Christ and the best of postmodern culture that resists absolutizing and totalizing metanarratives.

What do these five postfundamentalist evangelical theologians have in common? What makes Carl Henry, E. J. Carnell, Bernard Ramm, Donald Bloesch, and Clark Pinnock all "*evangelical* theologians"? They do not agree about basic theological methodology; some push universal canons of reason to the fore in theology, while others reject such and elevate divine revelation and faith over reason and evidence. They do not agree about the nature of divine revelation entirely; some insist on the primacy of propositions in revelation while others promote nonpropositional aspects of revelation such as incarnation, encounter, and narrative. They do not agree about the nature of Scripture; some argue for its verbal, plenary inspiration and strict inerrancy in all matters, while others view inspiration as dynamic and prefer infallibility to inerrancy. The diversity within evangelical theology becomes even greater when one includes other evangelical theologians in the list for comparison.

What makes them all evangelical is their common commitment to a supernatural life and worldview, the Bible as the supernaturally inspired and infallible Word of God, Jesus Christ as God and Savior, the triune, transcendent-immanent God of the Bible as creator of all things, salvation through conversion to Jesus Christ by repentance and faith and through grace alone, world transformation through evangelism and social action, and the cross of Jesus Christ (i.e., his atoning death) as the only hope for and means of reconciliation and redemption of lost humanity. Compared with many other groups of Christian theologians and movements within Christian theology, then, these five and all evangelical theologians have much in common. Together they form a distinct alternative to classical Roman Catholic theology and liberal Protestant thought, as well as to all the radical and liberationist theologies of the late twentieth century. Tensions within evangelical theology and among evangelical theologians threaten to dissolve that unity, however, and if they are not careful, they will

---

54. Clark H. Pinnock, *Tracking the Maze: Finding Our Way through Modern Theology from an Evangelical Perspective* (San Francisco: Harper & Row, 1990).

experience a balkanization of evangelical theology that will cause it to cease to exist as a relatively unified movement. The final portion of this historical essay will be a brief overview of those tensions within evangelical theology.

TENSIONS IN EVANGELICAL THEOLOGY

The postfundamentalist evangelical coalition was born with diversity, and yet some of its leaders—including its leading theologians—expected their own preferred theological orientations to dominate it. This is probably the most profound cause of tension within evangelical theology—the feelings of superiority and neglect among different types of evangelicals. Most of the early movers and shakers of the evangelical coalition in the 1940s and 1950s were theologically Reformed. That is, they looked back to Augustine, John Calvin, Ulrich Zwingli, Martin Bucer, and Jonathan Edwards as the great heroes of the evangelical faith. Bernard Ramm displayed this tendency to elevate Reformed theology over its alternatives in his *The Evangelical Heritage*. He almost totally ignored the contributions of non-Reformed theologians, such as the Anabaptists Balthasar Hubmaier and Menno Simons, the Pietists, John Wesley, Charles Finney, and other Arminian and free church theologians. Evangelical historian George Marsden has also highlighted the Reformed roots of Evangelicalism in his influential accounts of evangelical history. Many evangelical writers treat the subject as if Reformed theology is normative for Evangelicalism. All the while, of course, many evangelical lay people, pastors, and leaders, as well as influential evangelists and missionaries, are Arminian, Wesleyan, or Pentecostal. The National Association of Evangelicals includes at least as many non-Reformed member churches and denominations as Reformed ones.

In response to this bent toward Reformed thinking in evangelical theology, evangelical historian Donald Dayton has raised the argument that the "Pentecostal Paradigm" of evangelical history is just as likely and probably truer to the facts than the "Presbyterian Paradigm" of Marsden and others. The Pentecostal Paradigm refers to a view that authentic Evangelicalism and evangelical theology is revivalistic and at least implicitly Arminian, not Reformed.[55] The Presbyterian Paradigm refers to the view—opposed by Dayton but attributed to Marsden—that authentic Evangelicalism and evangelical theology is rooted in the Puritans and the Princeton School of theology. This debate and the hard feelings associated with it were raised to a new pitch of intensity with the founding of the Alliance of Confessing Evangelicals in the 1990s. Its publication, *Modern Reformation*, promotes the belief that authentic evangelical theology is indeed Reformed, or at least rooted in the Lutheran-Reformed (monergistic) Reformation and its doctrines of absolute divine sovereignty.

Tensions between conservative, aggressive Calvinist evangelicals and defensive Arminian evangelicals threaten to disrupt the uneasy harmony of the evangelical theological community. As long as Billy Graham is alive and well and able robustly to hold the evangelical coalition together in spite of all its diversity, these tensions remain just under the surface. Once the "Graham glue" dissolves with his retirement or death, it seems likely that at least the more dogmatic group of Reformed evangelicals and more defensive group of Arminian (including Wesleyan) evangelicals will break away from each other and disrupt the evangelical coalition.

Another tension within evangelical theology is between *reformist* and *traditionalist* evangelical theologians. Traditionalists favor a "forward to the past" program for

---

55. See Donald W. Dayton, "The Search for the Historical Evangelicalism: George Marsden's History of Fuller Seminary as a Case Study," *Christian Scholar's Review* 23, no. 1 (September 1993).

evangelical strength. That is, they regard reform and renewal as retrieval of tradition. Thomas Oden is a Methodist evangelical theologian who was formerly liberal and taught for many years at Methodist-related Drew Theological Seminary. In several volumes and numerous articles he has called for a rediscovery of the authority of the early church's teaching as a "consensual tradition" through which Scripture must be interpreted. His three-volume *Systematic Theology* (San Francisco: Harper & Row, 1987–92) is a compendium of early Christian teaching on all the traditional doctrinal loci of theology; he argues that the consensus of the church fathers and great creeds of Christendom must function for even Protestant Christians as a "rule of faith" alongside of Scripture.

Reformists favor a "new light" program for evangelical renewal. That is, they regard truth as continually breaking forth from God's Word, correcting tradition, and reforming the church and its theology. Pinnock is a reformist, as is Stanley J. Grenz, who has written numerous volumes of evangelical theology, including *Revisioning Evangelical Theology* (Downers Grove, IL: InterVarsity Press, 1993), which elevates "conversional piety" over doctrine as the essence of evangelical faith. Reformists believe that the constructive task of theology is never finished; traditionalists consider the only valid tasks of theology as instructional and critical. Traditionalists tend to be more concerned with evangelical identity and boundaries, whereas reformists are more concerned with diversity in unity through an evangelical community with a strong center but no definite boundaries. These two parties of evangelical theologians often fall into tension with each other.[56] Traditionalists tend to view reformists as soft on doctrine and relativistic with regard to truth; reformists tend to view traditionalists as dogmatic, reactionary, and irrelevant to contemporary issues and concerns facing Christians.

A third area of evangelical theological tension surrounds the nature of Scripture. Evangelical theologians have never reached complete agreement about this crucial matter. In 1977 influential evangelical theologian and editor of *Christianity Today* Harold Lindsell published a bombshell book, entitled *The Battle for the Bible* (Grand Rapids: Zondervan), that argued that belief in strict biblical inerrancy—including inerrancy in matters of history and cosmology—is an essential of evangelical faith. The book was written partly in response to an earlier work by evangelical theologian Dewey Beegle, entitled *Scripture, Tradition, and Infallibility* (Grand Rapids: Wm. B. Eerdmans, 1973), that argued that Scripture is simply not inerrant or infallible and that one can believe in its inspiration and authority without overlooking or denying its factual errors in matters unrelated to salvation. Lindsell disagreed most vehemently and identified evangelical scholars and institutions whom he considered less than authentically evangelical because they did not affirm inerrancy in the way he believed it must be affirmed. (Lindsell went so far as to posit six crowings of the rooster in the incident of Peter's denial of Jesus in order to harmonize the Gospel accounts!)

The fallout from the book was disastrous for evangelical unity. It helped propel the entire Southern Baptist Convention—America's largest Protestant denomination—into a twenty-year convulsion. Almost overnight evangelical organizations and institutions rushed to include inerrancy in their doctrinal statements, whether they understood precisely what it meant or not. Even Carl Henry disagreed with Lindsell about the status of inerrancy as an essential of evangelical faith; he considered it essential to *consistent* evangelical thought, but he did not agree that one must affirm it in order to be an evangelical. Between 1977 and the new millennium, controversy over

---

56. See Roger E. Olson, "The Future of Evangelical Theology," *Christianity Today* 42, no. 2 (February 9, 1998): 40–48.

inerrancy consumed evangelical attention and energies. Numerous high-level conferences were held to attempt to define the concept and bring about some degree of reconciliation among evangelical parties that disagreed about it. The flagship evangelical seminary, Fuller Theological Seminary, resisted any attempt to force it to put inerrancy into its statement of faith. The National Association of Evangelicals retained "infallible" rather than "inerrant" as its description of Scripture's trustworthiness. On the other hand, many evangelical denominations and institutions began to use inerrancy as a litmus test for inclusion and acceptance.

Few evangelical theologians are willing to say that Scripture errs, but many say that "inerrant" is a misleading term for Scripture in that it implies the imposition of an alien standard of accuracy on an ancient text and detracts from the humanity and historicity of Scripture. In other words, it simply is not consistent with the actual phenomena of the biblical text. For them, "infallibility" is a stronger term than "inerrancy," in that a phone book can be inerrant without being infallible. Scripture's purpose is to identify God and communicate God's will as well as God's mercy and grace to humanity. So long as it does that successfully, whether it is "without error in the original autographs" is irrelevant.

A fourth area of tension within evangelical theology revolves around the rather amorphous issue of "evangelical boundaries." That is, which Christians and theological ideas are legitimately evangelical and which, though they may claim to be evangelical, are not? This has also to do with evangelical uses of nonevangelical thought and with evangelical dialogue with nonevangelicals, including Roman Catholics, Latter-day Saints (Mormons), liberal Protestants (including process theologians), and proponents of modernism (culture shaped by the Enlightenment) and postmodernism (culture in reaction to modernism but still rooted in the Enlightenment). Postfundamentalist evangelical founders and early leaders were never sure about Evangelicalism's precise limits and boundaries. According to their separatistic fundamentalist critics such as Carl McIntire, they demonstrated a lack of discernment about this matter when they admitted Pentecostals into the National Association of Evangelicals. On the other hand, they excluded any and all denominations and organizations that held membership in the mainline, more liberal Federal Council of Churches (later known as the National Council of Churches). Throughout its first almost fifty years of existence the National Association of Evangelicals has rejected such dual membership, while including within its ranks groups that fundamentalists (and perhaps some conservative evangelicals) consider heterodox. When the Evangelical Theological Society was founded, it required affirmation of biblical inerrancy for membership and has retained that, while adding belief in the Trinity (perhaps to exclude non-Trinitarian Pentecostals). Most, if not all, of the evangelical coalition's leaders wanted to expand evangelical boundaries to include both Reformed and Arminian perspectives on God's sovereignty and salvation, while keeping Reformed theology at the center of the coalition calling most of the shots.

Gradually two distinct viewpoints on evangelical identity developed within the evangelical coalition. For lack of better terminology we will here refer to them as the "broad view" and the "narrow view." No value judgment is intended with this terminology. All evangelicals agree that if Evangelicalism is compatible with anything and everything—even within Christendom—it is a meaningless concept, and its hopes for being an agent of renewal are dashed. The narrow-view evangelical theologians and leaders wish to identify and hold firm boundaries around Evangelicalism in order to stave off the seemingly inevitable "drift" toward doctrinal compromise and pluralism that has (at least according to conservative evangelicals) undermined the Christian witness of all mainline Protestant denominations and most of their churches and institutions. The broad-view evangelical theologians and leaders wish to expand

Evangelicalism to include as many God-fearing, Jesus-loving, Bible-believing Christians as possible, while maintaining evangelical identity through a strong center of the movement. Narrow-view evangelicals fear that broad-view evangelicals will sell the soul of the movement through too much inclusion; broad-view evangelicals fear that narrow-view evangelicals will return the movement to fundamentalism. Of course, many evangelicals would not identify with either of these parties, but there are vocal leaders and thinkers within Evangelicalism who betray their sympathies by their responses to evangelical dialogue with nonevangelicals or to evangelical resolutions critical of greater diversity and inclusion within the movement.

The troubling issue of evangelical boundaries came up once again in the first year of the new millennium. The Evangelical Theological Society devoted its 2001 annual meeting to discussion about the matter and focused in particular on the open theism of Pinnock and others. Because several members of the ETS espoused that view of God and the future, it had become a matter of controversy within the ETS and the wider evangelical community. Several Reformed evangelical critics of open theism sought to exclude it and its proponents from Evangelicalism and the ETS by means of a resolution. The resolution that was passed by a majority of voting members of the society at its meeeeting in Colorado Springs in November 2001, however, stated only that God's knowledge of all events past, present, and future is certain and infallible. Much to the chagrin of some of the society's more conservative and fundamentalist members, open theists—including Pinnock—were not forced out. Whether their memberships will be dropped in the future, however, is uncertain.

Another boundary issue that creates tension within the evangelical theological community is related to evangelical appropriation of postmodern thought. This issue has been lurking in the background of evangelical discussion about boundaries throughout the 1990s and into the first decade of the new millennium, but it began to come to the foreground in 2001 at the ETS's annual meeting, devoted to evangelical boundaries. Controversy over evangelical uses of postmodern philosophy began with the 1995 publication of *Truth Is Stranger Than It Used to Be* (Downers Grove, IL: InterVarsity Press) by Canadian evangelical thinkers J. Richard Middleton and Brian J. Walsh. The authors claimed that postmodern philosophy's suspicion of all metanarratives (comprehensive worldviews) is compatible with the Bible's condemnations of idolatry and oppression. While affirming that the biblical narrative provides the one true metanarrative, Middleton and Walsh rejected any and all "totalizing metanarratives" on biblical grounds and argued that the Christian metanarrative is a liberating, antitotalizing one. Some evangelical critics felt they gave too much ground from under objective truth and accommodated too much to the relativistic spirit of the postmodern age. Sympathetic readers, however, discovered in *Truth Is Stranger Than It Used to Be* a refreshing departure from the conventional evangelical attacks on culture that are so often dependent on modern, Enlightenment modes of thinking.

The evangelical theologian who has done more than anyone else to engage postmodernity from an evangelical perspective is Stanley J. Grenz. In a series of lectures, papers, and books Grenz has presented a creative proposal for a postmodern evangelical theology that emphasizes the eschatological nature of truth and reality (drawing on the theology of Grenz's German mentor Wolfhart Pannenberg), the communal nature of Christianity (as opposed to modern individualism), and the narrative shape of revelation and the gospel message (using postliberal theologians such as Stanley Hauerwas). Grenz's systematic theology, *Theology for the Community of God* (Grand Rapids: Wm. B. Eerdmans, 2000), used the organizing theme of community to unite the various doctrinal loci and relegated the doctrine of Scripture to a section of the doctrine of the Holy Spirit. Like Middleton and Walsh and a variety of other postconservative evangelical thinkers who find an ally in some aspects of postmodernity, Grenz rejects Enlightenment foundationalist epistemology that seeks indubitable grounds for certainty outside of God's self-revelation in Jesus Christ and the narrative that identifies and makes him present to the believing community. Instead of viewing evangelical Christianity's essence as timeless truths in the form of revealed doctrines, he regards it as the experience of "conversional piety" that takes place within the believing Christian community shaped by the gospel story. As in the case of Middleton and Walsh, critics of Grenz's project object that it undermines the public, universal, propositional, and rational truth of the evangelical witness and ultimately succumbs to cultural relativism. Grenz and his defenders respond that such a critique is entirely based on outmoded Enlightenment (i.e., modernist) assumptions about the nature of truth and knowledge.

Some critics of evangelical engagement with postmodernity view the matter as a boundary issue and would like to restrict the evangelical community to those who reject postmodernism entirely. These narrow-view evangelicals are suspicious of evangelical appropriations of postmodern thought—however critical they may be—as dangerous, because they consider postmodernity irreducibly relativistic and worry that if the camel's nose of postmodernity is allowed under the evangelical tent, it will soon fill the whole tent and push out the objective truth of the gospel. Grenz and other broad-view evangelicals consider this concern overblown. Evangelicals have always appropriated elements of nonevangelical and even non-Christian philosophies—sometimes unwittingly. Conservative evangelicals such as Carl Henry and his followers used forms of foundationalism provided by Enlightenment thinkers such as Descartes and Locke and were heavily influenced by Scottish common sense realism—a British philosophy that responded to Hume's skepticism on the basis of a certain Enlightenment perspective. There is a great deal of interest in postmodernity among the younger evangelical students, pastors, and budding theologians. This greatly concerns many of the older evangelical thinkers who came to identify evangelical theology with the rational presuppositionalism and Reformed propositionalism of the leading evangelical thinkers of the 1950s. Some of them are mounting a concerted effort to enforce their narrow-view version of evangelical identity by portraying all postmodernity as negative deconstructionism that reduces to a relativistic ontology and pragmatic epistemology.

In spite of these points of tension within it and in spite of its diversity, evangelical theology has great vitality and significant unity. During the 1990s and into the first decade of the new millennium it has begun to emerge as a widely accepted legitimate theological alternative to mainline Protestant liberalism (e.g., process theology), liberationist theologies (e.g., radical feminism and Marxist-inspired Latin American liberation theology), and neo-orthodoxy (e.g., postliberal, Yale-New Haven theology). The future vitality and influence of evangelical theology will no doubt depend a great deal on harmony among evangelical theologians and the administrators who generally employ them in evangelical institutions. The greatest challenge facing them is striking the balance between unity and diversity within the evangelical theological community. Another challenge is retaining their basically conservative doctrinal identity while allowing and even affirming theological creativity within their ranks. At the moment most of the creative theological reflection and construction being done by evangelical theologians is taking place—and for the foreseeable future will be taking place—outside the power centers of conservative, establishment evangelical theological life (e.g., the Evangelical Theological Society and primary evangelical colleges and seminaries).

It seems that in order to break new ground in evangelical theology and think in fresh and imaginative ways, evangelical theologians must be free of the hindrances of ecclesiastical political conservatism and the fundamentalist habits of the mind that still regulate much of evangelical administration. Leading the way into Evangelicalism's theological reform are such young, innovate thinkers as Miroslav Volf, Stanley J. Grenz, Kevin Vanhoozer, Nancey Murphy, and John Sanders. Leading the way in maintaining the status quo of the "received evangelical tradition" and guarding Evangelicalism's traditional theological identity and boundaries are Millard Erickson, Wayne Grudem, Norman Geisler, and Al Mohler Jr. It would be to evangelical theology's great detriment if these thinkers and their followers ceased having dialogue with one another so that evangelical theology broke into two camps ignoring each other or even casting uninformed aspersions at one another. The future of evangelical theology depends on harmony, if not agreement, between these two groups of influential evangelical thinkers.

Movements and Organizations Related to Evangelical Theology

The Billy Graham Evangelistic Association

Without any doubt Billy Graham (William Franklin Graham) has been one of the most influential forces in the shaping of postfundamentalist evangelical *theology*. That is true in spite of the fact that he never earned a doctorate in theology or any other subject (although he has been awarded numerous honorary doctoral degrees) and he is not considered a theologian in any academic or professional sense. Nevertheless, the Baptist evangelist and his associated ministries virtually gave birth to the new evangelical coalition that arose out of separatistic *fundamentalism* in the 1940s and 1950s.

The Billy Graham Evangelistic Association (BGEA) was founded by evangelist Billy Graham and his associates Cliff Barrows, Grady Wilson, and George Wilson in 1950 in Minneapolis, Minnesota. Graham was serving as president of the Baptist-related Northwestern Schools (later renamed Northwestern College) in Minneapolis while traveling to preach at evangelistic rallies and campaigns across North America. The purpose of the BGEA was to serve as a corporate entity to handle funds raised for Graham's new radio evangelistic endeavor. The association's headquarters was established in downtown Minneapolis, where it remained until 2002, when Graham's son and successor as president of the organization, Franklin Graham, moved it to North Carolina, where the Graham family had lived and maintained a retreat center for decades.

Over the years the BGEA grew to become a massive and complex umbrella organization for numerous evangelistic endeavors related to the ministry of Billy Graham. The radio program that gave rise to the founding of the BGEA, *The Hour of Decision*, by 1954 was being broadcast by NBC on over eight hundred radio stations in North America alone. The same year that the BGEA was founded saw the birth of Billy Graham Films, later renamed World Wide Pictures, which eventually produced over two hundred films, some of which have been shown in secular movie theaters. A BGEA tabloid periodical entitled simply *Decision* grew to millions of subscriptions worldwide. The association also handles the arrangements and finances for Graham's evangelistic crusades, which, as of 2002, were still being held in major cities of the world.

One of the most significant events in the development of postfundamentalist Evangelicalism and its distinctive theology was the founding of its flagship periodical *Christianity Today*, which could not have happened without Graham and the BGEA. In his autobiography, *Just As I Am* (HarperSanFrancisco/Zondervan, 1997), Graham recounts the magazine's beginnings in his own mind in 1953. By that time, the evangelist and his associates were already networking with leading evangelical spokesmen to develop a "neo-Evangelicalism" free of the *separatism* and narrowness of fundamentalism but still basically conservative in theology. One such leading postfundamentalist evangelical was Harold John Ockenga, visionary and founder of the *National Association of Evangelicals* and president of the new Fuller Theological Seminary. With help from L. Nelson Bell (his father-in-law), Ockenga, philanthropist J. Howard Pew, and others, Graham founded *Christianity Today* in 1956. The founding editor was the man who eventually would be known as the "dean of evangelical theologians," *Carl F. H. Henry*. Although *Christianity Today* has never been a department of the BGEA, it began out of Billy Graham's ministry. This is just one example of numerous ways in which Graham and his organization deeply impacted the development of evangelical theology.

The influence of the BGEA on evangelical theology has been indirect. The BGEA never founded a seminary or theological publication, but it has touched virtually every corner of the evangelical community, including theological institutions and publications. It has initiated and funded many theological meetings that brought together evangelical theologians and leaders of different denominations for dialogue and cooperation. The primary impact of the BGEA on evangelical theology has been its breadth of theological vision, combined with its unwavering commitment to basic, historic Christian beliefs and values. It has served to soften some of the rough edges of conservative evangelical Christianity in North America and elsewhere, with the result that the evangelical coalition has included conservative Christians from various backgrounds and doctrinal orientations (e.g., Calvinist and Arminian). The BGEA's biblical and theologically conservative focus combined with ecumenical breadth has indelibly stamped the evangelical community and its theology.

Billy Graham, *Just As I Am* (San Francisco and Grand Rapids: HarperSanFrancisco and Zondervan, 1997).

The Charismatic Movement

Throughout the twentieth century, evangelical Christianity has included a Pentecostal contingent. (See the related article on *Pentecostalism*.) The Pentecostal movement began in the century's first decade–either in 1901 or in 1906, depending on which historians of the movement one believes. Pentecostalism stood out from other portions of Evangelicalism by promoting a particularly enthusiastic and emotional form of Christian *experience* marked by a "second definite blessing" subsequent to conversion, known as the *baptism of the Holy Spirit*, always accompanied by speaking in unknown tongues (glossolalia) after the pattern of the day of Pentecost (Acts 2). Pentecostals emphasized the contemporary, *supernatural* reality of all of the *gifts of the Holy Spirit* mentioned by the apostle Paul in 1 Corinthians 12, including miraculous divine healing and prophecy (which most Pentecostals interpret as divinely inspired

exhortative speech rather than foretelling the future). By midcentury the Pentecostal movement was by and large isolated from mainstream Christianity and even from other evangelicals, except for occasional cooperation with evangelistic endeavors such as *Billy Graham* crusades. The movement was divided into numerous sects and often exhibited legalistic and anti-intellectual tendencies. The predominant perception of Pentecostalism and its hallmark experience of speaking in tongues was one of fanaticism and otherworldly asceticism.

During the early 1950s, David Du Plessis, a Pentecostal minister from South Africa, began to attend meetings of the World Council of Churches—the worldwide ecumenical umbrella organization of denominations. Through his ecumenical contacts he began to spread the message of the "full gospel" (Pentecostals' term for their message of *Spirit baptism* accompanied by speaking in tongues and divine healing through prayers of faith) into mainline Protestant and Catholic churches. At about the same time and not coincidentally, Demos Shakarian, a California businessman of Armenian descent, founded the Full Gospel Business Men's Fellowship International on the same principles. From the mid-1950s to the mid-1960s a number of mainline Protestant ministers and leaders experienced the Pentecostal second blessing and spoke in tongues and remained in their churches and denominations. Dennis Bennett (Episcopalian), Larry Christenson and Herald Bredesen (Lutheran), and J. Rodman Williams (Presbyterian theologian) were among the earliest "neo-Pentecostals." (The term *neo-Pentecostal* is virtually synonymous with *charismatic*.)

Before 1959/1960 (the crucial years of the birth of the charismatic movement) Christians who spoke in tongues usually felt pressured to leave their denominations and join Pentecostal churches. Afterwards, many tongues-speakers managed to stay within their traditional denominations (including the Roman

Catholic Church, which embraced charismatics who remained faithful to traditional Catholic teaching and practice) and even to lead charismatic renewal movements within them. One of the largest and most influential mainline charismatic renewal movements has been the Lutheran Conference on the Holy Spirit centered in the Twin Cities of Minnesota. Every year thousands of Lutherans converge there to experience charismatic *prayer* and praise *worship*, speak in tongues, receive prayer for physical healing, and attend teaching workshops on subjects related to the gifts of the Holy Spirit.

The main theological difference between the charismatic movement (neo-Pentecostalism) and the classical Pentecostal movement (e.g., Assemblies of God) is that the latter insists on the "initial physical evidence of speaking in tongues" for the baptism of the Holy Spirit, whereas the former generally does not. Some charismatics affirm that Spirit baptism is always accompanied by speaking in tongues, and some do not. The vast majority of charismatics share with their more sectarian Pentecostal brothers and sisters the belief that speaking in tongues is a prayer language for every Christian that did not cease with the deaths of the first-century Christian apostles. There is no single, unified "charismatic *theology*." Most charismatics embrace the doctrinal perspectives of their own denominations or of their independent charismatic churches and simply add to them their belief in the present-day importance of the experience of Spirit baptism and of the supernatural gifts of the Holy Spirit, including speaking in tongues as a way of being spiritually edified and communicating with God beyond rational speech.

Most charismatics are evangelical in spirituality and theology. That is, they believe fervently in the hallmarks of evangelical Christianity such as *conversion* to Christ by *grace* through *faith* alone, *Jesus Christ* as God incarnate and Savior of the world, Scripture as uniquely authoritative in all matters of faith and practice, and the importance of *evangelism* and missions. Most are Trinitarian and affirm basic outlines of the historic Nicene faith of their churches. Few, however, have produced formal theological writings. Most of the books written by Charismatics have been testimonies of their own spiritual experiences and explorations of biblical materials related to the distinctive charismatic experiences. One exception is J. Rodman Williams, who first spoke in tongues while a theology professor at Austin Presbyterian Theological Seminary in Texas in 1965. Later Williams became a professor of theology at charismatic-related Regent University School of Theology in Virginia. Throughout the 1980s he produced a two-volume charismatic systematic theology entitled *Renewal Theology* (Grand Rapids: Zondervan) that focused on the theme of Holy Spirit renewal of individuals and *churches* including supernatural experiences (especially Spirit baptism) and the gifts of the Holy Spirit.

Vinson Synan, *The Century of the Holy Spirit: 100 Years of Pentecostal and Charismatic Renewal* (Nashville: Thomas Nelson, 2001); J. Rodman Williams, *Renewal Theology*, 1-vol. edition (Grand Rapids: Zondervan, 1996).

Dispensationalism The precise meaning, contours, and boundaries of the theological perspective known as dispensationalism are strongly disputed even by scholars who have studied it for decades. In its broadest sense, dispensationalism is any attempt to discern different "dispensations" or "economies" of *God's* saving plan and work in human history. In this broad sense, there have always been dispensationalists within Christianity. The medieval mystic and spiritual theologian Joachim of Fiore attempted to distinguish between three eras of history especially related to the persons of the *Trinity*. Nevertheless, modern dispensationalism began within the bosom of British Evangelicalism in the middle of the nineteenth century, and its most important interpreter, if not its founder, was Plymouth Brethren leader *John Nelson Darby*. Later proponents and interpreters of Darby's dispensational approach to biblical interpretation and *theology* included J. I. Scofield, editor of the influential *Scofield Reference Bible*, and Clarence Larkin, formulator of a series of charts of the history of biblical dispensations that became the basis for many evangelical prophecy conferences. During the twentieth century, dispensationalism of the Darby variety became the theological basis for a major conservative evangelical seminary—Dallas Theological Seminary—and was popularized by books written by Hal Lindsay (*The Late Great Planet Earth*) and Tim LaHaye (the *Left Behind* series). Its distinctive *eschatology* (view of the end of history) was also popularized by several motion pictures, including *Thief in the Night* and *The Omega Code*.

Dispensationalism interprets the Bible as revealing several distinct dispensations or economies of God's redemptive plan and work, the most important of which have to do with national Israel (the Hebrew people and the state of Israel) and the gentile Christian *church*. According to Darby and other dispensationalists, God's original plan of *salvation* for his chosen people, the Jews (Israel), was never abrogated, nor is the gentile Christian church successor to God's promises to them. God's redemptive plan and purpose has since Abraham been centered around the Jewish people, but when they rejected his Messiah Jesus, God turned to the gentiles with an offer of salvation by *grace* alone through *faith* alone apart from the Mosaic *law*. Dispensationalists view the "church age" (which has lasted two millennia now) as a "parenthesis" within God's overarching plan to save Israel and rule and reign with Jewish Israel in a literal one-thousand-year *kingdom of God* on earth after Christ returns (*premillennialism*).

Intrinsic to dispensationalism is a peculiar eschatology that is a variety of premillennialism. Dispensationalists believe that the final phase of this present age of history will end with a "secret rapture" of the church—God's gentile believers who have been saved by a special dispensation of grace apart from keeping the law of Moses. They will be taken away from the world into *heaven* (paradise). That secret event will inaugurate the great tribulation of seven years during which God will work through a series of catastrophic and apocalyptic events to turn Israel to Jesus Christ as her Messiah. Finally, at the end of the tribulation period, Christ will return visibly to defeat Israel's enemies and usher in his and Israel's earthly kingdom of one thousand years. Dispensationalists disagree about the details of this scheme of the future, but they agree that God's first and foremost focus has been and will be on Israel and that eventually gentile believers will be included in that plan in the millennial kingdom of God on earth.

Dispensationalism has had a tremendous impact on Evangelicalism and evangelical theology in the twentieth century. During the 1920s and 1930s virtually all fundamentalist evangelicals accepted some version of dispensationalism. Prophecy conferences focusing on that interpretation of the Bible and its related eschatology became a prominent feature of fundamentalism and remained a feature of some postfundamentalist evangelical churches and parachurch organizations. Clarence Larkin's dispensational charts (and variations on them) were carefully studied in fundamentalist and some conservative evangelical (including Pentecostal) Bible institutes and Christian education classes. The notes in the *Scofield Reference Bible* came to be considered second in *authority* only to Scripture itself by many conservative lay evangelicals.

Throughout the second half of the twentieth century many postfundamentalist evangelicals and especially postconservative evangelicals moved away from dispensationalism. Reformed evangelicals—with few notable exceptions—were never inclined to embrace it. During the 1950s and 1960s a few notable dispensationalist evangelical scholars defected from its ranks and published critical studies of its hermeneutics and eschatology. Most influential among the critics was Fuller Theological Seminary New Testament scholar George Eldon Ladd, whose *Crucial Questions about the Kingdom of God* (Grand Rapids: Wm. B. Eerdmans, 1952) convinced many evangelicals to abandon dispensationalism without abandoning premillennialism. Much to the chagrin of many evangelical scholars and pastors, in the 1960s dispensationalism gradually emerged as the informal orthodoxy of many, if not most, conservative evangelical lay people through the best-selling books of Dallas Theological Seminary graduate Hal Lindsay.

Some evangelical denominations and institutions are formally dispensational in hermeneutics and doctrine. Some promote it informally without requiring it for enrollment or membership. Some positively frown upon it, and a few (especially some Reformed evangelical organizations) regard it as a theological oddity at best and heresy at worst. In the last decade of the twentieth century, certain dispensationalist scholars began to develop "progressive dispensationalism" to counter some of the criticisms aimed at traditional Darby-style dispensationalism by evangelical scholars. Among other new emphases of progressive dispensationalism is one on social concern. A major criticism of traditional dispensationalism was that it neglected concern for this-worldly matters of *justice* and ecology because of its overwhelming focus on the imminent return of Christ in apocalyptic events. Progressive dispensationalism seeks to combine social conscience and concern for the present world with dispensational hermeneutics and eschatology.

J. Dwight Pentecost, *Things to Come* (Grand Rapids: Zondervan, 1965); Charles C. Ryrie, *Dispensationalism* (Chicago: Moody Press, 1995); Robert H. Gundry, *The Church and the Tribulation* (Grand Rapids: Zondervan, 1973).

The Evangelical Theological Society

The Evangelical Theological Society (ETS) is the primary academic and professional society of evangelical scholars. The society was founded by postfundamentalist evangelical theologians in 1949. They were concerned that *fundamentalism* had abdicated the life of the mind and had become theologically moribund. The stated purpose of the society was "to foster conservative Biblical scholarship by providing a medium for the oral exchange and written expression of thought and research in the general field of the theological disciplines as centered in the *Scriptures*." The founding president was theologian Clarence Bouma of Calvin College in Grand Rapids, Michigan. The founding officers and committee members represented a diverse range of evangelicals, including theologians from Wesleyan and *Arminian* institutions and denominations. The original membership was approximately one hundred, but the society grew to over over three thousand members (including associate and student members) by the beginning of the new millennium.

Membership in the ETS was originally limited to persons with the Th.M. or equivalent degree (or higher degree such as Ph.D. or Th.D.) who would affirm, "The Bible alone and the Bible in its entirety is the Word of God written, and therefore inerrant in the original autographs." Later the statement of belief was expanded to include "God is a *Trinity*, Father, Son and *Holy Spirit*, each an uncreated person, one in essence, equal in power and glory." The full requirement for membership ruled out many evangelicals (because not all believe in biblical *inerrancy*) and all Oneness Pentecostals (who hold to a non-Trinitarian, modalistic doctrine of the Godhead). The ETS holds an annual meeting immediately prior to the annual meeting of the larger and more inclusive American Academy of Religion/Society of Biblical Literature. It is usually held in a location close to the AAR/SBL meeting so that members of both can easily attend both. Many ETS members also belong to either the AAR or the SBL or both. The annual meeting of the ETS offers plenary addresses by notable evangelical scholars and sessions devoted to specific topics and paper presentations. The society publishes a quarterly scholarly journal entitled *The Journal of the Evangelical Theological Society* (*JETS*) (prior to 1969 entitled *The Bulletin of the Evangelical Theological Society*).

The ETS has maintained a high profile of influence within evangelical scholarly circles in spite of some controversies. The membership requirement of belief in inerrancy has been challenged on a number of occasions but has always been upheld by the membership. (The challenges have taken the form of requests for clarification and reconsideration.) The ETS's most significant controversies have revolved around alleged doctrinal deviations by members. What has come to be known as the Gundry affair rocked the ETS in 1983 and 1984. An influential and highly regarded member named Robert H. Gundry, a New Testament scholar at evangelical Westmont College in Santa Barbara, California, published a commentary on Matthew that employed redaction criticism and argued that the author of the Gospel used midrash in order to link Jesus' birth with Old Testament messianic prophecies. In effect, he argued that some of the events recorded in the infancy narratives did not actually happen. Certain influential members of the ETS proposed a resolution that would have led to Gundry's expulsion from the society for abrogating his membership affirmation of belief in biblical inerrancy. Gundry voluntarily resigned from the society rather than be the cause of division. It seemed that some members were

planning to leave the society and possibly found a new, rival evangelical scholarly group if Gundry was not expelled. Gundry's voluntary resignation forestalled that, but it also caused some moderate and progressive evangelicals to avoid the society. Some regarded the move against Gundry as evidence that the ETS catered to fundamentalists within its ranks.

Another controversy that shook the ETS arose in relation to the presence of open theists in its membership. (See the article on *Theism: Open Theism/Classical Theism*.) Open theists such as *Clark Pinnock* deny the exhaustive, infallible foreknowledge of God in favor of a view of God's omniscience as knowledge of everything actual as actual and everything potential as potential. For open theists the future is partly settled and partly unsettled or "open," and God can foreknow only the part that is already settled. In 1999 critics of open theism within the ETS began to agitate for examination of open theism with an eye toward ouster of open theists from the society. The annual meeting of 2001 was dedicated to the issue of evangelical *boundaries*, and open theism was treated as a test case. A resolution affirming the exhaustive and infallible foreknowledge of God (and thus against open theism) was proposed and passed, but open theists were not expelled from the society. Some members indicated dissatisfaction with the resolution because it went too far toward narrowing the theological breadth of the society, while others expressed dissatisfaction because it did not exclude open theists from membership.

In spite of its seemingly narrow doctrinal stance with regard to Scripture, the ETS is a relatively inclusive society. It includes members from Episcopalian, Pentecostal, and Seventh-Day Adventist churches and institutions. Many evangelical scholars are not members of the society. Some of them consider it just as theologically moribund as the fundamentalism ETS's founders left behind. At the same time, however, the society continues to grow in spite of controversy.

"Historical Background of the Evangelical Theological Society," *Records of the Evangelical Theological Society—Collection 243: 1949–1982*, at Wheaton College's Billy Graham Center (http://www.wheaton.edu/bgc/archives/guides/243.htm); Evangelical Theological Society official website: http://www.etsjets.org.

Fundamentalism Without any doubt fundamentalism is one of the most essentially contested concepts in late twentieth-century and early twenty-first-century religion. The media's tendency to use the term for virtually any and all religious individuals and groups perceived by journalists to be fanatical and militant has made it virtually useless. Many religious communities use the term as a pejorative label to marginalize those perceived to be too far to the "right"—that is, too conservative. Because of the label's negative implications, fewer and fewer people use it for self-description. However, fundamentalism once had a more objective and less polemical meaning. During the first three decades of the twentieth century, many, if not most, evangelical Protestants considered themselves fundamentalists, even though they were neither militant nor fanatical.

The fundamentalist movement began to take shape and gain influence within North American Protestantism in response to the rise of liberal Protestant theology in the 1890s and the first decade of the twentieth century, even though the label became widely used for the conservative reaction to liberal theology within Protestantism only in the second decade of the century and the 1920s. During the later decades of the nineteenth century, many American Protestant biblical scholars, seminary professors, and theologians began to adopt and use the higher-critical methods of biblical scholarship that arose in Germany earlier in the nineteenth century. They also began to urge Protestant theological accommodation to the new "modern" mind-set and worldview arising out of the Enlightenment and scientific revolutions. Two influential volumes of liberal Protestant theology appeared in 1901: Oberlin College president Henry Churchill King's *Reconstruction in Theology* and German church historian Adolf Harnack's *What Is Christianity?* Both books sought to adjust *theology* to the naturalistic worldview of much modern science and tended to reduce Christianity to a moral system centered around the teachings of Jesus stripped of everything miraculous. Fundamentalism was the conservative reaction to such phenomena. At first it was simply a retrieval and new assertion of the traditional beliefs of historic Protestant orthodoxy, with a decidedly polemical thrust against liberal doctrinal drift within Protestant (especially Presbyterian and Baptist) seminaries, colleges and universities, and denominational headquarters.

The precise year of fundamentalism's beginning is disputed. Some scholars trace it back to the Niagara Bible Conference that in 1878 issued a statement of basic Christian beliefs that formed the basis for later lists of "fundamentals of the faith." Five points asserted as essential to authentic Christianity against liberal doctrinal drift were the verbal *inerrancy* of Scripture, the divinity of *Jesus Christ*, the *virgin birth*, the substitutionary *atonement*, and the physical and bodily *return of Jesus Christ*. Between 1910 and 1915 a series of booklets called *The Fundamentals* was published and sent free of charge to thousands of Christian workers around the United States and Canada. These contained articles by well-known conservative Protestant scholars defending classical Christian beliefs against alleged liberal denials. Many historians of fundamentalism believe the movement took its name from those booklets. However, the first person to urge that conservative Christians call themselves fundamentalists was Curtis Lee Laws, editor of the conservative Protestant publication *The Watchman Examiner*, who in 1920 defined a fundamentalist as "a person willing to 'do battle royal' for the fundamentals of the faith." One year earlier an organization known as World's Christian Fundamentals Association was founded.

By the time of the famous Scopes trial (to test Tennessee's anti-evolution law) in 1925, fundamentalism was a well-known and widely discussed movement across denominational lines. The movement's leading celebrity spokesman was statesman William Jennings Bryan, and its leading theologian was *J. Gresham Machen*. Expelled from the mainline Presbyterian Church, Machen founded Westminster Theological Seminary and the Orthodox Presbyterian Church. Machen's *Christianity and Liberalism* (1923) declared liberal Protestantism a different religion from Christianity and called on liberals to leave Christian denominations and institutions. The two leading ministers of fundamentalism who crisscrossed the United States organizing the movement (which never was completely organized) and rallying laypeople and pastors to its cause were Minneapolis-based William Bell Riley and Fort Worth–based J. Frank Norris. These two men contributed a new tone and mood to fundamentalism as they became disillusioned with American Protestantism and called for separation from its doctrinally corrupt organizations and institutions.

Prior to 1925 fundamentalism was a broad-based conservative movement. After the debacle of the Scopes trial (on which the play *Inherit the Wind* is based), fundamentalism underwent a dramatic shift in mood and emphasis. Its leaders began to insist on *premillennialism* as one of the fundamentals of Christianity. J. Gresham Machen and most other Reformed fundamentalists were not premillennialists. Throughout the 1930s "biblical *separationism*" became the hallmark of fundamentalism as the movement's leaders called on conservative Christians to abandon all churches

and religious organizations even indirectly "tainted" by liberal thinking. The movement remained vigorous as it constructed its own network of churches, denominations, publishing houses, and colleges separate from mainline Protestantism and even separate from many evangelical institutions and cooperative endeavors. During the 1930s and 1940s fundamentalism became increasingly dogmatic about its own claims regarding Christian truth and right Christian practice. It appeared to outsiders—including many evangelicals—to be obscurantist, anti-intellectual, militant, and uncritical of its own crusades against culture and religion. The mantles of leadership of fundamentalism fell on three main spokespersons for the movement: Carl McIntire, Bob Jones Sr., and John R. Rice. For all their differences, these three together proclaimed a *gospel* of strict biblical inerrancy, literalistic interpretation of Scripture, and opposition to everything deemed liberal or progressive in American society and church life.

A major turning point in the history of fundamentalism came in the 1970s as certain younger leaders emerged to reassert fundamentalist influence in mainstream American life, including politics. In 1979 noted fundamentalist pastor Jerry Falwell of Lynchburg, Virginia, founded an organization called The Moral Majority, which promoted a conservative ethic of "family values" for American society. This gave rise to a variety of ministries and parachurch organizations that were lumped together by critics as "the religious right." While not all persons associated with that phenomenon called themselves fundamentalists, the ethos of the movement was embued by fundamentalist values—with a decidedly dampened emphasis on separatism. The separatistic mode of fundamentalism has been carried on into the twenty-first century by leaders of several denominations, including especially the General Association of Regular Baptist Churches (GARBC) and the Fellowship of Bible Baptist Churches. Numerous smaller denominations and networks across North America carry the fundamentalist separatistic torch symbolized by their refusal to cooperate with even other evangelicals—including *Billy Graham* —in any endeavor for any purpose. However, for the most part, late twentieth-century and early twenty-first-century fundamentalists have dropped that label in favor of "conservative evangelical." Like Jerry Falwell they have softened their separatism without compromising their firm commitment to what they consider to be the fundamentals of Christianity, including biblical inerrancy, often (perhaps not always) young earth *creationism* and anti-*evolutionism, dispensationalism,* and rejection of critical biblical scholarship.

Joel A. Carpenter, *Revive Us Again: The Reawakening of American Fundamentalism* (New York and Oxford: Oxford University Press, 1997); George M. Marsden, *Understanding Fundamentalism and Evangelicalism* (Grand Rapids: Wm. B. Eerdmans, 1991).

The Holiness Movement To a very large extent Evangelicalism and evangelical *theology* have been shaped by experiential movements within Protestantism. Such emphases on "personal encounter with *Jesus Christ*" and "receiving the *Holy Spirit*" were once labeled "religious enthusiasm" by critics. That was thought of as an insult in the eighteenth and nineteenth centuries. Today they would more often be considered simply movements for *church* renewal. Evangelicalism has always been influenced by such movements. One that placed its stamp forever upon evangelical Christianity is the Holiness movement that began in the nineteenth century among Methodists who looked back to John and Charles Wesley as the men who completed the reformation begun by Luther. The hallmark of the Holiness movement was and is equal emphasis on *sanctification* and *justifi-*

cation. Even more to the point, Holiness Christians believe that any true believer in Jesus Christ can *experience* a complete cleansing from original *sin* and from the "carnal nature" (sinful, fallen human nature) that "wars against the Spirit." This experience is known as *"entire sanctification,"* "eradication of the sinful nature," and "Christian perfection." Some Holiness Christians equate it with Spirit baptism—a "second definite work of grace" available to every believer. Holiness Christians base their theology of sanctification on John Wesley's classic *A Plain Account of Christian Perfection* and on the interpretation given to it by Methodist theologian John Fletcher. The motto of the Holiness movement is "Holiness unto the Lord," and these evangelical Christians preach and teach that each and every Christian believer can and should live a life empowered by God's Spirit that is free of willful sin and marked by perfect love.

The precise beginning of the Holiness movement is uncertain, but it seems to have arisen in the middle of the nineteenth century in the northeastern United States. The immediate background was the revivals, known as the Second Great Awakening, that swept through New England and New York and along the frontier in the first half of the nineteenth century. Out of that phenomenon came the revival ministry of *Charles Finney,* who preached a gospel of sinless perfection by *faith* and willpower. In the 1830s and 1840s groups of concerned Methodists began to break away from the mainline Methodist Episcopal Church because they regarded it as losing its original "fire" and "zeal" for Christian purity and *holiness.* One such group in New York became known as the Free Methodist Church; another one became the Wesleyan Holiness Church (later merged with another Holiness body to become the Wesleyan Church). In the 1830s a woman evangelist named Phoebe Palmer began an influential ministry in New England and New York that proclaimed a version of Christian perfection and focused on inward transformation by the Spirit of God. Some scholars argue that the actual birth of the Holiness movement was in the late 1860s with the founding of the "National Camp Meeting Association for the Promotion of Holiness." Methodist-based revivals and protracted camp meetings sprang up around the United States. Their central feature was experiential entire sanctification after personal *conversion* to Christ by *repentance* and faith. Such *experiences* were often emotional, so that some detractors coined the derogatory term "holy rollers" to describe the "holiness people."

Over the years the National Camp Meeting Association evolved into the National Holiness Association, which in 1971 became the Christian Holiness Association, an umbrella organization for cooperation among most of the Holiness denominations and organizations. The largest Holiness denomination in North America is the Church of the Nazarene. Others include the Salvation Army and the Church of God, Anderson, Indiana. All include in their confessional statements belief in entire sanctification as an experience of eradication of the sinful nature by the Holy Spirit such that the sanctified person is "perfected in love." These Holiness groups are *Arminian* in theology, as was John Wesley. They believe in the *free will* of human beings in spiritual matters and reject the Reformed doctrines of unconditional *election* (predestination) and irresistible *grace*. The Holiness movement has spawned a number of professional theological societies, the most notable of which is the Wesleyan Theological Society, which publishes the *Journal of the Wesleyan Theological Society* and holds regular meetings for scholarly exchange of ideas. The movement also gave rise to a number of Holiness colleges, universities, and seminaries. Its best-known seminary, Asbury Theological Seminary in Wilmore, Kentucky, supplies ministers for the Free Methodist and Wesleyan denominations, as well as for the United

Methodist Church. The Church of the Nazarene has several colleges and universities and a seminary in Kansas City, Missouri.

Theologically, Holiness Christians are evangelical, even though some avoid use of that label because they consider it too closely associated theologically with Reformed thought and rationalistic apologetics and theology. Nevertheless, in its broadest and historically correct sense Evangelicalism includes the Holiness movement and its related institutions. Holiness Christians are committed to the *authority* of the *Bible* as God's written Word, even though they do not always affirm its *inerrancy*. They confess the historic doctrines of the Christian faith, including the deity of Jesus Christ and the *Trinity*, and often fervently look forward to Christ's visible and imminent return. They tend to follow an *amillennial* eschatology rather than a *premillennial* or *dispensationalist* one. Holiness Christians eschew the Pentecostal distinctive of speaking in tongues, but most believe in and pray for supernatural divine bodily healing. They have often been accused of "otherworldly asceticism"—being so heavenly minded they are no earthly good. The same could be said, of course, of many evangelicals of a variety of denominational flavors. Holiness Christians have until recently (late twentieth century) tended to keep to themselves, without an explicit doctrine of separationism or sectarianism. During the later decades of the twentieth century, however, they merged more and more into the mainstream of evangelical life and thought. The movement's influence can be seen in various renewal movements that focus on experiencing God in a pure life of Christian discipleship marked by love. Also, Holiness groups were among the first American religious groups to object strenuously to slavery and to ordain women and grant women full equality in the life of the churches.

Charles Edwin Jones, *A Guide to the Study of the Holiness Movement* (Scarecrow Press,

1974); *Perfectionist Persuasion: The Holiness Movement and American Methodism: 1867–1936* (Lanham, MD: Scarecrow Press, 2002).

InterVarsity Christian Fellowship

Many twentieth-century evangelical theologians (both professional and otherwise) have been influenced by transdenominational parachurch organizations that seek to evangelize and disciple high school and college/university students. Some of the more prominent of these are Campus Crusade for Christ, Young Life, Youth for Christ, and InterVarsity Christian Fellowship (IVCF). IVCF has been especially active in theological education of Christians studying at secular institutions of higher learning and, of all the parachurch organizations for young people, it has been the most intellectually and theologically oriented. IVCF brings together leading evangelical scholars and college/university students and their IVCF campus program directors for weekend retreats and seminars. It facilitates serious biblical and theological discussions on campuses where it has chapters and promotes a biblically committed, theologically serious form of Christianity among its constituents. Many evangelical writers and thinkers were at some time in their early careers heavily influenced by IVCF lecturers and writers such as James Sire and John Alexander.

IVCF began at Cambridge University in England in 1877 as an intercollegiate Christian fellowship for spiritual and intellectual stimulation and formation. Its mission is "to establish and advance at colleges and universities witnessing communities of students and faculty who follow *Jesus Christ* as Savior and Lord: growing in love for God, God's Word, God's people of every ethnicity and culture and God's purposes in the world." The fellowship spread to Canada in 1928 and established its first chapter in the United States at the University of Michigan in 1937. It has chap-

ters on hundreds of college and university campuses in the United States and many more worldwide. It requires chapters and members to affirm a minimal statement of orthodox Christian belief that includes the full *authority* of Scripture without mention of biblical *inerrancy*. Like many evangelical parachurch organizations IVCF seeks to be as broad and inclusive as possible while maintaining the integrity of historic Christian belief and ethical practice. Most campus chapters meet regularly for *Bible* study (often using IVCF published materials), *prayer*, and *evangelism* training. The latter often involves a heavy dose of Christian apologetics aimed at answering skeptics' questions about Christian belief. IVCF is committed to the idea that Christianity includes a world and life philosophy (worldview) that, though perhaps not rationally provable, is consistent with *reason* and in fact illumines human life *experience* better than any competing worldview. It also believes and teaches that Christians may enter any legitimate academic or professional vocation and critically and constructively integrate their Christian worldview with it.

IVCF has spawned and maintains under its broad umbrella a number of related ministries that have profoundly influenced evangelical Christianity. Urban Projects helps Christian students become involved in inner-city ministries; the Urbana Conferences draws thousands of students to Urbana, Illinois, for a weeklong world missions conference every three years. InterVarsity Press is the fellowship's publishing house and has become one of the leading evangelical publishers in the world, with a strong line of scholarly and reference books dedicated to biblical studies and *theology*. The International Fellowship of Evangelical Students facilitates networking among evangelical college and university students throughout the world, and the Nurses Christian Fellowship is just one of several groups related to IVCF that seeks to help members of a particular profession continue to grow spiritually and theologically and integrate their Christian faith with their profession after college or university. Several evangelical luminaries gained influence and fame through the auspices of IVCF. John Stott, longtime pastor of All Soul's Church (Anglican) in London, has exercised tremendous influence over evangelical students' minds through his speaking and writing ministry, which has largely been promoted by IVCF and InterVarsity Press (IVP). *Francis Schaeffer*, founder of L'Abri Fellowship in Switzerland, also gained a wide audience through promotion of speaking and his writings by IVCF and IVP. James Sire of IVCF and IVP has influenced a large number of evangelical students and others through his lectures and books. These and other IVCF speakers and writers have in common a broad evangelical appeal that is clearly postfundamentalist in mood while vigorously promoting a conservative version of Protestant philosophy and theology. Especially Schaeffer and Sire have demonstrated Christianity's power to critique culture both prophetically and philosophically while strictly avoiding blanket condemnations of culture and urging readers and hearers to engage with secular and pagan culture.

IVCF has endured a number of controversies and emerged from them shaken but stronger. *Fundamentalist* critics of IVCF and its related organizations such as IVP have frequently reviled them for allegedly peddling a weakened version of the Christian *gospel*. During the 1980s some ultraconservative evangelicals went so far as to demonstrate outside IVP's headquarters in Illinois because of a book it published. Evangelical biologist D. Garth Jones's *Brave New People* dealt with a variety of controversial subjects related to bioethics and advocated a moderate Christian stance on abortion. Because of the controversy, IVP withdrew the book and was heavily criticized for that by more progressive evangelicals. IVCF's president Gordon

MacDonald resigned in 1988, which threw the fellowship into turmoil for a period of time during which it had five presidents in eight years. Critics of IVCF have accused it of being too distant from the local *churches* and of failing to propel students under its influence into local congregations. In spite of these controversies and problems, the fellowship has continued to grow and spread its influence for moderate evangelical Christian discipleship to new generations of students.

InterVarsity Christian Fellowship home Web site: http://www.ivcf.org; Keith and Gladys Hunt, *For Christ and the University* (Downers Grove, IL: InterVarsity Press, 1991); C. Stacey Woods, *The Growth of a Work of God* (Downers Grove, IL: InterVarsity Press, 1978).

The Keswick Movement   Evangelical Christianity has often focused its spiritual and theological energies on promoting and exploring the spirituality of inward transformation known theologically as *sanctification*. A large number of evangelicals have believed that *entire sanctification* or Christian perfection is a possibility before death. Methodist evangelist and founder John Wesley taught it, as did Second Great Awakening revivalist and theologian *Charles Finney*. The *Holiness movement* of the nineteenth century featured the reception of entire sanctification as a purifying *experience* of the *Holy Spirit* subsequent to Christian *conversion*. Some evangelicals of the late nineteenth century and early twentieth century came to believe in a "higher life" of perfect spirituality without a dramatic experience of being "baptized in the Holy Spirit" with the immediate result of eradication of the fallen, sinful nature. Some of the latter formed a renewal movement known as the Keswick Convention for the Promotion of Practical Holiness at Keswick, England, in 1875. The convention met annually to explore

Christian *holiness* and perfection through a distinctive, transforming experience of surrender to *Jesus Christ*. After the Second World War the movement spread out to other places in England and the United States while maintaining its annual retreats (three weekly meetings during the summer) in Keswick, England. While there is no unifying organization of all Keswick retreats and conferences worldwide, they are all influenced by the Keswick Conventions of Keswick, England.

Keswick spirituality emphasizes a fivefold message that focuses on an experience of "higher life": (1) the problem of indwelling *sin* within the Christian, (2) cleansing as prerequisite to being filled with the Holy Spirit, (3) absolute surrender to the lordship of Jesus Christ, (4) the Spirit-filled life, and (5) Christian service and ministry. The *theology* of Keswick spirituality is compatible with Reformed thought and therefore is not limited, as the Holiness movement tends to be, to *Arminian* and Wesleyan believers. It promotes a vision of Christian *sanctification* that is progressive rather than sudden (as in much Holiness thought) but also relatively perfectionistic in contrast to much traditional Protestant thought. The key to this spirituality is the experience of total surrender of the will to God, which is a "cross experience" in which one identifies with Christ's surrender to the Father. This experience of death of self results in an enduement or anointing with Holy Spirit power to live a holy, Christlike life. There is little or no emphasis on eradication of a sinful nature. Thus, the Keswick "fullness of the Spirit" is compatible with some degree of lifelong struggle against sin. The cross experience of self-surrender to *God* and reception of the Holy Spirit is to be constantly renewed through *Bible* study and *prayer*.

Keswick theology and spirituality profoundly impacted Evangelicalism in Great Britain and the United States, especially around the start of the twentieth century. Thousands of evangelical believers flocked to Keswick-style conferences and read Keswick books and magazines. An entire evangelical denomination—the Christian and Missionary Alliance (CMA)—was founded largely on the basis of Keswick teaching and experience. Most Keswick evangelicals remained in their own denominations and attempted to bring them spiritual renewal, often without mentioning Keswick by name. The movement's distinctive teaching became known simply as "higher life Christianity." The founder of the CMA was Presbyterian evangelist, hymn writer, speaker, and missionary Albert B. Simpson, whose influence on evangelical life extended far beyond the confines of that denomination. His "fourfold gospel" of Christ as "Savior, Healer, Baptizer with the Holy Spirit, and Coming King" greatly influenced early *Pentecostalism* and was enshrined in the name of one of its leading denominations—the International Church of the Foursquare Gospel. C. I. Scofield, editor of the *Scofield Reference Bible*, was not only a *dispensationalist* but also a Keswick Christian who communicated its principles about sanctification to millions through the notes of his study Bible. Keswickian ideas about spirituality have been promoted in Evangelicalism by persons not usually identified closely with the movement, such as Oswald Chambers, author of the extremely popular devotional book *My Utmost for His Highest*.

The Keswick movement and its distinctive spirituality have been criticized by many evangelicals for allegedly promoting anti-intellectualism, latitudinarianism (lack of high doctrinal demand), and quietism (lack of concern for the problems of the world). Some critics have accused it of focusing too heavily on one note of Christian experience—sanctification. Others have dismissed it as fanatical and perfectionistic, even though it is not at all emotional (unlike much of the Holiness movement) and does not teach "sinless perfection." The most common complaint is that Keswickianism inevitably leads to a belief in two classes of Christians—those who are merely converted and those who live a "higher life" of fullness of the Spirit in total submission and surrender to God through Jesus Christ. The same could be said of virtually any renewal movement and of Evangelicalism itself. The same complaint of divisiveness has often been leveled against evangelical Christianity by nonevangelicals within mainline Protestant denominations and churches.

Keswick Conventions' home Web site: http://www.keswickconv.com; J. C. Pollock, *The Keswick Story: The Authorized History of the Keswick Convention* (London: Hodder & Stoughton, 1964).

The Lausanne Conference   Evan-
gelicalism has always been missions-minded, and meetings of missionaries have been a frequent occurrence among evangelicals. Such meetings usually served as motivational and inspirational rallies, with glowing reports from missionaries returning from "foreign lands." Western Europe and North America often regarded missionary endeavors as extensions of colonization efforts in underdeveloped countries. Even well-intentioned evangelical missionaries often imposed Western culture on their converts in non-Western societies. For the most part, missionary conferences and conventions did little to question traditional missionary techniques, and indigenous people of non-Western cultures rarely had any influence in them. That changed in 1974 at the first Lausanne Conference, held in Lausanne, Switzerland. The initiator of the large, worldwide, multicultural missionary conference was American evangelist *Billy Graham.* The conference was the culmination of years of effort and preparation. It was to be the first such meeting of Western and non-Western evangelicals involved in missionary endeavor (broadly defined) in history. Its impact

on evangelical *theology* has been significant, although not yet fully assessed. It firmly inserted non-Western evangelical theologies, liturgies, and evangelistic methods into the evangelical movement and raised serious questions about Western dominance over evangelical life and thought.

Two thousand seven hundred evangelists and missionaries from numerous countries attended the conference, and several controversial papers were read. Rene Padilla and Samuel Escobar, both *InterVarsity Christian Fellowship* workers from Latin America, questioned the traditional evangelical division between *"evangelism"* and "social action" and especially Evangelicalism's overwhelming emphasis on the former to the neglect of the latter. A group of younger, third-world evangelicals at the conference prepared a declaration known as the Radical Discipleship Statement, which affirmed that *"God's* mission of love [is] to restore the world to wholeness through the Cross of Christ and him alone" and called for evangelical sociopolitical involvement on behalf of the poor and oppressed. Several non-Western evangelicals at the conference questioned the dominance of Western (European and North American) versions of the *gospel* in world evangelism and even labeled the Western-style message a "mutilated gospel." A few went so far as to call for a moratorium on Western missionary efforts and asked that indigenous Christians be allowed to evangelize their own countries without traditional missionaries from Europe and North America overseeing their work.

By and large, the calls for greater recognition of the need for a more positive approach to non-Western cultures and for greater integration of spiritual evangelism with social action were heard with respect by the conference's leaders. The conference produced a three-thousand-word document known as the Lausanne Covenant that confessed traditional evangelism's shortcomings, repented of them, and committed those affirming it to *prayer* and a new style of world missions and evangelism. The covenant contained fifteen specific articles dealing with renewal of evangelical thought and practice of evangelism around the world. The two that broke new ground for evangelicals were those on "Christian Social Responsibility" and "Evangelism and Culture." While some critics (especially fundamentalists) regarded them as relativistic (because they recognized the need to contextualize the gospel within cultures) and influenced by liberation theology, most evangelical missionaries and missiologists hailed them as major breakthroughs in modernizing world evangelism away from dualism between the "sacred" and the "secular" and toward a more holistic approach that respects cultures and the oppressed.

The Lausanne Conferences (a second one was held in Manila, the Philippines, in 1989) and Covenant opened the door of evangelical life and thought to greater recognition of non-Western Christians and forever changed the tendency to identify the gospel with Western cultural norms. Many of the evangelicals from the two-thirds world came to North America after the Lausanne Conference and spoke at Urbana missionary and evangelism meetings sponsored by Inter-Varsity Christian Fellowship and at other meetings and institutions. Exchanges between North American and non-Western evangelicals became more common, and North American theologians began to read and take seriously the writings of African, Asian, and Latin American evangelical thinkers. In the early twenty-first century Western Evangelicalism still has a long way to go before it is fully aware of the equality of non-Western cultures with Western culture, but the Lausanne Conference and the Lausanne Covenant paved the way for significant changes in attitude and approach among Western evangelicals.

Alan Nichols, ed., *The Whole Gospel for the Whole World: The Story of Lausanne II*

Congress on World Evangelism, Manila 1989 (Charlotte, NC: Regal Books, 1989); Rene C. Padilla, ed., *The New Face of Evangelicalism: An International Symposium on the Lausanne Covenant* (London: Hodder & Stoughton, 1976).

The National Association of Evangelicals

If there is one organization that symbolically unites and speaks for the evangelical community in North America, it is the National Association of Evangelicals (NAE). The NAE is a network of approximately fifty cooperating evangelical denominations and thousands of individual *churches*, ministries, educational institutions, and individuals. The combined constituent membership of the NAE is in the millions. And yet several notable evangelical groups do not belong to the NAE, including many African American evangelical churches (no predominantly black denomination has member status) and the 16-million-member Southern Baptist Convention. Nevertheless, the NAE functions as the voice of Evangelicalism in the public square. It includes a very diverse group of Christians—from Pentecostals to Reformed—but unites them around a common core of basic Christian beliefs and common concern for *evangelism* and social *redemption*.

The NAE grew out of the New England Fellowship in 1942 and 1943. Its founding meetings were held in St. Louis, Missouri (1942), and Chicago, Illinois (1943), with inspiration and organizational leadership from postfundamentalist leaders J. Elwin Wright and Harold John Ockenga. Fundamentalist leader Carl McIntire founded a rival, more separatistic and militant group of conservative Protestant denominations, ministries, and churches known as the American Council of Christian Churches just before the 1942 meeting to found the NAE. Some attempt was made to merge the two groups, but most who attended the founding meetings of the NAE felt that McIntire's group would be too narrow. The NAE was intended to include as broad a range of conservative Protestants as possible to rival the mainline, more liberally oriented Federal Council of Churches (later known as the National Council of Churches). The founders of the NAE wrote a very basic statement of belief that all member denominations and churches would have to sign. It affirmed the historic orthodoxy of Christianity (deity of Christ, *Trinity*) as well as the unique *authority* of the *Bible* (without mentioning *inerrancy*) and *salvation* by *grace* through *faith*. It intentionally avoided the doctrinal issues that fundamentalists had come to use to divide evangelical Christians from everyone else and even from each other. These included "biblical separationism" (from culture and liberal churches and ministers) and *premillennialism*. The NAE required member groups to leave or not join the Federal Council of Churches—a nod to Evangelicalism's fundamentalist (separatist) heritage. This exclusive membership requirement kept some evangelically inclined groups such as the Northern Baptist Convention (later the American Baptist Churches, U.S.A.) from joining the NAE. Among the founding leaders of the NAE were a Congregationalist (Ockenga), a Free Methodist, a Southern Baptist, a Presbyterian, and a Methodist. In a major rebuff to fundamentalists such as McIntire, the NAE voted to include Pentecostals. Eventually they came to be the single largest confessional "block" within the NAE, and the Assemblies of God, the largest predominantly white Pentecostal denomination, became the largest member denomination.

By 1948 the NAE had eighteen member denominations; by 2002 the number had grown to approximately fifty. In the intervening years the organization spawned a number of affiliated ventures including World Relief, a relief agency aimed primarily at alleviating hunger in underdeveloped countries, and the National Religious Broadcasters Association (which eventually separated from

the NAE). The periodical of the NAE is *United Evangelical Action*. Its headquarters was in Chicago until 2001, when it moved to a suburb of Los Angeles. It holds an annual national meeting as well as regional meetings for affiliated churches and ministries. The association has several commissions, including a theological commission composed of evangelical scholars who study theological issues and make recommendations for resolutions. The delegates to annual meetings of the NAE vote on various resolutions that speak to contemporary social and religious issues proposed by the board of directors, who represent a cross section of the member denominations. For the most part the NAE has existed and carried out its somewhat limited role peacefully. It has facilitated constructive dialogue and cooperation among its members, who come from very diverse theological orientations. Among the member denominations are Adventists (the Christian Advent Church), *Holiness* groups (Church of the Nazarene), Pentecostals (Assemblies of God), Reformed churches (Christian Reformed Church), and even a denomination previously widely considered by evangelicals a "cult"—the Worldwide Church of God. The NAE, then, represents a "broad tent" of evangelical goodwill and cooperation.

Throughout the 1990s the NAE suffered a series of setbacks that created some uncertainty about its future. The National Religious Broadcasters separated from it. The longtime president of the organization, Billy Melvin, retired and was succeeded by two ministers of member denominations often considered on the margins of evangelical life: the Assemblies of God and the Free Methodist Church. (Most of the leaders of the NAE and of Evangelicalism in general have come from Baptist or Presbyterian backgrounds.) Neither remained in the position very long. In 2001 the NAE was rocked by an inner controversy and struggle over the leadership of Free Methodist bishop Kevin

Mannoia, who tried to revive the struggling organization by proposing, among other changes, that the exclusivity rule of membership be dropped and that denominations such as the American Baptist Churches, U.S.A. be allowed to join and retain their membership in the National Council of Churches. Some of the more conservative members objected very strenuously. Soon Bishop Mannoia was out of the presidency, and an interim president was named. Some observers viewed the events as rooted in a struggle between the more open and moderate forces and the more conservative ones within the NAE.

In spite of some uncertainty about its future, the NAE continues to be a force for unity among evangelicals in North America. Its role in evangelical life has been one of aiding the emergence of Evangelicalism out of its fundamentalist past while maintaining a strong commitment to the authority of Scripture and to historic Christian orthodoxy. It has also been and continues to be the primary public voice of the post–World War II postfundamentalist evangelical coalition in American life.

The National Association of Evangelicals home Web site: http://www.nae.net; Joel Carpenter, *Revive Us Again: The Reawakening of American Evangelicalism* (New York and Oxford: Oxford University Press, 1997).

Pentecostalism   Pentecostalism forms a segment of the evangelical movement; some scholars claim it is the largest and fastest-growing segment worldwide. Without any doubt Pentecostalism has been one of the fastest-growing and largest religious phenomena to arise and grow to maturity within a single century. Although most Pentecostals embrace all of the beliefs of evangelical Christianity (some deny the classical doctrine of the *Trinity* while affirming the deity of *Jesus Christ*), they stand out as distinct from other evangelicals in their strong emphasis on an experience subsequent to conversion to Christ known as the *baptism of the Holy Spirit*, which they claim is always accompanied by speaking in unknown tongues (i.e., languages the speaker has not learned and does not understand). This doctrine of "initial physical evidence" forms the hallmark of classical Pentecostalism. (Neo-Pentecostals are *charismatics* who do not necessarily affirm that doctrine, although they do embrace and practice speaking in tongues as a special "prayer language.") Classical Pentecostals—of which there are somewhere between 10 and 15 million in North America and as many as 50 million in the world—insist that truly Spirit-filled Christians will speak in tongues and receive one or more supernatural *gifts of the Holy Spirit*, such as divine healing, ability to work miracles, *supernatural* knowledge ("word of knowledge"), prophecy (not "foretelling" but "forthtelling" or speaking for God in a special way). The term *Pentecostal* (not *Pentecostalist* as some mistakenly call it) comes from the events recorded in Acts 2 on the day of Pentecost, when the Jerusalem Christians received the *Holy Spirit* and spoke in tongues.

The Pentecostal movement began in the first decade of the twentieth century and grew out of the older *Holiness movement*. Although some early founders of Pentecostalism were Baptists and Methodists, most were strongly influenced by either the Holiness movement or *Keswick* spirituality and theology. Many of them had been touched by evangelist Albert B. Simpson, who founded the Christian and Missionary Alliance denomination, which believed in divine healing and other supernatural gifts of the Holy Spirit. Simpson's attitude toward speaking in tongues was "seek not; forbid not," but some of his followers believed it was proper for Christians to seek the gift of speaking in tongues and became Pentecostals. Some scholars trace the birth of the Pentecostal movement to Topeka, Kansas, in 1901. A Holiness revivalist named Charles Parham had founded a Bible institute there, and, so Pentecostal legend goes, a student spoke in tongues at midnight on January 1, 1901, thus signifying that the new century would be the fulfillment of biblical prophecies about the outpouring of the Holy Spirit in the last days. Pentecostals, like their Holiness cousins, regard themselves as always living in the "end times" just before Christ returns. Other scholars regard the true birth of the Pentecostal movement as happening in 1906 in Azusa, California, where a protracted revival took place under the leadership of African American Holiness preacher William Seymour. Hundreds, if not thousands, of Holiness Christians flocked to the Azusa Street Mission in Los Angeles, where the revival continued night and day for months. Many of them experienced speaking in tongues and returned to their home churches, converting them into Pentecostal congregations. A few Holiness denominations formally changed to adopt the new Pentecostal teaching and experience. Most notable is the Church of God in Christ, the largest predominantly African American Pentecostal denomination.

After 1906 several new Pentecostal denominations were founded. Out of a 1914 gathering of Pentecostal ministers from around North America in Hot Springs, Arkansas, came the Assemblies of God, which grew into the largest predominantly white Pentecostal group in North America. By the end of the century, it was one of the ten largest denominations in the United States, with well over one million members. (If one counts adherents and not only members, the Assemblies of God may have as many as three million followers in North America and millions more worldwide.) Pentecostalism was open to women ministers, and one emerged to found a new Pentecostal denomination in the 1920s. Aimee Semple McPherson, a traveling Pentecostal healing evangelist,

founded a church named Angelus Temple in Los Angeles, California, in 1923. Out of that in 1927 grew the International Church of the Foursquare Gospel, destined to become one of Pentecostalism's largest denominations. Other Pentecostal groups include the Pentecostal Holiness Church, the Church of God (Cleveland, Tennessee), and the United Pentecostal Church (which denies the orthodox Christian doctrine of the Trinity while affirming the deity of Jesus Christ). There are numerous smaller Pentecostal bodies. All are evangelical in doctrine and ethos (with the possible exception of the United Pentecostal Church and other non-Trinitarian Pentecostal groups, which are shunned by most evangelicals). Many of them joined the *National Association of Evangelicals* when it was founded in the 1940s. In 1948 some of them formed their own cooperative organization known as the Pentecostal Fellowship of North America (PFNA), which excluded the African American Pentecostal denominations. In 1994 the PFNA disbanded and was replaced by a racially inclusive organization called the Pentecostal and Charismatic Churches of North America.

Pentecostalism is regarded with some suspicion and even disdain by some other evangelicals. In fact, some evangelicals have been among its harshest critics. Some have accused it of being anti-intellectual, divisive, excessively emotional, and even heretical. However, by the end of the twentieth century the NAE's president was an Assemblies of God college president, and the largest evangelical churches in many North American cities were Pentecostal. Through the second half of the century Pentecostalism emerged from its sectarian shell into a major force in North American church life and within evangelical Christianity in particular. Its style of informal, enthusiastic worship and its emphasis on gifts of the Spirit have filtered into mainstream Evangelicalism. But mainstream Evangelicalism has also affected Pentecostalism; its distinctive practice of speaking in tongues and its "manifestations" of the Holy Spirit in healings, prophecy, and other supernatural events are becoming less prominent as features of Pentecostal worship. Many Pentecostal church members have never spoken in tongues and probably never will; their churches are evolving into generic evangelical churches in which the classical Pentecostal distinctives are verbally affirmed but nonfunctional.

Harvey Cox, *Fire from Heaven: The Rise of Pentecostal Spirituality and the Reshaping of Religion in the Twenty-first Century* (Reading, MA: Addison-Wesley Publishing Co., 1995); William W. Menzies, *Anointed to Serve: The Story of the Assemblies of God* (Springfield, MO: Gospel Publishing House, 1971); Vinson Synan, *The Century of the Holy Spirit: 100 Years of Pentecostal and Charismatic Renewal* (Nashville: Thomas Nelson, 2001).

Pietism-Revivalism   Evangelicalism and evangelical *theology* descend historically from the Pietist movement of the late seventeenth and early eighteenth centuries and the Revivalist movements of the eighteenth and nineteenth centuries. Pietism was a spiritual renewal movement that began with German Lutheran minister Philip Jakob Spener in Frankfurt and then Dresden in the late seventeenth century. His *Pia Desideria* (Pious Desires), the founding classic of the movement, was first published as a preface to an earlier spiritual classic entitled *True Christianity*, written by mystical Protestant writer Johann Arndt in 1675. A century and a half after the Protestant Reformation began, the reformation churches of Europe had by and large fallen into a state of spiritual lethargy; the theology of Protestantism had become dry and scholastic. Spener wanted a heartfelt experience of God to renew and refresh the vitality of Protestantism in Europe. In *Pia Desideria* he called for spiritual training and evaluation of ministerial candidates and for *church* discipline of openly sinning

members, as well as for an increase of *prayer* and *Bible* study among Christians. He emphasized the importance of union with Christ as well as the classic Protestant doctrine of *justification* by *faith* alone and wrote about the transformation of the "inner man" (heart, character, personality) of each person by the power of the *Holy Spirit*. Spener established *collegia pietatis* or conventicles (small groups) of "heart Christians" in his parish in Frankfurt. These groups were for the purpose of spiritual edification of lay people. Many of Spener's critics considered this a radical step and accused him of "enthusiasm" (virtually synonymous with fanaticism), which was an insult.

Spener was succeeded as leader of the Pietist movement by his own student August Hermann Francke, who taught theology at the Pietist University of Halle in Germany beginning in 1698. Francke stressed the importance of each Christian's having a "struggle of *repentance*" (*Busskampf*) that would lead to genuine *conversion* to Christ. He established a number of charitable organizations at Halle, including a missionary-sending agency, a publishing house, an orphanage, and a school for the children of people of all classes of society. Francke was succeeded as leader of Pietism in Germany by Spener's godson Count Nikolaus Ludwig von Zinzendorf. Zinzendorf, educated at the University of Halle, became the leader of a band of immigrant Pietists known as the Moravians, who settled on his estate. Zinzendorf and the Moravians emphasized a personal relationship with Jesus Christ as the essence of authentic Christianity. They sent missionaries to England, North America, and the Caribbean and greatly influenced John and Charles Wesley in London. Eventually the Pietist renewal spread to the Scandinavian countries, where strong Pietist movements took root and spread through immigration to North America. Many of Evangelicalism's leading denominations have roots in German and Scandinavian

Pietism (e.g., the Evangelical Covenant Church of America, the Evangelical Free Church of America, and the Baptist General Conference). Pietism did not reject doctrine or intellectual inquiry in theology, but it did and does emphasize *experience* of *God* over those. It is wary of doctrinal and theological controversies and follows the policy stated by one leading Pietist regarding the importance of doctrine: "In essentials unity, in nonessentials liberty, in all things charity." Above all, Pietism promotes heartfelt relationship with Jesus Christ as Savior, Lord, and friend.

Revivalism began with the evangelistic and church renewal careers of Methodist founders John and Charles Wesley and their friend George Whitefield in England and North America and with the Great Awakening in the North American colonies in the eighteenth century. There is no doubt that revivalism was influenced by Pietism, but the lines of connection and degree of dependency are matters of scholarly debate. The Wesleys and their friend Whitefield were Anglican ministers in England who traveled around preaching the *gospel* of conversion (repentance and *forgiveness*) to crowds of poor and working people in the open air. That sounds commonplace in the twenty-first century, but in the eighteenth century it was extremely controversial. Charles Wesley wrote hymns for mass revivals and for *worship* in the newly founded Methodist societies, which were at first simply renewal groups within the Church of England. John Wesley preached and wrote letters and commentaries on a wide variety of subjects, but his most notable themes were conversion-*regeneration* (the experience of being "born again" to Christ through the Holy Spirit) and *sanctification* (inward spiritual transformation into perfection). Whitefield was a powerful preacher who stirred thousands to repent and accept Christ as Savior and Lord. His preaching in the North American colonies sparked the Great Awakening, which was joined by Puritan

minister Jonathan Edwards and others in the 1740s.

The common theme of revivalism was and remains "You must be born again!" The message of a born-again experience (drawn from John 3) became the hallmark of revivalism and eventually entered into the stream of evangelical life. To revivalists, being born again involves heartfelt repentance for *sin*, trust in Jesus Christ alone for *salvation* (*forgiveness* and spiritual renewal), forgiveness by God, and union with Jesus Christ in the indwelling Holy Spirit. It may or may not be particularly emotional, but it is believed to involve a *supernatural* work of the *grace* of God within a person. This transcends mere "turning over a new leaf" and even being sacramentally justified through *baptism* and the *Lord's Supper*. Revivalists and many, if not all, evangelicals believe it is a dramatic change within a person's life brought about by the Holy Spirit.

Revivalism strongly influenced twentieth-century Evangelicalism and its *theology*. Many of the most influential fundamentalist preachers and leaders were revivalists. The entire *Holiness*-Pentecostal movement was and is revivalist to the core. The movers and shakers of the early postfundamentalist evangelical coalition that emerged in the 1940s and 1950s were all heavily influenced by Pietism and revivalism. *Billy Graham*, the most notable evangelical of the twentieth century, is a revivalist evangelist. Evangelicals who are not particularly drawn to the mass evangelism ethos of revivalism are heavily stamped by Pietism, which tends to be a quieter form of revivalism. Both emphasize spiritual experience without rejecting doctrinal confession. Some evangelicals are extremely wary of revivalism and have qualms about Pietism as well. They see both as too subjective and as leading to doctrinal decline and drift within evangelical churches. Many of the critics, like most evangelicals, were either raised in Pietist or revivalist homes and churches or were "saved" in them or both. And yet the critics believe that Pietism and revivalism need to be transcended in a more mature, less experiential and more intellectual, and perhaps liturgical form of evangelical Christianity. To be sure, Pietism and revivalism can be and often are distorted into religious forms of life that fall short of holistic Christian faith. The critics may be captivated by such distortions as seen in some religious television programming and in the books that crowd Christian bookstores' shelves. There is nothing intrinsically anti-intellectual or subjective about Pietism or revivalism, but as the critics point out, they need to be balanced by a more objective style of Christianity that gives due weight to doctrinal belief, corporate worship, and the value of the sacraments or ordinances.

Ted A. Campbell, *The Religion of the Heart: A Study of European Religious Life in the Seventeenth and Eighteenth Centuries* (Columbia: University of South Carolina Press, 1991); Frank Lambert, *Inventing the "Great Awakening"* (Princeton, NJ: Princeton University Press, 1999).

Princeton Theology Perhaps no single dynasty or school of *theology* has impacted Evangelicalism and evangelical thought more than what scholars routinely refer to as Old School Princeton Theology, which reigned virtually unchallenged at Princeton Theological Seminary (Presbyterian) in the nineteenth century and into the early twentieth century. Old School Princeton Theology (referred to here henceforth simply as Princeton Theology) was a scholasticized version of American Presbyterian Reformed (Calvinist) theology heavily influenced by post-Calvinian scholastic Reformed theologians such as the Swiss Calvinist systematizer Francis Turretin. In his *Institutiones theologiae elenchticae* (Elenctic Theology) (1679–85) Turretin argued that in order for *Scrip-*

ture to be fully authoritative, *God* must have inspired even the Hebrew vowel points that were added to the text by Jewish scholars known as the Masoretes. Protestant scholasticism sought to strengthen the *authority* and certainty of doctrines by placing them within a completely logical, comprehensive system of beliefs based entirely on Scripture and *reason*. Like medieval Catholic thinker Thomas Aquinas and unlike Luther and Calvin, the Protestant scholastics were fascinated, if not obsessed, by a philosophical style of theology that was uncomfortable with mystery and paradox. Turretin's systematic theology was used as the primary textbook at Princeton Theological Seminary for decades; the main systematic theologians there attempted to impart to American evangelical Christianity a rigorous, rational, comprehensive theological system that was also thoroughly biblical. Some scholars of evangelical theology have seen in the Princeton Theology evidence of a phenomenon they refer to as the "evangelical enlightenment" because of its emphasis on reason, consistency, and certainty.

The main thinkers of Princeton Theology were Archibald Alexander, Charles Hodge, Archibald Alexander Hodge (Charles' son named after his mentor), *Benjamin Breckenridge Warfield*, and *J. Gresham Machen*. Machen left Princeton when it departed from Protestant scholasticism (and perhaps also from Protestant orthodoxy) and founded Westminster Theological Seminary, which has carried on the Old School Princeton approach to evangelical life and thought throughout the twentieth century and into the twenty-first century. All of these theologians were staunchly conservative Calvinists and strong defenders of Scripture's *supernatural inspiration*, unique and unsurpassable authority as God's Word written, and *infallibility* and *inerrancy* in all matters, not only in matters related to *salvation*. However, unlike John Calvin, whose theology they claimed to follow, the Princeton theologians neglected the role of the *Holy Spirit* in the authority of Scripture. This was especially true of the later Princeton theologians A. A. Hodge, B. B. Warfield, and J. Gresham Machen.

The Princeton theologians attempted to combat nascent liberal Protestantism, which questioned the veracity and full authority of Scripture, by appealing to logical deduction: Scripture is God's Word; God does not lie or deceive; therefore Scripture cannot err. Of course, their expositions of this syllogism are sophisticated, but it provides the basic thrust of their view of Scripture. If the Bible could be mistaken about one thing, they argued, it could be mistaken about anything. They also sought to demonstrate that the various claims of Scripture's errancy could more often than not be countered. Where they could not, Scripture should be given the benefit of the doubt. The Princeton theologians contributed to evangelical Christianity a strong emphasis on the plenary (full) inspiration and inerrancy of the Bible and a tendency to be obsessed with rationally defending traditional Christian doctrines—especially about the Bible—against liberal skepticism and undermining of objective authority. Not all evangelicals agree with or follow this trajectory from the Princeton scholastic theologians, but evangelical thought as a whole cannot escape its influence.

The Princeton theologians sought to counter the rising tide of skepticism about objective truth and knowledge of reality as it really is (metaphysical knowing) by appealing to Scottish common sense realism—a philosophy that arose in the late eighteenth and early nineteenth century in response to Scottish philosopher David Hume's skepticism about metaphysical knowledge. Hume and the German philosopher Immanuel Kant together (in different ways) gave rise to a skeptical attitude toward knowledge of God and things theological even in theology. The nineteenth-century liberal Protestant theologians

exemplified by Albrecht Ritschl and Adolf Harnack cared little for knowledge of God in himself and tended to reduce Christian doctrine to moral attitudes about the *kingdom of God* as a social reality within history (the "fatherhood of God and brotherhood of man"). This "moralizing of dogma" arose in part, at least, out of skepticism about the possibility of human knowledge of realities such as the *Trinity*, the deity of *Jesus Christ*, and the bodily *resurrection* of Christ. The Princeton theologians turned to Scottish Common Sense Philosophy, which argued that human beings share certain basic experiences and cognitions that require no proof but are simply "common sensical." Such a reality would be cause and effect, which Hume had argued cannot be proven. Common sense philosophy, however, simply asserted that without certain beliefs rooted in common sense, life cannot be lived successfully and knowledge cannot be relied on. The Princeton theologians believed that the same approach could be taken to knowledge of God and other theological subjects. Where skepticism finds room for doubt, realism sees plenty of evidence and reason to believe in spite of lack of absolute proof.

Charles Hodge's systematic theology replaced Turretin's at Princeton in 1872. Eventually it became the "gold standard" for most conservative Reformed thinkers in North America, and it remains in print in the early twenty-first century. Its style of presenting Christian doctrine in a highly systematic framework that makes abundant use of deductive reasoning from Christian common-sense principles is emulated by many conservative evangelical theologians, and some of the most popular systems of evangelical theology are evidently inspired by Hodge. Hodge (and his disciples) left little room for ambiguity; in most matters of doctrine there is one and only one theologically correct doctrinal formulation, and all others are seriously defective if not heretical. In most cases that one correct formulation happens to be the one espoused by

Augustine in the early church and/or Calvin in the Reformation. Warfield did not produce a systematic theology, but instead wrote monographs on various theological subjects. His most influential book is *The Inspiration and Authority of the Bible*, which set forth his case for evangelical belief in and commitment to not only the supernatural plenary verbal inspiration of the Bible, but also its complete, technical, and detailed inerrancy in everything that it reports and teaches.

For Warfield and Machen and fundamentalists in general, the authority of the Bible depends on its very words being inspired by God. In other words, it is insufficient to believe that the authors of Scripture were inspired; unless the very words participate in the supernatural process that the New Testament calls *theopneustos* (inspiration), the Bible is unreliable. Of course, all of the Princeton theologians and most fundamentalists readily admit that only the original autographs were verbally inspired and inerrant. Many moderate and *progressive evangelicals* wonder how our current Bibles in any translation, or even in the reconstructed Greek texts, can be considered authoritative if only the original autographs were verbally inspired and inerrant and if those qualities are absolutely necessary for authority.

There can be no doubt that Princeton Theology profoundly influenced evangelical theology as it was at the turn of the century and as it evolved to become in the twentieth century. To be sure, not all evangelicals are impressed by Princeton Theology, but numerous leading evangelical theologians and apologists imitate the method of Hodge and Warfield. Their approach to theology is considered truly biblical and scientific in the best sense of the term by many conservative evangelicals. Others, however, view them as examples of accommodation to the Enlightenment because of their apparent obsession with absolute foundations of thought, truth within rationally coherent systems, and certainty of knowledge based on founda-

tions and systems as crucial to the success of modern Christianity.

———

Mark A. Noll, ed., *The Princeton Theology: 1812–1921* (Grand Rapids: Baker Book House, 1983); David Wells, "The Stout and Persistent 'Theology' of Charles Hodge," *Christianity Today* 18, no. 23 (Aug. 30, 1974): 10–15.

Progressive/Postconservative Evangelicalism

Throughout the history of postfundamentalist Evangelicalism (which spans the period after World War II) some evangelical scholars have argued that the established leadership of the movement has not moved far away from its fundamentalist roots. Some of the same dissidents within Evangelicalism have viewed as deleterious to the movement's health and progress the use of the old "right versus left" spectrum rubric for describing its theological diversity. Under the influence of postmodern ways of thinking, they have tried to abandon captivity to those categories, which they see as inextricably linked with modernity and with the old liberal-fundamentalist controversy of the 1920s through the 1940s. To such progressive and postconservative evangelicals, mainstream, establishment evangelical *theology* is still too closely tied to fundamentalist habits of the mind and to Enlightenment modes of thinking, such as insistence on rational certainty through logical coherence within a comprehensive system of propositional beliefs. Establishment evangelical theologians and leaders tend to view such dissenters as representatives of an "evangelical left wing" (i.e., liberal evangelicals) and as persons to be cautiously resisted. There is no single group or even network of such progressive and postconservative evangelicals. They have, however, tended to develop certain common traits and often have networked with each other to raise a common voice of concern against what they see as "maximal conservatism" and defense of the status quo among the gatekeepers of evangelical theology.

Progressive evangelicals trace their roots as a mood (not a movement) back to the emergence of postfundamentalist Evangelicalism out of fundamentalist Evangelicalism in the 1940s. For at least a decade that movement was known even by its proponents as neo-Evangelicalism, a name that was dropped once it became primarily a pejorative and polemical label used by fundamentalists against the postfundamentalist coalition. The leaders of postfundamentalist Evangelicalism began using the simpler label "evangelical" in spite of the fact that fundamentalists claim it as well. To outsiders (nonevangelicals) the difference between the two movements is often difficult to discern. Progressive evangelicals say that is because the difference is often slight and one of style rather than substance. Nevertheless, in the 1940s even such a notable conservative as *Carl F. H. Henry* seemed decidedly progressive to fundamentalists and to some of his own colleagues in the emerging neo-evangelical movement. That perception arose from his book *The Uneasy Conscience of Modern Fundamentalism* (Grand Rapids: Wm. B. Eerdmans, 1947), which criticized *fundamentalism* (broadly defined to include conservative evangelicals as well as strict separatists) for neglecting to develop a social concern for this world and its needs. Progressive evangelicals believe that conservative Evangelicalism stopped its progress out of fundamentalism some time after the publication of Henry's treatise and that it needs to continue. One of the leaders of progressive Evangelicalism has been Donald W. Dayton, a Wesleyan scholar who has taught at a variety of evangelical institutions, including a leading Baptist seminary. Together with several other "young evangelicals" (a label given them by sociologist of religion Richard Quebedeaux), Dayton developed a network of dissident, sociopolitically liberal, progressive evangelicals in the 1960s and

1970s. One book especially associated with that group of young evangelicals and their concerns is Dayton's *Discovering an Evangelical Heritage* (New York: Harper & Row, 1976). There Dayton attempted to demonstrate that in the nineteenth century evangelical Christians had been social reformers and that the movement had changed in the twentieth century as a result of the rise and influence of *premillennialism* and fundamentalism. In the 1970s a group of young evangelicals including Dayton produced and edited a magazine entitled the *PostAmerican*, which offered up cultural critiques of all things establishment and conservative in American social and religious life. Eventually the magazine evolved into *Sojourners*—a decidedly progressive publication edited by Jim Wallis and the Sojourners community of Washington, D.C.

The young evangelicals questioned conservative Evangelicalism's perceived obsessions with *authority* (e.g., defense of *inerrancy* of the *Bible*) and social conservatism (e.g., tendency to support the Republican party and condemn liberation theology and other sociopolitically progressive movements). They did not reject or seriously question historic Christian orthodoxy such as the doctrines of the *Trinity* and deity of Christ, but they argued that the evangelical establishment was overly concerned with orthodoxy at the expense of orthopraxis (right action). One of the enduring legacies of the young evangelicals group is the organization Evangelicals for Social Action (ESA), led by one of the luminaries of the young evangelical network—Ronald Sider, who wrote a manifesto of evangelical social concern entitled *Rich Christians in an Age of World Hunger* (4th ed. Nashville: Word, 1997). Another leader of ESA has been evangelical sociologist, speaker, and writer Tony Campolo. While establishment evangelical theologians and leaders such as Carl F. H. Henry have applauded the young/progressive evangelicals' concern for social transformation, they have also often strongly cautioned them about their seeming lack of concern for theological correctness and biblical inerrancy. To objective observers it seems that the difference between the older and younger evangelicals in the 1970s was primarily one of priorities and emphasis. None of the young evangelicals rejected biblical authority or any other distinctive belief of evangelical Christianity, although they were not particularly concerned with defending biblical inerrancy which they did not consider absolutely necessary.

Other evangelicals, not identified with the young evangelicals group of the 1960s and 1970s, expressed progressive views about Evangelicalism's identity and future in the 1980s and 1990s. Many of them were influenced by the earlier writings of evangelical theologian *Donald G. Bloesch*, who has identified himself as a "progressive evangelical" because of his openness to biblical criticism and his willingness to criticize rationalism within evangelical thought. The progressivism of Bloesch and some of his disciples came from their appreciation for the theological contribution of Karl Barth. Appreciation for Barth and uses of his theology within evangelical thought became a flashpoint of controversy within evangelical theological circles in the 1980s. Prior to that decade most evangelicals considered Barth's influence and legacy highly dubious— an attitude largely based on reading of highly negative secondary sources about Barth's theology. During the 1980s many evangelicals bothered to read Barth's *Church Dogmatics* and discovered there a much more evangelical Barth than they had read about. Because of his position outside of establishment Evangelicalism (teaching in a mainline Protestant seminary), Bloesch was able to open up Barth's evangelical side for both evangelicals and nonevangelicals.

In the 1990s Canadian Baptist theologians *Clark Pinnock* and Stanley J. Grenz developed their own versions of progressive and postconservative evangelical theology. They gained numerous admirers, friends, and supporters among younger evangelicals, while at the same time reaping a whirlwind of criticism from conservative evangelicals and neofundamentalists within Evangelicalism for allegedly being too open to doctrinal revision and for departing from the "received evangelical tradition" at a number of points. By the turn of the century (2001) the controversy was coming to a head within evangelical theological circles. Certainly influential neofundamentalist leaders within conservative Evangelicalism attempted to marginalize if not exclude Pinnock and Grenz and others who dared to question the *boundaries* of traditional evangelical scholarship and theology. Many ultraconservatives among evangelical theologians believed Pinnock was flirting with universalism as he developed his view of inclusive *salvation* and was compromising with process theology (*God* as ever changing and evolving with the world) as he developed his *open theism*. Grenz was criticized by some conservative evangelical leaders because he explored the common ground between postmodernity and Christian thought and argued for experiential spirituality (conversional piety) rather than doctrinal correctness as the enduring essence of Evangelicalism. What Pinnock and Grenz and their followers and admirers have in common is simply an openness to continue the evangelical reformation that began with the postfundamentalist or neoevangelical movement as it emerged out of fundamentalism in the 1940s. For them, evangelical theology is always reforming itself. For their critics, there are firm and hard boundaries around the "received evangelical tradition" that cannot be moved.

Gary Dorrien, *The Remaking of Evangelical Theology* (Louisville, KY: Westminster John Knox Press, 1998); Millard J. Erickson, *The Evangelical Left: Encountering Postconservative Evangelical Theology* (Grand Rapids: Baker Books, 1997).

Puritanism   After Pietism no movement has so strongly influenced Evangelicalism and evangelical theology as Puritanism. The Puritans of England and New England in the seventeenth and eighteenth centuries were in many ways the "evangelicals" of their day. They sought to complete the Protestant Reformation in English-speaking countries by restoring the New Testament *church* using Calvin's Geneva (both civil society and church) as model. They were not all of the same mind about how best to carry out that restoration, but they agreed on several crucial ideas and methods over against the established Church of England. Puritans agreed among themselves that the Church of England in the seventeenth and eighteenth centuries remained too close to its Roman Catholic roots and needed to be purified of "Romish" elements. Hence the label "Puritans." One of those elements they wished to purify was the Anglican Church's hierarchical polity, which centered around bishops in apostolic succession. The Puritans wished to have a presbyterian form of church government as established in the Reformed churches of continental Europe. Some of them became dissatisfied with that and created a congregational polity, which usually also involved some degree of separation of church and state. The Puritans also sought to have a genuinely pure "believers' church" or "gathered church," in which full members had not only to be baptized but also to recount their testimony of "acquisition of *faith*" (*conversion*) and demonstrate "signs of *grace*" (e.g., healthy family life and strong involvement in church and community). They rejected the "mixed assembly" model of church within the Church of England, in which all baptized persons were full members and participated in the *sacraments* regardless of lifestyle and often regardless of belief.

Nobody can say with absolute certainty who the first Puritan was. Some scholars trace Puritanism back to the Protestant reformers of England at the time of Henry VIII and his heirs Edward VI and Mary Tudor ("Bloody Mary") in the mid-sixteenth century. Such reformers included Thomas Cranmer, the architect of English Protestantism, and Nicholas Ridley and Hugh Latimer, who sought to turn England into a Protestant kingdom; all three were executed by the Catholic Queen Mary. Other scholars prefer to date the beginning of Puritanism later and regard the first true Puritan as Walter Travers of London, who openly opposed the Elizabethan Settlement that created Anglicanism as a combination of Catholic and Protestant elements within the Church of England. Travers and other anti-Anglicans opposed the imposition of the Book of Common Prayer on all English churches and sought to establish a national Presbyterian church similar in polity and *theology* to the Reformed churches of Switzerland, Holland, and Scotland. Their failure in the early seventeenth century led to a mass exodus of Puritans from England to New England, where many of them adopted congregationalism as their preferred form of church government. A few Puritans moved in an even more radical direction and adopted mystical or Anabaptist ideas and practices from radical reformation groups in Europe. The Baptist tradition began in England and Holland that way in 1608/1609. The Society of Friends (Quakers) also began as a radical offshoot of Puritanism. However, the main groups of Puritans rejected both Baptists and Quakers and often persecuted them.

The distinctive theological hallmark of Puritanism was federal theology, sometimes known as *covenant* theology. According to this interpretation of *Calvinism, God* relates to humanity through covenants or contracts in which God binds himself to people and promises them rewards or blessings if they fulfill certain conditions laid down by God. Every Puritan theologian gave his own spin to federal theology, so any account of it necessarily overgeneralizes.

In general, however, federal theologians among the Puritans regarded God as establishing two covenants with humanity—a covenant of works established with Adam and Eve, and a covenant of grace established with their fallen posterity. The *elect* (those *predestined* by God to eternal *salvation*) are those who keep the covenant of grace, which obligates fallen, sinful human beings to *repent* and believe in *Jesus Christ*. Under the covenant of grace God is obliged by his own decision in establishing the covenant to save those who repent and believe; the elect are known by their signs of grace. They demonstrate their election and make it certain by living lives to the glory and honor of God. For many, if not most, Puritans this meant prosperity as well as dedication to the church and community. Of course, since the Puritans were all Calvinists, they regarded the elect as eternally predestined by God to be in the covenant. The function of federal theology seemed to be to inject an element of synergism into a basically monergistic system of doctrine. (Synergism refers to cooperation, while monergism refers to one supreme foreordaining cause.) The covenant of grace has an absolute aspect in that God ultimately initiates it and decides who will be in it, but it also has a conditional aspect in that human persons must make choices and live lives of obedience to God to be and remain in the covenant. Federal theology also addresses the problem of assurance in Calvinist theology. How does one know he or she is elect? According to the Puritans, that dilemma is solved by examining one's life in the covenant or out of it. Children are saved by being in the covenant through connection with their saved parents; federal theology recognizes group salvation and not only individual salvation. Adults are assured of their election insofar as they joyfully keep the human side of the covenant of grace and see signs of grace in their own lives. Church elders inspect church attenders for signs of grace and allow only those who are showing them to become full members.

Modern Evangelicalism was born in the crucible of the Great Awakening in Great Britain and the American colonies in the 1730s and 1740s. Especially in North America, most of the preachers of the Great Awakening, such as Jonathan Edwards and Gilbert Tennent, were Puritans. Their Puritan theology, combined with revivalist passion, gave birth to North American Evangelicalism. Not all revivalists after the first Great Awakening were Puritans. Methodists most certainly were not. Many Baptists rejected Puritanism, just as they were rejected by Puritans. Nevertheless, the Puritan ethos spilled over into North American Evangelicalism and its theology in significant ways. Most of the leading evangelical theologians have been strongly influenced in some way by federal theology. This was certainly the case with Charles Hodge, the leading *Princeton theologian* of the mid-nineteenth century. The idea of a monergistic salvation combined with human participation has remained very strong in Evangelicalism. The Puritan ethos has also profoundly affected Evangelicalism's ethics, which has strongly emphasized voluntary obedience to God's commands (e.g., the Ten Commandments) not as means to salvation but as signs of election. At its worst, Puritanism could be stiflingly legalistic in imposing rigid lifestyle expectations on its followers. Dancing, consumption of alcohol, and working or even enjoying recreation on Sunday were often forbidden in Puritan homes and towns. Evangelicals adopted such stringent restrictions on lifestyle for centuries. Only in the later part of the twentieth century did many evangelicals begin to shed Puritan ethics in favor of a less rule-based and more principle-based approach to life.

Edmund S. Morgan, *Visible Saints: The History of a Puritan Idea* (New York: New York University Press, 1963); Leland Ryken, *Worldly Saints: The Puritans as They*

Really Were (Grand Rapids: Academie/ Zondervan, 1986); John von Rohr, *The Covenant of Grace in Puritan Thought* (Atlanta: Scholars Press, 1986).

Revivalism   *see* **Pietism-Revivalism**

The Third Wave Movement   One of the most recent movements to arise within and alter the course and character of Evangelicalism is the so-called Third Wave movement, identified and named by Fuller Theological Seminary professor C. Peter Wagner in 1983. Wagner was a missiologist and *church* growth expert at the flagship evangelical seminary when he began to notice and acquire interest in a new movement of independent churches and ministries throughout the world that are neither Pentecostal nor charismatic but emphasize "signs and wonders" such as those that characterized the ministries of *Jesus Christ* and the earliest apostles. One such minister was John Wimber, who led the best-known Third Wave denomination of churches, known as The Vineyard Fellowship, until his early death in 1997. During the 1980s Wagner and Wimber teamed to teach a course at Fuller Seminary entitled "The Miraculous and Church Growth." The emphasis of the course was Wimber's teaching of "power *evangelism*," which centered around miraculous signs and wonders, such as *supernatural* healing, supernatural knowledge, and exorcisms not only of individuals but also of entire geographical areas. The course seemed to meet a need among students and quickly became one of the most popular courses on campus, which led to a backlash from some faculty members and constituents. Nevertheless, the Fuller course gave the Third Wave movement notoriety, and it quickly spread throughout North America. By the turn of the century the Vineyard Fellowship alone had established eight hundred affiliated congregations in the United States and Canada. Other Third Wave groups include the Cal-

vary Chapels—an offshoot of the International Church of the Foursquare Gospel—and various independent congregations and ministries scattered throughout the world.

Three manifestations of the movement that brought it special attention in the later years of the twentieth century were the Toronto Blessing, the Kansas City Fellowship, and the Brownsville Revival. The first was a sustained revival at Toronto's Airport Vineyard church, which eventually left the Vineyard Fellowship. It featured an experience of "laughing in the *Holy Spirit*" that reminded many historians of bodily manifestations reported to have happened during the Great Awakenings. The second phenomenon, in a large charismatic church in Kansas City, featured the gift of prophecy in which certain apostles were believed to be able to guide their followers' lives with miraculous knowledge and verbal *revelations*. The third event was a protracted revival in Brownsville, Florida, near Pensacola. People traveled to an Assemblies of God church there from all over the world to experience a special transformation through an outpouring of a spirit of *repentance* that led many people to be "slain in the Spirit."

Scholars of the Third Wave movement point out its five distinctives. The first was contributed by John Wimber—power evangelism. According to Wimber and his followers and nearly all persons associated with the Third Wave movement, the best way to convert people to Jesus Christ is the way of the earliest apostles as recorded in the Acts of the Apostles—demonstrate *miracles* to them. The main way in which this happens is by "word of knowledge," supernatural revelation of things in peoples' lives that proves to them that *God* is encountering them and calling them to decision. The second distinctive is a rejection of the modern Western worldview which is based on *reason* and science and is biased against the supernatural. Third Wave Christians seek to bring to North America and Europe spiritual beliefs and phenomena already widely accepted in non-Western and developing countries and cultures. The third distinctive is belief that the *kingdom of God* is "already but not yet" and that its partial, anticipatory presence is manifested in miraculous signs and wonders that demonstrate Jesus Christ's lordship over powers and principalities of darkness (i.e., the devil and demons). The fourth distinctive is an emphasis on sickness as, often if not usually, a manifestation of *Satan's* power in a person's life that needs eradication through exorcism. Not all ill people are believed to be demon possessed, but illness is attributed to Satan's power and work and not merely to natural causes. Physical healing can come through rebuking Satan and his minions and casting them out of a sick person's body. The fifth distinctive is belief in and practice of spiritual warfare. Third Wave Christians believe that the world is locked in a cosmic struggle between God and God's forces and Satan and his forces. One tool in Christians' warfare is "spiritual mapping," which involves prayerful discernment of "territorial spirits" and powerful exorcisms of the same. Third Wavers believe that entire cities and countries can be under dominion of *evil* forces and that God and God's forces sometimes await believers' prayers before acting to conquer the evil powers.

The Third Wave movement must not be confused with classical Pentecostalism or with the neo-Pentecostal, charismatic movement. While there is much common ground, the Third Wave movement does not emphasize speaking in tongues nor does it reject it. Also, Third Wave Christians generally do abandon their mainstream denominations and churches (if any) and gather in independent congregations or in congregations associated with the Vineyard Fellowship or one of the Calvary Chapels. Many of these Third Wave churches have no formal membership other than a group of elders who minister with the pastoral staff. *Worship* services tend to be lengthy, emotional (often including spiritual dancing and falling on the floor in ecstacy), and aimed at inducing miraculous manifestations of some kind. While such worship used to be associated primarily with poorer people, Third Wave churches are often populated and visited by educated, middle- or upper-class people. Many of them attract university students, including graduate and professional students.

The Third Wave movement has injected a greater appreciation for the miraculous and supernatural into Evangelicalism, which at the beginning of the twenty-first century is much less prone than earlier to reject such signs and wonders out of hand. The fact that the movement came to public attention and grew through the course team-taught by John Wimber and C. Peter Wagner at Fuller Theological Seminary has given it an aura of respectability among many evangelicals. Also, in many cities of North America, the largest clearly and unequivocally evangelical churches (in terms of attendance) are Third Wave churches, and that cannot help but influence other evangelical churches and ministries. Thousands if not millions of evangelicals—including ministers—have traveled to Third Wave revivals (or "blessings") and returned to their home churches transformed. Finally, evangelical missionaries returning from developing countries report that the most vital forms of Christianity in those lands tend to be very similar to North American Third Wave churches. Postmodernity has broken down the hegemony of Western, rationalistic, naturalistic biases with regard to what is possible and what is not possible. All in all, then, the Third Wave movement has begun to transform evangelical Christianity in North America.

Lewis B. Smedes, *Ministry and the Miraculous: A Case Study at Fuller Theological Seminary* (Pasadena, CA: Fuller Theological Seminary, 1987); C. Samuel Storms, "A Third Wave View," in *Are*

Miraculous Gifts for Today? ed. Wayne A. Grudem (Grand Rapids: Zondervan, 1996); John Wimber and Kevin Springer, *Power Evangelism* (San Francisco: HarperCollins, 1986).

The World Evangelical Alliance

In 2002 World Evangelical Alliance (WEA) became the new name of the World Evangelical Fellowship, founded in 1951. It is the largest, most inclusive umbrella organization of evangelical organizations in the world. As of 2002 it had 120 member organizations. Most of them are national and regional cooperative groups of evangelicals, such as the *National Association of Evangelicals* (NAE) in the United States. The WEA has 3 affiliate groups and 101 associate organizations. Most of the latter are specialized missionary and *evangelism* or social action groups. The task of the WEA is to facilitate and coordinate fellowship and cooperation among all of these, which together have approximately 160 million constituents representing 111 countries. The alliance is sponsored primarily by evangelical Christians from developing, two-thirds-world countries, although many of its affiliated and associated organizations are headquartered in Europe and North America.

The WEA unites evangelicals of many different nations and denominations. Its required statement of faith is minimal, focusing only on basic beliefs of historic Christianity such as the *Trinity* and *return of Jesus Christ*. It does affirm the *inspiration, authority,* and *infallibility* of the *Scriptures,* but it does not mention inerrancy. The WEA publishes an article entitled "What Is an Evangelical?" by influential evangelical scholar Leon Morris. It focuses on *Jesus Christ* and his objectively atoning death (as opposed to the more liberal subjective, moral example theory of the *atonement*) as the central feature of evangelical confession. The alliance sponsors several commissions that bring attention to theological and practical issues such as women's rights and world evangelization. It seeks to avoid any dualism between spiritual *salvation* and social transformation without collapsing them together. The WEA's primary influence on evangelical theology is bringing the voices of non-Western evangelicals into the conversations of evangelical theologians. Its conferences and publications highlight the multicultural nature of world Evangelicalism and shed light on the degree to which traditional Western evangelical thought is influenced by European and North American (and modern) cultural patterns of thinking.

———

The World Evangelical Alliance home Web site: http://www.worldevangelical.org.

Key Figures
in Evangelical Theology

Donald G. Bloesch One of the most influential mainline Protestant theologians who is also an evangelical is Donald G. Bloesch (b. 1928), whose teaching and writing career at the Presbyterian-related University of Dubuque Theological Seminary in Iowa spanned nearly the last half of the twentieth century. Bloesch has been one of evangelical *theology's* most prolific and influential writers, producing dozens of volumes and scholarly articles as well as a number of hymns. Bloesch has always worked on the margin of the evangelical subculture, which has sometimes limited his influence, especially among hard-core conservative evangelicals who remain close to their fundamentalist roots. Bloesch is viewed by some of them with suspicion because he refers to himself as a "catholic evangelical," by which he means that he regards evangelical Protestant theology as part of the larger story of Christian theology that includes the entire visible, orthodox church going back to the apostles. In other words, he means to distance himself from sectarianism that cuts itself off from the historic tradition of Christianity by regarding it as apostate. Bloesch is decidedly Protestant, but he quotes with appreciation *church* fathers, medieval Christian thinkers, reformers of various traditions, and a wide variety of mediating and conservative modern theologians including Pietists and revivalists.

Bloesch is a member and minister of the United Church of Christ (UCC), which came into existence as an ecumenical merger of the older American Congregational Church and the Evangelical and Reformed Church. His family was part of the latter denomination, which has roots in the Lutheran-Reformed union of Germany and in the Reformed churches of Switzerland. That portion of the merger that created the UCC tended to be more conservative theologically than the American Congregational Church, which, though rooted in the Puritan movement, had become more liberalized. Bloesch has always considered himself relatively conservative compared to the theological center of gravity of his own denomination. However, he has never been in the thick of the fundamentalist-evangelical subculture of North America and so stands on the boundary between that and the Protestant mainline, speaking to both. His doctoral studies were conducted at the University of Chicago Divinity School, which was dominated by a form of liberal theology called religious naturalism. Process theology, a related form of liberal theology, was beginning to exercise influence there when Bloesch was a student. However, Bloesch associated with an evangelical student group and retained his basically conservative and Pietist Christian ethos throughout his student years. He received his Ph.D. from the University of Chicago after studying for a time with Karl Barth in Switzerland. When he embarked on his teaching career at the University of Dubuque Theological Seminary, he was well prepared to present to his students and the North American reading public a creative hybrid of warm-hearted Pietist Evangelicalism and Barthian neo-orthodoxy.

Among Bloesch's most important and influential books are *The Evangelical Renaissance* (1973), *Jesus Is Victor! Karl Barth's Doctrine of Salvation* (1976), *The Future of Evangelical Christianity: A Call for Unity Amid Diversity* (1983), *The Struggle of Prayer* (1988), *Essentials of Evangelical Theology*, 2 vol. (1978 and 1979); and his seven-volume magnum opus, *Christian Foundations* (first volume published in 1992). The latter two sets are Bloesch's two systematic theologies, although they are not especially systematic. That is, Bloesch is extremely wary of any imposition of a framework of human thought on *Scripture* and Christian doctrine. Unlike some other systems of Christian theology, his lacks any overriding, unifying theme. Both of his sets of systematic theology present the traditional loci of Christian doctrine in fairly traditional order without any dominating motif other than God's *revelation* of himself in *Jesus Christ* and Scripture. However, any careful reader of Bloesch's books cannot help but notice a negative theme that runs throughout—a stringent warning against the *authority* of *reason* and philosophy in Christian confession and theological reflection. Bloesch's approach to evangelical theology has always been nonapologetic. That is, unlike some evangelical theologians, he is actively disinterested in rationally demonstrating the rational superiority of Christian thought to all competing visions of reality. He believes that the best apologetic is a strong presentation of an intelligible account of divine revelation and Christian tradition that does *justice* to mystery (which is inevitable because of *God's* wholly otherness) and often expresses itself in paradoxes. Bloesch's appreciation for the contributions of Søren Kierkegaard, the nineteenth-century "melancholy Dane," and Karl Barth is noticeable throughout his body of writings. While he eschews irrationality, the Iowa theologian believes that the rationality of theology must be drawn from its own object, which is God and God's self-revelation, rather than from some secular standard of reasoning such as the modern Enlightenment or ancient Greek thought. His own substitute for the rage for rational certainty in evangelical apologetics and polemics is confidence in the truth of *gospel* brought about by the *Holy Spirit*. This method he labels (somewhat confusingly) "fideistic revelationism" because it bases Christian proclamation and confession on divine revelation, which is known to be true by the inner testimony of the Holy Spirit within the church as well as within the individual.

Bloesch's influence in postfundamentalist evangelical theology has been a moderating and mediating one. He has repeatedly criticized fundamentalist and conservative evangelical biblicism with its insistence on verbal *inspiration* and *inerrancy* as accommodation to modern rationalism (search for certainty

through rational foundations and logical deduction), while at the same time constructing his own progressive evangelical biblicism that affirms the authority of Scripture as the indispensable witness to and instrument of divine revelation, which, with all its flaws, is infallible for Christian knowledge of God and practice of the Christian faith. Bloesch's alternative to fundamentalist and conservative evangelical biblicism is what he calls a sacramental view of Scripture's authority in which the Bible is a *sacrament* (channel, means) of God's Word but not identical with God's Word, which is God's own self-communication centering uniquely in Jesus Christ. He compares Scripture to the glass and filament of a light bulb; God's Word is the light while Scripture is the medium of that light. While some critics have accused Bloesch of being neo-orthodox, his sacramental biblicism actually brings God's Word and Scripture closer together than does neo-orthodoxy. Bloesch is also moderating and mediating among evangelical theologians in that he draws on a rich variety of sources within the great tradition of Christian belief and teaching, including such diverse thinkers as early church father Tertullian, medieval scholastic thinker Anselm, Renaissance and Reformation mystics, Luther, Calvin, Anabaptists, Puritans, Pietists, and John Wesley. Bloesch affirms the Nicene (Trinitarian) faith of the Christian tradition and rejects all forms of liberal theology, while treating them with respect. He has been a harsh critic of radical feminist theology and especially of any replacement of the divine triune name of God as Father, Son, and Holy Spirit with gender neutral terms and of feminine language for God. And yet he is in favor of full equality of women with men in all areas of life including the church. For many moderate to progressive evangelical theologians, educated lay people, and pastors, Bloesch's theology has been a refreshing change from the often harsh polemics and divisive rhetoric that especially conservative evangelical theology has engaged in. His criticisms of other approaches to theology, spirituality, and *worship* are always based on careful understanding and are irenic even when they must pronounce a definite no.

Daniel J. Adams, ed., *From East to West: Essays in Honor of Donald G. Bloesch* (New York: University of America Press, 1997); Elmer M. Colyer, ed., *Evangelical Theology in Transition: Theologians in Dialogue with Donald Bloesch* (Downers Grove, IL: Inter-Varsity Press, 1999).

Edward John Carnell Edward John ("E. J.") Carnell (1919–67) was one of the very few watershed theologians in the early divide between *fundamentalism* and postfundamentalist Evangelicalism. He joined the faculty of Fuller Theological Seminary soon after its founding and served as its president from 1954 until 1959. Together with the seminary's founding president, Harold John Ockenga, and its most influential theologian, *Carl F. H. Henry*, Carnell attempted to "reform fundamentalism" by creating an intellectually respectable, theologically orthodox, nonseparatistic form of evangelical *theology*. Through his lectures and leadership of the flagship seminary of the new evangelical movement, as well as through a series of books, he influenced a generation of evangelicals struggling to find a new approach to conservative Protestant theology that would avoid the Scylla of fundamentalism and the Charybdis of liberalism. Among his best-known works are *An Introduction to Christian Apologetics* (1948), *A Philosophy of the Christian Religion* (1952), *Christian Commitment* (1957), and *The Case for Orthodox Theology* (1959). In general Carnell's concern was to defend a nonfundamentalist, nonsectarian version of evangelical Protestant thought using the tools of *reason*, human *experience*, *Scripture*, and tradition. His burden was primarily apologetic and sometimes polemical, and it can be said with some justifica-

tion that he represented an "evangelical enlightenment" that attempted to demonstrate rationally the intellectual superiority of conservative Christianity over the culturally accommodated liberal theology of mainstream Protestantism and the narrow and sometimes cultic separatism and obscurantism of much of fundamentalism.

E. J. Carnell was a wunderkind of the new Evangelicalism as it emerged out of fundamentalism in the early 1940s. He grew up in a fundamentalist Baptist pastor's home but began to turn away from fundamentalism (not from his Baptist heritage) while studying at Wheaton College, the flagship college of the postfundamentalist evangelical movement. At Wheaton he came under the influence of Reformed evangelical philosopher *Gordon Haddon Clark*, who convinced Carnell that the law of noncontradiction provided the magic key to the discovery of truth, even within the studies of religion and theology. For Clark and then for Carnell, truth is contained in factual propositions that are consistent with all other true propositions. In other words, truth is a coherent system of facts, and contradictions—including paradoxes (apparent inconsistencies)—are sure signs of error. That life and worldview (including theology) is most likely to be true that accounts for the largest scope of experience within a tight, logically coherent system. According to Clark and his disciples, Christianity, conservative Protestantism in particular, is that coherent system. Carnell attended conservative Westminster Theological Seminary after college and then earned doctoral degrees in philosophy and theology from both Boston University and Harvard Divinity School. His dissertations were rigorous scholarly critiques of two luminaries of modern Christian thought—Søren Kierkegaard and Reinhold Niebuhr. These caught the attention of Harold John Ockenga—the architect of the new postfundamentalist evangelical movement—and Carl F. H. Henry, who also earned a Ph.D. at Boston University.

As professor of philosophy and theology and then president of Fuller Theological Seminary, Carnell worked hard to develop a strong reasonable case for the truth of orthodox Christianity without relying on the tricks used by many fundamentalist preachers and writers of misrepresenting the competition and then knocking down the straw men they created. Carnell had studied in the nerve centers of liberal Protestant theology and knew the strengths and weaknesses of that approach to Christian thought and of other religions and philosophies well. Liberal Protestant theology often justified its revisionist approach to the reconstruction of Christian beliefs by appealing to common human experience over propositional *revelation* such as evangelicals find in Scripture. Carnell invaded the "enemies"' territory by also appealing to universal human experience and to logic to criticize liberal revisionism and defend orthodoxy. For example, in *Christian Commitment*, which some reviewers consider his magnum opus, Carnell used the universal human experience of objective valuing—judging some things objectively good and just and some things objectively *evil* and unjust—as the foundation for belief in the existence of a personal *God* as the ultimate source and judge of all values. Ultimately, he argued, Christianity provides the best (most coherent and comprehensive) account of human experience of valuing.

Perhaps the most controversial contribution of Carnell to the new Evangelicalism and its theology appeared in his 1959 volume *The Case for Orthodox Theology*, which was one in a three-volume set about the major forms of modern Christian thought. The other two were *The Case for Theology in a Liberal Perspective*, by liberal Methodist theologian L. Harold DeWolf, and *The Case for a New Reformation Theology* (referring to neo-orthodoxy), by Lutheran theologian William Hordern. Carnell's volume was to have been titled "The Case for Conservative Theology," but he preferred

the term *orthodox* to *conservative* because the latter could sound like a defense of a status quo and might imply something stale, rather than living and dynamic. Some have questioned whether "orthodox" is a better choice of terms for evangelical theology, which is what Carnell defended in his volume.

What stirred the most controversy was the Fuller president's attack on fundamentalism, which he described as "orthodoxy gone cultic" and "cunning pharisaism." His main criticisms of fundamentalism dealt with its sectarian separationism (which claimed that all mainline Protestant denominations, as well as the Roman Catholic Church, were apostate), which often arose out of concerns about secondary matters of the faith such as biblical *inerrancy* and *dispensationalist* hermeneutics. Carnell defended a moderate version of inerrancy, but argued that an intelligible evangelical biblicism would have to avoid wooden literalism in interpreting the Bible. He dismissed claims of absolute conflict between modern science—including evolutionary theory—and the Bible and argued for a greater openness by evangelicals to non-Christian scholarship, so long as it is not based on a hostile worldview. Many conservative evangelicals believed that Carnell has betrayed them in his stringent critique and even condemnation of fundamentalism. They detected in his book and in his leadership of Fuller an openness to significant revisions of doctrines they considered sacrosanct. With regard to the *virgin birth*, Carnell argued that it happened, not, however, as a miraculous means of *incarnation* or sinlessness but as a sign to Jesus' followers that he was the Messiah and Son of God.

Carnell's life was plagued with anxieties about many matters, including his legacy. Some scholars believe that he suffered from clinical depression caused by a chemical imbalance in the brain, but when he resigned his seminary presidency and then experienced what was then called a "nervous breakdown" in

1961, his friends believed he was over-worked and overly anxious about the lackluster reception of some of his books and about the harsh criticism his *Ortho-doxy* volume had received from conservative friends and colleagues. Carnell died of an overdose of sleeping pills in a hotel room in Oakland, California, in 1967. No one knows whether his death was accidental or suicide. He was only forty-eight. Just as he feared, all of his books went out of print and his influence in the birth of postfundamentalist Evangelicalism was largely forgotten for a time. During the 1990s, as scholars began to revisit that emergence of Evangelicalism out of fundamentalism, however, Carnell's importance to evangelical theology was rediscovered.

Gary Dorrien, *The Remaking of Evangelical Theology* (Louisville, KY: Westminster John Knox Press, 1998); George Marsden, "Edward J. Carnell," in *Makers of Christian Theology in America*, ed. Mark G. Toulouse and James O. Duke (Nashville: Abingdon Press, 1997), 484–88; Rudolph Nelson, *The Making and Unmaking of an Evangelical Mind: The Case of Edward Carnell* (Cambridge: Cambridge University Press, 1987).

Gordon Clark   *Carl F. H. Henry*, the "dean of evangelical theologians," declared his Wheaton College professor Gordon Haddon Clark (1902–86) one of the most able and influential Protestant philosophers. A generation of postfundamentalist evangelical thinkers was profoundly influenced by Clark, even if many of them later quarreled with aspects of his philosophy and some even repudiated it. When scholars of Evangelicalism and evangelical *theology* refer to the "evangelical enlightenment" they are often thinking of Clark and his general approach to defending the truth of Christianity, which he equated with the Reformed (Calvinistic) version of Protestantism. Clark believed that knowledge is linked with certainty, and

certainty is connected with logic. His entire career as a Christian philosophy professor was aimed at establishing the certain truth of Christianity's basic truth claims about reality and undermining, if not refuting, the truth of all competing worldviews and philosophies of life. Most of his disciples (almost all of whom were his students at one time) went on to become professors and writers in the fields of philosophy, apologetics, and/or theology, and they deeply stamped post-fundamentalist evangelical thought with a strongly rationalistic apologetic thrust.

Clark was born and raised in a Presbyterian minister's home and remained a devoted conservative Presbyterian (adhering to the Westminster Confession of Faith and Westminster Shorter and Longer Catechisms) his entire life. Clark stood on the boundary between the fundamentalism of *J. Gresham Machen* and the neoevangelicalism of the 1940s as it emerged out of *fundamentalism*. Like Machen, he left the mainline Presbyterian denomination to join the Orthodox Presbyterian Church but was denied ordination in the latter body because of a strong difference of opinion with its most influential philosopher and theologian, Cornelius Van Til, who succeeded Machen as the leading theologian at Westminster Theological Seminary. Clark, who believed the mainline Presbyterian church was falling into apostasy, then joined the Reformed Presbyterian Church. He graduated from the University of Pennsylvania with a Ph.D. in philosophy in 1929. His teaching career took him to Wheaton College, the flagship school of the postfundamentalist evangelical movement; Reformed Episcopal Seminary; Butler University; and Covenant College. During his sixty-year teaching career Clark wrote over thirty volumes and published numerous scholarly articles. His main works include *A Christian View of Men and Things* (1951), *From Thales to Dewey* (1956), and *Religion, Reason, and Revelation* (1961). While teaching at Wheaton College from 1936 to 1943 Clark vigorously promoted his own rather stringent version of Calvinism and his rigorously rationalistic philosophy. Both challenged the prevailing ethos of Wheaton, even as they stimulated many students, such as Carl F. H. Henry and *Edward John Carnell*. Wheaton's president terminated Clark at the end of 1943, and eventually Clark ended up teaching at a university related to the more mainline Disciples of Christ denomination (Butler University in Indiana). Nevertheless, his influence on evangelical thought remained strong until the 1960s. After that his influence was primarily through his students and disciples who adjusted and translated his philosophy.

Clark's philosophy has generally been considered a form of presuppositionalism, but it differed considerably from the presuppositionalism of his rival within the small world of conservative Reformed evangelical philosophy in the 1940s and 1950s, Cornelius Van Til of Westminster Theological Seminary. Some critics find the differences slight, but certainly Clark and Van Til and their disciples did not consider them so. Clark argued that every life and worldview, including every religion and theology, begins with certain often implicit unprovable presuppositions. Therefore, it cannot be irrational to start with such assumptions; otherwise there could be no rational philosophy at all. He rejected empiricism and its Christian apologetic offshoot evidentialism ("evidence that demands a verdict") because he believed the senses to be unreliable and historical information incapable of yielding certainty. He rejected strict rationalism because it claimed to work without presuppositions of content. Clark believed that rationalists were in denial about their presuppositions and argued that even the most rationalistic philosophies begin with certain unrecognized assumptions about logic and the mind's ability to grasp reality, using indubitable foundations such as "I think, therefore I am."

Clark believed that the Christian philosopher must unapologetically begin his or her philosophy (and that would include for him theology) with firm acknowledgment of the truth of *Scripture* as God's propositional, coherent self-revelation. That is, the *Bible* is the unquestioned starting point from which the Christian thinker must draw his or her conclusions about life and the world and meaning. Clark believed that the Bible constitutes a coherent system of truth about reality and that even reason's basic principles and methods can be derived from it. He virtually equated *God* with logic and claimed to find both in Scripture as the purest expression of God's thoughts. In the end, the Christian presupposition of the absolute truth of Scripture is justified by its ability to yield a more coherent and comprehensive account of human *experience* of reality than any other known presupposition. In fact, Clark argued, all the others ultimately yield nihilism (meaninglessness) when pressed by strict logic to their good and necessary consequences.

Clark was also a classical five-point Calvinist and did not hesitate to promote that particular Protestant theology as the only authentically Christian life and worldview. He taught that Scripture reveals God's absolute sovereignty, including God's freedom from any *law* (God is the author of all laws, so they do not apply to him in the same way they apply to creatures) and God's ultimate causation of everything that happens in nature and history including *sin* and *evil*. He argued that God is not morally responsible for the latter because he is not under any law; humans are responsible for the sins God foreordains they commit because they are under the law of God which forbids evil thoughts and actions. Clark taught the strongest possible vision of divine meticulous *providence*, in which everything that happens is the activity of God, even if only through secondary causes. Thus, in Clark's divine determinism, there is no true contingency in nature or history.

This is either the best of all possible worlds or the world necessary to arrive at the best of all possible worlds—even if we are unable to see how that can be in the midst of the evils of human history. Clark's legacy can clearly be seen in a certain strain of evangelical apologetics and theology. Carl F. H. Henry did not always agree entirely with Clark, who awakened him from his fundamentalist slumbers at Wheaton College, but he certainly based his own evangelical theology largely on Clark's general epistemological approach. Henry called his own version of it rational, biblical presuppositionalism. During the early years of his career as an evangelical philosopher and theologian, Edward John Carnell also worked with a version of Clark's philosophy, even if he later branched out from it into an apologetic that incorporated human experience. Clark's legacy to postfundamentalist evangelical theology is to provide it with one model of rigorously intellectual methodology. And yet, to some of his evangelical critics his model was fideistic—proceeding from blind faith in the truth of Scripture. Such critics are evidentialists who believe that all knowledge is based on empirical evidence and the mind's deduction of truth from it as well as on historical evidence, which cannot be divorced from empirical experience (e.g., historical artifacts). Clark and his disciples tend to be obsessed with certainty, and so long as their assurance of the veracity of Scripture holds out, their methodology yields it. Evidentialists are more concerned with probability. Both schools of evangelical philosophy represent what *Donald Bloesch* would call evangelical rationalism, which undermines the transcendence of God as incomprehensible mystery and reduces theology—which must embrace paradoxes—to philosophy.

"Memorials: Gordon Haddon Clark," *Journal of the Evangelical Theological Society* 29:1 (March 1986); Ronald H. Nash, ed., *The Philosophy of Gordon Clark* (Philadelphia: Presbyterian & Reformed Publish-

ing House, 1967); John W. Robbins, "An Introduction to Gordon H. Clark" at http://www.trinityfoundation.org.

John Nelson Darby One of the strangest and yet also most influential contributions to modern evangelical life and thought is that of Irish clergyman and *Bible* teacher John Nelson Darby (1800–82) who, more than any other individual, turned conservative Protestant *theology* in North America toward what is known as *dispensational premillennialism*. Most evangelicals of the nineteenth century and many in the twentieth century were and are believers in *amillennialism*—the identification of the *church* with the *kingdom of God* and denial of any literal thousand-year reign of Christ on earth at the end of history. A few have been *postmillennialists*. Because of Darby, many conservative evangelicals in the twentieth century, perhaps the majority, became dispensational premillennialists—espousing a view of *eschatology* virtually unheard of before his life and ministry. Darby's voluminous writings about biblical prophecy and the second coming of Christ and his peripatetic preaching and teaching all over Europe and North America set off a wave of Bible-prophecy conferences among conservative Protestants already being influenced in that direction by the rise of Adventism. Darby's influence on evangelist Dwight Lyman Moody in the late nineteenth century helped propel premillennialism into the spotlight of evangelical eschatological fervor. Popular study-Bible editor C. I. Scofield incorporated Darby's speculations into his study notes, and Clarence Larkin based his extremely influential Bible-history charts on Darby's interpretations of biblical apocalyptic and prophetic materials. Although Darby's name is hardly a household word among evangelicals, his influence has trickled down to the average evangelical pew sitter and many pastors through the enormously popular writings of Hal Lindsay and Tim LaHaye.

Darby was born in London to Irish parents in the last year of the eighteenth century. He was educated in law in Ireland and then turned to the ministry. Ordained a priest in the Church of England around 1825, he soon began to associate with a nameless group of Christians in Dublin who met in homes and were dissatisfied with conditions in the Anglican churches. Eventually he left the Church of England and became a member of the fledgling Plymouth Brethren movement, which eschewed clergy, church buildings, liturgy, and creeds. They met in homes, celebrated the *Lord's Supper* weekly, and worshiped in an extremely informal fashion with strong focus on biblical study and *evangelism*. The Brethren generally considered other churches apostate and called on all true Bible Christians to abandon them and become members of Brethren gatherings. Darby quickly rose to become the most influential leader of the movement. He was by far its best-known and most influential theologian and Bible scholar-teacher. The Plymouth Brethren (a name not used by the Brethren but only by outsiders) continue to exist in the twenty-first century although the group has fragmented and remained relatively small in numbers. Their impact on evangelical life and thought is far greater than their actual membership, largely due to Darby's promotion of two Brethren distinctives that he helped develop: ecclesiology and eschatology.

Brethren reject ecumenical interpretations of the church that emphasize an invisible body of Christ throughout history. They view the church as local and consisting of true believers only. Brethren churches are house churches (with a few exceptions that have occurred more often in the twentieth century) and expect all adult male members to serve as ministers. They view the marks of the true church as weekly celebration of the Lord's Supper and intense, correct Bible study and interpretation. In brief, their ecclesiology is sectarian. Their promotion of the idea that all true Christians should "come out and be separate" (from the apostate mainline churches) greatly affected the fundamentalist movement in the 1920s and 1930s.

The second distinctive that Darby is best known for is a peculiar eschatology, known as dispensationalism, that regards God's plan to save national Israel as not superceded by the gentile church and interprets the end of history through an allegedly literalistic interpretation of the Bible. According to dispensationalism the gentile church is an afterthought within God's redemptive plan, which always aims primarily at saving national Israel through her messiah, *Jesus Christ*. At the end of this present age God will "rapture" (take away) the gentile Christians who have been saved by God's *grace* apart from the *law* of Moses and bring Israel to *salvation* during a seven-year period of great tribulation, followed by the visible *return of Jesus Christ* and the establishment of his rule and reign on the earth for one thousand years. The term *rapture* comes from the Latin Vulgate Bible 1 Thessalonians 4:17. Nondispensationalist biblical scholars do not find any reference to a "secret rapture" in Scripture, nor do they believe God has two plans for salvation—one for Israel and one for the gentile church.

Dispensationalism entered into evangelical life and thought far beyond its humble beginnings among the Plymouth Brethren in the 1830s and 1840s. By the late twentieth century it was virtually taken for granted as the correct biblical interpretation of *God's* plans of salvation for Israel and the gentiles and of the end times (eschatology) by many, if not most, evangelicals. Reformed evangelicals have generally resisted it; they tend to view the church as succeeding Israel in God's plan of salvation through *Jesus Christ*. They also tend to interpret biblical apocalyptic literature nonliterally and regard the kingdom of

God as present already in and through the church. Some critics of dispensationalism within evangelical theology argue that it tends to promote an otherworldly ethos that denigrates nature and history as unimportant. They and others claim that dispensationalism simply finds in Scripture what is not in there—the so-called "secret rapture" of the church. Many critics point out that Plymouth Brethren–inspired *separationism*, sectarianism, and dispensationalism cut churches off from the great tradition of Christian thinking and teaching and contribute to a cultic mentality among conservative evangelicals. Evangelical dispensationalists, however, believe that Darby was a reformer who recovered lost truths of biblical Christianity.

The primary legacy of Darby is a network of dispensationalist ministries, writers, and educational institutions spread throughout the evangelical subculture in North America. One of the most prominent institutions related to his distinctive teaching about the Bible and the end times is Dallas Theological Seminary in Texas, a large independent evangelical (some would say fundamentalist) seminary that exists to promote dispensationalism. Its presidents and professors, such as Lewis Sperry Chafer and Dwight Pentecost, have interpreted and disseminated Darby's dispensationalism throughout North America and the rest of the world. Ironically, most Pentecostals have also adopted and promoted dispensationalism, although in a different way from Dallas Theological Seminary. The latter interprets it as Darby did—after a cessationist manner that views the *supernatural gifts of the Holy Spirit* as ceasing with the completion of the biblical canon. Pentecostals enthusiastically endorse dispensationalism without cessationism. One can also find dispensationalists spread throughout evangelical educational institutions and publishing houses.

_____

Robert C. Doyle, *Eschatology and the Shape of Christian Belief* (London: Paternoster Press, 1999); J. D. Hannah, "Darby, John Nelson (1800–1882)," in *The Dictionary of Christianity in America*, ed. Daniel G. Reid et al. (Downers Grove, IL: InterVarsity Press, 1990), 339–40; Dave MacPherson, *The Incredible Cover-Up* (Medford, OR: Omega Publications, 1980).

Charles G. Finney *Revivalism* has always been an important feature of Evangelicalism, and Charles Grandison Finney (1792–1875) is often regarded as the father of modern revivalism. His influence on revivalistic preaching and methods of mass *evangelism* is, for better or worse, incalculable. He was also a social reformer who worked tirelessly for the abolition of slavery and promoted equality of women with men. He gained notoriety in religious circles in both North America and Europe for allowing women to pray publicly and to take leadership roles in revivals and social reform activities. Finney was also a theologian who promoted a view of the relationship between *God* and individuals that has come to be known as moral government theology. It involved a radical revisioning of the doctrines of *sin* and *salvation* away from classical *Calvinism* (which formed the background of Finney's ministry in New England and New York) and toward a more moralistic and perfectionistic view of salvation. Admirers and critics agree that this father of modern revivalism changed the face of North American conservative Protestantism forever. To critics, he changed it by creating a form of religious life that is individualistic rather than centered around the *church*, focused on energetic endeavor rather than God's *grace* and power, and perfectionistic rather than realistic. To admirers, he introduced a Christianity optimistic about the potential and responsibility of human beings under God and free of the conundrums of classical Augustinian-Calvinism that seemed to hold human persons responsible for Adam's sin and God not responsible for the sin of humans that he foreordained. All agree that he was decades, and perhaps a century or more, ahead of his time in terms of his vision of social transformation.

Finney was born in Connecticut in 1792 and raised in Oneida and Jefferson Counties, New York, the setting for many nineteenth-century progressive social reform and evangelical-utopian movements. Second Great Awakening revivals frequently swept through that region, and Finney was caught up in one in 1821. He was serving as an apprentice attorney in Adams, New York, when he experienced a dramatic *conversion*. He spent a night in anxious *prayer* and *repentance* and then said to his client, "I have been given a retainer from the Lord *Jesus Christ* to plead his cause and I cannot plead yours." Finney sought ordination with the Presbyterian denomination and eventually switched to the more theologically flexible Congregationalist connection of churches. He began his ministry as a missionary, preaching in towns along the new Erie Canal in upstate New York, but soon gained such notoriety for his passionate preaching and for his listeners' emotional responses that he launched a series of protracted mass revivals in major cities such as Philadelphia and Boston. In 1832 he gained his own home pulpit at the newly established Broadway Tabernacle in New York City, while continuing to travel and hold evangelistic campaigns in the United States and Europe. He introduced what came to be called "new measures" into his revivals, including the so-called "anxious seat," where inquiring sinners sat near the pulpit before responding to the invitation to accept Christ. Often the audience's response to his fervent preaching was extremely emotional with people falling on the floor, writhing in sorrow for sin, crying out to God for *forgiveness*. Stories began to circulate about people experiencing dramatic spiritual transformations accompanied by physical manifestations even before Finney arrived to preach. Finney preached against slavery and denied the *Lord's Supper* to slaveholders. He argued that lack of social benevolence, manifested, for example, in dishonesty in business and slavery, hindered revivals and insisted that churches cooperating to support his endeavors oppose social sin as well as individual sinfulness.

In 1835 the newly established abolitionist Oberlin College in Ohio invited Finney to become its professor of systematic *theology*. He accepted and also pastored Oberlin's First Church, while continuing occasional traveling to preach at revivals. He served as Oberlin's president from 1851 to 1866 and helped the college move to the forefront of the abolitionist cause, becoming a significant stop along the Underground Railway. Finney encouraged students to engage in acts of civil disobedience so long as they were necessary to free slaves. While at Oberlin the evangelist wrote his most influential books, including a multivolume *Lectures on Systematic Theology* (1846–47). His *Lectures on Revivals of Religion* was published in 1835. Both books and his other writings challenged traditional Calvinist notions of *original sin*, depravity, *atonement*, salvation, and church renewal. Finney argued, for example, that revivals of religion (including church spiritual renewals) are not sovereign acts of God upon which humans must wait, but acts of God that can be initiated by humans through prayer, disinterested benevolence, and moral reform. He also encouraged careful planning and fiscal responsibility. All in all, Finney made revival sound like a business inspired by the *Holy Spirit*. He certainly denied the traditional Calvinist belief in monergism and encouraged instead belief in a synergistic cooperation between God and human persons in every area of life. His deviations from classical Calvinism and his focus on human activity in spiritual matters brought charges of heresy against Finney, but he managed to ride out the controversy with very little damage to his ministry or reputation.

Perhaps the most serious theological innovations in Finney's theology had to do with what has come to be called moral government theology by his twentieth-century evangelical followers. Finney rejected as irrational the classical magisterial Protestant doctrine of original sin inspired by early church father Augustine. He argued that a just God would not hold persons responsible for another person's (Adam's) sin, and so he rejected inherited guilt. But he also rejected inherited corruption and taught that original sin is nothing other than the bondage to sin incurred by individuals' own sinning, which creates a social network of *evil* influence. He rejected traditional Reformed beliefs about Christ's atonement and taught universal atonement, using the government theory of seventeenth-century Dutch Arminian statesman and theologian Hugo Grotius. In that view, Christ died not as a substitute punishment for humans' sins (which Finney believed would be unjust) but as a demonstration of God's righteousness and *justice* in the face of sin. Finally, and to his critics most seriously, Finney taught that human beings are fully capable and morally responsible to contribute to their own salvation by turning away from sin and entering into a life of disinterested benevolence. He affirmed the possibility of sinlessness by moral decisions alone. Where was God's grace in Finney's revised theology? He believed that grace formed the enabling background of all human moral and spiritual endeavor and the basis for forgiveness when people did sin, but sin is never necessary. Critics charge that Finney fell into the ancient heresy of semi-Pelagianism, if not into the worse one of outright Pelagianism. Even many Wesleyans rejected Finney's apparent lack of emphasis on the absolute necessity of God's *supernatural* grace for every good that humans have and do.

Finney's legacy in later American religious life—including Evangelicalism—cannot be overestimated. It may not be too much to claim that he was the most influential religious figure in nineteenth-century American religious life. The social gospel was inspired by his social reforming preaching and work. He virtually created mass evangelism as an organized industry and was followed in that by D. L. Moody, Billy Sunday, Aimee Semple McPherson, and *Billy Graham*. His lectures on *sanctification* and the *baptism of the Holy Spirit* form the deeper background for the rise of the *Holiness* and *Pentecostal movements* which took inspiration from his perfectionism and emphasis on divine indwelling power to live a life of Christian service. More abstractly, but just as significantly, Finney injected into conservative, evangelical Protestantism in North America an individualistic and moralistic impulse that endures into the twenty-first century. Largely thanks to Finney, the gospel in North America is an optimistic message of human perfectability that involves God but equally involves the human person's free choices and actions. This is so much a part of twentieth- and twenty-first-century Protestant life in North America that few are aware of how far it is from classical Protestantism.

Charles Hambrick-Stowe, "Charles G. Finney," in *Makers of Christian Theology in America*, ed. Mark G. Toulouse and James O. Duke (Nashville: Abingdon Press, 1997); Charles Hambrick-Stowe, *Charles G. Finney and the Spirit of American Evangelicalism* (Grand Rapids: Wm. B. Eerdmans, 1996); Keith J. Hardman, *Charles Grandison Finney: Revivalist and Reformer* (Grand Rapids: Baker Book House, 1990).

Billy   Graham   Hardly   anyone would dispute the claim that Billy Graham was the single most influential person in the post–World War II post-fundamentalist evangelical movement and coalition. Some scholars only half-facetiously identify an evangelical as anyone who loves Billy Graham. The same scholars and others who track the evangelical movement wonder what will become of it once Graham retires or dies. The "Graham glue" seems to be a major force holding it together. Billy Graham has never been a theologian, although he did study *Bible* and *theology* in college and wrote several books on theological subjects. He is best known as a world evangelist, missions trainer and organizer, ecumenist, founder and funder of Christian organizations, energetic motivator of Christians, and informal chaplain to presidents. According to annual polls he has ranked as one of the world's most admired men for decades. Graham and his associates have served as midwives helping to bring the new Evangelicalism into existence out of the older and more sectarian fundamentalist movement. They helped establish a number of Evangelicalism's most influential organizations, including *Christianity Today* and its affiliated publications (now known as Christianity Today Inc.). Wheaton College has on its campus the Billy Graham Center, which houses a museum of American *evangelism* that is virtually a shrine to Graham and his model evangelists throughout American history; Southern Baptist Theological Seminary in Louisville, Kentucky, has a Billy Graham center of evangelism and missions.

Billy Graham (William Franklin Graham) was born in 1918 in North Carolina. His parents were devout Christians and raised him in a fundamentalist Christian environment. He accepted *Jesus Christ* as his Savior at a tent revival held by evangelist Mordechai Ham when he was sixteen. After graduating from high school the young convert enrolled at fundamentalist Bob Jones College and then transferred to Florida Bible Institute. After graduating he attended Wheaton College, from which he received his bachelor's degree in 1943. There he encountered the budding postfundamentalist evangelical movement and made contacts that would serve him well as he supported that movement

throughout the 1940s and 1950s. After pastoring in Illinois for a few years, the young preacher embarked on an evangelistic career with a new youth-oriented evangelical organization known as Youth for Christ. The turning point into his fame came with his "Christ for Greater Los Angeles" evangelism crusade in 1949. Several celebrities were converted there, and William Randolph Hearst, the most powerful medial mogul in California at the time, ordered his people to "puff Graham." In 1950 Graham founded the *Billy Graham Evangelistic Association,* which spawned a number of influential evangelical organizations.

Throughout the 1940s and 1950s Graham and his associates had to wrestle with their fundamentalist heritage and constituency. They offended some of their strongest fundamentalist supporters, such as Bob Jones and John R. Rice, by insisting that their evangelistic meetings be absolutely and unconditionally integrated racially and by allowing nonevangelical Christians (e.g., mainstream Protestants and Roman Catholics) to cooperate with and support them. Graham even allowed mainline, somewhat liberal Protestant clergy to sit on the platform with him during some of his crusades. Much to the chagrin of fundamentalists, the evangelical evangelist insisted on creating a "broad tent" ministry and vision of authentic Evangelicalism and ignored their calls for "biblical separation" from all "compromisers of the gospel." This break between Graham and fundamentalists virtually required the construction of a new, postfundamentalist evangelical coalition, and Graham threw his support behind the one already under construction by men like Harold John Ockenga of Boston.

Graham's legacy to evangelical theology lies in his rejection of rigid, dogmatic, separatistic *fundamentalism* and his personal support for a broader, more inclusive, centrist evangelical vision of Christianity where there is plenty of room for diversity within basic biblical and historic orthodoxy ("generous orthodoxy"). Graham never wavered in his allegiance to the sole ultimate *authority* of the Bible in all matters of *faith* and practice. He has always been a "man of one book." And yet he never rejected the life of the mind, rigorous biblical scholarship, and theological reflection, insofar as they remained faithful to the Bible as God's inspired and infallible Word. He demonstrated a willingness to embrace Christians with whom he could not agree on secondary matters of doctrine and held back from condemning those who were not as certain as he about biblical *inerrancy*, the existence of *supernatural* beings (e.g., *demons* and *angels*), and the "soon *return of Christ.*"

The main difference between Graham and fundamentalists could be found in their attitudes toward secondary doctrinal matters, diversity among Christians, and the scope of authentic Christianity. Graham agreed with the fundamentalists on doctrine. He always preached the *gospel* of *salvation* through Christ's atoning death and *resurrection,* the need for personal *repentance* and faith in Christ, a *premillennial eschatology* and the Bible as God's inerrant Word. But he disagreed with the fundamentalists about the spiritual status of *churches* and ministers who were not as conservative as he. He also expressed somewhat controversial opinions that one would not expect to hear from a true fundamentalist. In an interview with a major variety magazine in 1978 the "pope of American Protestantism" confessed that he did not believe that everyone who did not hear and respond properly to the gospel of Jesus Christ in this life would be damned for all eternity. Graham's great prestige combined with his moderation created a space for evangelical theology to emerge from its fundamentalist shell and revision certain traditional conservative interpretations of Scripture and doctrine.

Billy Graham, *Just As I Am: The Autobiography of Billy Graham* (San Francisco and Grand Rapids: HarperSanFrancisco and Zondervan, 1997); L. A. Drummond, *The Evangelist* (Nashville: Word Publishing, 2001).

Carl F. H. Henry   *Time* magazine published a photo of evangelical theologian Carl F. H. Henry and labeled his thought "theology for the tent meeting." The headline writer was both right and wrong. Henry, often hailed as the dean of evangelical theologians in the second half of the twentieth century, wanted his theology to permeate American *revivalism* and give it a more solid, objective, and intellectual bent. However, his theology is not emotional; it does not appeal to *experience* as a source or norm for Christian belief. Henry built his entire reputation as postfundamentalist Evangelicalism's leading theologian on his clarion call for Christians to go "back to the *Bible*" as God's supernaturally verbally inspired and inerrant propositional *revelation.* Any departure from that, according to Henry, signals a serious decline of authentic Christianity into liberalism or folk religion. To liberals and some moderates Henry sounded like a fundamentalist; to fundamentalists he compromised too much with modern scholarship by recognizing some validity in certain methods of modern biblical criticism. For example, he defended new and updated translations of the Bible against fundamentalists' insistence on the sole validity of the King James Version of Scripture. Supported by the movers and shakers of the new Evangelicalism emerging out of *fundamentalism* in the 1940s and 1950s, Henry, ever the conservative, rejected narrow-minded separatism, anti-intellectualism, and angry divisiveness among evangelicals over secondary matters of *faith.* He criticized the fundamentalists' otherworldliness and neglect of social concern without affirming a social *gospel.* More than any other theologian Henry embodied and promoted the conservative yet nonfundamentalist vision of the new evangelical theology.

Carl Ferdinand Howard Henry was born to German immigrant parents in New York City in 1913. At the age of twenty he committed his life to *Jesus Christ* while working as a reporter on Long Island. Soon after that he enrolled at Wheaton College in Illinois, the flagship college of the Evangelicalism that was soon to emerge from fundamentalism. There he studied under philosopher *Gordon Clark* and became convinced of Clark's general approach to defending and explicating Christianity—an approach known as rational presuppositionalism. This highly philosophical approach to Christianity regards the *authority* of the Bible as the only presupposition that yields a comprehensive and coherent life and worldview. It emphasizes logic as the test of truth, while refusing to regard logic as an authority external to Scripture itself. Instead, logic is viewed as the expression of *God's* own nature, allegedly found in Scripture itself. After graduating from Wheaton with both the B.A. and M.A. degrees, Henry attended Northern Baptist Theological Seminary, where he earned a Th.D. (Doctor of Theology). He was ordained to Baptist ministry and then earned a Ph.D. in theology at Boston University, where he wrote a dissertation on Baptist theologian *Augustus Hopkins Strong* under liberal professors of the Boston Personalist school of theology. In 1948 Henry became one of the founding faculty members of Fuller Theological Seminary. In 1955 *Billy Graham* and Graham's father-in-law, L. Nelson Bell, invited Henry to become the founding editor of the new evangelical publication *Christianity Today*. He served in that capacity with distinction until 1968 and then became a lecturer-at-large for the evangelical world relief organization World Vision. In his retirement Henry continued to write, speak, and teach at a variety of evangelical colleges, universities, and seminaries. He died at his home in Wisconsin on December 7, 2003.

If Billy Graham is the "pope of Evangelicalism" Carl Henry was its head of the Holy Office (the Vatican's agency for protection of doctrine). That is, he oversaw and commented critically on virtually every theological movement within Christianity—including Evangelicalism—during his long career. When evangelicals wanted to know what the evangelical stance on something is or should be, they often turned to Henry. That was especially the case in the 1950s through the 1980s. Henry's published corpus is enormous; one can find within it opinions and pronouncements (some critics would say pontifications) on virtually any subject related to Christianity. His first theological book was *Remaking the Modern Mind* (1946), in which the young theologian—then still working on his doctorate—criticized modern secular thought and recommended a return to Christian foundations for Western society. The book that made him famous among the new evangelicals and infamous to fundamentalists was *The Uneasy Conscience of Modern Fundamentalism* (1947). There he called for a greater social awakening and activism among conservative Protestants. While he was editor of *Christianity Today* Henry published numerous columns and editorials on a wide variety of issues and established his reputation as the spokesman for postfundamentalist Evangelicalism. His magnum opus, the six-volume *God, Revelation, and Authority* (1976–83), includes essays on numerous topics related to Christian biblicism, apologetics, philosophy, theology, and culture. One of Henry's last books is *Toward a Recovery of Christian Belief* (Wheaton, IL: Crossway Books, 1990), which mercifully (for beginners) sums up his entire approach to theology.

According to Carl Henry, Christian thought must begin with two axioms or unprovable presuppositions: the ontological axiom of theism (God is the supreme person and ultimate reality) and the epistemological axiom (that God reveals himself in Scripture). Henry followed his mentor Gordon Clark in arguing vigorously that all life and worldviews begin with such axioms; there cannot be a presuppositionless system of thought about reality. The two Christian axioms are justified because, as it turns out, they provide the basis for a coherent and comprehensive account of reality—including human experience—unrivaled by any other system of thought. For Henry, the Bible delivers a presystematic comprehensive worldview that can be rationally understood and its propositions successfully arranged by the human mind into a coherent system of thought illuminating human experience better than any other philosophy or theology. For Henry, truth must be communicated through rational propositions, or it is meaningless. Divine revelation is primarily propositional, although Henry recognized the reality of nonpropositional revelation. The latter, however, he argued, cannot be given the same weight as propositional revelation in Christianity's cognitive truth content. Henry used this propositionalist and rational presuppositionalist approach to theology to critique nearly all other approaches and demonstrate that they lead to confusion and defection from orthodoxy. Any starting point for theology outside the Bible, Henry never tired of asserting, leads inevitably to chaos. Life's ultimate questions are answered successfully and satisfactorily in the Bible and in a rational system of theology drawn from it and not anywhere else.

Carl Henry's legacy to modern evangelical theology is enormous. Certainly not all evangelical theologians appreciate his contribution, but all must come to terms with it. That legacy is a strong affirmation of conservative Protestant orthodoxy as the only rationally defensible view of reality and of the verbally inspired and inerrant Bible as the only proper foundation for that orthodoxy. When questions began to arise around biblical *inerrancy* among moderate to progressive evangelicals and when Fuller Theological Seminary shed its affirmation of inerrancy in the 1960s, Henry launched a full-scale defense of

his own interpretation of inerrancy that some critics say kills it with the death of a thousand qualifications. Henry's argument was that if God is the ultimate author of Scripture—even through human authors—Scripture's content must be fully trustworthy. To say otherwise would be tantamount to questioning God's veracity. Other evangelicals, however, insisted on a stricter definition of inerrancy than Henry or questioned inerrancy altogether. Henry stood in the middle, insisting that, while one can be an inconsistent evangelical without affirming the Bible's inerrancy, one cannot do *justice* to the Bible as God's Word or to the coherence of Christianity in that denial. On the other hand, he questioned certain maximally conservative definitions and defenses of inerrancy that seemed to impose on Scripture twentieth-century standards of accuracy foreign to ancient culture and writing. Henry tried to moderate a growing quarrel over inerrancy among evangelicals in the 1970s and 1980s, but ended up contributing to division by offending ultraconservatives and progressives alike.

Millard Erickson, "Carl F. H. Henry," in *A New Handbook of Christian Theologians*, ed. Donald W. Musser and Joseph L. Price (Nashville: Abingdon Press, 1996); Carl F. H. Henry, *Confessions of a Theologian* (Waco, TX: Word Publishing Co., 1986); Bob Patterson, *Carl F. H. Henry* (Waco, TX: Word Publishing Co., 1983).

C. S. Lewis   Although he was neither a professional theologian nor a member of the evangelical network, Clives Staples Lewis (1898–1963) became a major influence on evangelical life and thought in the second half of the twentieth century. Most evangelical theologians consider him a popularizer, and yet many of them owe a great debt to Lewis, whose writings inspired and nurtured them spiritually and theologically. Lewis is probably quoted more often by evangelical speakers than any other single person after

Jesus Christ and the writers of *Scripture.* His book *Mere Christianity* (1952)—created out of a series of radio broadcasts delivered over the British Broadcasting Corporation during World War II—routinely tops the list of most admired and most influential Christian books. His series of children's allegories, *The Chronicles of Narnia,* has conveyed to thousands and perhaps millions of children profound Christian themes of *sin* and *redemption.* Lewis also wrote volumes of Christian apologetics that have been widely used as texts and supplementary readings in evangelical colleges, universities, and seminaries. Many evangelical scholars consider his *The Abolition of Man* (1943), *Miracles* (1947), and *The Problem of Pain* (1940) among the finest nontechnical works on Christian philosophy ever written. Wheaton College, arguably the flagship college of Evangelicalism, established the Marion E. Wade Center for C. S. Lewis studies in 1965; numerous other centers, institutes, societies, and journals devoted to the writings of Lewis have cropped up among evangelicals since his death on the same day that John F. Kennedy was assassinated in Dallas, Texas, in 1963 (November 22). Evangelical scholars debate Lewis's authorship of certain obscure texts attributed to him and spend a great deal of time, money, and energy exploring Lewis's legacy for modern and postmodern Christianity. Courses on C. S. Lewis's literature have been taught at many colleges and universities—including some secular ones—and several volumes of Lewis criticism have been published by evangelical scholars. All in all, it is safe to say that although Lewis was not a professional theologian or an evangelical in the usual sense of the word (he was a high-church Anglican with few if any connections to Evangelicalism), he has become an icon and oracle to evangelicals in the second half of the twentieth century and into the twenty-first century.

C. S. Lewis was born in Northern Ireland in 1898. His father was a relatively successful but highly neurotic business-man who sent Lewis and his brother to boarding school in England after their mother died when Lewis was a child. Raised in the Church of England, the young school boarder became an atheist in his teen years and graduated from Oxford University in philosophy and English literature after being injured fighting in World War I. He embarked on a career lecturing in English literature at Oxford and then accepted a chair in medieval and Renaissance English at Cambridge University in 1954. Some Cambridge colleagues opposed his appointment due to his popular Christian writings. Lewis had converted to Christianity in 1929—a process he described in his autobiography as one of being *Surprised by Joy* (1955). His journey back to the Christian *faith* of his youth (orthodox Anglicanism) seemed primarily intellectual, but as he looked back on it, the mature Cambridge don realized that *God* was pulling him irresistibly to himself. Although his *conversion* to Christ was not emotional or dramatic or even sudden, Lewis's testimony about it struck a chord with evangelicals who were already impressed with his writings about Christianity. In the 1950s evangelicals emerging from fundamentalism needed respectability desperately, and being able to claim C. S. Lewis—a well-known Cambridge professor and English literary celebrity—as one of their own was an irresistible temptation. It is doubtful that Lewis himself ever understood his passionate embrace by North American postfundamentalists.

Lewis's philosophy and *theology* were purposely nondenominational. He was not so much interested in defending Anglicanism as he was in promoting what he called "mere Christianity"—basic Christian beliefs and ideals that he saw threatened by modern, secular culture. His approach to defending and promoting the faith was through appeals to human *experience* and especially the moral experience of humanity. That is, rather than utilizing traditional *natural theology* with its so-called proofs for the existence of God, Lewis turned to human persons' awareness of being sinners accountable to Someone beyond nature or society. He attempted to show that only the orthodox Christian vision—highly colored by Platonism—explained human life in the world adequately. Without a transcendent, loving, and holy, personal God of righteousness, Lewis argued, human awareness of absolute value and desire for *forgiveness* and virtue could not be understood. Lewis appealed to the "sense of the divine" as well and led his readers to see that just as there would be no thirst if there were no water, so there would be no desire for God if God did not exist. Lewis knew that his apologetics fell far short of deductive or inductive proof of the truth of Christianity, but he believed that a strong rational case for it could be made, and he presented a sufficiently persuasive case through his books and essays that many skeptics accepted Christ and Christianity seemingly on the basis of reading C. S. Lewis alone. (Of course Lewis would be the first to claim that it was actually God the *Holy Spirit* who was drawing them through the instrumentality of his writings.) Lewis was most definitely not a fundamentalist, however, because he embraced the historic catholicity of the church and rejected a literalistic interpretation of all of Scripture. He also believed that non-Christian religions and myths could be vehicles of *grace*. Nevertheless, he was closer to *fundamentalism* (in the broadest sense of that term) than to liberal theology, because he harshly denounced cultural accommodation of Christianity to secularism, embraced a *supernatural* worldview (including *miracles*, which he defined carefully not as violations of natural law but as irregularities in God's activity in and through nature), and affirmed all the classical dogmas of orthodox Christianity, including the *Trinity*, the deity of Christ, and the saving *atonement* of Jesus Christ through his life, death, and bodily *resurrection*.

Lewis's legacy to evangelical theology is somewhat unusual. Unlike most of the other figures discussed in this section of this handbook, he did not offer any distinctive spin or twist to evangelical thought or engage in any controversy within it. His greatest influence was and remains on lay evangelicals and evangelical students who continue to devour his books a half century after most of them were written. He had a gift for conveying a reasonable explanation of seemingly mysterious Christian beliefs that many lay evangelicals and pastors find refreshing. He also presented an example of an intellectual engaged in the life of a major secular university holding high his Christian identity and vigorously criticizing the excesses of secular culture. This was different from the separatistic and often highly pejorative and obscurantist example of relating to secular culture often presented by fundamentalist combatants against modernity. The calm image of the British university don sitting in an overstuffed chair in his bachelor quarters, reading a book and puffing on a pipe while seemingly contemplating his next book defending orthodox Christianity, inspired many evangelicals to drop the narrowness and sectarianism of their fundamentalist past and enter into the cultural environment with confidence that Christianity can be defended without a fortress mentality, because it is simply true.

David Barratt, *C. S. Lewis and His World* (London: Marshall Pickering, 1987); Scott Burson and Jerry Walls, *C. S. Lewis and Francis Schaeffer* (Downers Grove, IL: InterVarsity Press, 1998); Michael Christenson, *C. S. Lewis on Scripture* (Nashville: Abingdon Press, 2002); Chad Walsh, *The Literary Legacy of C. S. Lewis* (Eugene, OR: Harvest Books, 1979).

J. Gresham Machen   "Highbrow *fundamentalism*" is one description of the theological contribution of J. Gresham Machen (1881–1937). In a time when fundamentalism was devolving into a militant, divisive, and separatistic movement, characterized all too often by anti-intellectualism and obscurantism, Presbyterian scholar and theology professor J. Gresham Machen stood out from the ultraconservative Protestant pack as a highly educated, cultured, scholarly defender of ultraorthodox Evangelicalism. His book *Christianity and Liberalism* (1923) may have been a jeremiad about the sad state of Protestant *theology*, but nobody accused it of being a shoddy or cheap criticism of the new liberal theology that was sweeping over the mainline Protestant seminaries. Leading secular commentator Walter Lippmann even endorsed the book and considered its main argument—that liberal Protestantism is a different religion from Christianity—largely convincing.

All too briefly the author of that influential critique of liberal theology and endorsement of Protestant orthodoxy stood out from the fundamentalist crowd of angry reactionaries and separatists, led by preachers such as William Bell Riley and J. Frank Norris and politicians such as William Jennings Bryan, as a beacon of light pointing toward a reasonable conservatism in theology. When postfundamentalist Evangelicalism began to emerge from fundamentalism in the 1940s and 1950s, some of its movers and shakers looked back to Machen as their model for moderate, intellectual conservatism. And yet, Machen was a fundamentalist, even if he did not fit the fundamentalist stereotype promoted by critics such as H. L. Mencken (who admired Machen even as he scathingly ridiculed fundamentalism's leaders). Like other fundamentalists, Machen practiced and promoted separatism from mainline Protestantism and established what even some evangelicals considered extremely conservative rival organizations to the ones he left.

Machen was born into an affluent, cultured Presbyterian home in Baltimore, Maryland. He graduated from Johns Hopkins University in 1901 and then studied at Princeton University and Princeton Theological Seminary, where he came under the influence of the great conservative Reformed theologian *Benjamin Breckenridge Warfield*—one of the last represenatives of the "Old *Princeton School*" of Reformed Protestant scholasticism. Machen studied New Testament and theology in Germany under leading liberal thinker Wilhelm Herrmann during the year 1905–06 and returned to teach at Princeton Theological Seminary, where he became a strong defender of Warfield's Old School *Calvinism*. He was ordained to the Presbyterian ministry in 1914 and became Professor of New Testament in 1915. His two major volumes of New Testament studies were *The Origin of Paul's Religion* (1921) and *The Virgin Birth of Christ* (1930). In these and other books he defended traditional Christian viewpoints and doctrines against the higher critical methods and conclusions of German and North American liberal Protestant thinkers.

Machen might have remained a fairly obscure conservative seminary professor, except that during the 1920s he took a strong stand against what he perceived to be encroaching debilitating liberal thought within his denomination and seminary. In *Christianity and Liberalism*, his manifesto, he declared that liberal Protestant theology and biblical scholarship had simply abandoned Christianity through radical revisions of classical Christian doctrines, such as the deity of Christ, Jesus' *virgin birth* and *resurrection*, and the *atonement*. In 1929 he resigned his position at Princeton and helped found the rival Westminster Theological Seminary in Philadelphia. In 1933 he helped found a rival Presbyterian mission board and in 1936 was suspended from ministry by his denomination. The same year he helped found a new Presbyterian denomination that eventually took the name the Orthodox Presbyterian Church. He died in Bismarck, North Dakota, on January 1, 1937, while drumming up support for the new denomination.

Machen's legacy to evangelical theology is complex. He certainly did not intend to contribute anything new to Christianity. Like Warfield, Machen valued tradition and regarded the Calvinism of the Old Princeton school as authentic Christianity not to be altered or adjusted. His legacy lies not in any new ideas but in his modeling of traditional, conservative, confessional Protestantism rigorously defended in a sophisticated manner without the antics or additions (e.g., *premillennialism* as a "fundamental of the faith") of the angry fundamentalists. In fact, some of his own disciples considered Machen too aloof from fundamentalist crusades against communism, alcohol, and tobacco, "godless *evolution*," and the ecumenical movement, and they broke away from his Westminster Theological Seminary and Orthodox Presbyterian Church to found hyperconservative rival institutions. And yet, when the new Evangelicalism began to emerge out of fundamentalism in response to that kind of hyperconservativism, Machen's own faithful heirs and disciples were not particularly helpful or enthusiastic. They have always felt that they represented true Evangelicalism and that the new Evangelicalism that looked to *Billy Graham* as its leader was too inclusive, was doctrinally weak, and put emotion and *experience* (e.g., "decisionism") over sound theology of the *gospel* and profound discipleship. Machen's legacy within evangelical theology is carried on by various groups of conservative Reformed evangelical thinkers and writers who eschew *revivalism* in favor of classical Reformed sacramentalism and confessionalism (e.g., the Nicene Creed and the Westminster Confession of Faith).

D. G. Hart, *Defending the Faith: J. Gresham Machen and the Crisis of Conservative Protestantism in Modern America* (Grand Rapids: Baker Books, 1994); Bradley J. Longfield, "J. Gresham Machen," in *Makers of Christian Theology in America*, ed. Mark G. Toulouse and James O. Duke (Nashville: Abingdon Press, 1997).

Thomas Oden   Relatively few liberal, mainline Protestant theologians with established reputations leave all of that behind publicly to join Evangelicalism. One notable example, however, is Thomas Oden (b. 1931), a liberal Methodist theologian who taught *theology* and *ethics* at Methodist-related Drew University Divinity School for many years. (He retired in the mid-1990s.) Oden's very public defection from the ranks of the liberals and just as public identification with evangelical theology (he joined the *Evangelical Theological Society*) was a momentous occasion and source of pride for many evangelicals. However, Oden never has fully fit the typical evangelical mold. His background is not in the evangelical movement and his postliberal, evangelical theological concerns and contributions aim at overcoming sectarianism as well as liberalism with a strong dose of patristic teaching.

Unlike many evangelicals and the evangelical movement as a whole, Oden regards the consensual teaching tradition of the undivided early church (roughly the first seven centuries) authoritative for Christian belief and witness in all ages and places. In other words, Oden considers himself catholic but not Roman Catholic. For him, authentic evangelical *faith* would be identical with the historic faith of the early *church* up until the division between East and West that occurred gradually in the centuries just before the official split of AD 1054. His call for Christians to return to early Christian sources outside the *Bible* is heard and heeded by many of his evangelical students and disciples.

Many evangelicals earned their Ph.D.'s under Oden at Drew in the 1980s and 1990s. Some have gone on to promote his agenda by writing for a project, inspired by Oden and published by

InterVarsity Press, known as the *Ancient Christian Commentary on Scripture* series —a twenty-eight-volume set of commentaries on books of the Bible focusing on the interpretations of early church fathers from Clement of Rome (late first century to early second century) to John of Damascus (seventh and eighth centuries). Oden is the general editor of the series, which reflects his passion for a renewal of early Christian teaching within Christianity. It is his antidote to what he regards as the poison of Enlightenment ideology within mainstream Christianity that manifests itself as liberalism and therapeutic emotionalism.

Oden was educated at the University of Oklahoma, Perkins School of Theology at Southern Methodist University, and Yale University, where he received his Ph.D. He is an ordained Methodist elder who spent most of his career teaching theology at Drew University Divinity School. His writings of the 1960s and early 1970s reveal a distinctly liberal persuasion. He describes himself as a "movement theologian" in those days, by which he means that he tended to follow fads and trends in theology. For a while he was fascinated by existentialism and wrote about German existentialist New Testament scholar and theologian Rudolf Bultmann under the spell of German existentialist philosopher Martin Heidegger. Then he turned toward therapeutic theology and wrote books on pastoral care, influenced by Carl Rogers and Sigmund Freud, that focused on transactional analysis and personal self-actualization.

In the mid-1970s the Methodist theologian became disillusioned with faddish theology, which he came to regard as shallow, and took a radical hermeneutical turn toward orthodox Christianity and a recovery of ancient Christian roots. In 1979 Oden published the book that signaled the hermeneutical turn toward orthodoxy: *Agenda for Theology: Recovering Christian Roots*. In that and its later revision, *After Modernity . . . What? Agenda for Theology* (1992), he criticized

modern and contemporary theology as guilty of moral relativism and reductive naturalism (among other things) and called for a turn in theology back to its ancient sources in the church fathers and creeds of the early church. Many of his colleagues and former students were shocked by the radical nature of Oden's reorientation and the harshness of his critique of his own and their liberal and liberationist theological mind-sets. But he gained an entirely new following among evangelicals disillusioned with both liberal accommodation to modernity and fundamentalist-evangelical *revivalism* and sectarianism that seemed shallow in its forgetfulness of the Christian heritage.

In 1987, 1992, and 1994 Oden published his magnum opus—a three-volume systematic theology promoting what he calls "paleo-orthodoxy." The three titles are *The Living God*, *The Word of Life*, and *Life in the Spirit* (San Francisco: Harper & Row). Throughout the volumes the author quotes early church fathers extensively, with a few references to the Protestant Reformers and almost no positive uses of modern theologians. The project attempts to uncover and reveal to modern readers the consensual teaching tradition of original Christianity as expressed by the Eastern and Western church fathers and councils up through the seventh century. It is clear that Oden believes that all truly important theological questions were answered by them then.

Oden's legacy to evangelical theology is difficult to predict, as his contribution is relatively recent and continuing and because he is something of an outsider to Evangelicalism. Although he joined the ETS and has served as a senior editor of *Christianity Today*, he is still identified more with conservative mainline Protestantism than subcultural Evangelicalism. He has never taught theology within a historically evangelical institution (except as a visitor), and he lacks the fundamentalist or revivalist roots that mark most evangelicals and give them their distinctive flavors. Nevertheless, he has entered and been welcomed within evangelical circles and has developed something of an evangelical following. His legacy will no doubt be through those evangelical disciples he likes to call "young fogeys" because they are not attracted to the new theological trends but rather gravitate to the ancient roots of Christianity ("paleo-orthodoxy"). If Oden has his way, they will reconnect Evangelicalism (and hopefully even mainstream Protestantism) with its catholic and orthodox roots in the church fathers and councils of the undivided church and regard with suspicion everything new in Christianity. Less clear is whether and how they will remain distinctively evangelical, which involves not rejection of ancient teachings of the church, but addition of a lively sense of special biblical *authority*, priesthood of believers, and conversional piety generally lacking in the postapostolic, pre-Reformation churches.

"An Interview with Thomas Oden," in *Modern Reformation* 4, no. 5 (September/October 1995); Thomas C. Oden, *Requiem: A Lament in Three Movements* (Nashville: Abingdon Press, 1995); Jeffrey C. Pugh, "Thomas C. Oden," in *A New Handbook of Christian Theologians*, ed. Donald W. Musser and Joseph L. Price (Nashville: Abingdon Press, 1996).

Clark Pinnock A few postfundamentalist evangelical theologians have dared to sail into uncharted waters and risk being ostracized by more conservative evangelical thinkers. One such courageous evangelical theologian is Clark Pinnock, who has reaped a whirlwind of criticism and condemnation from fellow evangelicals for daring to call for reform and revision in evangelical thinking about *God, Scripture*, and *salvation*. To some evangelicals he is a moving target who keeps changing his mind about important doctrines; to others he is a pioneer blazing new trails out

of the fundamentalist forest toward new horizons of evangelical thought. One leading evangelical theological popularizer has labeled Pinnock a heretic and condemned him as not even a Christian. On the other hand, an influential evangelical university professor and journal editor has written a laudatory book about Pinnock's theological "journey toward renewal" that hails him as a model of enlightened Evangelicalism. Few in the evangelical theological community seem indifferent to Pinnock; he tends to stir up strong reactions both positive and negative.

Pinnock was born in Toronto, Canada, in 1937. Although he was raised in a relatively liberal, mainline Protestant church and home, he came under the influences of a particularly godly grandmother and Sunday school teacher who led him into a deeper Christian *faith*. While in high school he became involved with a fundamentalist student group that both nurtured him in Christian spirituality and convinced him to align himself with an ultraorthodox style of Evangelicalism. Looking back on his teen years, the mature Pinnock described himself as a "teenage fundamentalist." After graduating from university in 1956, he pursued graduate studies at Manchester University in England with evangelical New Testament scholar F. F. Bruce. He remained there working as Bruce's teaching associate after he earned his Ph.D. in 1963. During this period he spent time at *Francis Schaeffer's* L'Abri Fellowship in Switzerland and came under Schaeffer's strong Calvinistic influence. He began to defend biblical *inerrancy* and unconditional *election* and identified himself with a very conservative strain in Baptist evangelical life. This brought him to the attention of resurgent conservative forces in the Southern Baptist Convention in the United States. In 1965 he was invited to join the faculty of New Orleans Baptist Theological Seminary, where he was to be in the vanguard of a budding conservative takeover of the

Southern Baptist seminaries. Later, and in the midst of significant changes in his own theological views, Pinnock taught at Trinity Evangelical Divinity School in Deerfield, Illinois, and at Regent College in Vancouver, Canada. In 1977 he became professor of systematic *theology* at Baptist-related McMaster Divinity College in Hamilton, Ontario, Canada, where he remained until his retirement in 2002.

Among Pinnock's notable early publications were *A Defense of Biblical Infallibility* (1967) and *Set Forth Your Case* (1967)—both very conservative monographs defending what he believed to be classical Christian doctrines. Other apologetic defenses followed those. During the 1970s Pinnock began to soften the edges of his ultraorthodoxy under the influence of a *charismatic experience* and a reconsideration of *Calvinism*. In 1974 he edited and published a collection of essays on Arminian theology entitled *Grace Unlimited* (Minneapolis: Bethany House). There he explained his disillusionment with Augustinian-Calvinist theology and especially the doctrine of God's absolute sovereignty, including unconditional election, limited *atonement*, and irresistible *grace*. Much later, in 1989, he edited a companion volume entitled *The Grace of God, the Will of Man: A Case for Arminianism* (Minneapolis: Bethany House), which carried further his critique of the monergistic interpretation of divine sovereignty. Pinnock's very public change of mind and heart from Old Princeton–style Calvinist orthodoxy to evangelical, Pietist *Arminianism* caused some of his friends to abandon him. Some of them became his harshest critics.

The year 1984 saw the publication of Pinnock's programmatic book on the Bible entitled *The Scripture Principle* (San Francisco: Harper & Row). There he criticized the *Princeton theology*–inspired view of Scripture as verbally inspired and technically *inerrant* and argued in favor of a more dynamic model of the divine and human authorship of the

Bible. In 1986 he published an essay entitled "God Limits His Knowledge," in an edited volume entitled *Predestination and Free Will* (Downers Grove, IL: InterVarsity Press). There he announced and explained his new "*open theism*" view of God's foreknowledge, in which God chooses to leave the future partly open so that even he cannot know it with absolute certainty. Pinnock saw this as both biblical and the logical consequence of Arminianism, which values *free will*. In *Tracking the Maze: Finding Our Way through Modern Theology from an Evangelical Perspective* (San Francisco: Harper & Row, 1990) the Canadian theologian expressed appreciation for some of the achievements of nonevangelical theologians and made positive use of the relatively new school of narrative theology. His movement away from strictly propositional views of divine *revelation* was becoming clearer. In 1992 he published *A Wideness in God's Mercy: The Finality of Jesus Christ in a World of Religions* (Grand Rapids: Zondervan). His trajectory away from an exclusivist or restrictivist view of salvation was becoming evident.

In 1994, together with four other open theists, he wrote *The Openness of God: A Biblical Challenge to the Traditional Understanding of God* (Downers Grove, IL: InterVarsity Press). His tendency away from *classical Christian theism* was being revealed. In 1997 Pinnock wrote *The Flame of Love: A Theology of the Holy Spirit* (Downers Grove, IL: InterVarsity Press), which drew on Eastern Orthodox and *charismatic* theologies and spiritualities to recover for evangelicals a strong doctrine of the *Holy Spirit*.

Finally, in 2001 he published his manifesto of open theism entitled *Most Moved Mover: A Theology of God's Openness* (Grand Rapids: Baker). All doubts about his revisionist tendencies were being removed. And yet, in and through all of these treatises calling for and mapping out reform in traditional evangelical ways of thinking about doctrinal issues, Pinnock remained firm in his commitment to basic Christian orthodoxy—the *Trinity*, the deity of *Jesus Christ*, the *inspiration* of Scripture, salvation by grace through faith, the bodily *resurrection*, and the visible *return of Christ*. Few evangelical thinkers have ever gone as far toward revising and reforming secondary doctrines while holding fast to and defending primary ones.

Needless to say, Pinnock's theological journey has brought upon him a whirlwind of controversy. Some of the fallout from it has touched the lives of his friends and sympathizers. In some conservative evangelical theological circles, expression of support for him can be the proverbial "kiss of death." Evangelical scholars—especially systematic theologians—have divided over him more than any other individual; this is one of his contributions to evangelical theology. He has forced it to examine itself and ask about its own adequacies to Scripture, tradition, *reason*, and *experience*. His intention has never been to create controversy or strife, but only to raise for reflection and new consideration questions about traditional doctrinal formulations. He has made clear in his essays responding to critics that he views theology as a pilgrimage rather than as defense of a fortress. He sees himself as a pioneer on a theological quest and has great difficulty understanding the degree of hostility expressed toward him by some of his critics—almost all of whom are former friends and associates.

Pinnock has almost single-handedly challenged the hegemony over evangelical theology of a highly rationalistic, propositional, Calvinistic form of systematic theology. He has forced the evangelical theological community's door open to Arminians and postconservatives like himself. Because of his thoroughly biblically faithful defenses of revised doctrines, it is impossible to exclude as nonevangelical everyone who doesn't toe the line according to "the received evangelical tradition." What Pinnock has accomplished is a demonstration of how

evangelical theology might shed the last vestiges of its fundamentalist heritage while remaining orthodox.

Two of Pinnock's revisions stand out as especially noteworthy in terms of his possible legacy to evangelical thought: his *inclusivism* with regard to non-Christians and his *open theism* with regard to God's foreknowledge. In *A Wideness in God's Mercy* the reformist evangelical theologian challenged the traditional conservative belief about the unevangelized. Basing his argument on God's character as well as on scriptural examples of persons who belonged to God's people without explicit expression of faith in the God of Israel or Jesus Christ, Pinnock argued for recognition of a hope for the scope of salvation beyond explicit Christians to those who have implicit faith in the Savior (Jesus Christ) whose name they do not know. The traditional view limits salvation to those who express explicit faith in Jesus Christ by name. To Pinnock, that view questions God's goodness and mercy. Why would a God of love limit his grace to the evangelized? And where does Scripture teach that? Pinnock rejects such restrictivism or exclusivism of salvation in favor of an inclusivist view that is very similar to Catholic theologian Karl Rahner's category of "anonymous Christians." They are persons who live lives of faith and love apart from knowledge of the Christian *gospel* of Jesus Christ. Both Rahner and Pinnock believe in a universal grace of God that can be resisted but that saves if not resisted. Like Rahner, Pinnock believes that even persons of non-Christian religions can be saved by the "light that they have." That is, by following the clues to God embedded in their own consciences, cultures, and religions, people have an opportunity to arrive at salvation, even if no Christian missionary reaches them with the gospel message of the crucified and risen Savior.

Pinnock's most controversial revision of traditional evangelical doctrine is his open theism (also known as the openness of God). In this view, God out of love freely condescended to give human beings the gift of free will. God wanted free partners to love him freely, not programmed beings who could not do otherwise. Genuine free will, according to Pinnock, is ability to do otherwise (libertarian freedom). Genuine love is always free and never compelled or predetermined. If human persons have such freedom, claims open theism, even God cannot know what they will decide to do with that freedom. Did God know with absolute certainty what Adam and Eve (humanity) would do when faced with the decision to obey God or seek to know good and *evil* for themselves? Not if they had genuine freedom in the matter. For free decisions and acts cannot be foreknown; the moment they are known, they are determined. The agent whose act is foreknown with absolute certainty is no longer a free agent with regard to that act, because he or she cannot do otherwise. For Pinnock this limitation of God's foreknowledge is voluntary. It is self-limitation out of love. Pinnock's critics have charged him with capitulating to process theology, a form of liberal philosophical theology in which God is dependent upon the world, but Pinnock strongly disagrees and criticizes both process theology and classical theism that asserts God's absolute immutability and impassibility.

Pinnock's legacy to evangelical theology is yet to be decided. As of 2003 it is a legacy of controversy. But so was Martin Luther's, and so was virtually every other reformer's. At the very least, he has launched a new evangelical theological movement that this writer has labeled "postconservative Evangelicalism." For Pinnock and other postconservatives, evangelical theology and spirituality are not primarily conservative but radical. That is, they challenge the status quo in the light of the divine Word of revelation in Jesus Christ as the supreme message of God's nature and character, and they seek to be reformed and always reforming. Postconservative

theology as exemplified by Pinnock lives by the belief that God always has more light to break forth from his Word; no human tradition is sacrosanct. For Pinnock and postconservatives, it is not enough to be postfundamentalist; authentic evangelical faith must shed its last vestiges of fundamentalism in maximal conservatism and defensiveness of human traditions (e.g., Old School Princeton Calvinism) and examine everything afresh in the light of new understandings of God's Word.

Barry L. Callen, *Clark H. Pinnock: Journey toward Renewal* (Nappanee, IN: Evangel Publishing House, 2000); Robert V. Rakestraw, "Clark H. Pinnock: A Theological Odyssey," *Christian Scholar's Review* 19 (March 1990): 3.

Bernard Ramm Every theological movement has its lesser-known but more influential thinkers. Albrecht Ritschl is not as well known or widely hailed as Friedrich Schleiermacher, and yet he was probably more influential in the formation of classical liberal Protestant *theology*. Emil Brunner worked under the shadow of his better-known Swiss counterpart in the neo-orthodox movement, Karl Barth, and yet in some ways he was more influential, especially in the English-speaking world. Hans Frei is not as well known as George Lindbeck and yet was the real power behind what has come to be called postliberal theology. Bernard Ramm has not gained as much attention as *Carl F. H. Henry* or *Francis Schaeffer*, but for many evangelical scholars he was the most creative and influential evangelical theologian of the second half of the twentieth century. Ramm was far from being liberal, but he was much more inclined to come to terms with the best of modernity than were Henry, Schaeffer, and most other postfundamentalist conservative evangelical thinkers. Ramm sought to build bridges between conservative Protestant thought and the larger culture's philosophies, scientific methods and discoveries, and humanities. Although he did not eschew *reason* or rationality, he was suspicious of approaches to Christian apologetics and theology that appealed to standards of verification outside of the Christian "pattern of *authority*," which for him centered around the dialectic of Word and Spirit. All in all, Ramm represents the beginnings of a move beyond postfundamentalism to postconservatism in evangelical theology. He was more interested in being faithful to the *gospel* and relevant to the culture than in parroting or defending traditional formulations of doctrine.

Bernard Ramm (1916–92) was born in Montana and gained a strong interest in science while in high school. At the University of Pennsylvania, where he pursued studies in physics and other sciences, he experienced a life-changing *conversion* to *Jesus Christ* and became an evangelical Christian. He felt called to the ministry and enrolled at the Eastern Baptist Theological Seminary in Philadelphia. After seminary he earned his Ph.D. in religion and philosophy at the University of Southern California. All through his theological studies he maintained a lively interest in the natural sciences and was convinced that conservative Christianity needed to be updated in their light. He developed a strong interest in apologetics and wrote some of his earliest papers and monographs on defenses of the *faith* in the modern world, so often hostile to classical religion. Ramm's career as a theologian took him to many evangelical colleges, universities, and seminaries. Most of them were Baptist institutions, as he was an ordained Baptist minister. He began his teaching career at the fundamentalist Bible Institute of Los Angeles (which later became the conservative evangelical Biola University) and finished it at the American Baptist Seminary of the West. In between he taught at California Baptist Theological Seminary, Bethel College and Seminary, Baylor University, and Eastern Baptist Theolog-

ical Seminary. He was a frequent speaker at student conferences sponsored by parachurch youth organizations and was noted as a passionate and articulate defender of biblical Christianity who was not afraid of any honest question.

Ramm wrote numerous books, beginning with *Protestant Biblical Interpretation* (1950) and ending with *Offense to Reason: A Theology of Sin* (1985). (His 1987 *God's Way Out* was a revision of the earlier *His Way Out*, published in 1974.) In between, he wrote such influential evangelical tomes as *Protestant Christian Evidences* (1953), *The Christian View of Science and Scripture* (1954), *The Pattern of Authority* (1957), *Special Revelation and the Word of God* (1961), *The God Who Makes A Difference: A Christian Appeal to Reason* (1972), *The Evangelical Heritage* (1973), *After Fundamentalism: The Future of Evangelical Theology* (1983), and *An Evangelical Christology: Ecumenic and Historic* (1985). Some of Ramm's volumes were widely used as textbooks in courses at evangelical Christian colleges and universities for many years; others were widely read, reviewed, and discussed. During the 1960s and 1970s especially he and Carl F. H. Henry were widely regarded as the two leading theological spokesmen for the evangelical movement.

Ramm's theological method evolved over the decades of his career. In its earliest stage it was similar to the approach of Fuller Theological Seminary's *E. J. Carnell*, in that it emphasized rational interpretations of historical and natural evidences and human *experience*. Ramm believed and argued that traditional Protestant Christianity could be rationally demonstrated to be the truest account of reality. Later, his theological methodology and approach to apologetics turned more toward the classical faith-seeking-understanding model, in that it left behind proofs and sought to focus more on a "synoptic vision" of reality illuminated by the Word of God and the *Holy Spirit*. The role of the inner testimony of the Holy Spirit grew in Ramm's theology and apologetics over the years as his confidence in the powers of reason to answer life's ultimate questions waned.

Ramm became more and more convinced that evangelical Christianity had fallen into obscurantism in resisting modernity and especially the discoveries of the sciences. In *A Christian View of Science and Scripture* (Grand Rapids: Wm. B. Eerdmans Publishing Co., 1954) he sought to integrate biblical **revelation** with modern science while debunking both naturalism and literalistic **creationism**. He developed an alternative to naturalistic evolution and young-earth creationism, called "progressive creationism," that kept God intimately involved in the beginnings and processes of life while allowing science to determine the age of the earth and mechanisms by which species evolved. Some critics saw this as capitulation to theistic evolution (which fundamentalists consider heresy), and others regarded it as incomplete acceptance of science. But Ramm's main concern was to resist evangelical obscurantism and maximal conservatism and emphasize what is really most important in Christian belief—not the "how" but the "who" of creation. He was also interested in opening the door for evangelicals to pursue studies in the natural sciences without shame or ostracism. To that end he argued that evangelicals must adjust their interpretations of the natural world to the "bare facts" of science (not every passing theory) and give up their fundamentalist habits of mind that cause them to resist science as the **devil's** territory.

Ramm's theological pilgrimage led him to appreciate the contributions of neo-orthodoxy, especially Karl Barth's theology, to evangelical thought. Once again, this was highly controversial. Evangelical theologians such as **Gordon Clark**, Cornelius Van Til, and Carl F. H. Henry had harshly criticized and sometimes condemned Barth's theology as a new form of modernism (liberal theology), because it allegedly did not affirm the full authority of the **Bible** as God's inspired and infallible Word. Ramm studied Barth carefully and decided that he had been misunderstood by his evangelical critics. He even went so far as to study with Barth in Switzerland in the late 1950s. In *Special Revelation and the Word of God* (Grand Rapids: Wm. B. Eerdmans Publishing Co., 1961) he attempted to set forth an evangelical view of revelation and Scripture that bridged the gap between Protestant orthodoxy and neo-orthodoxy. He strongly defended both the propositional and personal natures of divine revelation against those who would reduce it to one and neglect or reject the other. Later, in *After Fundamentalism* (San Francisco: Harper & Row, 1983), he embraced Barth's theology almost wholeheartedly, while still affirming (whether Barth did or not) the propositional aspect of some of divine revelation. However, Ramm agreed with Barth that the Word of God is found primarily in event—the event of Jesus Christ—and that Scripture is a witness to divine revelation, rather than identical with it.

Most importantly, Ramm recommended Barth's theology to evangelicals as possibly the only way out of the fundamentalist-modernist conflict. According to Ramm's interpretation of Barth, his is the only approach that takes equally seriously the Enlightenment and classical Christian orthodoxy, with its emphasis on the transcendence of God and God's Word. For Ramm this meant that evangelicals must abandon the last vestiges of unwarranted literalism arising out of suspicion and even hostility toward the Enlightenment and the modern mind and see with Barth that the gospel of Jesus Christ and the triumph of God's **grace** is the true center of evangelical faith and proclamation and not warfare against modernity.

Bernard Ramm's legacy to postfundamentalist evangelical theology is difficult to exaggerate. Numerous evangelical thinkers cut their teeth on Ramm's teaching and books and soaked in his spirit of moderation without mediocrity. He was a great mediating theologian—always seeking the truth in both sides of a disputed issue and building bridges wherever possible between Christians. His project was to strip away the last remaining vestiges of fundamentalism from evangelical theology while retaining its basically conservative character. This he did by returning to Protestant sources prior to fundamentalism and especially to the Protestant Reformers themselves. He also used neo-orthodoxy cautiously and critically in this endeavor. His enemies were religious obscurantism ("don't confuse me with the facts; my find is already made up") and anti-intellectualism more than liberalism and modernism. His basic conservatism shows up clearly in his last two books, on *Christology* and *original sin*. There he affirmed and defended classical formulations in the light of contemporary discoveries (e.g., in psychology and anthropology) without a hint of fundamentalist defensiveness or narrowness. (For example, he allowed for different models of orthodox, Chalcedonian Christology and of original sin.)

Gary Dorrien, *The Remaking of Evangelical Theology* (Louisville, KY: Westminster John Knox Press, 1998); *Perspectives in Religious Studies* 17:4 (winter 1990) (entire issue devoted to essays about Bernard Ramm).

Francis Schaeffer Evangelicalism's premier periodical *Christianity Today* published an issue picturing Francis Schaeffer on the cover with the headline *"Our* Saint Francis." Soon after he died, the same magazine published a cartoon showing the inimitable Schaeffer in lederhosen with his distinctive goatee arriving at the gates of heaven. Saint Peter examined a large ledger and declared "Francis Schaeffer . . . Oh, yes. Saint Thomas Aquinas would like to have a word with you." Devotees and critics of Schaeffer will readily recognize the reference. He had blamed the medieval "angelic Doctor" of Catholic

theology for most of the ills of modern skepticism and unbelief. Francis Schaeffer is not generally considered a true theologian, and yet he made a profound impact on evangelical life and thought through his teaching ministry called L'Abri Fellowship (headquartered just outside Lausanne, Switzerland) and books, which put evangelical publisher InterVarsity Press on the map and persuaded many young Christians being swept up in the early 1970s Jesus Movement to add a more intellectual and theologically serious dimension to their experiential *faith*.

Francis Schaeffer (1912–84) was born in Philadelphia and raised in a nominally Christian home. His parents were Lutherans, but the young Schaeffer was not raised in an evangelical environment. He converted to fundamentalist Christianity at age eighteen and entered Westminster Theological Seminary after graduating from Hampden-Sydney College. When Schaeffer enrolled at Westminster in 1935, it was a relatively new seminary founded by fundamentalist theologian *J. Gresham Machen* and his colleagues who were disillusioned with what they regarded as the drift of Princeton Theological Seminary toward liberal theology. At Westminster, Schaeffer came under the influence of ultra-conservative Reformed theologian Cornelius Van Til, who promoted a distinctive style of Christian philosophy and apologetics called biblical presuppositionalism. This view attempted to demonstrate the superiority of the Christian presupposition of the *authority* of the *Bible* as God's inerrant Word and the system of belief derived from it (Protestant Orthodoxy) over all other philosophies, *theologies*, and worldviews. When fundamentalist faculty member Carl McIntire left Westminster to found rival Faith Theological Seminary and the Bible Presbyterian Church to rival Machen's Orthodox Presbyterian Church, Francis Schaeffer went with him. He was the first person ordained to the ministry by the new fundamentalist denomination, which sent him and his wife Edith to Europe as missionaries. They settled in Switzerland, where Schaeffer began to dress in lederhosen like many of the older Swiss nationals.

In 1955 they resigned from their mission board and created their own missionary organization, which they called L'Abri, French for "shelter." Using an old Swiss chalet in a mountain village above Lake Geneva, they invited people with inquiring minds to come and stay with them and engage in reading and conversations about Christianity and culture. L'Abri grew into an international phenomenon as hundreds and then thousands of young people—many of them "hippies"—descended on the center and stayed for weeks at a time. It became an informal think tank for people who wanted to lecture, lead discussions, or simply engage in dialogue about a variety of subjects related to being Christian in the modern world.

Schaeffer's greatest influence was through his writings, which began out of his experiences encountering disaffected, countercultural young people from all over the world at L'Abri in the 1960s. His first book, published in 1968 under the title *The God Who Is There*, was quickly followed in the same year by *Escape from Reason* and then by *He Is There and He Is Not Silent* in 1972. In the 1970s he published more books criticizing secular culture and accommodated Christianity, including *Back to Freedom and Dignity* (1972), *How Should We Then Live? The Rise and Decline of Western Thought and Culture* (1976), and *True Spirituality* (1979). (Most of the books for which Schaeffer is best known were published by InterVarsity Press of Downers Grove, IL.)

His last book, published in 1984, the year he died while undergoing cancer treatment at Mayo Clinic in Rochester, Minnesota, was a jeremiad against Evangelicalism and evangelical theology, entitled *The Great Evangelical Disaster* (Wheaton, IL: Good News Publishers, 1984). While he still considered himself an evangelical, Schaeffer had come to believe that mainstream evangelical life and thought had seriously accommodated to the spirit of the age—a spirit that denied "true Truth." By "true Truth" Schaeffer meant objective truth that is not merely relative and that is essential to human dignity. He believed that Evangelicalism in the 1980s was succumbing to the modern and postmodern denial of objective truth in favor of market-driven *worship*, subjective spirituality, and therapeutic preaching and theology. He especially regarded the growing denial of strict biblical inerrancy as proof of Evangelicalism's "great disaster" and decried some evangelical leaders' reluctance to take a strong stand against abortion and euthanasia. In the end, Schaeffer's original *fundamentalism* reappeared after two decades of relatively irenic engagements in dialogue with people of various viewpoints. Many evangelicals who had been stimulated by his ministry at L'Abri and through his writings of the 1960s and 1970s were dismayed by his final words of outrage, which bordered on a total rejection of evangelical openness and seemed to amount to a new fundamentalist manifesto.

Francis Schaeffer's legacy to evangelical thought lies primarily in his Christian critiques of modern secular and increasingly pagan culture. He attempted to demonstrate through his writings that modern (some would now say postmodern) culture had fallen below a "line of despair," beginning with existentialism in the nineteenth century. For this he blamed, among others, the early nineteenth-century theological and philosophical antagonists G. W. F. Hegel and Søren Kierkegaard. Furthermore, Schaeffer speculated that all of the ills of modern culture with its alienation and despair could be traced back to Thomas Aquinas's bifurcation of knowledge into the natural and *supernatural* (gracious) spheres, which allegedly created a sphere of knowledge about *God*, the soul, and the world autonomous from God's special *revelation*. But more pertinent to Schaeffer's critique of modern culture were his attacks on existentialism and Enlightenment rationalism which both, in different ways, departed from the sure foundation of objective truth revealed in *Scripture* and sought security and answers to life's ultimate questions in human *experience* or *reason* divorced from faith. Schaeffer's approach to apologetics was to probe philosophical presuppositions of alternative worldviews to orthodox Christianity and attempt to show that all other presuppositions lead inexorably to despair, because they cannot secure objective meaning and hope. Basically, his argument was that modern people are faced with the choice between conservative Christianity and nihilism (nothingness, absurdity). His appeal was "back to the Bible" and "back to traditional Protestant Christianity" as the only antidotes to the poisons of modern subjectivism, which inevitably turn *humanity* in upon itself and lead to self-inflation and then self-excision. While many evangelical scholars agree with Schaeffer's overall point that only faith in God and obedience to God's Word ultimately preserve individuals and culture from despair, many would also say that Schaeffer's treatments of specific philosophers and cultural phenomena such as abstract art leave much to be desired. He did not seem to be thoroughly acquainted with the philosophies of Kierkegaard and Hegel, whom he blamed for the West's fall below the line of despair into nihilism.

The Francis Schaeffer Web site: http://www.francis.schaeffer.net; Thomas V. Morris, *Francis Schaeffer's Apologetics: A Critique* (Grand Rapids: Baker Books, 1987); Ronald W. Ruegsegger, ed., *Reflections on Francis Schaeffer* (Grand Rapids: Zondervan, 1986); Philip Yancey, "Francis Schaeffer: A Prophet for Our Time?" *Christianity Today* 23, no. 12 (March 23, 1979): 14–18.

Augustus Hopkins Strong

Throughout the first half of the twentieth century the single most influential voice in conservative, nonfundamentalist American Protestant *theology* was that of Baptist theologian Augustus Hopkins Strong (1836–1921). Long after his death his best-known and most influential book, *Systematic Theology* (first version 1886), which went through eight revisions, was still being used as the primary textbook in theology courses in evangelical colleges, universities, and seminaries across North America. It was also the model for many smaller volumes of introductory theology and thus influenced generations of evangelicals through its many imitations. Strong's three-volume final revision of *Systematic Theology* (*Systematic Theology: A Compendium*, often published as one volume of eleven hundred pages) was published in 1907 and was still in print in 2002 (Judson Press, 1985). Strong's systematic theology was moderately conservative, open to limited revisions of tradition in light of modern knowledge and philosophy, somewhat scholastic in methodology (highly systematic using deductive reasoning heavily), and mildly Calvinistic. Strong's other books went out of print long ago, but were widely read and discussed in the later nineteenth century and early twentieth century. His *Christ in Creation and Ethical Monism* (1899) included essays and lectures on a variety of subjects related to theology, philosophy, and culture, including some emphasizing *God's* continuing creative activity within the universe through the cosmic Christ immanent within everything. This represented Strong's alternative to liberal theology's emphasis on divine immanence that seemed to blur the distinction between God and the world. His *Philosophy and Religion* (1888 and 1912) sought to bring the two into creative mutual transformation without accommodation of the *gospel* to secular thought. The dean of evangelical theology, *Carl F. H. Henry*, wrote his Boston

University doctoral dissertation on *Personal Idealism and Strong's Theology* (published in 1951). Numerous other evangelicals struggling out of *fundamentalism* found in Strong's theology resources for a return to nonsectarian, nonseparatistic orthodoxy.

Augustus Strong was born into a prominent family in Rochester, New York. His father was the publisher of the city's daily newspaper and a faithful Baptist layman. The extended Strong family was one of the city's wealthiest and most influential families. The city's largest hospital is named after them. The young Strong graduated from Yale University in 1857 and from Rochester Theological Seminary (Baptist) in 1859. One of his first pastorates was in Cleveland, Ohio, where among his parishioners was John D. Rockefeller. In 1872 he joined the faculty of his alma mater, Rochester Theological Seminary, as its professor of systematic theology. Eventually he became the seminary's president, and to this day his bust is prominently displayed there. He remained at the seminary for forty years, until his retirement in 1912. After that he remained active in the affairs of the Northern Baptist Convention in spite of his increasing criticism of what he perceived to be its doctrinal drift toward liberalism.

Strong's legacy to Evangelicalism and evangelical theology has very little to do with his flirtation with idealist philosophy in his essays on Christ and ethical monism. Only a few distant echoes of it may be found in his *Systematic Theology*. Strong's legacy lies in his somewhat inconsistent view of *Scripture* and in his seemingly paradoxical view of God's sovereignty. His doctrine of Scripture evolved throughout the eight versions of his *Systematic Theology*. He always insisted that Scripture is God's inspired and inerrant Word, but he gradually redefined both concepts (*inspiration* and *inerrancy*) so that by the eighth edition (the one read by most evangelical students) he was emphasizing inspiration's dynamic and organic nature

over its verbal nature and describing inerrancy in terms of adequacy to God's and the author's purpose of conveying spiritual truths necessary for *salvation.* Inspiration came to mean God's communication to the authors of truths they could not realize on their own, leaving them to choose their own words under the superintending guidance of the *Holy Spirit.* By 1907 Strong was seeking to do full justice to the human authors as well as to the divine author of Scripture.

Fundamentalists, of course, were not satisfied with his accounts of inspiration or inerrancy and discarded his theology as hopelessly accommodated to modernism. Such was, of course, far from the truth. Strong always believed Scripture to be God's Word written, fully authoritative for all matters of Christian *faith* and practice. But he did not believe it had to be technically accurate in every detail or even literally true in all of its historical accounts in order to be God's Word. He allowed, for example, that the entire book of Jonah might be a parable. His account of Scripture became flexible enough not to break under the weight of historical and literary study of Scripture.

Strong's doctrine of divine sovereignty sought to remain as close as possible to classical Calvinism while emphasizing God's *justice* as the driving motive for his decrees and insisting that the decree of reprobation (that some be eternally lost) is permissive and not positive. That is, God reluctantly allows some to resist his *grace* to their eternal loss; he does not positively predestine them to *hell*. Strong's account of Protestant doctrine became the gold standard for those evangelicals of the first five or six decades of the twentieth century who were neither fundamentalists nor high Calvinists. The latter preferred the theology of Charles Hodge.

Beginning in the 1960s Strong's theology began to fall into neglect, even though some evangelical teachers continued to use it as secondary reading. Its style is old-fashioned and its approach is deductive. There are very few illustrations or applications in Strong's *Systematic Theology*, and the print is exceedingly small. Still, many evangelical pastors and more than a few theologians keep it nearby for ready reference when they need to quickly review a doctrine.

Carl F. H. Henry, *Personal Idealism and Strong's Theology* (Wheaton, IL: Van Kampen Press, 1951); Augustus Hopkins Strong, *Autobiography of Augustus Hopkins Strong* (Valley Forge, PA: Judson Press, 1981); Grant Wacker, *Augustus Hopkins Strong and the Dilemma of Historical Consciousness* (Macon, GA: Mercer University Press, 1985).

Benjamin Breckenridge Warfield

More than any other individual, Benjamin Breckenridge Warfield (1851–1921) passed on to twentieth-century evangelicals the Old *Princeton Theology* of his nineteenth-century mentors Charles Hodge and Archibald Alexander Hodge. Warfield influenced a generation of fundamentalists and conservative evangelicals with his staunch defenses of the plenary, verbal *inspiration* and *inerrancy* of the *Bible*. On the other hand, many twentieth-century fundamentalists and more than a few conservative evangelicals ignored the great Princeton scholar's rejections of literalistic interpretations of portions of the Bible such as the early chapters of Genesis. Contrary to many of the ultraconservatives who counted themselves his disciples, Warfield believed there could be some consonance between Darwin's theory of evolution and the Christian doctrine of *creation* and sought to demonstrate this using John Calvin's understanding of *God's* creative activity. While it would not be correct to categorize the great warhorse of Calvinist orthodoxy at Princeton as a theistic evolutionist, he certainly was not a young-earth creationist, and he defended those biblical interpreters and scientists who sought to integrate evolution (not naturalism) with *creationism*.

Warfield was born into a wealthy Virginia family of Presbyterians and given the finest private education money could buy. In 1868 he entered Presbyterian-related Princeton College and studied mathematics and natural science. After graduating with high honors in 1871, he traveled and studied in Europe and there decided to become an ordained minister in the Presbyterian church. Upon returning to America he enrolled at Princeton Theological Seminary and studied under Charles Hodge, whose theology he always tried to preserve and emulate. After studying in Europe again, Warfield pastored for a year and then began his teaching career at a seminary in Pennsylvania. In 1887 he succeeded Archibald Alexander Hodge as professor of didactic and polemical theology at Princeton Seminary. He remained there until his death in 1921. When he died, his protegé *J. Gresham Machen*, who also taught at the seminary, declared that the spirit of the Old Princeton went out of the seminary with Warfield's body. He was a passionate defender of Protestant orthodoxy and especially its Calvinist flavor. He promoted the theologies of Augustine, John Calvin, Jonathan Edwards, and Charles Hodge against all who would revise Reformed orthodoxy in the light of modern philosophy and culture. He refused to cooperate with an effort to revise the Westminster Confession of Faith within his own Presbyterian denomination. He steadfastly defended a high view of *Scripture* against the growing use of higher biblical criticism within Presbyterian seminaries and never wavered in his loyalty to the Calvinist doctrines of total depravity, unconditional *election*, limited *atonement*, irresistible *grace*, and *perseverance* (or preservation) of the saints (TULIP). On the other hand, as noted earlier, he accommodated somewhat to Darwin's theory of evolution and chastised the churches of his day for their continuing racial segregation. Like many great theologians, Warfield was something of an enigma.

Warfield was a prolific writer and editor; he produced numerous essays and monographs on theological subjects and edited the prestigious *Princeton Review* for thirteen years. Most of his books (many of which are edited collections of his essays) are still in print over a century after the essays contained in them were written. They are still widely read and studied in the twenty-first century, especially by Presbyterian and Reformed students and ministers. Most of them were written against the background and within the context of the growing controversy over higher criticism of the Bible and liberal Protestant theology within the mainline denominations and seminaries. They are, for the most part, polemical works aimed at exposing the heresies of liberals and higher critics and the alleged fanaticism of revivalists and especially Pentecostals (after the beginning of the twentieth century). A few are more devotional and homiletical in nature. Warfield's recognition as a theologian began when with Archibald Alexander Hodge (who was then teaching theology at Princeton Seminary) he coauthored an essay on "Inspiration" (of the Bible) for the *Presbyterian Review* in 1881. In it the two conservative theologians attempted to promote a reasonable doctrine of biblical inerrancy that would do justice both to Scripture's divine source and to the actual phenomena that contained apparent errors and contradictions. The authors argued that only the original autographs were perfectly free from all error and that errors in sources used by the biblical authors may not be considered errors in God's Word, even when they crept into the biblical autographs. They insisted that in spite of some apparent discrepancies and difficulties in the biblical writings, orthodox Christians should believe that since they are God's inspired Word, they must be (or have been) without any error even in matters not directly related to God and *salvation*.

Warfield followed the same general line of thinking about Scripture and *authority* in many of his later writings, such as are contained in *Revelation and Inspiration* (later revised as *Inspiration and Authority of the Bible*, edited by Samuel G. Craig [1948]), which contains ten essays explaining and defending the verbal inspiration and inerrancy of the Bible. In these and other articles the Princeton theologian attempted to answer all of the significant objections to these doctrines raised by critics, including the famous Scottish evangelical Presbyterian theologian James Orr, whom Warfield considered a friend and true Christian even though he did not believe in inerrancy. Against critics on both the right and the left, Warfield argued that both the evidences of Scripture (internal and external) and the inner testimony of the *Holy Spirit* establish that the whole of the Bible was supernaturally inspired by God through a "concursus" of divine and human activities; God prepared, guided, and superintended the human writers of Scripture so that they wrote the very words God wanted written without any diminution of their own personalities and powers as authors. That what they wrote is without error (with proper qualifications that take literature and textual transmission into account) is, according to Warfield, the testimony of Scripture to itself and logically necessary if it is God's inspired Word.

Warfield's legacy to twentieth- and twenty-first-century evangelical *theology* lies in his strong defense of a high view of Scripture, including plenary, verbal inspiration (without mechanical dictation) and inerrancy (of the original autographs). Numerous conservative evangelical defenders of those doctrines have relied heavily on Warfield's arguments. Warfield also contributed to at least one segment of modern Evangelicalism a strong emphasis on the rationality of Christian belief, which he believed could be demonstrated through the proper uses of evidence and logic. He argued that Christians believe in Christ because it is rational to believe in him, even though reasoning alone does not make one a Christian. According to Warfield, the Holy Spirit works to convince people of the truth of the *gospel* and of Christianity through evidence and never apart from or against evidence. While insisting that rational, philosophical apologetics cannot alone bring a person into a relationship with God, he averred that it is absolutely vital in establishing and spreading Christianity and that Christianity's success in the world has been due to its appeal to reason. He called Christianity "the Apologetic religion," by which he clearly meant that its truth is founded not on power ("the sword") or *experience* ("inner testimony of the Holy Spirit") but on rational persuasion. Warfield's approach to Christian foundations starkly conflicted with the approaches of other evangelicals. He was more than suspicious of all religious "enthusiasm," by which he meant appeals to inner experience, whether mystical or emotional, to establish spiritual and theological truth. He also had little use for the school of Dutch Calvinism (Abraham Kuyper and Herman Bavinck and their followers), whose proponents regarded all reasoning (including what counts as evidence) as determined by some prior religious or quasi-religious intuition. For Warfield, religious truth claims must be judged at the bar of universal reason. This by no means precludes recognizing that many people's ability to reason properly is adversely affected by *sin*. Certainly Warfield recognized the cognitive damage done by the fall and by individuals' sins. Nevertheless, he believed and taught that Christianity must be believed because it is true, and it is true because it is rational, and it is rational because it fits the facts of the world and is internally coherent. Warfield's religious epistemology, then, was classically foundationalist (with the exception that he did believe sinners' minds are clouded by sin, so that they are not as objectively rational as believers). He fit into and contributed heavily to what some scholars have called the "evangel-

ical Enlightenment" that emphasizes certainty, rationality, propositional communication, and scientific methods even in Christian theology. One segment of evangelical scholarship follows Warfield in this matter and finds rational proof of the truth of Christianity to be a crucial task of evangelical theology.

W. Andrew Hoffecker, "Benjamin B. Warfield," in *The Princeton Theology: Reformed Theology in America*, ed. David F. Wells (Grand Rapids: Baker Book House, 1989); Mark A. Noll, "B. B. Warfield," in *Handbook of Evangelical Theologians*, ed. Walter A. Elwell (Grand Rapids: Baker Books, 1993).

H. Orton Wiley Although most evangelicals (including theologians) have never heard of him, H. (Henry) Orton Wiley (1877–1961) is one of the most widely read and influential twentieth-century evangelical theologians—especially among non-Calvinists, Arminians within the large *Holiness movement*. The majority of evangelical scholars within the Wesleyan Theological Society reported in a 1984 survey that Wiley exerted the dominant influence on their scholarly work (reported in Mark A. Noll, *Between Faith and Criticism* [New York: HarperCollins, 1986]). For much of the twentieth century his three-volume magnum opus *Christian Theology* (Kansas City, MO: Beacon Hill Press, 1941) was the sole systematic theology listed in the Course of Study for Licensed Ministers in Church of the Nazarene colleges and universities. It has been widely used as the primary theology textbook in Nazarene and other evangelical Wesleyan seminaries. Like most other evangelical theologians Wiley was not aware of being an innovator; he sought only to pass along to his readers the evangelical tradition of his own particular heritage—the Holiness movement's evangelical Wesleyan theology of *conversion-regeneration* and *entire sanctification*. However, his theological writings sparkled with references to and quotations from a wide variety of theologians, including Europeans of the magisterial Protestant traditions. He was no narrow sectarian, but he had a wide acquaintance with Christian theology and sought from his own denominational vantage point to give his readers and students a grounding in a catholic (universal, apostolic) vision of Christianity. That was also John Wesley's concern in the eighteenth century. And, although he was passionately evangelical, Wiley was no fundamentalist. He criticized fundamentalism for its alleged tendency to put the inerrant letter of *Scripture* above the living relationship with *Jesus Christ*. He liked to remind his readers that Scripture itself testifies that "the letter killeth but the Spirit giveth life."

Wiley was born in Nebraska and moved with his family to California and then to Oregon. For a while after high school he worked as a pharmacist, and he then served as a minister in the United Brethren church. (The United Brethren was a Wesleyan denomination that merged in the twentieth century into the United Methodist Church.) While matriculating at the University of California (Berkeley) from 1905 to 1909, Wiley joined the new Church of the Nazarene and pastored one of its first congregations. He received the Bachelor of Divinity from Pacific School of Religion (Episcopal) in 1910 and became one of the first faculty members of the new Nazarene-related Pasadena College, which he served as president from 1912 until 1916, when he resigned to pursue a master's degree from the same seminary he had attended some years earlier. After receiving his master's degree, the young Nazarene scholar served briefly as president of the Northwest Nazarene College in Nampa, Idaho. Later he moved once again to be president of Pasadena College. At both institutions he was a bridge builder and peacemaker as the new denomination and its institutions struggled toward maturity through con-troveries over emotionalism, the life of the mind, the liberal arts, *theology*, and *worship*. Although he authored several books and numerous articles, Wiley's enduring contribution lies in his *Christian Theology* and its one-volume companion summary, which continue to be published by the Nazarene publishing house into the twenty-first century.

Wiley's legacy to evangelical theology lies in his transmission of a distinctly nonfundamentalist evangelical Wesleyanism to twentieth-century and later Protestants within the large and diverse Holiness movement. In his *Christian Theology* he refused to divorce Scripture from *experience* and insisted that while the former is the only authoritative and primary source of Christian theology, it is so because of its witness to the essential *revelation* of Jesus Christ. The *Holy Spirit* inspired the authors of Scripture and illumines its readers so that they are able to recognize it as God's Word pointing to Jesus Christ. Thus the truth contained in Scripture must be vitalized by the Spirit of God through a special experience of imparted spiritual life. For Wiley, then, theological truth is never merely propositional or rational; it is always also irreducibly personal. Its aim is never primarily the communication of information; it is always primarily the establishment of a relationship between the believer and the living God. *Reason* is a useful tool of interpretation, and propositions are inescapable in persuasion, but both are secondary to the experience of conversion-regeneration that results in *sanctification*. Transformation takes precedence over information. Wiley rejected the fundamentalist doctrines of verbal *inspiration* and absolute *inerrancy* of Scripture in favor of a more dynamic model of inspiration that he believed did greater justice to the human authors' personal involvement in the production of the Bible. For him, Scripture is infallible in all matters of faith and life but does not need to be technically without error in every area in order to be God's inspired Word.

Wiley was an evangelical synergist with regard to *salvation*. He rejected the Calvinist scheme of interpreting divine sovereignty (monergism) in favor of his own Holiness-inspired vision of Arminian theology, in which human beings cooperate with divine *grace* for salvation and Christian living. According to Wiley, human persons are sinful from birth (though not guilty of Adam's *sin*) and need the power of the grace of God to become free agents. Prevenient grace overcomes depravity and bondage of the will to sin and creates the human person's free agency; freed persons then must respond freely to the drawing of the Holy Spirit through the *gospel* of Jesus Christ by *repentance* and *faith*. When they do that, they receive "the birth of the Spirit" (conversion-regeneration), which frees them from the guilt of *sin*, and then are able also to receive the *"baptism with the Spirit,"* which brings instantaneous cleansing from the power of sin. Wiley believed in entire sanctifi-

cation, as did John Wesley. It is an act of the Holy Spirit within converted persons that frees them from desire to sin and from all willful sinning, but it does not involve complete moral perfection. Sanctified Christians will continue to err out of ignorance and weakness, but these are infirmities, Wiley argues. They are not sins in the same way that willful transgressions are sins. Thus, arguably, Wiley moved the Holiness doctrine of instantaneous entire sanctification closer to the mainstream evangelical concept of commitment to discipleship of Jesus Christ.

Gary Dorrien, *The Remaking of Evangelical Theology* (Louisville, KY: Westminster John Knox Press, 1998); Thomas A. Langford, *Practical Divinity*, vol. 1: *Theology in the Wesleyan Tradition* (Nashville: Abingdon Press, 1983, 1988); John R. Tyson, "H. Orton Wiley," in *Handbook of Evangelical Theologians*, ed. Walter A. Elwell (Grand Rapids: Baker Books, 1993).

Traditional Doctrines
in Evangelical Theology

Evangelical *theology* draws heavily on Reformation doctrinal wells and on Protestant sources after the Reformation, such as **Puritanism, Pietism** and *revivalism*. Much of evangelical doctrine is heavily influenced by Reformed theology; other evangelical interpretations of doctrine draw on Anabaptist and Wesleyan sources. The diverse sources of evangelical thought give rise to significant variety of doctrinal interpretation. Evangelicals exist within virtually every branch and denomination of Protestantism. Leading evangelical theologians represent this diversity, so that their expositions of doctrines also reflect it. Thus, there is no one, united evangelical doctrine of, for example, *faith*. Reformed evangelicals will tend to view faith as always a gift of God to communities (families, churches) as well as to individuals who receive it within those communities. Wesleyan and other Arminian evangelicals (e.g., Free Will Baptists) will tend to view faith as the human response to the divine initiative of calling, conviction, enlightenment, and enablement (prevenient *grace*). In spite of this difference of interpretation, however, all evangelicals agree that faith is the necessary instrumental cause of *salvation* and that it involves trust in **God** through *Jesus Christ*; they all eschew the more Catholic and Orthodox interpretation of faith as necessarily including faithfulness to the church's traditions and *sacraments*. Evangelicals also agree that while faith is salvation's instrumental cause (whether as gift or human response), it is not salvation's efficient cause. The efficient cause is grace alone.

So there is significant unity and significant diversity in evangelical interpretation of doctrines. Many traditional evangelical doctrines are also traditional doctrines of nonevangelical Christian traditions and communities. Some, however, are relatively distinctive to Evangelicalism. While other Christian traditions may use the term *conversion*, there is a distinctively evangelical doctrine of conversion that emphasizes a *supernatural* change in a person's life by God's grace through faith and *repentance*. Some nonevangelicals identify conversion with *baptism* and leave little or no room for a transforming life *experience* that involves a conscious decision of repentance toward God and faith in Jesus Christ. Some evangelicals believe in baptismal *regeneration*, but all evangelicals also insist that there is no full and complete salvation without a conscious decision of repentance and faith—even if it is interpreted theologically as a work of God in the person's life. Virtually any orthodox Protestant Christian who calls for conscious conversion to Christ through repentance and faith is an evangelical. Even the nature of conversion, however, is a matter of diversity among evangelicals. Some view it as a process that begins with baptism (especially in the case of infants), reaches a crisis in conscious repentance and faith, and evolves further through discipleship. Others view it as a momentary event and not at all as a process. All agree that it is not merely a sacramental event and process or a turning over of a new leaf; it is a transforming work of God that brings regeneration (being born again) and *justification* (*forgiveness* of sins and imputation of Christ's righteousness) in a special way.

Each of the delineations of doctrines here will focus on the distinctive evangelical interpretation, if one exists. If there is no distinctive evangelical interpretation, the exposition will describe the variety of beliefs about the doctrine among evangelicals and how that relates to nonevangelical traditions and interpretations. In many cases there will be very little difference between the evangelical view and the Reformed or Anabaptist or Lutheran view. In other cases evangelicals have developed a unique "spin" on the doctrine that one finds in other Protestant traditions only insofar as they have been touched by the evangelical movement. The suggestions for further reading that follow the articles include diverse evangelical viewpoints on the topics. Often a volume of systematic theology is cited, in which case there is a chapter in it on the specific topic of the article.

Amillennialism   Evangelical *theology* during the twentieth century developed a strong interest in *eschatology*. The evangelical movement as a whole seemed to be obsessed with the second coming of *Jesus Christ* and the events surrounding it; evangelical theology seeks to give some reasonable biblical understanding to evangelical eschatological fervor. One important root of evangelical interest in the end times and biblical prophecy concerning them is the Adventist movement of the mid-nineteenth century. The Adventists, including lay Baptist minister and biblical prophecy interpreter William Miller, sought to read the "signs of the times" in light of biblical apocalyptic literature. Miller and his followers identified 1844 as the date of the *return of Christ* and believed that Christ would establish his *kingdom* on earth over the nations after his return; he would rule and reign on earth for one thousand years, thus fulfilling the prophecies of Revelation 20. Miller's and the Adventists' *premillennialism* found a corresponding voice and emphasis in *John Nelson Darby* and the Plymouth Brethren movement in Great Britain. By the late nineteenth century, thousands of evangelicals in Great Britain and North America were attending Bible-prophecy conferences and spreading throughout evangelical Christianity belief in the imminent return of Christ, to be followed by his millennial (one-thousand-year) earthly rule and reign. Many other evangelicals of various denominational backgrounds throughout the nineteenth century and well into the twentieth century held to another millennial view: *postmillennialism*—the belief that Christ will return after a millennium on earth during which the nations would be Christianized. Influen-

tial Baptist theologian *Augustus Hopkins Strong* promoted postmillenialism. Both forms of *millennialism* competed with the more traditional amillennial understanding for the hearts and minds of evangelical Protestant Christians.

Amillennialism rejects belief in a literal millennial reign of Christ on earth during history. It is the belief that Christ's great kingdom within history is not social or political but spiritual. The early church father Augustine developed the amillennial view of the kingdom of God and of eschatology in his *The City of God*. According to Augustine (who was going contrary to a prevailing premillennialism among earlier church fathers especially in the Eastern, Greek-speaking Roman Empire) Christ's rule and reign is hidden within history in the *church*. The church of Jesus Christ is the kingdom of God that will be fulfilled and perfected when Christ returns to judge the world and create a new *heaven* and new earth. Thus, for Augustine, there will be no perfect earthly sociopolitical reign of Christ over the nations for a thousand years or any other period of time. Thus, amillennialism means "no millennium." Through the influence of Pope Gregory I (Gregory the Great) and later Catholic popes, bishops, and theologians such as Bernard of Clairvaux and Thomas Aquinas, amillennialism became the semiofficial view of the kingdom of God within history among Roman Catholics. The magisterial reformers such as Luther, Zwingli, and Calvin adopted it, and through them it became the semiofficial interpretation of the mainline Protestant churches. Some of the radical reformers, including some Anabaptists and later British sectarians, returned to the early premillennialism of the second- and third-century church fathers. Many of the British and North American Puritans adopted postmillennialism after it was proposed by British theologian Daniel Whitby in the eighteenth century.

Amillennialists neither hope for nor expect a "Christianization of the world" before Christ's return (postmillennialism) or a sociopolitical rule and reign of the returned Jesus Christ for a thousand years before the judgment and new heaven and new earth. They regard their view as a simpler if less literal interpretation of biblical literature about the end times, supported by numerous biblical passages that identify the kingdom of God with the spiritual presence of Christ among his people. Many amillennialists hold to a preterist or historicist rather than futurist interpretation of biblical apocalyptic literature. Preterism views Revelation and other apocalyptic literature as referring to events now in the past, such as the fall of Rome and persecution of Christians by the Roman emperors. Historicists view them as referring to recurring historical patterns such as the occasional rise of dictators who persecute God's people. All evangelicals believe in Christ's second coming in the future, but amillennialists do not believe that all of the events described in Revelation and other apocalyptic portions of Scripture are to be taken literally as referring to future events before and after Christ's coming. For amillennialists, the biblical prophecies about a utopia when righteousness will fill the earth and **Satan** will be bound refer either to the church itself or to the new heaven and new earth to be established by **God** after the return of Christ and great judgment.

Amillennialism was without doubt the majority view of evangelical Protestant theologians in the eighteenth and nineteenth centuries. They followed Augustine closely in their interpretations of biblical eschatological literature and in their views of the church as the kingdom of God on earth within history. Many evangelical hymns express an amillennial perspective. The well-known and beloved song "When the Roll Is Called Up Yonder" refers to the time when "time shall be no more"—immediately after Christ returns. One of the most influential theologians of Protestant orthodoxy who influenced the evangelical movement

and its theology during the nineteenth century was Princeton Seminary theologian Charles Hodge, who steadfastly opposed both postmillennialism and premillennialism and advocated an Augustinian amillennial interpretation of the kingdom of God and the end times events biblically prophesied. During the twentieth century postmillennialism waned in popularity as belief in the gradual Christianization of the nations became more difficult to envision. Premillennialism gained great popularity among evangelicals during the late twentieth century; some commentators suggested that its dispensational form (see *Dispensationalism*) became an unofficial "evangelical orthodoxy" regarding eschatology. Yet amillennialism remained an influential evangelical interpretation of the kingdom of God and reign of Christ into the twenty-first century, especially among Reformed evangelicals and traditional, mainline Baptists (Northern and Southern as well as English). Two evangelical theologians who breathed new life into amillennialism for evangelicals in the late twentieth century were Anthony Hoekema of Calvin Theological Seminary and Stanley J. Grenz.

Robert G. Clouse, ed., *The Meaning of the Millennium* (Downers Grove, IL: InterVarsity Press, 1977); William E. Cox, *Amillennialism Today* (Nutley, NJ: Presbyterian & Reformed Publishing, 1992); Millard Erickson, *Contemporary Options in Eschatology* (Grand Rapids: Baker Book House, 1987); Stanley J. Grenz, *The Millennial Maze: Sorting Out Evangelical Options* (Downers Grove, IL: InterVarsity Press, 1992).

Angels Evangelicals believe in a normally invisible, spiritual world populated by creatures of **God** called angels, because the biblical narrative mentions that world and its inhabitants often, Christian tradition includes belief in them as God's agents, and numerous Christian men and women have experienced them in some way throughout history. There is no distinctive evangelical doctrine of angels, but evangelicals may be among the only Protestants left who adamantly insist that angels—God's created, spiritual and invisible agents—are real and not merely personifications of cosmic forces or legendary beings of ancient Middle Eastern lore. Evangelicals agree with the basic contours of the Roman Catholic doctrine of angels, although they do not share with Catholics much of the latter's traditional lore about them. According to most evangelical theologians, angels were created before humans, and some portion of them fell away from *heaven* in a rebellion led by the archangel Lucifer. Lucifer and the fallen angels are opponents of God's creative and redemptive plan and activity; Gabriel and Michael, the only two angels named in *Scripture*, lead a heavenly host of messengers who carry out God's bidding in *creation*. Scripture says very little about angels' nature or about the hierarchy of the angelic ranks. It is more revealing of their activities, which include carrying messages to humans, protecting human beings in certain circumstances, ministering to Christ and prophets, worshiping God, and possibly overseeing the historical developments of certain nations. Evangelicals believe that angels are not created in God's image and are not subjects of God's redemptive plan and purpose; they are instruments that serve and worship God. How many angels can dance on the head of a pin was a topic of discussion in medieval *theology*, but most evangelical theologians eschew such speculation and settle for a minimal doctrine of angels. Most evangelical theologians do not believe or teach that every person has a "guardian angel" or that territorial spirits (especially assigned good and bad angels over nations and countries) control the destinies of communities or history. Such folk theological ideas of angels detract from the sovereignty of God and have little or no warrant in Scripture.

One particular segment of the evangelical community tends to place more weight on the doctrine of angels than do other evangelicals. The *charismatic movement* emphasizes the *supernatural* character of God's ways with humans in history and seeks to retrieve and renew the supernatural worldview and life of the early church as recounted in the book of Acts. There angels intervened to rescue Peter from execution. Charismatics note that there are many seemingly mysterious references to angels in the Bible and that while it may be impossible to develop a detailed, systematic theology of angels ("angelology"), Christians should not give up too quickly on paying any attention to them. Some charismatics read books like *Angels on Assignment* and believe that it is possible for Spirit-filled Christians to command angels to cooperate with them in carrying out God's mission in the world. Some charismatic Christians practice "spiritual warfare," which often involves corporate praying to defeat fallen angels who are trying to undermine God's purposes in the world and praying to strengthen good angels in their warfare against *Satan* and his minions. Noncharismatic evangelicals are generally more reluctant to address angels or pay very much attention to them at all, because there is very little if any scriptural basis for it. Nevertheless, all evangelical theologians admit and even emphasize the existence of angels even if they do not become involved with angels in any way.

Wayne E. Caldwell, "Angelology and Demonology: Intelligent, Nonhuman Creatures," in *A Contemporary Wesleyan Theology: Biblical, Systematic, and Practical*, vol. 2, ed. Charles W. Carter (Grand Rapids: Zondervan, 1983), 1043–97; Millard Erickson, *Christian Theology*, vol. 1 (Grand Rapids: Baker Book House, 1983); Billy Graham, *Angels* (Nashville: Word Publishing, 2000); Stanley J. Grenz, *Theology for the Community of God* (Grand Rapids: Wm. B. Eerdmans, 2000); Charles Francis

Hunter, et al., *Angels on Assignment* (Pittsburgh: Whitaker House, 2000).

Atonement   One of the hallmarks of evangelical Christianity is crucicentrism–special focus and emphasis on the cross of *Jesus Christ* as saving event. Evangelical preachers have specialized in either dramatically portraying the sufferings of Jesus on the cross for the *sins* of the world or carefully expounding the intricate details of the doctrine of the propitiatory sacrifice of Christ. While evangelical theology cannot claim any unique contribution to the doctrine of the atonement, it has often given it special attention and sometimes insisted on a particular interpretation as the only fully orthodox one. Evangelical theologians of the mid-twentieth century argued over the proper translation of the Greek word *hilasterion*, used by Paul to describe Christ's reconciling work in his death. (The word itself refers to the mercy seat in the tabernacle and temple Holy of Holies, where the blood of sacrifice was sprinkled on the Day of Atonement.) Should it be translated "propitiation" (appeasement of God's wrath) or "expiation" (covering of sins)? More conservative evangelical theologians and fundamentalists have insisted that it must be translated "propitiation" while more moderate and progressive evangelical theologians have often supported the Revised Standard Version's translation "expiation."

The word *atonement* simply means *reconciliation*. Some scholars believe English Bible translator William Tyndale created the word to describe reunion between *God* and *humanity* in salvation by Christ's death: "at-one-ment." Be that as it may, the English word *atonement* is simply synonymous with reconcilation. Many modern English Bible translations use one word or the other to translate *hilasterion* (rather than the less familiar words *propitiation* and *expiation*). The issue is the doctrine more than the term. The majority of evangelical theologians

have followed the classical Reformed *theology* of the atonement, which views Christ's work as providing a substitutionary punishment for the sins of either all humanity or only the elect. Reformed theologians interpret the scope of Christ's substitutionary death as extensive only with the elect (those predestined by God's decree to *salvation*), whereas Wesleyan and other Arminian theologians view it as universal in scope. In both cases, conservative evangelical theologians have tended to follow some version of Anselm's satisfaction theory, as it was adjusted by Calvin and the post-Calvinian Reformed theologians in what has come to be known as the penal substitution theory. According to this account of the work of Christ on the cross, Jesus Christ suffered the wrath of God against sin and endured the punishment due to sinful humanity. This was an act of God's love and *justice*; God's *holiness* demanded that sin be punished and God's love desired that humanity (or the elect) be forgiven. Christ's sinless, undeserved death was a voluntary act of passive obedience that satisfied the demands of God's holiness and assuaged God's wrath; it is imputed by God to those who receive Christ by *repentance* and *faith* in *conversion*.

Some evangelical theologians are uncomfortable with this strongly objective interpretation of the atonement that portrays it as a transaction between Christ and God (or between God and God). The idea that God must have his "pound of flesh" because of humanity's disobedience and that God's wrath must be and was assuaged by Jesus Christ seems to make God cruel and bloodthirsty and implies that human beings are mere objects in the process of atonement. The love of God for sinful humanity and the participation of human persons in the reconciling process seem lost in the traditional penal substitutionary doctrine.

In the early decades of the twentieth century, several British evangelical thinkers attempted to revise the strongly objective imagery of the traditional Reformed doctrine to emphasize Christ's voluntary sacrifice, the representative nature of his sacrificial death (as opposed to substitionary punishment), and the love of God as the motive in the atonement (rather than justice or wrath). These theologians—R. W. Dale, P. T. Forsyth, and James Denney—all emphasized the vicarious and representative nature of Christ's sacrificial death more than its nature as substitutionary punishment. Many twentieth-century evangelical theologians on both sides of the Atlantic (and later in other parts of the world) adopted the British Congregationalists' approach because it was less forensic and more participatory and because it portrayed God as less like the proverbial Shylock and more like a heavenly Father. This led many of them to prefer expiation to propitiation as the appropriate description of atonement.

In the last few decades of the twentieth century, some evangelical theologians expressed dissatisfaction with traditional and revisionist Reformed models of the atonement, preferring instead more distinctly human and social understandings of why Christ died and how it made salvation possible for alienated humanity. Baptist theologian Fisher Humphreys suggested a step beyond the vicarious sacrifice theory of the British Congregationalists, in which God in Christ suffers therapeutically for fallen, alienated humans much as a therapist experiences vicarious suffering in helping an emotionally distraught patient return to health and wholeness; Humphreys points out further that all *forgiveness* involves suffering—especially when the person being forgiven has committed a terrible act of betrayal against the person forgiving. Humphreys and other evangelical theologians use modern psychological experiences and insights to illuminate the meaning of the cross in relation to reconciliation between God and humanity.

Joel Green and Mark Baker, two Wesleyan theologians, attempted to update the doctrine of the atonement and at the same time return to some of its forgotten or neglected biblical roots (e.g., in images of reconciliation) by looking at non-Western, third-world Christian contexts for interpreting atonement. Their focus was less on guilt and propitiation of wrath than on shame and resolving its stigma. They drew on Asian cultures to explain how identifying and suffering love can banish shame and how humanity's shame for disobeying God is overcome in the reconciling act of Christ, who demonstrates love in a supreme act of identification with sinners in their shame. Reformed evangelical critics of these newer approaches to understanding the atonement accuse them of losing sight of the necessary dimensions of human guilt, divine condemnation, and forensic justice. They view the newer approaches as too subjective and even humanistic. Defenders of the newer approaches point to biblical descriptions of the cross as God's identification with sinners in Jesus Christ and as involving repentant sinners in its saving power through relationship and community.

In spite of disagreements about the nature of the atoning work of Christ, evangelicals agree that it is the only ground and hope for human salvation. They all reject pluralism that regards salvation as possible through several or many saviors and lords. According to evangelical thinkers, in concert with evangelical piety in general, the cross of Jesus Christ is the reconciling event that makes it possible for God and humans to enjoy a restored relationship of peace. Furthermore, they agree that it is a divine act that creates a new situation for both God and humans, rather than merely a moral example that encourages and enables humans to repent and reconcile themselves to God. They steadfastly oppose any attempt to interpret Christ's death as merely tragic martyrdom or "divine child abuse." The cross stands at the center of evangelical piety and proclamation as saving act of God, even if its explanation varies somewhat from theologian to theologian.

Donald Bloesch, *Jesus Christ: Savior and Lord* (Downers Grove, IL: InterVarsity Press, 1997); Peter Taylor Forsyth, *The Work of Christ* (London: Hodder & Stoughton, n.d.); Joel B. Green and Mark D. Baker, *Recovering the Scandal of the Cross: Atonement in New Testament and Contemporary Contexts* (Downers Grove, IL: InterVarsity Press, 2000); Fisher Humphreys, *The Death of Christ* (Nashville: Broadman Press, 1978); Ronald Wallace, *The Atoning Death of Christ* (Westchester, IL: Crossway Books, 1981).

Authority Evangelical theology concentrates on religious authority; some critics might say evangelical theologians are obsessed with issues of authority for belief. Authority is warrant for belief and practice; it has to do with sources and norms for doctrine and *theology*. To what sources and norms should Christian theologians appeal in settling controversies about correct belief? How is right belief—orthodoxy—established? What norms exercise control in these matters? Evangelical theologians are concerned with right authority because they are concerned with truth and avoiding error, especially heresy. They are influenced by the decline of mainstream Protestant theology into liberal theology and by *fundamentalism's* reaction against that drift and decline. Evangelical theologians are not indifferent to doctrine: they believe that what people believe about *God, Jesus Christ,* and *salvation* (and related matters) really matters. Some are concerned with constructing coherent systems of doctrine—systematic theologies—that are biblical, reasonable, and relevant to contemporary modes of thought. The importance of right authority looms large in these matters. All evangelical theologians reject the modern establishment of Enlightenment *reason* and universal human *experience* as the supreme norm for Christian theology; they also reject the postmodern destruction of the "house of authority." But they are not unanimous in their vision of the proper pattern of authority for theology.

As Protestants, evangelical theologians look to the dialectic of Word and Spirit as the supreme pattern of authority for right religious belief. According to Luther, Zwingli, Calvin, and other first-generation Reformers, the *Holy Spirit* authorizes Holy Scripture through a process called *inspiration* and also illumines the minds of Scripture's readers. Apart from the Spirit of God, the *Bible* is just a dead letter because of the darkening of the hearts and minds of human readers. However, the Spirit ties himself inextricably to the written Word, so that there is no authoritative *revelation* outside of it. Virtually all evangelical thinkers agree with this basic approach to authority in theology. Spirit-inspired and Spirit-illumined Scripture is the ultimate source and norm for theological reflection and construction—*sola scriptura*. (Contrary to a misunderstanding, *sola scriptura* does not mean that Scripture is the only source; it means that Scripture is the sole supreme source—the *norma normans* [norming norm] of Christian thought about God, salvation, etc.) At the same time, Scripture is not an authority in and of itself; it is authoritative as witness to God; it derives its authority from the Spirit of God. Most evangelical theologians then appeal to something like the so-called Wesleyan Quadrilateral to fill out the pattern of authority for theology: Scripture, tradition, reason, and experience. The quadrilateral is not an equilateral; Scripture is supreme, with the other three sources and norms serving as tools of interpretation of Scripture. Some evangelical theologians emphasize tradition more than others; some emphasize reason over tradition. Few appeal to experience to establish truth.

Two general approaches stand out as competing in evangelical theology's search for a proper approach to fleshing out the pattern of authority that centers around Word and Spirit. One approach, championed by *Carl F. H. Henry* and followers, emphasizes the role of reason in carrying out the tasks of theology. For Henry, Scripture is a coherent, intelligible, propositional revelation of God. The Holy Spirit works through the illumined rational mind of the Christian theologian to establish a coherent system of revealed truths based on the foundation of Scripture. Logic plays a crucial role in eliminating inconsistencies which are sure signs of error. Truth is signaled by comprehensiveness and coherence within the system of doctrine. The second approach is championed by *Bernard Ramm, Donald G. Bloesch,* and other evangelical thinkers in the Pietist tradition of "heart Christianity." For them, faith plays the leading role in theology, followed by reason; paradox is expected in theology, because it deals with revealed mysteries that transcend human comprehension. Whereas the first approach emphasizes the objectively given written Word, sometimes to the neglect of the Spirit, the second approach emphasizes the role of the Spirit in contemporary theological work, while affirming the written Word as the highest court of appeal. The second approach refuses to separate Word from Spirit and argues that the Spirit working within the Christian community leads toward correct interpretations of the Word. The first approach seeks rational certainty and consistency; the second seeks practical spiritual application and comfort with mystery and ambiguity. These two approaches frequently clash, as adherents of the first view adherents of the second suspiciously for signs of irrationality, while the latter view the first for signs of rationalism and reduction of mystery. In fact, the two approaches balance one another and offer each other correctives.

One of the most controverted topics in evangelical theology has to do with the role of tradition in theology. Most evangelical theologians regard the Great Tradition of ancient and Reformation Christianity (church fathers and Reformers) as a secondary norm—a *norma nor-*

mata (normed norm)—in theology. Its light is "reflected glory" from Scripture, and it is open to correction from fresh biblical study. It serves as a fallible guide to Christian thinking and interpretation of Scripture. Other evangelical theologians seek to elevate the ancient Christian consensus of the church fathers to a status alongside Scripture as its authoritative interpretive lens. Thomas Oden coined the label *paleo-orthodoxy* to describe this approach to authority. The consensus of the church fathers is inviolable for evangelical thought; it serves as a magisterium for controlling theological reflection. Critics of Oden's paleo-orthodoxy worry that it undermines *sola scriptura* and the Reformation principle of the *church* (and its theology) as "reformed and always reforming."

Donald G. Bloesch, *A Theology of Word and Spirit: Authority and Method in Theology. Christian Foundations,* vol. 1 (Downers Grove, IL: InterVarsity Press, 1992); Carl F. H. Henry, *God, Revelation, and Authority,* (6 vol.), (Waco, TX: Word, 1976–83); Thomas Oden, *The Rebirth of Orthodoxy: Signs of New Life in Christianity* (San Francisco: HarperSanFrancisco, 2003); Bernard Ramm, *The Pattern of Authority* (Grand Rapids: Wm. B. Eerdmans, 1957).

Baptism   Baptism is the universal rite of initiation into the Christian *church*. The vast majority of Christian traditions initiate children or converts into the church by means of water—either immersion into water, sprinkling of water on the head, or effusion (pouring) of water over the person being baptized. Most churches baptize in the name of the Father, Son, and *Holy Spirit*; a few baptize in the name of Jesus. Most evangelicals practice water baptism; the Salvation Army and the Evangelical Friends (Quakers) are the exceptions; they interpret *conversion* as *Spirit baptism* and do not use water or have a separate ceremony of water baptism for initiation into the church. Other evangelicals draw on various Protestant traditions for their practice and interpretation of water baptism. Some baptize infants by sprinkling; some baptize believers only, by effusion or immersion. Whatever the preferred mode, virtually all evangelicals agree that baptism is by itself insufficient for complete *salvation* and does not convey *grace ex opere operato* (by virtue of the act itself). Evangelicals emphasize the personal dimension of salvation, which must include a conscious decision of *repentance* and *faith,* even for persons who were baptized as infants. The heart of evangelical Christianity is conversion; some evangelicals view it as a process that begins with baptism (even of infants) and culminates in a profession of faith followed by a life of Christian discipleship to *Jesus Christ.* Others interpret it as a momentary *experience*—a "crisis experience"—to be followed by baptism as an act of commitment to Christ and his church.

Many evangelicals in the Lutheran, Reformed, Anglican (Episcopal), and Methodist traditions retain the classical rite of infant baptism and the traditional understanding of baptism as a *sacrament*—a visible means of grace. Their nonevangelical counterparts may emphasize the sufficiency of baptism for full insertion into authentic Christian life. Evangelical paedobaptists (infant baptizers) insist, however, that the baptized child, made a Christian by baptism, must later experience conversion. That may be at confirmation, or it may be by walking the aisle and "accepting Christ" in a revival-like church service. In any case, the evangelical paedobaptist interpretation is that baptized children have great advantages spiritually over nonbaptized children but must accept Jesus Christ by an act of repentance and faith at some point, often called the "age of accountability" or "awakening of conscience." An example is John Wesley, who along with the Church of England believed in baptismal regeneration of infants but who also believed all fall away from grace and into need of personal repentance and faith sometime later. He universalized this situation for all persons who live beyond childhood. Evangelicals of sacramentalist and paedobaptist traditions may express this differently, but they agree that baptism itself does not guarantee authentic Christian existence or salvation and that every person must have his or her own "personal encounter" with Jesus Christ in an experience of conversion.

Many evangelicals reject infant baptism in favor of believer baptism. For them, the only valid baptism is of persons already converted to Jesus Christ by conscious, free repentance and faith. Baptism, then, is an act of commitment (to discipleship of Christ) and a symbol of entrance into the body of Christ; it is not salvific but an "outward sign of an inward work." The "inward work" is *regeneration.* For these evangelicals, baptism is not a sacrament (in the traditional sense of means of grace) but an *ordinance*—a rite ordained by Christ for perpetual observance by the church until his return. The other ordinance is the *Lord's Supper.* (Some evangelicals add footwashing as a third ordinance.) Believer baptism is practiced by Anabaptists (e.g., Mennonites), Pentecostals, members of the Evangelical Free Church, the Churches of Christ and Independent Christian churches, and Baptists of all varieties. They defend their departure from the tradition of infant baptism by pointing to its absence from the New Testament and earliest churches after the New Testament. They also point to the great twentieth-century Swiss theologian Karl Barth, who defended believer baptism in *Church Dogmatics* IV/4 (Edinburgh: T. & T. Clark, 1969). Of course, evangelical paedobaptists defend their practice by pointing to circumcision for inclusion in the people of God (baptism replacing it in the church) and to Jesus' imperative to let children come to him "for of such is the *kingdom* of heaven." They also point to apparent household baptisms in the book of Acts.

For the most part, evangelicals, including theologians, have learned to coexist and even cooperate with one another in spite of profound differences over baptism, the Lord's Supper, church government, *predestination* and *free will*, and other controversial matters. A few denominations of evangelicals have even settled the controversy over baptism by including both practices. The Evangelical Covenant Church of America requires pastors (with some exceptions) to baptize either infants or believers; the parents decide whether to have their children baptized. Many Evangelical Free Church congregations and independent evangelical churches do not require baptism for membership. Some Baptist and Anabaptist congregations have begun accepting infant baptisms as valid for church membership. Evangelical theologians struggle with the drift toward marginalization of the sacraments within the vast evangelical network, which has a genericizing effect. Many of them seek ways to accommodate diverse points of view without discarding or neglecting baptism as the essential rite of initiation into Christian existence.

Donald Bridge and David Phypers, *The Water That Divides: The Baptism Debate* (Downers Grove, IL: InterVarsity Press, 1977); Paul S. Fiddes, ed., *Reflections on the Water: Understanding God and the World through the Baptism of Believers* (Macon, GA: Smyth & Helwys, 1996); Paul King Jewett, *Infant Baptism and the Covenant of Grace* (Grand Rapids: Wm. B. Eerdmans, 1978).

Baptism of the Holy Spirit   *see* Spirit Baptism

Bible/Scripture   Evangelical theology specializes in the doctrine of Scripture. Evangelicals revere the Bible as God's uniquely inspired and authoritative book; for them it is the supreme source and norm for Christian *faith* and practice. Some evangelicals insist that the Bible must be inerrant—without error in

the original autographs (the manuscripts written by the prophets and apostles who wrote the books of the Bible). All agree that it is in some sense infallible; there is no higher court of appeal for determining right doctrine and right living for Christian individuals and communities. It is infallible, evangelicals believe, because it is uniquely inspired by God (2 Timothy 3:16). Because it is inspired and infallible, it is authoritative and normative; as God's written Word it forms the unique, supreme source and norm for Christian belief. Many evangelicals, such as *Carl F. H. Henry* (the "dean of evangelical theologians"), regard modern nonevangelical theology's demotion of Scripture from that exalted status as the root of every other theological problem that plagues it. Evangelical theology, then, rests on a "Scripture principle" that requires every theological assertion that bears the label "Christian" to justify itself according to Scripture, which, to evangelicals, is the sixty-six inspired books of the Protestant canon and no more or less. Evangelicals have produced numerous volumes defending the canon of the Bible, the Bible's special, *supernatural inspiration*, its *infallibility*, and its *authority*. It is almost a requirement that an evangelical theologian write at least one book on the Bible. That has held true from *Benjamin Breckenridge Warfield's* Inspiration and Authority of the Bible (Phillipsburg, NJ: Presbyterian & Reformed, 1980) to Clark Pinnock's *The Scripture Principle* (San Francisco: HarperSanFrancisco, 1984). Evangelicals do not believe their Scripture principle is a recent discovery or invention; it is the foundation of Protestant orthodoxy itself. They believe that Luther, Calvin, and all the other Protestant Reformers held the same basic view of the role of Scripture—that it is supremely authoritative for Christian faith and practice.

Beyond that basic consensus about the Bible, evangelical theologians stake out varying positions regarding the Bible's nature, accuracy, and interpretation. One issue that has bedeviled evangelical theology and often caused great dissension and controversy in the ranks of the theologians is *inerrancy*. Is the Bible without error? Many evangelical theologians distinguish between "infallibility" and "inerrancy" and argue that Scripture can be and is inspired and authoritative for faith and practice, while being flawed in terms of accuracy of details in history and cosmology. Its *infallibility*, then, is functional—it does not fail to communicate truth about *God* needed for salvation and Christian living. Other evangelical theologians insist that inerrancy is necessarily implied by inspiration and infallibility. They argue that if Scripture is to be trustworthy at all, it must be inerrant in every detail. This debate took place between evangelical theologians Warfield and James Orr in the late nineteenth and early twentieth centuries; it was an ongoing disagreement about Scripture between theologians who agreed on most other points of doctrine. Warfield defended inerrancy, while Orr (a Scottish Presbyterian theologian who wrote against liberal theology) argued that Scripture can be and is inspired and authoritative without being inerrant.

The controversy erupted within evangelical theological ranks again in the 1970s with the original publication of Dewey Beegle's *Scripture, Tradition, and Infallibility* (Pryor Pettengill, 1988) (which was itself a revision of Beegle's earlier book *The Inspiration of Scripture*). Beegle attempted to demonstrate Orr's claim by showing that Scripture contains errors (e.g., contradictions) in history and cosmology that cannot reasonably be explained by appeal to mistakes of copyists. His motive was not to tear down faith in Scripture or its authority but to show that belief in the Bible's inspiration and authority does not depend on its strict inerrancy. This set off a furor among conservative evangelical thinkers that came to expression in Harold Lindsell's *The Battle for the Bible* (Grand Rapids: Zondervan) in 1976.

Lindsell argued that Scripture's authority depends on its strict, detailed, and technical inerrancy and that evangelical identity depends on that vision of the Bible's accuracy. Numerous articles and books poured forth on all sides of the issue in the late 1970s and throughout the 1980s. A summit meeting held in Chicago promulgated the Chicago Statement on Inerrancy, which tried to calm the troubled waters of evangelical theology by setting forth a reasonable definition of inerrancy. Many evangelical scholars felt that the statement killed inerrancy with the death of a thousand qualifications; others viewed it as a reasonable resolution to the debate.

By the 1990s a rough consensus was emerging among evangelical theologians that Scripture must be considered inerrant in some meaningful sense, but that its inerrancy must not be defined using modern, scientific standards of accuracy. Evangelical theologians as diverse as *Bernard Ramm, Clark Pinnock*, Millard Erickson, and Stanley Grenz all affirmed inerrancy, while noting that Scripture is not a scientific textbook or a book of cosmology; its accuracy is tied to its ancient context and to authorial intent. That is, the writers of Scripture were not attempting to give flawless performances in statistics, and the Bible contains much literature that is intended not to convey information but to provoke decision or describe God poetically. Inerrancy, then, became basically synonymous with infallibility, though many evangelical scholars continued to use the former term, even as they qualified it in many ways. It is safe to say that few, if any, evangelical theologians who describe Scripture as inerrant think even the original autographs were accurate by modern standards in matters of historical record or cosmological description. Nevertheless, even moderate and progressive evangelical thinkers are loath to reduce Scripture to being only "partially infallible" (i.e., only those parts pertaining to salvation) or merely spiritually and morally inspiring. Many evangelical theologians of the early twenty-first century refuse to describe Scripture as inerrant at all; in some circles the term *inerrancy* has become a political shibboleth emptied of serious theological content. So much confusion and controversy surrounds the word and the concept that many shy away from it entirely, while continuing to describe the Bible as God's uniquely inspired and authoritative book.

The concept of Scripture's inspiration is also a matter of some disagreement among evangelical theologians. Especially those who view the Bible as inerrant tend to interpret inspiration as extending to the very words of the original autographs. This is known among evangelicals as "plenary, verbal inspiration." In other words, all of Scripture is equally inspired, and inspiration is the quality of its words as being "God-breathed" (*theopneustos*). Evangelical scholars such as Millard Erickson strongly distinguish this from divine dictation—a view of Scripture held by some church fathers (e.g., Origen) but eschewed by nearly all evangelicals. According to Erickson and like-minded evangelical theologians, God guided the minds of the authors so that they chose the very words God wanted written, but the process left their personalities intact. Their conscious processes were not overridden by inspiration but put into its service. Other evangelical theologians, such as Clark Pinnock, prefer a dynamic view of inspiration in which God gave the authors of Scripture divine wisdom and guidance without directing them to exact words. Inspiration is a quality of the authors and not of the words. Advocates of dynamic inspiration insist that it does greater justice to the phenomena of Scripture than does verbal inspiration, which cannot account for the sometimes odd writing style of Paul, who left sentences unfinished and lashed out angrily at his opponents. All evangelicals use the analogy of *incarnation* for Scripture: just as Jesus Christ had two natures, so Scripture has two natures—divine and

human. (Of course this is only an illustrative analogy; no evangelical thinks the Bible is God incarnate!) Scripture is the product of both the Holy Spirit and human authors. The authors were more than mere secretaries of the Spirit, and their words or ideas are more than mere human expressions. A *perichoresis* (interpenetration) of divine wisdom and human expression appears in Scripture, with the divine aspect being dominant without displacing the human aspect.

Millard Erickson, *Christian Theology*, vol. 1 (Grand Rapids: Baker Book House, 1983); Clark Pinnock, *The Scripture Principle* (San Francisco: Harper & Row, 1984); Bernard Ramm, *Special Revelation and the Word of God* (Grand Rapids: Wm. B. Eerdmans Publishing Co., 1961); Jack B. Rogers and Donald K. McKim, *The Authority and Interpretation of the Bible: An Historical Approach*, with a new epilogue (Eugene, OR: Wipf & Stock Publishers, 1999).

Christology   Christology is belief about the person of *Jesus Christ*; it is also the study of the person of Jesus Christ or of doctrine about him. Evangelical Christianity is intensely Christ-centered; so it is natural that evangelical theologians have focused reflection on Jesus Christ. To a great extent, however, they have affirmed the early, ancient Christian consensus held also by the Protestant Reformers—that Jesus Christ is the *incarnation* of God the Son, the second person of the *Trinity*, one person who exists with two natures. This is the doctrine of the hypostatic union, affirmed by the Council of Chalcedon in AD 451 and enthusiastically reaffirmed and defended by two leading evangelical theologians: *Bernard Ramm* in *An Evangelical Christology—Ecumenic and Historic* (Vancouver, BC: Regent College Publications, 1993) (originally published 1985) and *Carl Henry* in *The Identity of Jesus of Nazareth* (Nashville: Broadman Press, 1992). Both Ramm and Henry found little to add to the doctrine of the hypostatic union; most of their reflections explored its ancient and contemporary meaning and defended it against revisionist Christologies, such as those offered by liberal theologians Norman Pittenger (*The Word Incarnate* [Digswell Place, UK: James Nisbet & Co., 1959]) and John A. T. Robinson (*The Human Face of God* [Philadelphia: Westminster Press, 1973]). The general consensus of evangelical theologians has been and remains the classical two-natures doctrine of the incarnation (which is affirmed by most of the major Protestant confessional statements such as the Westminster Confession of Faith) even though some evangelical thinkers have attempted to supplement it with other points of view. Only a few have challenged it as faulty.

One debate that continues about Christology within evangelical theological circles is over the so-called kenotic Christology. Kenotic Christology (based on the Greek word for "emptying," used in Philippians 2:7) suggests that the eternal Son of God divested himself of the knowledge and use of his attributes of glory in order to enter fully into human experience. Kenoticists affirm that while Jesus Christ was God incarnate, one divine person of two natures, he did not have complete awareness or use of such divine attributes as omniscience, omnipotence, and omnipresence, due to a voluntary self-limitation. This idea, first developed by German theologian Gottfried Thomasius of Erlangen in the eighteenth century, was elaborated further by British thinkers Charles Gore, H. R. Mackintosh, and P. T. Forsyth. Forsyth, an evangelical mediating theologian, softened the corners of kenotic Christology by asserting that the Son of God did not divest himself of any divine attributes, but only retracted them from activity to inactivity for the sake of true humanity in the incarnation. Kenoticists, including some evangelical theologians, agree that Jesus Christ is both truly human and truly divine, but that he did not depend on his divine nature for his sinless life and *miracles* but relied

entirely on his Father and the *Holy Spirit.*

Kenotic Christology—emphasizing the need to take with utmost seriousness Jesus' true *humanity*, including limited consciousness—has made significant inroads among evangelicals, while other evangelical theologians have resisted and criticized it. (Unfortunately its evangelical critics often misunderstand it as suggesting that Jesus was not fully and truly divine.) Canadian evangelical theologian Russell F. Aldwinckle relied on kenotic Christology in his 1976 response to liberal and especially process Christology entitled *More Than Man: A Study in Christology* (Grand Rapids: Wm. B. Eerdmans, 1976). Aldwinckle's successor *Clark Pinnock* has also employed the theme of kenosis in explicating the incarnation and Christology. Evangelical critics of kenotic Christology include *Donald Bloesch*, Millard Erickson, and Stanley Grenz. And yet, in most cases, the criticisms are aimed at an extreme form of kenotic Christology not representative of the milder forms espoused by Forsyth, Vincent Taylor, Aldwinckle, and other evangelical kenoticists, who do not claim that the Son of God renounced or gave up any attributes but only retracted his power and glory in order to grow in stature and wisdom and favor with God and humanity.

The debate over kenotic Christology continues in evangelical theology. As recently as the mid-1990s heresy charges were thrown by conservative evangelicals at more moderate and progressive ones who dared to use the kenotic motif in writing about the incarnation. Those evangelicals who reject kenosis (except as the servant existence of Jesus Christ) interpret Jesus Christ as possessing two consciousnesses—one human and one divine. This model of Christology is promoted and defended by evangelical philosopher Thomas V. Morris in *The Logic of God Incarnate* (Ithaca, NY: Cornell University Press, 1986). According to this model, Jesus Christ possessed two distinct minds or consciousnesses because he possessed two natures; he was able to "switch" between them at will. Evangelical kenoticists believe this implies Nestorianism—the heresy of a divided person of Jesus Christ.

Two evangelical theologians who have attempted to push the frontiers of Christology are Clark Pinnock and Stanley Grenz. Both affirm that Jesus Christ is truly God and truly human, but they are dissatisfied with the classical expression of that belief in Chalcedonian Christology (hypostatic union). They are not so much interested in rejecting it as in supplementing it with new and more helpful thought forms. People today, they argue, are not as tuned as ancient people were to the substance ontologies of Greek metaphysics, and the times call for a new expression of the doctrine of Jesus Christ's humanity and divinity. In *Flame of Love: A Theology of the Holy Spirit* (Downers Grove, IL: InterVarsity Press, 1996) Pinnock draws on the ancient Spirit Christology of the second-century church fathers and suggests that Jesus Christ be viewed not as the incarnation of the Spirit but as the man fully possessed ("filled") by the Spirit. He does not deny but affirms the incarnation of the Son of God in Jesus Christ; his use of Spirit Christology aims rather at emphasizing Jesus' reliance on the Holy Spirit for carrying out his divine mission. Jesus was, then, the fully and perfectly Spirit-filled and Spirit-empowered human person who led the way for the rest of human persons into Spirit-restored humanity in the image of God. This seems more of a supplementation rather than a revision of classical Christology.

Grenz argues in *Theology for the Community of God* (Grand Rapids: Wm. B. Eerdmans Publishing Co., 2000) that classical incarnational Christology falls short biblically and logically and revises it using the eschatological ontology (the future as the locus of being) of German theologian Wolfhart Pannenberg. According to Grenz, Jesus Christ is the Logos, who is not to be thought of as preexisting and then "descending" into

human history but as revealing God and therefore belonging to the eternity of God by virtue of his *resurrection*. This Christology emphasizes Christ's unity with God rather than the incarnation of the Son of God into humanity. Jesus did not "become God," as in adoptionism, but he is one with God because of what happened with him in history. He belongs to the future, where God resides as the power determining the past and present, and therefore he belongs to the triune being of God as the second person of the Trinity. The main difference between this Christology and classical Christology lies in its denial of a *logos asarkos*—discarnate or preincarnate Logos or Son of God. For Grenz, Jesus Christ *is* the Logos, the second person of the Trinity. Whatever tensions or problems may exist in Pinnock's and Grenz's Christology, they are not so much revisions of the hypostatic union as restatements of that basic christological vision in new terms.

Donald G. Bloesch, *Jesus Christ: Savior and Lord* (Downers Grove, IL: InterVarsity Press, 1997); Donald G. Dawe, *The Form of a Servant: A Historical Analysis of the Kenotic Motif* (Philadelphia: Westminster Press, 1963); David F. Wells, *The Person of Christ: A Biblical and Historical Analysis of the Incarnation* (Westchester, IL: Crossway, 1984).

Church   The evangelical movement consists of Protestant Christians of many different denominational backgrounds. Evangelical ecclesiology (doctrine of the church) is extremely diverse; little consensus exists among evangelical theologians about the government of the church, *worship*, or the *sacraments*. The vast majority of evangelical thinkers come from and work within particular ecclesiological traditions and often defend them against a late twentieth-century and early twenty-first-century trend toward a generic evangelical model of the church. That is, the evangelical movement experienced and is experiencing a swift but little-noticed drift toward a generic doctrine and practice of the church based on the independent, community-church model; many evangelical churches are entrepreneurial rather than rooted in tradition or accountable within denominational structures. The "megachurch movement" and the "church growth movement" have both contributed to this trend, as have the numerous contacts between evangelical leaders within parachurch organizations and events.

Evangelical theologians tend to resist this trend and emphasize the theological nature of the church, including its ties to particular traditions. Most often evangelical theologians do this within a particular ecclesiological perspective rather than a general evangelical one; this gives rise to tremendous diversity about the nature and character of the church within evangelical theology. Reformed evangelical thinkers describe the church in Reformed and Presbyterian terms as free congregations tied by *covenant* bonds of heritage and accountability to each other within a relatively loose hierarchical structure. They stress the office of elder while playing down the offices of deacon and bishop. Episcopal evangelicals stress the hierarchical structure of the church and its catholicity (ideal unity with the universal church throughout time and space) and support the historical episcopate of apostolic succession of bishops. Baptist and other free-church evangelicals emphasize the autonomy of the local congregation, which is the locus of the church (as opposed to transcongregational universal church), as they also affirm the voluntary nature of church membership, which is for believers only. Many Pentecostals and charismatics follow a new model of the church that harks back to the fivefold office of church leadership in the New Testament: pastors, teachers, apostles, prophets, and elders. They also tend to support the radical independence of local congregations led by prophets or pastor-teachers and not accountable to anyone outside themselves.

All evangelical theologians agree that the church (however more precisely defined and described) is the primary locus of spiritual *experience*, growth, and discipleship and that the marks of the true church are unity, apostolicity, catholicity, and *holiness* (as stated in the Apostles' Creed). Many agree with Swiss theologian Emil Brunner that beneath these marks the essence of the church is fellowship rather than institution. Institutional form exists for the sake of fellowship, and fellowship exists for the sake of the glory of *God* and the spiritual edification of the individual Christian within community edification. The church exists to carry forth the presence of *Jesus Christ* in the world and accomplish his *kingdom* task and mission there. The outer form of the church, then, is its structure, which may be somewhat flexible. Some high-church and confessing evangelicals of the Episcopal and Reformed-Presbyterian traditions, however, react against this emphasis on fellowship and mission in favor of a greater stress on the church's visible and institutional unity around bishops and/or doctrinal, confessional purity.

It is possible to identify four major models of the church in evangelical theology. The first is the traditional free church model; evangelical Baptists and Anabaptists such as Stanley Grenz and James McClendon explicate this model within a late modern and postmodern cultural context. The second is the traditional Reformed and Presbyterian model; conservative confessing evangelicals in the Calvinist traditions, such as Michael Horton and David Wells, promote this model. The third model is the hierarchical and episcopal model defended by evangelicals "on the Canterbury Trail," such as Robert Webber, who has influenced a generation of evangelicals in favor of this traditional model. The fourth model is the radical, entrepreneurial, and independent model espoused by many Pentecostals, charismatics, and fundamentalists. This model finds very little theological support, and is developed and lived primarily by evangelists and independent pastors, whose influence through the church growth, megachurch, and *charismatic movements* is spreading throughout Evangelicalism. This gives rise to a backlash by evangelical theologians who turn to new forms of the first three traditional ecclesiological models in order to limit the influence of the fourth one.

The first model—espoused and developed in different ways by Grenz and McClendon—focuses ecclesiological reflection on the voluntary nature of church membership and participation and on the priesthood of believers within Christian community. McClendon calls this the "baptist" (with a small "b") model of the church and sees it as rooted in the Anabaptist vision of the Radical Reformation and consistent with the postmodern emphasis on individual identity forged in community. For him, as well as for Grenz, the apostolicity of the church resides in its embodiment within community of the New Testament *gospel* proclaimed by the apostles, rather than in a historical episcopacy or formal, visible ties with the ancient, ecumenical church. The second model—explicated and defended in various ways by Horton and Wells—emphasizes doctrinal confession (creeds and confessions of faith) and discipline as the essence of the church; the true church exists when and where correct doctrine is taught—the ancient, ecumenical creeds and appropriate Reformation confessions are affirmed by the people—and where the sacraments are rightly administered in a disciplined manner. These evangelical thinkers challenge the doctrinal drift and informal, "easy-believism" and experientialism of much of the contemporary evangelical movement. Robert Webber argues for the third model, which emphasizes the unity of the church around historical, hierarchical leadership and liturgy. Its catholicity is especially important, which leads some evangelical theologians into a greater appreciation for the authority of the

church fathers and identification with churches under the *authority* of bishops in apostolic succession. No evangelical theologians embrace the fourth model; it is anathema to most of them. Even most Pentecostal theologians prefer the first, traditional model (perhaps as amended and updated by Grenz and McClendon) to the entrepreneurial model, in which an individual or very small group owns the church much as a business person establishes and owns his or her own business enterprise. And yet that fourth model has quickly become accepted in many sectors of Evangelicalism in the the late twentieth and early twenty-first centuries.

Veli-Matti Kärkkäinen, *An Introduction to Ecclesiology: Ecumenical, Historical, and Global Perspectives* (Downers Grove, IL: InterVarsity Press, 2002); James Wm. McClendon Jr., *Doctrine: Systematic Theology II* (Nashville: Abingdon Press, 1994); Dale Moody, *The Word of Truth: A Summary of Christian Doctrine Based on Biblical Revelation* (Grand Rapids: Wm. B. Eerdmans, 1981); Robert Webber, *Evangelicals on the Canterbury Trail: Why Evangelicals Are Attracted to the Liturgical Church* (Harrisburg, PA: Morehouse Publishing, 1989); David F. Wells, *No Place for Truth, Or Whatever Happened to Evangelical Theology?* (Grand Rapids: Wm. B. Eerdmans, 1993).

Conversion   Evangelicals are noted for their emphasis on *salvation,* and especially the initiating event of salvation—conversion. The appeal of evangelists, "You must be born again," is closely associated with the evangelical movement, as are slogans and phrases such as "I found it!" and "the four spiritual laws" that play up the need for personal *repentance* and *faith.* If the evangelical movement is about anything, it is about the call to conversion to Christ. The best-known example of this to the modern mind is evangelist *Billy Graham's* mass appeal and the responses of thousands who stream forward at his evangelistic crusades to "receive Christ as their personal Savior." Evangelical theologians have devoted much reflection to the subject of salvation, and conversion is salvation's initial or crucial event. It is the event—evangelical theologians agree—in which an individual responds to the call of *God* with repentance and faith and receives from God *regeneration* (being "born again") and *justification* (*forgiveness* and declaration of righteousness). Not all Protestant theologians describe conversion in precisely that way, but evangelicals do.

For evangelicals, conversion to Christ may be part of a process, but it is not identical with *baptism*, nor is it merely turning over a new leaf. It is a transforming work of God in which a person receives the gift of the *Holy Spirit* and becomes a new creation in Christ Jesus; the old life devoted to *sin* and under condemnation begins to pass away and the new life of *reconciliation* with God and release from the power of sin begins. This all happens as soon as one repents, asks God for forgiveness, and trusts in *Jesus Christ* alone for salvation. This is how evangelicals read the New Testament. This is largely what makes them evangelicals, distinct from so-called mainline Protestants, who by and large adopt either belief in salvation through *sacraments* or Horace Bushnell's "Christian nurture" model of salvation by being born and raised in a Christian *church* and family (i.e., salvation by Christian education). Without eschewing sacraments or Christian education, evangelicals insist that authentic Christian life comes into existence through personal conversion, even if that is the culmination of a process that begins with infant baptism and/or Christian nurture.

This evangelical idea of conversion as an *experience* not identical with baptism or confirmation of baptism can be traced back to the Anabaptists of the sixteenth century, who rejected baptismal regeneration and belief in salvation by *covenant* inclusion in the collective people of God and proclaimed a gospel of repentance

and faith—even for those who were already baptized Christians. Balthasar Hubmaier and Menno Simons both wrote about the necessity of conversion through repentance; they insisted that in order to become a Christian in the full sense, one had to acknowledge that one is a wretched sinner and guilty and begin to make "amendment of life" through faith in Christ and faithfulness to his teachings. Later, the continental Pietists and the English Puritans also stressed personal conversion as necessary for salvation. During the Great Awakening of the 1730s and 1740s, preachers like John Wesley, George Whitefield, and Jonathan Edwards called for conversion on the part of people already within the church as well as by those outside it. Much to the dismay of many of his Anglican colleagues in ministry, Wesley preached the necessity of a radical conversion *experience* by the *grace* of God through personal repentance and faith, even on the parts of persons—like himself—who were rightly baptized, raised within the church, and even ordained to priesthood. The Great Awakening gave birth to the modern evangelical movement with its hallmark of the call to conversion. *Revivalism* continued to sustain the evangelical movement through the ministries of great evangelical preachers such as *Charles Finney*, Dwight L. Moody, Billy Sunday, Aimee Semple McPherson, and Billy Graham.

Although evangelicals agree that conversion is necessary for authentic Christian existence, theologians explain it in different ways. Some of the deepest divisions among evangelical theologians relate to the so-called *ordo salutis* or "order of salvation." What is the relationship between conversion (including regeneration and justification) and other aspects of the process of full salvation? What does God do, and what does the human person do? How is baptism related to conversion, and is conversion a momentary event or a process? These and other questions receive different answers from evangelical theologians. One group views conversion as primarily a work of God (monergism), while another group sees it as the human person's response to God's call, enabled by grace (synergism). Both groups of evangelical thinkers affirm that conversion is both God's work and the human person's work, but they lay the emphasis on different aspects. Reformed evangelical theologian Anthony Hoekema argued that conversion—repentance and faith—is what human persons do in response to regeneration by the Holy Spirit. In true Calvinist fashion he placed regeneration—the Spirit's transformation of the individual including freedom from bondage of the will to sin—prior to repentance and faith; only persons born again by the Spirit of God can repent and trust in Christ. Only the elect (those predestined by God for salvation) are regenerated, and they are regenerated irresistibly by grace. Yet, also in true Calvinist fashion, Hoekema (with other Reformed evangelicals) affirmed that conversion is also a work of God; God causes conversion to happen. Finally, still in true Calvinist fashion, he said that conversion is also the work of the human person. Conversion is a paradox of grace as expressed in Philippians 2:12. However, Hoekema and other Reformed evangelical theologians emphasized the efficacy of the work of grace in conversion.

Arminian (including Wesleyan) and Anabaptist evangelicals are synergists; they point up the work of the human person in conversion, without neglecting the priority of grace. *Thomas Oden,* an Arminian-Wesleyan evangelical theologian, views conversion also as a work of God's grace and human response, but in typical Arminian fashion he places the emphasis on the free human response; repentance and faith are what humans do in response to God's calling, convicting, and enabling grace. But that grace is resistible. Therefore, the human response is crucial and determinative. Grace is not effectual but enabling; only

with free human consent does it become effectual. Thus, for Arminian evangelicals (including Oden), regeneration does not precede repentance and faith; it follows from them. Those who respond to the prevenient grace of God with repentance and faith are regenerated and justifed simultaneously. *Sanctification* follows conversion in both evangelical accounts.

Other differences of opinion exist about conversion among evangelical thinkers. Some view conversion as a process that begins with infant baptism. (In adults who have not been baptized, the rite of baptism follows conversion.) For most Reformed evangelicals, baptism initiates a child into the covenant between God and the church; it parallels the rite of circumcision in the covenant between God and Israel. Conversion is the fulfillment of baptism with personal repentance and faith and may be identified with confirmation, although in truly evangelical Reformed communities confirmation would then not be routinized; its personal nature would be emphasized. Revivalist evangelicals tend to regard conversion not as the culmination of a process but as a radical turning from sin and condemnation to new life in Jesus Christ. Children are viewed as innocent, or as persons to whom the guilt of *sin* is not imputed by God for Christ's sake, until they reach the "age of accountability" and sin willfully and presumptuously. Then they require repentance. In the revivalist tradition of evangelical thought, conversion is more experiential than progressive. In spite of these differences of opinion, all evangelical theologians embrace conversion as necessary for full, authentic Christian initiation.

Anthony A. Hoekema, *Saved by Grace* (Grand Rapids: Wm. B. Eerdmans, 1989); Thomas C. Oden, *The Transforming Power of Grace* (Nashville: Abingdon Press, 1993); Peter Toon, *Justification and Sanctification* (Westchester, IL: Crossway Books, 1983); David E. Wells, *The Search for Salva-*

tion (Downers Grove, IL: InterVarsity Press, 1978).

Covenant   Biblical *theology* has long recognized the importance of the covenant theme for hermeneutics; throughout the Old Testament *God* enters into covenants or contracts with individuals such as Abraham and with communities such as Israel. Christian theology has traditionally regarded God's redemption of humanity through Christ the fulfillment of a covenant of *grace*. Evangelical biblical scholars and theologians traditionally draw heavily on this covenant theme to explain the flow of the biblical history or drama of *redemption*. The story of God's interaction with *humanity* beginning with Adam is the story of covenant relationships initiated by God, established according to God's will and conditions, and entered into by human beings. The early church father Irenaeus of Lyons made use of covenant imagery in his theory of *salvation* as recapitulation, and medieval scholastic theologians incorporated covenant concepts into their speculative accounts of salvation.

Evangelical theology, however, has been most heavily influenced by a strain of covenant theology sometimes also known as federal theology, developed in the sixteenth century on the basis of the Reformed Protestant thinkers Zwingli, Bullinger, Calvin, and Beza. They and other Reformed (i.e., non-Lutheran) Protestants made use of the covenant theme to express God's sovereignty and human responsibility in salvation. Most non-Lutheran evangelical theologians are influenced by that Reformed approach to biblical theology, hermeneutics, and soteriology (doctrine of salvation); for them covenant best expresses the divine-human relationship in history in its beginning, development, and consummation. God approaches human persons with offered contracts or covenants that entail rights and responsibilities; God alone sets the conditions of

these covenants and invites humans into them. Covenants imply a voluntary self-binding of God in relation to humans; God is obligated to bless those who keep the conditions of the covenant and judge those who violate them. God's human partners in the covenant relationship are also obligated to obey the conditions of the covenant such as keeping the *law* or repenting and trusting in the provided Redeemer (*Jesus Christ*) alone for righteousness. Jesus Christ is viewed by most evangelical covenant theologians as the perfect covenant-keeper (and more), whose active and passive obedience to the law is imputed as righteousness to those who through the covenant of grace embrace him by *repentance* and *faith*.

While some Arminian evangelical theologians make use of covenant theology and even elements of the federal theology closely connected with it, for the most part evangelical covenant and federal theologians work within the Reformed and Presbyterian traditions. For some of the latter, "covenant" is the central theme of Reformed theology. (Here "Reformed" will be used to include classical, conservative Presbyterian theology.) If one looks at all the churches of the World Alliance of Reformed Churches, the one thing they all have in common (beyond historical-theological connection with the Swiss Reformers mentioned above) is some form of covenant/federal theology (even if that is muted in the more liberalized denominations). Evangelical covenant/federal theology looks back especially to the authors of the Heidelberg Catechism—a major Reformed document—Zacharius Ursinus and Caspar Olevianus, who posited covenants of law and grace (or *gospel*) in redemption history. Later Reformed theologians such as Hermann Witsius and Johannes Cocceius developed this perspective on the unity of the drama of redemption further, as did the Puritan divines such as William Perkins, Thomas Cartwright, and Thomas Hooker. In more recent times Presbyterian and Reformed theologians

Charles Hodge and Louis Berkhof fine-tuned the theory for nineteenth- and twentieth-century Reformed evangelicals in North America. Contemporary evangelical covenant/federal theology is promoted and debated especially by theologians closely associated with Westminster Theological Seminary, such as John Murray, Meredith Kline, and Michael Horton. While there is no unanimity among covenant/federal theology's thinkers—past or present—certain constant themes unite them as a relatively cohesive movement, in contrast to other evangelical theologians of the Arminian, revivalist, Pentecostal and *Holiness* traditions (who may occasionally make some use of covenant theology but do not adopt federal theology as the ruling hermeneutical tool for explicating biblical history and theology).

Covenant/federal theologians read *Scripture* and view salvation history as organized around two covenants between God and humanity—the covenants of law and grace. Some theologians affirm a third covenant between God the Father and God the Son, who became incarnate as Jesus Christ. However, the essence of covenant/federal theology lies in the idea that God established a covenant with Adam, the first human, progenitor and "federal head" of the human race, such that God would bless him and his posterity if he perfectly obeyed God's law. This is the covenant of law. When Adam failed, God justly (according to the covenant) imputed his guilt to all of humanity, such that they deserve eternal death. However, without abrogating the law covenant (which always remains in effect), God mercifully offered fallen humans a new covenant, the covenant of grace. According to the new covenant, everyone who repents and has faith in God's promise of a Savior and who (after Christ's death and *resurrection*) believes in Jesus Christ will have Christ rather than Adam as his or her new federal head. The active and passive obedience of Jesus Christ (his sinless life and atoning death) is then imputed as righ-

teousness to those who enter into the new covenant by faith alone; they are then united with Christ, given new birth from the *Holy Spirit* (regenerated), and justified by God the Father. All of this in spite of the fact that they are lawbreakers, disobedient to the covenant of law and worthy of eternal damnation. Instead of condemnation, through the new covenant they receive eternal life and blessing from God, because of the benefits of Christ's life and death imputed to them. They are nevertheless still obliged to obey the law of God given to Adam and then renewed through Moses. That they cannot and do not have to (because of the new covenant) is the gospel, which does not abolish the law but only the condemnation it causes because of disobedience.

Reformed theologians regard covenants as both conditional and absolute (unconditional). That is, they are absolute in that God creates them and offers them to human beings. Their conditions are unconditional, so far as human participants are concerned. They are also absolute, in that God foreordains and decrees which groups of people and even which individuals will keep them (unconditional *election*). They are conditional, in that human persons are responsible freely to enter into them and keep the obligations they impose. Reformed theologians admit that a paradox lies at the heart of covenant/federal theology as it is explicated by the Puritans and their contemporary theological heirs. Some non-Calvinist and revisionist Calvinist covenant/federal theologians have attempted to relieve the paradox by interpreting the keeping of covenants by humans as conditional and not absolute. Puritan divines Richard Baxter and John Goodwin were Arminian federal theologians; Hendrikus Berkhof is an example of a revisionist Calvinist theologian who also interprets the covenants as conditional without rejecting the sovereignty of God. However, among evangelical theologians covenant/federal theology is viewed as the special province of relatively strict followers of the Puritan and Presbyterian divines of, for example, the Westminster Confession of Faith and the Westminster Shorter and Longer Catechisms, which enshrined this hermeneutic confessionally.

Louis Berkhof, *Systematic Theology* (Grand Rapids: Wm. B. Eerdmans, 1996); Michael Horton, *Covenant and Eschatology: The Divine Drama* (Louisville, KY: Westminster John Knox Press, 2002); John Murray, *Redemption Accomplished and Applied* (Grand Rapids: Wm. B. Eerdmans, 1984).

Creation   Evangelical theology agrees enthusiastically with the traditional Christian beliefs about creation: *God* created the universe (all that exists outside of God) ex nihilo (out of nothing); creation is good, but not God (or made of divine substance); creation is fallen under a curse due to the rebellion of sentient, moral creatures (*angels* and humans). These ideas may seem antiquated by modern liberal theological standards, but evangelicals affirm them as biblical and orthodox. In this they stand in agreement with the early church fathers, medieval theologians, Reformers, and Protestant orthodox thinkers. In contrast to much folk religion (even among evangelicals), evangelical theologians also affirm with the classical Christian tradition that creation is benefit. That is, creation is an act of God's love and *grace* that came into existence by God's power and *providence* with purpose—to glorify God and bestow blessings on creatures. Evangelical theologians reject any entanglement of creation with God or vice versa (panentheism), as they also reject any separation between God and creation; creation is neither a prison of God nor a godless reality. These beliefs about creation comprise a surprising consensus across the board among evangelical thinkers. They are loath to give up any of these ideas, as they form the backbone, as it were, of the classical Christian worldview.

Any compromise of them tends to lead toward some heresy, such as deism, pantheism, or panentheism. All evangelical theologians endorse this classical Christian doctrine of creation.

Devilish diversity appears in the details of the doctrine of creation, however. Evangelicals fall into significant diversity and sometimes conflict with regard to working out the details of the classical Christian doctrine of creation; occasionally the conflict has divided evangelicals from each other. While all evangelicals view creation as purposeful, they do not agree about the main purpose of God in creation. Heirs of eighteenth-century Puritan theologian and preacher Jonathan Edwards agree with him that "The End for Which God Created the World" is God's own glory. The created cosmos came into existence and is sustained by God in order to manifest his attributes for his own good pleasure. Following Calvin, these Reformed evangelical thinkers view the universe as the "theater of God's glory" that reveals his majesty to those with minds and hearts regenerated by the *Holy Spirit*. One conservative Reformed evangelical thinker who promotes this idea of the purpose of creation is apologist-theologian R. C. Sproul, whose many books presuppose and often promote Edwards's idea of creation as manifestation of divine glory. Other evangelical theologians prefer the creation purpose proposed by Karl Barth and Jürgen Moltmann—two of the most influential and prolific twentieth-century Protestant thinkers: according to them, the purpose of creation is *covenant* and love. That is, creation came into existence by God's grace and power as the expression of God's inner-Trinitarian love between Father, Son, and Holy Spirit. It exists to manifest God's love and to bestow blessings on human creatures made in God's own image and called by God into covenant relationship. Progressive evangelical thinker *Clark Pinnock* prefers this idea of creation, as do many evangelical theologians, especially of the Arminian-Wesleyan tradition. Both groups of evangelical scholars agree that creation is absolutely free on God's part; there was no necessity imposed on God from within or from outside to create the universe.

Another area of disagreement among evangelical thinkers with regard to creation has to do with the thorny problems of the universe's age and the evolutionary development of life forms, that is, with reconciling the Genesis accounts of creation (especially chapters 1 through 3) with modern sciences. Most evangelical theologians and preachers of the eighteenth and early nineteenth centuries agreed roughly with Irish Archbishop James Ussher's chronology of creation, which declared the year of creation as 4004 BC. This was based on a literal interpretation of the chronologies of Genesis. Some conservative evangelical apologists and theologians reacted negatively to claims of the greater antiquity of the earth made by geologists in the first half and middle of the nineteenth century. They were even more offended by Charles Darwin's suggestions about the *evolution* of life forms on earth over great ages of time through a mechanism known as natural selection. Conservative Princeton Theological Seminary theologian Charles Hodge rejected Darwin's ideas about biological development and preferred the traditional belief in creation of human beings de novo relatively recently. He argued vociferously for the literal, historical existence of Adam and Eve in an earthly paradise (Eden) only a few thousand years before Christ. Conservative evangelical apologist *Francis Schaeffer* picked up Hodge's reactionary view toward scientific revisions of traditional Christian beliefs about creation chronology and argued for *Genesis in Space and Time* (Downers Grove, IL: InterVarsity Press, 1972) by which he meant a literal Adam and Eve, a literal garden of Eden, and so on.

Fundamentalist evangelicals elevated the battle against "godless evolution" (Darwinism and later neo-Darwinism)

to the status of a Christian ideological crusade and broke fellowship with Christians (including evangelicals) who compromised with the newer views of creation brought about by modern science. Such "scientific creationists" follow the teachings of ultraconservative evangelical engineer and apologist Henry Morris, whose anti-evolutionary writings explain the evidence of the antiquity of the earth by appeal to a catastrophic flood (viz., Noah's flood). According to most fundamentalist evangelicals, God created the universe about ten thousand years ago in a literal week of twenty-four-hour days; all biological species came from the hand of God, and none developed through natural selection or anything like it. The propaganda produced by the scientific creationists has flooded the popular evangelical market via radio programs, Bible institutes, seminars, and books, so that both evangelical lay people and nonevangelicals tend to identify that view as evangelical orthodoxy.

In fact, however, the vast majority of evangelical scholars and theologians reject young-earth creationism and seek a more moderate approach to reconciling Genesis with science. All evangelicals reject sheer naturalistic Darwinism, of course, but some view the Genesis creation accounts as saga (nonliteral expressions of events that took place in space and time), and others view them as poetry or liturgical literature. Few take them entirely literally. Many want to incorporate belief in a real, historical progenitor couple (Adam and Eve) into a scientifically informed interpretation of Genesis so that they were prehominid animals into whom God breathed the breath of life so that they became living beings in God's image with souls.

One of the most popular theories of creation among evangelical theologians is progressive *creationism*—a very broad view and possibly more of a family of views than one solid belief about creation. A major promoter of this approach to reconciling Genesis with science was evangelical theologian **Bernard Ramm,** whose book *The Christian View of Science and Scripture* (Grand Rapids: Wm. B. Eerdmans, 1954) remains a classic of evangelical literature into the twenty-first century. According to Ramm and other progressive creationists, God created the universe aeons before Christ (geology and not the Bible sets the date of creation) but worked through gradual processes to bring about life forms on it. Progressive creationists interpret the "days" of creation as ages of time; allow for some element of evolutionary development of species; reject natural selection as the entire explanation for the emergence of biological life forms; and regard God as the one who occasionally "steps into" the immanent processes of emergence to produce entirely new forms of life such as human beings. Most progressive creationists accept the idea that humans evolved biologically, while rejecting reductionism of human persons to evolved biological organisms. They believe in a supernatural act of God in giving humans souls and the *image of God*. Progressive creationists can point back to conservative evangelical thinker **Benjamin Warfield,** who, after Charles Hodge and in the same seminary, argued for a reconciliation of Darwin's evolutionary theory with the Bible and traditional Christian belief. Warfield was without doubt one of the most stalwart and astute defenders of the *inerrancy* of the *Bible*.

Very few evangelical theologians adopt theistic evolution, but some evangelical scientists have defended it as a viable option for evangelical interpretation of Genesis and creation. A controversy erupted at evangelical Calvin College in the 1980s when Calvin science professor Howard Van Til defended theistic evolution. The American Scientific Affiliation—which requires members to hold doctorates in science and confess biblical inerrancy—came to Van Til's defense, as did a number of moderate and progressive evangelical theologians. Theistic evolution—belief that humans and all life forms evolved through natural selection guided by God—is a minority view among evangelical theologians, but few consider it heretical unless it denies any element of *supernatural* involvement by God in the creation process or reduces human persons to biological organisms. The debate about origins continues within evangelical circles into the twenty-first century.

Many evangelical apologists are attracted to nontheological evidences and arguments against naturalism, including neo-Darwinian evolutionary theory. Evangelical law professor Philip Johnson's books arguing against naturalism and naturalistic evolution on evidentialist ground are extremely popular among evangelical students, pastors, and some theologians. A movement to promote belief in "intelligent design theory," based on scientific and mathematical probabilities against naturalism, is gaining popularity among evangelicals. The best-known evangelical thinker associated with that movement is William Dembski. Theologians tend to view these projects as helpful but not crucial in the development and defense of a biblical and orthodox doctrine of creation.

David A. S. Ferguson, *The Cosmos and the Creator: An Introduction to the Theology of Creation* (London: SPCK, 1998); James M. Houston, *I Believe in the Creator* (Downers Grove, IL: InterVarsity Press, 1980); David N. Livingstone, *Darwin's Forgotten Defenders: The Encounter between Evangelical Theology and Evolutionary Thought* (Vancouver, BC: Regent College Publishers, 1984).

Demons *see* **Satan/Devil/Demons**

Devil *see* **Satan/Devil/Demons**

Election/Predestination Because the terms are biblical concepts, all evangelical theologians embrace and use *election* and *predestination*. *Election* is especially used by the apostle Paul in, for example, Ephesians 1. *Predestination* is used, among other places, in Romans 8. In concert with Protestant *theology* in general, evangelical theology holds that *God* is sovereign in *salvation*; God chooses to save and initiates salvation. *Election* is the term usually used by evangelical theologians to describe God's initiative and special calling with regard to those who are to be saved. *Predestination* is the term usually used for God's foreknowledge and/or foreordination of individuals to either salvation or damnation. *Predestination* and *foreordination* are synonyms in Reformed evangelical theology; *predestination* and *foreknowledge* are synonyms in Arminian evangelical theology. In both cases God is the superior partner in the *covenant* relationship with those who are saved. Evangelical theologians believe that God elects himself to be the Savior of the world in *Jesus Christ* and chooses to have a people for his name in covenant relationship. Israel and the church are God's elect peoples; they are chosen by God in his sovereignty, *grace,* and mercy. Evangelical theologians also believe that God predestines individuals to be in the covenant through *repentance* and *faith* or to be condemned for all eternity due to unbelief. All of that is to say that, for evangelical theology in general, God is the sovereign one who alone enables salvation; if anyone is saved, it is because God sovereignly made that possible and provided everything necessary for it to be the case.

This consensus contradicts both ancient and modern Pelagianism and semi-Pelagianism, both of which undermine God's sovereignty in salvation and imply that salvation is at least in part a human achievement. Pelagianism follows a fourth- and fifth-century British monk and opponent of Augustine, Pelagius, who insisted that humans are not depraved but fully able to obey God's *law* without *supernatural,* assisting grace. Pelagianism was condemned by the third ecumenical council at Eph-

esus in 431, and all evangelical theologians second that condemnation. Semi-Pelagianism follows certain post-Augustinian theologians (the Massilians) who averred that while salvation is God's work, humans can initiate the process. The Western second synod of Orange in 529 condemned that, and evangelical thinkers agree that God alone initiates and makes possible salvation by his grace. Election and predestination are the positive, biblical expressions of the antithesis of Pelagianism and semi-Pelagianism in theology; salvation is entirely God's work and achievement to which human persons can add nothing.

In spite of profound agreement about the basic meanings of election and predestination as expressions of God's sovereignty in salvation, evangelical theologians fall into sharp disagreement with each other over their precise interpretations. The situation is the same in the early twenty-first century as it was in the middle of the eighteenth century, when the evangelical movement was being forged in the fires of the Great Awakening, and John Wesley and George Whitefield went their separate ways over different interpretations of election and predestination. Evangelicals still find it difficult to cooperate and have full fellowship due to the same differing interpretations. It is possible to identify three distinct approaches to election among evangelical thinkers. The first one is the classical Calvinist approach, sometimes called "sovereign grace" theology by its advocates, whose theological hero is Jonathan Edwards. This was also Whitefield's approach. The second one is the classical Arminian approach as taught by John Wesley and his heirs. The third approach is one that appeals to paradox and combines elements of the first two theological interpretations of election and predestination.

Classical Reformed (Calvinist) evangelicals define election and predestination as unconditional decrees of God that effactually result in saving grace or reprobation in the lives of individual human persons apart from any genuinely free choices they make. Their choices (especially with regard to salvation) are determined by God, who bends their wills so that their decisions and actions conform to the foreordained plan and purpose of God. These evangelicals, including Charles Hodge, *Benjamin Warfield*, *J. Gresham Machen*, *Francis Schaeffer*, R. C. Sproul, James Montgomery Boice, and John Piper, flatly reject human *free will* as ability to thwart the will of God; God takes no risks and assures by his sovereign power that certain individuals will be included in the covenant people of God and others will be included in the mass of perdition to everlasting damnation in *hell*. All this is for God's glory, even though it may be impossible for mortals to perceive how the damnation of a significant portion of *humanity* glorifies God. These evangelicals believe that any other account of election and predestination undermines God's glory as the sovereign one and detracts from the sheer graciousness of salvation. If persons can truly resist the grace of God, then those who do not resist can boast, in which case salvation would not be sheer gift. These evangelicals have a tendency to cast aspersions at their non-Calvinist colleagues in the evangelical theological community, frequently labeling them semi-Pelagians.

The second approach defines election corporately; God sovereignly chooses to have a people for his name, and he works to save them. Predestination is simply God's foreknowledge of people's free choices with regard to salvation. This is the classical Arminian account of these doctrines. (Jacob Arminius was a seventeenth-century Dutch theologian who affirmed human free will and ability to cooperate with saving grace, against the prevailing *Calvinism* of Holland in his day.) Arminian evangelicals begin with God's universal love for humanity as their first principle and interpret election and predestination in light of that. They do not begin with humanity and freedom, as some Calvin-

ist evangelicals allege. For Arminians, God's love is simply incompatible with unconditional election or irresistible grace within a nonuniversalist scheme. In other words, so long as hell is in the picture, as it is for the vast majority of evangelicals, for God to select some fallen persons to everlasting punishment, apart from any free choices they make, is inconsistent with any account of love, including God's. To avoid impugning God's character, then, Arminian evangelicals interpret election and predestination as conditional and grace as resistible. This is the interpretation held by a significant portion of evangelical thinkers, including *Thomas Oden*, *Clark Pinnock*, Dale Moody, Fisher Humphreys, Jonathan Wilson, and Roger Olson. They avoid semi-Pelagianism by affirming human depravity as helplessness apart from supernatural, assisting grace (prevenient grace) and the divine initiative in salvation. Grace always convicts, calls, enlightens, and enables sinners before they repent and believe. There is a sense, then, in which God regenerates the will of the fallen person before he or she converts, but *conversion* is his or her work enabled by God. This is, of course, what offends Reformed evangelicals who believe that any truly contingent role of the human person in salvation makes salvation a work and not a gift.

The third approach arises because many evangelicals are unable to accept either of the first two interpretations of election and predestination. Proponents of the third approach refer to the "paradox of grace" and affirm that salvation is both a sheer gift and a free human response, without attempting speculatively (as they put it) to smooth out the tensions. J. I. Packer is one of the best-known and most influential supporters and promoters of this third way. He appeals to "antinomy" to resolve the problem; God is absolutely sovereign in salvation through election and predestination, but humans also have the ability from God freely to accept or reject offered salvation. *Donald Bloesch* also appeals to paradox and rejects extremes of Calvinism and *Arminianism*; for him salvation is wholly God's work and at the same time occurs only with free human response. There can be little doubt that this third way is one of the most popular approaches for educated lay evangelicals and evangelical preachers; one hears it expressed (often in a somewhat vulgarized way) in evangelical sermon illustrations and popular evangelical discussions of this seemingly intractable dilemma. Evangelical proponents of the first two approaches are not satisfied with appeal to paradox and antinomy, however, because it comes perilously close to embracing contradiction and thus reducing theology to incoherence. God's grace is either resistible or not resistible; there is very little room for paradox there. Election is either individual or corporate; predestination is either conditional or unconditional. The debate goes on among evangelical theologians and is likely to continue forever or, as evangelicals like to say, "until Christ returns." In the meantime, evangelicals struggle to maintain rough unity as a movement in spite of this and other deep fractures.

David Basinger et al., *Predestination and Free Will: Four Views of Divine Sovereignty and Human Freedom* (Downers Grove, IL: InterVarsity Press, 1986); Anthony A. Hoekema, *Saved by Grace* (Grand Rapids: Wm. B. Eerdmans, 1989); Thomas C. Oden, *The Transforming Power of Grace* (Nashville: Abingdon Press, 1993); J. I. Packer, *Evangelism and the Sovereignty of God* (Downers Grove, IL: InterVarsity Press, 2001).

Eschatology Evangelicals have often specialized in eschatology—the study of the *kingdom of God,* especially in relation to the future, including Christ's return to earth, the *resurrection* of all people, judgments of individuals and nations, and the completion of

God's plan for the *redemption* of *creation.* These are just some of the subjects dealt with under the category of eschatology in theology generally. Evangelicals have tended to focus on details of biblical prophecy of the future and of the events surrounding the *return of Christ.* Popular books and movies by evangelical authors about eschatology appeared on the market and sold to general audiences beginning in the 1960s. By the 1990s certain types of evangelical speculation about the end of the world and the return of Christ had entered into popular culture through the writings of Hal Lindsay and Tim LaHaye. Much popular evangelical eschatology is apocalyptic in nature; it draws heavily on biblical books such as Daniel and Revelation and seeks to interpret their apparently predicted catastrophes. In this, evangelicals follow closely the pattern set by Adventists and Plymouth Brethren of the nineteenth century, including William Miller, *John Nelson Darby,* and Ellen G. White.

Most evangelical theologians consider it unfortunate that evangelical eschatology is virtually equated, both in the popular mind and by evangelical lay people and pastors, with this florid, speculative, apocalyptic vision of the future. Evangelical theologians generally regard eschatology as dealing with much more than apocalyptic events of the future; for them it includes the entire doctrine of the rule and reign of God, especially as it is completed in the future, and also the destinies of individuals after death. Most evangelical theologians are quick to say that eschatology is also about the presence of the kingdom of God within history and that it includes the study of the anticipations of the future consummation of God's cosmic plan within the *church* in history.

Evangelical theologians share a basic consensus about eschatology with many nonevangelical Christians, including the church fathers of the first four to five centuries of Christianity, the Protestant Reformers, and post-Reformation Protestant leaders and thinkers. Their diversity also reflects that history of Christian thinking about eschatology. Some of the early church fathers, such as Irenaeus, were apocalyptic in their thinking about the future and looked forward to an imminent and violent end of history, leading up to the visible return of *Jesus Christ*. Others, like Origen, believed in a progressive realization of the kingdom of God within history and eschewed catastrophic and apocalyptic focus in eschatology. Augustine developed what has come to be known as *amillennialism,* whereas most of the earliest church fathers were premillennialists, as were many of the Radical Reformers of the sixteenth century. All in all, then, there is unity and variety in Christian theological reflection about the future, and that unity in diversity is reflected in evangelical thought.

Evangelical thinkers stand together in rejecting liberal Protestantism's tendency to demythologize and existentialize eschatology. That is, most evangelical theologians believe the future end of history does include fabulous events, hardly imaginable, that are metaphorically described in biblical apocalyptic literature. They agree among themselves that people who die before the general resurrection prophesied in Scripture will be raised and enter into everlasting punishment or everlasting fulfillment in *heaven*. They all also believe that Jesus' prayer, "Thy kingdom come, thy will be done on earth as it is in heaven," will be answered by God in the future and that God's perfect will and plan for human history will be revealed and fulfilled either on earth or in a new heaven and new earth. Some evangelical thinkers focus on eschatology more than others; some seem downright shy about the matter and try to avoid it because biblical *revelation* contains it primarily in symbols and metaphors. But they all believe that God's promises of cosmic *redemption* (e.g., Romans 8:18–24) will be fulfilled by God in surprising ways that surpass natural or human possibilities.

Like William James's nature, evangelical eschatology at times seems like a blooming, buzzing confusion. There are numerous conflicting opinions, and equally evangelical denominations and institutions have completely contrary visions of the end times. The one major debate within evangelical theology about the future of individuals ("life after death") is over the so-called intermediate state. Most evangelical thinkers stand firmly with the majority Christian consensus in believing that people who die in a state of grace go directly to the place Jesus called paradise—a place of rest and peace with God and Jesus Christ, where they await the bodily resurrection. Unbelievers go to an opposite place of hopelessness to await judgment at the resurrection. Some evangelical theologians reject any conscious intermediate state and believe that the biblical references to the dead as "asleep" should be taken very seriously. The dead literally know nothing at all; they are unconsciously waiting to be raised at the last day, when Christ returns. Sometimes known as "soul sleep," this is the doctrine of life after death taught by all branches of the Adventist movement. More popular among evangelical thinkers is the idea that the dead do not so much sleep (i.e., wait unconsciously) as go directly into the resurrection as they leave the temporal order of duration and succession and enter into God's future immediately upon bodily death. This is the view espoused by evangelical thinker Stanley Grenz and others.

Of much greater controversy is the evangelical diversity about the fulfillment of the kingdom of God in the rule and reign of Jesus Christ. Will Christ reign as Lord over earth in a one-thousand-year "millennial kingdom" within history? That is the view held by premillennialists, who point to Revelation 20 and to several important church fathers for support. Premillennialist evangelicals (and most premillennialists are evangelicals) believe that Christ will return to earth at a particularly low point in world history and destroy the powers and forces of the antichrist, who will be persecuting God's people. Then he will establish his earthly kingdom for one thousand years, during which time Satan will be bound. At the end of the millennium, all the dead will be raised, the nations will be judged, and the universe will be renewed. "Heaven" is what comes after that—the new heaven and new earth described by John in Revelation 21. Postmillennialist evangelicals (and most postmillennialists are evangelicals) look for a Christianization of the world before Christ's return to renovate creation and join earth with heaven. Amillennialists reject any earthly, historical rule and reign of Christ except secretly, spiritually in the hearts and minds of the people of God. The church, then, is the kingdom of God.

Evangelical theologians stopped arguing over these differences in the middle of the twentieth century, when they realized that all views could be supported from Scripture and wished to move away from the fundamentalists who were insisting that only a certain brand of *premillennialism* was acceptable for evangelicals. Nevertheless, many conservative evangelical theologians still present their particular theories about the end times, including the order of events predicted in biblical apocalyptic literature such as the so-called tribulation period and the antichrist. Almost all fundamentalist evangelicals insist on belief in a so-called secret rapture of the church that will inaugurate the end times; it is supposed to happen mysteriously at the beginning or in the middle of the seven years of great tribulation leading up to the second coming of Christ—the *parousia*. This theory, linked closely with dispensationalist hermeneutics and popularized in evangelical novels, is widely identified by the popular mind with evangelical eschatology. Many moderate and progressive evangelicals do not accept it at all, and Reformed evangelicals by and large reject it. It is the view of the end times propagated by many con-

servative evangelical and fundamentalist institutions, such as Dallas Theological Seminary, Moody Bible Institute, and Biola University.

Many evangelical theologians have been profoundly affected by the rise in the 1970s and 1980s of the eschatological *theology* and theology of hope associated with German theologians Wolfhart Pannenberg and Jürgen Moltmann. Many moderate and progressive evangelical thinkers studied with one of them and sought to incorporate their insights into evangelical eschatology. Pannenberg and Moltmann eschew both apocalyptic visions of the future as catastrophic and liberal visions of the future as progressive improvement through social action and education. They draw on the philosophy of hope of German revisionist Marxist philosopher Ernst Bloch, who speculated that the future of the world—ultimate, universal history at its end—is the power that determines the present and past without destroying freedom or contingency. Evangelicals combine the idea of the future coming of God in his kingdom with the biblical scholarship of evangelical George Eldon Ladd, who emphasized Christian existence "between the times" (of the first coming of Christ to inaugurate his kingdom and the second coming to fulfill it) to develop a distinctively evangelical eschatology that uses the promises of God for the future redemption of all creation to energize redemptive activism within history. In agreement with Pannenberg and Moltmann (who are very different thinkers in some regards), and drawing on Ladd's New Testament scholarship of the kingdom of God these evangelicals view the kingdom of God as both already and not yet. They place primacy on God's coming out of the future into the present, determining history together with human partners who are filled with the Spirit of God in the church, to realize the eschatological kingdom partially and proleptically now. In this evangelical theology, there is no reductionism of the future (as in liberal thought) to development; at the same time, this evangelical eschatology resists obsessive identification of God's eschatological kingdom with future apocalyptic and catastrophic events. Christ will return bodily—on that all evangelicals agree—but some evangelical thinkers prefer to view Christ as present in and through the church, which is his eschatological community of transformation already within history living from the power of the future, when God will be all in all (or everything to everyone). *Reconciliation,* then, is not only something to be waited for, but also something to be achieved in the power of the Spirit within history in light of the future reconciliation to be established by God at Christ's return. Evangelical thinkers who draw on Ladd's insights and the theologies of Pannenberg and Moltmann include Miroslav Volf and Stanley Grenz.

Robert C. Doyle, *Eschatology and the Shape of Christian Belief* (Carlisle, UK: Paternoster Press, 1999); Millard Erickson, *Contemporary Options in Eschatology* (Grand Rapids: Baker Book House, 1987); Stanley J. Grenz, *Theology for the Community of God* (Grand Rapids: Wm. B. Eerdmans, 2000).

Ethics Evangelical ethics seeks to ground values, virtues, and moral principles, as well as right behavior, in divine *revelation;* more specifically it seeks to be biblical ethics without falling into literalism or legalism. This approach stands in contrast to modern utilitarianism and all forms of exclusively consequentialist ethical thinking. Consequentialism solves moral dilemmas by examining the consequences of decisions and behaviors; utilitarianism is that form of consequentialist ethical reflection that regards the greatest happiness for the greatest number of people as the summum bonum—the highest good to be sought and, insofar as possible, achieved. Evangelical theologians and ethicists view consequentialism and

especially utilitarianism as inexorably relativistic; moral norms are reduced to guides to possible outcomes, and all rules are thereby relativized. Absolutes other than, for example, greatest possible happiness are undermined if not dissolved. Evangelical thinkers almost universally view secular, nonreligious ethics and moral philosophy as relativistic and thus essentially unreliable because manipulable and changing. And they are not particularly enthusiastic about Kantian deontological absolutism, which seeks to ground ethics in self-evident or rationally discernible principles such as duty. Kant's categorical imperative, which dictates living only according to maxims that could rationally be universalized (e.g., always treat other persons as ends in themselves and never as means to ends), rests entirely on immanent insight; it is anthropocentric and ignores divine commands that transcend *reason.*

Evangelical ethical reflection and guidance rests on divine commands; almost all evangelical ethical thinkers appeal to commands of *God* found in *Scripture* as ultimate norms, even if they also seek to demonstrate their rationality and ethical flexibility and fruitfulness for normal human living. Evangelical ethical living, then, is basically obedience to God, rather than conduct based on rational calculation of consequences or on performance of reasonable, self-evident duty, even if these can provide some help in fleshing out the demands of obedience to God in concrete situations. Almost all evangelical thinkers regard the twin principles of love and *justice* as the two supreme and irreducible, nonnegotiable commands of God in Scripture. Other commands are secondary to love and justice; rules abound in Scripture and ought not to be cavalierly dismissed as impossible or irrelevant, but their relevance and application to moral decision making and concrete action are subordinate to and governed by love and justice, which are absolutes because they are grounded in the nature of God himself. The task of evangelical ethical reflection is to apply love and justice to moral dilemmas and to guide moral decision making and action in specific situations where divinely revealed rules do not clearly and unequivocally apply. (Most evangelical ethicists agree that many rules in Scripture are aimed at specific people in specific situations and are not universally relevant. Others may be "counsels of perfection" not meant to be carried out blindly by all in every situation.)

Some evangelical ethicists—especially in the Reformed tradition—appeal to "*creation* mandates," which are discerned through careful examination of nature (including human nature) in the light of God's word in Scripture. Reformed thinkers view creation as a revelation of God that can be properly understood only by persons regenerated by the *Holy Spirit* and illuminated to see and understand God's revelation in nature. Such mandates of creation include cultural creativity and procreation; creation orders placed in the world by God for fulfilled human living include marriage, family, and government. Reformed evangelical thinkers do not regard the creation mandates and orders of creation as separate from divine commands in Scripture; they do not supercede or take precedence over love and justice. Such mandates and orders provide concrete structures for living lives of love and justice in the world, especially in view of the fall of *humanity* into sin. Other evangelical ethical thinkers, often influenced by the Radical Reformation, prefer to emphasize ethics of *redemption* over ethics of creation; many would attempt to combine the two. The ethics of redemption focuses attention on the *kingdom of God* in its proleptic presence and eschatological fulfillment and seeks to derive ethical mandates from the promised kingdom of God, when God's will will be done on earth as in *heaven*. Reformed ethics, then, tends to stress order, whereas redemption ethics tends to emphasize transformation.

Evangelical ethics includes more diversity in theory and method (beyond obedience to divine commands of love and justice) than in concrete recommendations and prohibitions. Virtually all evangelical ethicists affirm the sanctity of human life and condemn abortion on demand (e.g., as birth control), but some base it on biblical materials that command respect for human life (e.g., that humans are created in *God's image*), while others base it on a metaphysical vision of *humanity* within the creation between God and nature. Some, of course, combine the two perspectives for a stronger case. Virtually all evangelical ethicists affirm the normativity of heterosexual, monogamous marriage as the foundation of faithful and fulfilling family life, but some base it on biblical exhortations, while others base it on an apprehension of the created order. Some, of course, combine the two approaches. In the overall scheme of things, evangelical ethical thinkers tend to be conservative; most affirm the possibility of just war, defend capitalism, and reject homosexual behavior as immoral. Areas of disagreement and debate among evangelical ethicists include the roles of women in society, family, and church; the justice of capital punishment; and the rightness of uses of technology in biomedicine. Some follow the French Christian ethicist Jacques Ellul in cautioning against technology as inherently masterful (tending toward idolatry), whereas others are more optimistic about the potential of technology for glorifying God and establishing relative love and justice in society. Some evangelical ethicists view feminism with suspicion as a manifestation of the modern rage for autonomy, whereas others regard it as a positive, if sometimes misguided and extreme, movement for love and justice manifested through greater equality.

In spite of significant disagreements over specific ethical advice, evangelical ethical thinkers agree that secularism, situational ethics, relativism, and disregard for human life are intimately related and that only a theocentric (God-centered) moral vision can provide the foundation or horizon for the good life. Most affirm some kind of graded or differentiated absolutism over against all forms of relativism. That is, the glory of God is the ultimate good, and love and justice are the twin principles for guiding human behavior toward God's glory. Rights, values, and duties are negotiable in light of the absolutes of love and justice, and all rules serve love, justice, and their attendant values. How should ethics be taught and inculcated? In the late twentieth century and into the early twenty-first century, evangelical ethicists began to debate whether the moral life is grounded in intellectual formation or inculcated virtues. Under the influence of theologian and ethicist Stanley Hauerwas, many evangelical ethicists began to argue in favor of virtue rather than knowledge as the basis of the moral life; ethics is authentic only when it flows from the virtuous life. That takes shape only in virtuous communities that shape and form individuals' values and behaviors. These evangelical thinkers reject the modern and ancient maxim that "to know the good is to do the good" and argue instead that doing the good (love and justice) holds primacy over knowing precisely what the good is. Being good precedes knowing good; obedience yields understanding. Critics of this approach charge that it is vulnerable to postmodern relativism; knowing precedes doing, and understanding shapes behavior.

Donald G. Bloesch, *Freedom for Obedience: Evangelical Ethics in Contemporary Times* (San Francisco: Harper & Row, 1987); Stanley Grenz, *The Moral Quest: Foundations of Christian Ethics* (Downers Grove, IL: InterVarsity Press, 1997); Carl F. H. Henry, *Christian Personal Ethics* (Grand Rapids: Wm. B. Eerdmans, 1957); Dennis Hollinger and David P. Gushee, "Evangelical Ethics: Profile of a Movement Coming of Age," *Annual of the Society of Christian Ethics* 20 (2000): 181–203; Richard J. Mouw, *The God Who Commands* (Notre Dame, IN: University of Notre Dame Press, 1990); Lewis Smedes, *Mere Morality: What God Expects from Ordinary People* (Grand Rapids: Wm. B. Eerdmans, 1983).

Evangelism   Evangelicals believe in and practice evangelism—the proclamation of the *gospel* of *Jesus Christ* in order to facilitate *conversions* to Jesus Christ and to Christianity. They are committed to fulfilling the Great Commission of Jesus Christ to his disciples recorded in Matthew 28:18–20, and they do not believe this commission is fulfilled only through programs for social improvement or individual relief. These may be part of evangelism, but evangelism cannot be reduced to them. Telling the story of *God's* love, mercy, and *grace* revealed in Jesus Christ and his death on the cross and the message of *forgiveness, reconciliation* with God and restoration of true *humanity* through *repentance* and belief in the cross of Christ is an essential part of true Christian evangelism. The goal of evangelism is conversions of people to *faith* in Jesus Christ; membership in Christian *churches* may be a secondary goal of evangelism. Whether a person or group can be truly evangelical and not support this kind of evangelism is doubtful; the evangelical movement stemming from European *Pietism* and the Great Awakenings has always been marked by evangelistic efforts to spread the gospel to those who have not yet heard it. Some hyper-Calvinists rejected early missionary endeavors by evangelicals among them, on the ground that God does not need human instruments to save the elect and that missionary endeavors (especially "soliciting faith" indiscriminately) implicitly deny God's sovereignty in *salvation*. William Carey and other eighteenth- and nineteenth-century evangelicals gave great impetus to the evangelical movement by establishing the first foreign missions boards; Baptists who supported such cooperative programs for international and home missions became known as Missionary Baptists (especially but not only in the South), while those who rejected them (mostly Primitive Baptists and other hyper-Calvinists) are usually not considered evangelicals even if their doctrinal beliefs are orthodox.

The nineteenth century is known in some circles as the century of missions; it was a period of unprecedented efforts throughout the world to evangelize people groups that had not yet converted to Christianity. Evangelical organizations for evangelism at home (within the United Kingdom and the United States) and abroad (usually to countries considered underdeveloped and not yet Christianized) exploded in number and strength. American evangelical writer and speaker Albert B. Simpson founded a denomination based almost entirely on the missionary ideal—the Christian and Missionary Alliance. Most Protestant denominations founded mission boards and sent missionaries to "unreached people groups" (a late twentieth-century term), especially in Asia and Africa.

Mainline Protestant missionary activity underwent a dramatic change in the early and mid-twentieth century, when the goal of evangelism shifted from conversions to relief through education and development. Evangelicals were dissatisfied with this change and founded their own rival missionary boards, which often led to splits within mainline Protestant denominations. What was at stake (e.g., in Presbyterian theologian *J. Gresham Machen's* founding of a rival missionary agency to the mainline Presbyterian board of foreign missions) was a theological principle—the nature of salvation. Evangelicals saw universalism undermining evangelistic efforts for conversion and insisted that since *hell* is a very real possibility for personal des-

tiny, evangelism must remain focused on spreading the gospel, in order to facilitate conversions to faith in Christ. Post-fundamentalist Evangelicalism carried on this strong emphasis on evangelism for conversions after World War II and eschewed missionary work that did not include church planting, gospel preaching, publication of *Bibles* in indigenous languages, and other efforts toward converting people. One of the largest missionary societies in history is the evangelical Wycliffe Bible Translators, which focuses on providing Scriptures in all languages. This is a distinctly evangelical movement because it combines Bible translation and dissemination with relatively conservative doctrine and strong belief in the importance of conversion for salvation.

If evangelism is one of the adhesives holding Evangelicalism together, there are theological solvents threatening to weaken its uniting power. While all evangelical theologians strongly affirm evangelism, they disagree among themselves about particular methods and motives. Reformed evangelicals are often critical of "indiscriminate evangelism," where evangelism is defined as "solicitation of faith." In other words, because Christ did not die for every person, it is theologically incorrect to hold mass evangelistic rallies and campaigns (such as have been a major feature of the evangelical movement since mass evangelism was founded by *Charles Finney* in the early nineteenth century), where all people present are equally invited to accept Christ, who died for their sins. Reformed evangelicals believe true evangelism is right proclamation of the gospel; getting the gospel message right is as important as getting it out (to the world beyond the church). Evangelism is restricted to correct proclamation of the gospel—that Christ died for the elect and that whosoever believes in him will be saved. Reformed evangelicals also tend to focus on the cost of conversion in discipleship; conversion is not by "cheap grace," and authentic Christianity is not "easy believism" but costly discipleship. Conversion to Christ must result in participation in the sacramental community of God's people, the church, which is a disciplined body of confessing Christians. Reformed evangelical theologians believe that the offer of God's free grace through repentance and faith (conversion) is a "well-meant offer," even if not all hearers are elect and therefore will not be regenerated by the grace of God unto conversion. However, it is important not to solicit faith indiscriminately so that everyone is equally invited to repent and believe as if everyone were capable. Only the elect will be drawn effectually by the *Holy Spirit*; the non-elect will reject the well-meant offer of God's grace because the Spirit does not regenerate them so that they can believe and receive salvation.

Arminian evangelicals find the Reformed theology of evangelism problematic. They believe that it undermines the universality of the gospel message and places too many conditions on solicitation of faith. Following the teachings of John Wesley, Arminian evangelical theologians of evangelism believe that prevenient grace—the calling, convicting, enlightening, and enabling power of God through the Holy Spirit—reaches people by means of proclamation of the gospel and that proclamation may and should include invitation to all hearers to repent and believe unto salvation. In this evangelical viewpoint, then, there is no limitation on the potential number of persons who may be saved; Christ died equally for all persons, and all are invited to be converted. This theology places more emphasis on the urgency of soliciting faith through "witnessing" and "invitations" (to repent and believe in Jesus Christ). Such proclamation and faith-solicitation is indiscriminate, urgent, passionate, and unconditional (except for the necessity of repentance and faith). The motive for missions and evangelism, then, is that such activity gives people the opportunity to enjoy the temporal and eternal blessings of

reconciliation with God, and all who hear have that opportunity. Reformed evangelicals believe the motive for missions and evangelism is obedience to Christ's command and believe that God already has chosen an elect people who will respond to proclamation of the gospel message.

Other issues related to evangelism that create some division among evangelical theologians have to do with contextualizing the gospel culturally, including social transformation in evangelism and the role of miraculous "signs and wonders" in evangelism. Harvey Conn of Westminster Theological Seminary pioneered in the area of culturally contextualizing the gospel and missionary methods. In his view (and the view of many other evangelical missiologists), evangelists must avoid imposing European or American values and lifestyles (especially individualism and materialism) on non-Western people. Western cultural baggage must be separated from the proclaimed gospel and from the churches planted in non-Western cultures. Indigenous forms of Christianity must be allowed to develop and flourish, up to the point of syncretism. Ultraconservative evangelicals have tended to be suspicious of syncretism in all culturally contextualized evangelistic efforts.

Some evangelicals, such as sociologist and evangelist Tony Campolo, have argued strongly that "soul-winning" (conversions) and church planting are not sufficient for holistic evangelism and that evangelical missions must aim at transforming people's social, economic, and political lives. Latin American liberation theology has influenced some evangelical missionaries to attempt to "conscienticize" converts to the true causes of their poverty and oppression. Many conservative evangelicals reject that and restrict evangelism to proclamation of the gospel and planting of gospel-centered churches.

Finally, some evangelicals of the so-called *Third Wave movement,* such as the late John Wimber and evangelical sociologist-anthropologist Charles Kraft and missiologist C. Peter Wagner, call for "power encounters" to facilitate evangelism. They endorse "spiritual warfare" as a form of missionary activity. These methods focus on use of supernatural *gifts of the Holy Spirit* and powerful *prayer* against "territorial (evil) spirits" that hinder the spread of the gospel. Many evangelicals believe this methodology focuses too much on human work and undermines awareness of the sovereignty of God in evangelism. Clearly, then, evangelicals do not agree uniformly about the theology or methods of proper evangelism, but they do agree that converting people to Jesus Christ by calling them to repent and believe in the gospel (i.e., trust in Christ and his death on the cross for reconciliation with God and fulfilled human life) is an essential aspect of authentic Christian life in obedience to God who is "not willing that any should perish, but that all should come to repentance" (2 Peter 3:9 KJV).

William J. Abraham, *The Logic of Evangelism* (Grand Rapids: Wm. B. Eerdmans, 1989); Milton J. Coulter and Virgil Cruz, eds., *How Shall We Witness? Faithful Evangelism in a Reformed Tradition* (Louisville, KY: Westminster John Knox Press, 1995); David Watson, *I Believe in Evangelism* (London: Hodder & Stoughton, 1999); John Wimber, *Power Evangelism* (New York: HarperCollins, 1993).

Evil   One of the most intractable problems in Christian *theology* and philosophy of religion is the problem of evil. What is evil and why does it exist in a world created and ruled by a perfectly good and all-powerful *God*? Evangelicals are orthodox Christians; they believe in the classical concept of God rooted in the biblical narrative and the great tradition of Christian belief: God is personal, infinite, transcendent-immanent, holy, good, loving, faithful, and self-existent. Furthermore, evangelicals believe, God

is omnipotent, omniscient, and omnipresent. How then can evil exist in God's world? The problem is as old as Christianity itself and older. Evangelicals agree with the Protestant orthodox tradition of theology that *Satan* is a real, created being given entirely over to evil and that evil is whatever opposes God or is not willed by God. Evangelicals emphasize the power and involvement of Satan in history in varying degrees; some virtually ignore Satan, and others revel in speculation about Satan and spiritual warfare against that personal power of darkness.

Most evangelical theologians would agree with British evangelical theologian Michael Green, who was asked to write a volume on Satan in a theological series in which all books' titles began with *I Believe in. . . .* Rather than write *I Believe in Satan*, he chose the title *I Believe in Satan's Downfall*. In other words, evangelical theologians are reluctant to place Satan on the same level as God; their *faith* is solely in God. They believe in Satan's existence and the existence of evil, but they do not believe in Satan in the same way they believe in (i.e., place trust in) God. They prefer to write and speak about the end of evil rather than the origin or nature of evil; biblical *revelation* points to Satan's downfall and evil's demise in the glorious triumph of God when Christ returns. However, there can be no avoiding the fact that evangelical theologians and philosophers of religion also resist any reduction of evil (or Satan) to poor human choices, a "not-yetness" of evolutionary development (e.g., of human nature out of and beyond its animal heritage), or ignorance. Evil is irreducible. It cannot be explained as merely an epiphenomenon of something else. To many nonevangelicals this sounds as if evangelicals do believe very strongly in evil, but to evangelicals this is simply biblical realism. The greater truth is that evil cannot and will not triumph in the end; it will be conquered and set aside in the *redemption* of *creation*.

Most evangelical theologians work in the general Augustinian tradition of Christian thought; the fourth- and fifth-century North African bishop and *church* father Augustine provides the general framework for their life and worldview insofar as that builds on and goes beyond what is explicitly stated in *Scripture*. Augustine was influenced by the Neoplatonic tradition of Greek philosophy and drew on it to explain the reality of evil to Christians and pagans alike. In contrast to the Manichees—a religious sect Augustine knew by intimate acquaintance—Augustine believed that evil is very real and powerful but lacks ontological substance. Their worldview was dualistic—good versus evil. Augustine drew on an old Platonic and Neoplatonic idea of *mē on* (nonbeing or nothingness). According to Augustine, evil is not a substance with positive being, nor is it unreal; it has the status of nonbeing, a negative power that resists the power of being. For Augustine, evil is the absence of the good, but it is not absence in the sense of unreality or nonexistence. The "absence" that evil is is very powerful—like the power of a vacuum. Evil is to good what darkness is to light; good has real being that is rooted in God's own eternal being, but evil exists as privation. For Augustine and for most evangelical theologians, this explains why evil's existence in the world does not call into question God's goodness. God did not create evil; evil exists due to the misuse of *free will*. According to Augustine and many evangelical thinkers, the only evil thing is an evil will and that is not a substance but a twist or distortion in something otherwise good (free will).

Both Reformed and Arminian evangelical theologians regard evil as nonbeing or absence of the good. Both draw on Augustine's explanation of evil, though Arminians place more emphasis on its origin in free will than do Reformed thinkers. Even Reformed evangelicals, however, appeal to the corruption of creaturely nature (angelic and human) to explain the source of evil; evil does not originate in God or in any created essence or substance but in a corruption of otherwise good nature. Arminians insist that corruption originates in an original free rebellion against God and the good; Reformed evangelicals usually refuse to speculate and simply say that it originates in an original corruption that is beyond explanation. Reformed thinkers tend to see evil as an instrument of God in *providence*; God did not create it and is not stained by it but does use it to accomplish a greater good. As one Reformed evangelical thinker puts it, this world (with all its evil) is the best world on the way to the best of all possible worlds (in the future *kingdom of God*). God deemed it better to have a world with evil in it than to have a world with no evil in it, but he is not the author of *sin* or evil. Their origin is beyond human knowing, even though God foreordained them and rendered them certain by withholding the necessary grace for creatures to avoid falling into corruption. Arminian theologians regard this explanation of evil as inherently flawed, as it inevitably makes God the author of sin and evil, regardless of Reformed intentions and claims. Arminians view evil—even gratuitous evil—as part of the creaturely fall and curse, which originate in rebellion against God's goodwill and commands. Evil exists because God allows it to exist—probably in order to allow the probationary creation to play out in freedom until God intervenes to abolish evil and make his people truly free in the restoration of the shattered *image of God*. Both Reformed and Arminan evangelical thinkers take evil with all seriousness and urge that people face the world realistically and avoid reducing evil to something natural.

Some evangelical theologians are dissatisfied with the Augustinian tradition of understanding evil and argue instead for a view of evil as having positive ontological status. That is, they prefer to view it as a substance that invades God's good creation and corrupts it. One such evangelical thinker is Gregory A.

Boyd, whose trilogy on a "spiritual warfare world view" challenged the entire Augustinian tradition in evangelical theology. In the second volume of the trilogy, *Satan and the Problem of Evil*, Boyd critiques the Augustinian tradition in theodicy (defense of the ways of God in the face of evil) as trivializing evil and also making God the author of evil. (The latter accusation is aimed particularly at the Reformed tradition of Augustinian theology that emphasizes meticulous providence.) According to Boyd and some other evangelical thinkers who wish to call evangelicals to spiritual warfare against Satan and demons, evil is a surd—an inexplicable substance in creation. Its origin cannot be explained. To Augustinian evangelicals this implies a Manichean dualism, but Boyd denies that evil is on the same level with God or that there are two equal powers in the universe. Evil is subordinate to God, even if its origin cannot be explained. It is a power of resistance to God that resides in the universe, and God will eventually conquer it. Human beings are invited by God to participate in that conquest through *prayer*. For Boyd and like-minded evangelicals, evil exists in the world because God chose to limit himself in the historical process. He literally cannot abolish evil without undoing the project that includes as a necessary element (on the way to the consummation of God's kingdom) human free will to cooperate with evil, whose orchestrator is Satan. Classical evangelicals in the Augustinian tradition explain evil differently by appealing to evil's role in God's providence. While God does not create evil or wish it to exist in the world, its corruption is part of the plan of God to redeem creation. All agree that evil is God's enemy that really does exist—not merely as illusion or ignorance, but also as power.

Gregory A. Boyd, *Satan and the Problem of Evil* (Downers Grove, IL: InterVarsity Press, 2001); Stephen Davis, ed., *Encountering Evil: Live Options in Theodicy*

(Louisville, KY: Westminster John Knox Press, 2001); Paul Helm, *The Providence of God* (Downers Grove, IL: InterVarsity Press, 1994); Michael Peterson, *Evil and the Christian God* (Grand Rapids: Baker Book House, 1982).

Experience   Evangelicals specialize in experiential religion or what was called "experimental religion" in the eighteenth century. Opponents of eighteenth-century evangelicals during the Great Awakenings often dismissed them as enthusiasts, a term of opprobrium similar to fanatics. They were known as Christians who sought spiritually transforming experience and not only correct doctrine and right *worship.* Two of Evangelicalism's founders wrote volumes defending and exploring evangelical experience of God. Jonathan Edwards penned *On Religious Affections* in order to defend the profoundly emotional elements of *revivalism,* as well as to criticize their excesses and offer criteria for distinguishing true from false religious feelings. Religious experiences and feelings that do not result in benevolence for beings are false, whereas those that awaken love in action for **God** and fellow creatures are likely to be true. John Wesley wrote *A Plain Account of Religious Perfection* to explain his doctrine of *entire sanctification* in a moment—a hallmark of the Methodist revivals and movement. For Wesley as for Edwards, love is the criterion of true sanctification, and "Christian perfection" is nothing else than being "perfected in love." Yet both Edwards and Wesley acknowledged that authentic Christianity necessarily involves experience such as Wesley's own heart being "strangely warmed," which brought an inner sense of assurance of God's love.

Some kind of *conversion* experience became the distinguishing feature of early Protestant Evangelicalism, and it has remained so ever since. The distinctive message of evangelical preaching has been "You must be born again";

evangelicals have stressed the inward experience of God over merely "historical faith." And yet there is no evangelical doctrine of experience as such. Rather, experience is tied inextricably to the doctrine of *salvation*, including conversion, *regeneration, sanctification*. Evangelicals believe that salvation includes experience in the dimension of transformed affections (regeneration as the "expulsive power of a new affection" —*A. H. Strong*) and a "personal relationship with *Jesus Christ.*"

Because evangelical folk religion revels in experiential Christianity, evangelical theologians have been reticent with regard to subjective and inward religious experiences; they often prefer to write about the objective work of God in *election* and *justification*. In the late twentieth century and the early twenty-first century one of the most popular evangelical books has been *Experiencing God,* by Baptist minister Henry Blackaby and Claude V. King (Nashville: Broadman Holman, 1998). The book and its study guide have been used by thousands of churches. They have focused on the subjective side of evangelical *faith*— experiencing God in an individual, personal relationship through *Scripture* reading and *prayer*. This is the main appeal of Evangelicalism to millions of North Americans and people around the world. Evangelical theologians often criticize the tendency toward anti-intellectualism and neglect of doctrinal confession in such courses and in popular evangelical religion generally. And yet most evangelical theologians write at least one book on the subject of religious experience.

Among the best known and most influential in contemporary evangelical theology are *Donald G. Bloesch's The Struggle of Prayer* (Colorado Springs, CO: Helmers & Howard, 1988) and Stanley J. Grenz's *Revisioning Evangelical Theology* (Downers Grove, IL: InterVarsity Press, 1993). Bloesch's book, dedicated to "Puritan father Richard Sibbes," is a study of what the author calls prophetic prayer. According to him, the essence of true evangelical prayer is not contemplation (wordless prayer) but petition. Bloesch promotes the continuing struggle of petitionary prayer in the life of the individual evangelical Christian and the evangelical *church*. For him, evangelical experience is an I-Thou relationship between the Christian and his or her heavenly Father through the Son Jesus Christ and in the power of the *Holy Spirit*. Such experience may not yield constant or reliable spiritual feelings, but it is life-transforming, resulting in the fruit of the Spirit (love, joy, peace). Grenz's book is less devotional than theological; in it the author discusses "convertive piety" as the true heart of evangelical Christianity. That is, not doctrine but a certain spirituality rooted in the experience of conversion (being "born again" by the Spirit of God) lies at the center of evangelical Christianity as its defining and identity-creating feature. Doctrine is secondary language that serves the experiential dimension of Christianity. The true core of Evangelicalism is the experience of regeneration—becoming a new *creation* in Christ Jesus by God's grace through *repentance* and faith. That results in a life of sanctification or growth into the image of Christ. For both Bloesch and Grenz, doctrine is essential to evangelical identity, but orthodoxy is second to orthopathy for identifying authentic Christian faith.

All evangelicals believe in the experience of conversion, including regeneration, whether they highlight subjective feelings or not. Especially Reformed evangelicals tend to play down the subjective aspects of evangelical experience and emphasize the objective work of God in electing, calling, and regenerating people. Few, however, would deny the value of feelings of peace in *reconciliation* with God and assurance of salvation stemming from the gift of conversion. Evangelicals rooted in the revivalist traditions (Wesleyan-*Holiness*, Pentecostal and *charismatic*) specialize in explorations of postconversion Christian experiences such as the second blessing subsequent to regeneration. Many evangelicals refer to it as the *baptism of the Holy Spirit*; some equate it with entire sanctification in a moment (Wesley's "perfection in love"). Evangelicals steeped in the *Keswick movement* appeal to the cleansing experience of total commitment through "death to self" and encourage struggling Christians to "crucify" their selves with Christ in an act of identification with his self-sacrifice for *humanity*. In the second blessing, such evangelicals agree, the Holy Spirit takes control of the individual's life in a new way that brings spiritual power for serving God. Often the second blessing is sought fervently with prolonged praying ("tarrying for the gift of the Holy Spirit") and sometimes with fellow believers laying hands on the seeker's head and shoulders and praying for that person to receive the blessing of the Holy Spirit. Pentecostals believe the Spirit baptism happens when the seeker speaks in unknown tongues; other experiential evangelicals look for evidence in transformed personalities and works of righteousness. Such experientialism embarrasses some evangelicals, who label it fanaticism or subjectivism; others call it the "full gospel" and view with suspicion mainstream evangelicals who eschew such *supernatural* and expressive experiences.

Most evangelicals would agree that authentic Christian experience—whatever precise shape it takes—is especially related to the Holy Spirit. Unfortunately, because of perceived excesses of emphasis on the Holy Spirit and spiritual experiences of an emotional nature among some evangelicals, many evangelicals have virtually ignored the Holy Spirit except as the third member of the *Trinity*. Many evangelical theologians have relied heavily on a rational-propositional account of Christianity as a system of correct, coherent doctrines to explain evangelical faith. They would do well to remember that even John Calvin spoke glowingly of the "inner testimony of the Holy Spirit" as crucial to knowing God

and understanding Scripture. For Calvin and the best of Reformed theology since the sixteenth century, the indwelling of the Holy Spirit and the Spirit's work of illumination of the heart and mind of the believer were a foundation of evangelical faith. While Reformed theology has rarely emphasized subjective feelings or elevated them to a criterion of authentic Christian existence, it traditionally knows the proper place of experience of God and Jesus Christ through the Holy Spirit within the believer. There is, then, no true divorce between Reformed and Wesleyan Evangelicalism at this point; both contain an experiential impulse even if it is not highly emotional, merely subjective, or antidoctrinal.

———

Frederick Dale Bruner, *A Theology of the Holy Spirit: The Pentecostal Experience and the New Testament Witness* (Grand Rapids: Wm. B. Eerdmans, 1970); Donald A. Thorsen, *The Wesleyan Quadrilateral: Scripture, Tradition, Reason, and Experience as a Model of Evangelical Theology* (Indianapolis: Light and Life Communications, 1990); Robert Alexander Webb, *Christian Salvation: Its Doctrine and Experience* (Ashburn, VA: Hess Publications, 1998); Dallas Willard, *Renovation of the Heart: Putting on the Character of Christ* (Colorado Springs, CO: Navpress, 2002).

Faith   Every evangelical child learns in Sunday school that faith means "Forsaking All I Trust Him." Faith plays a central role in evangelical devotion and exhortation. It also figures prominently in evangelical hymnody and *worship*. Numerous songs in evangelical hymnals extol the power and virtue of faith: "My Faith Looks Up to Thee," "Faith of Our Fathers, Living Still," "Faith Is the Victory," "Living By Faith." Evangelical *theology* also focuses attention on faith. Three volumes of the multivolume work of Dutch evangelical theologian G. C. Berkouwer contain "faith" in their titles: *Faith and Justification, Faith and Perseverance,* and *Faith and Sanctification.* Evangelicalism stems from the Protestant Reformation, which was energized by the three *solas,* one of which was *sola fide*—by faith alone. Together with all Protestants, evangelicals believe and teach that human beings cannot merit *salvation* and that salvation in all its aspects and dimensions is received "by *grace* through faith alone," not through works of righteousness. In this sense, faith is trust in *Jesus Christ* and his atoning death on the cross for righteousness and *reconciliation* with God. Another sense of faith, however, is belief. Evangelicals talk about confessing and proclaiming the faith, by which they mean the *gospel* of Jesus Christ and its immediate ramifications (basic orthodoxy). Finally, some evangelicals believe in a special, *supernatural* gift of faith mentioned by the apostle Paul in 1 Corinthians 12; especially Pentecostal and charismatic evangelicals seek the gift of faith as supernatural ability to believe in answers to *prayers* and to pray with power and supernatural results. It is closely related to the gift of *miracles.* In this sense, faith is confident expectation of special acts of God in response to prayers for healings, resolutions of crises, salvation of souls, and resources for the work of the *church.*

Evangelical theologians follow Protestant tradition in distinguishing between three dimensions of faith in relation to salvation: *notitia, assensus,* and *fiducia.* Evangelicals emphasize the third aspect of holistic faith, *fiducia,* which is heartfelt trust in Jesus Christ. *Notitia* is knowledge of certain facts about *God,* Jesus Christ, and the gospel. For example, evangelical thinkers normally affirm that holistic faith necessarily includes some understanding of Jesus Christ as God's Son and of his death on the cross for the *sins* of the world. (How much a person must know in order to be saved is a matter of some debate among evangelical theologians; some restrict salvation to those who explicitly hear the gospel of Jesus Christ, and others include as possibly saved

even persons who never hear the gospel explicitly preached but who arrive at an implicit understanding of the gospel through the "lights" of reason, conscience, and nature.) *Assensus* refers to the stage of faith that transcends mere propositional-cognitive knowledge and understanding in a motion of the will and mind to embrace the truth of the gospel for oneself. But evangelicals argue that merely giving assent to the truth of the gospel only makes one a "professing Christian" and not an authentic Christian. John Wesley and other early evangelicals distinguished between mere "professors" and those who went further to become "real Christians" by an act of the heart (transcending mind and will) called *fiducia. Fiducia* refers to a surrender of the self in total trust and commitment to the gospel. For evangelicals this is the crucial step that renders faith salvific; grace is the effectual cause of salvation, but faith as trust is its instrumental cause.

Evangelical theologians disagree about whether faith is a gift of God or an act of the human person. Many evangelicals would say it is both, but most incline one way or the other—toward emphasizing its nature as gift or its nature as a free human response to the call of God through the gospel. Evangelicals in the Lutheran and Reformed traditions tend to treat faith as gift, while those in the Arminian-Wesleyan traditions tend to treat it as human response to prevenient grace. Lutheran and Reformed evangelicals argue that if faith is salvation's instrumental cause and a human response, it is a meritorious work, and in that case salvation is not sheer gift of grace; they see Protestantism itself as at stake in saying faith is a gift. Arminian-Wesleyan evangelicals regard faith not as a work but as reception of gift; it is not a meritorious work but only an acknowledgment of sin and need of grace. They argue that if faith is a gift and not a free human response to the initiative of prevenient and resistible grace, the urgency of evangelism (especially as solicitation of faith) is undermined. Evangelical activism hangs on belief that *repentance* and faith are grace-enabled but free responses of hearers of the gospel.

Other debates over the nature of faith occasionally stir controversy within the evangelical theological community. Some evangelicals insist that authentic, holistic faith involves commitment to the lordship of Jesus Christ and to being his disciple in every aspect of one's life; others regard faith as bare, empty trust in Jesus Christ for *forgiveness* through his atoning death on the cross. For the latter evangelicals, commitment is a step beyond faith. The former tend to view authentic faith as faithfulness or at least as inward commitment to faithful obedience to the way of Jesus Christ; the latter view faithfulness as part of *sanctification,* which is distinct from the faith of *justification.* This is probably a false debate; both sides agree more than they acknowledge. Few, if any, evangelicals believe that faith can be entirely divorced from commitment to faithful following of Jesus Christ. The only question is how much that commitment must be present at the beginning of *fiducia* in order for it to receive the saving grace of God and result in reconciliation with God. Evangelicals also disagree about the certainty or assurance of faith. Is authentic faith compatible with doubt? Finally, evangelicals diverge over the question of faith's power to alter the circumstances of one's life. So-called "positive faith" charismatics emphasize faith's ability to appropriate health and prosperity; the majority of evangelicals do not consider health and prosperity fruits of faith or their lack as evidence of weak faith.

Donald G. Bloesch, *Essentials of Evangelical Theology,* vol. 1: *God, Authority, and Salvation* (San Francisco: Harper & Row, 1978); Larry D. Hart, *Truth Aflame: A Balanced Theology for Evangelicals and Charismatics* (Nashville: Thomas Nelson, 1999); R. Larry Shelton, "Initial Salvation: The Redemptive Grace of God in Christ," in *A Contemporary Wesleyan Theology,* vol. 1: *Biblical, Systematic, and Practical* (Grand Rapids: Francis Asbury Press, 1983), 469–516.

Forgiveness Evangelical theologians understand forgiveness in much the same way as other traditional Protestants. Forgiveness presupposes offense; humans offend *God's holiness* and love by disobedience. The doctrine of *sin* underlies the doctrine of forgiveness, and the doctrine of forgiveness is part of the larger doctrine of *salvation* and is usually treated under *justification.* For evangelicals, divine forgiveness is a conditional act of God's mercy in response to human *repentance*; it is God's act of reconciling humans to himself on the basis of love. Only because *Jesus Christ* offered his sinless life as a perfect sacrifice can God forgive sinners; the sacrifice of Christ was not a bid to persuade a reluctant God to forgive humans but God's own act of love and *justice* aimed at providing the basis for forgiveness. All evangelicals agree that in its fullest sense divine forgiveness of sin is wholly God's merciful gift and at the same time only received by sinners upon repentance. Some evangelicals believe—following the Anabaptists and Arminians (e.g., John Wesley)—that God sovereignly forgives the guilt of inherited sin (Adamic sin) that fell upon all humanity at the fall. This is one evangelical reading of Romans 5. This forgiveness is also only possible because of Christ's sacrificial death; evangelicals are people of the cross, who emphasize the cross event as the foundation of all salvation. Even those who believe the guilt of *original sin* is not imputed to infants for Christ's sake believe that people who grow to maturity need to repent of their own willful embrace of inherited sin in conscious acts of rebellion against the *law* of God.

Evangelicals place forgiveness at the center of salvation; the appeal of evangelists and evangelical preachers has always been to repent and believe for the forgiveness of sins. Of course, the larger issue surrounding forgiveness is *reconciliation* with God, which is more holistic than forgiveness; it involves being united with Christ and entering into a relationship of friendship with God. In spite of tremendous agreement about forgiveness, evangelical theologians disagree about some of its aspects, mainly its conditional dimensions. Is the offer of divine forgiveness universal? Is God an equal opportunity Savior? Or are only the elect offered forgiveness because provision for it was made only for them by Christ's death on the cross? Is forgiveness full and free at *conversion* (which involves repentance and *faith*)? Can forgiveness be lost by presumptuous sinning (e.g., refusing to forgive others) after conversion?

These issues divide evangelical theologians, and the fault line runs generally between Reformed and Arminian (or Wesleyan) theologies. Reformed evangelicals believe that divine forgiveness is provided only for the elect and that only they will be forgiven. This is based largely on the Reformed interpretation of John 14–17 and Romans 9–11. The elect are forgiven either at *baptism* as infants (in which case they need to confirm the *grace* of forgiveness by conscious repentance and faith later in life) or at conversion; in either case God assures that they will do what is necessary to be forgiven. Some Reformed theologians believe all of the elect were fully and freely forgiven by God when Christ died on the cross. Baptism and repentance simply appropriate that unconditional forgiveness for the elect person's life. That they will be baptized and that they will repent is rendered certain by God. Arminian and Wesleyan evangelical theologians view forgiveness much more conditionally. Christ's death on the cross provided the possibility of forgiveness for all who repent and believe in Jesus Christ as Lord and Savior. The "cost" of forgiveness is fully paid; only those who repent receive the benefits of that price paid at the cross.

Reformed evangelicals believe that the truly forgiven cannot fall away into condemnation; forgiveness is guaranteed by *election*, irresistible grace, and the grace of *perseverance*. Arminian and Wesleyan theologians question the unconditional eternal security of every believer; forgiveness is always conditional, and those who reject grace by sinning presumptuously without repentance are in danger of losing divine forgiveness and entering once again into condemnation.

Evangelical theologians agree that the result of divine forgiveness is a restored relationship with God marked by reconciliation. Another result is the promise of eternal life with God in *heaven* after the *resurrection*; those who repent are counted as forgiven and will be treated so at the judgment, even though they sin a thousand times a day (in thought if not in deed). One of Evangelicalism's greatest appeals is the gratuity of forgiveness; evangelicals (like most traditional Protestants) believe and proclaim that forgiveness cannot be earned or lost (even if some believe it can be rejected). Another benefit of forgiveness is ability to forgive others; evangelicals believe that the lifestyle of forgiving is made possible for those who are aware of being forgiven. The only condition for forgiveness of others is that one is forgiven; a fully restored relationship must await repentance and willingness to change.

Evangelical moral philosopher Lewis B. Smedes gained renown for his writings and lecturing on divine and human forgiveness in the last decades of the twentieth century. He explored the dynamics of human forgiveness and promoted its therapeutic value for persons who have been abused and betrayed. Smedes closely connected human forgiveness with divine forgiveness, as did Protestant theologian Reinhold Niebuhr earlier. Both rejected any easy forgiveness as unrealistic and counterproductive, but both associated real forgiveness with the realism of the cross and the awareness of *evil* and need of forgiveness within one's own personality.

The central message of Evangelicalism with regard to forgiveness, then, is that it is possible only in light of the cross of Jesus Christ and that it requires awareness of one's own guilt and shame and the painful *experience* of repentance and the joy of being forgiven by God. Contrary to much late twentieth-century and early twenty-first-century pop culture, evangelical *theology* rejects self-forgiveness as central to personal wholeness. Self-forgiveness depends on cosmic forgiveness, which is a completely gratuitous act of a merciful God through the pain of the sacrifice of the cross of Jesus Christ.

Millard Erickson, *Christian Theology,* vol. 3 (Grand Rapids: Baker Book House, 1985); Anthony A. Hoekema, *Saved by Grace* (Grand Rapids: Wm. B. Eerdmans, 1989); L. Gregory Jones, *Embodying Forgiveness: A Theological Analysis* (Grand Rapids: Wm. B. Eerdmans, 1995); Lewis B. Smedes, *Forgive and Forget: Healing the Hurts We Don't Deserve* (Waco, TX: Word Publishing, 1984); Miroslav Volf, *Exclusion and Embrace: A Theological Exploration of Identity, Otherness, and Reconciliation* (Nashville: Abingdon Press, 1996); Marsh G. Witten, *All Is Forgiven: The Secular Message in American Protestantism* (Princeton, NJ: Princeton University Press, 1993).

Freedom/Free Will Free will has always been one of the most controverted topics of evangelical *theology*. At the movement's beginnings during the Great Awakenings of the 1730s and 1740s, its major movers and shakers (John Wesley, George Whitefield, and Jonathan Edwards) disagreed strongly about human free will. Wesley and his Methodists affirmed it; Whitefield and Edwards and the Puritan-influenced revivalists denied it. In the nineteenth century Charles Spurgeon of London rejected free will in favor of absolute divine sovereignty, while *Charles Finney* embraced free will and seriously compromised divine sovereignty. The Methodists and offshoots in the *Holiness*

movements affirmed free will; the *Princeton theologians* denied it. One of Evangelicalism's most influential turn-of-the-century thinkers was Baptist theologian *Augustus Hopkins Strong,* who rejected free will in favor of unconditional *election* and irresistible *grace.* His main Southern Baptist counterpart, E. Y. Mullins, attempted to hold free will and divine sovereignty together. Throughout the twentieth century the controversy between Arminian and Calvinist evangelicals waxed and waned. At times evangelicals set it aside for the sake of cooperation and unity; at other times they argued and divided over the issue.

In the last decades of the century, certain Reformed theologians founded organizations to promote belief in divine sovereignty among evangelicals; to some extent they argued against free will. Two such organizations are the Alliance of Confessing Evangelicals and Christians United for Reformation. Among Southern Baptists the leading Calvinist appeal is made by the Founders Ministries, which holds an annual conference and publishes a journal. Arminians, who believe in free will, have not organized in the same way, but they are represented by Wesleyan, Holiness, and, Pentecostal organizations and publications. During the 1980s evangelical theologian *Clark Pinnock* edited two volumes of essays by various evangelical thinkers expounding and defending evangelical *Arminianism* and belief in freedom of the will (evangelical synergism): *Grace Unlimited* (Minneapolis: Bethany House, 1975) and *The Grace of God and the Will of Man* (Minneapolis: Bethany House, 1995). Two conservative Baptist Calvinist theologians responded by editing a volume of essays attempting to refute evangelical Arminianism. The two theologians are Bruce Ware and Thomas Schreiner, and their volume is titled *Still Sovereign: Contemporary Perspectives on Election, Foreknowledge, and Grace* (Grand Rapids: Baker Book House, 2000).

Throughout the final decade of the twentieth century and into the first decade of the twenty-first century, evangelical theology in North America fell into caustic debate over the issues of *God's* sovereignty and human free will. The debate was sparked by Pinnock's conversion from *Calvinism* to Arminianism and his subsequent development (together with other evangelical theologians) of *open theism*, which he considers consistent Arminian theology. Pinnock published several essays and books promoting Arminianism and open theism. Conservative evangelical Calvinists responded with vitriolic attacks not only on open theism but also on belief in free will generally. One leading evangelical Calvinist spokesperson declared Arminians "barely Christian." A new round of the old struggle between monergism (belief in God as the all-determining reality) and synergism (belief in divine-human cooperation) was underway within the evangelical theological community.

Most evangelical thinkers affirm free will; disagreement arises over the nature of free will. Monergists such as traditional Calvinists (Reformed thinkers) believe that humans are in a condition of bondage of the will to *sin*. They stand in the tradition of Augustine, Luther, and Calvin in affirming that due to the fall of *humanity* and subsequent corruption of human nature, people are only free to sin. As Augustine put it, before the fall Adam and Eve were able not to sin, but after the fall they and all their posterity are unable not to sin. Monergists claim that even sinners in bondage of the will to sin have a kind of free will, ability to do what their strongest dispositions incline them to do. The disposition to sin is the strongest disposition, apart from *supernatural*, irresistible grace. Human persons are free to sin, but they are not free to cooperate with grace. Thus, *regeneration* must precede *conversion*. Some Reformed thinkers affirm a limited free will after regeneration, while others deny any libertarian free will at all. (Libertarian free will is ability to do otherwise, to choose between alternative options.)

Arminian evangelicals believe in libertarian free will; the will is truly free only when the person is able to choose between alternatives. That is, free will is ability to do otherwise (than one does). Arminians believe not in unlimited free will but in situated free will. That is, humans are creatures, and therefore they do not possess absolute freedom of will. They cannot choose anything or everything. They can choose only among a limited range of options, and in many cases their choices are governed by nature and/or nurture. Evangelical Arminians affirm original sin and inherited corruption including bondage of the will to sin. However, they believe that God's prevenient grace revives the will and gives sinners the ability to choose to cooperate with grace unto *salvation*. The only cooperation that counts is bare acceptance of justifying and regenerating grace through *repentance* and *faith* in *Jesus Christ*. Arminians believe that humans have freedom of choice in most areas of life and that God's sovereignty does not override or control human decisions in most cases.

Evangelical monergists argue that synergism seriously compromises the *gospel* of salvation as a free gift of grace by making it dependent on human response. They also claim that synergism reduces God's sovereignty and majesty and elevates human power of free decision to a competitor with God. Some have even gone so far as to label free will an "idol" worshiped by Arminians. A few particularly aggressive evangelical monergists have labeled Arminianism heresy. Evangelical synergists such as Arminians and Anabaptists reject these accusations and give all glory for salvation to God alone; the free human response is grace-enabled and not a good work. It is mere, empty reception of the offer of the gift of salvation. They appeal to divine self-limitation to explain God's sovereignty in relation to human freedom. God chooses not to control all events but to share history making with humanity. Arminians accuse monergists of making God the author of sin and *evil* (thus impugning the character of God) and of making humans automatons in the process of salvation. They believe that responsibility, and especially culpability, for sin resulting in damnation must be tied to libertarian freedom. If one is not able to do otherwise, they argue, what justice is there in condemning that person? Most Arminians believe that God supplies sufficient prevenient grace for anyone to accept the mercy and grace of God; people are condemned for resisting the light that God gives them through conscience and nature, if not through the proclamation of the gospel.

David Basinger and Richard Basinger, eds., *Predestination and Free Will: Four Views of Divine Sovereignty and Human Freedom* (Downers Grove, IL: InterVarsity Press, 1986); F. Leroy Forlines, *The Quest for Truth: Answering Life's Inescapable Questions* (Nashville: Randall House, 2001); Thomas Oden, *The Transforming Power of Grace* (Nashville: Abingdon Press, 1993); R. C. Sproul, *Chosen by God* (Carol Stream, IL: Tyndale House, 1994).

God, Existence and Nature of

Evangelical *theology* affirms the existence of the personal, transcendent and immanent, holy, and loving God of the *Bible* and the broad sweep of Christian tradition. It is a theocentric rather than an anthropocentric theology; with the Westminster Shorter Catechism, evangelical theology believes that the chief end of *humanity*—and therefore of theology—is to glorify God and enjoy him forever. In this, evangelical theologians agree with classical Orthodox, Catholic, and Protestant theology. If evangelical theology in general has its own spin on traditional Christian belief in God, it may be an emphasis on God's personal nature. Evangelicals view God as relational; having a relationship with God lies at the heart of evangelical religion. One way in which many evangelical

thinkers express this is by highlighting the traditional Christian idea of God as the living God. That is, God is not static, immobile, wholly other, remote, otiose, or irrelevant. The God of evangelical faith is a living, speaking, revealing, and interactive God who calls humans to decision and relationship with him. Of course, this vision of God's dynamic quality is inseparable from belief in God's triunity; God can and does relate intimately with creatures (and especially humans who are created in God's *image*) precisely because God is a community of three persons. Evangelicals all affirm the doctrine of the *Trinity*, but the focus here will be on evangelical belief about God's existence and nature.

Evangelical theologians tend to avoid *natural theology*. There are exceptions to that general rule, but most evangelical thinkers are suspicious of purely rational proofs of the existence of God insofar as they are disconnected from special divine *revelation* and *faith*. At best, evangelicals believe, natural theology is an apologetic tool that should play no role in developing Christian thinking about who God is and about God's will and ways. Evangelicals believe in general revelation; they do not agree with Karl Barth's radical rejection of natural theology, which borders on denying any revelation of God in nature. However, with John Calvin they believe that general revelation does humans little good in their "search for God" because of the cognitive ramifications of original sin. Because humans are fallen into sin and their minds are darkened by sin, the unregenerate human mind is little more than a factory of idols. Especially Christian theological endeavors to know God and understand God's attributes should be based on special revelation including especially *Jesus Christ* and the Bible. *Carl F. H. Henry*, the "dean of evangelical theologians," published a six-volume work on knowledge of God with the general title *God, Revelation, and Authority* (Waco, TX: Word, 1976–82). In volume one, entitled *God Who Speaks and*

Shows (1976), the author criticizes all approaches to knowledge of God that do not begin with the *authority* of the Bible. Finding theology's starting point in general reason, natural evidences, or human *experience* (or any combination) is, according to Henry, doomed to failure if one is interested in knowing the true and living God. While reason and philosophy can provide some help in theological thinking, Henry argues, autonomous human reasoning cannot reach God; in order for God to be known, God must condescend to reveal himself. He has done that in Jesus Christ and Holy Scripture, which must be presupposed by theology as authoritative sources and norms. Henry is critical of natural theology because it ends up forcing divine revelation to meet secular criteria of thought.

Most evangelical theologians follow a line similar to Henry's, although some place more emphasis on natural theology as a servant of theology based primarily on special revelation, and some emphasize human spiritual experience more than he does. Norman Geisler borrows heavily from the thought of Thomas Aquinas in his approach to the doctrine of God's existence and nature; for him natural theology, including the proofs for the existence of God, plays a major role in Christian theology, even though it cannot by itself bring anyone into a saving encounter with God. *Donald Bloesch* is an evangelical theologian who especially eschews natural theology and places more stress on human experience of God through an encounter with Jesus Christ in the *Holy Spirit*. In this he is influenced by *Pietism*. Even Bloesch, however, will not abide any elevation of experience to an authoritative role alongside Scripture. Universal knowledge that God exists through an inner awareness (*sensus divinus*) is acknowledged by most evangelicals, as it was by Luther and Calvin in the sixteenth century, but knowledge of who God is and what God wants with us is reached only as God reveals himself. All evangelicals agree that Scripture is the special, authoritative Word of God through which people arrive at knowledge of God beyond that God exists.

Most evangelical theologians embrace some form of classical Christian theism that draws on the early church fathers' and medieval Christian theologians' reflections about God. A few evangelical theologians argue that this vision of God's nature is inconsistent with evangelical theology's general rejection of natural theology, because it is heavily influenced by philosophy. These evangelicals agree with Pascal that "the God of the philosophers is not the God of Abraham, Isaac and Jacob." The majority of evangelical thinkers, however, see little inconsistency between classical Christian theism in broad outlines and the biblical portrayal of God. Still, many who defend classical Christian theism adjust some of its traditional descriptions of God's attributes to bring them more closely into line with the biblical revelation of God as personal. According to classical Christian theism, God is self-sufficient, spiritual (as opposed to bodily or physical), eternal, immutable, omnipotent, omnipresent, and omniscient. These are the so-called absolute or incommunicable attributes of God, because God alone possesses them and they cannot be shared with creatures.

Some versions of *classical theism* add that God is infinite, simple (not composed of parts), and impassible (incapable of suffering). Some evangelical theologians who otherwise affirm classical theism debate one or more of these three attributes on biblical and/or logical grounds. The Westminster Confession of Faith states that God is "without body, parts or passions." Most Reformed evangelical thinkers agree and emphasize God's transcendence and otherness from creatures who are physical, composite, mutable, and subject to suffering. Nineteenth-century Reformed theologian Charles Hodge defended classical theism, including these attributes, in his three-volume *Systematic Theology* (Grand

Rapids: Wm. B. Eerdmans, 1973). More recently conservative evangelical theologian John Feinberg has defended a somewhat qualified version of classical theism in *No One Like Him* (Wheaton, IL: Crossway, 2001). Besides the so-called incommunicable attributes of God, classical theists describe God in terms of certain communicable or transitive attributes. They are also sometimes called the moral attributes, in contrast to the metaphysical attributes. These include God's goodness, love, *justice*, mercy, wisdom, faithfulness, and truthfulness.

All evangelical theologians reject panentheism, which views God as eternally existing in a mutually interdependent relationship with **creation**. Panentheism is regarded as heresy by almost all evangelical thinkers, because it denies *creatio ex nihilo* and therefore also that creation and **redemption** are acts of divine **grace**. It radically revises the biblical and historical vision of God as transcendent over the world and imports the world (as creation) into God's own being. However, some evangelical theologians believe that the God of classical theism is not much better than the God of panentheism; if the latter is too dependent and weak, the former is too impersonal and despotic. How can the God of classical theism be the compassionate God of the biblical narrative, they ask?

Reformed thinkers James Daane and Nicholas Wolterstorff raised theological and philosophical objections to certain aspects of classical Christian theism in their essays in *God and the Good*, edited by Clifton Orlebeke and Lewis Smedes (Grand Rapids: Wm. B. Eerdmans, 1975). Daane argued that God is not impassible and immutable but capable of being affected by human decisions and actions; Wolterstorff offered God's temporal everlastingness as an alternative to the traditional notion of God as timeless (simultaneous with all times). Donald Bloesch developed a "biblical-classical synthesis" that sought to take more seriously than classical theism the biblical motif of God's personal relationship with the world without discarding classical theism entirely. According to Bloesch, Greek and Hebrew ideas of God can be combined in Christian theology with the latter dominating. He states in *God the Almighty: Power, Wisdom, Holiness, Love* (Downers Grove, IL: InterVarsity Press, 1998; part of his seven-volume *Christian Foundations* series) that while God enjoys independence from the world, God makes himself vulnerable to pain and suffering in the world. He clearly does not mean only in the human nature of Christ. Bloesch and other evangelical thinkers, then, break from certain aspects of classical theism, such as impassibility, that seem to remove God too far from involvement in the affairs of humans.

The most significant controversy about the doctrine of God in evangelical thought in the late twentieth and early twenty-first centuries has to do with what is called **open theism**. In 1994 five evangelical thinkers (three theologians and two philosophers) published a book entitled *The Openness of God* (Downers Grove, IL: InterVarsity Press, 1994), which fell like a bombshell on the evangelical theological scene. *Clark Pinnock*, Richard Rice, John Sanders, William Hasker, and David Basinger denied the exhaustive and infallible foreknowledge of God while affirming God's omnipotence and omniscience. They argued that God limits himself in relation to creaturely *free will* so that he does not know future free decisions and actions. God's omniscience is simply his knowing all that there is to know; future free decisions and actions are unknowable.

This view, later called open theism, created a divisive controversy among evangelicals, with some declaring it heresy and others defending it as a legitimate evangelical opinion. Clark Pinnock and John Sanders published other books expounding and defending the open view of God, and evangelical theologian Gregory Boyd joined them with his own monographs on the subject, such as *God of the Possible* (Grand Rapids: Baker, 2000).

Critics of open theism responded with a spate of articles and books arguing that according to biblical revelation God cannot learn and that open theism amounted to little more than a form of panentheism. Open theists responded to their critics by exposing the Greek philosophical influences on conventional theism and playing up the fact that in the biblical narrative God is said to have changed his mind numerous times. How is it possible to change one's mind if one already knows in advance what the new state of mind will be? The open theists argued that their view of God is more consistent with biblical revelation and the evangelical practice of petitionary *prayer*. In 2002 the Evangelical Theological Society voted to investigate the memberships of two open theists. Various evangelical organizations and institutions declared that they would not employ open theists. On the other hand, major evangelical publishers printed books and articles by open theists, and a number of evangelical institutions declared they had no problem with employing them. Generally the fault line of the controversy runs along traditional Reformed versus Arminian line, although some Reformed thinkers have defended open theism as a legitimate option and a few Arminians have criticized it.

James K. Beilby and Paul R. Eddy, eds., *Divine Foreknowledge: Four Views* (Downers Grove, IL: InterVarsity Press, 2001); John W. Frame, *No Other God: A Response to Open Theism* (Phillipsburg, NJ: Presbyterian & Reformed Publishing, 2001); Christopher Kaiser, *The Doctrine of God: An Historical Survey* (Westchester, IL: Crossway Books, 1982); Ronald H. Nash, *The Concept of God: An Exploration of Contemporary Difficulties with the Attributes of God* (Grand Rapids: Zondervan, 1983).

Gospel   The word *evangelical* comes from a Greek word for "good news" or "good message." *Gospel* comes from an old English word for "*God's* story" or "the message of God." Thus, "evangelicals" are people of the gospel—of the good news of God's story or message. Proclaiming the gospel is a hallmark of evangelicals; Evangelicalism is a movement to recover and promote the gospel of *Jesus Christ*. Many evangelical theologians are concerned that evangelicals get the message *right* as well as get it *out*. A favorite saying among them is "If we are to get the gospel out [to the world], we had better get it right." Surprisingly, however, there are few evangelical theological treatises on the nature of the gospel; many evangelicals assume the content of the gospel and reflect very little about it. Others—especially fundamentalists—are notorious for overdefining the gospel and separating from those who disagree about any element of their interpretation of it.

Generally speaking, however, evangelicals understand the gospel through the lens of *Pietism*—the Protestant renewal movement that swept through Europe in the late seventeenth and early eighteenth centuries and that influenced the revivalists of the Great Awakenings, such as John Wesley, George Whitefield, and Jonathan Edwards. According to Pietism—which is decidedly Protestant theologically—the gospel is the good news that God accepts into reconciled relationship and imparts new spiritual life to anyone who repents and trusts in Jesus Christ. Persons do not have to earn any part of *salvation*; it is a free gift given to those who accept it by repenting and believing (trusting) in the *atonement* of Jesus Christ on the cross. Implied in this is the full and free salvation accomplished by Jesus Christ in his death on the cross. Furthermore, Pietism affirms, God accepts into a personal relationship with himself all converted sinners and shares his life with them in intimate union with Jesus Christ. All this is by *faith* alone and excludes works of righteousness (i.e., meritorious works that earn or establish salvation).

The basic elements of the gospel according to evangelicals, then, include

God's love, God's initiative in the salvation of sinners, Christ's atoning death, *reconciliation* with God, and spiritual rebirth (*regeneration*) by *grace* through faith, and the promise of eternal blessedness with God in *heaven* for those who accept God's free mercy. Throughout the 1990s some evangelical theologians became concerned that the gospel was being diluted in many evangelical churches and parachurch organizations and by some evangelical theologians. They suspected that it was being oversimplified for "spiritual seekers" and weakened into a feel-good message of cheap grace and easy-believism. They also worried about the influences of secular humanism and popular psychology and spirituality, which collaborated to make the gospel a human-centered, therapeutic message of self-realization and problem-solving. In 1999 a group of fifteen evangelical theologians met to carve out a unifying evangelical statement of the gospel; it was signed by one hundred and fourteen evangelical (including some fundamentalist) scholars, pastors, writers, and leaders (in addition to the drafting committee). The list of signers included persons from a broad spectrum of evangelical theological orientations and communities, including Reformed (Calvinists), Pentecostals, Wesleyans, Anabaptists, Baptists, Presbyterians, and Episcopalians. The statement, "The Gospel of Jesus Christ: An Evangelical Celebration," was published as a special insert by *Christianity Today* in its June 14, 1999, issue. Several ecumenical evangelical meetings were held to celebrate and discuss the statement, and at least one volume of essays exploring it was published. *Christianity Today* published a follow-up article, entitled "The Gospel in Brief," that gave voice to other evangelicals who did not necessarily sign or wholeheartedly agree with the lengthier statement (February 7, 2000).

"The Gospel of Jesus Christ: An Evangelical Celebration" begins with a preamble, continues with a lengthy exposition of the gospel itself, and closes with a theologically fussy statement of "Affirmations and Denials" that reads like a list of anathemas against those who disagree with points allegedly implied by the gospel. Readers of the entire statement may notice a difference of tone and texture between the gospel exposition—which is relatively irenic and generic—and the affirmations and denials, which rely heavily on a very traditionalist Reformed system of *theology*. According to the exposition of the gospel, "The heart of the Gospel is that our holy, loving Creator, confronted with human hostility and rebellion, has chosen in his own freedom and faithfulness to become our holy, loving Redeemer and Restorer." It continues by emphasizing Jesus Christ as the sole Savior of *humanity* and salvation, offered freely to all who trust in him. It highlights the Reformation doctrine of imputed righteousness, the belief that even saved persons have no righteousness of their own—even as a gift of God implanted in them—but are clothed only in Jesus Christ's righteousness. The statement balances the objective, forensic aspects of salvation with the more subjective, interior aspects and affirms that salvation is entirely a work of the Trinitarian God received by sinners as a free gift by faith. Few evangelicals would disagree with anything in the statement's exposition of the gospel; it expresses what most, if not all, evangelicals have always believed and taught. Some evangelicals in the Anabaptist and Wesleyan traditions may have qualms about the strongly forensic doctrine of alien, imputed righteousness and may prefer to talk about the working of God's righteousness within persons producing *holiness* of life.

Problems appear in the second half of the statement, which expresses eighteen affirmations and denials. To some evangelical critics this portion of the "Celebration" reads like a mini–systematic theology; a summation of Reformed dogmatics. Affirmation and denial number eight says,

We affirm that the atonement of Christ by which, in his obedience, he offered a perfect sacrifice, propitiating the Father by paying for our sins and satisfying divine *justice* on our behalf according to God's eternal plan, is an essential element of the Gospel. We deny that any view of the Atonement that rejects substitutionary satisfaction of divine justice, accomplished vicariously for believers, is compatible with the teaching of the Gospel.

Some evangelicals are uncomfortable with the language of Christ "propitiating the Father" by his death on the cross, because it implies a division between the love and the justice of God and between the Son and the Father. They prefer to speak of Christ's "expiation" of our sins through his death. Both are valid English translations of the Greek word *hilasterion*, which Paul uses for the reconciling atonement of Christ's death on the cross. However, propitiation implies assuaging wrath, while expiation implies covering of sin. Many evangelicals find the latter more compatible with God's love manifested in the cross and believe the former is inextricably tied to a medieval view of God as a bloodthirsty feudal tyrant.

Most objectionable to many evangelicals, however, is the statement that the "substitutionary" and "satisfaction" theories of the atonement are normative for the gospel itself. No particular theory or model of the atonement is universally binding in the history of the *church* universal; only some denominational confessional statements elevate Anselm's and/or Calvin's theory of the atonement to *status confessionis*. Many evangelicals would prefer to distinguish clearly between the gospel itself and systematic theological and particular confessional interpretations of the gospel. Luther defined the gospel simply as "nothing but the preaching about Christ, Son of God and of David, true God and man, who by his death and resurrection has overcome for us the sin, death and *hell* of all who believe in him" ("Preface to the New Testament, 1546," in Timothy F.

Lull, ed., *Martin Luther's Basic Theological Writings* [Minneapolis: Fortress Press, 1989], 115). Many evangelicals agree wholeheartedly.

Roger E. Olson and Gabriel Fackre, "Evangelical Essentials? Reservations and Reminders," *Christian Century* 116, no. 23 (Aug. 25–Sept. 1, 1999): 816–19; R. C. Sproul, *Getting the Gospel Right: The Tie That Binds Evangelicals Together* (Grand Rapids: Baker, 1999); "What's the Good News? Nine Evangelical Leaders Define the Gospel," *Christianity Today* 44, no. 2 (Feb. 7, 2000): 46–51.

Grace   Every evangelical child learns in Sunday school that grace is "God's Riches At Christ's Expense." Evangelical theologians sometimes cringe at such easy-to-remember but misleading memory devices. Evangelical *theology* wishes to emphasize that there is no division or conflict between *God* and *Jesus Christ*; grace is the unmerited favor of God expressed in Christ and communicated through the *Holy Spirit*. The evangelical doctrine of grace is heavily indebted to the Protestant Reformers, including especially Luther, Calvin, and the Anabaptists. It is also influenced by the twists and turns of post-Reformation theology, including especially the Puritans and the early Methodists. Evangelical theologians agree with the Protestant Reformation that grace is not an ontologically transforming substance or energy conveyed through the *sacraments* ex opere operato—by virtue of the act itself (apart from faith). Rather, grace is a power and a relationship; it is legal and personal in nature. Grace is simply God's love and favor toward persons that cannot be earned; it is sheer gift. It is rooted in God's love and serves both God's glory and human spiritual fulfillment. The aim of grace is to reconcile sinners with God and restore in them the *image of God*.

For evangelicals grace lies at the heart of the *gospel*—the good news—from which the evangelical movement derives its name. (*Evangelical* means "of the gospel" or "of the good news.") The good news is that God bestows *salvation* with all its benefits and blessings fully and freely apart from merit; it cannot be earned or deserved but must be accepted as totally free gift from God. Some evangelicals talk about a *covenant* of grace that God established with fallen *humanity* after it failed to keep the covenant of works. Unlike the covenant of works, the covenant of grace requires nothing except *repentance* and *faith*. Upon repentance and faith (*conversion*) sinners are fully forgiven and given the gift of the Holy Spirit for union with *Jesus Christ*. They are adopted as sons and daughters of God and made joint heirs with Christ to receive God's blessings in *heaven*. Evangelicals reject any idea of required "grace boosters"— rituals or performances or works that must be observed in order for grace to have its full effect and that can increase God's grace in one's life. Grace cannot be increased by human religious performance; it can increase only according to need and that only by God's free offer and presence received.

In all of this, evangelicals reject what they understand to be the doctrines of grace found in Roman Catholic folk religion, if not in official Roman Catholic theology. Dialogue between evangelicals and Catholics has helped to overcome certain misunderstandings about grace on both sides. However, generally speaking, evangelicals are reluctant to dissect and categorize grace into various types such as justifying grace and purifying grace. This is more typical of scholastic theology and associated especially with medieval Catholic thought. Rather, evangelicals view grace as one power and relationship with varying functions. The two main distinctions are prevenient grace and saving grace.

All evangelicals believe that grace precedes and enables even the *initium fidei*—the beginning of faith. If a person is converted to Christ and becomes saved (regenerated, justified, etc.), it is

only because God's prevenient grace called, convicted, enlightened, and enabled him or her to receive Christ by faith. This rules out Pelagianism and semi-Pelagianism, which to different degrees place the initiative of salvation on the human side. In evangelical theology, as in Protestant theology generally, God initiates *reconciliation* and restoration in Christ and through the Holy Spirit. Because of bondage to *sin*, human persons apart from *supernatural* empowering and regenerating grace cannot and will not exercise even the beginning of a goodwill toward God. Evangelical theology places a great deal of emphasis on Ephesians 2:5–10, which speaks of the natural person's death in "trespasses and sins" and the free gift of salvation, of which no person may boast. Salvation, the apostle teaches, is not of ourselves but entirely of God. Another crucial passage is Philippians 2:12–13, which teaches that God is at work in anyone who is working out their salvation; that is a reference to prevenient (assistant and enabling) grace. Evangelicals believe that not only salvation but also *creation* itself is of grace. Creation is sheer gift for the glory of God and benefit of humanity. It both contradicts nature (as fallen under a curse) and fulfills nature (as it was originally intended). The proper response to grace is gratitude that results in works of love, but works of love in no way boost or increase grace.

Evangelicals disagree among themselves about several issues of the doctrine of grace. The most significant controversy is whether grace is resistible or irresistible. This debate is rooted in the old Calvinist-Arminian controversy. Some evangelical theologians, who side with the followers of sixteenth-century Reformer John Calvin, argue that God's grace is always effectual and cannot be resisted or thwarted. Prevenient grace, in this account, is given only to those who are elected for salvation unconditionally; it bends their wills to repent and believe in Jesus Christ. *Regeneration* and faith are gifts prior to conversion; only in this way can salvation be completely a gift that is not at all earned even by the right decision. The decision is itself a product of grace.

Other evangelicals prefer to follow the teachings of James Arminius and John Wesley that prevenient grace overcomes the deadness of the will due to sin and sheds light into the sinner's heart and mind but leaves intact his or her ability to resist. Prevenient grace assists in every good decision and action, but it does not usurp the role of *free will*. Rather, free will is itself a gift of grace. The act of the free will to receive saving grace for reconciliation with God through repentance and faith is the person's own contingent, not determined or coerced, act. These evangelicals place a great deal of emphasis on decision and appeal to hearers of the gospel to make the right decision and act upon it (e.g., walk down an aisle to pray a "sinner's *prayer*" with the minister or evangelist and then be baptized). To Calvinist evangelicals this appears semi-Pelagian; it appears to place the initiative in salvation on the human side. However, Arminian evangelicals insist that even the right decision is enabled only by God's grace; apart from grace no person seeks after God.

Michael S. Horton, *Putting Amazing Back into Grace: Embracing the Heart of the Gospel* (Grand Rapids: Baker, 2002); Samuel J. Mikolaski, *The Grace of God* (Grand Rapids: Wm. B. Eerdmans, 1966); Thomas Oden, *The Transforming Power of Grace* (Nashville: Abingdon, 1993).

Heaven Evangelicals love to sing about heaven; that may not be as true in the twenty-first century as it was in the nineteenth and early twentieth centuries. However, the hymnody of heaven has left a lasting impression on evangelical consciousness and *theology*. Songs such as "When We All Get To Heaven" and "In the Sweet By and By

(We Shall Meet on That Beautiful Shore)" were sung enthusiastically in evangelical revivals and Sunday evening *church* services. Some critics of evangelical piety have labeled it "otherworldly asceticism" because of its emphasis on paradise (life with Christ after death) and heaven (the eternal state of blessedness with *God* after the *resurrection*). Many evangelicals were poor and disenfranchised in the eighteenth and nineteenth centuries, and heaven was their only hope for peace, health, and happiness. In the twentieth century evangelicals increasingly entered the mainstream, and the focus of evangelical folk religion gradually shifted from the hope of heaven to problem solving on earth. Nevertheless, nearly all evangelicals—including scholars and theologians—believe fervently in life after death, including existence with Christ in a blessed state of fulfillment. Evangelical theologians have generally tried to observe Reinhold Niebuhr's caveat against wanting to know too much about the furniture of heaven or the temperature of *hell*, but occasionally they have delved into speculation about the nature of the life beyond the grave. It is always rooted in the biblical witness, even if it is sometimes influenced by nineteenth-century spiritualism and ancient Greek philosophy.

The evangelical theological consensus about heaven is that those persons who die in a state of *grace* (i.e., forgiven and reconciled with God by grace through *faith*) are promised life everlasting in God's presence and in the presence of their Savior *Jesus Christ*. This belief is shared by most traditional Christians, and evangelical theologians hold fast to a semiliteralism about the future state of the saved. Of course, they eschew folk images of heaven such as Saint Peter at the "pearly gates" and people becoming *angels* and floating around strumming on harps. These have no basis in *Scripture*, but evangelical theologians do believe that the biblical imagery of golden streets and gates of pearl points to a surplus of joy and fulfillment that cannot be described. Heaven will be a real place, even if only in a dimensional and not geographical sense. Evangelical theology does not picture heaven as a specific geographical location in the universe but as a dimension unseen by ordinary human sensory capacities. Jesus spoke about his Father's "house" with many "rooms" (sometimes mistranslated "many mansions") and promised to return to take his disciples to be with him there. This and other biblical promises of eternal satisfaction with God after death play a very prominent role in evangelical *eschatology*.

Evangelical theology does not include belief in purgatory as a vestibule of heaven; those who die in Christ go directly into paradise (the intermediate "heaven" between bodily death and the *resurrection*) to be with Christ (per Christ's own promise to the thief dying on the cross beside him) and eventually are taken into the fullness of the "new heaven and new earth" after Christ's return to earth and the general resurrection of the dead and great judgment. Most evangelical theologians distinguish between paradise and heaven. *Paradise* is derived from a term for oasis; Jesus used it to describe the abode of the righteous after death before the resurrection. Evangelical theologians believe that very little can be known about paradise; it is simply a pleasant, restful, nonbodily but conscious existence in God's holy and loving presence. Evangelical theologians view "heaven" as the fulfillment of paradise after the *return of Christ* and resurrection of the dead. The righteous dead in paradise will be taken into heaven, which is viewed as a restored earth—freed from the curse brought about by the fall of *humanity* into *sin*—where they will *worship* God and reign with Christ forever. There they will be fulfilled in God's own *image* as they were meant to be before the fall into sin intervened. It will be a place of transformed physicality—a bodily existence without corruption, decay,

or death. People will still be human beings, but they will be glorified as Jesus Christ was glorified sometime after his resurrection.

Some evangelical theologians reject the intermediate paradise state in favor of a belief in immediate translation into heaven. That is, they regard those who died in a state of grace as already (from their perspective) enjoying the fullness of heaven; death takes them immediately there. This presupposes a stark contrast between earthly, historical time and eternity. These evangelical theologians are impressed by the argument that a dualism between body and soul is a foreign element of Greek thought, alien to biblical religion. There is no disembodied existence; humans persons are embodied souls rather than souls wearing bodies. Without bodily resurrection there is no conscious existence of human beings. Very few evangelical theologians accept the Adventist view of "soul sleep," which implies an unconscious state of the dead before the resurrection. Evangelicals who deny the intermediate state prefer to picture the dead in Christ as already in the resurrection enjoying the bliss of heaven. The rest of us will join them there. Other evangelicals point out the difficulties with this vision of the future; it contradicts Paul's assurance to the Thessalonians that the dead will not precede the rest of us in resurrection but we will all be raised together (1 Thess. 4:15–18). It also has difficulty accounting for Jesus' promise to the thief on the cross beside him and for Paul's testimony about a man (himself) who was taken up into paradise temporarily and returned (2 Cor. 12). Because of biblical passages such as these, most evangelical theologians accept the idea of an intermediate, nonbodily, conscious state of the dead that is not the fulfillment of biblical promises or the blessed hope of believers but a waiting for future heavenly existence.

A few evangelical theologians regard heaven as a renovated creation; the physical universe and perhaps especially the earth will be transformed by God into a perfect habitat for resurrection bodies. They base this on Romans 8:18–25; the creation itself will be liberated from its bondage to decay. Such evangelicals believe that there will be some kind of union or communion between the dimension where God dwells (also called heaven) and the transformed world. This is symbolized in John's vision in Revelation 21, where the heavenly city descends to earth and there is "a new heaven and a new earth." Evangelical scholars admit it is difficult or impossible to describe this future reality, but they agree that it will be the perfect fulfillment of what the garden of Eden in Genesis symbolized— a state of fellowship between creatures and God free from sin and death. Many other evangelical thinkers view heaven proper as a totally new reality after earth passes away in a prophesied conflagration. Heaven will be that dimension where God and Christ now dwell, populated by glorified human persons with resurrection bodies as well as by angels. In either case, evangelical theologians agree, heaven will be beyond the best imaginings of earthly minds and the fulfillment of every good potential possessed by creatures. Best of all, it will be free of temptation and filled with the glory of God; people will realize their chief end as described in the Westminster Shorter Catechism: "to glorify God and enjoy him forever."

A. J. Conyers, *The Eclipse of Heaven: Rediscovering the Hope of a World Beyond* (Downers Grove, IL: InterVarsity Press, 1992); John Gilmore, *Probing Heaven: Key Questions on the Hereafter* (Grand Rapids: Baker, 1989); Anthony Hoekema, *The Bible and the Future* (Grand Rapids: Wm. B. Eerdmans, 1979); Peter Toon, *Heaven and Hell* (Nashville: Thomas Nelson, 1986); Jerry L. Walls, *Heaven: The Logic of Eternal Joy* (New York and Oxford: Oxford University Press, 2002).

Hell Evangelicalism has a reputation in some quarters for overemphasizing "hellfire and brimstone." That reputa-

tion comes from a caricature of revivalist preaching, which is (like all caricatures) partly true. Evangelical founder Jonathan Edwards preached about "sinners in the hands of an angry God," and nineteenth-century frontier revivalists warned listeners of the torments of hell and begged them to "turn or burn." Evangelical theologians have not been as enthusiastic about hell as the caricature would suggest, and yet they all include it in their reflections on biblical *revelation* and systematic truth. Most evangelical thinkers are reluctant to talk or write very much about the "temperature of hell"; they try to avoid overliteralization and speculation in their accounts of the "destiny of the wicked." Yet they believe in hell and see it as integral to the message that Evangelicalism proclaims and by which evangelicals live.

While many mainstream and especially liberal Protestant and Catholic theologians relativize or deny hell, evangelical theologians preserve it without celebrating it. Hell is for them a necessary aspect of God's *justice* and human sinfulness, and it is clearly taught in Scripture; Jesus talked more about hell ("Gehenna") than any other person in the *Bible*. Especially the New Testament is filled with references to a "lake of fire," into which *Satan* and his minions and followers will be cast, and to Hades as the underworld where the wicked who reject God's mercy await their final fate in the lake of fire. While some nonevangelical theologians may view these as an empty threat or holdovers from primitive religious thought, evangelicals regard them as pointers to the very real possibility of total and eternal loss of spiritual fulfillment and hope for *reconciliation* with God.

More debate about hell than about *heaven* exists within evangelical *theology*. While all evangelical theologians agree that hell is real and everlasting, they do not all agree on the nature of its punishment. Is hell physical torment? Is it everlasting suffering or annihilation? Do those who die outside of God's *grace* go directly to hell, or do they go some-where to await judgment and con-signment to hell, or are they in an unconscious state until then? These are the main questions that divide evangeli-cal thinkers about hell. Some evangelical theologians view hell as spiritual rather than physical or even quasi-physical torment. After all, how do souls or nonphysical, *resurrection* bodies suffer physically? Most evangelical thinkers agree that fire is a symbol of hell's suffering, but some view it as a symbol of a spiritual torment such as eternal, hopeless separation from *God*. Persons in hell will be locked up in their self-centeredness and pride and allowed to exist eternally knowing that they missed eternal blessedness, satisfaction, and ful-fillment in heaven. *C. S. Lewis's* allegory of hell, *The Great Divorce*, has influenced many evangelical theologians to regard hell as God's last, painful refuge for those who would not be happy in God's presence. In consigning people to hell, then, God says, "Not my will but thine be done." For such theologians hell's door is locked on the inside. This view of hell comports better with God's love and mercy than a more traditional vision of hell borrowed from medieval writer Dante. Other evangelical thinkers remain closer to the medieval tradition and interpret hell as endless quasi-physical torment.

Some evangelical theologians are attracted to annihilationism, the belief that hell is the extinction of the wicked as a last act of God's justice and mercy—a kind of capital punishment. Maverick evangelical theologian *Clark Pinnock* has endorsed this idea, and relatively conservative, standard evangelical pas-tor and theological writer John Stott of England has raised it as a valid possibil-ity. Annihilationists point out that Scrip-ture often refers to hell as death (e.g., "the second death," Rev. 20:14) and as destruction. They also appeal to the logic of God's nature; if God is love and good-ness, how could he allow any of his crea-tures to suffer eternally without hope of

redemption? Pinnock regards the God of eternal suffering a tyrant and a sadist; the God of annihilationism is more mer-ciful. Critics of annihilationism point to Scriptures that refer to hell as including endless suffering (e.g., gnashing of teeth and the smoke of their torment rising forever). They argue that capital punish-ment is not God's method of dealing with rebels; God respects the life he has given so much that he will not take it away. Fortunately, this debate between annihilationist evangelicals and other evangelicals has remained civil and respectful. However, in the last days of the twentieth century and in the early twenty-first century, some conservative evangelical leaders began to imply that annihilationism might be heresy. Many oppose it in part because it is the stan-dard belief of Adventists, who they con-sider cultists.

Many evangelical theologians believe that hell proper is the lake of fire that Jesus called Gehenna and that John saw in his Revelation (chapter 20). Satan and his angels will be cast there, and every-one who followed them rather than trusting in Jesus Christ will go with them. The wicked dead are in Hades awaiting its emptying into the lake of fire (Rev. 20). Hades is not hell but a holding cell (so to speak) for hell (just as paradise is a place of waiting for heaven). The pre-cise nature of Hades is no clearer than that of Gehenna, and some evangelical theologians do not believe in it; they view the dead as unconscious or as already (by some twist of time) in hell proper. How-ever, Revelation 20:14 prophesies that death and Hades will be emptied into hell (the lake of fire) after the great judg-ment of all people and nations. Further-more, Jesus' story of the rich man and Lazarus implies that he believed in an intermediate state of conscious suffering for those who die outside of God's mercy and grace.

William Crocket, ed., *Four Views on Hell* (Grand Rapids: Zondervan, 1992); Peter Toon, *Heaven and Hell* (Nashville: Thomas

Nelson, 1986); Jerry L. Walls, *Hell: The Logic of Damnation* (Notre Dame, IN: University of Notre Dame Press, 1992).

Holiness One major submovement within Evangelicalism is the *Holiness movement*. It arose among disaffected Methodists in the middle of the nineteenth century; they believed that the mainline Methodist church in America (the Methodist Episcopal Church) had lost its original fervor and zeal for Christian perfection as taught by Methodist founder John Wesley in the eighteenth century. Various Holiness revivalists traveled around the United States establishing revivals ("protracted meetings") and churches. Eventually several denominations emerged; the best known are the Church of the Nazarene, the Wesleyan Church, and the Free Methodist Church. The Salvation Army also has roots in the Holiness movement. The distinctive witness of this movement is *entire sanctification* as a normal Christian *experience* by the *grace* of *God*. That is, Holiness evangelicals believe and teach that every Christian can attain Christian perfection of life interpreted as "perfection in love." This is a gift of the *Holy Spirit* received by *faith* and often accompanied by emotional manifestations. Many Pentecostal churches and denominations began within the Holiness movement and believe in three distinct blessings—*conversion, sanctification,* and Holy *Spirit baptism* accompanied by speaking in tongues. Non-Pentecostal Holiness evangelicals believe in two blessings—conversion and entire sanctification—and do not embrace speaking in tongues. The Holiness and Pentecostal movements possess no monopoly on holiness, however, and most evangelical Christians believe that holiness of life and character is a mark of authentic Christianity. Unlike Holiness evangelicals, however, they regard sanctification as a process of growth in holiness and not as a momentary event of being entirely cleansed from the corrup-

tion of *sin*. Some Holiness evangelicals believe the second blessing involves eradication of the fallen, sinful nature such that the sanctified Christian no longer struggles against "the world, the flesh, and the *devil*."

Most evangelical theologians are careful to point out that holiness is not first and foremost a moral achievement but God's own attribute of being set apart from *creation* both metaphysically and morally. Holiness designates God's deity; God is holy because he is other than anything finite, limited, and prone to imperfection. But God's holiness is not a morally neutral condition; it includes God's perfect righteousness. God's holiness is his "wholly otherness" from creaturely finitude and impurity. Holiness is, however, one of God's transitive or communicable attributes; it can be shared in limited degree with human persons, in part because they are created in God's *image*. Thus, evangelical thinkers agree, human beings can become partially holy through the grace of God and the power of the indwelling Holy Spirit.

Most evangelical theologians think of holiness as a progressive state that begins at conversion; conversion includes *regeneration*—the event of being "born again" by God's Spirit and becoming a new creation in Christ Jesus. As one evangelical Baptist theologian of the early twentieth century declared, regeneration is "the expulsive power of a new affection." The born-again person is given a new love for new things that expels love for sin. Jonathan Edwards considered regeneration a gift of God that altered the affections so that persons gain a "benevolence for being." In any case, evangelicals believe regeneration is the beginning of sanctification, which is attainment of holiness. In sanctification the person's inward condition is gradually changed to conform to his or her position as reconciled with God in *Jesus Christ*. Evangelical theologians almost uniformly regard holiness as conformity to the character of Christ; Jesus Christ is the model of human holiness. It includes submission to the will of God, dedication to God's cause (i.e., the *kingdom of God*), conformity to Christ (i.e., doing what Jesus would do), and the fruit of the Spirit listed by Paul in Galatians—especially love, joy, and peace. Evangelicals do not believe human persons can ever attain God's own metaphysical, divine holiness, but they do believe in the empowering presence of God's Spirit to help "yielded Christians" become increasingly like Jesus Christ. Evangelicals influenced by the *Keswick movement* define holiness as death to self and consecration of life to Jesus Christ; they view it as involving experiences of the cross in which a person identifies with the crucified Christ "nailing self to the cross with him" and allowing Jesus to replace the self that has died. Although this is not the same perfectionism as that of the Holiness movement, it is another kind of perfectionism.

Evangelical theologians disagree about the extent to which a person can become holy before death and resurrection and whether holiness is attainable in a moment. Holiness evangelicals and some Keswick-inspired evangelicals believe passionately in entire sanctification and holiness as a normal achievement in the Christian life. They look back to John Wesley's teaching in *A Plain Account of Christian Perfection*, which includes the possibility of entire sanctification in a moment. Wesley was careful to point out that by "entire sanctification" he did not mean metaphysical perfection as freedom from all error and temptation. Rather, he taught it as "perfection in love," in which sanctified persons would always act out of right motives driven by love. According to Wesley and contemporary Holiness evangelicals, this is a gift and not a human achievement; it can only be attained as God imparts it as transforming grace into human lives. It can be lost, and it waxes and wanes. Keswick perfectionism also views holiness as a gift but emphasizes that believers need to

desire it and seek it; it arrives at the apex of a process of dying to self through focusing on the sacrifice of Christ on the cross. From then on, the consecrated person lives for others, as Christ died for others. This, Keswickians believe, is a "higher" or "deeper" Christian life than ordinary Christian life that settles for *forgiveness* and *reconciliation* with God by faith.

Most evangelical theologians reject any kind of Christian perfection before death and glorification with Christ in the resurrection; only then will we be fully like him. Before then, they argue, holiness is a process of gradually "putting on Christ," which means becoming Christlike in character and conduct through pursuit of holy living in the power of the Holy Spirit. This involves *prayer, worship, Bible* study, devotional life, helping others, and committing all of life to God. Perfectionist evangelicals appeal to Jesus' admonition to "Be perfect, therefore, as your heavenly Father is perfect" (Matt. 5:48 NRSV). Nonperfectionist, gradualist evangelicals appeal to Paul's self-description in Romans 7, which they take to be an account of the normal Christian life as struggle between sin and obedience to God.

Evangelicals offer different descriptions of holiness. All agree that it is closely related to God's own character as revealed in Jesus Christ. Many emphasize that it involves being separated from all that is profane and related to that which is sacred—God's will and cause. For them it is not first and foremost a moral condition so much as a missional position of being dedicated to the kingdom of God. Christians are holy to the extent that they sacrifice themselves to the cause of God. Other evangelicals view holiness primarily as obedience to God's *law*, understood as love for God and neighbor, but also as the moral codes of the Old Testament Ten Commandments and New Testament teachings about morality. Many evangelicals understand holiness as manifesting the fruit of the Spirit listed by Paul in Galatians 5: love, joy, peace, patience, kindness, generosity, faithfulness, gentleness, self-control. Some Reformed evangelicals, such as **Donald G. Bloesch,** view holiness primarily as profound faith that is on its way to perfection of faith. These differences in evangelical *theology* are primarily differences of emphasis; most evangelicals would agree that all of these visions of holiness play some role in defining it. The disagreement is over the core or heart of holiness.

A major controversy broke out between conservative evangelical theologians in the 1990s over whether holiness is a requirement for salvation. What came to be known as the lordship controversy was in fact just another round in the old antinomian debate among Protestants. Two evangelical scholars associated with Dallas Theological Seminary published monographs arguing that it is possible to be fully and truly justified (saved by grace) without Christian holiness as submission to the lordship of Jesus Christ. The most noted proponent of this view, evangelical Zane Hodges, believed he was simply defending the classical Protestant doctrine of salvation by grace alone against those who base salvation partly on human moral achievement. Proponents of lordship salvation responded with a number of books and articles arguing that authentic salvation cannot exist apart from consecration of life to the service of Jesus Christ as Lord, manifested in living a morally pure life actively obedient to the teachings of Jesus. California evangelist and pastor John MacArthur led the forces of lordship salvation against Hodges and others who rejected it. Although the debate was not explicitly over "holiness," it did revolve around it. One side argued that holiness is a minimally necessary sign of salvation; the other side explained holiness as a second stage of Christian life that is more or less optional for salvation. Most evangelicals view the truth as lying between these two extremes; for them holiness is a nat-ural and inevitable result of authentic Christian conversion. It is not a requirement for receiving or keeping salvation, but it is a sure sign of salvation already present by grace. The difference lies in attitude toward holiness: having to attain it versus getting to receive it.

Donald L. Alexander, ed., *Christian Spirituality: Five Views of Sanctification* (Downers Grove, IL: InterVarsity Press, 1989); Donald G. Bloesch, *Essentials of Evangelical Theology,* vol. 2: *Life, Ministry, and Hope* (New York: Harper & Row, 1979); William M. Greathouse, *Wholeness in Christ: Toward a Biblical Theology of Holiness* (Kansas City, MO: Beacon Hill Press, 1998); J. C. Ryle, *Holiness: Its Nature, Hindrances, Difficulties, and Roots* (Moscow, ID: Charles Nolan Publishers, 2001).

Holy Spirit   Evangelical *theology* is Trinitarian theology; it includes belief in three divine persons inseparably united in nature: one *God* in three persons, blessed *Trinity*. Evangelical theologians regard the Holy Spirit as the third person of the Trinity and as the divine person who testifies of *Jesus Christ* and redeems forgiven human beings from the corruption of the fall. That is, in the economy of *salvation* the Holy Spirit has the special functions of witnessing within human minds and hearts that Jesus Christ is Lord and that *Scripture* is the inspired Word of God and of transforming those who repent and believe in Jesus Christ into the *image* of Christ. Of course, many other works are especially attributed to the Holy Spirit in classical Christian theology and by evangelical theologians: enduing believers with power for service, illuminating their minds to understand Scripture, drawing people to the *gospel,* and enabling them to choose *grace* in spite of the bondage of the will to *sin,* imparting the gifts and fruit of the Spirit to believers. Many evangelical theologians also regard the Holy Spirit as especially involved in *creation* as the person of God who gives life, brings order out of chaos, and creates anticipations of the eschatological glory of the future **kingdom of God** and new **heaven** and earth. Some believe that the Holy Spirit's function within the eternal being of God (immanent Trinity) is that of bond of love between Father and Son.

Evangelical theology follows classical Christian orthodoxy on many aspects of the doctrine of the Holy Spirit, usually without staking out a particular position vis-à-vis the debate between Eastern Orthodoxy and the Roman Catholic church about the procession of the Holy Spirit. Does the Holy Spirit eternally proceed from the Father and the Son, or only from the Father? This is the so-called *filioque* controversy that contributed to the division between Eastern and Western halves of Christendom in AD 1054. Evangelicals are not particularly interested in it. They are especially interested in the functions of the Holy Spirit, however, because the Holy Spirit is so closely associated with salvation in Scripture and in the Great Tradition of Christian belief.

Evangelical theologians emphasize that the Holy Spirit is a person and not merely a force or power of God. This is, of course, consistent with classical Trinitarian belief, but evangelicals fear much of Christianity has relegated the Holy Spirit to the status of a presence of God in the world and muted the Spirit's full personal nature. Of course, debates about that exist even within evangelical Christianity. Pentecostals, for example, often accuse other evangelicals of neglecting the Holy Spirit, especially the Spirit's full personhood and continuing presence as giver of **supernatural** gifts to the **church**. In reaction against **Pentecostalism,** some evangelicals have neglected the Holy Spirit. For the most part, however, evangelical theology includes a robust belief in the third member of the Trinity, while refusing to give as much attention to the Holy Spirit as is given to Christ. That is because Jesus taught in John 15:26 that the Spirit (*parakletos,* Comforter) will witness to him.

All evangelicals believe that the Holy Spirit is both fully divine—sharing equally in the eternal being of God with the Father and the Son—and personal— one who can and does relate to others with purpose and freedom. The Spirit is *perichoretic* with the Father and the Son in their eternal intimacy as they indwell and interpenetrate one another. The Spirit is equal with the Father and the Son even though the Spirit is voluntarily subordinate to them in the economic Trinity, which is the eternal, immanent community of the Godhead at work in history for the salvation of human persons. The Spirit plays a role in creation as the source of life and one who brings order out of chaos; the Spirit inspires prophets and speaks through them and also inspires the authors of Scripture and superintends their writing. The Spirit fills believers for power to overcome sin and serve Jesus Christ in the world. The Spirit convicts, calls, enlightens, and enables sinners and draws them to Jesus Christ through the proclamation of the gospel. The Spirit unifies the church and empowers it to be a force for good in the world. Above all, evangelicals believe, the Spirit is the Spirit of Christ, who brings the risen, exalted Jesus Christ into Christians' lives and unites them with him.

In spite of tremendous agreement about the Holy Spirit evangelicals debate some aspects of the doctrine of the Spirit among themselves. One debate revolves around the Spirit's role within the eternal, immanent Trinitarian life of God. Evangelicals like Stanley J. Grenz who follow the Augustinian tradition with regard to the Spirit's being in the Trinity describe it as love, especially as the love that binds the Father and the Son together. To the Spirit is especially attributed the quality of love; thus the Spirit also goes forth from the Trinitarian community as the power of transforming love in the church and in the world. Some evangelical thinkers consider this speculative and bordering on a diminution of the Spirit's full personhood in comparison with the Father and Son.

They prefer to view the Spirit as the person who proceeds eternally from the Father through the Son, just as the Son is generated by the Father. This is a more hierarchical view of the Trinity and according to its critics tends to subordinate the Spirit to the Father and the Son, even in the immanent Trinity. This debate about the structure of the Trinity and the role of the Spirit erupted among evangelicals in the context of the controversy over the role of women in family, church, and society. Some evangelical theologians believe the woman should graciously submit to her husband, just as the Spirit and Christ submit to the Father even within God's eternal being; other evangelicals reject hierarchy with the immanent life of the Trinity and view subordination as purely temporal and economic.

Another area of disagreement and sometimes conflict within evangelical thinking about the Holy Spirit relates to the experience of *baptism of the Holy Spirit* or filling of the Holy Spirit. All evangelicals believe that the Holy Spirit is given to believers at conversion; it is part of *regeneration* that the Holy Spirit comes to dwell within believers to make them "new creations in Christ Jesus." There is no significant difference in that between evangelicals and other Christians except that evangelicals tend to view the indwelling of the Holy Spirit as at conversion rather than as at *baptism* or confirmation. Some evangelicals, however, insist that the "fullness of the Spirit" is received later in an experience and event called variously the "baptism of the Holy Spirit" and the "infilling of the Holy Spirit." They base this on the fact that at the end of John's Gospel Jesus imparted the Spirit to the disciples but told them to go and wait in Jerusalem for the descent of the Holy Spirit upon them, giving them power for witness throughout the world. Those who believe that the infilling of the Spirit comes later, after conversion, point out that throughout the book of the Acts of the Apostles, people already born again by the Spirit

of God who are followers of Jesus Christ receive the Holy Spirit in special fillings for service. These infillings of the Spirit are accompanied by signs and wonders, such as speaking in tongues and prophesying. During the nineteenth century many Methodists and some Baptists came to believe in the "second blessing" after conversion and "tarried" for the infilling of the Spirit. They were inspired theologically by the writings of John Wesley's follower John Fletcher and by the revivalist teachings of *Charles Finney*. The *Holiness movement* developed a doctrine of a "second blessing" of being filled with the Holy Spirit for *entire sanctification*; Pentecostalism grew out of the Holiness movement in the last decade of the nineteenth century and first decade of the twentieth century and identified speaking in tongues as the "initial, physical evidence" of the second blessing called baptism of the Holy Spirit. Some Baptists and Presbyterians adopted a milder form of belief in the subsequence of the infilling of the Holy Spirit through the *Keswick movement* in England, which spread to Canada and the United States around the turn of the century. Throughout the twentieth century a debate raged within Evangelicalism about the nature of the infilling of the Spirit; many evangelicals insist that it is simply another term for the *experience* of conversion-regeneration, and others teach that it is a distinct experience available to all authentic Christians but only actually possessed by those who seek for and receive it from God.

Gary D. Badcock, *Light of Truth and Fire of Love: A Theology of the Holy Spirit* (Grand Rapids: Wm. B. Eerdmans, 1997); Frederick Dale Bruner, *A Theology of the Holy Spirit* (Grand Rapids: Wm. B. Eerdmans, 1970); Sinclair B. Ferguson, *The Holy Spirit* (Downers Grove, IL: InterVarsity Press, 1996); Veli-Matti Kärkkäinen, *Pneumatology: The Holy Spirit in Ecumenical, International, and Contextual Perspective* (Grand Rapids: Baker, 2002); Clark Pinnock,

Flame of Love: A Theology of the Holy Spirit (Downers Grove, IL: InterVarsity Press, 1996).

Humanity Evangelical *theology* focuses its attention and energies on matters directly related to *salvation*; humans are the objects of *God's* salvation and, at least according to many evangelicals, participants in salvation. Therefore, evangelical theology has traditionally placed great weight on the proper understanding of humanity. The psalmist asked God, "What is man that thou art mindful of him?" (Ps. 8:4 KJV). The answer was that God made human beings somewhat lower than the heavenly beings and crowned them with honor and glory. And yet the psalmist also declared that all humans have gone astray; they have missed the mark of God's true intention and calling for them. Evangelical theologians seek to keep these two emphases in proper balance: humans are glorious in that they are created in God's image and endowed with gifts above even those of the heavenly beings (*angels*?). As evangelical thinker *Francis Schaeffer* liked to say, "God don't make no junk!" On the other hand, evangelicals equally emphasize, humans are all fallen from their lofty *creation* and have become depraved, corrupted, sinful, and alienated from God and from their true nature. In all of this, evangelicals follow the general outlines of classical Protestant theology closely. *Sin* has become second nature to humans whose first nature is a reflection of God's own glorious nature. They are created "to glorify God and enjoy him forever," as the Westminster Confession of Faith expresses the "chief end of man," but apart from special *grace* they are incapable of doing either one.

If there is any distinctive theological note about humanity in evangelical theology, it is that union with Christ by *faith* through the *Holy Spirit* in the "inner man" (an old Pietist term for the heart—the seat of the affections and core

of the personality) transforms sinful persons in community now so that they do not have to await the perfection of the eschaton to begin to reflect God's perfect image in Jesus Christ. Evangelicals emphasize *regeneration* and *sanctification* at least as strongly as *justification*; human persons can be more than forgiven. They can also be transformed by grace through faith. This injects a note of optimism into evangelical anthropology, but it is an optimism of grace and not an optimism of human potential apart from grace.

Evangelical anthropology distinguishes between two aspects of the doctrine of humanity: the human *constitution*, that is, what uniquely marks human nature, and the human *condition*, that is, the actual life of humanity. Ironically, most evangelical theologians would agree with neoliberal Protestant Paul Tillich, who declared humans "essentially good but existentially estranged." Evangelicals draw their account of human essence and existence primarily from *Scripture*; they eschew heavy dependence on modern psychology, sociobiology, or anthropology for thick description of humanity. These sciences may contribute something helpful to Christian understanding of humanity, but they tend to be reductionist in their accounts. That is, they tend to reduce humans to either nature (biological conditioning) or nurture (social conditioning) and neglect or reject any transcendent dimension to humanity. Evangelicals insist that biblical *revelation* is the basis for Christian belief about the ultimate realities of human nature and *experience*.

In biblical theology human beings cannot be understood apart from their relationship with God, and sin cannot be reduced to ignorance or fear. There is a mysterious dimension to humanity in biblical revelation; human persons cannot be captured in natural categories or imprisoned in historical forces alone. They have godlike qualities while being both finite and fallen. The human constitution, then, is described by evangelicals using two biblical categories—body/spirit duality and *image of God*. Popular evangelical folk piety often misunderstands these as dualistic (physical versus spiritual) and as grossly physical. That is, evangelical lay people often misinterpret Scripture as promoting a view of human persons as godlike spirits imprisoned in physical bodies. A kind of rough Gnosticism pervades evangelical folk religion in spite of the best efforts of evangelical theologians. Evangelical lay people often interpret the image of God as a likeness of countenance or as the spiritual (spirit-possessing) quality of humans in contrast to angels and animals. Again, evangelical theologians strive to correct these notions.

Most evangelical theologians regard human persons as composite unities of physical and immaterial realities. (Older theologians often said "physical and immaterial substances," but most modern evangelicals shy away from calling body and soul substances.) One of the oldest debates in evangelical anthropology revolves around whether human persons are *dichotomous* or *trichotomous*, that is, is the constitution of human persons a unity of two or three realities? Body and soul/spirit or body, soul, and spirit? Are these separable realities? Popular evangelical belief tends to assume that humans are trichotomous beings, made up of three distinct and even separable substances: body (physical), soul (life force, personality), and spirit (aspect that relates to God). This trichotomous constitution scheme goes back to some of the early *church* fathers such as Tertullian and has been promoted among evangelicals in the twentieth century by writers such as Watchman Nee of China. The majority of modern evangelical scholars prefer the dichotomous view of the human person: humans are unified bodies and soul-spirits. That is, they believe that biblical anthropology knows no real ontological distinction between "soul" and "spirit," so that these are synonymous terms for that aspect of the human person that transcends physicality. It is the dimension of personhood that makes humans more than animals, even as they are less than God.

The soul/spirit is not a "spark of the divine," as in Gnosticism, or naturally immortal, as in Greek philosophy and religion. Most evangelical theologians believe it does survive bodily death and awaits reunification with the body in the *resurrection*; other evangelical scholars consider that too dualistic and prefer to believe that body and soul/spirit are inseparable. An increasingly popular view among evangelical theologians is "holistic dualism" promoted by John W. Cooper and Ray S. Anderson. These and other evangelical theologians emphasize the unity of the human person, whether or not soul and spirit are distinguishable aspects and whether or not the physical and nonphysical dimensions of the human person are separated temporarily at death. Holistic dualism views the soul as the whole person, expressed physically in the body and spiritually in the spirit. These all belong together; the human person—soul—is an embodied spirit and a spirited body.

Evangelical theologians have never come to consensus about the image of God or the precise nature of the fallen condition of humanity. They agree that humans are unique in creation in that they alone reflect God's glory in what is called in the *Bible* the "image of God." The Genesis account of creation specifically refers to both male and female as created in God's image and likeness, and most evangelical scholars consider *image* and *likeness* synonyms (Hebrew parallelism). A few follow Emil Brunner in distinguishing between the formal image and the material image so that the fall into sin destroyed only the material image, not the formal image. The image of God, however precisely that is understood, is the basis for human dignity and worth; evangelicals insist strenuously on the intrinsic value of each human person because of the image of God. Some understand that as the spiritual dimension of humanity, while others view it as the intellect (reason) or moral capacity (conscience).

Toward the end of the twentieth century a popular interpretation gaining ground among evangelical theologians is that the image of God refers to relationality; humans are created for relationships, just as God exists in community as three persons united by a single essence. Stanley Grenz, among other evangelical thinkers, has especially stressed this link between the image of God in humans as being-for-community and God's own sociality within the eternal Trinitarian community. A few evangelicals have interpreted the image of God as "dominion-having." It is a task of "tending the garden" of creation and encompasses all that is required for nurturing nature and creating culture. Leonard Verduin and others who are interested in developing an ecologically sensitive theology have worked on this interpretation of the image of God. In any case, whatever it means specifically, the image of God plays an important role in evangelical anthropology.

Evangelical theologians are united in belief in human total depravity due to the universal fall into sin at humanity's origins. Not all evangelical scholars take every aspect of the fall narrative in Genesis 3 literally, but all are agreed that humanity is all together and altogether fallen into sin, with the result that a curse has come upon humanity and nature and their relationship. Humans are born sinners; sin is their second nature due to the rebellion of the first couple (or of everyone, as symbolized by Adam and Eve in the narrative). Not all evangelicals believe that infants inherit the collective guilt of humanity, but all agree that every child (except Jesus Christ) born into the world since the beginning is born with a corrupted, depraved human nature that makes actual transgressions that bring guilt inevitable. When condemnation appears in the individual is a matter of debate among evangelicals, but that condemnation comes upon all who reach the age of awakening of conscience (or "age of accountability") is beyond debate. That is why all mature persons stand in need of *conversion* even if they were baptized as infants.

Evangelicals in the Reformed tradition tend to underscore the total depravity of every human individual, such that there is in him or her no spark of goodness or natural ability to seek or find God. Total depravity is absolute incapacity in spiritual matters. Wesleyan evangelicals are not entirely comfortable with the language of total depravity; they prefer to describe natural, fallen humans apart from grace as totally deprived. In the end, however, the difference is slight. In both cases and for all evangelicals, human persons after the fall are completely disabled spiritually and stand in need of *supernatural*, assisting *grace* even to initiate a goodwill toward God. Equally important for evangelicals is belief that in spite of original sin and total depravity (or the state of being totally depraved) human persons are capable of being transformed by the grace of God into beings who reflect God's glory and Christ's character, even if only imperfectly, until they are glorified in the eschatological *kingdom of God*.

Ray S. Anderson, *On Being Human: Essays in Theological Anthropology* (Grand Rapids: Wm. B. Eerdmans, 1982); George W. Carey, *I Believe in Man* (Grand Rapids: Wm. B. Eerdmans, 1977); John W. Cooper, *Body, Soul, and Life Everlasting* (Grand Rapids: Wm. B. Eerdmans, 1989); Stanley J. Grenz, *The Social God and the Relational Self* (Louisville, KY: Westminster John Knox Press, 2001); H. D. McDonald, *The Christian View of Man* (Westchester, IL: Crossway, 1981); Bernard Ramm, *Offense to Reason: A Theology of Sin* (Vancouver, BC: Regent College Publishers, 2000).

Image of God   Evangelicals believe that human value and dignity lies in the *imago dei*—the image of God. That is, human persons are created in the image and likeness of God as stated in Genesis 1:26–27. Evangelicals share this belief with all other Christians; there is nothing peculiar or unique about the evangelical interpretation of *humanity's* special relationship with God as created in God's image. That is not to say, however, that evangelical theologians have not contributed distinctive notes to Christian theological anthropology. Especially in the last decade of the twentieth century and first decade of the twenty-first century, they have focused attention on the relational aspects of the *imago dei*—that human persons are created for community and thus reflect the communal nature of the triune God. In this, evangelical thinkers build on themes of Karl Barth's *theology* and extend them forward in conversation with the communitarian movement. The irony in evangelical theological emphasis on the communal nature of the image of God lies in the fact that popular evangelical folk religion tends to stress the individualistic dimensions of human existence, especially of spirituality. Evangelical theologians decry the "Jesus and me" distortion of evangelical theology in revivalistic and popular pietistic Protestantism and in response develop the communitarian picture of human existence in the *imago dei* as existence for others.

Evangelical theology has not always emphasized the communal and relational aspects of the *imago dei*, however. *Carl F. H. Henry*, the "dean of evangelical theologians," together with his philosophical mentor *Gordon Clark*, held out for the more traditional idea of the image of God in humanity as an ontic aspect of the human person identical with that which makes him or her higher than animals and reflective of God's own nature. For them, and for many evangelical thinkers in the twentieth century, the *imago dei* is the substantial soul combined with intellect as capacity for rational thought and moral discernment. This trend in evangelical anthropology

reflects the influence of medieval scholasticism (e.g., Thomas Aquinas) and post-Reformation orthodoxy (Protestant scholasticism). It is heavily indebted to Aristotelian philosophy and anthropology. As the *Bible* nowhere actually defines the *imago dei*, it is left to theologians to discern what that might be. No council of the *church* ever declared it, so theologians have always speculated about it, and there is great diversity in interpretation throughout church history. Henry's evangelical vision of the *imago dei* is classical and very close to the traditional Catholic view. It stands in continuity with much Protestant orthodoxy as well.

Some conservative evangelical theologians have attempted to expand it to include all that makes human beings personal—volition, creativity, and so forth, in addition to reason and moral judgment. For Henry and those who follow his lead, one virtue of identifying the *imago dei* with having a rational soul and conscience lies in the fact that this links humans with God, who is spirit and mind as well as the standard of morality in *holiness*. This means also, then, that the *imago dei* survived the fall of humanity, even though with damage. For Henry and other conservative evangelical thinkers, this helps explain humanity's accountability for the evidence of God in nature, and it promotes their agenda of regarding Christianity as objectively cognitive and not subjectively spiritual or inward. The *gospel*, then, appeals to the reasoning intellect and to the conscience; people are capable of responding to and knowing God because they are rational beings with souls who have moral awareness of their own fault and guilt and need of redemption.

Other evangelical thinkers have followed a more Augustinian and less Aristotelian (and scholastic) approach to defining the *imago dei*. For them, as for Augustine, the image and likeness of God (a Hebrew parallelism and not a reference to a dualism) refers to a function or calling of the human person, rather than to a substantial core of humanity's nature. It is not so much having a soul or possessing rational powers as being in relationship with God and being called by God to take up and fulfill a certain function together with God. Dutch Reformed theologian G. C. Berkouwer has strongly influenced evangelical theology in the second half of the twentieth century. For him, the *imago dei* is conformity to the character of Christ in and through fellowship with God; it is a matter of calling and function rather than of natural equipment. Even Adam was intended by God to reflect the character of Christ—an apparent but not actual anachronism, as Christ is the purpose of *creation* itself.

The *imago dei* is revealed in *Jesus Christ* and especially in his obedient, *covenant* relationship to God his Father which establishes his fellowship with God. So humans possess the image of God in embryo through their creation but it only comes to partial fruition in their *redemption* by Christ through the *Holy Spirit* within the context of the church. This explains how and why humans were created in God's image and likeness (in fellowship with God) but fell away from it; the process of growing into that image and likeness was interrupted by *sin*. This echoes early church father Irenaeus's notion of the image and likeness of God in humanity even though that was dualistic in its strong distinction between the two terms. For Berkouwer and evangelical theologians who follow him, the image of God is being imparted through Christ; it is not an always already present reality in humanity, even if it is a potential always already present in humanity. This basically Berkouwerian view has been extended and adjusted by Scottish evangelical theologian Philip Edgcumbe Hughes in the late twentieth century. For him as for Berkouwer and many evangelical thinkers, the *imago dei* lies primarily in Jesus Christ and secondarily in humans as their destiny.

One of the most interesting and influential evangelical contributions to theo-logical anthropology in the area of explicating the meaning of the *imago dei* lies in Leonard Verduin's idea that the image of God lies in a task rather than a substance or relationship. For him and others who follow his lead, the *imago dei* is "dominion-having." That is, God gave to the first humans and to all humanity the assignment and power to care for the garden of creation. Adam and Eve (and by extension their posterity) were to take dominion over the creation. God's assignment to Adam to name the animals is a clue to this interpretation of the *imago dei*. Verduin's interpretation of the image of God has gained popularity because of the ecological crisis and its direct application to that. For him, dominion does not mean domination but care. Humans are created cocreators with God in caring for nature. Sin distorts the image of God into domination over and abuse of nature; in redemption the human relationship with nature is being restored. The appeal of this interpretation of the *imago dei* is obvious in a context of environmental concern, but many critics have pointed out that it lacks positive biblical support and has little or nothing to do with the vocation of Jesus Christ and the specific call to discipleship in the New Testament.

In 1964 evangelical scholar Russell Phillip Shedd published *Man in Community: A Study of St. Paul's Application of Old Testament and Early Jewish Conceptions of Human Solidarity* (Grand Rapids: Wm. B. Eerdmans), which promoted the idea that human beings exist in and for community. This helped launch a new trend in evangelical thinking about the *imago dei* that also borrowed from the writings of Karl Barth, Dietrich Bonhoeffer, Jürgen Moltmann, and Wolfhart Pannenberg. The communitarian movement, centered around philosopher Amitai Etzione, also contributed much to the new emphasis on the relational nature of the image of God in evangelical theology. Among those who have developed the relational view in evangelical circles are Stanley Grenz and

Miroslav Volf. For them and other evangelical thinkers who work along the same lines, the *imago dei* is not a substance or a task but true community. That is, Adam and Eve and all humans are created for each other; Adam was not good alone but needed a counterpart to be fully and truly human. So all humans exist in cohumanity; true humanity is never isolated, individualistic or self-centered. The true theological ideal of the person is not isolated selfhood but self-in-community. Grenz and Volf connect this idea of the image of God with the Trinitarian being of God; for them God is first and foremost community and not immutable substance or transcendental self. There is no "source of divinity" within or behind the three persons in their perichoretic (coinherent) coexistence; their divinity lies precisely in their relationships with each other. So humans are created to be fulfilled as humans only in relationship with God and with other humans and (some would say) with nature. Jesus Christ reveals this in his own need for fellowship and dependence upon the Father and the Holy Spirit. The church is the context for fulfillment of the *imago dei*.

Ray S. Anderson, *On Being Human: Essays in Theological Anthropology* (Grand Rapids: Wm. B. Eerdmans, 1982); Stanley J. Grenz, *The Social God and the Relational Self: A Trinitarian Theology of the Imago Dei* (Louisville, KY: Westminster John Knox Press, 2001); Philip Edgcumbe Hughes, *The True Image: The Origin and Destiny of Man in Christ* (Grand Rapids: Wm. B. Eerdmans, 1989); Leonard Verduin, *Somewhat Less Than God* (Grand Rapids: Wm. B. Eerdmans, 1970).

Incarnation Evangelical *theology* has tended to focus on issues related to epistemology and soteriology: the nature of *revelation*; reason and *faith*; biblical *inspiration* and *authority*; and *conversion, regeneration, sanctification,* and the Christian life. It has often adopted the great themes of orthodox

Christian dogma, such as the *Trinity* and *incarnation,* with little or no adjustment. Evangelicals have traditionally affirmed these orthodox doctrines on the basis that they are scriptural as well as part of the Christian consensus. *Jesus Christ* stands at the center of evangelical faith as Savior and Lord, and all evangelicals warmly affirm his ontological (as opposed to merely functional) divinity; the classical doctrine of two natures (hypostatic union) carved out by the church fathers at the Council of Chalcedon (AD 451) is usually embraced by evangelical scholars. Both *Carl Henry* and *Bernard Ramm*, luminaries of post-fundamentalist evangelical theology, insist on classical incarnational *Christology* as fundamental to authentic Christianity and reject all attempts radically to revise it in light of modern sensibilities: "Only people who hold to the traditional view of the incarnation have the right to the name of Christian. The retoolers or reworders of the message of the New Testament do not deserve the name of Christian" (Bernard Ramm, *An Evangelical Christology: Ecumenic and Historic* [Nashville: Thomas Nelson, 1985, 179]; see also Carl F. H. Henry, *The Identity of Jesus of Nazareth* [Nashville: Broadman Press, 1992]). In contrast to Eastern Orthodoxy and some portions of Anglicanism, however, evangelical thought has not exploited the dogma of the incarnation as thoroughly as possible. Orthodox and Anglican theologians are noted for placing the incarnation of *God* in Jesus Christ at the center of speculative and dogmatic theology. The idea of the cosmic Christ uniting with *creation* through the historical event of the incarnation of the Logos in *humanity,* thereby divinizing creation, seems highly speculative and sometimes even slightly pagan to many evangelicals. Only in the late twentieth century have some of them begun to appreciate and make some use of the universal metaphysical dimensions of the incarnation.

Evangelical reflection on the incarnation has focused on problems related to

Jesus Christ's true humanity. For the most part Evangelicalism has taken Christ's deity for granted; the greater problem is reconciling his authentic human nature and existence with his presupposed divine nature and existence. That is not to say evangelicals have totally ignored the apologetic problem of establishing Jesus' deity in a skeptical culture; many evangelical apologists have focused a great deal of attention on making belief in it intelligible, if not rationally certain. It is only to say that in systematic theological reflection most attention has been given to the task of explaining how the transcendent, holy, and metaphysically perfect God could be human, creaturely, vulnerable, and subject to suffering and death.

Some evangelical thinkers such as *Donald Bloesch* are more than willing to embrace the incarnation as Kierkegaard's absolute paradox and eschew all attempts to soften the tension or make it rationally intelligible. For Bloesch, who is strongly influenced by *Pietism* and by twentieth-century dialectical theology, the reality of the incarnation is a basic datum of revelation and of Christian faith that must simply be embraced by faith without rational explanation or support. Jesus Christ is the God-man who was and is truly human and truly divine through the inexplicable process known as incarnation. He preexisted his earthly journey as Jesus Christ in the eternal immanent Trinity as the second person, the Logos and Son of the Father. He entered into true human existence through the virgin Mary and lived a life that was both human and divine. All attempts to explain that existence undermine its glorious majesty as mystery. For Bloesch and others like him, the incarnation is a mystery to be adored rather than a problem to be solved. Although Bloesch recognizes some validity in the Eastern Orthodox and Anglican speculative cosmic Christology, he cautions against infringing on the historical particularity of the incarnation in the man Jesus Christ.

Many evangelical theologians have been attracted to kenotic Christology as it was mediated to the English-speaking world by the British theologians H. R. Mackintosh and P. T. Forsyth in the early part of the twentieth century. Kenotic Christology attempts to soften the paradox of the incarnation by appealing to Paul's statement about Jesus Christ's self-emptying or self-limitation (kenosis) in Philippians 2:5–11. This is a distinctly Protestant form of speculative Christology, but its proponents regard it as justified by *Scripture*. According to it, the preexistent Word (Logos, Son of God), who is eternally equal with the Father and the *Holy Spirit* in the immanent Trinity, laid aside his use of the divine attributes of glory in order to enter fully into human existence. Evangelical kenotic thinkers such as Russell Aldwinckle, Fisher Humphreys, C. Stephen Evans, and Ronald Feenstra deny that the Logos of God divested himself of any divine attributes, but they insist that the only way in which he could "become human" as Jesus Christ (as opposed to merely take on an impersonal human nature) was voluntarily to restrict even his full and constant consciousness of his eternal equality with God in order to grow "in wisdom and stature, and favor with God and man" (Luke 2:52 KJV).

These evangelical thinkers affirm the basic Chalcedonian framework of Christology (hypostatic union), while eschewing the ancient option of regarding the human nature of Christ as *anhypostasia*—impersonal. Russell Aldwinckle turned to the ancient Christian theologian Leontius of Byzantium's concept of the *enhypostatic* nature of the humanity of Christ to explain how he could have two natures and yet be one integrated person. According to Leontius and his modern interpreter Herbert Relton, Jesus Christ's humanity had no independent personal existence apart from the incarnation as hypostatic union with the Logos, but it was given personal existence in union with the person of the

Logos. Thus, Jesus Christ's humanity was not impersonal (as church father Cyril of Alexandria implied), but was personalized through the incarnation. Just as the human nature was personalized, so the divine nature was limited to the humanity without being altered ontologically. That is, it remained divine while its mode of being was restricted. The upshot is that for many evangelical theologians Jesus Christ, although God incarnate, was not functionally omnipotent, omnipresent, or omniscient; he received his powers from the Holy Spirit in and through his earthly relationship with God his Father. The attributes of glory were retracted from actuality into potentiality (to use the language of P. T. Forsyth favored by Russell Aldwinckle).

Many evangelical theologians do not favor kenotic Christology and prefer to explain the incarnation as the eternal Word's assumption of a full and true human nature, without any alteration in the Word's eternal divine being. Evangelical theologian Millard Erickson criticizes kenotic Christology for allegedly infringing on the immutability of the divine nature. (It is doubtful whether that criticism applies to the Forsyth-inspired type of kenotic Christology.) According to Erickson and many other conservative evangelical thinkers, the incarnation is analogous to a three-legged race: the Son of God (God the Son) joined a human nature to himself, thereby hobbling, as it were, his earthly existence without altering his nature in any way. This seems to imply two consciousnesses in Christ, which is indeed what evangelical thinker Thomas V. Morris affirms.

For Morris and several other evangelical theologians and philosophers, Jesus Christ was God incarnate in that he possessed two equally essential minds—one divine and one human—in one person. This explains, for example, how Jesus Christ could be incapable of temptation (let alone *sin*) and at the same time be tempted. His divine consciousness was free from temptation while his

human consciousness was buffeted by it. His human consciousness grew in wisdom while his divine consciousness was always omniscient. Of course, even his divine consciousness was limited by its union with the creaturely consciousness of the man Jesus, but that limitation was not a self-emptying or restriction of knowledge or power. Rather, it was merely an associational limitation; the divine knowledge and power of the Son of God was through the incarnation "tied," as it were, to a human being. According to Morris, the person of the Son of God was the unifying link between the divine consciousness and human consciousness; he could and did draw on both as needed without being a "split personality." The personality of Jesus Christ was the person of the Word, the Son of God, while the two consciousnesses were (and still are) aspects or tools of that one personality. The viability of this view of the incarnation depends on the viability of the distinction between "person" and "mind" so that one person can possess two minds without being divided.

A few evangelical theologians have sought to cut the Gordian knot of traditional incarnation and two-natures Christology, which seems inevitably to imply a dual personality of Jesus Christ. Stanley Grenz draws on the eschatological ontology of German Lutheran theologian Wolfhart Pannenberg to express a high Christology without "descent Christology." That is, for Grenz (as for Pannenberg), Jesus Christ was not the incarnation of a preexistent, nonhuman (or prehuman) eternal divine Son of God. Picturing Jesus Christ's union with God in that manner leads inevitably to the conundrums of classical Christology and to the either/or of kenotic or two-minds Christologies, both of which are fraught with difficulties. According to Grenz's alternative, "as this man Jesus is God" (to borrow Pannenberg's phrase). In other words, through his full and unique revelation of God that culminates in the *resurrection,* the man Jesus

Christ is demonstrated to belong eternally to the deity of God.

There is no *Logos asarkos*—Word without flesh—but only the man Jesus Christ, who through his unique relationship with the Father in history is the Logos that unites God with creation. He demonstrates the distinct purpose of God in creation and reveals the Father's glory. He is the self-realization of the glory of God within history who thus brings about the **kingdom of God** and establishes the rule of God proleptically (before its time). The incarnation, then, is the preappearing (anticipatory realization) of the eschatological realization of the deity of God in his manifest rule over creation. As such, Jesus Christ belongs to the eternity of God, which is, from the human perspective in history, eschatological. His resurrection establishes and manifests it. While some conservative evangelicals who are committed to a classical incarnational Christology have criticized Grenz's reformulated Christology as implicitly adoptionistic, they have not grasped the eschatological orientation of its underlying ontology. In this perspective, God is the Power of the Future whose deity is his eschatological rule and reign; to be its historical, proleptic realization is to belong to it. Jesus' deity is his union with God. As this man, Jesus is God.

Russell F. Aldwinckle, *More Than Man: A Study in Christology* (Grand Rapids: Wm. B. Eerdmans, 1976); Peter Taylor Forsyth, *The Person and Place of Jesus Christ* (London: Independent Press, 1909); Stanley J. Grenz, *Theology for the Community of God* (Grand Rapids: Wm. B. Eerdmans, 2000); Thomas V. Morris, *The Logic of God Incarnate* (Ithaca, NY: Cornell University Press, 1986); Cornelius Plantinga and Ronald Jay Feenstra, eds., *Trinity, Incarnation, and Atonement: Philosophical and Theological Essays*, Library of Religious Philosophy, vol. 1 (Notre Dame, IN: University of Notre Dame Press, 1990); David F. Wells, *The Person of Christ: A Biblical and Historical Analysis of the Incarnation* (Westchester, IL: Crossway, 1984).

Infallibility/Inerrancy   Few doctrinal subjects have generated as much heat (and some would say so little light) among evangelicals as the issue of biblical accuracy. The controversy has waxed and waned for decades and perhaps centuries (depending on how far back one dates Evangelicalism). Two theological terms have come to be especially associated with evangelical debate over the Bible's accuracy: infallibility and inerrancy. How they are related to one another is controversial; some evangelicals insist they are synonyms and others strongly distinguish between them. Evangelical belief about the Bible is rooted in a common commitment to the plenary (complete), **supernatural** inspiration of the sixty-six books of the Protestant canon. Evangelicals have never arrived at full consensus about the nature of inspiration. (See related articles in this handbook: **authority, Bible, inspiration, revelation**.) Nevertheless, all evangelicals agree that Holy Scripture is uniquely the product of a special operation of the **Holy Spirit** through prophets and apostles called in English inspiration. This doctrine derives especially from 2 Timothy 3:16, which says Scripture is *theopneustos*, "God-breathed," but also from 2 Peter 1:20–21. It is also rooted in the traditional Jewish reverence for Scripture.

The great Jewish first-century philosopher Philo of Alexandria believed the Hebrew Bible was dictated by **God**. Several Christian church fathers such as Origen agreed. Protestants have generally shied away from a dictation model of the production of **Scripture**, while holding on to belief that the entirety of the Bible is divinely inspired in a manner that transcends mere illumination of humans' minds. Whether that process of divine inspiration extends to the very words of Scripture, so that they are to be considered God's words, or whether inspiration involves the authors only, so that they wrote divine ideas in their own words, is a matter of disagreement among evangelicals. Naturally, how one views inspiration will likely affect his or her interpretation of the extent of biblical accuracy.

Evangelical theologians agree that inspired Scripture is uniquely authoritative for religious belief and practice, because it is in a sense unparalleled by any other book—God's Word in written form. This high regard for the Bible is a hallmark of Evangelicalism, and no evangelical theologian has dared to call it into question. Furthermore, in order to protect the Bible's special authority the vast majority of evangelicals affirm the Bible's accuracy in a special way; that is, they consider it infallible. Since God is its ultimate author, it cannot fail to communicate God's message of *salvation* accurately, even if the reception of that communication is often faulty due to human finitude and fallenness. Thus, according to the evangelical theological consensus, the Bible is infallible as well as inspired; inspiration guarantees its infallibility. According to over three hundred evangelical scholars who signed the 1978 Chicago Statement on Biblical Inerrancy, "*Infallible* signifies the quality of neither misleading nor being misled and so safeguards in categorical terms the truth that Holy Scripture is a sure, safe and reliable guide in all matters." Some evangelicals would like to amend the end of the definition with the addition "related to *faith* and practice." Nevertheless, no evangelical scholar would contest Scripture's infallibility in the broadest sense of the word. They recognize that the Bible's authority requires its infallibility and that its quality of being inspired by God leads necessarily to the conclusion that it is infallible.

However, debate among evangelical theologians and biblical scholars erupts over several secondary matters related to infallibility. Is the Bible infallible in matters not related to salvation or Christian living? That is, does its flawless communication of truth extend beyond faith and practice to matters of history and cosmology? Is its infallibility plenary in the same way that its inspiration

is said to be plenary? Also, does infallibility require inerrancy? Is it possible to affirm that Scripture is infallible but not inerrant? The Chicago Statement distinguishes infallibility and inerrancy while linking them inseparably. *Inerrancy* is defined as "the quality of being free from all falsehood or mistakes," and it is said that it "safeguards the truth that Holy Scripture is entirely true and trustworthy in all its assertions." The statement explicitly mentions facts related to history and cosmology as inerrant ("free from all falsehood and mistakes") when found in the Bible.

The *Evangelical Theological Society* requires prospective members to affirm biblical inerrancy; so do many evangelical organizations and institutions. The *National Association of Evangelicals'* statement of faith, however, does not mention inerrancy. Fuller Theological Seminary's confessional statement affirmed inerrancy until the early 1960s, when it was altered to omit that, while retaining a strong affirmation of biblical authority and trustworthiness. This change at Fuller Seminary was the catalyst for an uproar among evangelicals in North America. Some (certainly not all) decried the seminary's deletion of inerrancy from its statement of faith as the beginning of a slippery slope into neo-orthodoxy, if not liberal theology. Others applauded it as a liberation from the last vestiges of *fundamentalism*. In 1963 evangelical scholar Dewey M. Beegle published *The Inspiration of Scripture* (later revised and republished as *Scripture, Tradition, and Infallibility* [Grand Rapids: Wm. B. Eerdmans]), in which he argued that it is possible to believe in the supernatural, plenary inspiration of the Bible while admitting that it contains factual errors in matters of history and cosmology. In 1976 influential evangelical theologian Harold Lindsell published his bombshell book *The Battle for the Bible* (Grand Rapids: Zondervan), which created a firestorm of controversy because it accused specific evangelical institutions, organizations, and persons of declension from authentic evangelical faith because they denied biblical inerrancy in relation to facts of history and cosmology. Lindsell laid down the gauntlet and urged such "partial infallibilists" to recant or leave the evangelical fold. He argued that if Scripture contains any errors, it cannot be trusted and is not authoritative.

In 1978 the International Council on Biblical Inerrancy met in Chicago and began a ten-year project to produce an evangelical theological consensus about the Bible's accuracy. Its main product is the Chicago Statement on Inerrancy, which became for many conservative evangelicals the gold standard for defining biblical accuracy and even for determining who is authentically evangelical. The heart of the statement is that Scripture is both infallible and inerrant and that its inerrancy extends to all of its factual assertions. However, the statement presented a list of qualifications that seemed to many critics to kill inerrancy with the proverbial death of a thousand qualifications. For example, according to the statement the Bible's inerrancy is consistent with discrepancies in reports of the same events (e.g., in the Gospels) and with approximations in records of numbers. It is also said to be consistent with "phenomenological language" about nature.

A careful examination of the statement shows that the authors, if not all of the signers, intended to allow for errors in the Bible by modern, technical standards of accuracy. They simply denied that the Bible's accuracy should be judged by modern standards and held the authors to no higher standard of accuracy than their own cultures and intentions would entail. That is, since they were not attempting to give flawless performances in statistics, for example, inaccuracies in numbers are not to be considered errors. Many evangelicals who had dared to question strict, technical inerrancy and had come under fire from Lindsell (who signed the Chicago Statement) cried, "Foul!" because the

statement—which seemed aimed at them—affirmed their own view of Scripture's infalliblity (sans inerrancy) while calling it "inerrancy." And yet some of them were being barred from evangelical ranks because they were perceived as out of step with the Chicago Statement. The controversy continued long after 1978 and promises to plague Evangelicalism into the foreseeable future.

Each evangelical theologian who writes on the subject of biblical accuracy seems to have his or her own unique twist to the subject, but in general two main views have emerged within the evangelical subculture and among evangelical theologians. On the right side of the spectrum are those who, like Lindsell, insist that Scripture is completely, strictly true and accurate in all of its assertions of fact—spiritual, theological, historical, and cosmological. These theologians hark back to the leading lights of Protestant orthodoxy and scholasticism, especially to the nineteenth-century Princeton theologians Archibald Alexander, Charles Hodge, A. A. Hodge, and *Benjamin B. Warfield,* who responded to growing mainline Protestant liberal skepticism about the Bible with a strong reaffirmation of its supernatural inspiration, unique authority, and factual infallibility. These theologians—including *Carl F. H. Henry, Francis Schaeffer,* and Millard Erickson—regard inerrancy as extending only to the original autographs upon which all biblical texts are based. Therefore, they acknowledge, there may be and probably are some factual errors in all existing Bibles. They also, in varying ways, restrict biblical accuracy to standards of accuracy appropriate to biblical literature (i.e., genre), cultural context, and authorial intent. They agree among themselves that the Bible is infallible because it is inerrant, and it is both because its ultimate author is the Holy Spirit; to claim that any factual statement of the Bible is false is implicitly to call into question the Holy Spirit's veracity.

Evangelical adherents of the second position, on the left of the evangelical spectrum (i.e., further away from fundamentalism) consider the strict inerrancy position fraught with problems. What good are inerrant autographs that do not exist? How is inerrancy with so many qualifications different from infallibility without inerrancy? The second position views Scripture as wholly infallible but inerrant only in spiritual and theological matters. That is, the whole of the Bible is God's inspired Word and infallibly communicates God's truth about himself and about salvation; it does not fail to render a true account of God's will and ways. Nevertheless, incidental errors of history and cosmology do not affect Scripture's infallibility or authority.

Evangelical theologian *Donald Bloesch* writes that "Scriptural inerrancy can be affirmed if it means the conformity of what is written to the dictates of the Spirit regarding the will and purpose of God. But it cannot be held if it is taken to mean the conformity of everything that is written in Scripture to the facts of world history and science" (Donald G. Bloesch, *Holy Scripture: Revelation, Inspiration, and Interpretation* [Downers Grove, IL: InterVarsity Press, 1994], 107). Even though Bloesch here affirms inerrancy in one sense, elsewhere he and other scholars who hold a similar view express preference for infallibility. Bloesch uses an analogy, drawn from the Swiss theologian Emil Brunner, that compares reading Scripture with an old vinyl record and a dog listening to the megaphone of an old Victrola record player (the RCA Victor logo). The dog hears and recognizes "his master's voice" in spite of the scratches and imperfections on the record. So it is with the Bible; we need not go to great lengths to try to explain away the obvious human and cultural imperfections in the text of the Bible. In spite of them, it is God's infallible and authoritative Word to *humanity*, which is able to hear God's voice in it in spite of its humanness.

This view of Scripture's accuracy harks back to Scottish turn-of-the-century (ninetenth to twentieth) evangelical theologian James Orr, who debated inerrancy with Warfield and yet affirmed plenary inspiration and a general infallibility of Scripture, and to Dutch theologian G. C. Berkouwer, who held virtually the same position as Orr. Neither of these two scholars has ever been considered "neo-orthodox" or "liberal," and yet their view of biblical accuracy is the one behind the moderate or progressive evangelical affirmation of infallibility without inerrancy.

G. C. Berkouwer, *Holy Scripture*, trans. Jack B. Rogers (Grand Rapids: Wm. B. Eerdmans, 1975); David S. Dockery, *Christian Scripture: An Evangelical Perspective on Inspiration, Authority, and Interpretation* (Nashville: Broadman & Holman Publishers, 1995); Robert K. Johnston, *Evangelicals at an Impasse: Biblical Authority in Practice* (Louisville, KY: Westminster John Knox Press, 1979); Clark Pinnock, *The Scripture Principle* (San Francisco: Harper & Row, 1984); Jack B. Rogers and Donald K. McKim, *The Authority and Interpretation of the Bible* (New York: Harper & Row, 1979).

Inspiration Evangelical *theology* has specialized in the doctrine of *Scripture*. For many, if not most, evangelical theologians, a sound doctrine of Scripture is foundational for the entire structure of authentic Christian belief and practice; if the foundation is unsound, the structure will eventually fall. Most evangelicals believe that much mainline, liberal Protestant theology represents a series of serious declensions from authentic, historical, classical Christianity because of its deviation from a high view of Scripture. *Carl F. H. Henry*, the "dean of evangelical theologians," specialized in tracing out this connection between the loss of a high view of Scripture and the subsequent rise of liberal theology among Protestants. (See his six-volume series *God, Revelation, and Authority* [Waco, TX: Word, 1976–84].) According to most evangelical theologians, the linchpin of a sound doctrine of Scripture is a correct view of its inspiration, its *"God*-breathed"—*theopneustos* (2 Tim. 3:16)—quality. There is nothing new or distinctive about Evangelicalism's affirmation of this special quality of Scripture. "Given by inspiration of God" (KJV) and "inspired by God" (NRSV) are simply English translations of the Greek *theopneustos*, which is a combination of the words for "God" and "breath." Literally, according to 2 Timothy 3:16, Scripture is given by God's breath or God's breathing out. This is clearly an idiom or metaphor for a process of God's operation in producing Scripture. Nevertheless, the early church fathers, medieval theologians, and Reformers all equally affirmed that Scripture is the product of a special, unique, *supernatural* process involving God's initiative and guidance and human participation on some level. Inspiration means that God is Scripture's ultimate author, even if the human prophets and apostles are its penultimate authors. Evangelicals have expended tremendous energy exploring, expounding, and defending divine inspiration of Scripture in order to guard Christian theology against the defections from classical Christianity into liberal, pluralistic thought characteristic of the efforts of many post-Enlightenment theologians.

According to most evangelical theologians, Scripture is to be understood first and foremost as *revelation*; inspiration is a secondary but especially important doctrine about Scripture. *Bernard Ramm* speaks for most evangelical thinkers when he writes that "inspiration derives its life and substance from revelation. Revelation is prior in point of time to inspiration, and is the more important of the two doctrines. While it is the function of revelation to bring to the sinner a soteric knowledge of God, it is the function of inspiration to preserve that revelation in the form of tradition and then in the form of *graphē* [Scripture]" (Bernard Ramm, *Special Revelation and the Word of God* [Grand Rapids: Wm. B. Eerdmans, 1961], 175–76). However,

few Christian theologians have ever denied a special link between the Bible and revelation; the doctrine of inspiration is much more disputed, especially in the modern, Western world and churches.

According to Henry, Ramm, and other evangelical theologians, the *authority* of Scripture depends on its being a form or "modality" (to use Ramm's language) of special revelation and on its being supernaturally inspired by God. In response to modern challenges to supernatural inspiration, and in order to protect Scripture's authority as the primary modality of revelation for Christian belief and practice, then, evangelicals have concentrated much attention on the doctrine of inspiration. Again, Ramm speaks for most evangelicals in expressing a basic conviction about inspiration's meaning: "Inspiration, then, is the Holy Spirit securing for the Church the Christian *graphē* [Scripture] in such a form that the Church may trust its verbal form as an adequate, authentic, and sufficient vehicle of special revelation" (*Special Revelation*, 179). For evangelicals, then, inspiration is the connecting link between the Bible as special revelation from God and its authority; without inspiration it can hardly be either one. Evangelicals believe it must be both in order for secure, objective truth to be available for Christian proclamation and teaching as well as for devotion and spirituality.

A problem arises, however, when evangelicals attempt to explicate the nature of the process called inspiration. How it works is not explained anywhere in Scripture, and various models have been proposed and strongly held throughout *church* history. Many church fathers, including the great Origen, believed that inspiration involved dictation of the very words of Scripture by the *Holy Spirit* to the human authors. The Protestant Reformers tended to back away from that mechanical view of inspiration and affirm the human element in Scripture, while emphasizing the divine role in its production. The post-Reformation theologians of Protestant orthodoxy and scholasticism played up the divine initiative and superintendence of Scripture, while acknowledging that the human authors were something more than mere secretaries of the Holy Spirit.

With the rise of freethinking and biblical criticism in the late eighteenth century and early nineteenth century, many liberalized Protestant philosophers and theologians highlighted the human role to account for the diversity of Scripture and to explain the apparent discrepancies being noticed in the biblical text. During the later nineteenth century and early twentieth century, the Princeton theologians Archibald Alexander, Charles Hodge, A. A. Hodge, and *Benjamin B. Warfield* drew on the heritage of Protestant scholasticism (especially Francis Turretin) to provide certainty about biblical truth to increasingly doubtful European and North American Christians. They developed the "plenary, verbal inspiration" theory (which they considered more than a theory), which has remained a major interpretation of Scripture's unique nature as God's Word among evangelicals. Other conservative Protestant theologians developed a more dynamic and content-oriented interpretation of inspiration that they believed fit the phenomena of Scripture better than the plenary, verbal view, while at the same time providing a solid foundation for Scripture's authority in a time of uncertainty. Among these theologians were *Augustus Hopkins Strong,* James Orr, and G. C. Berkouwer. These two traditions within evangelical thought in the twentieth century account for the diversity of views about inspiration among evangelicals and also for much of the debate about Scripture among evangelicals (e.g., *infallibility* versus inerrancy, etc.).

Very few evangelical thinkers espouse a dictation model of inspiration. Only the most conservative, even fundamentalist, evangelical theologians explicitly appeal to a dictation process as the correct interpretation of inspiration. Few, if any, evangelical theologians embrace the so-called "illumination theory" of inspiration popular among liberal scholars: "the *Bible* is inspired insofar as it is inspiring" and it is inspiring because the human authors' minds were illumined by the Spirit of God. The mechanical dictation model undermines the human character of the Bible and simply does not fit with the data of the biblical text, which shows the marks of human personality, culture, and writing style. The illumination model undermines the divine character of Scripture and reduces the difference between it and other great writings to one of degree and not of kind. The result is a serious relativizing of Scripture's authority and consequent doctrinal pluralism in the churches.

There are only two models left, and evangelicals divide between them: the plenary, verbal inspiration theory and the dynamic, concursive inspiration theory. The first was basically spelled out by the *Princeton theologians,* while the second one is constructed out of the contributions of Strong, Orr, and Berkouwer (as well as other moderate evangelical and mediating theologians). A major evangelical defender of the plenary, verbal model of inspiration is Millard Erickson, whose three-volume *Christian Theology* (Grand Rapids: Baker Book House, 1983) has been and remains a major instructional tool for evangelical professors and students in the later decades of the twentieth century and first decade of the twenty-first century. According to Erickson, the process of inspiration extends to the very words of the Bible without suspending the human contribution in Scripture's production. For him, the Bible is both human and divine in a way analogous to *Jesus Christ* (although it is not to be worshiped, of course). Inspiration means that God prepared humans to write Scripture and led them to freely choose the very words in their own vocabularies that would best convey God's intended meaning. The words were the human authors' own, even if they could not have chosen other words. Underlying Erickson's view of inspiration is a monergistic view of God's sovereignty, in which God renders everything certain without coercing free agents to act against their wills. Something like middle knowledge (the view that God knows what every creature would freely do in any given set of circumstances) seems to underlie Erickson's "modified Calvinist view" of the entire God-*creation* relationship. God renders everything certain—including the very words of the Bible—without violating creaturely freedom. According to Erickson and other conservative evangelicals, this is different from the mechanical dictation view of inspiration, in that it affirms rather than denies the human participation in inspiration; the human authors were more than secretaries of the Holy Spirit, even though they freely wrote precisely what the Holy Spirit wanted written, down to the very words. This, they believe, is the only way to preserve Scripture's full and true authority; any other model of inspiration inclines toward rendering Scripture's authority relative. Only this view can form the foundation of biblical infallibility and inerrancy so necessary to certainty of its truth.

Other evangelicals prefer the dynamic, concursive model of inspiration, because they are impressed with the marks of human authorship all over the biblical texts. They believe that the plenary, verbal model amounts to dictation, even if not "mechanical" dictation. In the end, these evangelical scholars claim, verbal inspiration as expounded by Erickson and most other proponents reduces the human authors to secretaries even if conscious ones. Why would the Holy Spirit render certain some of the strikingly strange things in the Bible such as the imprecatory Psalms and Paul's wish that the Judaizers in the Galatian churches would "emasculate themselves"? A major proponent of dynamic, concursive inspiration is Scottish evangelical biblical scholar and theologian

I. Howard Marshall, who compares inspiration with the concursive work of God in continuing creation of the universe. Just as a full Christian understanding of nature requires two complementary angles of vision—one seeing nature as ruled by natural laws and processes and the other seeing it as governed by God who is active in special ways as well as always active in general ways—so a full Christian understanding of inspiration requires two complementary angles of vision toward Scripture. On the one hand, God is the ultimate author of Scripture, such that the product ultimately comes from him. On the other hand, it comes from him in various ways, including human collection and editing of sources. *Clark Pinnock* also promotes a version of the concursive-dynamic view of inspiration in *The Scripture Principle* (San Francisco: Harper & Row, 1984). Scripture is the product both of divine initiative and guidance through the people of God leading to the production of a normative text for the community and of human use of divine gifts such as prophecy, insight, imagination, and wisdom. For both Marshall and Pinnock (who happen to be Arminians), then, inspiration is a cooperative effort of God and human writers, even as God is the ultimate partner in the process. Some progressive evangelical theologians go so far as to say that the concursive-dynamic inspiration model means that only the ideas found in Scripture are inspired, while the words are solely the human authors'. This seems to be the view espoused by the great Baptist theologian Augustus Hopkins Strong in his *Systematic Theology* (Valley Forge, PA: Judson Press, 1907), and it finds echoes in the writings of Bernard Ramm and *Donald Bloesch,* although the latter emphasizes that the words of the human authors are "taken up" by the Spirit of God and used for a divine, salvific purpose.

David S. Dockery, *Christian Scripture: An Evangelical Perspective on Inspiration, Authority, and Interpretation* (Nashville:

Broadman & Holman, 1995); Donald K. McKim, *What Christians Believe about the Bible* (Nashville: Thomas Nelson, 1985); I. Howard Marshall, *Biblical Inspiration* (Grand Rapids: Wm. B. Eerdmans, 1982).

Jesus Christ Evangelicals tend to be Jesus-centered in their piety; popular evangelical devotional literature focuses a great deal on the spirituality of a "personal relationship with Jesus Christ" that begins with *conversion* and grows in intensity throughout one's lifetime. Evangelicals also talk much about "Christian discipleship," which involves following Jesus Christ in daily life and emulating his character. Books such as the ever-popular *In His Steps* by Charles Sheldon remain influential among evangelicals into the twenty-first century; many imitations of that volume have been written by evangelicals, and bookshelves at evangelical Christian bookstores carry numerous titles related to the theme of imitating Jesus Christ. In the 1990s a popular trend began among evangelicals of wearing bracelets (and later other jewelry) with the initials "WWJD" on them. The letters stand for "What would Jesus do?" the subtitle of Sheldon's classic of popular folk religion published in the late nineteenth century.

Evangelical *theology* has focused more on the classical doctrine of the person of Jesus Christ than on Jesus-centered spirituality and piety. (See the articles on *Christology* and *incarnation*.) However, evangelical scholars have produced numerous volumes about the life of Jesus that undergird at least some popular evangelical Jesus piety. Especially evangelical New Testament scholars have written and continue to write scholarly monographs and trade books defending the historicity of the Gospels against the demythologizing approaches commonly found among more liberal biblical scholars. For most of the twentieth century, evangelical scholars were content by and large to develop their own biographies of Jesus, independent of the various skeptical "quests for the historical Jesus" being carried on by liberal scholars and separate from the religious existentialist rejections of the importance of the historical Jesus, in favor of concentration on the "Christ of faith" encountered by *faith* in the proclamation of the *gospel*.

Liberal scholars have conducted at least three distinct quests for the historical Jesus. The first one was influenced by Hegelian philosophy and sought to reduce Jesus to the religious ultimate who brought opposing religious impulses of *humanity* into unity. That first quest was closed by the great missionary scholar Albert Schweitzer, whose 1906 classic *Quest of the Historical Jesus* shattered the liberal dream of discovering their own image (of the ideal religious person) hidden behind the apocalyptic and supernatural legends and myths of the New Testament Gospels.

The second quest was led by disciples of German New Testament scholar Rudolf Bultmann in the middle of the twentieth century. Bultmann and other existentialists practically despaired of separating the Jesus of history (Jesus as he actually was apart from the *kerygma*—proclamation—about him developing by the early *church*) from the Christ of faith (Jesus as proclaimed by early Christian prophets and apostles and as encountered by faith in the moment of decision provoked by the proclamation of the cross). They concentrated on the Christ of faith to the detriment of knowledge about the historical Jesus. Leaders of the new quest for Jesus, such as Günther Bornkamm and Hans Conzelmann, sought a much more modest knowledge of Jesus (than was hoped for by the first questers) and attempted to reunite the Jesus of history with the Christ of faith. They retained existentialist elements borrowed from Bultmann and combined them with new research into the Gospels in order to discover at least some minimal and relatively reliable factual knowledge about Jesus.

The third quest for the historical Jesus arose in the later decades of the twentieth century among a new group of New Testament scholars influenced by political theology and bent on deconstructing the traditional images of Jesus in favor of a political Jesus who spoke against power. The Jesus Seminar gained notoriety in the 1980s and 1990s for attempting to determine which sayings of Jesus in the Gospels were actually uttered by Jesus and which were put into his mouth by various groups of Jesus' followers in the later first century. Scholars such as Robert Funk, John Dominic Crossan, and Marcus Borg contributed to the third quest, which turned out to be radically reductionist in its results; Jesus appeared from it as a wandering Jewish cynic or sage who challenged the hierarchical political and religious powers of his day.

All three quests for the historical Jesus worked from naturalistic presuppositions and tended to assume the unreliability of the New Testament Gospels as historical documents. For example, many involved in these liberal quests assumed that any saying of Jesus that reflects a problem situation in the life of the early Christian community must not have been uttered by Jesus during his lifetime; they may have been uttered by Christian prophets speaking on behalf of Jesus (thus, the "Christ of the community") and read back into the mouth of the historical Jesus in the oral stages of the Gospel traditions. Most of the questers simply relegated *miracles*— including the *virgin birth* of Jesus and his bodily *resurrection*—to the status of legend and myth.

Evangelical scholars began earnestly responding to the quest for the historical Jesus during its third manifestation. Before that, very few evangelical scholars approached the quests with anything more than dismissive disdain, which was typical of the fundamentalist reaction to anything and everything in liberal theological and biblical scholarship. An exception is the very influential *A*

Short Life of Christ, by Fuller Seminary New Testament scholar Everett F. Harrison (Grand Rapids: Wm. B. Eerdmans, 1968). Harrison attempted to take seriously some of the critical scholarship of the previous century and respond to it from a supernaturalist but somewhat critical perspective. He attempted to demonstrate that a generally reliable life of Jesus could be developed out of the Gospel sources in spite of problems with those sources. He did not treat the Gospels as straightforward biographies as was typical of much conservative scholarship before. And yet Harrison and other postfundamentalist evangelical New Testament scholars launched a project of countering the reductionistic portrayals of Jesus in liberal scholarship by showing that their skepticism was entirely unnecessary and that internal and external historical evidences collaborate to support the traditional image of Jesus Christ as Messiah, Savior, and Lord. Other semicritical evangelical lives of Jesus followed Harrison's, including Donald Guthrie's magisterial *Jesus the Messiah* (Grand Rapids: Zondervan, 1982).

These evangelical lives of Jesus differed from traditional evangelical approaches in that they took seriously some of the assured results of modern biblical scholarship—even as developed by liberal scholars. For example, instead of treating the Gospels as straightforward biographies that could be perfectly harmonized, the new evangelical Jesus scholars accepted the critical conclusion that the Gospels are documents intended for witness and guidance for the early churches and therefore reflect the faith of the early church in Jesus as the Son of God. They are not neutral historical documents, and they are highly selective with regard to information about Jesus. Furthermore, their chronologies and accounts of Jesus' sayings and stories about his life cannot be harmonized in every instance.

These new evangelicals scholars were much less sanguine about the possibility of a "biography of Jesus" and about discovering the "consciousness of Jesus" than were most conservative scholars before them. Nevertheless, they rejected the naturalistic worldview underlying the liberal quests for the historical Jesus and concluded that there is no reason to doubt the general veracity of the Gospels with regard to what Jesus said and did, even if that veracity must be qualified when it comes to details of the order of events and exact words uttered by Jesus. They were willing to settle for the *ipsissima vox* of Jesus (his "voice"), rather than insisting on having the *ipsissima verba* (his exact words).

When the third quest for the historical Jesus began to arise among radical New Testament scholars in the 1980s, especially when the Jesus Seminar began to gain influence through the media, several evangelical scholars stepped forward to counter them. During the 1990s a spate of books appeared from evangelical scholars' pens criticizing the presuppositions and methods of the third questers and of the Jesus Seminar. The most influential and widely acclaimed evangelical Jesus scholar of the late twentieth century and early twenty-first century is Ben Witherington III, who produced a number of articles and books promoting a relatively traditional view of Jesus Christ's historical reality against the radical portraits of the third questers. His *The Jesus Quest: The Third Search for the Jew of Nazareth* (Downers Grove, IL: InterVarsity Press, 1997) provided evangelicals with a critical account of the Jesus Seminar and other deconstructionist and reconstructionist approaches to the Gospels and to knowledge about Jesus. Witherington engaged the third questers seriously and strictly avoided ridicule or dismissive arguments that begged critical questions about the Gospels. No one could accuse him of being a fundamentalist reactionary, and yet his own critical approach to the Gospels—allied closely with the works of British New Testament scholar N. T. Wright—resulted in a strong scholarly defense of a fairly traditional (or classical) account of Jesus Christ as one who was conscious of his special call from God, who knew himself to be Israel's messiah and the one sent by God to redeem the world, and who rose bodily from the dead. Jesus was not merely a wandering Palestinian cynic or sage or magician but the Son of God.

Evangelicals believe that even if the Gospels are not biographies of Jesus (and most evangelical scholars now agree they are not), and even if they contain problems of chronology and different descriptions of the same events, they are relatively reliable portraits of Jesus Christ. They also believe that the historical Jesus and the Christ of faith cannot be separated; the Christ experienced as Savior and Lord by the early church was the very same Jesus who had walked among the disciples, died on the cross, risen from the dead, and ascended into *heaven* and who will return at the end of the age. According to evangelical theology, a sound "Christology from below" based on the historical experience of the disciples and early Christian apostles combined with contemporary communal experience of Jesus Christ in the worship and piety of the church can and does yield justified belief that Jesus Christ is God the Son, the second person of the *Trinity*, whose life is to be imitated, teachings to be followed, and return to be expected.

Gregory A. Boyd, *Cynic, Sage, or Son of God?* (Grand Rapids: Baker, 1995); Joel B. Green and Max Turner, eds., *Jesus of Nazareth: Lord and Christ* (Grand Rapids: Wm. B. Eerdmans, 1994); Carl F. H. Henry, ed., *Jesus of Nazareth: Savior and Lord* (Grand Rapids: Wm. B. Eerdmans, 1966); Robert H. Stein, *Jesus the Messiah: A Survey of the Life of Christ* (Downers Grove, IL: InterVarsity Press, 1996).

Justice   Evangelicals agree that true justice is rooted in God's character— *God's* righteousness—and revealed through the Word of God in *Scripture*. A favorite saying among evangelicals is that "humanity's fairness is not God's justice," which means that there is a transcendent and spiritual dimension to true justice that can only be revealed; it cannot be captured by examination of strictly immanent impulses in *creation*. Unfortunately, the saying has sometimes been misused by popular preachers and teachers on the evangelical circuit to demean fairness and to counter demands for justice on the part of oppressed people. The true meaning of the maxim is that genuine justice is found in the cross of *Jesus Christ* and through God's *justification* of sinners in spite of their sinfulness because of the action of God in the cross. "Humanity's fairness" does not comprehend the restorative justice of the cross, which manifests the *grace* and mercy of a loving God; humanity's justice (as fairness) is often retributive or distributive only. God's justice includes a retributive and a distributive element, but is most fully revealed in the restorative work of Christ's death on the cross, which sets aside the deserved punishment of sinners and renders them righteous in spite of their continuing sinfulness. (See the article on **justification**.)

Unfortunately, evangelical reflection on justice as an ethical norm has not always been centered around the *gospel* of the cross of Jesus Christ; it has often drawn from philosophical sources more than from biblical ones. There is no unified evangelical understanding of justice as an ethical norm; most evangelical reflection on *ethics*—including social ethics—has been based on the concept of obedience to God's commands. Nevertheless, post–World War II postfundamentalist evangelical thought has begun to develop a conversation about social justice—something often regarded by conservative Christians as the preserve of liberal "social gospelers," who allegedly neglected individual and organizational obedience, in favor of secular standards of fairness for all, derived from utilitarian ethics. Some historians

of Evangelicalism consider *Carl F. H. Henry's The Uneasy Conscience of Modern Fundamentalism* (1947) the first manifesto of postfundamentalist evangelical *theology* and ethics. (It was re-released by Wm. B. Eerdmans in 2003.) In that little volume, the "dean of evangelical theologians" challenged fundamentalism's tendency to ignore issues of social justice in favor of almost exclusive focus on personal ethics and support for the social status quo in North America. Henry did not advocate any radical social change, but he questioned the prevailing social conservatism of fundamentalism and Evangelicalism and pointed the way toward a more activist role in social transformation for theologically conservative Christians and churches. Later, in the 1960s, Henry defended capitalism and private property against "creeping socialism" in mainline Protestant social ethical teachings. Evangelicals have by and large opposed socialism (to say nothing of communism!) and have been significantly allied with conservative causes. Many evangelicals would consider true justice to be identical with right order in society; without order there can be no peace or justice.

In 1973 a group of progressive evangelicals met in Chicago to found the organization Evangelicals for Social Action. One product of the first meeting was the Chicago Declaration of Evangelical Social Concern, which called evangelicals to consider their own "uneasy conscience" with regard to issues of social justice. A major mover and shaker of this movement has been evangelical theologian and social ethicist Ron Sider, whose 1977 *Rich Christians in an Age of Hunger* raised questions about evangelical complacency about world hunger and poverty in America and challenged conservative Protestants to become more actively involved in promoting quality of life and not only pro-life causes. Sider followed *Rich Christians* (republished in a twentieth-anniversary edition by Thomas Nelson, 1997) with various volumes and articles explicating an evangelical "seamlessly pro-life ethic," including *Just Generosity: A New Vision for Overcoming Poverty in America* (Grand Rapids: Baker, 1999). For Sider and many other progressive evangelicals associated with Evangelicals for Social Action, justice is to be understood not primarily as retributive (to each what is deserved) but even more as distributive (to each what is needed) and even restorative (to each opportunity to reach his or her potential).

Such a vision of justice is rooted in the biblical concept of *humanity* in the *image of God* as well as in the *incarnation*, in which God took on humanity in order to restore fellowship with God to those who had forfeited it and deserved damnation. Evangelicals for Social Action does not envision social justice in terms of revolutionary, forced redistribution of wealth (as in some liberation theology) but in terms of fundamental equality of opportunity and assurance that basic life needs are met for all people by the church (charity) but also by society (welfare).

Evangelicals for Social Action is only one evangelical advocacy organization for justice; there are many others focusing on specific issues and causes. Evangelical organizations exist to promote justice for nature (environmental justice), prisoners (Prison Fellowship), women (Christians for Biblical Equality), and many other specific issues. Of course, so-called "pro-life" and "compassionate conservative" groups of evangelicals would also envision their programs as justice-centered, even though they are not traditionally categorized as "peace and justice" groups. Tremendous diversity exists among evangelicals, and even among evangelical scholars, about the nature of justice. Views range from so-called compassionate conservatism on the right to sympathy with liberation theology on the left. In between are evangelicals who sympathize with views of justice as radically different as John Rawls's and Ayn Rand's. By and large, however, most evangelical theologians regard true justice as that order of society that will be established in the *kingdom of God*—a social order marked by peace and plenty and centered on Jesus Christ's example and message about love for God and neighbor. Disagreement enters when evangelical scholars debate how far that eschatological social reality can be realized within history under the conditions of *sin*. In that discussion, evangelicals express a "scattered voice" with a wide range of beliefs about what social justice looks like in the everyday world of sin, crime, poverty, oppression, and war.

Klaus Bockmuehl, *Evangelicals and Social Ethics* (Downers Grove, IL: InterVarsity Press, 1979); James Skillen, *The Scattered Voice: Christians at Odds in the Public Square* (Grand Rapids: Zondervan, 1990).

Justification Evangelical *theology* is a form of Protestant theology; many evangelical theologians would argue it is the contemporary expression of the truest impulses of original Protestant theology as expressed by Luther, Calvin, and the English Reformers such as Thomas Cranmer. Especially Reformed evangelicals place a great deal of emphasis on justification by *grace* through *faith* alone as the soul of the Christian *gospel*—the good news from which Evangelicalism gets its name. To proclaim the gospel is to proclaim *reconciliation* with God through Christ alone by *God's* grace apart from works; it is by faith—defined as trust—alone that sinful people may find peace with God and enter into eternal life. Every evangelical child learns in Sunday school that justification means "just as if I'd never sinned." Evangelical theologians often go further and place stress on Luther's doctrine that not only are repentant sinners who trust in Christ alone forgiven; they are also, and perhaps more importantly, declared righteous by God because of Christ's active and passive obedience, which is imputed to them on account of their faith.

Noted evangelical theologian J. I. Packer (both Anglican and Reformed) expresses the classical doctrine of justification for many evangelicals: "Our *sins* were reckoned (imputed) to Christ, so that he bore God's judgement on them, and in virtue of this his righteousness is reckoned ours, so that we are pardoned, accepted, and given a righteous man's status for his sake. Christians in themselves are sinners who never fully meet the *Law's* demands, nonetheless . . . 'they are righteous because they believe in Christ, whose righteousness covers them and is imputed to them.' On this basis, despite all the shortcomings of which they are conscious, believers may be sure of eternal *salvation*, and rejoice in hope of the glory of God" (*Here We Stand: Justification by Faith Today* [London: Hodder & Stoughton, 1986], 91–92). To a very large extent, evangelical theologians agree heartily with this strongly forensic (declaratory, legal) concept of justification, and all evangelicals (whether they agree with the forensic description or not) agree that justification as reconciliation with God is entirely a work of God by grace appropriated by faith alone at the moment of *conversion*. All who accept Christ through *repentance* and faith are made right with God because of what Christ accomplished by his life (active obedience) and death (passive obedience).

Evangelicalism is a diverse phenomenon and classical, magisterial Protestantism is one major element in it. Often Reformed evangelical thinkers tend to regard that element—drawing heavily on the perspectives of Calvin and other Reformed theologians—as normative for authentic evangelical faith and thought. However, Wesleyans (including Holiness and Pentecostal evangelicals) and Anabaptists (including Mennonites and evangelical Brethren groups) have not always expressed salvation in forensic terms; the strong Reformed doctrine of imputed righteousness does not find expression in those forms of evangelical theology as enthusiastically as in Reformed evangelical thought. That is especially true when it is linked with Luther's idea of "alien righteousness," in which human persons receive no inward transformation into truly righteous persons. Wesleyans and Anabaptists emphasize *regeneration*—the impartation of transforming grace into the converted person's life—more than justification. They do not deny justification, but they are often uncomfortable with the strongly legal and forensic imagery used by Reformed evangelicals. It sounds to them as if Christians' righteousness is a legal fiction, and they fear it could lead to moral and spiritual lethargy on the parts of persons who expect no inward righteousness to transform their affections.

Reformed evangelicals, of course, do believe that the grace of regeneration—simultaneous with justification at conversion—is transformative, but they wish to distinguish strongly between saved persons' positional relationship with God, which is based entirely on God's declaration of them as righteous, and their conditional salvation, which involves a gradual growth in obedience to the law of God by God's grace planted in their hearts. John Wesley, the founder of the Methodist tradition and a great hero to many evangelicals, affirmed justification by grace through faith alone, and he also embraced imputed righteousness, but he was unwilling to consider all righteousness "alien." For him and for his evangelical heirs, the **Holy Spirit** imparted at conversion-regeneration works righteousness (Christlike character) in the lives of Christians; they do not rely only on a legal declaration that they are righteous. God actually causes them to become righteous with Christ's righteousness in their "inner man" (affections, heart, core of personality).

This difference of opinion about justification occasionally erupts into controversy between evangelical scholars who by and large came to live with this difference of interpretation and others in their evangelical coalition after World War II. In the last decade of the twentieth century, heated debate over the nature of justification threatened to divide evangelical scholars in North America, and the controversy continues into the twenty-first century. In 2003 the prestigious Wheaton Theology Conference was devoted to airing evangelical differences about justification; some scholars presented stringent defenses of the classical Reformed doctrine, while others—especially New Testament scholars—argued just as stringently for a modified understanding of the same doctrine. Numerous books and articles appeared by evangelical theologians and biblical scholars in the 1990s and early years of the twenty-first century exploring the biblical and theological foundations for the classical Protestant concept of justification and examining possible new perspectives.

In the 1990s several notable evangelical scholars, including Anglican J. I. Packer and Southern Baptist Timothy George (both senior theological advisors to evangelical publication *Christianity Today*), entered into dialogue with North American Roman Catholic theologians and biblical scholars about the nature of justification, a doctrine which Protestants have traditionally viewed as the sine qua non of the theological difference between Catholic and Protestant communities. The dialogue resulted in a document entitled "Evangelicals and Catholic Together," which expressed agreement about the doctrine of justification by grace through faith. In 1997 the same group of evangelical and Catholic theologians produced a second statement entitled "The Gift of Salvation," which pushed the agreement further. Some evangelicals hailed the dialogue and the two statements as groundbreaking; others condemned them as a sellout of the gospel by the evangelical partners in the dialogue.

In 1999 *Christianity Today* published a document entitled "The Gospel of Jesus Christ: An Evangelical Celebration," which purported to be a consensus statement about the gospel signed by scores of noted evangelical theologians, biblical scholars, and leaders. The declaration included a high Reformed expression of justification by grace through faith alone, including imputation of Christ's righteousness. Some critics saw the manifesto as a slap at the evangelical-Catholic position papers, even though some of the evangelicals who had been involved in writing them also signed "The Gospel of Jesus Christ." A number of evangelicals—including New Testament scholar Robert Gundry—published critiques of "The Gospel of Jesus Christ" that focused on its doctrine of justification, which seemed to them one-sidedly forensic. How Wesleyans and Anabaptists could sign it in good faith without compromising their own historical theologies of salvation was a puzzle to many observers; and yet several prominent Wesleyans and Anabaptists did sign it.

Evangelical scholars who question the whole idea of justification as imputation of Christ's righteousness have relied heavily on the explorations of Pauline theology in the writings of British Anglican bishop and scholar N. T. Wright. Wright argues that one looks in vain for a forensic doctrine of justification (especially "alien righteousness") in Paul's writings. Instead, what one finds is salvation through the faith of *Jesus Christ* reproduced in the believers; sinners are justified by the faith of Jesus Christ, which they have by embracing the gospel proclamation of the cross and *resurrection*. By no means does Wright or any of his evangelical followers regard justification as by works of righteousness, but they do increasingly see it as involving a subjective element of inward transformation.

This development in contemporary scholarship finds an echo in the Finnish school of Luther studies, which came to the attention of North American evangelicals in the late 1990s. According to this school of thought, even Luther did not rely exclusively on a forensic concept of justification as alien righteousness imputed to sinners who remain entirely inwardly sinful. Rather, according to the Finns, Luther paradoxically also embraced a concept of union with Christ at conversion in which justified persons receive God's righteousness inwardly, so that they are transformed by the same grace that justifies them. These challenges to the classical Reformed doctrine of justification heartened Wesleyan and Anabaptist (as well as other) evangelicals who have always been suspicious of the biblical foundation of the Reformed doctrine.

By the early years of the twenty-first century many North American evangelical theologians and biblical scholars began to revise the classical Reformed doctrine of justification so that it includes a more relational understanding of reconciliation with God by grace through faith, such that Christians' righteousness is not merely declaratory but also ontological in and through union with Christ (so that his righteousness is shared) and inwardly transforming, so that justified persons are also persons being made truly righteous. Reformed evangelicals are pushing back with a robust reassertion of the strongly forensic doctrine of justification found in classical accounts of Luther's and Calvin's soteriologies.

Kenneth J. Collins, *The Scripture Way of Salvation: The Heart of John Wesley's Theology* (Nashville: Abingdon Press, 1997); Robert H. Gundry, "Why I Didn't Endorse 'The Gospel of Jesus Christ: An Evangelical Celebration,'" *Books and Culture* 7, no. 1 (Jan./Feb. 2001): 6–9; Alister McGrath, *Iustitia Dei: A History of the Christian Doctrine of Justification*, 2nd ed. (Cambridge: Cambridge University Press, 1998); Thomas C. Oden, *The Justification Reader* (Grand Rapids: Wm. B. Eerdmans, 2002); Peter Toon, *Justification and Sanctification* (Westchester, IL: Crossway, 1983); James R. White, *The God Who Justifies* (Minneapolis: Bethany House, 2001).

Kingdom of God   Evangelical *theology* reflects the same diversity about the meaning of kingdom of God that one finds in Protestant theology generally. All Protestant Christians acknowledge the rule and reign of *God* in some sense; only liberal revisionists reduce it entirely to a myth. Even they, however, regard God's rule and reign as real in the hearts and lives of persons who live according to the impulses of love represented by *Jesus Christ* in his life and death. Some evangelicals follow church father Augustine, whose concept of the kingdom of God in *The City of God* held sway in medieval Catholic thought and is still extremely influential in both Catholic and Protestant thinking. According to Augustinian Christianity, the kingdom of God exists secretly in the world wherever the true *church* of Jesus Christ worships and serves. It is God's invisible city hidden among the cities (kingdoms) of humans. It is spiritual, even if its teachings and practices influence the political arrangements of human communities. The kingdom of God is never identical with any historical sociopolitical arrangement; its fulfillment will be realized only in the eschaton, when Christ returns triumphantly to establish it in the heavenly city, the new Jerusalem. This is why evangelicals (and others) can sing, "I love thy kingdom, Lord (the house of thine abode)," and "Jesus shall reign (where'er the sun does its successive journeys run)." On the one hand, the kingdom of God is already, in the lives of Christians and in the life of the church of Jesus Christ. On the other hand the kingdom of God is future, in the visible rule of Christ over *creation* after his return to earth. Evangelical New Testament scholar George Eldon Ladd, who educated a generation of evangelical scholars in his classes at Fuller Theological Seminary in the 1960s and 1970s, emphasized the paradoxical nature of the kingdom of God as "already but not yet." For most evangelicals this is standard Christian belief; the kingdom of God now is the church suffering and militant, and the kingdom of God future is the church triumphant in the eschatological return of Christ.

Differences of opinion about the kingdom of God exist among evangelicals and have much to do with their interpretations of the so-called millennium or one-thousand-year reign of Christ mentioned three times in Revelation 20. Amillennialists expect no literal one-thousand-year sociopolitical rule and reign of Christ within history; for them the kingdom of God is spiritual until the new *heaven* and new earth are created after Christ's return, when it will be visibly manifest outside of history and beyond creation as we now know it. Postmillennialists look forward to a historical kingdom of God during a millennium of peace and righteousness immediately prior to Christ's return to earth. This will appear due to the evangelistic and social work of the people of God; Christ will return to a Christianized world. Premillennialists believe in a literal one-thousand-year earthly rule and reign of the risen and glorified Christ after his return to earth; the whole world will be under the rule of Jesus Christ during the last epoch of history. All three of these perspectives normally acknowledge that the kingdom of God has both a present dimension (hidden, spiritual) and a future dimension (visible, manifest) and that there is some continuity as well as discontinuity between these dimensions. These views of God's kingdom are not unique to evangelicals; they may be found in earlier church history.

Postmillennialism is the most recent of the three; during its first two centuries of existence (eighteenth and nineteenth centuries), it was promoted almost exclusively by evangelicals (e.g., Puritans). In the early twentieth century it was taken up by liberal social gospel theologians, but World War I tended to dispel belief in a historical utopia brought about by humans. Evangelical theology has contributed one distinctive note to the doctrine of the kingdom of God. Some premillennialists—known as dispensationalists—believe that the kingdom of God is primarily if not exclusively future. For some (if not most) dispensationalists, the kingdom of God is identifiable with the future millennium on earth, when Christ will bodily rule the world from Jerusalem. The present dimension of God's kingdom is muted in this theology, which heavily emphasizes the future. For many dispensationalists the kingdom of God is political; it was established first with David the king of Israel. Israel forfeited it through disobedience and unbelief, but it will be restored and fulfilled when Jesus returns as the successor of David to rule and reign the whole earth in a renewed Davidic kingdom in which the Jewish people—who will accept Christ as their messiah—will play a special role. The Jewish temple will be rebuilt in Jerusalem, and Jesus the Messiah will reign over people of every tongue and race who will come there to offer him homage. The Jews will be vindicated as God's chosen people, and they will be Jesus' administrators over his worldwide kingdom. These speculations, though common among some dispensationalists, are not affirmed by all evangelicals. Not even all premillennialists agree with the dispensationalist scenario of the future. All dispensationalists are premillennialists, but not all premillennialists are dispensationalists.

George Raymond Beasley-Murray, *Jesus and the Kingdom of God* (Grand Rapids: Wm. B. Eerdmans, 1994); George Eldon Ladd, *The Gospel of the Kingdom* (Grand Rapids: Wm. B. Eerdmans, 1959); J. Dwight Pentecost, *Thy Kingdom Come: Tracing God's Kingdom Program and Covenant Promises throughout History* (Grand Rapids: Kregel, 1995); Howard A. Snyder, *Models of the Kingdom* (Nashville: Abingdon Press, 1991).

Law   In *theology*, *law* usually refers to the law of *God*—all of the commandments and precepts that express the moral will of God for all people. It does not usually refer to human laws or to the ceremonial laws of Israel, even insofar as they were delivered by God through Moses. Distinguishing clearly between these three meanings of *law* is not always simple, but Christian theologians generally do strive to focus their attention on those commands they perceive to be divine and universal. Evangelical theology has no distinctive interpretation of the law of God; the range of views held by evangelical scholars corresponds to the Protestant range of interpretations. However, by and large, evangelical thinkers have worked out of the Reformed theological tradition, and for Reformed theology divine law has three distinct offices or functions. Luther had limited the functions or roles of the law of God to two: to limit general human sinfulness expressed in civil disorder and crime (a civil use of the law) and to reveal human wickedness and helplessness apart from grace. The first use of the law applies to magistrates in the secular arm of society. Luther was a law-and-order man when it came to civil society; he believed the *gospel* could be propagated only where civil order prevailed. Therefore, he taught that civil magistrates should enforce the Ten Commandments. He also believed that even Christians are incapable of keeping the law of God perfectly, so it is of no use as a standard for spiritual behavior. Spirituality is a matter of the heart, so even outward performance of the law of God would not guarantee true righteousness. The law, then, was given to drive people to Christ in *repentance* and *faith*. Luther explicitly denied the so-called third use of the law that Calvin and other Reformed Protestants affirmed: the law as code for Christian behavior. The Reformed branch of Protestantism has always believed that even though Christians may not be able to keep the law perfectly, they should strive with the help of the *Holy Spirit* to conform to its standards as much as humanly possible.

For the most part, evangelicals have followed the Reformed view of the law

and have believed and taught that regenerate people (those born again of God's Spirit) should keep the law of God as expressed in the Ten Commandments and in Jesus' summarization of it in the famous love commandment insofar as possible. Jesus' perfect obedience to the divine law in his sinless life and atoning death is imputed to repentant sinners who throw themselves on the mercy of God so that they are reckoned by God as law-keepers, even as they fall short of perfect obedience. The law is to be preached not as a means to *salvation* but as a standard for God-pleasing living. Sometimes, of course, popular Evangelicalism has fallen into a legalistic interpretation of the law of God, in which divine commandments such as "keep the Sabbath" are rendered as burdensome obligations and duties. Evangelical theologians have gone out of their way to explain that all laws of God are meant for human well-being as well as for God's honor and glory. Keeping the law of God is the means to a full and happy life, the "chief end" of which is to "glorify God and enjoy him forever" (Westminster Shorter Catechism). Many evangelical thinkers urge that lawkeeping be viewed not as a burden imposed but as a privilege granted and that proclamation of the law include promise of power from the Holy Spirit. Every proclamation of the law must be followed by proclamation of the gospel of *forgiveness* and *grace*.

Although evangelicals agree that lawbreaking (breaking the *covenant* of works established by God with *humanity*) is the cause of the alienation between God and humans and the source of guilt that brings condemnation, and even though they agree that divine law is a standard to live by, they do not agree about the extent to which it is possible for regenerate people to keep the law of God. Reformed theology is pessimistic about even the saintliest Christians' ability to keep the law of God; as soon as a person thinks he or she is living up to one part of God's law (e.g., "Love the

Lord your God with all your heart"), he or she discovers dimensions of the law (e.g., "Love your neighbor as yourself") yet unfulfilled. There is always a gap between duty and performance to be filled by grace through faith.

Wesleyan evangelicals believe it is possible for regenerate persons to keep the law of God fully and perfectly in the power of the Holy Spirit. John Wesley wrote *A Plain Account of Christian Perfection* in order to explain and defend his doctrine of **entire sanctification,** in which Christians empowered by God's Spirit act always only out of love. They may commit sins of omission, but they no longer sin presumptuously by willfully violating known and understood laws of God. *Holiness* evangelicals— including many Pentecostals—believe momentary entire sanctification followed by a life of perfect love for God and fellow humans is a real possibility for all Christians. They seek a "second blessing" (after **conversion**) that cleanses them of the corruption of **sin** and purifies their hearts so that they will only to love and please God; they are perfected in that they no longer knowingly act out of any other motive but love. For Wesley and his followers, such a state of being "perfected in love" is perfect fulfillment of the law of God as it was summarized by Jesus. Reformed evangelicals view human nature before **resurrection** as incapable of moral perfection; the law always remains a source of condemnation and guidance, even as the condemnation is set aside by grace through faith (because of Christ's obedience on the repentant sinners' behalf) and the guidance expresses an impossible ideal.

One controversy involving different attitudes toward the law of God became divisive among evangelical theologians in the late twentieth century: the so-called *lordship salvation* controversy. Zane Hodges, then a professor at Dallas Theological Seminary, published *Absolutely Free! A Biblical Reply to Lordship Salvation* (Grand Rapids: Zondervan, 1989), which argued that genuine Christian conversion frees a person entirely from any obligation to keep the law of God; Christians may and perhaps should seek to please God by living according to the law of love, but they cannot suffer condemnation for failing to do so. They are fully and freely liberated from the law by *justification* by grace through faith. Any other interpretation, Hodges and his supporters argue, leads back into works righteousness, which is what the apostle Paul denounced in Galatians and other epistles. The other side was represented primarily by California pastor and evangelist John MacArthur, but many evangelical scholars chimed in with him. According to lordship salvation theology, even Christians—justified by grace as they are—are obligated to strive to the best of their ability with God's help to keep the divine law. Any other view, they argue, is antinomianism, a heresy rooted in ancient gnostic Christianity. Lordship salvation views the law of God—especially as expressed by Jesus—as the duty of every Christian believer, such that flouting it may lead to apostasy or proof of false faith. (Of course, many evangelicals who follow this view of the matter believe it is impossible for genuine saving grace to be lost; real apostasy never happens. For them, the point of lordship salvation is to warn against "cheap grace," which is false Christianity.) MacArthur's manifesto of lordship salvation was published as *The Gospel According to Jesus* (Grand Rapids: Zondervan, 1994).

Donald G. Bloesch, *Essentials of Evangelical Theology,* vol. 2: *Life, Ministry, and Hope* (San Francisco: Harper & Row, 1979); Kenneth Grider, *A Wesleyan-Holiness Theology* (Kansas City, MO: Beacon Press, 1994); Wayne G. Strickland and Walt C. Kaiser, eds., *Five Views on Law and Gospel* (Grand Rapids: Zondervan, 1996).

Lord's Supper Evangelicals have not concentrated a great deal of theological attention on the **sacrament** of the Lord's Supper. Free-*church* evangelicals (especially Baptists and Pentecostals) do not consider it a sacrament in any traditional sense; for them it is not so much a means of grace as a commemoration of Christ's death. They prefer to call it an *ordinance* because, together with baptism, it was ordained by Christ for perpetual observance by the church until he returns. Evangelicals in the sacramentalist church traditions (especially Episcopal and some Reformed churches) do consider the Lord's Supper a sacrament. For them it is more than a meal of remembrance; it is also a channel of *grace* whereby the faith of believers is strengthened. Few, if any, evangelicals consider the Lord's Supper salvific in the sense that it conveys saving grace automatically; evangelical sacramentalists view the Lord's Supper as a sacrament only when observed with *faith* and normally in the community of the worshiping people of God.

Most evangelicals believe there is some "real presence" of Christ in the communion celebration, although they interpret that differently. The Roman Catholic doctrine of transubstantiation, whereby the bread is believed to become the actual body of Christ and the wine the blood of Christ, is virtually absent among evangelicals; many reject it vehemently. A few evangelicals (especially in high-church Episcopal contexts) believe in consubstantiation, which is closely associated with Luther's teaching regarding the Lord's Supper. That is the idea that Christ's risen and glorified body is "in, with, and under" the elements of bread and wine.

Most evangelicals divide between two other concepts of Christ's presence in the meal. Those in the classical Reformed traditions (Presbyterian, Christian Reformed, Reformed Church in America, etc.) believe with Calvin that Christ's personal presence is mediated by the *Holy Spirit* such that believing partakers receive a greater intensity of union with Christ in the Lord's Supper. Although there is a mystical presence of Christ, Christ's body remains in *heaven* where it is localized after the *resurrection* and ascension.

Most evangelicals in the free churches view Christ's presence in the Lord's Supper as purely spiritual; they do not think they are being mystically united with Christ through eating the elements, but they do believe that the Holy Spirit uses the communion service to make Christ more vividly present in the minds and hearts of the participants. In this, they follow Calvin's predecessor in the Swiss Reformation, Ulrich Zwingli. Thus, free-church evangelicals tend to be Zwinglian in their interpretation of the Lord's Supper, while many evangelicals in the magisterial, Reformed Protestant churches tend to follow a Calvinist interpretation. For all evangelicals, the Lord's Supper is a time of self-examination and renewed repentance, as well as an opportunity for new commitment to Christ and the Christian community. At their best, there is only a hair's breadth of difference between these two majority views among evangelicals, even though at times the two sides have overemphasized that difference.

For the most part, evangelicals have simply agreed to disagree about the precise meaning of the Lord's Supper; the doctrine is left to the individual traditions and denominations, and Evangelicalism as a multidenominational movement holds no particular view other than it is an important observance for all Christians. (Two relatively small groups sometimes associated with Evangelicalism do not observe the Lord's Supper or water *baptism* at all: the Society of Friends [Quakers] and the Salvation Army. Evangelical Friends and members of the Salvation Army are usually included in the broad evangelical community in spite of their neglect of the sacraments or ordinances.) Some evangelicals celebrate the Lord's Supper weekly; others celebrate it only monthly or even only quarterly. Some evangelicals open the celebration of the Lord's Supper to everyone present; others close it to all but members of the congregation.

The most common practice is "open communion," which means that everyone who has accepted Jesus Christ as Lord and Savior is welcome to participate with the congregation. Some observe it in ecumenical settings, while others believe it is only for the local congregation. Some use wine, and others use only grape juice. Tremendous variation exists in the details. In all of this, evangelicals reflect the diversity of Protestantism generally. Evangelical theology has contributed little that is new or distinctive to the understanding of the Lord's Supper.

Evangelical theologian Stanley J. Grenz has attempted to breathe new life into evangelical celebration of the Lord's Supper by emphasizing its association with history, eschatology, and community. For him, the ordinance has three distinct orientations by which it establishes the individual believer's identity in relation to the community of God's people. It reenacts the history of salvation that focuses, especially for Christians, on the crucifixion of *Jesus Christ*; it directs believers' attention to the future fulfillment of the *kingdom of God* when Christ returns; it expresses the unity of all believers in the one body of Jesus Christ. In all of this the Lord's Supper constitutes the church as eschatological community in which Christ is present. It thereby also establishes the individual believer's identity in Christ through participation in the community that is Christ's body. For Grenz, then, the Lord's Supper is not a "mere symbol" but an identity-creating act of commitment in which both believers and the triune God are equally active.

Christopher J. Cocksworth, *Evangelical Eucharistic Thought in the Church of England* (Cambridge: Cambridge University Press, 1993); Vernard Eller, *In Place of Sacraments: A Study of Baptism and the Lord's Supper* (Grand Rapids: Wm. B. Eerdmans, 1972); Stanley J. Grenz, *Theology for the Community of God* (Grand Rapids: Wm. B. Eerdmans, 2000); Fred D.

Howard, *Interpreting the Lord's Supper* (Nashville: Broadman Press, 1966); Gordon J. Keddie, *The Lord's Supper Is a Celebration of Grace: What the Bible Teaches about Communion* (Darlington, UK: Evangelical Press, 1999).

Millennialism The secular media focused a great deal of attention on the phenomenon of millennialism around the turn of the century (2000/2001). Some of that attention was given to evangelical folk religion, especially as reflected in popular books and movies about the return of Christ. Millennialism is nothing new among evangelicals; nor is it limited to folk religion and popular images. A significant portion of evangelical Christians have always been strongly millenarian in hope and expectation about the future. Millennialism in the largest sense is any secular or religious expectation of a future historical era of peace and righteousness. Secular utopianism is often included under the rubric of millennialism. Religious millennialists believe that a messiah will come to establish a righteous utopia on earth, during which the whole earth will be filled with the knowledge of *God*. Christian millennialism (sometimes also known as chiliasm) looks forward to a literal fulfillment of Revelation 20, which mentions a thousand years during which *Satan* will be bound and Christ will rule and reign over the whole world. Millennialists look also to Old Testament prophecies of a messianic age at the end of history, during which nature as well as the nations will be at peace. Isaiah 11's depiction of the peaceable kingdom is one such biblical prophecy.

Evangelical millennialism can be dated at least to the eschatological speculations of Puritan Daniel Whitby, who in the eighteenth century developed the idea now known as *postmillennialism*. The majority of medieval theologians and Protestant Reformers (including Luther and Calvin) were amillennialists, in that they did not believe in a historical utopia; they believed perfect peace and righteousness would be established only in the new heaven and new earth after the judgment of God. Whitby and his followers predicted a Christianization of the entire world before Christ's return; it would be a virtual historical and earthly utopia, insofar as all the peoples of the earth would repent and begin to live according to the divine-human *covenant* established by God with Israel and perfectly revealed in *Jesus Christ*. Most of the Puritan divines after Whitby adopted postmillennialism, and it became a driving force for world evangelism and social reform in Great Britain and North America in the nineteenth century. World War I tended to diminish such millenarian optimism, and after World War II *premillennialism* virtually replaced it as the majority view among American evangelicals. Premillennialism is historical pessimism; it interprets the kingdom of God as a thousand-year reign of Christ on earth, after the great catastrophes of the "great tribulation period" described in the book of Revelation and after Christ returns to defeat the antichrist and his forces. Premillennialism has been popularized in graphic novels about the end times by evangelical authors. Many evangelical theologians are premillennialists; many others are amillennialists. A few carry on the tradition of postmillennial hope. (See the articles that deal with these three eschatological perspectives on the nature of the kingdom of God: *amillennialism,* postmillennialism, premillennialism.)

Because so many evangelical Christians in North America are premillennialists (whether they know that theological term or not), the mass media have at times virtually equated Evangelicalism with premillennial expectation. Millennialism of that type has become an informal orthodoxy among many (if not the majority) of evangelical lay people who have drunk deeply at the wells of popular writings about the end times by evangelical authors. In reaction to this popular evangelical millennialism, many evangelical theologians have shied away from writing much about the "furniture of heaven or the temperature of *hell,*" especially about the details of the future return of Christ, tribulation, judgment, and kingdom of God. Many of them grew up in churches that hosted annual prophecy conferences in which evangelists would use fabulous charts of history and the future to inculcate pessimism about the present and immediate future and to find hope only in the millennial reign of Christ after his catastrophic return to earth. Many moderate to progressive evangelical thinkers exercise great reserve and modesty of claims to knowledge because of that overheated eschatological atmosphere of their youth.

Many of them have been attracted to the eschatological speculations of the German theologians of hope, Wolfhart Pannenberg and Jürgen Moltmann. Especially Moltmann offers a new and, to many, improved version of millennialism that takes up the fundamentalist and evangelical realism about history and the hope for historical utopia and combines them with an anti-apocalyptic eschatology. For Moltmann and his evangelical followers, millennialism does not lead to inaction in the present, because there is continuity between the present and the future Sabbath of God, which will be a renewal of this world at the end of history. Only God can establish his millennial utopia (which may or may not be a literal one thousand years), but humans are called to be God's partners in preparing the world for it by working for peace and *justice*. At the end of the twentieth century and beginning of the twenty-first century, many evangelical theologians began to discover a new way to be millenarian without apocalyptic pessimism and hope for *redemption* only through violence. At the same time, however, popular folk Evangelicalism descended further into those negative aspects of traditional premillennialism through the best-selling books and popular movies of the *Left Behind* series, based on the eschatological speculations of fundamentalist writer Tim LaHaye.

Robert G. Clouse, ed., *The Meaning of the Millennium: Four Views* (Downers Grove, IL: InterVarsity Press, 1977); Gary DeMar, *End Times Fiction: A Biblical Consideration of the* Left Behind *Theology* (Nashville: Thomas Nelson, 2001); Robert C. Doyle, *Eschatology and the Shape of Christian Belief* (Carlisle, UK: Paternoster Press, 1999); Stanley J. Grenz, *The Millennial Maze: Sorting Out Evangelical Options* (Downers Grove, IL: InterVarsity Press, 1992).

Miracles All evangelicals—including evangelical theologians—believe in the *supernatural* power of *God* and in divine interventions (or unusual acts of God) that lack natural explanations. Supernaturalism is part and parcel of the evangelical Christian worldview, just as it has always been an integral part of the classical Christian perspective. Only with the rise of Enlightenment rationalism, naturalism, and skepticism did much of Protestant Christianity turn away from belief in miracles to a demythologizing interpretation of biblical history based on a naturalistic outlook on the universe. Naturalism is the relatively modern belief that nature is a closed and uniform network of causes and effects ruled inexorably by mathematically describable natural laws. In this there is no room for singular miracles; many liberal Protestants have combined this modern worldview with supernaturalism by positing that the universe itself is the one and only miracle. Evangelicals have retained classical Christian belief in miracles, even as they have often fallen under the influence of naturalistic impulses by relegating miracles to "biblical times" and/or to "primitive cultures." Many evangelicals, however, revel in belief in contemporary miracles. None espouse explicit naturalism as a worldview.

Evangelical theologians insist—often against popular evangelical folk belief —that miracles are not "violations of natural laws" or "divine interventions into nature." These popular definitions of miracle create tremendous tensions between Christian supernaturalism and modern science, which works with a generally naturalistic view of physical reality. British Christian apologetics writer *C. S. Lewis* dispelled this mistaken notion of miracle in his book *Miracles* (San Francisco: HarperSanFrancisco, 2001). Evangelical theologians and philosophers of religion such as Colin Brown of Fuller Theological Seminary have also worked against it. According to evangelical theology, a miracle is not a violation of natural law but an extraordinary act of God, who is the author of nature. In other words, a correct definition of miracle depends on a sound view of God's relationship with nature. God is not to be viewed as remote and uninvolved in the course of nature except in instances when he chooses to interfere in an otherwise autonomous and unbroken chain of natural causes and effects set over against God and God's agency. God's immanence requires that nature be viewed as in some sense God's activity even if it is acknowledged as having a relative autonomy within the realm of God's overall providential action. Thus, a miracle is nothing other than an unusual use of natural laws—which are really only regularities of God's activity in and through the natural world— intended to reveal God in a special way, or to rescue people from calamity, or both. Evangelicals insist that belief in miracles cannot be irrational within an overall belief in an omnipotent God and that so long as miracles are not defined as violations of autonomous natural laws and God's immanence is correctly understood, there is no necessary conflict between belief in miracles and the scientific enterprise.

Evangelicals are united in belief that miracles occurred in biblically narrated *salvation* history. Especially the *virgin birth* and bodily *resurrection* of *Jesus Christ* are universally considered miracles by evangelicals; they are not dismissed as legends or demythologized as existential events in the self-understandings of the disciples of Jesus. That is not to say that evangelical scholars are naive literalists; many of them handle miracle stories in the *Bible* critically and do not regard all of them as literal events in history. However, the text, not philosophy, is what determines it. Evangelicals view the world through biblical lenses; for them "the text [of the Bible] absorbs the world," which means that instead of interpreting the Bible through the modern metanarrative, they strive to view modernity and all other culturally conditioned perspectives through the biblical narrative and its worldview. The biblical narrative portrays nature and history as activities of God involving spiritual powers beyond normal human perception, and it depicts the world as open to acts of God that cannot be reduced to natural causes and effects. Where evangelicals disagree among themselves is over the extent to which miracles still occur. Especially Pentecostals and so-called *Third Wave* evangelicals passionately believe in contemporary miraculous "signs and wonders," often brought about through fervent *prayer*. Many other evangelicals adopt a perspective known as cessationism, in which miracles ceased with the demise of the apostolic age and the completion of inspired Scripture.

Cessationism relies heavily on the explanations offered by influential Reformed evangelical theologian *Benjamin Warfield* of the Old *Princeton School* of conservative Protestant *theology*. In his *Counterfeit Miracles* (Edinburgh, UK: Banner of Truth, 1996) Warfield, while acknowledging the freedom of sovereign God to do anything, advocated a highly skeptical attitude toward modern claims of the miraculous—even among Christians—and encouraged belief that, for the most part, miracles ceased with the end of the apos-

tolic age. Warfield was trained as a scientist before becoming a theologian; some critics have suggested that he was trying to reconcile biblical Christianity with scientific methodological naturalism—which would be highly ironic, given his penchant for opposing modernism in every form. Especially dispensationalist evangelical thinkers adopted cessationism and taught that miracles belong to earlier dispensations of God's economy, not to the present *church* age, during which God chooses to work through the written word and *gospel* proclamation, rather than through special signs and wonders.

Pentecostalism began with claims of miraculous utterances (speaking in tongues) and built on earlier belief in supernatural healing through prayer and *faith* among Holiness revivalists. Although most evangelicals tended to look down on Pentecostals and Holiness people throughout much of the twentieth century, eventually belief in miracles returned among mainline evangelicals in the later part of the century. The Third Wave movement began among non-Pentecostal evangelicals with belief in John Wimber's message of "signs and wonders" accompanying authentic evangelism. John Wimber was founder of the evangelical Vineyard Fellowship of Churches and author of a number of books on evangelism and Christian living that advocated expectation of miracles. Another Third Wave network is the vast Calvary Chapels movement, which grew out of Pentecostalism. By the 1990s some mainstream evangelical theologians were beginning to endorse the new message of signs and wonders. A course in signs and wonders was taught at Fuller Theological Seminary for several years; Fuller Seminary professor of missiology C. Peter Wagner adopted belief in contemporary miracles as a normal part of evangelical activism. Conservative evangelical theologian Wayne Grudem edited and contributed to the symposium *Are Miraculous Gifts for Today?* (Grand Rapids: Zondervan, 1996) and answered the question with an emphatic yes. He joined the Vineyard Fellowship and promoted greater acceptance of miracles, including supernatural healing, prophecy, and speaking in tongues among conservative, mainstream evangelicals.

By the end of the twentieth century cessationism no longer held the grip on non-Pentecostal evangelical thought that it once did. And yet evangelical theology in general continues to lack a doctrine of miracles as such. Only Baptist theologian Gregory A. Boyd seeks to develop a sustained theological account of the supernatural as integral to evangelical life and thought in his "spiritual warfare worldview" trilogy published by evangelical publisher InterVarsity Press. Mainstream evangelical theology dominated by classical Reformed thought continues to pay lip service to miracles—as real events in biblical history—while not seeing miracles as part of God's contemporary providential activity.

Gregory A. Boyd, *God at War: The Bible and Spiritual Conflict* (Downers Grove, IL: InterVarsity Press, 1997); Colin Brown, *Miracles and the Critical Mind* (Waco, TX: Word, 1984); R. Douglas Geivett, ed., *In Defense of Miracles: A Comprehensive Case for God's Actions in History* (Downers Grove, IL: InterVarsity Press, 1997).

Natural Theology Natural theology is the attempt to discover valid knowledge of *God* through *reason* alone, without any aid from special *revelation* or appeal to *faith*. Stated another way, natural theology is the attempt to gain knowledge of God from general (universal) revelation without any reliance on special (particular) revelation. Natural theology traditionally uses philosophy as an aid in finding natural knowledge of God. Roman Catholic *theology* places emphasis on natural theology; medieval scholastic theologian Thomas Aquinas believed that God's existence can be proven through

reason using one or more of five arguments, all of which rely heavily on Aristotle's philosophy. Catholic theology is profoundly influenced by Thomas Aquinas's natural theology, whereas Protestant theology generally eschews it. Luther believed that every person knows that God exists but denied that anyone can gain true knowledge of God's nature, character, or will from reason alone. That is not because God is not revealed in nature but because of a defect of human reason; it is corrupted by *sin*. The same approach was taken by Calvin, who argued that everyone has a "sense of the divine" but lives contrary to it. Without the special "lens" of the *Holy Spirit* given through Christian *conversion*, the human mind is nothing but a factory of idols. Natural theology yields idolatry rather than truth about God. Both Luther and Calvin based their antipathies toward natural theology largely on Romans 1 and on their biases against Catholic thought. In the twentieth century, Protestant theologian Karl Barth also strongly rejected natural theology; he blamed it for virtually every distortion of modern Christianity. Not all Protestants are opposed to any and all uses of natural theology, however. A minority have seen it as an ally in defending the faith against the onslaughts of skepticism and fideism (blind faith).

Evangelical theologians have been divided over natural theology. All evangelical thinkers believe in general revelation as God's universal self-testimony in nature, conscience, and perhaps also in universal history. However, they also believe in the universal fall of *humanity* into sin, with profound cognitive consequences. Most evangelical theologians are interested in making Christian belief intelligible to contemporary secular people bereft of strong Christian foundations. These interests and commitments create cognitive dissonance within evangelical thinkers and sometimes conflict between them. The gamut of evangelical opinions about natural theology ranges from almost Barth-like defiance in

Donald Bloesch to moderate acceptance and use in Norman Geisler, who is sometimes accused of being an evangelical Thomist. Many perspectives exist on a spectrum between these two influential evangelical thinkers and writers.

Bloesch works out of a theological orientation heavily influenced by the mainline Protestant Reformers Luther and Calvin, Catholic and Protestant mystics and Pietists, British Congregationalist theologian P. T. Forsyth, and dialectical theologians Barth and Emil Brunner. He also holds Catholic philosopher Blaise Pascal and nineteenth-century Danish existentialist philosopher Søren Kierkegaard in high regard. For Bloesch, the authentic Christian is a knight of faith who trusts in God's Word against the onslaughts of skeptical reason. "The heart has reasons the reason knows not of" (Pascal). Bloesch believes that the fall of humanity into sin has so clouded the human mind and will that they are incapable of grasping the truth about God that shines in nature, apart from a special inner testimony of the Holy Spirit that accompanies *regeneration*. Furthermore, God is so transcendent and personal that he cannot be revealed by nature, which is immanent and impersonal. Finitude and fallenness make natural theology useless, as do God's *holiness* and personal nature. A person (or personal community such as the triune God) can be known only through encounter and not through nature. Bloesch argues that while it is the task of Christian theology to make the Christian message intelligible, it has no assignment to prove the existence of God or even establish the rational credentials of the *gospel* through appeal to reason alone. The best defense of the gospel is its faithful and sound proclamation. Like Barth, Bloesch worries that any reliance of Christian theology on secular reasoning will inevitably cause an accommodation of the gospel to culture.

Norman Geisler believes that Christian apologetics as defense of the faith is an essential component of Christian scholarship in a secular, skeptical world. Furthermore, nature and grace must not be pitted against each other, for both are from God. Finally, although human sinfulness clouds thinking about spiritual matters, humans are not so fallen that an appeal to reason cannot be used as a tool of the Holy Spirit to draw them into the orbit of the gospel message. For Geisler and many other rational evangelical apologists, Christianity is more reasonable than any competing worldview, and belief in God is a major component of Christianity that can be proven through reason alone, without any special pleading by appeal to special revelation or faith. Geisler relies on forms of Thomas Aquinas's five ways of proving the existence of God. Especially relevant is the cosmological argument in its appeal to final, ultimate causation. The universe is inexplicable without an ultimate cause upon which it is dependent, because no part of the universe or the universe as a whole explains its own existence. A necessary, eternal, omnipotent being is essential for the universe to exist; belief in the universe without a divine first cause upon which it is dependent is irrational. Neither Geisler nor any other evangelical apologist believes that natural theology alone is salvific; in order to know God personally and salvifically, special revelation and faith are required. But natural theology can serve both as a defense of the rationality of foundational Christian beliefs and as a propaedeutic to faith in Jesus Christ. Like the law of Moses to Israelites, it can drive modern, skeptical people to *repentance* and faith.

Certainly Bloesch and Geisler do not represent the only two evangelical positions with regard to natural theology. During the 1950s and 1960s *Edward John Carnell* wrote several volumes of Christian apologetics that modestly incorporated aspects of natural theology. In contemporary terminology his work would be called "fundamental theology," in that it attempted to lay a foundation for specific Christian doctrine in reason and human experience. Carnell especially found an ally in universal human experience of morality; apart from God, objective morality cannot exist. Only God can explain objective values and standards of truth, beauty, and goodness; apart from belief in God, these become subjective—mere matters of taste and convention. Evangelical theologian **Bernard Ramm** wrote a Christian appeal to reason that articulated a "synthetic vision" of human life and *experience* that could not be adequately explained without belief in God. Both Carnell and Ramm strove mightily to avoid both the Scylla of irrational fideism and the Charybdis of rationalistic natural theology; their accounts of natural theology (or fundamental theology) were not aimed at proving Christianity true and tried to avoid basing its reliability on secular standards of evidence and reason. Both attempted to establish the reasonableness of Christian belief as an aid to persons open to Christianity whose minds had been clouded by hostile arguments based on secular philosophies of modernity.

During the last decades of the twentieth century, Reformed epistemology gained influence among evangelicals beyond the traditional boundaries of the Christian Reformed and Dutch Reformed communities. It is especially associated with the works of Reformed evangelical philosophers Nicholas Wolterstorff and Alvin Plantinga, both of whom rejected natural theology while arguing that Christianity has rational warrants for its basic truth claims. The essence of Reformed epistemology is the claim that belief in God is "properly basic"; the burden of proof does not lie on the believer but rather on the denier. The modern mind is captivated by the idea of "religion within the bounds of reason alone," whereas Reformed epistemology argues for "reason within the bounds of religion," in that every worldview or philosophy of life functions as a quasi-religion that involves fundamental faith commitments or basic beliefs.

Such basic beliefs cannot be proven or disproven; they are fundamental commitments that determine what counts as evidence and reasons for believing. Critics of Reformed epistemology accuse it of being a sophisticated form of fideism, while its defenders argue that any other approach to religious knowledge inevitably undermines the irreducible quality and autonomy of religion by placing it at the mercy of a nonreligious test of truth. Reformed epistemologists believe that there are reasons for Christian belief; Christianity has sufficient rational warrants to justify believing in its truth. However, they reject the project of submitting Christian truth claims to non-Christian and nonreligious criteria as if they would be neutral and objective.

Donald G. Bloesch, *The Ground of Certainty* (Eugene, OR: Wipf & Stock, 2002); Bruce Demarest, *General Revelation: Historical Views and Contemporary Issues* (Grand Rapids: Zondervan, 1982); Gordon Lewis, *Testing Christianity's Truth Claims* (Chicago: Moody Press, 1976); Bernard Ramm, *The God Who Makes a Difference: The Christian Appeal to Reason* (Waco, TX: Word, 1972); Nicholas Wolterstorff, *Reason within the Bounds of Religion* (Grand Rapids: Wm. B. Eerdmans, 1984).

Ordinances   *see* **Sacraments**

Original Sin   *see* **Sin**

Parousia   *see* **Return of Christ**

Perseverance   Many evangelicals believe that once a person is truly converted to *Jesus Christ,* he or she is guaranteed eternal *salvation*; it is not possible to lose authentic salvation. In theological language, apostasy is not a possibility for the genuinely converted; *grace* is inamissible. This doctrine is sometimes called eternal security or simply the security of the believer. It is supposed to bring assurance and relief from anxiety over one's eternal destiny, once one has repented and trusted in Christ alone for salvation. Advocates of unconditional perseverance rely on biblical and theological arguments. They point to passages such as Romans 8:38–39, which states that nothing can separate believers from the love of *God*. Many also refer to the doctrine of *election* (predestination) and argue that if all for whom Christ died are saved because they are so foreordained, they cannot be lost. The unconditionally elect must persevere because they will be preserved by God's grace. They can no more discard salvation than they could earn it. Calvinists prefer to call the doctrine of perseverance the doctrine of preservation; it is God who perseveres for true believers— the elect—by preserving them from whatever might cause them to fall away from grace. Unconditional perseverance or preservation does seem to follow logically from foundational beliefs of the Reformed system of *theology*; if persons are totally depraved such that salvation can only come by unconditional election (predestination) through irresistible grace, then losing salvation would seem to be a logical impossibility unless God is capricious and reneges on his own electing choice of some individuals. Reformed evangelicals believe he never does that. Many evangelicals—especially Baptists—believe in unconditional eternal security of true believers without basing it on a Calvinist foundation. For them, belief that true believers will persevere or be divinely preserved from permanently falling away from grace is based not on systematic theology but on biblical promises.

Many evangelicals reject the doctrine of unconditional perseverance of the saints on both biblical and theological grounds. Some add experiential evidences to support their contention that some genuinely converted persons do actually fall away and die outside of a state of grace. They point to biblical examples such as Saul, the first king of Israel, from whom the Spirit of God withdrew to be replaced by an evil spirit. They also point to historical and contemporary examples of Christians who commit apostasy as examples of the danger the apostle Paul warned about in Galatians 5:4 (falling from grace by living according to the *law*) and the author of the Epistle to the Hebrews cautioned against in chapter 6. Opponents of the doctrine of unconditional security of believers are usually also opponents of the Calvinist scheme of unconditional election and irresistible grace and argue that without those beliefs it is unreasonable to trust in unconditional perseverance. Just as persons cooperate in their own initial salvation by receiving the gift of grace through *repentance* and *faith*, so they can freely reject the grace of God to their own destruction. Grace is resistible even after it is received. Some evangelical groups have taken this to an extreme so that eternal security seems to be replaced by eternal insecurity; repentance and even renewal of conversion is necessary after every willful sin. However, few evangelical theologians espouse such an extreme position. Those who, like Southern Baptist theologian Dale Moody, argue against the doctrine of unconditional perseverance secure assurance by saying that falling away from grace is never an accident; it can happen only through willful and wanton rejection of the grace of salvation. Thus, their belief is not in insecurity of believers but in their conditional security; they are secure only in Christ. If they choose to leave Christ behind, they have no assurance of salvation.

Many mistakenly believe that the evangelical division over the doctrine of unconditional perseverance falls along the Calvinist-Arminian dividing line. It does not, even though most Calvinists accept the doctrine and most Arminians reject it. Some Arminians—especially in Baptist communities—passionately defend belief in eternal security even though it seems somewhat inconsistent with other Arminian commitments. (*Arminianism* is belief in the *free will* cooperation of persons with the grace of God in salvation.) Some evangelicals believe in the "impossible possibility" of total apostasy in spite of not being Arminian in their theology. Lutherans especially often paradoxically combine belief in amissible grace (grace from which one call fall) with belief in predestination. To a very large extent, this difference of opinion among evangelical theologians is handled irenically; very seldom does it erupt into open conflict or controversy in evangelical circles, even though occasionally individual denominations and institutions may struggle over it. Dale Moody, a highly regarded professor of theology at Southern Baptist–related Southern Baptist Theological Seminary in Louisville, Kentucky, for over twenty-five years, had his teaching privileges revoked, in part due to his vocal criticism of the Southern Baptist doctrine of unconditional eternal security of all true believers. Occasionally a Pentecostal or Nazarene minister or theologian will decide that the doctrine is true, creating conflict between him or her and the denomination. In multidenominational evangelical contexts, however, the general attitude is one of irenic toleration of diverse opinions.

G. C. Berkouwer, *Faith and Perseverance,* trans. Robert D. Knudson (Grand Rapids: Wm. B. Eerdmans, 1958); Daniel P. Corner, Vic Reasoner, and L. D. Savage, *The Believer's Conditional Security: Eternal Security Refuted* (Washington, PA: Evangelical Outreach, 2000); I. Howard Marshall, *Kept by the Power of God: A Study of Perseverance and Falling Away* (Minneapolis: Bethany House, 1969); Dale Moody, *Apostasy: A Study in the Epistle to the Hebrews and in Baptist History* (Macon, GA: Smyth & Helwys, 1997); J. Matthew Pinson and Stanley N. Gundry, eds., *Four Views on Eternal Security* (Grand Rapids: Zondervan, 2002).

Postmillennialism Some evangelical theologians believe that the *kingdom of God* will be a historical utopia on earth in which the world will be Christianized through evangelism and social transformation. This will occur before Christ returns. Thus, the *return of Christ* will be postmillennial. This eschatological interpretation of history and final events stands in contrast to the more traditional amillennial view, which regards the kingdom of God before Christ's visible return as spiritual (nearly identified with the *church*), and *premillennialism,* which believes the kingdom of God will be an earthly utopia after Christ returns, yet before the final judgment and new *heaven* and new earth are established. (See the articles on *millennialism, amillennialism,* and premillennialism.) Postmillennialism is a minority view among evangelicals since World War II; before World War I many evangelicals in Great Britain and North America were postmillennialists, as were many liberal theologians. As historical pessimism replaced social optimism in church and society, most Christians turned to premillennialism, which believes the historical situation of *humanity* will become progressively worse until Christ intervenes to conquer the forces of *evil* and establish his kingdom on earth. Postmillennialists view history more optimistically and look forward to a great *conversion* of Jews and Gentiles throughout the world leading to a long period of peace and *justice*. Some of them think the millennium may already have begun.

Postmillennialism is absent from church history before Daniel Whitby, who propogated his new interpretation of biblical *eschatology* in 1703; soon afterwards many, and eventually most, Puritans and revivalists of the Great Awakening accepted it and taught that the godly millennium would arise in the New World and spread around the earth from there. Hymns such as "We've A Story to Tell to the Nations" and "Rise Up, O Men of God" express postmillennial hopes and dreams. Whitby based his interpretation of history and the kingdom of God on a preterist understanding of biblical apocalyptic literature; he believed that most of the references to calamity had already been fulfilled (e.g., in the fall of the Roman Empire) and that many of the references to Christ's coming were gradually being fulfilled within history in and through the church's penetration of society with Christian beliefs and values. Postmillennialists rely on gradualist passages about the kingdom of God in the New Testament, such as Jesus' comparison of the kingdom with a seed growing into a tree. Of course, they fully recognize that there will be ups and downs in the history of the kingdom as it dawns within history, but they are optimistic that the power and *grace* of God working through the church will gradually turn the darkness to dawning and the dawning to noonday bright.

Although postmillennialism fell on hard times after the two world wars of the twentieth century, several notable evangelical theologians continued to espouse it straight into the twenty-first century. Most of its proponents are conservative Reformed thinkers with deep roots in *Calvinism* of the Puritan variety. A major defender of postmillennialism in the twentieth century was conservative Presbyterian theologian Lorraine Boettner, whose volume *The Millennium* (Phillipsburg, NJ: Presbyterian & Reformed Press, 1992) influenced many evangelicals to hold onto *faith* in the intrahistorical kingdom of God as a sociopolitical reality appearing before Christ's return. In 1987 noted evangelical theologian John Jefferson Davis of Gordon-Conwell Theological Seminary published a defense of postmillennialism entitled *Christ's Victorious Kingdom: Postmillennialism Reconsidered* (Grand Rapids: Baker). Other evangelical postmillennialists include *Donald Bloesch*, Keith Matthison, and Kenneth L. Gentry. During the 1990s and into the first decade of the twenty-first century, postmillennialism made something of a comeback among evangelicals through a spate of books by these and other evangelical scholars. That is true especially

among those attracted to resurgent Puritan-style Reformed theology. The year 2003 was the three-hundredth anniversary of the births of both John Wesley and Jonathan Edwards, two of Evangelicalism's greatest heroes who are highly regarded by evangelical theologians. Edwards was a major proponent of postmillennialism as was Wesley and his brother Charles. Evangelical celebrations of their lives and three centuries of influence increased interest in postmillennialism as a viable option for evangelical eschatology.

Most evangelical postmillennialists such as Donald Bloesch, however, do not expect the preparousia millennial kingdom of God to be a utopia. They are chastened by the horrors and catastrophes of the twentieth century and the likelihood of more of the same in the future. They believe that the kingdom of God in history may not include a total Christianization of the world but rather a permeation of the *gospel* into all cultures and societies with transforming results for world peace and unity. Christ will return to a world filled with faith even as it is mixed with sin and sorrow (which is the case in the church throughout history). Bloesch expresses his own version of postmillennialism (within the context of a strongly modified amillennialism) this way: "The millennium is best understood not as a condition already actualized in all its power and efficacy but as a drama that is being unfolded on the screen of history as the church penetrates the darkness of the world" (*Essentials of Evangelical Theology*, vol. 2: *Life, Ministry, and Hope* [San Francisco: Harper & Row, 1979], 199). One significant appeal of postmillennialism is the motivation it provides for Christian activism, and evangelicals are especially activist in their various efforts at *evangelism* and social transformation. One significant problem with postmillennialism for many evangelicals is its tendency to postpone the parousia (return of Christ) whereas most evangelicals believe in the "imminent return of Christ."

Robert G. Clouse, ed., *The Meaning of the Millennium: Four Views* (Downers Grove, IL: InterVarsity Press, 1977); Millard Erickson, *Contemporary Options in Eschatology* (Grand Rapids: Baker, 1988); Keith A. Mathison, *Postmillennialism: An Eschatology of Hope* (Phillipsburg, NJ: Presbyterian & Reformed Press, 1999).

Prayer   Evangelicals emphasize devotional life; the life of spirituality is crucial to evangelical *faith*. Prayer plays a significant role in evangelical devotions and in evangelical *worship*. Virtually all evangelicals—including theologians—believe that *God* hears and answers prayer. This has the status of an axiom for most evangelicals' life of faith. In evangelical churches and parachurch organizations children are taught how to pray; most evangelical churches hold weekly prayer meetings, and many reserve time during their worship services for meditation, contemplation, petition, and intercession. Prayer is without any doubt a cornerstone of evangelical piety. And yet evangelical *theology* has produced little in the way of formal, critical reflection on the phenomenon of prayer. It is for the most part simply taken for granted and left to devotional writers to explicate. Evangelical bookstores are crammed with books on prayer, including titles like *Pray and Grow Rich* and *The Prayer of Jabez*, best-selling evangelical books of the 1970s and 1990s respectively. The shelves also include more down-to-earth handbooks on prayer. Most evangelicals shun formulaic prayers in favor of spontaneity in prayer, but they welcome help from persons experienced in prayer, who give advice about how to persevere in prayer and what to do when prayers go unanswered.

Evangelical theologians are mainly concerned with the nature of true prayer, which must be distinguished from false interpretations of prayer. They also examine the problem of prayer's efficacy; does prayer make a difference in the way things go? Can prayer change the mind of God? Why pray if God already knows or has foreordained everything that is going to happen? No evangelical theologian discourages praying; all support the general practice of prayer and affirm that God hears and answers prayer. Problems and differences arise as they attempt to describe what the best kind of prayer is and answer whether prayer actually makes a difference.

Two evangelical thinkers who approach the nature of true prayer differently are *Donald Bloesch* and Richard Foster. Both have deep roots in Protestant piety and spirituality. Bloesch is a Pietist who believes that the essence of authentic Christianity includes a deep personal relationship between the believer and God that cannot be reduced to doctrinal confession or participation in *sacraments*. For him prayer is essential to authentic Christian life and at the core of what it means to be evangelical. Richard Foster is a member of the Friends (Quaker) tradition who also has deep roots in Pietism and emphasizes the life of spirituality as the true heart of evangelical life and faith. His books *Celebration of Discipline* (San Francisco: HarperCollins, 1988) and *Prayer: Finding the Heart's True Home* (San Francisco: HarperSanFrancisco, 1992) profoundly influenced a generation of evangelicals to turn toward the mystical, contemplative traditions of Christianity and to view prayer as more than petition or supplication. Foster advocates wordless praying—a form of meditation or contemplation in which the person communes with God apart from explicit meaningful communication. Due to Foster's influence, a revival of interest in mystical traditions and practices arose within Evangelicalism in the 1980s and 1990s. Foster was less interested in explaining how prayer works than in encouraging the practice of prayer for more profound, transforming communion with God.

Bloesch, on the other hand, regards "prophetic praying" as the essence of true evangelical prayer; for him the center of prayer is not contemplation (he is quite critical of wordless praying) but petition. In *The Struggle of Prayer* (Colorado Springs, CO: Helmers & Howard, 1988) Bloesch argues that true Christian prayer always involves encounter and even confrontation between the person—who is a sinner—and the holy God who is a person. Bloesch is influenced in his spirituality not only by **Pietism** but also by Emil Brunner's theology of I-Thou encounter; he has little use for mystical approaches to spirituality that move in the direction of pantheism or blur the distinction between the soul and God. For him, meaningful prayer always involves words. Meditation may play a role in evangelical prayer, but it cannot be useful apart from intelligible communication.

Another difference between evangelical thinkers revolves around the issue of whether prayer actually alters the course of events. Does prayer change the mind and will of God? Most evangelicals would say that prayer plays a role in bringing about what God always already wills; it is a foreordained means to a foreordained end. Thus, in all humility before the sovereignty of God, Christians should always pray, "If it is your will." This is the approach taken by Reformed evangelicals, but it is shared—perhaps paradoxically—by Arminians, who do not believe in meticulous **providence** but affirm **free will**. The majority of evangelical Christians, whether Reformed or Arminian, strongly believe in God's control over history, including individuals' lives.

Yet, as some evangelical thinkers have pointed out, much evangelical prayer implies that petition to God can change God's mind and the course of events from what was to happen to something else. Especially open theists (who deny the exhaustive and infallible foreknowledge of God) point to the biblical story of King Hezekiah of Judah, who, in Isaiah's time, was told he would soon die (2 Kings 20). He petitioned God for extension of life; God relented and gave

him fifteen more years. Open theists point to this and numerous other examples in the biblical narratives of prayer causing God to "repent" (relent) and argue that prayer is not merely a foreordained means to a foreordained end but a means provided by God for humans to influence him in his providential activity. Evangelical philosopher and spiritual writer Dallas Willard advocates this view of prayer in *The Divine Conspiracy* (San Francisco: HarperSanFrancisco, 1998), against the idea that God is a "great unblinking cosmic stare" whose ways cannot be changed by human petition. Rather, he argues, God allows himself to be affected by his creatures while maintaining his sovereignty; answers to prayers are not guaranteed, but prayer may change the mind and will of God because God allows it to. Open theists such as **Clark Pinnock** and John Sanders heartily agree and point out that evangelical theology—especially the doctrine of God—needs to be adjusted to fit evangelical spirituality and prayer.

More traditional evangelical thinkers have responded to open theism in two ways. First, they argue that "prayer never changes God; it only changes us." Second, they say that prayer does make a difference in that God commands it and foreordains it as his chosen means to accomplishing his purposes. In other words, petitionary prayer does not alter what God has already determined to do, but what he has already determined to do often includes prayer as part of the process leading to the goal he has in mind. The main purpose of prayer, however, is not to alter God's mind or ways, but to bring humans into harmony with the plan of God in which they are allowed to participate through prayer. This is the Reformed doctrine of prayer accepted by most evangelicals, including those who consider themselves more Arminian than Calvinist.

Terrance Tiessen, *Providence and Prayer: How Does God Work in the World?* (Downers Grove, IL: InterVarsity Press, 2000).

Predestination   *see* Election

Premillennialism   Many evangelical Christians believe that *Jesus Christ* will return to earth after a seven-year great tribulation and establish his rule and reign—the *kingdom of God* on earth—for a thousand years. They base this on a literal interpretation of Revelation 20, as well as on Old Testament prophecies of a utopia on earth during a messianic period in the future (e.g., Isaiah 2 and 11). This vision of the future is known as premillennialism because it asserts that Christ will return before the millennium (a thousand-year utopia at the end of history). Several early church fathers, including Irenaeus and Tertullian, were premillennialists. Many of the Radical Reformers, including some Anabaptists, were also premillennialists. It remained a minority view among Christians until the twentieth century, when seeds planted in the fertile soil of North American *revivalism* in the 1830s and 1840s by Adventist prophets and by British Plymouth Brethren grew to fruition in an explosion of evangelical end-time fervor. In the 1890s and early years of the twentieth century, *Bible* prophecy conferences grew in popularity among evangelicals. Most of these promoted premillennial expectation. In the 1920s leading fundamentalists added premillennialism to the list of "fundamentals of the faith."

Before then, *postmillennialism* and *amillennialism* had held sway among conservative Christians; they were being swept aside as especially fundamentalists and evangelicals embraced premillennialism (also known historically as chiliasm). The growth of premillennialism corresponded with the increasingly pessimistic view of history after the two world wars. Popular evangelical preachers and writers urged their followers to win as many souls as possible before the second coming of Christ, so that they would be resurrected to rule and reign with him in his millennial kingdom on earth.

Evangelical theologians distinguish between two types of premillennialism: historic and dispensationalist. The former is continuous with the chiliasm of the early church fathers and Radical Reformers; the latter is a relatively new spin on premillennialism that began with evangelical sects in Great Britain in the 1830s and 1840s. Especially *John Nelson Darby*, a founder of the Plymouth Brethren movement, interpreted biblical apocalyptic literature and eschatological passages of Paul's epistles as referring to a "secret rapture" of all true believers in Jesus Christ before the seven-year-tribulation period immediately preceding the parousia (second coming of Christ). *Dispensationalism* includes much more than that, of course, but as a unique and innovative form of premillennial expectation, this is its distinctive contribution. It was popularized among evangelicals through the footnotes of the wildly popular *Scofield Reference Bible* and later by the writings of Hal Lindsay, author of *The Late Great Planet Earth* and other volumes of popular evangelical apocalyptic literature. Dallas Theological Seminary—a leading evangelical institution—specializes in dispensationalism. Historic premillennialists such as evangelical theologian Millard Erickson and evangelical New Testament scholar Robert Gundry reject dispensationalism's two-stage view of the *return of Christ*, especially the idea of a secret rapture of the church. They find no warrant for it in *Scripture* and argue that it is so novel in terms of the Great Tradition of Christian belief that it is unlikely to be true. They believe that Christians alive at the end stage of history will experience the great tribulation; the rapture will be simultaneous with the parousia. Believers in Jesus Christ will be caught up in the air (literally or figuratively) to meet Christ as he returns. Then they will reign with him during his millennial kingdom, during which *Satan* will be bound. The earth will be a virtual utopia under the benevolent rule of Christ and his people—Jews and gentile Christians, all who have accepted him as Lord and Savior before his return.

Most evangelicals who believe in premillennialism do not consider it an essential of the *gospel* or necessary to sound Christian *theology*; they relegate it to the realm of opinion or interpretation. Only some fundamentalists regard it is as crucial Christian belief. And yet many evangelical denominations include it in their doctrinal statements and require ministers, if not church members, to affirm it as true. This is especially the case with Pentecostals, conservative Baptists (primarily in the North), and many independent evangelical churches. Critics of premillennialism argue that it is too literalistic in its interpretation of Revelation 20; thousand years is often used in Scripture as a symbol for a special era of history. They also claim that all of the biblical materials claimed as support by premillennialists can adequately be explained through either amillennialism or postmillennialism and that belief in the one-thousand-year rule of Christ on earth is superfluous to the history of *salvation.* What is accomplished during it that is not being accomplished through the *church* before the end or that will not be accomplished in the new *heaven* and new earth after Christ's return and the great judgment? In other words, critics—including many evangelical theologians—view the millennium of premillennialism as a wholly unnecessary appendage to an otherwise successful history of salvation. Finally, critics of premillennialism say that it undermines concern for the present; focus on a future utopia brought about by Christ alone through *supernatural* intervention tends to cut the heart out of evangelical efforts for social transformation.

Premillennialists respond by pointing out that Revelation 20 is quite specific about the millennium of the future and Christ's role in binding Satan (when else would Satan be bound?) and ruling the world righteously. The purpose

of the millennium is to fulfill God's promises to his people—both Israel and the church—and to vindicate Christ's messiahship. It will reveal the will of God for the world in an era of peace and *justice*. Furthermore, belief in a future utopia on earth is no more likely to hinder efforts for social transformation now than is belief, shared by all evangelicals, in a future new heaven and new earth. In fact, premillennialists argue, belief in the millennial kingdom of peace and justice provides a vision for contemporary social transformation according to the will of God. Believers in the millennium should not sit idly by allowing the present world to go to *hell* in the proverbial handbasket but they should be working for Christ's kingdom to anticipate its fulfillment when he returns.

Millard Erickson, *Contemporary Options in Evangelical Eschatology* (Grand Rapids: Baker, 1988); Brian Hebblethwaite, *The Christian Hope* (Grand Rapids: Wm. B. Eerdmans, 1985); Robert H. Gundry, *The Church and the Tribulation* (Grand Rapids: Zondervan, 1973); George Eldon Ladd, *Crucial Questions about the Kingdom of God* (Grand Rapids: Wm. B. Eerdmans, 1952); Dwight Pentecost, *Things to Come* (Grand Rapids: Zondervan, 1965).

Providence   Providence is the exercise of *God's* sovereignty over nature and history; it is God's governance over the affairs of his *creation*. Evangelicals affirm the sovereignty of God along with the classical Christian tradition; together with Eastern Orthodox, Roman Catholic, and orthodox Protestant traditions of all denominations, evangelicals confess that God is Lord and that nothing in his world escapes his control. As one evangelical theologian expresses it, if there is one maverick molecule in the universe, God is not God. This is simply a contemporary, pithy expression of Jonathan Edwards's strong doctrine of God's sovereignty. Most evangelicals would agree, even if they would extend the explanation of God's providential governance to include freedom and contingency in the universe. A favorite saying among evangelicals is that "God is in control." Put somewhat more theologically, "Man proposes but God disposes." Evangelicals are fond of assuring themselves and others that the God of the *Bible* knows what he is doing and his plans cannot be thwarted by creaturely resistance. This doctrine gives meaning to the otherwise chaotic events of nature and history. What appear to be accidents are actually the workings of God's secret will.

Yet not all evangelicals are comfortable with such a monergistic doctrine of providence. (Monergism is belief in the single active, causal agency of God overriding all others.) Although meticulous providence has a long and respectable history among evangelicals, and even many non-Reformed evangelicals tend to fall back on it as a default position in the face of calamities, some evangelicals resist attributing *sin, evil,* and disaster to God's will and power. Even evangelicals who embrace the micromanaging image of the God of meticulous providence generally hesitate to regard God as the author of evil. Evil arises from the corrupt intentions of fallen human hearts, not from God's perfectly loving and benevolent will. God controls all events—including evil—by allowing them; he does not cause evil even if he does will it in the same way that he wills the good. Evil, Reformed evangelicals say, is the necessary dark side of the greater good that God is working out in creation, and why it must exist is beyond our ability to grasp. God does not cause it, but he does will it in order that he may bring good out of it (Romans 8:28). Evangelicals working out of the Arminian tradition express God's sovereignty in relation to sin, evil, and calamity differently. They believe that although nothing can happen without God's permission and even concurrence (because God's creating and sustaining power is necessary for every action by a creature), sin, evil, and calamity are not willed or caused by God

in the same way as are the benefits of creation. God does not positively will them, but he does will to permit them for the sake of creaturely freedom. Arminians distinguish between God's sovereignty de jure (by right) and de facto (in actuality); the former is always the case while the latter is eschatological. God is not yet fully in control of whatever is happening; yet nothing that happens falls outside God's governing rule. He is in charge but not yet fully in control. This is due to a self-limitation on God's part. God chooses to give creatures *free will* such that they can resist and even temporarily thwart God's perfect will, but he retains overall control of the course of history. A favorite analogy of Arminian evangelicals was provided by evangelical author A. W. Tozer in the popular *The Knowledge of the Holy* (San Francisco: HarperSanFrancisco, 1978). A ship's captain is in charge of the ocean liner as it crosses the Atlantic from New York to Liverpool, but he does not control everything that happens below deck on the journey. The destination and arrival are predestined, but specific events on board during the trip are not, and they may even be contrary to the will of the captain. So it is with God on the journey of history to its consummation in the *kingdom of God.*

Reformed evangelicals reject the Arminian distinction between God's sovereignty de jure and de facto because it appears to them to loosen God's grip on the world he has created and transfer power and control from God to creatures. Arminian evangelicals reject Reformed theology's meticulous providence because it cannot avoid implying that God is the author of sin and evil, thereby impugning God's character. It also seems to undermine the responsibility of humans for the evils they commit in history, if they could not do otherwise. Evangelicals have generally agreed to disagree about this matter. Individual denominations and organizations within the evangelical community may hold one view or the other (or even some paradoxical hybrid view), but cooperation and fellowship across confessional boundaries has for the most part characterized Evangelicalism in spite of profound differences of interpretation such as this.

Some views, however, seem to strain that peaceful cooexistence. On the Reformed side, some evangelical thinkers such as R. C. Sproul and John Piper have raised objections from Arminians by seeming to attribute evil to God. Sproul and Piper (and some other Calvinists among evangelicals) wish to be completely consistent in their accounts of God's sovereignty and therefore push meticulous providence to (what Arminians consider) an extreme; Sproul occasionally implies that any other view of God's sovereignty than meticulous providence amounts to atheism. While many Reformed thinkers would nuance God's relationship with evil by emphasizing the instrumentality of secondary causes, these and some other conservative evangelical thinkers strongly assert God's governing role in whatever happens, including (according to John Piper) terrorists' acts. However offensive these viewpoints may be to many modern sensibilities, they find precedents in the strong affirmations of God's sovereignty in Ulrich Zwingli, John Calvin, and especially Jonathan Edwards; Piper and Sproul would be quick to add Paul the apostle. Some Arminian evangelicals worry that this seemingly extreme view of providence gives excuse to those who do evil—that they, like *Satan*, are merely instruments in the hand of God. Furthermore, Arminians object, why would Jesus have taught his disciples to pray to God, "Thy kingdom come; thy will be done on earth as it is in heaven," if God's will is always already being done?

On the other side, some Arminian evangelicals have attempted to take with utmost seriousness the moral distance between God and evil by asserting that God is by no means providentially in control of everything that happens. John Sanders, an influential open theist who believes that God does not know the future exhaustively and infallibly, argues that God takes risks in history. In fact, creation itself was a risk of God. (In this he finds precursors in well-known German theologian Helmut Thielicke, who affirmed a risk-taking God, and influential Scottish theologian Thomas Torrance, who coined the phrase "openness of God.") According to Sanders and other open theists, God limits himself in relation to creation such that he does not even know with absolute certainty what humans are going to do with the gift of free will. He remains omnipotent even if he is not omnicausal, however, and therefore is able to respond to whatever humans do, resourcefully to bring good out of it. Open theism's account of divine providence is highly qualified and, according to Reformed critics, so diminishes God's sovereignty that it virtually disappears. Open theists, however, respond that God is sovereign because he is able to guide history to its predetermined goal in God's kingdom and to draw even human acts of sin and evil into his good plan. They argue that their God is more powerful and resourceful and glorious than the all-determining God of *Calvinism's* meticulous providence, precisely because he has to respond to challenges from creatures, whereas Calvinism's God simply controls everything.

The tensions within evangelical *theology* over providence are illustrated in two volumes published by evangelicals in the 1990s. On the Reformed side, in *The Providence of God* (Downers Grove, IL: InterVarsity Press, 1993) British evangelical philosopher Paul Helm argued for meticulous providence and adamantly rejected the risk-taking view of God held by many Arminians, and especially by open theists, as unbiblical and incoherent. On the Arminian side, Baptist theologian E. Frank Tupper developed *A Scandalous Providence: The Jesus Story of the Compassion of God* (Macon, GA: Mercer University Press, 1995) out of a careful narrative reading of the Gospels and out of his own and others' *experiences* of sickening calamity. According to Tupper, God did not slaughter the infants of Bethlehem; Herod did. God limits himself in relation to history and allows much that he does not will and that is even against his will. Tupper argues that the God of the Bible is not a do-anything-anytime-anywhere God but a loving God who grieves over innocent suffering; in every tragic situation God does all that God can do to relieve suffering and stop evil. What God can do is embedded in the particularities of individual situations; sometimes God can act miraculously to prevent or stop evil, and sometimes he cannot. Only God knows the calculus that explains it. For Tupper and many other evangelicals, any other view renders God monstrous.

Benjamin Wirt Farley, *The Providence of God* (Grand Rapids: Baker, 1988); John Sanders, *The God Who Risks: A Theology of Providence* (Downers Grove, IL: InterVarsity Press, 1998); R. C. Sproul, *Almighty over All: Understanding the Sovereignty of God* (Grand Rapids: Baker, 1999); R. K. McGregor Wright, *No Place for Sovereignty: What's Wrong with Freewill Theism* (Downers Grove, IL: InterVarsity Press, 1996).

Rebirth   *see* **Regeneration**

Reconciliation   In general, reconciliation simply refers to *salvation*; it is *God's* work for and in *humanity* bringing them back into fellowship with himself. It is the restoration of a broken relationship through Christ's atoning death and *faith* in him. More specifically it refers to the result of justification. (See the article on *justification*.) When human persons are justified by *grace* through faith because of *Jesus Christ's* active and passive obedience to God in his life and death, the result is reconciliation between God and them. The guilt and condemnation of *sin* are set aside, and they are reckoned as righteous in

God's sight. Evangelicals especially love to emphasize the mediatorship of Christ in restoring fellowship between God and humanity; he is often depicted as the bridge that crosses the chasm between people and God created by sin. Many evangelicals agree that even God needed reconciling with humanity due to his *justice* and wrath provoked by sin. God provided it in Jesus Christ; when he died on the cross God's wrath was assuaged and his heart was reconciled with humanity. All that remained for salvation to be actualized was humanity's response of *repentance* and faith. Some evangelicals are uncomfortable with the idea that God needed to be reconciled; they believe that since God's nature is love, wrath is not a hostile attitude in God toward sinners but the effect of God's love when it is resisted and rejected. Reconciliation, then, is entirely something that happens to humans when they respond appropriately to God's offer of mercy and grace. (See the article on *atonement*.)

Leon Morris, *Apostolic Preaching of the Cross* (Grand Rapids: Wm. B. Eerdmans, 1984); Leon Morris, *The Atonement: Its Meaning and Significance* (Downers Grove, IL: InterVarsity Press, 1984); Clark H. Pinnock and Robert C. Brow, *Unbounded Love* (Eugene, OR: Wipf & Stock, 2001).

Redemption   The concept of redemption plays an important role in evangelical preaching and doctrinal teaching; in its widest sense it is virtually synonymous with *God's* action for *humanity's* salvation in all its aspects. One often hears or reads in evangelical language of "God's plan of redemption," which usually means the entire scope of God's plan, purpose, and activity for human *salvation*, focusing especially in *Jesus Christ's* life, death, and *resurrection*. A narrower and more specific sense of the term refers to the atoning death of Christ and especially that dimension of atonement by which God through Christ's death rescued humanity from the condemnation of *sin* through some kind of legal or financial transaction. This is biblical imagery drawn from the marketplaces of Greek and Roman cities and especially from the slave markets where family members could buy back slaves from their masters. The apostle Paul uses this imagery in Ephesians 1:17, 14 and 4:30, as well as other places in his epistles. The early *church* fathers developed the biblical imagery of sacrifice as redemption into a theory of Christ's saving atonement in which humanity had fallen into slavery to *Satan* through the fall of Adam and Eve, and God had to pay Christ as a ransom to redeem them from Satan's legal hold. Most evangelicals do not follow the church fathers that far in using the language of redemption, and especially evangelical theologians know well that there is no biblical justification for regarding Christ's death as a ransom paid to Satan. Nevertheless, the language and imagery of redemption and of Christ as redeemer is found in much evangelical hymnody, devotional literature, and preaching. For the most part, it is simply one way of expressing Christ's atoning work for human salvation. (See the article on *atonement.*)

John Murray, *Redemption Accomplished and Applied* (Grand Rapids: Wm. B. Eerdmans, 1984); W. Graham Scroggie, *The Unfolding Drama of Redemption*, 3 vol. in one (Grand Rapids: Kregel, 1995); John Stott, *The Cross of Christ* (Downers Grove, IL: InterVarsity Press, 1986).

Regeneration   Of all the dimensions and aspects of *salvation,* evangelicals especially love to emphasize regeneration, which is more popularly known as "being born again." In classical Protestant orthodoxy, holistic salvation includes an entire *ordo salutis* (order of salvation): *election,* calling, *conversion,* regeneration, *justification, sanctification,* and glorification. Some theologians would fold regeneration and justifica-

tion into conversion; others (especially Reformed thinkers) insist that regeneration precedes conversion (which includes *repentance* and *faith*). The details of the order of salvation are much disputed by conservative Protestant theologians; it is one of the most divisive issues within evangelical thought. However, all evangelicals agree that a crucial aspect of salvation too often neglected by other Christians is the experience of being born again or becoming a new *creation* in *Christ Jesus.* They point to Jesus' words to Nicodemus in John 3 about being born again and also to the apostle Paul's teaching to the Ephesians about becoming new creations by God's *grace* through faith. Evangelicals believe that genuine salvation always includes an internal transformation by the *Holy Spirit*; it cannot be reduced to a legal pronouncement by God about a person's righteousness in Christ by faith. Baptist theologian *Augustus Hopkins Strong* defined regeneration as "the expulsive power of a new affection" and connected it and justification as two moments of one event called conversion. True conversion, evangelicals insist, cannot happen without both regeneration's inward cleansing and empowerment and justification's *forgiveness* and imputation of righteousness. Regeneration is the beginning of a process called sanctification, which is growth in righteousness that is completed in Christian perfection. Some evangelicals believe that process of inward perfection can happen before death, while most believe it happens only in the *resurrection* (glorification).

While all evangelicals believe fervently in the *experience* of regeneration, they disagree among themselves about such details as when and to whom regeneration can happen and what precisely is involved in it. Roman Catholics and some magisterial Protestants (especially Lutherans and Episcopalians) believe in baptismal regeneration; being born again of the Spirit of God involves an inward cleansing from sin and awakening to God that can happen to infants when they are baptized within a context of faith. (The Roman Catholic Church does not believe faith is required; *baptism* can effect regeneration *ex opere operato*—automatically by virtue of the sacrament itself when properly performed by a priest. But even Roman Catholics believe resistance to the grace of baptism can invalidate the sacrament, and faith in the hearts and minds of the parents, godparents, and church members is a valuable asset to the child being baptized.) Most evangelicals are uncomfortable with baptismal regeneration; they believe that being born again necessarily involves a personal decision of repentance and faith. That is, conversion to Christ must be conscious and involve some level of personal commitment; it cannot be performed for someone by a priest or minister. They point to all the instances of conversion in the New Testament; in every case the person coming to Christ in faith is able to express sorrow for sin and trust in Christ for salvation. All the commands about salvation involve decision and commitment.

So what about infant baptism? Many evangelicals practice infant baptism, but most consider it parallel with the Hebrew rite of circumcision in the *covenant* between God and Israel; it is the *church's* rite of initiation of children into the fellowship of the body of Christ. Some evangelicals would go so far as to consider infant baptism regenerative, in the restricted sense that it inserts the child into Christ's body, thus effecting an ontological change. It may even wash away *original sin*. (Evangelicals who practice infant baptism stand in various church traditions that explain its effect differently.) However, all evangelicals—including those who practice infant baptism—believe that every person must come to his or her own personal decision of repentance and faith and embrace Christ consciously and willingly. This conversion is more than a mere rite of confirmation of baptism. It is a personal response to the call of God and involves

a sense of guilt for personal sins and profound desire to be forgiven and accepted by God. It involves trust in Christ alone for *reconciliation* with God and adoption into God's family by the Holy Spirit. Some evangelicals believe this experience of conversion including new birth and forgiveness necessarily manifests itself in a struggle of repentance that involves emotions. Especially Pentecostals and many Baptists expect converts to walk down an aisle and pray with the evangelist or pastor. High-church evangelicals in the Episcopalian and Presbyterian traditions usually do not expect such emotional conversions, but they nevertheless welcome and encourage persons coming to Christ in faith (even if baptized as infants) to acknowledge they are sinners and need Jesus Christ for pardon and cleansing.

Reformed evangelicals believe that regeneration as spiritual awakening and empowerment happens before repentance and the outward expression of faith (conversion). It may seem simultaneous with these, but because of total depravity no sinner would ever be converted to Christ without God's effectual calling, irresistible grace, and inward regeneration by the power of the Holy Spirit. Especially the latter may happen chronologically simultaneously with conversion, but theologically a distinction must be made between regeneration and conversion. Conversion is what human persons do in response to God's call and regeneration. (Of course, for Reformed theologians even the human response is a gift of God!) That is why, for many Reformed evangelicals, regeneration may begin at infant baptism, even if its completion arrives only just before conversion. Still, even for Reformed evangelicals, being born again is something that necessarily involves an experience of repentance and faith. For them, however, regeneration precedes and effects the experience rather than following from it. Again, the issue has nothing to do with time; "before" and "after" here are not chronological but logical terms, having to do with relationships of causation. The convert and observers may notice no difference between the elements of conversion; they come in a package all at once, so to speak. Theologians insist on distinguishing between the elements of conversion and putting them in the right order in relation to each other, in order to preserve the sovereignty of God (Reformed) or the necessity of *free will* decision in cooperation with God's prevenient grace (Arminian).

Helmut Berkhardt, *The Biblical Doctrine of Regeneration*, trans. O. R. Johnston (Downers Grove, IL: InterVarsity Press, 1978); Anthony A. Hoekema, *Saved by Grace* (Grand Rapids: Wm. B. Eerdmans, 1989); Hugh Dermot McDonald, *Salvation* (Westchester, IL: Crossway, 1982); Robert E. Picirilli, *Grace, Faith, and Free Will: Contrasting Views of Salvation* (Nashville: Randall House, 2002); Timothy L. Smith, ed., *Whitefield and Wesley on the New Birth* (Grand Rapids: Zondervan, 1986).

Repentance   Evangelical *theology* is rooted in three distinct but related Protestant soils: *Puritanism, Pietism,* and revivalism. All three strongly emphasize the necessity of repentance for *salvation,* and all three view repentance as a personal struggle involving sorrow for *sin* (contrition), confession of sinfulness (confession), and amendment of life (change of mind and behavior). For the most part, evangelicals have adopted this general perspective about repentance. They deny that contrition alone is sufficient for true repentance; sorrow for sin is only one step in the repenting process. On the other hand, confession of sinfulness and of known sins is necessary but insufficient without genuine contrition. Finally, contrition and confession without amendment of life are incomplete repentance; true repentance always involves commitment to embark upon a life of rising above sin as much as possible by *God's* help.

Evangelicals love to point out that the Greek word for repentance in the New Testament is *metanoia,* which implies a turning around. In other words, repentance is not merely an expression of sorrow for sin (being a sinner and sinning) but also a definite change in the direction of one's life. Otherwise, evangelicals claim (often relying on Dietrich Bonhoeffer's classic *The Cost of Discipleship*) *grace* would be cheap; "costly grace" means that salvation cost God the life of his Son *Jesus Christ* and that persons seeking salvation must bear the cross of true repentance in amendment of life.

It should be clear by now that evangelicals consider **conversion,** of which repentance is an integral element, more than "turning over a new leaf." Conversion involves a radical change in one's life. This is crucial to the ethos of Evangelicalism, and most evangelical theologians agree with it heartily, although they may not always be enthusiastic about some of the details of the struggle of repentance as portrayed by popular evangelical authors and speakers. Emotion, theologians point out, is not the issue; the important issue to emphasize is change of mind, heart, and behavior. Furthermore, in contrast to assumptions often made by evangelicals in the pews and the pulpits, theologians emphasize that genuine repentance—like all of conversion—is a gift of God and not a work achieved by human beings.

Reformed evangelicals argue that all descendants of Adam (except Christ, of course) are so totally depraved that apart from a special work of God in their lives, they would never repent. They base this on Romans 3:11, which includes the claim that no one seeks after God. Unless God intervenes and creates repentance and faith in the person's life, he or she will never turn from sin to God in conversion. This happens to the elect when they are supernaturally regenerated (born again, made new creatures) by the **Holy Spirit.** Conversion—including holistic repentance—follows from regeneration.

Evangelicals of the Arminian persuasion agree that true repentance, like true faith, is a gift of God, but they believe it is resistible and that its reception necessarily involves a cooperation by the person who repents. By his prevenient (going before) grace God calls, convicts, enlightens, and enables the sinner to repent and believe; the sinner then must respond to the Spirit's work by allowing it to change his or her life, and that change takes the aspect of repentance and faith. These are not works that merit salvation (contrary to some Reformed anti-Arminian polemics), but simply what it means to accept the gift of salvation. Both Reformed and Arminian evangelicals equally regard repentance as a work of God that manifests itself in the sinner's contrition, confession, and life amendment; the difference lies in whether or not the sinner called by God could resist so that repentance and faith are aborted.

One group of evangelical theologians has rejected the idea that repentance is necessary for salvation; they are in the minority among evangelicals. Zane Hodges and others label the strong emphasis on repentance, including amendment of life, "lordship salvation" and criticize it as a new form of legalism. Their perspective is that conversion involves only *faith*; they point to the apostles' answer to the Philippian jailer who asked, "What must I do to be saved?" The answer did mention repentance, but only "believe in the Lord Jesus" (Acts 16:31). Hodges and others who resist so-called lordship salvation (which argues that true salvation necessarily involves allowing Jesus Christ to be Lord of one's life in obedience to his will) end up going against the entire history of evangelical theology. They believe that repentance is valuable and necessary for *sanctification*—the process of becoming mature as a believing Christian—but not for conversion to Christ (including *regeneration* and *justification*). This leads to the idea that there are two classes of Christians—those who have merely believed in Christ so that their sins are forgiven, and those who are not only forgiven but also becoming disciples of Jesus Christ. Only the latter must repent. The majority of evangelicals stand somewhere between extreme lordship salvation (which seems to imply a dependence of salvation on active obedience if not perfection) and Hodges's reaction against it. Most believe that holistic repentance is necessary for salvation, but one can be saved without yet being an obedient disciple of Jesus Christ in every area of life. Most evangelicals say that all genuinely saved persons will inevitably move toward and into obedience as they grow and mature in the faith. The only two absolutely necessary conditions for salvation, however, are repentance and faith. (See the article *Lordship Controversy*, in section on issues in evangelical theology.)

William Douglas Chamberlain, *The Meaning of Repentance* (Grand Rapids: Wm. B. Eerdmans, 1954); Anthony A. Hoekema, *Saved by Grace* (Grand Rapids: Wm. B. Eerdmans, 1989); Thomas Oden, *The Transforming Power of Grace* (Nashville: Abingdon, 1993); Richard Owen Roberts, *Repentance: The First Word of the Gospel* (Wheaton, IL: Crossway, 2002); Thomas Watson, *Doctrine of Repentance* (Edinburgh, UK: Banner of Truth, 1988).

Resurrection   Resurrection can refer either to Jesus' resurrection from death, to other humans' resurrection, or to both. In Christian *theology* generally the two are distinguished but closely related; Jesus' resurrection happened two days after his crucifixion (according to the New Testament Gospels and the book of Acts); everyone else's resurrection, though like his (1 Corinthians 15), will occur in the future when *Jesus Christ* returns. Evangelicals enthusiastically agree with classical Christian orthodoxy that both are actual events in space and time; they are not legends or myths but great acts of *God* in outer world history (not merely inward, subjective history). Evangelicals stand against the modern tendency to demythologize resurrection as merely the restoration of *faith* in Jesus' mission in the hearts and minds of the disciples (Bultmann and Tillich). Most evangelicals would consider anyone who denied the reality of resurrection not authentically Christian; for them this is a nonnegotiable, watershed issue, because *Scripture* is so clear about it and also because *salvation* is at stake. The apostle Paul told the Corinthians (chapter 15) that if Christ was not raised their faith is in vain, and he connected their future resurrection closely with Christ's as promise and fulfillment.

For evangelicals, Christ's resurrection necessarily includes the empty tomb; it was a bodily resurrection, not merely an example of the universal truth of life after death. They take seriously Luke's account of the reality of Christ's resurrection body, while admitting that Paul refers to Christ's and our future resurrection bodies as "spiritual bodies." Evangelicals agree that this should not be interpreted as mere immortality; there is real continuity as well as discontinuity between the body that is buried and the body that is raised to transformed existence fit for eternal life in *heaven*. Some evangelicals insist on emphasizing the literal resurrection. Of course, theologians point out, this is a problem, because if something is "literal" that means it is just like something else, and resurrection is not exactly like anything else in nature or history. All evangelicals agree that even if "literal" is not the best adjective to describe the resurrections, they are nevertheless objectively real and not merely visions or ghostlike apparitions.

Some evangelical apologists have gone to great lengths to prove the historical objectivity of the resurrection of Jesus, believing that this can establish the truth of Christianity in a world of skepticism. Books such as Frank Mori-

son's *Who Moved the Stone?* (Grand Rapids: Zondervan, 1977) and Josh McDowell's *Evidence that Demands a Verdict* (San Bernadino, CA: Here's Life Publishers, 1979) are extremely popular among evangelicals; how much influence they have exercised outside of evangelical circles is uncertain. Most evangelical theologians are somewhat skeptical of the power of proofs to create faith and point out that the resurrection of Jesus had a revelatory quality to it; that is to say, that some persons who witnessed it (or saw Christ afterwards) did not recognize him or did not believe, in spite of seeing him. This has no bearing whatsoever on the historical reality of the bodily resurrection of Jesus. It is simply to say that rational proofs may be of little value in convincing skeptics.

Evangelical theologians influenced by existentialism and neo-orthodoxy especially object to rationalizing the faith with historical or logical proofs. *Donald Bloesch* is one such evangelical thinker who warns against attempting to establish the truth of the faith through reason alone apart from faith in God's revelation; for him the resurrection is knowable only through an inner witness of the *Holy Spirit* that brings one into encounter with the living Jesus Christ. Stanley J. Grenz, a former student of German Lutheran theologian Wolfhart Pannenberg, believes that the resurrection is historically verifiable. Grenz believes that while the resurrection may not be amenable to proof (what constitutes proof is problematic in a postmodern age), it is true beyond a reasonable doubt, even if some element of *revelation* is necessary to attain certainty of it. Grenz, though not an apologist so much as a constructive evangelical theologian, offers a bridge between the naively rationalistic ultraconservatives among evangelicals and those who tend to fall into a fideistic antirationalism that may put the *gospel* into a ghetto of faith.

Evangelicals have disagreed among themselves about the exact nature of the resurrection. While all affirm its bodily nature, they do not describe that in the same way. This has sometimes given rise to sharp debates and even accusation of heresy and overliteralism. The older fundamentalist movement, out of which post–World War II Evangelicalism grew, insisted on the physicality of the resurrection and occasionally described it in ways that sounded like corpse resuscitation. This was in reaction to liberal Protestants, who often tended to interpret the resurrection in purely spiritual terms so that it was hardly different from the Greek idea of immortality of souls. In response to fundamentalist literalism, many evangelicals pointed out that Jesus' resurrection body had special qualities such as ability to walk through solid doors (John 20). Fundamentalists argued back that the resurrected Jesus of Luke 24 declared that he had "flesh and bones" and ate fish with the disciples. Nevertheless, the more progressive evangelicals insisted that Jesus' body after the resurrection could not be grossly material, because it would never die again. Therefore, it could not be a resuscitated corpse like the body of Lazarus. If that were the case, it would be subject to death.

The debate waxed and waned until it came to a head in the 1990s at Trinity Evangelical Divinity School and its parent denomination, the Evangelical Free Church of America. New Testament professor Murray J. Harris wrote *From Grave to Glory: Resurrection in the New Testament* (Grand Rapids: Zondervan, 1990), which defended the bodily resurrection both of Jesus and believers but argued that resurrection bodies are transformed bodies without normal physicality or materiality. He affirmed the empty tomb of Jesus and that in the general resurrection of the eschaton believers' graves will be empty, but he exploited Paul's term for the resurrection of the body *soma pneumatikon*—"spiritual body"—to underscore the discontinuity as well as continuity between bodies that die and bodies that are raised by the power of God. Harris's colleague Norman Geisler

charged him with holding an unorthodox view of the resurrection. The matter went all the way to the annual meeting of the Evangelical Free Church, which exonerated Harris; Geisler left Trinity and founded a new seminary. *Christianity Today* published an editorial calling the controversy "the mother of all muddles" (just after the first Gulf War, which Iraqi president Saddam Hussein labeled "the mother of all battles"). Many evangelicals lined up on one side or the other, while others sat out the debate because of the clear truth on both sides and what many considered the negative spirit in which it was started and conducted.

Most evangelical scholars agree with Harris that Jesus' resurrection body and our future resurrection bodies will be both continuous and discontinuous with the bodies that die, but they agree with Geisler that because of the overwhelming tendency of liberal theologians to reduce the resurrections to myth or apparitions and to reduce resurrection to immortality of souls, evangelicals need to stress the bodily nature of the resurrection. Harris would not disagree. The only real question is how grossly physical the resurrected bodies are.

Stephen T. Davis, *Risen Indeed: Making Sense of the Resurrection* (Grand Rapids: Wm. B. Eerdmans, 1993); Norman L. Geisler, *The Battle for the Resurrection* (Nashville: Thomas Nelson, 1992); George Eldon Ladd, *I Believe in the Resurrection of Jesus* (Grand Rapids: Wm. B. Eerdmans, 1975).

Return of Christ (Parousia) Evangelicals confidently hope for and expect the return of *Jesus Christ*. For them this future event is not mythology but realistic expectation based on Jesus' *resurrection* and promise to return, as well as on the eschatological and apocalyptic chapters and books of the New Testament that refer, however obliquely, to Christ's Parousia (return or reappearing). They believe that Jesus Christ is still the incarnate Son of *God*, messiah of all *humanity*, Savior and Lord and that only when he returns will his *kingdom* be fulfilled. Evangelical folk religion overflows with odd symbols of the second coming of Jesus Christ, including bumper stickers that read "In Case of Rapture This Car Will be Driverless" and books with titles like *88 Reasons Why Christ Will Return in 1988*. This popular fascination with the return of Christ and events surrounding it has seeped out of Evangelicalism and into popular culture, with entire series of novels based on an evangelical vision of the end times and films based on those novels.

Evangelical theologians tend to be more sober about the return of Christ and events related to it in biblical prophecy. They realize that apocalyptic imagery is notoriously obscure and that there are many seemingly contradictory references to the final events of history in the *Bible*. Sorting it all out and making sense of it all is not easy; only a few hardy souls among evangelical theologians have attempted to present systematic visions of *eschatology*. Nevertheless, all evangelical thinkers agree that Christ will return to the earth he left after his resurrection and that his kingdom will then be consummated either in a millennium on earth or in a new *heaven* and new earth for eternity.

Many evangelicals refer to the return of Christ as imminent, by which they mean it can happen at any time and will happen soon. Especially conservative evangelicals live in hopeful (and sometimes fearful) expectation of the return of Christ at any time. Many believe the first stage of the Parousia will be a "secret rapture" of true believers, followed by a seven-year era of great tribulation on earth, during which an antichrist will rise up and rule the world. The second stage of the Parousia will follow the seven-year tribulation and will be visible and public. Christ will descend from heaven to defeat the antichrist in open warfare at the battle of Armaggedon. This scheme has been popularized throughout Evangelicalism by books associated with *dispensationalism*—a scheme of biblical hermeneutics introduced and promoted by Plymouth Brethren and later by fundamentalists of various denominations. It has become virtually orthodox belief about the end times among conservative evangelicals; theologians working out of Dallas Theological Seminary in Texas have especially developed and promoted it in books such as *Things to Come* by Dwight Pentecost (Grand Rapids: Zondervan, 1965). Other evangelicals find this scheme too pretentious with regard to human ability to know exactly what biblical apocalyptic literature means; many have accused it of distorting the biblical testimony about the return of Christ by introducing completely foreign elements such as "secret rapture."

For the most part evangelical theologians have agreed to live according to a code of modesty and humility with regard to knowledge of the details of the return of Christ; very little caustic controversy has existed within postfundamentalist Evangelicalism about this doctrine. All agree that Christ will return, but there is very little expectation that evangelical theologians will insist on anything more than that for authentic evangelical *faith*. Fundamentalists, on the other hand, tend to require belief in a literal millennium after Christ's return (see the article on *premillennialism*), if not in a secret rapture preceding a seven-year tribulation.

In evangelical theology Christ's return signifies the triumph of righteousness over evil and God's vindication of his Son and his kingdom in the face of rejection and denial. It also signifies the beginning of the consummation of God's redemptive plan for the world; Christ will return to establish God's reign to the detriment of *sin, Satan*, and *evil* powers and principalities. The nations will be judged according to God's standards of righteousness and *justice*; people will be consigned to *heaven* or *hell* according to their *faith* in Christ and/or lives of obedience to God's will. The world will be renewed through a transformation of nature to abolish the rule that life is possible only through death. Eventually, because of his return, death itself will be put to death, and God will dwell with his people in everlasting peace and harmony. This utopian vision is the surrounding context of the evangelical hope for the return of Christ; only then will humanity be fulfilled, nature be released from the curse brought about by sin, and God's righteous love and faithfulness be revealed to all.

In the past, much evangelical preaching and teaching focused on this eschatological hope; a great deal of evangelical hymnody exulted in it. During the later years of the twentieth century, as Evangelicalism came of age and evangelicals entered into the mainstream of North American society, attention to the eschatological hope waned. Yet belief in the return of Christ remained a cornerstone of evangelical theology, even as expectation of its imminence diminished.

The main difference of opinion about the Parousia within evangelical theology has to do with the so-called "rapture of the *church*." Scripture nowhere uses the term "rapture," but it has come to designate the ascension—literally or figuratively—of all believers in Jesus Christ to meet him when he returns. The apostle Paul refers to this gathering to meet Christ on the "day of the Lord" in both 1 and 2 Thessalonians. Evangelicals fervently believe that they will meet Christ when he returns, but they do not all agree on when that will happen or how. Some evangelicals expect to be "raptured" before Christ's visible and public return; they base this on a series of passages in the New Testament that supposedly teach that true believers will be taken away before the end stage of history during which God's wrath will be poured out on the earth ("the great tribulation"). Other evangelicals think this expectation is unfounded; they believe the rapture (a term they seldom use) will

be part of the one event of Christ's return in glory to establish peace and justice. Instead of being literally caught up in the air to meet Christ as he comes, they look forward to a mysterious gathering of followers of Christ to be with him when he returns. This will include all who have died in fellowship with God through Christ as they are raised and united with the entire body of Christ (the church) in this rapturous reunion and celebration. When Christ returns, then, the suffering church militant will become the church triumphant.

For evangelicals, Christ's return symbolizes the universality of his lordship and the unity of the invisible church of his followers. Humanity, now divided into warring factions under different and competing lords, will be unified in declaring Jesus Christ Lord to the glory of God. Christianity's exclusive claim that "Jesus [alone] is Lord!" will be vindicated as true. The church, now fragmented into numerous sects, will be drawn together around her Savior and Lord so that its mystical unity will be made visible. Both of these meanings of the return of Christ have ethical implications for the present; if humanity is to be united in the future, all people are to be treated as equal now, for they all equally have one Lord. If the church is to be unified in the future, we should strive for unity now—spiritually if not institutionally. The return of Christ is the basis for present ecumenical cooperation and fellowship. Finally, the blessed hope of Christ's return energizes evangelical activism in evangelism and social transformation. Evangelicals want their Lord to return to a world already as suited for his habitation and rule as possible, and they want as many people as possible prepared for Christ's return in judgment and mercy.

G. C. Berkouwer, *The Return of Christ*, trans. James C. Van Oosterom (Grand Rapids: Wm. B. Eerdmans, 1972); Brian Hebblethwaite, *The Christian Hope* (Grand Rapids: Wm. B. Eerdmans, 1985); George

Eldon Ladd, *The Blessed Hope* (Grand Rapids: Wm. B. Eerdmans, 1980); John F. Walvoord, *The Blessed Hope and the Tribulation* (Grand Rapids: Zondervan, 1976).

Revelation   Evangelical theologians have always been fascinated by the issue of divine revelation. Here *revelation* refers not to the final book of the *Bible* but to *God's* communication to humans. In its broadest sense, revelation includes all the ways in which God discloses something to creatures; it excludes only what they can discover and know by themselves without any divine disclosure. Christians have always believed that God has revealed himself uniquely and unsurpassably in *Jesus Christ*; they have also generally believed that God reveals himself in special events of history, through prophets and apostles, in nature and through conscience, and in inspired Scripture. Some Christians would extend the category of revelation to include guidance through dreams, visions, deep spiritual impressions, and perhaps even the universal human *sensus divinus*—sense of the divine. Normally Christian theologians, including evangelicals, distinguish between two types of divine revelation—general and special (or universal and particular). General revelation is God's disclosure of himself or something about himself (e.g., his existence) through the natural world, including humans themselves (e.g., conscience). The Catholic tradition has emphasized this general revelation more than the Protestant tradition; according to most Catholic theologians, it makes possible a natural knowledge of God through reason and evidence alone. Protestants are traditionally more wary of the value of general revelation as they confess the fallenness of *creation*, including the cognitive effects of the fall on human reason. According to both Luther and Calvin, humans have a bare knowledge that God exists implanted within them, but general revelation yields no true natural knowledge of God

because of the *sin* that infects human understanding. They base this on Romans 1, which says that although God is revealed in his handiwork, people prefer to *worship* the creation rather than the creator and thus are guilty. Evangelicals generally follow the classical Protestant line with regard to general revelation and emphasize special revelation, which is God's particular, historical disclosure of himself and possibly information about himself through prophets, apostles, inspired Scripture, and so forth. This is different from general revelation because it is not universally available at all times; it is remedial revelation due to humans' inability to know God through nature alone. Evangelicals begin theology with the assumption God has provided a special revelation that is sufficient for salvation; whatever human beings need to know in order to have a right relationship with God and receive God's *grace* may be found in special revelation. Thus revelation becomes a very important category in evangelical theology; it is the ground and basis for all true knowledge of God.

Evangelical *theology* in the twentieth century has developed its doctrine of revelation in a context of conflict over the nature of divine disclosure. John Baillie's *The Idea of Revelation in Recent Thought* (New York: Columbia University Press, 1956) summed up the consensus of most modern liberal and neo-orthodox theologians with the axiom that there are no revealed truths but only truths of revelation. In other words, according to Baillie, for modern Christian thinkers divine revelation is not propositional; God reveals *himself* and not truth claims about himself. Revelation comes in and through great saving acts of God in history such as the exodus and, of course, Jesus Christ, who is God's supreme self-disclosure. For much of nonevangelical twentieth-century theology, then, it became axiomatic that revelation is personal (e.g., I-Thou encounter) and not propositional (i.e., communicated in objective truth claims).

Of course, there are as many different interpretations of revelation among modern theologians as there are modern theologians. For Karl Barth, revelation—God's Word—is always act; it has the nature of event. For Wolfhart Pannenberg, it takes the form of universal history. For Emil Brunner, it is the divine-human encounter that occurs when the message of the cross confronts individuals with the call to decision. All these modern views of revelation have in common an aversion to propositional revelation—revelation as communication of information. Scripture, then, is not revelation but an instrument of revelation or a human record and interpretation of revelation. (Karl Barth did include Scripture as one form of God's Word, but subordinated it to revelation itself, which is Jesus Christ.)

Evangelicals have wrestled with these modern views of divine revelation and found them weak if not useless for the critical and constructive tasks of theology; doctrine can hardly be examined or developed out of nonpropositional revelation. By and large evangelical theologians have sought to preserve the traditional view of Protestant orthodoxy that divine revelation comes through the very words of Scripture by means of the process called *inspiration* and that the Bible does not merely contain revelation or become revelation in an existential moment of encounter but is itself divine revelation. *Carl Henry*, "dean of evangelical theologians" in the post–World War II era, spent much of his career attempting to demonstrate the necessity of propositional revelation by exposing the incoherence of any other view. His six-volume *God, Revelation, and Authority* (Waco, TX: Word, 1976–84) is a sustained defense of propositional revelation against all competing interpretations of the nature of revelation. According to Henry and his followers among evangelicals, unless God has given a propositional disclosure of himself, we are bereft of true knowledge of God. Historical events and existential encounters are use-

less as revelation without interpretation in meaningful statements. Without the latter it is impossible to have Christian doctrine unless it is understood merely as humanly contrived interpretations of events and encounters, in which case doctrine lacks *authority*. The result of modern theology's attempt to reduce the meaning of divine disclosure to subjective interpretation is doctrinal pluralism in which Christianity becomes compatible with anything and everything.

Some evangelical theologians have gone further than Henry in arguing for propositional revelation, and some have hesitated to regard revelation as primarily propositional. The latter find some value in modern theology's emphasis on nonpropositional revelation, while preserving belief that some revelation communicates truth claims. British evangelical thinker Paul Helm represents those who go beyond Henry. According to Helm, the very concept "revelation" includes the idea of "proposition." There can be no nonpropositional personal disclosure. If a person is disclosed, that disclosure always involves truth statements about the person—especially if the person is invisible! Helm uses sophisticated analytical philosophy (analysis of language) to attempt to reduce the very idea of nonpropositional divine revelation to an absurdity. If God is Spirit and invisible, how, Helm asks, is it possible for him to reveal himself through acts and encounters with humans totally apart from saying something about himself to them? In the end, Helm argues, nonpropositional revelation of God is an oxymoron. Not very many evangelical theologians agree with Helm; they are more inclined to agree with Henry that revelation is primarily propositional while containing nonpropositional elements.

Bernard Ramm, however, attempted to soften the rationalistic implications of Henry's view of divine revelation. He believed that the emphasis on divine revelation as intelligible disclosure of information about God tended to turn

Christianity into philosophy and neglect the historical and existential elements of the divine-human relationship. According to Ramm, divine speaking (communication of information) is only one modality of special revelation; others include divine condescension, historical event, and incarnation. While Ramm agreed entirely with Henry that revelation must include a propositional element to interpret historical events and existential encounters, he did not elevate propositions to the status of essence of divine revelation. Ramm expressed the view of many moderate to progressive evangelicals in *Special Revelation and the Word of God* (Grand Rapids: Wm. B. Eerdmans, 1961):

> The disjunction presented so frequently in modern theology between revelation as either "information" or "encounter" is false. The historic version of revelation is frequently misrepresented as if it were merely a revelation of information. Such a view is not difficult to run through with a sword. But on the other hand to represent revelation as only encounter or as only event is also defective. A professed knowledge of God which is not rooted in historical event at the critical junctures is but powerless abstraction; and historical events without a powerful interpreting word of God are opaque occurrences. The structure of special revelation calls for a hard event and a hard word of interpretation. There cannot be a hard event with a soft interpretation. (158)

Both Henry and Ramm, together with most evangelical theologians, focused attention on past revelation; for them revelation is a category that primarily includes only God's acts in the history of Israel and the early church, inspired prophetic utterances and teachings of Jesus and the apostles, and inspired Scripture. While they and most evangelicals acknowledge that revelation was progressive, they are reluctant to widen the category of revelation to include postcanonical developments. Conservative evangelical theologians often greatly fear subjectivism and there-

fore close off revelation with the completion of the biblical canon, in order to avoid doctrinal confusion and chaos.

Progressive evangelical thinker *Clark Pinnock*, however, expands the category of revelation to include contemporary illuminating experiences of the *Holy Spirit*. Surely, he argues, God has not stopped revealing himself to people; it is of the nature of personal relationship that persons reveal themselves to one another. While insisting on the primacy of Scripture for doctrine and theological reflection, Pinnock allows for present events of revelation. The nature of revelation is "epic story of *redemption*"; God is the author, prime actor, and teller of the grand narrative of *salvation* unfolding through history. The story is not yet finished, even if Scripture as normative criterion for discerning its plot is complete. The same Holy Spirit who inspired the biblical authors is at work in the lives of Christians, in the *church*, and in history today. The Spirit is guiding Christ's followers into all truth, so revelation cannot be relegated to the past. Pinnock's view of revelation is somewhat influenced by the *charismatic movement* as well as by narrative theology; it is appealing to many evangelicals within the Pentecostal, charismatic, and *Third Wave movements* of Evangelicalism, who are just as concerned for vital fellowship with God as they are with objective doctrinal truth. Pinnock serves as a bridge between them and the more conservative evangelical thinkers, who emphasize the rationality of revelation and theology; to the charismatics he points to the primacy of inspired canon for discerning present revelation and to the conservative theologians he points to the present work of the Holy Spirit revealing not new truths but the contemporary reality of the epic drama of redemption.

Paul Helm, *The Divine Revelation* (Westchester, IL: Crossway, 1982); Leon Morris, *I Believe in Revelation* (Grand Rapids: Wm. B. Eerdmans, 1976); Clark Pinnock, *Track-*

ing the Maze (San Francisco: HarperSan-
Francisco, 1990).

Sacraments/Ordinances

There is no evangelical doctrine of sacraments or ordinances; evangelicals generally follow the doctrines of their own denominations regarding these rites of the *church*. As Protestants, evangelicals observe only two: *baptism* and the *Lord's Supper*. A few evangelicals observe washing of feet as an ordinance; they tend to be in the Anabaptist tradition (Mennonites and Brethren). A few evangelicals do not practice any ordinances, even baptism and the Lord's Supper; this neglect is restricted almost entirely to the Salvation Army and the Evangelical Friends (Quakers). The vast majority of evangelicals follow various Protestant beliefs and practices and have no distinctive shared evangelical interpretation of the rites. Evangelicals in the Episcopal churches embrace infant baptism and believe that when *faith* is present (e.g., in the hearts of the parents and congregation), it initiates the child into the body of Christ. On the other hand, many evangelical Methodists believe infant baptism is simply a dedication of the child to Christ. Baptists, Pentecostals, and many other evangelicals baptize only believers—persons old enough to confess faith consciously and publicly. Very few evangelicals regard baptism as salvific in any final or full sense; they highly value conscious *conversion* to *Jesus Christ* and at most view baptism as an initiation rite into the church. Presbyterians and Christian Reformed evangelicals believe infants and adults who are baptized enter into the *covenant* relationship between *God* and his people. Tremendous diversity exists about baptism, but most evangelicals eschew any idea that it saves apart from a conscious conversion *experience* including *repentance* and faith.

The same situation exists with regard to the Lord's Supper; evangelicals reject transubstantiation (the Catholic doctrine that the bread and wine become the body and blood of Jesus Christ), but they embrace a variety of Protestant interpretations and practices. Some consider it a true sacrament, in the sense that it conveys *grace* that strengthens faith. Others regard it as a memorial meal that focuses attention on the death of Jesus Christ for sins. Some observe the Lord's Supper (or Eucharist) weekly, while others observe it only monthly or quarterly. In general, the evangelical movement has not emphasized the sacraments or ordinances very strongly.

On the other hand, they have often experimented with them in ways that shock some evangelicals and many nonevangelicals. For example, many evangelical leaders will baptize new converts at conferences, revivals, camps, and other meetings outside the church. The same will often celebrate the Lord's Supper in ecumenical contexts. Evangelicals in denominations that restrict the rites to church settings are often dismayed by the seemingly frivolous or indiscriminate attitude revivalist evangelicals take toward them.

Generally speaking, evangelicals divide into two broad camps with regard to the sacraments/ordinances. High-church evangelicals (mostly Episcopalians but also some in the Reformed traditions) place great value and emphasis on them as channels of God's grace and connect them as closely as possible with conversion. They also tend to restrict them to the context of the congregation gathered in faith under the leadership of church officers (priests, elders, and/or deacons). High-church evangelicals emphasize the vertical dimension of the sacraments; the communicants' relationship with God is strengthened as they observe the ceremonies rightly to the glory of God, whose presence is mediated in a special way through these rites of the church. Low-church evangelicals (e.g., Baptists, Pentecostals, Holiness Protestants, and Anabaptists) tend to regard the ordinances not as sacraments but as symbolic acts of commitment. They restrict them to followers of Jesus Christ, but they often allow them to be observed virtually anywhere and anytime. Low-church evangelicals stress the horizontal dimension of the ordinances; the communicants' relationship with God is strengthened as God's presence is felt in a special way in the communal observance of these symbolic acts of memory, commitment, and hope.

Especially Reformed theologians (in the Calvinist tradition) have chided evangelicals at large for neglecting and/or trivializing the sacraments. Articles to this effect have appeared in a number of journals and magazines dedicated to exploring and promoting the classical Reformed understanding of the church. According to Reformed evangelicals, the sacraments form an intrinsic part of the *worship* of the church and the church's identity as the body of Christ is inextricably bound up with their correct observance. They should be viewed as gifts of God to the church and not as human ceremonies to stimulate religious feelings; they are observed not merely out of obedience to Christ, who instituted them, or in order to deepen spiritual experiences. God is the giver and receiver of the sacraments, which mediate union between believers and Christ within the covenant relationship between the elect and the sovereign God. Reformed evangelical theologians worry that many evangelicals—including some within Reformed churches who have been seduced by popular evangelical folk religion—reduce the sacraments to religious symbols contrived and celebrated by humans for their own pious feelings. This is especially true, they argue, when anyone can lead in their observance anywhere and at any time, as is the case in many evangelical parachurch gatherings.

At the other end of the spectrum stand many Pentecostals, who believe that the ordinances should be open to all who confess faith in Jesus Christ and may be observed indiscriminately. Pentecostal leader Jack Hayford has led the way in opening the Lord's Supper to all persons present at any Christian event where it is being observed—regardless of their beliefs and commitments. The theory behind this evangelical view is that the Lord's Supper and baptism are celebrations of the *salvation* of Jesus Christ open to all; baptism should be observed as publicly as possible as a witness to the world about the grace of Jesus, and the Lord's Supper should be celebrated by everyone within any worship context as a witness to the cross event as the basis of salvation. These are two radically different evangelical perspectives on the sacraments—one churchly and oriented to worship, and the other public and oriented to evangelism.

Salvation   The *experience* and doctrine of salvation lie at the heart of evangelical *faith*; evangelical theologians expend much energy exploring the nature of salvation. *Salvation* literally means "wholeness" or "being made whole." It is closely related to healing in the fullest sense—spiritual, emotional, and physical wholeness. In Christian theology, salvation designates especially a right relationship with God that results in everlasting life in *heaven*. It includes, however, a host of moments or aspects that give rise to speculation and controversy among evangelical theologians. Terms such as *election*, prevenient *grace*, calling, *conversion, regeneration, justification,* and *sanctification* are used to identify these elements of what theologians call the *ordo salutis* or "order of salvation." They are all biblical concepts, but *Scripture* offers no system of placing them in relationship to each other or to the whole process of salvation. That task is left to theologians, and evangelical theologians have specialized in it. It is commonplace to hear evangelical theologians say that Christians have been saved, are being saved, and will be saved. That is, if a person is saved, there are three time dimensions to it: past, present, and future. Almost all evangelicals would agree that the past dimension (for an already-saved person) includes election and calling as well as conversion, including justification and regeneration. Sanctification is the present dimension, and the future dimension is glorification. (See the articles on some of these aspects of salvation in this handbook.)

Evangelical theologians agree wholeheartedly with classical Protestantism that initial salvation is a onetime event that includes a complete *reconciliation* between *God* and the person who repents and believes on *Jesus Christ*. That reconciliation event of peace with God happens at the moment of justification and is synonymous with it. God forgives the person and imputes righteousness to him or her. Pardon for the guilt of original sin and actual sins is granted completely and cannot be increased by acts of love, which flow naturally from a converted life. Regeneration is the other side of the coin of conversion; at the moment the person who repents and believes is reconciled with God—justified—he or she is made a "new *creation* in Christ Jesus." That is, in the words of Baptist theologian *Augustus Hopkins Strong*, the person receives inwardly the "expulsive power of a new affection." The *Holy Spirit* enters his or her life and creates a new impulse away from *sin* toward *holiness* of life in Christlikeness. The person is empowered by the Holy Spirit to rise above love for sin and to enjoy life to the glory of God. This is initial salvation—reconciliation in justification and the new birth of regeneration—which results in the process of sanctification, or increasing righteousness of life.

Virtually all evangelicals agree that conversion—repentance and faith associated closely with justification and regeneration—is the crucial aspect of salvation and that every person needs it for peace with God and eternal life with him in heaven. This is the basis of evangelical efforts at world *evangelism*. It is not so that there will be fewer "heathens" and more "Western Christians," but so that all people will have opportunity to know the joy and peace of reconciliation with God and the inward cleansing from sin that comes with the indwelling of the Holy Spirit. Evangelicals also agree that a truly converted life will experience sanctification, which is the outgrowth of regeneration; the Holy Spirit within continues to renew the regenerate person in the *image of God* (corrupted by the fall of humanity into sin and by actual sins) and in Christlike character. The end result of the process of sanctification is glorification, which comes in the *resurrection* and in heaven. Evangelical theologians agree that all of this is a gift of God and not a reward for merit; that is, evangelicals stand in the classical Protestant tradition that rejects any idea of salvation involving works of righteousness that merit God's gracious favor and the gift of the Holy Spirit.

This salvation is entirely "by grace through faith" and not "of works" (Eph. 2:8–10). There is no room for saved persons to boast, even if others are not saved, because salvation is from beginning to end a sheer gift of the grace and mercy of God. All evangelical theologians agree with this even if at times evangelical folk religion forgets it and falls into the heresy of semi-Pelagianism, which implies that salvation is a cooperative effort initiated and partly earned by human goodwill toward God. All evangelical theologians reject semi-Pelagianism, the bane of their existence as theologians within the evangelical context. Much evangelical preaching and piety implies that human beings must initiate the process of salvation by exercising a goodwill toward God. A popular evangelical illustration—rejected by evangelical theologians—is that God casts a vote for the sinner and *Satan* casts a vote against him or her and salvation depends on how the sinner votes. Evangelical theologians reject such semi-Pelagian analogies for salvation and insist that even the *initium fidei*—beginning of faith—is made possible by God, whose prevenient grace calls, convicts, enlightens, and enables sinners who hear the *gospel* message to repent and believe.

Controversy arises among evangelical theologians over several issues related to the order of salvation. Can genuine salvation ever be lost? Does God unconditionally elect and irresistibly bend the wills of converted persons, or do sinners confronted with the gospel message have the freedom to resist the grace of God? Does regeneration precede conversion (in terms of cause and effect), or does conversion include or result in regeneration? These are all issues related to the larger Calvinist-Arminian debate that has raged off and on within Evangelicalism for centuries. From its very beginnings in the Great Awakening of the 1730s and 1740s in Great Britain and the American colonies, the evangelical movement has been divided between those who follow John Calvin's theology (often as it was later developed by Puritans) and those who follow the theology of Jacob Arminius (often as it was later developed by John Wesley).

Calvinist evangelicals generally (with some variations) hold to the so-called "five points of *Calvinism*" remembered by the acrostic TULIP, which stands for total depravity, unconditional election, limited *atonement*, irresistible grace, and [unconditional] *perseverance.* According to them, persons are saved by God alone, apart from any cooperation on their part. They may feel that they have cooperated with the grace of God, but in fact even their decision to repent and believe was not only enabled but caused by God's effectual grace. They were chosen by God for salvation (unconditional election) and effectually, irresistibly drawn to conversion. They were regenerated (born again) by the Holy Spirit before they repented and believed. All this is necessary because due to original sin, all people are totally depraved—"dead in trespasses and sins"—and must be given new birth spiritually before they can even begin to exercise a goodwill toward

God. Thus, for Calvinist evangelicals, regeneration of the elect precedes conversion (repentance and faith) and even justification, even if all happens in a moment. The deep background to salvation is the mysterious electing will of God, which chooses some persons to be saved and passes over others who are left to their deserved damnation. During the Great Awakening, Jonathan Edwards of New England and George Whitefield, among others, preached and wrote on the basis of a Calvinist understanding of salvation. Today some evangelical Calvinists reject limited atonement—the idea that Christ died only for the elect—while others accept it as a necessary part of the system of Calvinist doctrine.

During the Great Awakening, John and Charles Wesley—founders of the Methodist tradition—embraced the Arminian understanding of salvation. Arminius had taught that persons are enabled by grace to freely receive salvation, but they are free to resist grace and reject the offer of salvation. Persons are fallen into sin and need salvation as a gift from God, but they are not totally depraved in the classical Calvinist sense. Wesley preferred to say that they are deprived of what is necessary for righteousness and thus stand in need of grace. Arminius and Wesley believed that *election* is conditional and that predestination is synonymous with foreseen faith. They rejected limited atonement and insisted that Christ died for all people. They affirmed that persons are always free to resist the grace of God and that perseverance in God's grace is not guaranteed to anyone; it depends on remaining in Christ by faith. Arminian evangelicals believe in the "will freed by grace" rather than in "*free will*" as that is popularly understood. Because people are sinners, they are not naturally free to find and accept God's salvation, but they are free to reject it when it is offered. Their wills are in bondage to sin until they are freed by grace which normally happens through encountering the gospel of Jesus Christ.

God takes the initiative by extending prevenient grace—grace that goes before salvation and enables sinners to accept it freely. If they do accept salvation by repentance and faith (conversion), they are reconciled with God (justification) and born again spiritually (regeneration). The only thing they contribute to their own salvation is lack of resistance to and free acceptance of God's grace; all else is sheer gift.

Calvinist evangelicals are not satisfied with this Arminian account of salvation; they regard it as tantamount to meriting salvation, because the person has to make a free decision to accept or reject it. Arminians respond that mere acceptance of a gift is not the same as earning it. Clearly these are very different perspectives, and evangelicals view salvation according to one perspective or the other, but all agree that salvation is a gift of God's grace, received by faith and not earned, and that it is a *supernatural* work of God for and in those who believe in Jesus Christ, not a human achievement (e.g., "turning over a new leaf") or something already possessed by everyone.

Anthony Hoekema, *Saved by Grace* (Grand Rapids: Wm. B. Eerdmans, 1989); H. D. McDonald, *Salvation* (Westchester, IL: Crossway, 1982); Clark Pinnock, *The Grace of God and the Will of Man* (Minneapolis: Bethany House, 1995); Gordon T. Smith, *Beginning Well: Christian Conversion and Authentic Transformation* (Downers Grove, IL: InterVarsity Press, 2001).

Sanctification   Sanctification refers to the present dimension of *salvation,* in which persons already converted to *Jesus Christ* are growing in Christian maturity and increasing in personal *holiness.* The term itself is related to holiness; both signify being set apart for sacred use and service. Sanctification, then, is the gradual *experience* of being set apart by the *Holy Spirit* for service to *God,* and that involves inward transfor-

mation into Christlike character. Like all other Protestants, evangelicals believe that initial salvation is a complete *reconciliation* with God, as well as an inward change away from an orientation to love of self and *sin* toward a new life orientation to love of God and righteousness. This is called *regeneration* or being born again. It does not bring perfection; it is simply the beginning of a process that eventually yields perfection of character. Perfection is interpreted as complete likeness to Jesus Christ, perfect reflection of his character of love. Most evangelicals believe perfection—the goal of sanctification—is achieved (or received) only in the eschaton, when believers are raised to new life fit for *heaven.* Some evangelicals, however, believe it can be accomplished before death. This is the main point of controversy about sanctification within evangelical theology. However, significant consensus exists among evangelicals about sanctification.

On the popular level of grassroots Evangelicalism, the essence of sanctification is developing a "personal relationship with Jesus Christ" through daily devotions involving *Scripture* reading and prayer. Books with titles like *Experiencing God* line the shelves of evangelical Christian bookstores; most evangelical churches and parachurch organizations hold classes on strengthening one's personal relationship with Christ. The roots of this go back to the Pietist movement of the late seventeenth and early eighteenth centuries in Europe; later the Puritans and revivalists from the Great Awakening onward spoke and wrote much about this idea of a personal relationship with Christ. Evangelical theologians tend to refer to the same idea of sanctification as intimacy with God or conversional piety— the life that grows out of *conversion* to Christ and is marked by ever deepening *repentance* and *faith.* Some evangelical theologians emphasize the role of the *law* of God in sanctification, while others stress the indwelling Holy Spirit; in either case the ideal is voluntary obedience to God's will and way from the heart filled with love for God and the "things of God."

Evangelicals disagree among themselves about whether it is possible to arrive at perfect obedience to God's law of love ("Love the Lord your God . . . and your neighbor as yourself") before death. Can sanctification be complete in this life? Reformed evangelicals (and those influenced by Reformed theology) believe sanctification is a process of growth that is completed only after death in the glorification that comes at the *resurrection*. That is, only in heaven will anyone be perfectly Christlike (except Christ himself, who is always already perfect in character, reflecting the glory and love of God). Reformed evangelicals believe that human depravity due to inherited sin as well as "the world, the flesh, and the *devil*" retain their hold over even converted Christians so long as they live in the fallen world under the curse brought about by the primeval fall of *humanity* into sin. While that hold may be loosened by the believer's regeneration and while progress may be made toward true obedience to God, complete perfection is impossible under the condition of mortality. The normal Christian existence is marked by being *simul justus et peccator*—being sinner and righteous at the same time. It is a paradoxical condition of being positionally perfect in God's sight by *grace* through faith, while being conditionally sinful due to the remnant of sin still remaining "in the flesh" (i.e., in the fallen human nature not yet transformed in the resurrection). For Reformed evangelicals, sanctification involves continual realization of one's sinfulness and renewal of repentance and total reliance on the grace and mercy of God. Sanctification, then, is as much an outgrowth of *justification* as of regeneration. Repentance remains a necessary aspect of sanctification, even for the most mature Christian. The context for sanctification is the *church*—the company of the elect—where new life in

Christ is being imparted through word and *sacrament*, as well as through fellowship, *prayer*, and study. Sanctification is measured in terms of the "signs of grace" manifested in the life of the believer, including love that is demonstrated in service.

Evangelicals in the Wesleyan tradition (including Holiness and many Pentecostal believers) believe that the process of sanctification can be completed in earthly life prior to death and resurrection. John Wesley taught this in *A Plain Account of Christian Perfection* (written in stages through various revisions in the mid-eighteenth century), as well as in sermons, letters, and notes on the biblical texts. The early Methodists proclaimed Christian perfection as being "perfected in love" and expected it as a normal part of Christian existence. Wesley made clear that he did not mean "sinless perfection" is possible if that would exclude all sins of omission or errors of judgment. For him and for his followers—who are numerous among evangelicals—*entire sanctification* is simply purity of motive with love as the always determining intention in every action and relationship. This is a gift of the Holy Spirit and not a human achievement; many Wesleyans equate it with *baptism of the Holy Spirit* as a second blessing after conversion. Wesley believed that entire sanctification—Christian perfection—could happen "in a moment."

During the nineteenth century the various groups associated with the *Holiness movement* of radical Wesleyans emphasized this experiential dimension of sanctification and encouraged people already converted to Christ to seek it at revival meetings. It was often accompanied by emotional manifestations of weeping and sometimes falling. Many Holiness evangelicals became Pentecostals when that movement swept across North America in the first decade of the twentieth century. Not all Pentecostals believe in entire sanctification or Christian perfection; many (such as the Assemblies of God) follow the Reformed view of sanctification as a process completed only after death. Especially in the Southern parts of the United States, however, many Pentecostals embrace the momentary experience of total cleansing from sin; they speak of "three blessings"—conversion, sanctification, and baptism of the Holy Spirit with speaking in tongues. Wesleyan evangelicals insist that the perfection they experience in entire sanctification (whether momentary or not) has nothing to do with infallibility, and it does not preclude the need for continuing repentance. Wesley made clear in his writings that even the perfected Christian is only "perfect in love" and still needs to repent of errors of judgment that arise out of living under the curse in a fallen world.

G. C. Berkouwer, *Faith and Sanctification*, trans. John Vriend (Grand Rapids: Wm. B. Eerdmans, 1952); Wilbur T. Dayton, "Entire Sanctification," in *A Contemporary Wesleyan Theology: Biblical, Systematic, and Practical*, vol. 1, ed. Charles W. Carter (Grand Rapids: Zondervan, 1983), 521–69; Peter Toon, *Justification and Sanctification* (Westchester, IL: Crossway, 1983).

Satan/Devil/Demons   Some evangelicals—especially Pentecostals and charismatics—focus much attention on *evil* spiritual powers; they believe that Satan, also known as the devil, is an ontologically real (as opposed to symbolically real) personal presence and power in the world opposing *God*. They also believe in demons as Satan's invisible spiritual agents in the world. Such belief is not limited to evangelicals, however; C. S. Lewis's most popular book, *The Screwtape Letters*, was an imaginative account of demons and their interference in human lives. Nevertheless, in the modern religious context, almost only Roman Catholics and evangelical Protestants believe in the distinct and literal reality of these personal forces of evil in the world. Some evangelicals practice "spiritual warfare," which involves

using special types of *prayer* to defeat the plans of Satan and his minions. Other evangelicals prefer to leave such battle to God and focus their attention on God alone. Evangelicals are united in their belief that Satan and demons are real; they are not merely personifications of human evil. They are not merely symbols of the social forces that oppress people (à la Walter Wink's account of "the powers").

Evangelical theologians tend to be more cautious in their descriptions of Satan and demons than are many writers of popular evangelical literature who portray them using imagery drawn from medieval narratives such as Dante's *Divine Comedy* and Milton's *Paradise Lost*. Evangelical theologians note that in Scripture Satan is described as an angel of light and not as a lizard-skinned, dragonlike humanoid with a sharp tail, horns, and a pitchfork. Demons are nowhere described in Scripture; their role in biblical narratives seems only to be carrying out Satan's strategies. Evangelical theologians believe in Satan's power and in demonic possession, but they avoid giving such subjects major attention in their theologies. The *Bible* is relatively silent about their origin or nature; that they are fallen angels is a matter of reverent speculation and is widely believed by evangelicals.

In evangelical *theology*, as in Scripture, Satan's primary role is as the tempter and accuser of humans. Nowhere is all *sin* or evil attributed to him; he has limited powers and is not able to cause people to sin. Especially Reformed evangelical theologians view Satan and demons as God's instruments. As Luther put it, Satan is God's devil. In other words, Satan is not a god over against God limiting him. God does not have to deal with Satan as if he were an equal, opposite force. Rather, the sovereign maker of heaven and earth controls Satan and allows him to wreak just as much havoc in human history as is necessary for God's ultimate purpose, which is to glorify himself by defeating sin and evil and redeeming the fallen world. There is a sense, then, in which Satan and demons do God's bidding.

Reformed evangelical theologians caution, however, that God is not stained by the guilt of what Satan does and is not responsible for the evil that comes about because of Satan's and demons' work. God's intentions are pure and holy; Satan's are corrupt. God used Satan to bring about the cross of Christ, but it was Satan who inspired it and bears responsibility for crucifying the Son of God. Satan plays a role in God's *providence*, even if he is not aware of it. Critics of the Reformed view argue that it undermines the biblical injunctions to resist the devil; why resist God's instrument? Also, it stains God with the evil done by Satan, since Satan does only what God foreordains and controls. Reformed theologians may use the language of permission when writing about God's control of Satan, but in the end what they really mean is that Satan also does God's will.

Non-Reformed evangelical theologians prefer to view Satan as a mad dog on a long leash rather than as God's instrument; for them there is no sense in which Satan is "God's devil," except that he is a creature of God who went bad. Nevertheless, God limits the evil that Satan is able to do; demons can cause only as much chaos and havoc as God allows. Yet Satan and demons are real opponents of God's plan and purposes. They seek in every way possible to frustrate God's project of redeeming the fallen world. Moral evil comes about as a result of humans' willing or unwitting cooperation with the demonic strategies and activities. Especially Pentecostal, *charismatic*, and *Third Wave* evangelicals emphasize the role of the demonic in the evils that make life in the world so dangerous and difficult.

In *Satan and the Problem of Evil: Constructing a Trinitarian Warfare Theodicy* (Downers Grove, IL: InterVarsity Press) evangelical theologian Gregory A. Boyd goes beyond most evangelical theologians in portraying Satan and demons as a powerful force for evil directly involved in tragedy, calamity, horrors, and egregious acts of sin. Without absolving of responsibility humans such as Hitler, Boyd comes close to endorsing the folk religious saying "The devil made me do it." He attributes great autonomy and power to Satan and argues that events such as the Holocaust cannot be understood apart from demonic instigation and power. Boyd reads the biblical narratives in this manner; to him (and to many Pentecostal, charismatic and Third Wave evangelicals) they are more consistent with third-world cultures' worldviews than with modern, Western perspectives on nature and history, which tend to be corrupted by post-Enlightenment naturalism. According to him, the Bible portrays Satan as the "god of this world" and Christians as soldiers in a war against Satan and his demonic forces. The war, of course, is not conducted with any worldly weapons but with spiritual weapons of prayer and *worship* and service. Exorcism is a necessary but all too often neglected weapon of spiritual warfare. Critics accuse Boyd of coming too close to dualism, but he argues that Satan is not equal with God. Satan is a creature whose origins are unknown to us, and he is not omnipotent. God is self-limiting for the sake of creaturely freedom. Therefore, in the era before the eschatological victory of God over Satan, it appears that the world is ruled by two deities—God and Satan—when in fact God, the superior ruler, has given Satan a limited realm of freedom and control. Boyd interprets the biblical book of Job as justification for this view; there God allowed Satan to wreak havoc in the realm of Job's family. That is a microcosm of the world, which is a macrocosm of Job's family. Until the end, when Satan is finally and completely defeated, Boyd argues, the partial defeat of his plans and strategies depends to a very great extent on the prayers of God's people. This is what is called "spiritual warfare" and can take the form of identifying Satan's hand at work in specific evil trends through spiritual discernment and targeting them with special efforts of collective, concerted prayer.

In spite of serious disagreement about God's role in Satan's activities and Satan's power temporarily to thwart the will of God, evangelical theologians are agreed that Satan is also God's creature and therefore finite. He is not omniscient, omnipotent, or omnipresent. His mode of being is spiritual rather than physical, and therefore he is able to move quickly across the face of the earth; he uses agents called demons to carry out his evil schemes. He is not able to force anyone to sin or commit evil acts, but he can and does tempt people and inspire evil in society. His successes depend to a very great extent on human cooperation (which is usually unwitting, even if intentional) and completely on divine permission. Most evangelical theologians caution against paying too much attention to Satan and demons. Worship, including prayer, belongs to God alone, and God will take care of Satan. The best defense against the wiles of the devil is being filled with the *Holy Spirit* collectively as well as individually. Evangelicals stand against two extremes in this area of doctrine: the semioccult tendency of some Christians to become obsessed with the devil and demons manifested, for example, in the phenomenon of "speaking against the devil," and the liberal tendency of some Christians to deny the real ontological existence of Satan and demons and attribute evil to a "superpersonal kingdom of evil" that consists of powerful social forces of injustice and oppression.

Michael Green, *Exposing the Prince of Darkness* (Ann Arbor, MI: Servant Publications, 1981; originally published with the better title *I Believe in Satan's Downfall* and still published under that title in Great Britain by Hodder & Stoughton); Erwin W. Lutzer, *The Serpent of Paradise: The Incredible Story of How Satan's Rebellion Serves God's Purposes* (Chicago: Moody

Press, 1996); Sydney H. T. Page, *Powers of Evil: A Biblical Study of Satan and Demons* (Grand Rapids: Baker Books, 1995).

Scripture *see* **Bible**

Sin/Original Sin Many nonevangelicals associate the evangelical movement with hellfire and brimstone preaching, epitomized in Jonathan Edwards's famous sermon "Sinners in the Hands of an Angry God." There is some truth to that stereotype of Evangelicalism; evangelicals have always believed in the irreducible and universal reality of sin in human existence. Of course, not all evangelical preaching is focused on sin or the wrath of *God*; evangelical sermons run the gamut of topics, and in the later part of the twentieth century many conservative evangelical scholars complained that therapeutic preaching ("How to live life more successfully and be happier in ten easy steps") was replacing sermons about sin, *repentance*, and *salvation* in evangelical *churches*.

Evangelical *theology*—in contrast to some popular evangelical folk religion—very firmly holds to the classical Christian doctrine of original sin, carved out by Augustine in his debates with Pelagius in the early fifth century. They do not all agree with every aspect of Augustine's or Luther's or Calvin's doctrine of original sin, but they all affirm that sin is a more fundamental human condition than ignorance or negative social conditioning or corruption of the gene pool or even individual acts of willful disobedience to God's revealed will. Evangelical theologians believe that all human *evil* derives from a basic evil condition called "sin" or "original sin" into which all humans (except *Jesus Christ*) are born and that plagues them throughout life. Humans since the fall of *humanity* into sin are damaged goods; sin is second nature to them (their first nature being the *image of God*). Evangelical theologians believe that this universality of sin that creates alienation between humans and God and between humans and other humans stems from an original fault of disobedience at the beginning of the human race; because the first ones sinned by a voluntary act of disobedience, all their descendants (except Jesus Christ) inherit that fault as corruption that leads inevitably to guilt. (Some evangelical theologians believe that guilt is inherited, but many do not.) This doctrine of original sin and inherited depravity forms the foundation for evangelical preaching and teaching about salvation; everyone is a sinner—even if their lives seem outwardly moral and even saintly—and stands in need of God's mercy and *grace*, which is received through repentance and *faith*.

Reformed evangelicals follow Augustine, Calvin, and the Puritans closely in insisting that the first person's fall into sin brought corruption and condemnation on the whole human race. They agree with the old Puritan adage that "In Adam's fall we sinnéd all." For them, every baby born (except Jesus) is both totally depraved and condemned by the *justice* of God. This leads inevitably to open rebellion against God in maturity, but even children are full-fledged sinners who are destined for *hell* apart from God's mercy, which they may have (if they are among the elect) through their inclusion in the people of God by baptism and the faith of their parents. This is based on the Augustinian and Calvinist reading of Romans 5, which seems to imply that all humans were included in Adam as the federal head or representative of the human race. His breach of *covenant* with God brought condemnation on all of his descendants. They are born "dead in trespasses and sins" until they are awakened by the regenerating grace of God and forgiven by the mercy of God through Jesus Christ. Sin's spiritually deadening effect is so profound that people are unable even to cooperate with the grace of God; the elect are chosen by God and saved apart from any free decision they make. The decision to repent and believe follows the regenerating act of God, which overcomes the spiritual death of original sin and imparts new spiritual life. Most Reformed evangelicals regard pride (self-idolatry or "refusal of creatureliness") as the essence of original sin; it is an attitude and disposition rather than an overt act of disobedience. This strong Augustinian account of sin is passed into evangelical theology through Jonathan Edwards; many Reformed evangelicals consider him the faithful conduit and creative interpreter of the biblical doctrine of sin.

Many evangelical theologians consider the Augustinian and Edwardsian doctrine of sin too harsh; they prefer the kinder, gentler perspective of John Wesley, who was more influenced by the Eastern church fathers than by Augustine. For Wesley and his evangelical heirs, sin is an original fault and fundamental condition; it cannot be reduced to individual, conscious acts of willful transgression of the *law* of God that might all be avoided by sheer determination. Such reduction is the essence of semi-Pelagianism, which is regarded as heresy even by non-Reformed evangelicals. According to Wesleyan evangelical theologians, however, original sin does not include condemnation, and inherited corruption leads not to total depravity but to deprivation of spiritual strength and ability. Children are not born guilty of Adam's sin. Evangelicals in the Wesleyan tradition (or influenced by Arminian theology in general) disagree with the Augustinian and Reformed interpretation of Romans 5; they point out that the Greek text, which Augustine did not use (he used a flawed Latin translation), nowhere implies that all sinned in Adam or that condemnation spread to all because Adam sinned. Rather, the text says that sin and death spread to all because all sin. Thus, these evangelicals believe that the guilt of sin that alienates people from God derives only from intentional sinning. Any guilt associated with original sin, they argue, was set aside and covered by the atoning death of Jesus Christ. Inherited depravity implies total evil, and Arminian-Wesleyan evangelicals do not believe the *image of God* can be obliterated.

Thus, some spiritual ability remains in spite of the fall of humanity into sin. It is distorted by sin, so that apart from special grace no person is capable of avoiding culpable sinning. Transgression that brings condemnation is inevitable and normally occurs immediately at the "age of accountability," so that persons of awakened conscience who know they stand guilty before God and are alienated from him by their willful transgressions need to repent and embrace the mercy of God in Jesus Christ by faith in order to be saved. Infants are innocent and go from death into paradise; sin is not imputed to them for Jesus' sake. Arminian-Wesleyan evangelical theologians tend to interpret the essence of original sin less as pride than as selfishness or self-centeredness. By this they mean focusing on one's own self-interest to the neglect of community and the common good. In the end, this is not far from the Reformed idea of sin as pride. Both involve idolatry of self.

In spite of different interpretations of original sin, evangelicals agree that sin is a fundamental human condition derived from a primeval fall of humanity. (The extent to which Adam and Eve are to be taken literally as the spiritual progenitors of the race is a matter of some disagreement among evangelical scholars; conservative evangelicals tend to insist on it, while moderate and progressive evangelicals believe it is possible to consider them symbolic figures. All evangelicals believe in a historical fall and reject reductions of the fall to mythology.) Although humans are "essentially good" (because created in God's image), they are since the fall existentially estranged from God and from each other because of the sinful disposition they inherit from their progenitor Adam. God's antidote to this flawed human condition is the proclamation of the *gospel* of Jesus Christ. Whenever and wherever the word of God is rightly preached and taught, God's gracious provision for overcoming the deadening effects of sin is implemented; people are set free from bondage of the will to sin and enabled to repent, believe, and begin to live lives pleasing to God, even if not free from all sin.

Evangelicals freely admit that their doctrine of sin—rooted in biblical revelation and the classical Christian tradition—is an offense to reason. Sin is the "mystery of iniquity" that cannot be solved by social engineering or individual turning over of new leaves. And yet evangelicals love to say that even though it is a mystery, it is the only empirically provable doctrine of Christianity (G. K. Chesterton). Only this account of the human condition fits the facts of human existence; evil cannot be eradicated by human intentionality and invention. It is irreducibly rooted in the fallenness of humanity, and its only solution is the *supernatural* grace and mercy of God. Furthermore, only this account of sin makes possible a full understanding of *redemption*. Evangelical theologian *Bernard Ramm* quoted O. Hobart Mowrer to this effect: "Just so long as we deny the reality of sin, we cut ourselves off, it seems, from the possibility of radical redemption (recovery)" (*Offense to Reason: The Theology of Sin* [San Francisco: Harper & Row, 1985], 150).

Henry Blocher, *Original Sin: Illuminating a Riddle* (Grand Rapids: Wm. B. Eerdmans, 1997); Cornelius Plantinga Jr., *Not the Way It's Supposed to Be: A Breviary of Sin* (Grand Rapids: Wm. B. Eerdmans, 1995); David L. Smith, *With Willful Intent: A Theology of Sin* (Wheaton, IL: Victor Books, 1994).

Spirit Baptism/Baptism of the Holy Spirit

Spirit baptism or baptism of the Holy Spirit is a technical term in evangelical *theology*; it refers to a specific act of *God* in the life of a follower of *Jesus Christ*. Although some Christians associate it with water *baptism*, it is not synonymous with it. Spirit baptism is that event in which the *Holy Spirit* of God—the third member of the *Trinity*—fills a repentant, believing person's existence, with the result that he or she is "filled with the Holy Spirit." The term comes from the New Testament *Gospel* narrative in which John the Baptist tells his listeners that Jesus will baptize them with the Holy Spirit. This is the only mention of a Spirit baptism in the Bible, but many Christians—including many evangelicals—use the term for the more frequently mentioned phenomenon of believers in Jesus Christ being filled with the Holy Spirit for *holiness* of life and power for service to God and his *kingdom*. The book of Acts frequently says that the disciples and apostles were "filled with the Spirit" as they manifested miraculous signs and wonders and performed *miracles* and preached the gospel boldly. All evangelicals believe in being filled with the Holy Spirit; many use the term baptism of the Holy Spirit for the initial filling. Disagreement arises among evangelicals over when that initial filling or baptism of the Spirit occurs and to whom it occurs. Disagreement also exists over the signs or evidences of Spirit baptism.

The early evangelical movement of the eighteenth and nineteenth centuries was inextricably connected with *revivalism*. Many of the great revivalists and theologians associated with revivalism believed that *conversion* to Christ was insufficient for fulfilled discipleship of Jesus Christ. Many evangelicals in the Wesleyan tradition, including all in the Holiness churches, believe that *sanctification*—holiness of life leading to Christian perfection—takes a quantum leap in a radical "second blessing" after the first blessing of conversion-*regeneration*. The born-again *experience* ushers one into *reconciliation* with God and a new affection for the "things of God." However, another experience equated with Spirit baptism ushers one into a higher dimension of Christian living freed from the domination of the "flesh" (fallen human nature). John Wesley's favored theologian John Fletcher seems to have been the first evangelical to distinguish between conversion and Spirit baptism, equating the latter with a special sanctification experience. The great nineteenth-century evangelical revivalist *Charles Finney* taught a similar second blessing experience of Spirit enduement with power for holiness and service. In the late nineteenth century and early twentieth century, numerous evangelical leaders promoted Spirit baptism subsequent to conversion as a catalyst into fulfilled Christianity. R. A. Torrey (first president of BIOLA—Bible Institute of Los Angeles) and A. B. Simpson (founder of the Christian and Missionary Alliance movement) were among the influential evangelical speakers and writers who promoted subsequence of Spirit baptism. The standard Protestant view—common among evangelicals past and present—is that Spirit baptism is simply another label for regeneration, the "expulsive power of a new affection" (*A. H. Strong*) that occurs at conversion (also known as "being born again").

The difference is between those who believe that all authentically converted Christians are Spirit-baptized or Spirit-filled and those who believe in a two-tier Christianity: those who are merely converted and those who are both converted and Spirit-baptized. In 1901 the Pentecostal movement was born out of the *Holiness movement* and in 1906 it burst into prominence in the evangelical scene in North America with the Azusa Street Revival, which lasted months in Los Angeles. *Pentecostalism* teaches as official doctrine that Spirit baptism is a second baptism subsequent to conversion, and it adds that speaking in tongues always accompanies it as the "initial, physical evidence." Pentecostals base this on the Pentecostal narrative in Acts 2 and on the several instances in the book of Acts in which speaking in tongues (unknown languages) occurred when people were filled with the Spirit. Critics argue that the Pentecostal doctrine cannot be proven from Scripture, which nowhere says that speaking in tongues always accompanies Spirit baptism and that the need for an initial, physical evidence for a spiritual experience is based on modern need for certainty.

Four views of Spirit baptism exist among evangelicals. The first one is found primarily in sacramental circles such as among evangelical Anglicans and Episcopalians. There Spirit baptism is equated with water baptism; the Spirit of God comes into a person being baptized when *faith* is present. The second view is the standard evangelical Protestant view that Spirit baptism is the infilling of the Holy Spirit at conversion-regeneration. All true Christians are baptized in the Holy Spirit; there is no subsequent experience that catapults some Christians into a higher or deeper dimension of Christian living. The third view is the one held by Holiness evangelicals (radical Wesleyans who believe in entire sanctification and Christian perfection) and evangelicals in the "higher life" movement closely associated with the *Keswick movement* and its extensions. They believe that Spirit baptism is a second blessing subsequent to conversion-regeneration that is available to every authentic Christian and should be sought for fervently. It brings fullness of the Spirit for power to overcome sin and to serve God's kingdom effectively. Prior to Spirit baptism, Christians are forgiven but ineffective; after it, they are transformed into effective disciples of Jesus Christ no longer bound to "the world, the flesh, and the devil" but triumphant servants of Christ against whom the gates of *hell* cannot prevail. The fourth view is held by Pentecostals who add to the third view the doctrine that Spirit baptism is always accompanied by the evidence of speaking in tongues. Both the third and fourth views include that only Spirit-filled believers receive and manifest the gifts of the Holy Spirit mentioned by Paul in 1 Corinthians 12.

Pentecostal evangelicals believe that standard evangelicals are missing that dimension of Christianity that propelled the early *church* into a force that turned the world upside down. Standard evangelicals believe that Pentecostals create an elitist vision of Christianity and impose their own experience on everyone without biblical warrant. To a very great extent, persons who hold these different views of Spirit baptism within the evangelical movement have learned to work together in organizations such as the *National Association of Evangelicals*, but especially Pentecostals stand apart from other evangelicals in their emphasis on the experience of Spirit baptism accompanied by speaking in tongues as the sine qua non of completed Christianity.

A few evangelical theologians have attempted to bridge the gap between Pentecostals and standard evangelicals. A major player in this mediating effort is progressive evangelical theologian *Clark Pinnock*, whose life was touched by the *charismatic movement* and then by the *Third Wave movement* in the 1980s and 1990s. He remains a member of a mainstream Baptist church, while reaching out to Pentecostal and other more radical evangelical groups and individuals. According to Pinnock, there is truth in both sides; conversion-regeneration is the initial infilling of the Holy Spirit and may be equated with Spirit baptism. On the other hand, there is always more to experience of the Holy Spirit's inwardly transforming power in a Christian's life. Although "baptism of the Holy Spirit" should be reserved for conversion-regeneration (since the New Testament says that there is only one baptism and that all are baptized into one body), there can be and perhaps should be many "infillings of the Spirit" throughout Christian life. With regard to speaking in tongues, Pinnock affirms its validity as a spiritual experience and says that while it is normal, it is not the norm. In other words, not everyone must speak in tongues in order to be Spirit-filled, but every Spirit-filled Christian is a candidate for the gift of speaking in tongues as the Spirit assigns the gifts. Evangelical churches should be more open to that phenomenon and not quench the Spirit by excluding it; Pentecostals should drop their insistence that everyone speak in tongues in order to be regarded as Spirit-filled or Spirit-baptized.

Frederick Dale Bruner, *A Theology of the Holy Spirit* (Grand Rapids: Wm. B. Eerdmans, 1970); James D. G. Dunn, *Baptism in the Holy Spirit* (London: SCM, 1970); Gary B. McGee, ed., *Initial Evidence: Historical and Biblical Perspectives on the Pentecostal Doctrine of Spirit Baptism* (Peabody, MA: Hendrickson, 1991); Clark H. Pinnock, *Flame of Love: A Theology of the Holy Spirit* (Downers Grove, IL: InterVarsity Press, 1996); Max Turner, *The Holy Spirit and Spiritual Gifts* (Peabody, MA: Hendrickson, 1996).

Supernatural   Many people equate the concept of the supernatural with *miracles* or paranormal *experiences*. As this handbook contains an article on miracles, here *supernatural* will be treated in its more theological sense. Modern Christian *theology* can be divided into two categories, natural and supernatural. Under the spell of the Enlightenment and scientific revolutions, some liberal theologians have jettisoned the whole idea of the supernatural in favor of a naturalistic theology. The latter is any approach to theology that assumes a worldview in which the only reality is nature—a closed, causal network governed by laws that are in theory scientifically describable. Naturalism does not exclude the possibility of forces within the universe that lie outside the parameters of what is already known and understood. It does not rule out the reality of *God*. However, the God of naturalistic theology is either remote from the universe, not interfering in its physical functions, or else bound inextricably with the universe so that his activity is limited to and by natural laws. In almost every case, naturalistic theology is forced into a

dualism between mind and matter such that God works within consciousness but not in the physical realm. Evangelical theology rejects naturalism and naturalistic theologies in favor of the more classical worldview, which regards divine activity as including supernatural (or supranatural) acts that cannot be accounted for or limited by scientifically describable laws of nature and that take place in the physical processes of nature and history and not only in consciousness.

In the broadest sense, supernatural designates whatever transcends nature. Evangelicals believe that God is supernatural; God cannot be limited to the natural universe. God existed before it and has existence independent of it. *Grace*—the divine favor and transforming energy—cannot be forced by nature. In this evangelicals agree with classical Catholic theology as well as Protestant orthodoxy. Contrary to Catholic thought, however, most evangelicals believe that supernatural grace—the favor and power of God—tends to contradict nature in its fallen state. Nature has come under a curse because of the primeval fall of *humanity,* and that includes intellect and will. Catholic theology views the supernatural and natural realms as complementary; grace fulfills nature. Evangelical theology tends to view them as in tension; grace corrects and transforms nature. The challenge in this is to overcome the threat of dualism. If God is the creator, then there must be one reality in two dimensions. God and *creation* (nature) must not be confused, but neither should they be so separated as to make creation a reality alongside of and opposite God.

Evangelical theology has not reflected on this problem as deeply or thoroughly as it should. A task of relating the two realms of one reality to each other stands before evangelical metaphysics. How exactly does God work in the world without violating nature's relative autonomy? How does nature possess its own integrity without violating the divinity of God as sole maker of heaven and earth? In any case, evangelicals agree with the classical Christian tradition (going back at least to Thomas Aquinas in the medieval era) that nature and supernature must be coordinate but distinct realms of reality. Nature must not be allowed to swallow the supernatural, and the supernatural must not be allowed to obliterate or demean the natural. Many evangelical thinkers view nature and the supernatural as two dimensions or aspects of God's sovereign activity. God is just as involved in nature as in the supernatural, and yet they cannot be collapsed into each other. Miracles belong to the supernatural realm, but they must not be viewed as violations of the laws of nature. Rather, they are intersections of the supernatural with the natural; they signify special and unusual activities of God, whereas natural events signify regularities of God's activity.

Examples of the supernatural include miracles, special answers to *prayer*, *conversion, sanctification*, the presence of Christ in the *sacraments, resurrection*, and perhaps even life itself. Can conscious life come from material existence and physical laws? Can *redemption* come from nature or even a grace embedded in nature? Evangelicals agree that it cannot. Evangelical theology is based on a supernatural worldview that is largely assumed and rarely explicated or defended in depth or detail. In evangelical theology God is the creator and redeemer who transcends physical nature and its laws; his activity includes extraordinary events within the fabric of nature and history that cannot be accounted for scientifically and are thus not part of that fabric itself. As good as nature is (because one mode of God's creative activity and an object of redemption), it cannot circumscribe or limit the divine activity, which is free, gracious, purposeful, and powerful beyond physical laws and forces.

Thomas V. Morris, *Our Idea of God: An Introduction to Philosophical Theology*

(Downers Grove, IL: InterVarsity Press, 1991); Ronald H. Nash, *The Concept of God: An Exploration of Contemporary Difficulties with the Attributes of God* (Grand Rapids: Zondervan, 1983); James Orr, *The Christian View of God and the World* (Grand Rapids: Kregel, 1989).

Theism   In its broadest sense, theism is any belief in *God*; it usually indicates monotheism—belief in a single God, who is the supreme being over all *creation*. With the exception of a few radical theologians of the late twentieth century and early twenty-first century, all Christians—including evangelicals—have been and are theists and share with Jews and Muslims that religious perspective on ultimate reality. (See the article in this handbook on *God* for more details on the evangelical doctrine of God.) Here, theism indicates not belief in God in general, but the specifically Christian view of God's nature and attributes often known as "classical Christian theism," which developed over centuries of Christian theological reflection on *Scripture, reason*, and *experience*.

Classical Christian theism is rooted in the second-century Christian apologists who attempted to communicate what Christians believe about God to educated Greek and Roman elites, using concepts from Greek and Roman philosophy. Church fathers such as Clement of Alexandria, Origen, and Augustine contributed heavily to the development of classical Christian theism. The high point of its evolution came with the medieval scholastic philosophers and theologians such as Anselm and Thomas Aquinas, who attempted to use logic and Greek philosophy (especially Plato and Aristotle) to create a highly coherent system of Christian beliefs about God. During the Protestant Reformation, Luther reacted negatively to this correlation of biblical religion with Greek philosophy; during the post-Reformation era French Catholic thinker Blaise Pascal declared that "the God of the philosophers is not the God of Abraham, Isaac, and Jacob." This was an expression of his opinion of classical theism, even though he agreed with many of its tenets insofar as they could be demonstrated from Scripture.

In the twentieth century classical theism found both defenders and detractors among Christian theologians. Swiss theologian Emil Brunner scorned the speculative nature of theism and attempted to strip Christian theology of all extra-biblical elements without falling into *fundamentalism*. He argued that theism tends to subordinate God's personal nature and the I-Thou encounter between people and God and to stress instead God's absolute, transcendent nature, which leads to a vision of God as impersonal being itself. On the other hand, during the Reformation Calvin made some critical use of theism, and later English Protestant theologians found great value in it. Among other modern Protestant theologians, E. L. Mascall defended and further explicated classical Christian theism. Process theologians such as Charles Hartshorne and John Cobb worked to develop a "neoclassical" or revisionist Christian theism, while conservative Catholic and Protestant theologians defended traditional or conventional concepts of God against such revisions.

The twentieth century brought about a crisis for classical theism; many Christian theologians believed it was no longer possible to believe in the conventional portrayal of God stemming from the *church* fathers and medieval scholars due to changes in the modern worldview and because of the Holocaust. Some theologians declared God dead, by which they often meant the concept of God in classical theism is dead.

Classical Christian theism is not a monolithic system, but there are certain common features that appear across time and cultures. Theism portrays God as the self-sufficient, eternal, immutable (unchanging) perfect being who makes *heaven* and earth and rules over them with absolute sovereignty. For theism, God's being is perfect and complete, and the universe adds nothing to it. God is *actus purus*—pure actuality with no potentiality. God is not dependent in any way on the creation, even if he does interact with it. Some theists argue that God genuinely interacts with the world without being changed by that interaction, and other theists argue that God cannot be affected by creation. For most theists, God's relationship to the world is timeless; God's life is not just everlasting (without beginning or end) but also in some sense timeless. All temporal moments are simultaneously before the eyes of God. God is omnipotent, omniscient, and omnipresent, as well as the perfect standard of truth, beauty, and goodness. The concept of perfection appears everywhere in theism and seems to underlie it; the God of theism is perfect in every way—morally and metaphysically—so that nothing can add anything to his already complete and blissful existence, power, knowledge, and sovereignty.

During the Middle Ages Anselm worked rigorously to develop a logically coherent account of God and correlate that with biblical *revelation*. According to Anselm, God cannot be compassionate, because to feel compassion is to be moved by something outside of oneself. Therefore, Anselm argued, compassion is not an attribute of God, but a feeling humans have when they contemplate God's great mercy. In the words of the seventeenth-century Westminster Confession of Faith, God is "without body, parts or passions." Many defenders of classical Christian theism—including many evangelicals—attribute impassibility to God. They believe that God is incapable of any suffering including mental and emotional anguish. The biblical narratives that portray God as grieving are labeled "anthropomorphic" and attributed to the condescended nature of revelation. In contrast, twentieth-century Protestant theologian Dietrich Bonhoeffer declared that "only the suffering God can help," and even many conservative evangelical theologians wondered aloud whether impassibility is taking God's absoluteness too far.

By and large evangelical theology has relied heavily on some version of classical Christian theism for its doctrine of God. This has usually been done without overt reliance on medieval scholastic theology; most evangelical theologians prefer to believe that they are drawing their portrayal of God directly from Scripture, even if they happen to find support also in church tradition and logic. One of the most influential books about God among evangelicals has been A. W. Tozer's *The Knowledge of the Holy: The Attributes of God: Their Meaning in the Christian Life* (San Francisco: HarperSan-Francisco, 1998), a popular exposition and defense of a version of classical theism. The author, a popular evangelical speaker and writer, borrowed heavily on Catholic and Puritan sources to explicate approximately twenty attributes of God, including incomprehensibility, self-sufficiency, infinitude, immutability, wisdom, goodness, *justice, holiness,* and sovereignty. Few, if any, evangelicals would dispute these attributes or the general portrait of God found in Tozer's book.

On the other hand, many popular evangelical books about God emphasize God's personal nature, and the personal relationship with God lies at the heart of evangelical religion. Evangelicals have not reflected sufficiently on how to correlate these two impulses in their theological perspective on God: God's wholly otherness and God's intimacy with his people. The personal encounter with God and prayer that affects God are crucial elements of evangelical devotional life and of evangelical proclamation and teaching, but conservative evangelical theologians often dwell at length on God's transcendence and absoluteness in a way that seems to undermine the possibility of a personal relationship with God (insofar as personal relationship indicates interaction). Most evangelical theologians adhere

firmly to the Westminster Confession's negative theology of God "without body, parts or passions." Some even argue that divine simplicity is one of God's crucial attributes that makes him God. Others believe that is extrabiblical, speculative, and logically unnecessary and that it may conflict with belief in the *Trinity.* For the most part, however, evangelical theologians have endorsed classical theism, even if they have questioned particular attributes such as impassibility and simplicity.

In 1975 two Reformed evangelical thinkers raised serious questions about classical theism that opened a Pandora's box of controversy among evangelical theologians. James Daane asked "Can a Man Bless God?" (*God and the Good: Essays in Honor of Henry Stob,* ed. Clifton Orlebeke and Lewis Smedes [Grand Rapids: Wm. B. Eerdmans, 1974], 165–73) and answered in the affirmative. In other words, the Fuller Seminary professor of theology argued, God is not entirely self-sufficient in the classical scholastic sense of aseity—inability to be affected by anything outside of himself. For Daane and others who came to agree with him, the God of the biblical narrative is capable of being "blessed" by human *worship* and good deeds so that his life is in some way enriched. Nicholas Wolterstorff, writing in the same volume about "God Everlasting" (181–203), argued that the conventional view of God as timeless is biblically and logically flawed. He presented an alternative view of God's eternity as everlastingness, in which God has no beginning or end, but is temporal with creation. Of course, both Daane and Wolterstorff affirmed God's self-sufficiency apart from creation, but they envisioned God as self-limiting in relation to creation, so that God's attributes have to be understood in relation to God's voluntary self-restriction.

Arminian evangelical theologian *Clark Pinnock* similarly challenged some aspects of classical theism beginning in the early 1980s, when he announced his intention to develop a "neo-classical theism" (a term he dropped because of its use by process theologians for their revisionist understanding of God). In 1986 Pinnock first publicly announced his view that God limits himself in relation to creation so that he does not know the future exhaustively and infallibly. This came to be known over the next two decades as "*open theism*" or "openness of God theology." Several noted evangelicals joined with Daane, Wolterstorff, and Pinnock in questioning classical theism's influence in evangelical thought and revising the evangelical portrait of God in order to underline God's personal nature and God's goodness. Throughout the 1990s evangelical open theists such as John Sanders, William Hasker, Gregory Boyd, and David Basinger joined Clark Pinnock's project and added their own spins to it. Conservative evangelical critics thought they detected heresy in this new view of God and created a stir among evangelicals by calling it a serious defection from classical, biblical theology. Some defenders of open theism responded by saying that evangelical theology is not tied normatively to any particular system of thought but is required by *sola scriptura* (Scripture as the ultimate source and norm of faith and practice) to remain open to revisions in doctrine, insofar as they are based on faithful biblical reflection. The open theists pointed to the biblical narratives that portray God as changing his mind in response to prayer and grieving over the waywardness of his people and averred that such a God cannot be the God of philosophical theism.

By the first years of the twenty-first century, evangelical theology in North America was in a turmoil over this controversy, with the *Evangelical Theological Society* contemplating expelling open theists from its ranks. Supporters of open theism argue that its conservative critics are elevating classical theism to a position of *authority* alongside of or even over Scripture; conservative critics of open theism disagree and claim that

open theism is not only inconsistent with classical theism but also with Scripture itself. The question that lingers over all of this debate is how authoritative classical theism is for evangelical theology; that has not been settled and probably will not be settled for a long time. Some evangelical theologians are committed to the basic contours of the scholastic view of God, while others are more than willing to discard some major portions of it.

John S. Feinberg, *No One Like Him: The Doctrine of God* (Wheaton, IL: Crossway, 2001); Christopher B. Kaiser, *The Doctrine of God* (Westchester, IL: Crossway, 1982); Thomas V. Morris, *Our Idea of God: An Introduction to Philosophical Theology* (Downers Grove, IL: InterVarsity Press, 1991); Ronald H. Nash, *The Concept of God: An Exploration of Contemporary Difficulties with the Attributes of God* (Grand Rapids: Zondervan, 1983); Clark H. Pinnock, *Most Moved Mover: A Theology of God's Openness* (Grand Rapids: Baker Books, 2001).

Theology   Theology is not, of course, a doctrine, but doctrine develops through theological reflection. Evangelical theologians agree unanimously that theology is inevitable and even necessary and that if conducted properly, it is a very positive aspect of Christian *faith* and life. Not all evangelicals agree. Evangelical theologians know all too well that there is an antitheological bias in many evangelical *churches* and organizations and that many individuals prefer their folk religion to sound theological reflection. This situation is not unique to Evangelicalism, of course; it exists in virtually every religious movement and form of life. There is always some tension between the scholars and the laity in religions; Evangelicalism is no exception. However, the anti-intellectual stream in evangelical life is exacerbated by the movement's populist roots in *revivalism*. Evangelical theologians strive to educate their constituents regarding the value of theological reflection and doctrine, with some success here and there. Evangelical thinkers agree among themselves that proper Christian theology is rooted in the biblical texts and is authoritatively governed by them as God's *revelation* in written form. They agree also that *Jesus Christ*, as *God* incarnate, holds supreme *authority*, but for the most part they believe that authority is delegated to the inspired biblical writings and that humans are submitting to Jesus' authority when they submit to *Scripture's* authority. Theology, then, is reflection on Scripture that seeks to correlate its teachings with contemporary human *experience*. Experience, however, is not authoritative in the same way as Scripture; it serves as tool of interpretation, along with reason and tradition.

Many evangelical theologians adhere to the method of theology known as the Wesleyan Quadrilateral—Scripture, tradition, *reason,* and experience—with wide variations in how the four elements are used. All agree that the quadrilateral is not an equilateral; Scripture is supreme. Some elevate the Great Tradition of historic Christian belief and/or the "received evangelical tradition" to a status almost alongside Scripture, while others eschew a normative role for tradition and view it as one guidance mechanism among several. In general, evangelical theologians in the Anglican, Lutheran, and Reformed traditions tend to view tradition—however that is precisely defined—as authoritative, while those in the Anabaptist, Baptist, and Pentecostal traditions do not. Some evangelical theologians regard logic as authoritative in the critical and constructive tasks of theology, while others revel in paradox and dialectical thinking. Experience is generally viewed with some suspicion by evangelical theologians because of the tendency within revivalism to emphasize it; many evangelical theologians are wary of allowing experience to play any normative role in the tasks of theology. Nevertheless, virtually all would admit that it is inescapable and always plays some part in reflection.

The main watershed regarding theology in evangelical thought lies along the line that separates the highly systematic, propositional approach to theological reflection from the more experiential and existential approach. *Carl F. H. Henry,* the "dean of evangelical theologians," has built his reputation on his project of demonstrating the coherence of evangelical Christian theology. According to Henry and many other conservative, generally Reformed evangelical thinkers, one of theology's primary tasks is to develop, using logic, an architectonically perfect system of beliefs out of the biblical texts. Beginning with the reasonable presuppositions of God's existence and the authority of Scripture, Henry and other rational presuppositionalists seek to correlate all biblical teachings with each other in a perfectly coherent system; the law of noncontradiction rules the method. The truth of the pattern of theology constructed is based on its superior coherence to all alternative worldviews, philosophies of life, and theologies. The presuppositions are validated by the coherence of the system they yield; the falseness of other, rival systems of thought is demonstrated by the incoherence of the systems that are built on them. Experience plays little role in this approach to theology, and paradox is eschewed as a sure sign of error. This does not mean that God is perfectly comprehensible or that no mystery remains in theology's account of God. Rather, mystery is the limit of intelligibility, and the latter must be pursued as far as the human mind—enlightened by the Spirit-inspired Word of God in Scripture using basic laws of logic that are rooted in God's own being—can take it. Henry and others who follow this approach view other approaches as ending in subjectivism, which undermines theology's public voice and dilutes the truth value of theology's assertions.

The second evangelical approach is also biblicist in that it begins with

Scripture, but it takes more seriously the necessity of the cognitive help of the *Holy Spirit* in knowing that Scripture is God's Word and in interpreting it and developing a system of doctrine from it. *Bernard Ramm,* among other evangelical thinkers, argued for a pattern of authority centering around the dialectic of Word and Spirit. In this he could and did appeal to John Calvin, who argued that apart from the "inner testimony of the Holy Spirit" it is impossible to know oneself or God truly and also impossible to receive and use Scripture as God's inspired Word. For Ramm and other evangelicals who take this path of theological method, the communal, collective spiritual experience of the faithful people of God and the inner guidance of the Spirit of God in the individual believer play an indispensable role in theology. That does not mean that individuals can simply fabricate doctrine out of subjective spiritual impulses, but it does mean that spirituality is crucial for correct theology. An unbeliever cannot do Christian theology correctly; theology is the project of the Spirit-enlivened and Spirit-led people of God.

Stanley J. Grenz has especially argued for this experiential approach to evangelical theology. For him the biblical witness is the ultimate authority for evangelical theology, but reception and use of that witness always depends on spiritual devotion that is communally shaped. *Donald G. Bloesch* is another evangelical theologian who eschews the highly rationalistic, dogmatic approach of the Henry-style presuppositionalists. Like Grenz, Bloesch sees Evangelicalism as primarily rooted in *Pietism,* the seventeenth- and eighteenth-century movement of "heart Christianity" in Europe and later Great Britain and North America. The Pietists regarded theology as secondary language; it traces out the workings of the Holy Spirit in Scripture and in the life of the people of God. The demonstration of truth in theology is not primarily in its rational intelligibility but in "the Spirit and power." That theology

is likely to be true that arises out of genuinely Spirit-transformed community life centered around the person of Jesus Christ and faithful to the biblical witness. Because "the heart has reasons the reason knows not of" (Pascal), it is not suprising when theological reflection gives rise to paradoxes. The intellectual tasks of theology can never exhaust or penetrate the mysterious *holiness* and intimate presence of the Thou who encounters us in Jesus Christ through the biblical narratives and within the *worship* of the church.

All evangelical theologians agree that doctrine is essential to the life of the church and to the identity and vitality of Christianity; they also agree that theology is essential to the development and defense of sound doctrine. Finally, they also agree that biblical revelation is the foundation of evangelical theology; for evangelicals, theology is reflection on Scripture in the light of tradition, reason, and experience. Differences of opinion arise over the roles of tradition, logic, and experience in theology and doctrine, as well as over the value of paradox and mystery in theological systems.

During the last decade of the twentieth century and into the first decade of the twenty-first century, evangelical theologians fell into debate with one another over theology's relationship with postmodernity and especially over dialogue between evangelical theology and postliberal theology, a form of postmodern theology. Postmodernity views reason with suspicion and has little use for architectonically perfect systems of truth; it rejects claims to objectivity and univocal grasp of reality. Postliberal theology—launched by Yale theologians Hans Frei and George Lindbeck in the 1980s—claims that theology is an intratextual discipline and that doctrine does not describe extratextual reality in some objective or univocal way. Theology is reflection on biblical narrative, and doctrine provides the rules that govern Christian speech about God. Some evangelical theologians have found an ally in postliberalism, insofar as it takes the biblical narratives very seriously and does not seek to impose a system on them. Other evangelical theologians worry that any dialogue between evangelical theology and postliberal theology may lead to a new subjectivism and ahistorical interpretation of the Bible. They are concerned that postliberal theology leads into "story theology," in which the narratives are disconnected from real history and related only to persons' "inner histories" as guides and representations. The controversy over postliberal theology within evangelical theology is at the cutting edge of evangelical debate about the nature of theology in the early years of the twenty-first century.

Stanley J. Grenz, *Revisioning Evangelical Theology: A Fresh Agenda for the 21st* Century (Downers Grove, IL: InterVarsity Press, 1993); Carl F. H. Henry, *Toward A Recovery of Christian Belief* (Wheaton, IL: Crossway, 1990); Henry H. Knight III, *A Future for Truth: Evangelical Theology in a Postmodern World* (Nashville: Abingdon, 1997); Timothy R. Phillips and Dennis L. Okholm, eds., *The Nature of Confession: Evangelicals and Postliberals in Conversation* (Downers Grove, IL: InterVarsity Press, 1999); D. H. Williams, *Retrieving the Tradition and Renewing Evangelicalism: A Primer for Suspicious Protestants* (Grand Rapids: Wm. B. Eerdmans, 1996).

Trinity There is no distinctively evangelical doctrine of the Trinity; evangelicals by and large accept the historical (Nicene) doctrine of the Trinity. A few evangelicals reject the classical Christian doctrine of the Trinity in favor of modalism (Sabellianism), which regards the three persons of the Trinity as modes or manifestations of the one supreme person of *God*. These are so-called Oneness Pentecostals. Many evangelicals do not consider them authentically evangelical because of this doctrinal aberration, but they exist nevertheless on the fringes of the evangelical subculture around the

world and are evangelical in many respects. The vast majority of evangelical theologians insist that the orthodox doctrine of the Trinity is crucial to authentic evangelical doctrinal belief; Oneness Pentecostals and others who deny it are banned from membership in the *National Association of Evangelicals* and the *Evangelical Theological Society*. Evangelicals share the doctrine of the Trinity with most other Christians and have no distinctive spin on it. Nevertheless, evangelical scholars have made some contributions to the doctrine of the Trinity, and within evangelical theological circles certain debates about the Trinity are ongoing.

The classical, orthodox doctrine of the Trinity shared by evangelicals with nearly all Christians is that God is one divine substance (*ousia*) (monotheism) but three distinct (not separate) persons (*hypostaseis*). This is true immanently in God from eternity, as well as economically in God's self-*revelation* and activity in *salvation* history. The Father, Son, and *Holy Spirit* together form one God, even as they remain forever distinct persons; the Father is not the Son, and the Son is not the Holy Spirit, and the Spirit is not the Father. Yet all are inseparably united in essence. Baptist theologian *Augustus Hopkins Strong* summed up the evangelical doctrine of the Trinity early in the twentieth century using the acrostic TRIUNE: Three recognized as God; Regarded as distinct persons; Immanent and eternal, not merely economical or historical; United in essence; No inequality; Explains all other doctrines yet itself inscrutable. With this, few evangelicals would disagree even if the doctrine of the Trinity is largely functionless in evangelical folk religion.

Some debate exists among evangelical theologians about the unity of the three persons in the Godhead. Some evangelical theologians prefer to use the so-called social analogy of the Trinity articulated especially effectively by British theologian Leonard Hodgson in the middle of the twentieth century. It has roots in the Greek fathers of the church (especially the Cappadocians). According to this analogy, the unity of the three persons is an organic unity like that of an especially close community of human persons. The unity of substance is a bond of love, not a metaphysical reality that overwhelms or overshadows the distinctness of the three persons.

This social analogy is used by Stanley J. Grenz, who explicates the Trinity in relation to the *imago dei* (*image of God*) in human persons; both are social realities. Just as Father, Son, and Holy Spirit draw their eternal identities from relationship with the other members of the Trinity, so human persons find identity in relationship with God and other human persons. Grenz draws heavily on the phenomenology of community life to develop an account of the Trinity that supports the idea of the Christian life as a life in community. Human persons reflect God and reach their own identity and fulfillment by living in community with and for others and finding their identity in and through loving relationships. God is not an isolated monad in the heavens who manifests himself in three ways or has three dimensions (such as memory, consciousness, and will) but a community of persons open to others. Grenz's view of the Trinity is very close to Hodgson's social analogy, while depending explicitly on the reflections of Wolfhart Pannenberg and correlating closely with the Trinitarian *theology* of Jürgen Moltmann.

Some evangelical theologians are uncomfortable with the social analogy because it seems to them close to tritheism—the heresy of three gods. They draw on the Trinitarian theology of Augustine, which emphasizes the oneness of God's subjectivity and substance. This is the so-called psychological analogy of the Trinity very strongly preferred by those evangelical theologians impressed by classical theism's understanding of God's simplicity of being. For these evangelicals, the divine Trinity is not a community but a single subjectivity with three dimensions or aspects that can properly be called "persons" in the sense of the Greek word *hypostaseis*— "subsistences." The only ontological difference between Father, Son, and Holy Spirit lies in their relationships of origin. The Father generates the Son eternally; the Spirit proceeds forth from the Father eternally; the Father stands above the Son and Spirit as the fount or source of divinity of the entire Godhead. In another analogy, the Spirit is the bond of love that unites the Father and the Son. In any case, according to these theologians, there is no real distinction or difference of activity of the persons of the Trinity; all are equally involved in every relationship toward what is outside of God. These theologians are concerned to protect and preserve monotheism within Evangelicalism, and they eschew any hint of polytheism. They believe the social analogy smacks of polytheism.

Another area of some controversy among evangelical theologians has to do with whether hierarchy exists within the Trinitarian life. Some evangelical theologians argue for the monarchy of the Father; for them the Son and Spirit are eternally subordinate to the Father, who is their head in the sense of ontological source and *authority*. These evangelicals often use this vision of the Trinity to favor hierarchy of men over women in families and churches. Opponents of hierarchy within the immanent Trinity (the eternal Trinity) argue that it is nowhere supported in *Scripture*, where the Son and Spirit are treated as equal with the Father in every way except for voluntary submission within salvation history. Furthermore, they respond, the monarchy of the Father reduces the Trinity to subordinationism (Arianism), which is a heresy. In that case, the Son, who became *Jesus Christ* in the incarnation, is not fully divine. Some of these evangelical theologians view the egalitarian, communal Trinity as justification for egalitarian life within families and churches. The doctrine of the Trinity has thus become entangled with a debate about gender roles in families, churches, and society.

Some evangelicals who believe strongly in subordination of women to men base that in part on 1 Corinthians 11:3, where it is said that Christ is the "head" (*kephale*) of every man, the husband is the "head" of the wife, and God is the "head" of Christ. They read this as instruction about hierarchy in the Trinity and in the family. Egalitarian evangelicals, who believe in mutual submission of husbands and wives, reject the argument on the ground that elsewhere Paul urges that husbands and wives submit to each other (Eph. 5:21) and declares that in Christ there is "neither male nor female" but Christians "are all one" (Gal. 3:28 KJV). For egalitarian evangelicals, Paul's obscure reference to God as the head of Christ must refer to economic subordination for the purpose of *incarnation* and *atonement*; otherwise, apologies are due to Arius, who was condemned as a heretic in the fourth century for teaching that Jesus Christ is not equal with the Father.

Kevin Giles, *The Trinity and Subordinationism: The Doctrine of God and the Contemporary Gender Debate* (Downers Grove, IL: InterVarsity Press, 2002); Stanley J. Grenz, *The Social God and the Relational Self: A Trinitarian Theology of the Imago Dei* (Louisville, KY: Westminster John Knox Press, 2001); Cornelius Plantinga and Ronald Jay Feenstra, eds., *Trinity, Incarnation, and Atonement: Philosophical and Theological Essays* (Notre Dame, IN: University of Notre Dame Press, 1990); Peter Toon and James D. Spiceland, eds., *One God in Trinity: An Analysis of the Primary Dogma of Christianity* (Westchester, IL: Cornerstone Books, 1980); Peter Toon, *Our Triune God: A Biblical Portrayal of the Trinity* (Wheaton, IL: Victor Books, 1996); Miroslav Volf, *After Our Image: The Church as the Image of the Trinity* (Grand Rapids: Wm. B. Eerdmans, 1998).

Virgin Birth   Evangelical *theology* is deeply committed to the reality of the virginal conception, more commonly but somewhat incorrectly called "virgin birth," of *Jesus Christ*. This commitment arises out of Evangelicalism's belief in the trustworthiness and *authority* of the *Bible*, which mentions Jesus' virgin birth in two Gospels, and also from Evangelicalism's fundamentalist roots. Classical Christianity of all branches—Eastern Orthodox, Roman Catholic, and orthodox Protestant—has always adhered firmly to belief that Mary was a virgin when she conceived Jesus and that his conception and birth were a *miracle* brought about by the *Holy Spirit*. During the nineteenth century and especially in the early decades of the twentieth century, some liberal Protestant theologians began to express doubts about the reality of the virgin birth; they tended to reduce it to legend or myth because it is not mentioned by any New Testament writer other than Matthew and Luke and it is similar to many ancient Greek and Roman stories about the births of heroes. Furthermore, it does not comport with the modern bias against the miraculous. Liberal theologians found it relatively easy to dismiss the virgin birth without damaging their own understandings of the divinity of Christ (which tended to be functional rather than ontological).

In the early decades of the twentieth century, conservative Protestants looked for a litmus test to distinguish between sound and heretical theologies within the North American Protestant context of the liberal-fundamentalist dispute consuming the *churches* in the aftermath of the rise of liberal theology. Many conservatives believed that the doctrine of the virgin birth of Christ could function as such a litmus test; no liberal would affirm it, and no conservative would deny it. The first article in the first volume of the series *The Fundamentals* (Chicago: Testimony Publishing Company, n.d.), by Scottish evangelical theologian James Orr, was entitled "The Virgin Birth of Christ." Orr argued against the liberal denial of the virgin birth and for the classical doctrine on biblical and theological grounds. For example, like many other conservative theologians, Orr believed that Christ's sinlessness was proof of his virgin birth; if he had been conceived in the normal biological manner, he would be a sinner like everyone else. This, of course, presupposes that there is something like a hereditary *sin* gene that is passed down through the act of sexual procreation. Not all conservative theologians believe that, even though Augustine taught it and many Christian theologians have assumed it throughout church history. Fundamentalists—the conservatives among the conservatives in the Protestant reaction against liberal theology—placed great stress on the literal truth of the virgin birth in order to identify and exclude liberals from their denominations. The great fundamentalist thinker *J. Gresham Machen* in 1930 published a scholarly volume defending and explicating the virgin birth (*The Virgin Birth of Christ* (New York: Harper). Like Orr he emphatically denounced the liberal treament of the doctrine as a myth or legend and argued that without this miracle of conception and birth Jesus Christ would not be sinless, let alone the *incarnation* of God. For the most part, conservative evangelicals have accepted this point of view.

In 1959 Fuller Seminary president and evangelical theologian *Edward John Carnell* published in *Christianity Today* a dissenting view of the virgin birth ("The Virgin Birth of Christ," *Christianity Today* 4:4 [Dec. 7, 1959], 9–10; later published in Carnell's *The Case for Biblical Christianity*, ed. Ronald H. Nash [Grand Rapids: Wm. B. Eerdmans, 1969]). There the moderately progressive evangelical critic of *fundamentalism* ("orthodoxy gone cultic") argued that while the virgin birth is true and an important confession for all Christians, it is not the miraculous explanation of Christ's sinlessness. If his sin-

lessness was caused by his being virginally conceived (that is, not inheriting sinful corruption from the male through sexual procreation), it would not be a great moral achievement or example but a given. Carnell argued that the purpose of the virgin birth was not to bring the sinless Son of God into the world, as if it could not happen any other way, but to serve as a sign of Jesus' uniqueness to his family and disciples. Some fundamentalist critics viewed Carnell's interpretation as tantamount to denial of the virgin birth, even though Carnell made his own belief in it crystal clear. Ultraconservative evangelicals considered Carnell's denial of the virgin birth as guarantee of Christ's sinlessness a serious deviation from the traditional interpretation and a step down a slippery slope toward denial of both the virgin birth and sinlessness (if not deity) of Jesus Christ. For the most part, however, moderate to progressive evangelicals came to agree with Carnell that *original sin* and Jesus' sinlessness cannot be biologically explained and that the traditional interpretation was based largely on Augustine's low view of the sex act as inherently *evil* and somehow the conduit of both the corruption and guilt of original sin from Adam to his posterity.

Donald G. Bloesch, *Jesus Christ: Savior and Lord* (Downers Grove, IL: InterVarsity Press, 1997); Robert G. Gromacki, *The Virgin Birth: A Biblical Study of the Deity of Jesus Christ* (Grand Rapids: Kregel, 2002); Howard Hanke, *The Validity of the Virgin Birth* (Grand Rapids: Zondervan, 1963).

Worship   The last quarter of the twentieth century witnessed what some commentators on the evangelical scene labeled the worship wars. Evangelical *churches* were racked by controversy over worship styles varying from liturgical to traditional to contemporary to charismatic. "Seeker-sensitive" worship burst on the evangelical church scene, with critics decrying it as thinly disguised religious entertainment. At the same time, many evangelical churches began experimenting with ancient liturgies drawn from Celtic and Greek sources. It would be difficult to imagine anything more diverse than worship among evangelical churches in North America. Storefront Pentecostal and huge suburban megachurches often share an enthusiastic, revivalistic format, while some inner-city and small-town Baptist churches look to Episcopalian patterns for renewal. What makes a church evangelical has little to do with its worship style; it is virtually impossible to generalize about worship when referring to evangelical churches and religious organizations.

It might be safe to say that, compared with so-called mainstream Protestantism, evangelical churches tend to experiment with worship more often and are often more flexible than churches tied to denominational worship books and traditions. Evangelical theologians often decry Evangelicalism's trendiness and faddishness, especially with regard to worship. And yet that seems to explain some of the movement's continuing vitality and growth. Evangelicals have been especially adept at appealing to youth by incorporating their sensitivities and desires into worship. This is in part what has led to the so-called worship wars, where many evangelical churches have divided over innovations in worship. Many have avoided splits simply by holding two or more worship services on Sunday (or one on Saturday evening and another on Sunday). Often one is "traditional," with hymns and litanies and a thirty-minute expository sermon, while the other is "contemporary," with "praise and worship choruses," skits, liturgical dance, and a fifteen-minute dialogue sermon. Other evangelical churches have settled for "blended worship" that incorporates diverse worship styles into a single service.

Evangelical *theology* is just as divided over the true nature of worship

as evangelical churches are divided over worship styles. All evangelical theologians agree that worship's primary purpose is to glorify *God*, but beyond that, much disagreement exists about its secondary and tertiary purposes. Differences of opinion also exist about how best to glorify God in worship. Evangelical theologians in the Reformed tradition tend to be highly critical of any type of worship that seems human-centered. They disdain therapeutic, entertaining, or evangelistic worship. For them, all worship should focus on the glory of God in praise and adoration, and for many of them worship must be disciplined; it should be led by persons whose beliefs and life are conformed to the standards of a network of churches under the rule of *Scripture* and the historic Reformed confessions (e.g., the Heidelberg Catechism and the Westminster Confession of Faith). In the late twentieth century a group of mostly Reformed evangelical theologians organized to promote traditional, disciplined worship among evangelicals. Taking the name The Alliance of Confessing Evangelicals, they produced the magazine *Modern Reformation*. Some theologians associated with the Alliance and the magazine wrote and signed a document entitled The Cambridge Declaration, which decried, among other things, the deterioration of modern evangelical worship into entertainment. These and other traditionalists among Reformed evangelical thinkers are not so concerned about a particular format or liturgy, but they eschew unbridled experimentation in both theology and liturgy and call for evangelicals to return to styles of worship that focus attention on God, not on human need and desire.

A second group of traditionalist evangelicals look to former Wheaton College professor Robert Webber for leadership. Webber taught theology and worship at Evangelicalism's flagship educational institution for many years and influenced numerous serious-minded evangelical thinkers and leaders to associate themselves with the high-church pattern of worship and polity, and especially with the Episcopalian denomination. Webber's concern, however, was not with any denomination but historical continuity with the ancient Christian churches and their forms of worship and common life. According to Webber and his numerous students and followers, independent, entrepreneurial church life and worship weakens the churches by separating them from their common roots in apostolic and ancient Christianity. Webber and his cohort of evangelicals interested in church renewal emphasize the unity of the church across time and cultures and seek to overcome the rootlessness of modern evangelical church life by retrieving the historic episcopate and liturgical traditions. While most evangelical churches do not observe the traditional pattern of the church calendar and its seasons, Webber encourages them to discover its rich resources for renewal in order to overcome the trivialization he sees taking place in much *revivalism* and contemporary worship.

Both the Reformed and Webberian traditionalists among evangelicals emphasize the vertical dimension of worship, while at the same time seeking to preserve a role for the horizontal dimension. Their common concern is to reconnect evangelical worship with historic catholic and Protestant traditions and to overcome shallow evangelical worship that shifts with every wind of culture. They see much evangelical worship as accommodationist. The church, they believe, ought to be an anchored ship in the rolling and shifting seas of modern and postmodern culture. Its anchor should be deeply sunk in the bedrock of ancient and Reformation Christian traditions.

Not all evangelical thinkers agree with the traditionalists. A third group of evangelicals includes Pentecostals and charismatics, who readily adjust worship style to fit the needs of contempo-

rary spiritual seekers. A leading Pentecostal-charismatic writer, speaker, and liturgical reformer is Jack Hayford, pastor of the large and influential Church on the Way in Van Nuys, California. Hayford agrees with traditionalists that the horizontal (Godward) dimension must be preserved in all worship; the purpose of worship is always to glorify God. However, how people glorify God in worship cannot be captured in historical, liturgical patterns. God is glorified in the life-transforming encounter with God in *Holy Spirit*–filled, enthusiastic worship that is informal and open to spontaneous manifestations of spiritual gifts. Lying behind Hayford's pastoral concerns about worship are Pentecostal-charismatic theologian J. Rodman Williams's reflections on Spirit-filled worship. Williams is a former Presbyterian seminary theology professor who became charismatic and eventually joined the faculty of Regents University, a charismatic evangelical graduate school in Virginia Beach, Virginia. Williams combines the horizontal and vertical dimensions of worship by emphasizing the prophetic quality of authentically Spirit-filled worship, in which the Holy Spirit is given sovereign freedom to speak and act for the benefit of the worshiping community.

Hayford and Williams eschew the crass antics of many television evangelists who promote the "gospel of prosperity" and promise people health and wealth in return for donations. They do not, however, want to throw the baby of enthusiastic worship out with the bathwater of fanaticism. Worship in this pattern of evangelical life tends to be open, flexible and spontaneous. It is not particularly concerned with being catholic or disciplined. Hayford, for example, invites everyone present in his worship services to participate in the ordinance of the Lord's Supper without restriction or limitation. Although he belongs to the Pentecostal Foursquare Gospel denomination, he does not limit worship leadership to that tradition; a Spirit-inspired ecumenism is what he and other Pentecostal evangelicals seek and practice. To more conservative and traditionalist evangelicals, however, this appears chaotic and confusing, because precise boundaries and strong historical connections are not in focus.

A fourth evangelical pattern of worship may be seen in the so-called seeker-sensitive movement led by the Willow Creek Community Church of suburban Chicago. Numerous evangelical churches in North America and increasingly around the world have joined that church's network in order to emulate its style of community outreach and worship. Pastor Bill Hybels is advised by evangelical theologian and former Wheaton College professor Gilbert Bilezikian, who emphasizes the need for contemporary evangelical churches to adjust to the needs of post-modern spiritual seekers and not be bound by traditional patterns of worship or promote eccentric and often off-putting styles of worship that are unintelligible to increasingly post-Christian suburbanites. Seeker-sensitive churches offer worship services at nontraditional times such as Saturday evenings and Sunday afternoons in order to accommodate the schedules of their constituents. Worship in seeker-sensitive churches accommodates to modern and postmodern people's brief attention spans by offering brief skits instead of lengthy sermons. It is often characterized by a blend of musical selections that imitate popular styles of music with spiritual messages. To critics, seeker-sensitive worship is shallow entertainment that has little to do with traditional Christian liturgy. Some have even gone so far as to label it "McChurch."

Admittedly, seeker-sensitive churches offer low-demand worship *experiences* to visitors, but they defend themselves by saying that the primary worship services are outreach and evangelistic tools,

while more mature Christians are offered deeper worship experiences in smaller settings. Commitment to the church runs high among a few adherents, and more are drawn into that inner circle through the popular public worship services that often attract hundreds if not thousands. The theological defense of seeker-sensitive worship is that God is glorified in building up his kingdom on earth, and increasingly secular and pagan city dwellers and suburbanites simply will not darken the doors of churches that worship with ancient rites in minor keys and whose ceremonies are exotic and foreign to them. Continuity with ancient and Reformation patterns of church life and worship are less important to the leaders of the evangelical seeker-sensitive church movement than evangelism and growth.

All evangelicals agree that worship's primary purpose is to glorify God. How is God glorified in worship? What kind of worship glorifies God? These are the questions that give rise to diversity among evangelicals. Traditionalists argue that God is most glorified in historically rooted Christian rituals and in confessionally disciplined leadership that provides clear boundaries around the worshiping community. God is glorified when the worship of the church is distinctively Christian and not accommodated to the demands and desires of constantly changing culture. God is glorified when human fulfillment is regarded as secondary to praise and when that fulfillment is seen as arriving precisely in submission to the traditions of the church. Pentecostal-charismatics argue that God is most glorified in Spirit-filled worship that is flexible, spontaneous, and open to everyone, regardless of confessional boundaries. The unity of the Spirit transcends the unities of strict confessional identity and historic episcopacy. Renewal rather than discipline glorifies God. Seeker-sensitive evangelicals argue that God is most glorified in evangelistic growth and expansion of the gospel of the *kingdom of God* into culture.

Marva J. Dawn, *Reaching Out without Dumbing Down: A Theology of Worship for the Turn-of-the-Century Culture* (Grand Rapids: Wm. B. Eerdmans, 1995); D. G. Hart and John R. Muether, *With Reverence and Awe: Returning to the Heart of Reformed Worship* (Phillipsburg, NJ: Presbyterian & Reformed, 2002); Jack W. Hayford, *Worship His Majesty: How Praising the King of Kings Will Change Your Life* (Ventura, CA: Regal Books, 2000); Robert E. Webber, *Ancient-Future Faith: Rethinking Evangelicalism for a Postmodern World* (Grand Rapids: Baker Books, 1999); J. Rodman Williams, *Renewal Theology: The Church, the Kingdom, and Last Things* (Grand Rapids: Zondervan, 1992).

Issues in
Evangelical Theology

Arminianism   *see*
Calvinism/Arminianism

Baptism of the Holy Spirit/Gifts of the Holy Spirit   Evangelical theologians and leaders have long disagreed among themselves about the existence and nature of a so-called baptism of the Holy Spirit as a "second definite work of grace" after *conversion*. They have also argued over the *supernatural* gifts of the *Holy Spirit* sometimes known as the charismata. The latter include supernatural healings, speaking in tongues, prophecy, and *miracles*. Although these *experiences* and manifestations are usually associated with *Pentecostalism* and the *charismatic movement*, they and the controversy about them predate the twentieth century and those specific movements that arose during it. As there are numerous specific theological and spiritual positions held about the baptism of the Holy Spirit (sometimes referred to as the infilling of the Spirit) and the supernatural gifts of the Spirit, we will here have to generalize and simplify; it will be impossible to discuss all the diverse views held about them among evangelicals.

Some evangelicals believe that after conversion to Christ (including *regeneration* and *justification*) by *grace* through *repentance* and *faith*, a person may experience a "second blessing" or second definite work of grace that propels him or her into a higher dimension of Christian life. (A few evangelicals believe in three blessings or definite works of grace, but it will not be possible to deal with that minority view here.) Some of those who believe in a second definite work of grace known as baptism of the Holy Spirit believe it is always accompanied by the phenomenon of speaking in unknown tongues. They are Pentecostals. (Some charismatics also believe it.) Other evangelicals believe in only one instantaneous and definite work of grace, and that is Christian initiation as conversion; they identify conversion-regeneration with the baptism

of the Holy Spirit. Some evangelicals believe that all the gifts of the Holy Spirit mentioned in the New Testament (e.g., in 1 Cor. 12) are available to Spirit-filled Christians today; other evangelicals believe that some of the supernatural gifts of the Spirit, such as speaking in tongues and healing, ceased in the first century and have not been available since the apostles died and all of inspired *Scripture* was written. The latter view is known as cessationism.

The identification of a second blessing after conversion began among followers of John Wesley in the late eighteenth and early nineteenth centuries. Two of the most important figures in Methodism in the late eighteenth century were John Fletcher and Joseph Benson. Fletcher especially influenced North American Methodism and its offshoots through his writings about *sanctification* and the Holy Spirit. Wesley had taught the doctrine of *entire sanctification* and this was interpreted by some of his followers—and especially Fletcher—as an instantaneous eradication of the sinful nature by means of an experience of "receiving the Holy Ghost." Unlike Wesley, Fletcher and some other of Wesley's followers distinguished between believers "baptized with the Pentecostal power of the Holy Ghost" (a reference to the day of Pentecost birth of the *church* recorded in Acts 2) and those Christian believers who are not yet filled with that power (like the apostles before the day of Pentecost). Ever since Fletcher, a significant minority of evangelicals have held that distinction and emphasized and promoted an experience of enduement with power from the Holy Spirit subsequent to conversion, in which believers receive the power of the Holy Spirit for supernatural spiritual service to *Jesus Christ* and the church. For them, all Christians are indwelt by the Holy Spirit, but only some Christians are filled with the Holy Spirit.

During the nineteenth century, this view of Christian initiation as involving two steps and stages caught on among followers of the *Holiness movement* and, later, among some followers of the *Keswick movement*. The Holiness movement was an offshoot of Methodism among American revivalists that gave rise to a variety of new denominations, including the large Church of the Nazarene and the smaller Wesleyan and Free Methodist groups. The Keswick movement was a "higher Christian life" movement among Christians, first in Great Britain and then in North America, who did not believe in instantaneous entire sanctification as eradication of the sinful nature (the hallmark of the Holiness movement) but did believe in a higher (or deeper) experience of entire consecration of life to God. By the beginning of the twentieth century, some influential evangelical speakers, educators, writers, and evangelists were promoting the experience of baptism of the Holy Spirit as a second definite blessing after conversion for all true Christians. They included A. B. Simpson, R. A. Torrey, and J. Wilbur Chapman. Nineteenth-century revivalists *Charles Finney* and D. L. Moody both had laid the foundation for this wider movement of "second blessing Christianity" by embracing a two-stage interpretation of Christian experience.

The Pentecostal movement burst on the American evangelical scene in the first decade of the twentieth century. Its hallmark is the doctrine and experience of speaking in unknown tongues (glossolalia) as the "initial physical evidence" of the baptism of the Holy Spirit. According to classical Pentecostals (as distinct from charismatics), only persons who speak in tongues like the apostles on the day of Pentecost are genuinely filled with the Holy Sprit. The second blessing is always accompanied by that sign. This is the distinctive teaching of Pentecostal denominations such as the Assemblies of God, Church of God in Christ, Church of God (Cleveland, Tennessee), and the International Church of the Foursquare Gospel. The Pentecostal doctrine and practice split the movement of higher-life Christians in Amer-

ica. A. B. Simpson criticized it, as did many other evangelical leaders. The Holiness movement split over it. The Pentecostal Church of the Nazarene, founded in 1905, dropped the word *Pentecostal* after the Azusa Street Revival of 1906 that gave impetus to the budding Pentecostal movement. Many evangelicals refused not only the classical Pentecostal emphasis on speaking in tongues but also the entire distinction between two blessings of Christian initiation. The vast majority of evangelicals have always identified Spirit baptism with conversion-regeneration and taught that all true Christians are filled with the Spirit of God.

Pentecostalism did not invent or rediscover the supernatural gifts of the Holy Spirit; throughout the nineteenth century many revivalists prayed for divine healing of sick bodies. The entire Holiness movement believes in and practices prayer for physical healing. However, most evangelicals—including Holiness revivalists—have believed that speaking in tongues, prophecy (except as powerful preaching of the gospel), and miracles (i.e., ability to work miracles by faith) ceased when the early church emerged out of its infancy after the deaths of the apostles and the completion of the canon of Scripture. Princeton evangelical theologian *Benjamin Breckenridge Warfield* wrote essays attacking Pentecostalism's "counterfeit miracles" and argued for cessation of the supernatural gifts of the Spirit after the first century. *Dispensationalist* evangelicals relegated supernatural signs and wonders—including speaking in unknown tongues—to the age of the early church.

During the first decade of the twentieth century, however, Pentecostalism brought about a new awareness of and emphasis on the present-day reality of supernatural experiences and manifestations of the Holy Spirit. It teaches that every Spirit-filled Christian receives one or more gifts of the Holy Spirit, in addition to speaking in tongues, as the sign of Spirit baptism. (Classical Pentecostals distinguish between two kinds of speaking in tongues: the sign and the gift. The sign is a *"prayer* language" unknown to the person praying and is universal among Spirit-filled Christians; the gift is a specific gift of the Holy Spirit for only some Spirit-filled believers and is for the edification of the church. When exercised in the church, the gift of speaking in tongues must be accompanied by a manifestation of the gift of interpretation of tongues.) Pentecostals simply reject the arguments of cessationists; they find no convincing biblical basis for it. They find that their own experience fits with New Testament narratives—especially in the book of the Acts of the Apostles—and teachings about the Holy Spirit, Christian initiation, and the Spirit's gifts (e.g., in 1 Cor. 12 and 14).

Especially dispensationalist, fundamentalist evangelical theologians have been harshly critical of both the doctrine of a second baptism of the Holy Spirit after conversion (which is not unique to Pentecostals) and the Pentecostal interpretation and practice of the gifts of the Spirit. Conservative evangelical preacher John MacArthur's book *Charismatic Chaos* (Grand Rapids: Zondervan, 1992) well represents the hard-line cessationist attack on these ideas and practices. Other evangelical critics have also sought to undermine the doctrines of a Spirit baptism subsequent to conversion and of speaking in tongues as the sine qua non of fullness of the Holy Spirit. A classical scholarly critique of both is Presbyterian evangelical theologian Frederick Dale Bruner's *A Theology of the Holy Spirit* (Grand Rapids: Wm. B. Eerdmans, 1970). Like many other evangelical critics of higher-life Evangelicalism and Pentecostalism, Bruner points out that the New Testament affirms only one baptism of the Spirit and equates that with the reception of the Holy Spirit at conversion. Although believers in the subsequence of the baptism of the Holy Spirit—including classical Pentecostals, with their distinctive views about speaking in tongues and supernatural gifts of the Holy

Spirit—are now the fastest-growing part of the postfundamentalist evangelical coalition, they are regarded by the majority of evangelical theologians as holding a false interpretation of the Holy Spirit and Christian initiation. Rarely, however, does one hear non-Pentecostal evangelicals condemning them as fanatics, "holy rollers," or demonically deluded, as happened in the past. Only the most conservative fundamentalists—a tiny minority of evangelicals—continue to criticize and shun Pentecostals in that manner, which was once common.

Donald W. Dayton, *Theological Roots of Pentecostalism* (Grand Rapids: Zondervan, 1987); Vinson Synan, ed., *The Century of the Holy Spirit: 100 Years of Pentecostal and Charismatic Renewal* (Nashville: Thomas Nelson, 2001); Max Turner, *The Holy Spirit and Spiritual Gifts* (Peabody, MA: Hendrickson Publishers, 1996).

Boundaries of Evangelicalism   A

recurring controversy among evangelical theologians and leaders centers around the issue of Evangelicalism's identity, sometimes framed as a debate about the movement's boundaries. The 2001 annual international meeting of the *Evangelical Theological Society* in Colorado Springs, Colorado, dealt with this issue as its central theme. Several plenary addresses and seminar presentations contributed to the ongoing evangelical scholarly debate about the limits of evangelical *theology*. This was not the first time evangelical theologians and leaders have engaged in such examination of evangelical identity and flexibility, unity and diversity. The whole fundamentalist controversy of the early decades of the twentieth century had the same problem as its focus: What are the "fundamentals" (essentials) of authentic Christianity (Evangelicalism)?

The debate in its different forms and stages always is sparked by some perceived threat to evangelical identity. The early fundamentalists felt authentic

Christianity was being threatened by creeping liberal Protestant theology and higher criticism of the *Bible*. Later, separatistic fundamentalists believed Evangelicalism was being undermined by conservative Protestants who would not abandon mainline denominations and who accommodated to modern science (theistic evolution and progressive *creationism*) and secularism. In the 1970s postfundamentalist Evangelicalism was divided by controversy over the *inerrancy* of the Bible. A "battle for the Bible" was launched by conservative evangelicals who were scandalized by abandonment of inerrancy by some progressive evangelicals. In the 1990s and first years of the twenty-first century, some conservative evangelicals perceived a threat to evangelical orthodoxy in the rise of *open theism*—the belief that *God's* knowledge of the future is self-limited because of human *free will*. This led to the 2001 consideration of evangelical boundaries by the Evangelical Theological Society, which declared by means of a resolution that evangelical theology affirms God's unlimited foreknowledge. In effect, open theism was ruled out of bounds for authentic evangelicals by the voting members of the society. (Only a minority of the society's members voted on the resolution.) Other evangelicals, however, disagreed and continue to press for greater inclusion of minority theological perspectives among evangelicals. Some object to the concept of definite boundaries to evangelical theology and argue instead for identification of evangelical Christianity by its center and not by boundaries.

The problematic underlying the continuous debate among evangelicals over boundaries is the movement's lack of a magisterium. There is no headquarters of Evangelicalism, no evangelical equivalent of the Roman Catholic Sacred Congregation for the Doctrine of the Faith. There certainly is no evangelical pope. Of course, that is true of Protestantism in general, but many Protestant denominations have developed confessional statements and required candidates for ordination and professors of theology to swear an oath of allegiance to them. No such magisterium—formal or informal, human or written—unites all evangelicals. Evangelicalism is a movement and not an organization; it is a loose coalition and network of diverse Christian churches, ministries, institutions, and organizations with certain common concerns.

The issue of evangelical boundaries arises when an individual evangelical or group of evangelicals decides that some other individual or group among evangelicals is guilty of heresy and wishes to demonstrate to evangelicals with power (administrators, publishers and editors, influential executives of evangelical organizations) that limits have been transgressed and someone should be excluded (fired or not hired, not published, generally blackballed within the coalition). Of course, individual evangelical organizations such as the *National Association of Evangelicals* and the Evangelical Theological Society set their own boundaries and use them in making decisions about membership. But these do not decide the identity or boundaries of authentic Evangelicalism for everyone. Nevertheless, many evangelical leaders look to them for general guidance in deciding what evangelical boundaries may be. Some evangelical colleges, for example, wish to hire only evangelical faculty members. Who are they? The colleges' administrators may watch decisions about evangelical boundaries being made by the NAE, ETS, and other evangelical organizations. But there is no central group of leaders who meet even occasionally to determine evangelical boundaries. Some have attempted to speak on behalf of all evangelicals, but they are usually greeted with strong dissent by others.

The only semieffective appeal in determining evangelical boundaries is to "the received evangelical tradition." One attempt to identify this rather amorphous phenomenon (beliefs, practices), edited by evangelical theologian Kenneth Kantzer, was *Evangelical Affirmations* (Grand Rapids: Zondervan, 1990), a volume of essays on evangelical doctrines and themes by a variety of evangelical scholars. There have been other, briefer, attempts to identify and gain wide agreement about evangelical identity and boundaries, including Celebration of the Gospel, a statement published in *Christianity Today* in 1999. It was signed by numerous evangelical scholars, but many others declined to sign it, citing its heavily Reformed (Calvinistic) tone and its exclusion of certain minority opinions (e.g., *inclusivism* of salvation) as incompatible with authentic evangelical *faith*.

Some evangelical theologians believe it is possible to distill and identify a set of beliefs that constitute "the received evangelical tradition" out of the writings of the sixteenth-century Reformers, later Protestant orthodox thinkers, and nineteenth- and twentieth-century conservative Protestants. Often, however, these accounts of the received evangelical tradition appear to be biased toward some particular strain of evangelical theology, such as the Old School *Princeton Theology* of Charles Hodge and *B. B. Warfield*. Strains more associated with the Anabaptist, *Holiness*, and Pentecostal movements often are neglected, if not totally ignored, in such accounts. This has led to a debate between those evangelicals who regard authentic Evangelicalism as normatively Reformed (in the broad sense of deriving from the magisterial Protestant heritage) and those who regard it as normatively revivalist. Evangelical historian Donald W. Dayton has dubbed these two accounts of Evangelicalism's essence the "Presbyterian paradigm" and the "Pentecostal paradigm." They could also be labeled the Puritan paradigm and the Pietist paradigm. The latter approach tends to view evangelical boundaries less in terms of theological correctness (orthodoxy) than in terms of experience (orthopathy) and is uncomfortable with

firm boundaries that exclude people using strict doctrinal tests.

For much of its existence the post–World War II postfundamentalist evangelical alliance has been held together by the dominating influence of *Billy Graham*, who—while never rejecting the importance of doctrine—tended to emphasize the importance of the *experience* of *conversion* and love of the Bible as the hallmarks of authentic evangelical Christianity. With Graham's gradual retirement in the late twentieth century and early twenty-first century, the evangelical movement may be entering an identity crisis. Discussion of evangelical identity and boundaries is heating up as never before. Every creative and innovative proposal for reconsideration and reconstruction of traditional interpretations of doctrine is met by a conservative response that seeks to exclude; this is greeted by a reaction that decries the narrowing of boundaries, because they are always identified in terms of some particular strain of evangelical life and thought. In 2002 a group of 110 evangelical scholars and leaders signed a document, entitled "The Word Made Fresh: A Call for a Renewal of the Evangelical Spirit," intended to counter the Evangelical Theological Society's 2001 attempt to marginalize or exclude open theism and to caution against future attempts to narrow the boundaries of evangelical theology. The statement called for greater openness to nontraditional views within evangelical theological circles and for an irenic spirit among those who feel compelled to debate them.

Many *progressive* evangelicals believe that Evangelicalism (as distinct from a particular denomination or organization) does not need definite, identifiable *boundaries* such as "inerrancy" (which is one example of an often proposed boundary); they suggest that such a loose affiliation needs only a strong *center* of common commitment and experience. With such a powerful center of gravity, the boundaries can be fluid and flexible. All evangelicals agree that commitment to the supreme *authority* of Scripture (under God) as God's uniquely inspired written Word is a part of such an enriched center. Not all agree that inerrancy or even plenary verbal *inspiration* is a valid boundary of authentic evangelical faith. Some conservative evangelicals would like substitutionary *atonement* to be a boundary of evangelical theology; others reject that as a definite boundary, but affirm that commitment to *salvation* through the cross of *Jesus Christ* is part of Evangelicalism's core and that various (not all) theories of the atonement are compatible with it.

Donald G. Bloesch, *The Future of Evangelical Christianity: A Call for Unity amid Diversity* (Garden City, NY: Doubleday & Co., 1983); Gary Dorrien, *The Remaking of Evangelical Theology* (Louisville, KY: Westminster John Knox Press, 1998); Stanley J. Grenz, *Renewing the Center: Evangelical Theology in a Post-Theological Age* (Grand Rapids: Baker Academic, 2000).

Calvinism/Arminianism   When the postfundamentalist evangelical coalition emerged in the 1940s and 1950s, a conscious decision was made to include both Calvinists (persons of the Reformed theological persuasion) and Arminians (persons who believe in *freedom of the will* and reject unconditional predestination) on an equal basis. Some of the founders of the coalition were raised as Arminians (e.g., within the Wesleyan *Holiness movement*), and others were raised as Calvinists. Some converted from one to the other earlier in life. The *National Association of Evangelicals* has included both theological persuasions since its founding; among its first member denominations were Pentecostal and Wesleyan-Holiness denominations, as well as traditionally Reformed-Calvinist denominations.

This cooperation was a relatively new development in the history of evangelical Protestant Christianity, which had been divided between these two theological parties since the eighteenth-century Great Awakening, during which John Wesley and his fellow Methodist evangelist George Whitefield went their separate ways, due to firmly expressed differences about the nature of divine sovereignty and the freedom of the human will in matters pertaining to *salvation*. Wesley affirmed an Arminian position, while Whitefield viewed the Calvinist position as more biblical. Throughout the nineteenth century Calvinist and Arminian evangelicals tended to remain separate. During the early twentieth-century *fundamentalist movement*, some Calvinists and Arminians found common cause in fighting liberal *theology* and evolution.

The founders of the postfundamentalist evangelical alliance in the 1940s decided it was high time to overcome this deep division among equally God-fearing, Bible-believing, Jesus-loving Protestant Christians. That is not to say, however, that the debate died out completely. Most evangelical theologians are committed to one historic Protestant perspective regarding God's sovereignty and salvation to the exclusion of the other. Many would admit that the other party is evangelical, but many would also claim that the other's theology is defectively evangelical. The old debate between Wesley and Whitefield (which was also between other Great Awakening evangelists and theologians) has resurfaced from time to time among twentieth-century evangelicals and threatens to continue to divide evangelicals into the twenty-first century.

The roots of this internecine evangelical rivalry between two theological orientations go back to the early seventeenth century in Holland. There a Protestant theologian named Jacob Arminius (d. 1609) openly quarreled with a colleague at the University of Leiden over the doctrines of unconditional *election*, limited *atonement*, and irresistible *grace*. Arminius strongly denied these distinctives of Calvinist theology and was harshly criticized for it by many

Protestant theologians and political leaders of Holland and other Protestant countries. The controversy continued after Arminius's death; some of his followers published a document called The Remonstrance (they were called the Remonstrants) that rejected five points of classical Calvinist theology: total depravity, unconditional election, limited atonement, irresistible grace, and perseverance of the saints, later remembered using the acrostic TULIP.

The Reformed ministers and theologians responded at the Synod of Dort (1618–19) by affirming these as orthodox and condemning the Remonstrants as heretics. Arminian theology spread to Great Britain and North America, where it was opposed by the Puritans. The first Baptist communities were divided by this controversy. The General Baptists embraced Arminian theology of universal atonement and free will while the Particular Baptists confessed Calvinist doctrines. Presbyterians and most Congregationalists have been on the Reformed side of the debate. Methodism and its offshoot Holiness and Pentecostal groups have been solidly Arminian. Many evangelical denominations rooted in European *Pietism*, such as the Swedish Covenant and Free Mission movements (now the Evangelical Covenant Church and the Evangelical Free Church of America), decided to allow both Arminianism and Calvinism within their ranks.

The uneasy truce between Calvinists and Arminians within the postfundamentalist evangelical coalition after World War II broke down from time to time. Very rarely has the old polemical label "heresy" been hurled by either side at the other, but occasionally spokespersons for each side have indicated strong and lively disagreement with the other side. Most of the rhetoric of exclusion or marginalization has come against Arminianism by Calvinist evangelicals. In response, some Arminians have raised their voices in harsh criticism of Calvinism.

One eruption of this recurring controversy occurred in the 1990s with the founding of two organizations of Reformed evangelical theologians: the Southern Baptist Founders Conference and the Alliance of Confessing Evangelicals. The former sought to return Southern Baptists to their alleged Calvinist roots; the latter is a multidenominational organization to promote classical magisterial Protestant orthodoxy, including a strong belief in divine sovereignty. Most of its movers and shakers are Calvinists. Members of the Alliance promulgated "The Cambridge Declaration," which unequivocally identified authentic evangelical faith with the sovereignty of God's grace in salvation and rejected Arminian belief in cooperation of the human will with grace in salvation. One influential evangelical speaker and writer declared that Arminianism was "barely Christian" and that was due only to a "felicitous inconsistency" (between affirmation of God's sovereignty and salvation by grace alone on the one hand and belief in human free will on the other hand).

Arminian evangelicals responded coolly to these assaults on the authenticity of their evangelical status. One evangelical author penned an article for *Christianity Today* with the title "Don't Hate Me Because I'm an Arminian" (September 6, 1999). Because Reformed theology is widely considered normative for evangelical theology by leading evangelical thinkers and administrators, many Arminians do not use that label, preferring instead to call themselves "moderately Reformed" (which Arminius considered himself) or to avoid either label. Many Calvinist evangelicals prefer to call their theology Reformed, as they do not view it as exclusively linked with one sixteenth-century Protestant Reformer. The debate between these two camps of evangelical theologians is likely to continue to ebb and flow as long as the evangelical coalition lasts.

David Basinger and Randall Basinger, eds., *Predestination and Free Will: Four Views of Divine Sovereignty and Human*

Freedom (Downers Grove, IL: InterVarsity Press, 1986); Michael S. Horton, "Evangelical Arminians: Option or Oxymoron?" *Modern Reformation* 1, no. 3 (May/June, 1992); Douglas Jacobsen, "The Calvinist-Arminian Dialectic in Evangelical Hermeneutics," *Christian Scholar's Review* 23 (spring 1993); Alan P. F. Sell, *The Great Debate: Calvinism, Arminianism, and Salvation* (Grand Rapids: Baker Book House, 1982).

Creation/Evolution   Ever since shortly after Charles Darwin published his theory of natural selection (macroevolution) and applied it not only to nonhuman animals but also to humans in *The Descent of Man* (1871), conservative Protestants in North America have debated whether it is compatible with belief in the *authority* of Scripture and with Christian orthodoxy. Evangelicals have always been concerned with both of those norms and thus have debated *creation* and evolution throughout most of the twentieth century. During the late nineteenth century evangelical responses to evolution were not uniform. Charles Hodge of Princeton Theological Seminary was set against evolution and declared it incompatible with the Christian doctrine of creation.

On the other hand, Hodge's successor as professor of theology at Princeton, *Benjamin Breckenridge Warfield*, who was trained in the natural sciences, believed it was possible to reconcile evolution and creation so long as the former was not naturalistic. That is, according to Warfield, so long as evolutionary theory did not rule *God* out of the picture of creation, it could be consistent with Genesis and the orthodox Christian belief in creation. God would simply be seen as working in and through processes that appear to be natural to the investigative scientist. The Christian—including Christian scientists—would see those processes as activities of God. The great turn-of-the-century Baptist theologian *Augustus Hopkins Strong* of Rochester Theological Seminary agreed with War-

field's assessment of evolution and creation and attempted to explicate evolution in terms of God's (and Christ's) immanence within the world of nature.

Thus arose within evangelical Christianity a strain of theistic evolution—an attempt to reinterpret the doctrine of creation (including human origins) as involving aeons of divine activity in and through the process of natural selection. Warfield, Strong, and other theistic evolutionists believed that evolution, stripped of naturalistic biases, could support belief in intelligent design within creation. In other words, for them it had apologetic value.

Not all conservative Protestants in America agreed with Warfield, Strong, and other theistic evolutionists. The *fundamentalist movement*, which grew out of conservative Protestant orthodoxy in reaction to liberal theology, in the 1920s began a crusade against "godless evolution." The two leading fundamentalist ministers in America, J. Frank Norris of Texas and William Bell Riley of Minnesota, were pastors of large, influential, archconservative Baptist congregations. They and their fundamentalist friends and followers began to link opposition to evolution with belief in the *Bible* and with traditional Protestant orthodoxy. Riley hosted antievolution meetings at his church and invited a leading fundamentalist of the day—politician William Jennings Bryan—to speak. In the early 1920s Riley's and Norris's antievolution show went on the road and attracted a great deal of attention.

Many people began to equate opposition to evolution with fundamentalism. In 1925 the famous Scopes "monkey trial" in Dayton, Tennessee, was widely viewed as a contest between secular and progressive thought (liberal theology, science, the American Civil Liberties Union, and agnostics like prosecuting attorney Clarence Darrow) and fundamentalism (Bryan and conservative preachers around the country). The trial was the first event broadcast live nationwide on radio. The outcome was a devastating public relations blow to fundamentalism. Afterwards, fundamentalists began to develop a separate subculture in America that would be untouched by godless evolution and secular ridicule, such as was heaped on them by popular columnist H. L. Mencken. From 1925 on, fundamentalists strongly opposed evolution and called for authentic Christians to resist and condemn all attempts to reconcile the Christian doctrine of creation with evolution.

The evolution versus creation controversy entered into the postfundamentalist evangelical scene in spite of attempts to squelch it. Many postfundamentalist evangelical leaders and theologians believed it was counterproductive and sought to allow within the evangelical coalition a range of opinions about the nature of God's creative activity and evolution. In his classic evangelical treatment of the subject, *The Christian View of Science and Scripture* (Grand Rapids: Wm. B. Eerdmans, 1954), evangelical theologian **Bernard Ramm** tried to quench the fires of the debates over the age of the earth, evolution, and the proper interpretation of Genesis 1–3. He warned fundamentalists and conservative evangelicals who wished to impose antievolutionism and young-earth creationism on all evangelicals that it is just as possible to sin to the right as to the left. He argued that the Genesis accounts of creation are open to a variety of valid interpretations and that equally orthodox and evangelical Christians can legitimately disagree about evolution, so long as they do not accommodate to the philosophy of naturalism, which reduces life to chemistry. Ramm set the tone for many evangelicals by urging that the heat of this controversy be cooled and that evangelicals enter fully into the natural sciences and not demonize them. For his own part, Ramm endorsed a mediating view of creation and life's origins called "progressive creationism."

Among evangelicals in the twentieth century, one finds three main views of creation and how best to reconcile the biblical narratives of creation with modern geological evidence and evolutionary theory. No evangelical believes in evolutionary naturalism, which is tantamount to atheism. The three views are special creationist theism (sometimes known as young-earth creationism or scientific creationism), evolutionary theism (described by one evangelical science professor as "fully gifted creation"), and progressive creationism.

Special creationist theism is promoted by several conservative evangelical institutions and organizations, including the Creation Science Research Institute, which grew out of the work of scientist Henry Morris and theologian John Whitcomb, who coauthored two books in the 1960s and 1970s that attempted to demonstrate the scientific credentials for belief in a young earth (created only about ten thousand years ago). The two books were *The Genesis Flood* (Grand Rapids: Baker, 1979) and *Scientific Creationism* (Waco, TX: Word, 1974). According to Morris, Whitcomb, and other so-called scientific creationists, the Bible and objective scientific evidence (stripped of controlling naturalistic assumptions and methods) point to a world created in a relatively short time (perhaps a literal week of six days of twenty-four hours each) only a few thousand years ago (as they believe a literal interpretation of Genesis indicates). The geological evidence of great age can be accounted for by the catastrophic universal flood of Noah's time recorded in Genesis. Young-earth creationists tend to believe and argue that this is the only view of creation compatible with a biblically serious Christianity; all other views are wholly unnecessary and perhaps heretical accommodations with godless evolution. Many other evangelicals believe young-earth creationism amounts to obscurantism with regard to modern scientific evidence and that it interprets the biblical creation narratives too literally.

The opposite option within evangelical *theology* is *theistic evolution*. Though not particularly popular within evangelical theology, it has always had its defenders among evangelical scientists, including many in the American Scientific Affiliation, a large and influential organization of natural scientists (all with earned doctorates) committed to biblical authority. One evangelical defender of theistic evolution is Calvin College science professor Howard J. Van Till, whose books, including *The Fourth Day: What the Bible and the Heavens Are Telling Us about Creation* (Grand Rapids: Wm. B. Eerdmans, 1986), have created controversy within evangelical circles because of the author's scientific and theological perspective on God's creative activity through evolutionary processes. According to Van Till, science and Scripture together confirm that God created the world in an unformed state and instilled in it every necessary capacity for "self-organization" and "transformation." Life evolved through a process very much like Darwin's natural selection, but its emergence was not an accident. It was the natural outworking of impulses planted in nature by the Creator. Many evangelicals, especially fundamentalists, believe this is not an adequate account of *humanity's* unique status of being created in the *image of God*. They insist on a special creation of humans if not of nonhuman life forms.

The middle way within evangelical theology, *progressive creationism*, combines some elements of special creationist theism and theistic evolution. Progressive creationism, championed by evangelical theologian Bernard Ramm, finds many adherents among evangelical theologians. It is simply the belief that the age of the earth is irrelevant to evangelical orthodoxy and that God's creative activity must have taken place through both processes and special creative acts. It leaves open the details for science to fill in. It rejects a naturalistic interpretation of creation and argues that although processes guided by natural law (e.g., natural selection) may account for the appearance of some

life forms, they cannot exhaustively explain the emergence of humanity. Occasionally God had to "step into" the processes and create something de novo (completely new—not emergent from something already existing). (Of course, progressive creationist evangelicals know full well that "step into" is metaphorical language; God is always already intimately involved in nature. "Step into" simply designates a new act that goes beyond sustaining and guiding processes already in motion.) According to Ramm and other progressive creationists, this view of the origins of life and the emergence of species integrates the undeniable facts of evolution with the authoritative affirmations of Scripture and is fully consistent with biblical, historic Christian orthodoxy. Of course, in order to make this work, progressive creationist evangelicals must interpret the creation narratives nonliterally, while at the same time taking them very seriously. They must also resist the temptation to accept Darwinian and neo-Darwinian accounts of the evolution of species without significant adjustments in the light of theological and hermeneutical necessities. Progressive creationism is satisfying neither to young-earth creationists, who view it as too close to theistic evolution, nor to theistic evolutionists, who regard it as too close to young-earth creationism.

David N. Livingstone, *Darwin's Forgotten Defenders* (Grand Rapids: Wm. B. Eerdmans, 1987); Bernard Ramm, *The Christian View of Science and Scripture* (Grand Rapids: Wm. B. Eerdmans, 1954); Del Ratzch, *The Battle of Beginnings* (Downers Grove, IL: InterVarsity Press, 1996).

Ecumenism/Separatism   One of the oldest and most heated debates among fundamentalists and evangelicals in the twentieth century was over the issue of separation from mainline, historic Protestant denominations and from all doctrinal impurity. Here, ecumenism designates evangelical catholic-ity—the belief in the universality of the true *church* and desire for unity among all authentic Christians. Separatism describes evangelical sectarianism—the desire for purity of doctrine above, and even against, unity of Christians. All evangelicals believe in both *unity* and *truth* and at least pay lip service to both the oneness of Christ's Body, the church of *Jesus Christ*, and doctrinal cor-rectness. The debate within Evangelical-ism has revolved around the issue of whether the mainline, historic Protestant denominations are apostate or on the precipice of apostasy, or whether they are flawed but redeemable.

Many, if not most, of the evangelical denominations in America were founded as a result of some serious dissatisfaction with a mainline Protestant denomina-tion. During the nineteenth and early twentieth centuries, many *Holiness* groups broke away from the Metho-dist Episcopal Church (the ancestor of today's United Methodist Church, which is a union of the Methodist Episcopal Church and the Evangelical United Brethren Church). They believed it had fallen into "lukewarm" spirituality and theological ambiguity. They wanted to reemphasize the Wesleys' doctrines of *conversion* and *sanctification*. During the twentieth century the Northern Baptist Convention (now known as the American Baptist Churches, U.S.A.) splintered into numerous smaller Baptist conventions and conferences over issues related to liberal *theology* and *funda-mentalism*. Most of the newer Baptist denominations believed the older North-ern Baptist Convention had become infected by liberal theology. New Presby-terian denominations have emerged out of the mainline Presbyterian churches over the same issues, and Lutherans have also been affected by this fragmen-tation process. In almost every case, the reason for the founding of the new evan-gelical denomination had to do with alleged doctrinal drift toward liberalism within the parent organization.

Throughout the 1920s and 1930s fun-damentalists loudly promoted "biblical separationism" from all liberal, secular, and heretical teachings and practices and argued that all of the historic, main-line Protestant denominations were infected with them. Some evangelicals wanted to stay within their denomina-tions and try to reform them. This was one of the reasons for the emergence of postfundamentalist Evangelicalism—the desire to at least allow evangelicals to remain in their mainline churches and work to reform them.

Many of the founders of the *National Association of Evangelicals* (NAE) in the 1940s were members and ministers of mainline Protestant bodies such as the American Congregational Churches (now part of the United Church of Christ after the merger with the Evangelical and Reformed Synod), the Northern Baptist Convention, the Presbyterian Church in the United States, and the Methodist Episcopal Church. Ironically, very early in its history the NAE voted to restrict membership to those denomina-tions not affiliated with the more liberal, mainline Federal Council of Churches (later called the National Council of Churches). Individuals and congrega-tions were allowed to hold membership in the NAE, even though their denomi-nations were barred because of their membership in the FCC. Some evangeli-cals have always suspected that this rule is evidence of lingering fundamentalism within the postfundamentalist coali-tion. Some individuals, churches, and denominations that call themselves evangelical could just as legitimately be called fundamentalist, except that the term has gradually been limited to those few conservative denominations and churches that eschew cooperation and fellowship even with the NAE and with *Billy Graham* and his ministries.

There are degrees of separatism among conservative Protestants, includ-ing evangelicals. During the 1990s one mainline Protestant denomination decided that it is both ecumenical and evangelical and began talks with the NAE toward membership, even though it is a longtime member of the National Council of Churches (NCC). In 2000 a new president of the NAE openly called for the abolition of the rule forbidding dual affiliation with his organization and the NCC. Within weeks of his announcement he was forced to resign. The NAE was not prepared to admit NCC-related denominations. On the other hand, the NAE has always been much more inclusive than its fundamentalist counterpart, the American Council of Christian Churches (also founded in the 1940s by Carl McIntire). In the 1990s it extended full membership to the Worldwide Church of God, founded by Herbert W. Armstrong. That group, long considered a cult by many evangelicals, after the founder's death shed its cultic aspects and embraced orthodox Christianity. Nevertheless, many people were surprised and even shocked by the NAE's embrace of a movement that continued to have some unusual (not heretical) practices and beliefs. The NAE includes approximately fifty denominations representing a wide variety of doctrinal orientations from Anabaptist to dispensationalist to Holiness to Pentecostal to Calvinist. The exclusion of the ecumenical and evangelical mainline Protestant denomination and the forced resignation of NAE's president convinced some moderate and progressive evangelicals that Evangelicalism has not yet fully emerged out of its fundamentalist background of separatism.

Catholic-ecumenical evangelicals, including *Donald G. Bloesch* and Robert Webber (longtime professor at Wheaton College), value the unity of the church and view Evangelicalism as a renewal movement within the larger universal church throughout the ages. They see no need to abandon mainline Protestant denominations so long as there is hope for their renewal. Bloesch, a minister of the United Church of Christ, taught for many years at a Presbyterian-related seminary. Webber, an Episcopalian, influ-

enced an entire generation of evangelicals to join him on the "Canterbury trail" toward the historic episcopacy. Both of them cherish the ancient and Reformation roots of evangelical Christianity and seek to retrieve and renew the Great Tradition of Christian teaching and *worship*. They eschew sectarianism that celebrates division from the historic churches and revels in separation. In 1977 Robert Webber and a group of forty evangelical scholars representing a number of denominations and theological traditions met to write a manifesto of catholic-ecumenical evangelical Christianity called "The Chicago Call." It proclaimed the importance of ancient Christian doctrinal and liturgical roots and decried a trend among evangelicals toward rootless, ahistorical Christianity. In 1994 groups of Roman Catholic and evangelical Protestant theologians met to write a document entitled "Evangelicals and Catholics Together," which recognized profound differences between their two branches of Christianity but agreed that both Roman Catholics and evangelical Protestants can be authentically Christian. That was followed by continuing dialogues between representatives of both groups with eventual agreement on the doctrine of *justification* by *grace* through *faith* alone.

Catholic-ecumenical Evangelicalism is rejected by many conservative evangelicals who believe that evangelical renewal must be carried out in separation from the historic mainline churches —both Catholic and Protestant. Separationist evangelicals—including all fundamentalists—value doctrinal purity (if not perfection) above continuity with the Great Tradition of historical, organized Christianity. For them, the true church is marked by apostolicity (continuing in the teaching of the New Testament apostles) and *holiness* more than by universality (catholicity). Some of them directed harsh criticism at the evangelical signers of the "Evangelicals and Catholics Together" document, on the ground that it ignored the issues that divided the church at the time of the Reformation and the differences that still exist between Roman Catholic theology and practice and Protestant faith and life. For separationist evangelicals, the motto is the biblical call to "come out from among them, and be separate" (2 Cor. 6:17). Even mainline Protestant organizations are regarded with strong suspicion because of their liberal theological tendencies and inclusiveness of diverse beliefs and practices.

Sometimes this suspicion extends to evangelical denominations, institutions, and ministries, insofar as they are allegedly insufficiently separated from Roman Catholicism and liberal, mainline Protestantism. A leading advocate of evangelical separation and even sectarianism was fundamentalist leader Carl McIntire (1906–2002), founder of the Bible Presbyterian Church, Faith Theological Seminary, and the American Council of Christian Churches. Together with other ultraconservative evangelicals and fundamentalists, he convinced many listeners and readers to view the entire ecumenical movement in all its forms and manifestations as apostate and even possibly communistic. Some less extreme conservative evangelicals reject McIntire's hard-core separationism (which shuns cooperation in Billy Graham evangelistic endeavors because of the cooperation of Catholics and mainline Protestants) but practice their own kind of separationism by means of humanly constructed walls of division that make fellowship with other evangelicals and the larger Christian world nearly impossible. For example, many conservative Baptist groups regard *premillennialism* as a hallmark of authentic biblical faith. One such denomination has a binding statement of faith in which the last article—on *eschatology* (last things; *return of Christ*)—is twice as long as any other article, including ones on *Scripture*, Christ, and *salvation*.

Two leading evangelical advocates of sectarian separationism were followers of fundamentalist leader William Bell Riley in Minnesota: Richard V. Clearwaters and Ernest D. Pickering. They founded and led Central Baptist Theological Seminary of Minneapolis after Riley's death and proclaimed the importance of evangelical separation from all doctrinal impurity and from secularism. For them, as for all separationists, Christian fellowship depends on knowledge of faithfulness. Ministers, evangelists, church organizations, and denominations suspected of being in fellowship with doctrinally unfaithful (heretical or apostate) ministers, evangelists, church organizations, or denominations are to be shunned. This policy was spelled out by Ernest Pickering in *Biblical Separation: The Struggle for a Pure Church* (Schaumburg, IL: Regular Baptist Press, 2001). Clearwaters's and Pickering's more moderate evangelical counterparts in the Conservative Baptist Association (CBA) (another split off from the Northern Baptist Convention) did not argue for separation so much as simply practice it, while gradually entering into the mainstream of evangelical life. The CBA and other conservative evangelical denominations practice organizational separation from liberal Protestantism, while cooperating with a broader spectrum of Protestants (than Clearwaters, Pickering, and their followers) in evangelistic and social causes.

Evangelicalism and evangelical theology have no unified perspective about the nature of the church or about ecumenical cooperation or separation. These matters are not heavily disputed within the evangelical coalition, and those who have very strong views about them generally do not participate in it. The implicit view of most evangelicals is demonstrated through their practice of forming distinctly evangelical denominations and churches apart from mainline Protestant groups and at the same time engaging in fellowship and cooperation with a variety of Christians—especially other evangelicals—beyond their own denominations. And yet many evangelicals hold on to their mainline

Protestant identities and church memberships and strive to reform their denominations and ecclesiastical organizations from within. Every major mainline Protestant denomination in America has at least one evangelical renewal group functioning within it.

Epistemology: Faith/Reason   One of the most controverted areas of evangelical thought is theological epistemology—how one knows the truth status of truth claims about *God*. Does theology have foundations? If so, what are they? What roles do *reason* and *faith* play in apprehending and demonstrating the truth of these foundations and the truth status of beliefs derived from them? Is there a general, natural knowledge of God? Or is true knowledge of God based only on special *revelation* and faith in God's Word? Can the existence of God and the *resurrection* of *Jesus Christ* be rationally proven? If so, how? If not, on what is belief in them based? These are some of the questions surrounding theological epistemology; many more could be mentioned.

In order to make this topic somewhat manageable, we will here focus on the issue of *apologetics*: justifying Christian truth claims. For the most part, evangelicals have been interested in vigorous Christian apologetics, and evangelical scholars have produced an avalanche of volumes on the subject during the movement's post–World War II existence. Some of these volumes, however, would best be described as polemics against apologetics. That is, not all evangelical scholars believe the apologetic endeavor is valid; some regard it as positively detrimental to authentic Christian faith. Others view it as essential to the task of following Christ's Great Commission to make disciples of the nations. Evangelical scholars fall into three main categories with regard to theological epistemology and apologetics: evidentialism, rational presuppositionalism, and fideistic revelationism. These are not always the terms used by the proponents of these approaches, but they well describe clearly discernible approaches to defending the truth of Christianity. There are other approaches, but most of them appear upon close inspection to be versions of one or more of these.

Evidentialism is without doubt the most popular approach to theological epistemology and apologetics among the evangelical laity. This is largely due to the influence and popularity of the writings of evangelical apologist Josh McDowell, whose two-volume *Evidence That Demands a Verdict* (San Bernadino, CA: Here's Life, 1972) has made a profound impact on popular Evangelicalism. According to McDowell and more philosophically sophisticated evangelical evidentialist apologists such as R. C. Sproul and John Gerstner, basic Christian truth claims can be demonstrated to be true by appeals to the observed facts of nature and history. While *sin* may cloud the human mind's objectivity, there is no fundamental ambiguity in the pattern of evidences that point to the existence of God, truth of the Christian Scriptures, and deity of Jesus Christ. Persons who look at the evidences for these Christian truth claims and do not conclude that the truth claims are true are simply not looking hard enough, or they are blinded by their moral preferences. That is, they choose not to be fully rational about these matters, because the conclusions they would have to draw would challenge their moral choices (e.g., not to repent and accept the lordship of Jesus Christ).

Evidentialists make use of the a posteriori arguments for the existence of God, which are the ones developed especially by medieval Catholic philosopher and theologian Thomas Aquinas. Thomas's "five ways" point to the necessity of God for the existence of the contingent world and for the teleological character of nature, which shows evidences of purpose and design. According to these arguments for God's existence, only the reality of God explains the phenomena of nature. Evidentialists also believe that the bodily resurrection of Jesus Christ can be demonstrated historically true to a high degree of probability. For them, it is true beyond a reasonable doubt. They point to the otherwise inexplicable birth of the Christian movement and to the Jerusalem authorities' failure to discover and display Jesus' dead body. Evangelical evidentialists believe that sufficient evidence for the truth of Christianity exists to require any rational person to believe; the only reason some do not believe after considering the evidence is that their judgment is clouded by sin and their preference for a life devoted to self and pleasure over a life dedicated to the mission and cause of Jesus Christ.

Evangelical *rational presuppositionalists* reject appeals to evidence as too weak to support the full truth of Christianity. Evidence at best yields probability; it cannot deliver certainty. Christian commitment demands certainty. Furthermore, presuppositionalists argue, evidence is always judged according to certain assumptions about reality; a person who presupposes that God does not exist will always find some way to explain away evidence for his existence. The so-called proofs of the existence of God rest on presuppositions about the nature of the world that cannot themselves be proven true. Furthermore, evidentialism fails to take seriously the cognitive damage caused by sin; sinful persons simply cannot discover God and Jesus Christ as Lord and Savior by means of investigation of evidences. As the Reformer John Calvin noted, the mind of the sinner is nothing but a factory of idols.

Rational presuppositionalism is the dominant view of theological epistemology and apologetics among evangelical scholars. (Evidentialism is much more popular in the pews and pulpits.) It takes several forms, but all share the belief that all thinking—including proving or justifying truth claims—begins with unprovable assumptions or "control beliefs." Reformed epistemologists such

as Nicholas Wolterstorff and Alvin Plantinga call these "properly basic beliefs," and they count among them belief in the reality of God. They argue that belief in God's existence is "properly basic" in the same way as belief that other minds exist. People are rationally justified in believing these things; proof is not required. Evangelical biblical presuppositionalists such as Cornelius Van Til, *Carl F. H. Henry*, and *E. J. Carnell* argued that not only the existence of God but also the *authority* of the *Bible* are rationally justified presuppositions. Every belief system (and belief systems are inescapable) begins with at least one unprovable authority. For Henry, Christianity begins with two basic axioms— the ontological axiom of the reality of a God who speaks and shows, and the epistemological axiom of the authority of divine revelation and especially the Christian Scriptures. The Christian can and must begin with these two assumptions and be guided by them throughout his or her thinking, but they are not incorrigible a priori assumptions. They stand the test of coherence. Persons are finally and fully justified in using them as control beliefs precisely because they fruitfully yield a comprehensive and coherent system of beliefs about the world that satisfactorily answers life's ultimate questions.

Evidentialists strongly disagree and have been known to label evangelical presuppositionalists "naked fideists." (That is, they claim that presuppositionalists believe by blind faith and discard reason.) Presuppositionalism is not fideism, however, because it does not appeal to a "leap of faith" to justify Christianity's truth claims; it appeals ultimately to the test of coherence (inner consistency). Christianity is true because it is the most coherent (and perhaps the only coherent) system of beliefs about reality. Most presuppositionalists would also argue that it fits the facts of experience better than any competing belief system. But they do not put much stock in "facts," as they are always "facts" only according to some belief system that begins with assumptions that are not simply factual in the ordinary sense of being experienced and demonstrable.

Fideistic revelationism is a term coined by evangelical theologian **Donald G. Bloesch** to describe his own preferred theological method and approach to apologetics, which is shared by a number of evangelicals. Evidentialists and rational presuppositionalists reject it as antithetical to the apologetic task because it does not appeal to reason but to faith or, more correctly, to the inner testimony of the **Holy Spirit**. Evangelical fideistic revelationists such as Bloesch reject evidentialism and rational presuppositionalism because they base the truth of Christianity on non-Christian foundations and thus subject Christianity's truth claims to secular, and therefore alien, criteria. Put bluntly, they drag Christianity before the bar of human reason and demand that it prove its credentials before it may be believed. Furthermore, fideistic revelationists argue, God's transcendence and human finiteness and fallenness make it impossible and even irreverent to demonstrate the truth of the *gospel* to human reason. Christian truth, they point out, is often packaged as paradox, which is anathema to the rationalisms of evidentialism and biblical presuppositionalism. In *The Ground of Certainty* (Grand Rapids: Wm. B. Eerdmans, 1970) and other books, Bloesch argues that the truth of Christianity is based on God alone and is apprehended by the human mind by the special influence of the Holy Spirit, which confirms as true the deposit of divine revelation in Holy Scripture. While empirical tests and the criterion of coherence may help someone come to believe in the gospel of Jesus Christ, they fall far short of establishing Christianity's gospel as true and may actually undermine its truth by forcing it to conform to secular standards of reason. Truth about God transcends secular reasoning; it is supernatural truth that cuts across ordinary human mental activity

and challenges persons to decide for or against it in a leap of faith. Bloesch and other evangelical fideists owe a great debt to the Danish philosopher Søren Kierkegaard, but they also appeal all the way back to Luther and Calvin, who eschewed objective reason in favor of the inner testimony of the Holy Spirit as the proper foundation for Christian belief.

In what sense, then, is fideistic revelationism a form of apologetics? Some argue that it is not. However, it argues that, once made, the leap of faith (which is actually a work of the Holy Spirit upon the mind and soul of the person who believes) turns out to be the entrance into a perspective on reality that illumines experience better than any other one. While this cannot be demonstrated empirically or logically, it is existentially experienced as true. Christian evangelists can point to their own experience and its cognitive advantages (e.g., satisfaction with regard to the meaning of life, etc.) and appeal to open-minded seekers to allow the Holy Spirit to give them inner certainty of the truth of the gospel as they repent, trust, and resolve to obey the gospel of Jesus Christ. The best apologetic, then, is intelligible and winsome witness to the gospel.

Steven B. Cowan, *Five Views on Apologetics* (Grand Rapids: Zondervan, 2000); Gordon R. Lewis, *Testing Christianity's Truth Claims* (Lanham, MD: University Press of America, 1990); Ronald B. Mayers, *Balanced Apologetics: Using Evidences and Presuppositions in Defense of the Faith* (Grand Rapids: Kregel Publications, 1996).

Eschatology: Millennialism/Non-millennialism

Evangelicals have traditionally loved to speculate about the end of the world (or end of this present age of world history). They are fascinated with biblical apocalyptic literature and reading the "signs of the times" to discern when *Jesus Christ* is going to return. But this is not true of all evangelicals in the same way or to the same degree. Many evangelicals in the Reformed theological tradition avoid eschatological speculation and reject detailed examination of apocalyptic literature and attempts to find the signs of the times in contemporary history. Nevertheless, because of the overwhelming interest in this subject among so many evangelicals, even Reformed critics of "eschatological fever" have to come to terms with it and explain their own positions regarding the *return of Christ* and the end of world history. All evangelicals, of all tribes and flavors, believe in the visible, bodily, glorious return of Jesus Christ to this earth. They all believe in subsequent judgment and a new *heaven* and new earth. None demythologize or totally historicize eschatology so that these are merely symbolic representations of existential experiences or historical processes. Beyond that bare, minimal consensus, however, evangelicals have little in common with regard to the details of the future. Some embrace *premillennialism;* some believe in *postmillennialism;* many promote *amillennialism.* Some evangelical denominations and institutions require leaders, if not all members, to confess belief in Christ's premillennial return; many do not. There are pockets of evangelicals who regard premillennialism as heterodox. The majority of evangelicals view postmillennialism as an oddity at best, and most have probably never met one of its few evangelical adherents.

The revival campaigns of late nineteenth-century evangelist Dwight L. Moody brought Adventism and premillennialism into the evangelical mainstream. Before that, the vast majority of evangelicals, going back to the Great Awakenings, were either amillennialists or postmillennialists. That is, they believed that the millennial *kingdom of God* is identical with the *church* and the march of Christianity through world history (a view going back at least to Augustine and possibly to Origen in the early church) or that it will be a Christianization of the world

order prior to Christ's visible, bodily return (Parousia).

Amillennialists identify Revelation 20's references to a thousand years during which *Satan* will be bound symbolically with the gradual triumph of the *gospel* of Jesus Christ through the church and its spiritual transformation of men and women and of society. The millennium, then, is a spiritual reality and not a temporal, political one. For amillennialists such as the early church father Augustine and the Reformers Martin Luther and John Calvin, the invisible, universal church of Jesus Christ spread out throughout time and space is the kingdom of God, and the church age between Christ's first and second advents is the "millennium." The biblical references to the establishment of a restored, perfected Davidic kingdom and to a renewed *creation* where the lion and lamb lie down together are to the new heaven and new earth after Christ's return in judgment. They are not referring to an earthly, temporal, political reign of Christ for one thousand years after his return and before the universal judgment and new heaven and new earth, as in premillennialism.

Postmillennialists, such as Jonathan Edwards in the eighteenth century and Reformed theologian Loraine Boettner in the twentieth century, view the millennium as a period of time (not necessarily precisely one thousand years) within world history during which the structures of society throughout the world will be permeated with the gospel and the whole earth will live according to principles of love and *justice.* This will be the time when Jesus Christ shall reign over the earth. Then comes the return of Christ, judgment of the nations, and a new heaven and new earth.

Evangelical premillennialists are divided into two camps: those dispensationalists who believe in a two-stage Parousia (return of Christ) and those who do not. The former interpret biblical apocalyptic literature as referring to a "secret rapture" (the word *rapture* comes from the Latin Vulgate translation of the Bible) of all true believers in Jesus Christ before a seven-year tribulation period that will immediately precede the visible, triumphant return of Christ. According to the dispensationalist premillennialists, the tribulation period will be a time when God will save all Israel (Jews) through persecution at the hands of an antichrist and his sidekick the false prophet ("Great Beast"). Gentile Christians will be gone—having been raptured before the tribulation began. (Some dispensationalists place the rapture in the middle of the tribulation.) Near the end of the tribulation period, a great war called the battle of Armageddon will be fought between the forces of the antichrist and the people of God (Israel?) and Christ himself and his angels and raptured saints. Then Christ will rule and reign on the earth for one thousand years before the final judgment and new heaven and new earth. Historic premillennialists reject the concept of a secret rapture and believe that Jews and gentile believers alike will suffer through the tribulation or die martyrs' deaths during it. Then Christ will return publicly and visibly to conquer *evil* powers that persecute God's people and establish a peaceable kingdom for a thousand years.

These four interpretations of the kingdom of God and of the eschatological events are all held and taught by various evangelicals. During the rise of *fundamentalism* in the 1920s, most fundamentalists embraced premillennialism. Many came to regard its dispensationalist interpretation as orthodox Christianity. Pentecostals by and large teach and preach dispensationalist premillennialism without implying that other views are heretical. Premillennialism has made significant inroads into Evangelicalism in America throughout the twentieth century. Hal Lindsay's books, such as *The Late, Great Planet Earth* (Grand Rapids: Zondervan, 1970), and Tim LaHaye's *Left Behind* novel series have given tremendous impetus to dis-

pensational premillennialism. In the 1960s and later, several influential evangelical scholars disputed belief in a secret rapture (two-stage Parousia) and promoted historic premillennialism as the biblical and historical eschatology for evangelicals. Among them are Fuller Theological Seminary New Testament scholar George Eldon Ladd, Robert Gundry of Westmont College, and evangelical theologian Millard Erickson. They all appeal to a relatively literal interpretation of Revelation 20 and to the lack of clear biblical references to any secret rapture to establish their historic premillennial eschatology. They also point out that belief in a secret rapture was unheard of before the middle of the nineteenth century.

Evangelical amillennialists such as Anthony Hoekema and Stanley J. Grenz argue that all of the biblical allusions to an earthly rule and reign of Christ—including Revelation 20—can naturally be interpreted symbolically as referring to the church and to heaven. They question the need for an earthly political rule of Christ for one thousand years. Evangelical postmillennialists such as Loraine Boettner and John Jefferson Davis of Gordon-Conwell Theological Seminary point to the biblical promises of the growth of the kingdom of God in Jesus' parables, as well as to Revelation 20's references to a time of peace and justice on earth when Satan will be bound, to defend their hopeful vision for the Christianization of the world before Christ returns.

No evangelical denomination or major organization requires belief in postmillennialism for leadership or membership; some would probably exclude its adherents from leadership roles. It is widely considered aberrant belief by conservative evangelicals because of its optimism about human persons playing a role in bringing about the kingdom of God. And yet postmillennialists can point to no less a saint of evangelical Protestantism than Jonathan Edwards as a model. Many evangelical denominations include "the premillennial return of Jesus Christ" (or similar wording) in their confessional statements, and a few include specific reference to a secret rapture of all true believers. Most evangelical denominations, churches, and institutions leave this whole area of doctrine in the category of opinion and refuse to establish one view as the only acceptable one. Nevertheless, with the continual avalanche of evangelical books, articles, television sermons and lessons, and movies about the end time, this controversy is likely to continue among evangelicals for many years.

Robert G. Clouse, ed., *The Meaning of the Millennium: Four Views* (Downers Grove, IL: InterVarsity Press, 1977); Robert C. Doyle, *Eschatology and the Shape of Christian Belief* (Carlisle, UK: Paternoster Press, 1999); Stanley J. Grenz, *The Millennial Maze: Sorting Out Evangelical Options* (Downers Grove, IL: InterVarsity Press, 1992).

Evangelism: Restrictivism/Inclusivism

Evangelicalism prides itself on being a missionary movement reaching out to persons who have never heard the *gospel* of *Jesus Christ* with the good news of *salvation* and with support for their physical needs. Anything that threatens the missionary and *evangelism* impulse is regarded by most evangelicals—including theologians—as a challenge to evangelical identity. At the same time, however, Evangelicalism prides itself on presenting to the world a message of genuine good news of a *God* who is loving as well as just, compassionate and forgiving as well as righteous. The question of the destiny of those who never hear the gospel of Jesus Christ has been discussed and debated among Christians for centuries; it is certainly not a controversy unique to evangelicals. It has entered into evangelical conversation in a new and often divisive way in the post–World War II era, how-

ever, and at the turn of the millennium the issue of the possible salvation of the unevangelized is one of the most hotly debated questions among evangelical scholars. How can a loving, merciful, and compassionate God send to *hell* for eternity everyone who, through no fault of his or her own, fails to hear the Christian message of Jesus Christ as Savior? And yet, how can a righteous and holy God simply forgive people who do not repent and believe in his Son? Does not the *Bible* restrict salvation to those who call upon the name of the Lord Jesus Christ? On the other hand, does it not teach a wideness in God's mercy that extends to those who serve the poor and needy, even if they have never heard of Jesus Christ?

Evangelical scholars have divided into two main camps over this issue: the restrictivists (sometimes called exclusivists) and the inclusivists. Virtually no evangelical theologians embrace universalism (belief that all will eventually be saved and hell emptied) or pluralism (belief in more than one Savior through whom people may be saved). Some evangelical thinkers prefer to remain agnostic with regard to the destiny of the unevangelized. They simply place the matter in God's hands and trust in his justice and mercy to do what is best with them. Inquiring minds are often not satisfied with that solution, however, and many, if not most, evangelical theologians locate themselves in one of the two main categories of restrictivism or inclusivism.

Although this issue has been bubbling just below the surface of evangelical discussion for decades and perhaps centuries, it broke through the surface into full-blown controversy, including some hostility, with the publication of evangelical theologian **Clark Pinnock's** book *A Wideness in God's Mercy* (Grand Rapids: Zondervan, 1992). The same year saw the publication of another book that contributed to the controversy: evangelical theologian John Sanders's *No Other Name: An Investigation into the Destiny of the Unevangelized* (Grand

Rapids: Wm. B. Eerdmans, 1992). Both books promoted the *inclusivist* position that persons who never hear the gospel of salvation before death are not automatically destined to perdition. Pinnock argued that some and perhaps many of the unevangelized may be saved on the basis of God's character; the God of the New Testament, though wrathful against *sin*, is a God of love and *justice* who is not willing that any should perish but wants all to come to salvation. Surely God provides some witness to himself in nature and culture and a way for persons who never receive the Christian message via a missionary or Bible to *repent*, believe, and be saved. According to Pinnock and other inclusivists, every person created in the *image of God* possesses some degree of prevenient (enabling but resistible) *grace*; this is often referred to as "the light they have." In other words, the light of the Word (Logos, Son of God) came into the world and enlightens everyone to some extent. If people follow the light of the Logos (cosmic Christ) by seeking out and obeying the clues to their own sinfulness and God's righteousness embedded in conscience, the natural world, and culture, they may find salvation. If they do, inclusivists aver, it is the salvation won for them by Jesus Christ through his life, death, and *resurrection*. Nobody will be saved without Christ, but some may be saved without explicit knowledge of Jesus Christ.

Inclusivists point out that this view is not a new teaching; it has been around in the Christian churches for centuries, and hints of it may be found in the early church fathers and at least some of the Reformers. John Wesley certainly believed it, and the evangelical hero *Billy Graham* espoused it in an interview with *McCall's* magazine in 1978. *C. S. Lewis*, a mentor to many evangelicals through his writings, clearly embraced a version of inclusivism. Nevertheless, many conservative evangelicals reacted strongly against Pinnock's and Sanders's recommendations of

inclusivism. Some of them charged it with universalism—a charge that both denied vigorously. Neither Pinnock nor Sanders nor any other evangelical inclusivist has embraced or promoted unqualified universalism of salvation. More often, critics accused inclusivism of being on a slippery slope toward universalism and of denying clear biblical teachings about the exclusivity of Jesus Christ, whose name is the "only name" given under heaven on earth by which people may be saved. Inclusivists respond by denying that their view leads to universalism and by arguing that seemingly restrictivist biblical passages are open to other interpretations. For example, people can be saved by Jesus Christ and his name without explicitly hearing of him; their full salvation is in *heaven* when they will hear of him and gladly embrace him as their Savior, whose name they did not know.

Restrictivism is the view that only persons who hear the gospel message and repent of their *sins* and trust in Jesus Christ for *forgiveness* will be saved. Its supporters base this belief on a pattern of New Testament passages that seem to restrict salvation to those who hear and believe (e.g., Rom. 10:14). They point out that believing inevitably implies at least some knowledge of God and Jesus Christ—for example, that God is one and that Jesus Christ died and rose from the dead. To restrictivists, inclusivists seem to empty salvation of any cognitive content; one can be saved and not know anything about God or Jesus Christ. Many restrictivists also appeal to the danger that any other view may inevitably undermine the urgency of evangelism and missions. If there is any chance that people may be saved without them, Christians will be less prone to give and go to deliver the message of the gospel and call people to repentance and *faith*. Another argument used by restrictivists to defend their position is that it is the traditional Christian view of salvation and certainly the view of the "received evangelical tradition." Why else would Evangelicalism have developed such an urgency in its appeals to support missionary endeavors?

Restrictivists can point to a line of supportive sayings and teachings in church fathers, Reformers, and modern evangelical preachers and teachers. Restrictivists acknowledge that their view may be interpreted as harsh and unloving, but, they remind critics, the issue is not which view is attractive, but which one is biblical. Some evangelical restrictivists regard inclusivism as antithetical to authentic Evangelicalism and label it heterodox or even heretical. Ronald Nash, a leading apologist for restrictivism, suggests that inclusivism leads inevitably to universalism, because it regards the unevangelized as already saved by Christ unless they explicitly reject that salvation. Whether evangelical inclusivists believe that is debatable, however, and the charge of universalism misses the mark entirely so long as inclusivists explicitly affirm hell and deny universal reconciliation.

The debate between evangelical inclusivists and restrictivists heated up around the turn of the millennium. The *Evangelical Theological Society* hosted a scholarly discussion of the subject at its 2002 annual meeting. The Southern Baptist Convention increasingly aims its theological artillery at inclusivism. In return, inclusivists press their case that restrictivism is not the traditional evangelical view by pointing to John Wesley, Billy Graham, and C. S. Lewis and arguing that these men's lives of evangelism (Lewis through his writings) undermine the claim that inclusivism is antithetical to missions. At times the rhetoric on both sides, with charges of gnosticism and universalism, has become overheated. In the midst of the debate, some evangelical scholars opt for the agnostic position, and others choose to believe in a postmortem encounter between the unevangelized and Jesus Christ, where the unevangelized will be asked to repent and believe. This option—taken by *Donald Bloesch* and Gabriel Fackre, a main-

line Protestant theologian sympathetic with Evangelicalism—satisfies neither inclusivists nor exclusivists. To both camps it appears speculative and unnecessary, if not unbiblical.

———

Dennis L. Okholm and Timothy L. Phillips, eds., *More Than One Way? Four Views on Salvation in a Pluralistic World* (Grand Rapids: Zondervan, 1995); John Sanders, ed., *What About Those Who Have Never Heard? Three Views on the Destiny of the Unevangelized* (Downers Grove, IL: InterVarsity Press, 1995).

Evolution   *see* Creation

Gender Roles: Complementarianism/Egalitarianism   The evangelical movement has generally been led by men, but women have always contributed much to its vitality. While most evangelical denominations and *churches* have not ordained women to professional ministry and have discouraged or disallowed women pastors, most have commissioned women as missionaries and many have included women evangelists. Especially the *Holiness* churches and movements have allowed women leaders, and some Pentecostal denominations were founded by women. One of the most influential women in twentieth-century North American religious life was Aimee Semple McPherson, founder of the International Church of the Foursquare Gospel, a member denomination of the *National Association of Evangelicals*. Several other evangelical denominations have had women leaders as well. On the other hand, most evangelical bodies have relegated women's leadership roles to women's organizations (e.g., missionary-supporting unions), Sunday schools, and foreign missions.

During the 1960s and 1970s a number of evangelical women began to question this situation and call for full equality of women with men in evangelical organizational life. They noticed that women were rising to positions of leadership in mainline Protestant organizations and that women were playing increasingly visible roles in the burgeoning *charismatic movement*. The women's liberation movement swept across North America and Europe in the 1960s and 1970s; evangelical women called for a reconsideration of traditional gender roles in evangelical homes, churches, and organizations. Among the most influential voices in this regard were two women. In 1974 Nancy Hardesty, a professor at evangelical Trinity College, and Letha Scanzoni, an evangelical writer, published a manifesto of evangelical feminism entitled *All We're Meant to Be: Biblical Feminism for Today* (Grand Rapids: Wm. B. Eerdmans). The authors argued that the traditional evangelical view of male headship and domination over women in families and churches is seriously flawed, both in terms of biblical interpretation and the ethics of *justice*. They averred that concerns of moderate feminists are supported by Scripture and called for equality of women with men in every aspect of life. The book created a furor among evangelicals as it was widely read, discussed, reviewed, applauded, and condemned. One major evangelical publication named it the best book of the year.

The book unleashed an evangelical women's movement with two organizational centers: the Evangelical Women's Caucus and Christians for Biblical Equality. The former is more radical and the latter more conservative, but both energetically lobby for women's equality with men among evangelicals. Throughout the 1980s and 1990s evangelical women poured into evangelical seminaries and sought traditional ministerial degrees and ordination. By the end of the century, most evangelical denominations had to deal in some way with the question of women's ordination and women as senior ministers of churches; some went further and passed resolutions for or against ordination of women, women pastors, submission of wives to husbands, and male leadership in families and churches.

The rise of evangelical feminism and the movement for equality of women with men (egalitarianism) provoked a traditionalist reaction among conservative evangelicals. In 1987 a group of conservative evangelicals calling themselves the Council on Biblical Manhood and Womanhood met in Danvers, Massachusetts, and promulgated the Danvers Statement, a manifesto of evangelical traditionalism with regard to gender roles. According to the view espoused there—labeled "complementarianism" by its formulators—males and females are equal in God's sight with regard to personal dignity and *salvation*, but they are not equal with regard to divinely assigned roles in families and churches. Some roles of leadership are reserved for men. The traditionalists based this claim on biblical passages such as 1 Timothy 2:8–15, Ephesians 5, and 1 Corinthians 11. Evangelical egalitarians had already dealt with these passages by means of a hermeneutic of cultural accommodation, which argues that the apostle Paul assigned women roles subordinate to men because of the churches' precarious situation in a hostile cultural environment that was scandalized by women's leadership in religious groups, often equating that with fertility cult rituals. They pointed to Galatians 3:28, which says that "in Christ" there is "neither male nor female" (KJV), and to the leadership roles of women in the ministries of Jesus and Paul. In 1991 leading evangelical traditionalists John Piper and Wayne Grudem edited a massive volume promoting complementarianism entitled *Recovering Biblical Manhood and Womanhood*. It was named book of the year by *Christianity Today*.

Throughout the 1990s the two organizations and their contrasting agendas competed for the hearts and minds of evangelicals. At many evangelical meetings one could find booths of both the Council on Biblical Manhood and Womanhood and Christians for Biblical Equality, promoting complementarianism and egalitarianism respectively. A major defeat for the egalitarian agenda came in the Southern Baptist Convention's (SBC) revisions of the Baptist Faith and Message in 1998 and 2000. Earlier versions had said nothing about gender roles or women in ministry, but in 1998 the SBC made gracious submission of wives to husbands a matter of doctrine, and in 2000 it effectively made belief in women pastors heresy. Moderate Baptists in the South rejected these changes and continued to ordain women and encourage them to enter into all levels of church leadership. Attempts to duplicate that defeat for egalitarianism in several evangelical denominations met resistance, and the issue continues to be divisive among evangelicals into the twenty-first century.

Although individual evangelical scholars vary widely in their interpretations of the biblical and traditional teachings about gender roles, two main views tend to dominate evangelical thinking. *Complementarianism* insists that women and men are fully equal in God's sight and that women must not be in any way demeaned or dehumanized by men. The Danvers Statement explicitly says that women should not be expected to follow any authority—including husbands—into *sin*. Male headship and *authority* is not unqualified. Men and women are given different roles and gifts for service and leadership within homes and churches, however, and women are to submit graciously to the loving authority of men. Men are to take the lead in families and churches and exercise caring authority over children, wives, and other women; only men are allowed to preach the *gospel*, receive ordination to gospel ministry, and hold offices of deacon, elder, and pastor. Complementarians base this inequality of roles on New Testament passages such as 1 Corinthians 11:2–13, which refers to the man as the "head" (*kephale*) of the wife. They argue that "head" here signifies authority.

Egalitarians object that the Greek word for head can have two or more con-notations and that authority is only one of them. They point to the entire passage, which, they claim, complementarians conveniently ignore. The passage calls for men to pray and prophesy with heads uncovered and for women to pray and prophesy with heads covered. Do complementarians follow this command? Most do not. If women are to be submissive and never teach men or exercise authority over men in the church, why does the apostle permit them to prophesy? However prophesy is interpreted, it would seem to be a form of exercising authority at least as strong as preaching or teaching. Egalitarians find similar problems with all of the complementarian interpretations of New Testament passages regarding male and female roles, and they point to the fact that the New Testament also permits slavery and discourages slaves from seeking their freedom. Do complementarians affirm slavery whether in North America or Africa? Generally speaking, they do not. Egalitarians suspect inconsistency in complementarian hermeneutics.

The *egalitarian* viewpoint is that although the genders are different biologically and perhaps sociologically (that is, they are socialized differently), they are fully equal partners "in Christ." That is, there should be no more distinction between men and women in the sacred spheres of home and church than there is between Jew and Greek and slave and free. Christ came to tear down walls of separation. Even though the New Testament in places allows for such walls to remain for a time for the sake of the gospel in a hostile culture, they should not remain today. Just as slavery was opposed and abolished, in spite of biblical permission for slavery, so domination of women by men should be abolished. Egalitarians argue that permanent, fixed authority of men over women is intrinsically dominating and demeaning to women; no amount of qualifying it can take away its sting. To argue that women must submit to men's authority in family life and in churches is to place them in positions of inequality and subject them to domination and control by men. For egalitarians, this is unjust and contrary to the liberating spirit of Christ, in which all of Christ's disciples are his friends. Complementarians regard the egalitarian view and agenda as seriously subverted to secular culture's movement against all authority outside the self. They see it as evasive of *Scripture's* clear meaning and authority and view it as dangerous to the health of evangelical families and churches, if not to the gospel itself.

Craig Blomberg et al., eds., *Two Views on Women in Ministry* (Grand Rapids: Zondervan, 2001); Robert G. Clouse and Bonnidell Clouse, eds., *Women in Ministry: Four Views* (Downers Grove, IL: InterVarsity Press, 1989); Stanley J. Grenz with Denise Muir Kjesbo, *Women in the Church: A Biblical Theology of Women in Ministry* (Downers Grove, IL: InterVarsity Press, 1995).

Gifts of the Holy Spirit   *see* **Baptism of the Holy Spirit**

Homosexuality   Many observers of the evangelical theological scene regard the issue of homosexuality as the one looming on the horizon with which evangelicals will have to deal in new ways. Traditionally, evangelicals and conservative Catholic, Eastern Orthodox, and Protestant Christians have rejected not only homosexual practices as sinful and intolerable among Christians, but also homosexuals themselves as especially corrupt sinners to be avoided. It was not unusual in the 1950s and later to hear evangelical ministers condemn homosexuals as *demon*-possessed and homosexual orientation (same-sex desires and attractions) as not only unnatural and disordered but sinful and a cause of eternal damnation.

A series of events in mainline Christianity and among evangelicals in the 1960s through the 1990s caused some evangelical leaders and scholars to reconsider some of the traditional rhetoric about homosexuality and homosexuals; the same events deepened traditional abhorrence in other evangelicals. At the turn of the millennium, evangelical leaders and the vast majority of evangelical theologians held firmly to the traditional view that sexual relations are sinful outside of heterosexual, monogamous marriage. The traditional fundamentalist and conservative evangelical attitude toward homosexual orientation, however, was beginning to show signs of weakening in some quarters, as some evangelical scholars called for greater compassion toward gay men and women and for acceptance of those believers who struggle with same-sex attraction and erotic feelings.

Those evangelicals who wished to abolish all discrimination against practicing homosexuals in the church by ordaining them and blessing homosexual unions left evangelical *churches* and organizations and joined more liberal mainline Protestant ones. In some cases, evangelicals formed new churches and organizations as safe havens for homosexual Christians. Most evangelical leaders feel so strongly about the issue that evangelicals who openly embrace a "welcoming and affirming" position with regard to practicing homosexuals in the church are generally forced out of Evangelicalism. And yet the same evangelical leaders who exclude "welcoming and affirming" advocates from evangelical institutions often express compassion for gays and lesbians and advocate a position of "welcoming but not affirming" homosexuals in churches.

The first significant crack in the wall of evangelical opposition to homosexuality as an especially heinous sin came in 1978 with the publication of *Is the Homosexual My Neighbor? Another Christian View* (New York: Harper & Row) by evangelical feminists Letha Dawson Scanzoni and Virginia Ramey Mollenkott. (The book was revised and updated in 1994 under the title *Is the*

Homosexual My Neighbor? A Positive Christian Response [San Francisco: HarperSanFrancisco].) The book fell like a bombshell among evangelicals. It argued that homosexuals should not be singled out for special condemnation and that they should be accepted by Christians even if their *sin* (practice of same-gender genital sex) cannot be condoned. Just as Christians follow the motto "Love the sinner; hate the sin" with regard to many sins, so they should follow it with regard to homosexuals and homosexual behavior. The book raised a serious challenge to the common evangelical practice of treating homosexual relations as a special category of sinful behavior and homosexuals as beyond care and concern. Many evangelical critics (to say nothing of fundamentalists!) perceived the book to constitute a subtle break in the solid evangelical front against the steadily increasing social acceptance of homosexuality. Other evangelicals welcomed the book as a needed corrective to evangelicals' tendency to treat homosexuals as untouchables in society and unwelcome even as visitors in churches. It created a discussion that had hardly existed among evangelicals before 1978.

In 1994 another bombshell fell among evangelicals concerning the issue of homosexuality. Just as many evangelicals were raising their voices against the flood of calls for acceptance of homosexuals within the mainline Protestant churches, a well-known and influential evangelical personality publicly announced his gay lifestyle. Mel White, former professor of communications at Fuller Theological Seminary and ghostwriter for Jerry Falwell, Pat Robertson, *Billy Graham,* and other fundamentalist and evangelical notables, published his memoirs, *Stranger at the Gate: To Be Gay and Christian in America* (reprint edition; New York: Plume, 1995). White, who became dean of a gay cathedral in Dallas, Texas, and leading spokesperson for a growing gay Christian movement, strongly condemned evangelical discrimination against homo-

sexuals such as himself. He recounted his own story of functioning within the evangelical community while struggling with his secret homosexual orientation and lifestyle. He chastised his former evangelical friends, colleagues, and employers (for whom he ghostwrote books and sermons) for what he regarded as their uncharitable attitudes and actions toward gays and lesbians in America. White joined and was ordained to ministry by the theologically conservative (some would say evangelical) gay denomination the Fellowship of Metropolitan Community Churches, founded in the 1960s by Pentecostal minister Troy Perry. Another organization of gay evangelicals pressing for full acceptance of practicing homosexuals within the evangelical movement is Evangelicals Concerned, which publishes books and articles promoting full equality of homosexuals in Christian communities and sponsors support groups for gay Christians throughout North America.

By and large, the evangelical establishment turned its back on Mel White, Troy Perry, and other openly gay evangelicals. Professors and employees of evangelical colleges and universities who openly advocate a "welcoming and affirming" policy for homosexuals in evangelical churches and organizations are disciplined and sometimes fired from their positions. Leading fundamentalist spokespersons openly condemn the "gay agenda" and express very little compassion for Christians struggling with homosexual desires, other than to tell them they can be delivered through *prayer* and Christian counseling. Some notable fundamentalist and conservative evangelical television and radio speakers frequently blame gays in America for an assortment of social problems, including terrorism, as God's judgment in response to social tolerance of sexual perversion. The highly charged rhetoric on both sides led some evangelical scholars to call for a middle way between "welcoming and affirming" and outright exclusion of all persons with homosexual orientations.

Two examples of what some consider an enlightened evangelical approach to the issue of homosexuals and homosexuality in evangelical churches and organizations were published in the 1990s. In 1995 Thomas E. Schmidt, a professor at evangelical Westmont College in southern California, published *Straight and Narrow? Compassion and Clarity in the Homosexuality Debate* (Downers Grove, IL: InterVarsity Press); in 1998 noted evangelical theologian Stanley J. Grenz published *Welcoming but Not Affirming: An Evangelical Response to Homosexuality* (Louisville, KY: Westminster John Knox Press). Both books examined the biblical, theological, psychological, and social aspects of the issues surrounding homosexuality and concluded that the traditional evangelical rejection of homosexual practice is correct. Both also argued, however, that homosexuality is not an especially heinous sin but is in the same category as other sexual sins such as adultery. Thus, the authors suggested, evangelicals should stop singling out homosexuals as a particularly condemnable group of persons and welcome them into the church to hear the *gospel* and receive the church's ministry on an equal footing with all other sinners. However, both authors also concluded that Christian churches and organizations should not affirm the homosexual lifestyle—including monogamous same-gender unions—because it is positively disordered compared with God's revealed norms for sexual behavior. Both presented biblical and theological arguments against ordination of practicing gays and lesbians, as well as against blessing of homosexual unions, while calling for love and compassion toward persons struggling with a homosexual orientation and lifestyle.

Persons on both ends of the spectrum of the homosexual debate were dissatisfied with Schmidt's and Grenz's proposals. Gay and lesbian Christians welcomed them as a step in the right direction, but pressed for full equality with heterosexuals in Christian and evangelical churches, denominations, and organizations. Many conservative evangelicals, especially fundamentalists, regarded such welcoming policies as dangerous accommodations to the secular social and liberal theological trajectory toward tolerance of all sexual lifestyles based on mutuality and love. Nevertheless, an evangelical consensus based on the kind of scholarship presented by evangelical theologians such as Schmidt and Grenz seemed to be emerging around the turn of the millennium. The new consensus is best expressed by the title of Grenz's book: "welcoming but not affirming." Many evangelical churches and organizations express open-door policies with regard to even practicing gays and lesbians, and most welcome nonpracticing homosexuals (i.e., persons with a homosexual orientation who are living celibate lives). Few, however, ordain persons living or condoning homosexual lifestyles or allow them to hold church offices. The questions of membership and employment as other than clergy are still very much disputed among evangelicals; no clear consensus has emerged. Many churches follow a "Don't ask; don't tell" policy, and others deny membership and employment to persons who are suspected of being active and practicing homosexuals. As the secular social pressure to grant full equality to homosexuals in every area of society mounts, evangelicals will have to revisit this issue and decide exactly where they stand with regard to it. It seems reasonable to expect that eventually it will become a focus of significant theological and ecclesiastical discussion and debate among them; it may be the issue "on the horizon."

John J. Carey, *The Sexuality Debate in North American Churches: 1988–1995* (Lewiston, NY: Edwin Mellen Press, 1995); Keith Hartman, *Congregations in Conflict: The Battle over Homosexuality* (New Brunswick, NJ: Rutgers University Press, 1996); Ernie Zimbelman, *Human Sexuality and Evangel-*

ical Christians (Lanham, NY: University Press of America, 1985).

Lordship Controversy: Faith Alone/Faith and Submission

The Protestant Reformation of the sixteenth century is often regarded by evangelicals as the deep background for their own form of Christianity; evangelicals are Protestants profoundly influenced by the later renewal movements of *Pietism* and *revivalism*. One of the most important ideas of the sixteenth-century Protestant Reformation of the *church* was *justification* by *grace* through *faith* in *Jesus Christ* alone. For centuries evangelicals have affirmed that Reformation principle and judged theologies by it. For example, many evangelicals have declined to extend recognition to Seventh-Day Adventists because they are believed to fall short of full acceptance of justification by faith alone—*sola fide*. (In fact, Seventh-Day Adventists are not completely united among themselves about that doctrine; all affirm *salvation* by grace alone, but some believe grace is received by faith alone and some believe salvation by grace requires obedience to the moral *law* of God.) In general, Evangelicalism as a movement heartily affirms the Protestant doctrine of salvation as a free gift of God received by faith as trust in Christ alone.

But evangelicals have also sung "Trust and Obey" and often promoted a rigorously moral lifestyle labeled otherworldly asceticism by some sociologists of religion. They usually eschew use of alcoholic beverages (or at least any degree of drunkenness), sexual intercourse outside of traditional marriage, use of mind-altering drugs, "lustful entertainment" (pornography and anything bordering on it), and even legal dishonesty. Most evangelical denominations have their own distinctive prohibitions that mark them off from the rest of the world such as Sabbath (Sunday) observance or abstinence from tobacco

or even dancing. In a world of declining moral standards and behavior, how should evangelicals who cherish obedience to God's Word view salvation? Can one live a life of disobedience to God's moral commands and still be saved? What about discipleship to Jesus Christ? Can one be saved and not be a disciple or at least be in the process of learning better how to imitate and follow him? Is submission to the lordship of Jesus Christ in every area of life a requirement for true reconciliation with God and eternal life? Or must one only have heartfelt trust in Jesus Christ in order to be fully and truly saved? This set of questions has arisen repeatedly throughout evangelical history, but it came to the foreground of evangelical theological attention in the so-called lordship controversy of the 1980s and 1990s in North America.

What must one do to be saved? No question is dearer to the hearts of evangelicals, all of whom believe that human persons are in need of salvation by God and that the *gospel* of Jesus Christ addresses the most profound issues of human existence. All evangelicals agree with the Protestant Reformers Luther and Calvin that the New Testament gospel proclaims the good news that all one must do to be saved is believe on the Lord Jesus Christ—that is, have faith in him alone. They also all agree, however, that *repentance* is a necessary aspect or dimension of genuine, saving faith. What must a person's life be like in order for salvation to be genuine?

In 1988 evangelical (some would say fundamentalist) evangelist, pastor, and writer John MacArthur published a scathing attack on "easy-believism" or "cheap grace" (a term coined by German theologian Dietrich Bonhoeffer) that proclaims a gospel devoid of the demand that persons saved by the grace of God through faith alone make Jesus Christ Lord of all of life. In the book, *The Gospel According to Jesus* (Grand Rapids: Zondervan, 1994), the California pastor affirmed that a person who is truly saved will always make continual progress in personal submission to the lordship of Jesus Christ and that willful, persistent, habitual disobedience to the moral law of God revealed through Christ and in the rest of the New Testament proves the inauthenticity of faith. A truly disobedient person cannot be saved, even if he or she appeared to make a genuine profession of faith in Jesus Christ. MacArthur scoured the New Testament for evidence of this strict demand of submission to the lordship of Christ and came up with numerous seemingly clear passages supporting his view. Contrary to some of his book's critics, he did not deny the security of true believers; as a good Calvinist he affirmed it. Rather, what the author denied was that genuine salvation by grace through faith alone could be consistent with presumptuous sinning against the will of God made known in Christ. A person who does not grow in discipleship to Jesus Christ simply never did have genuine saving faith.

The response to MacArthur's diatribe against easy-believism and cheap grace was swift and from a somewhat unexpected source. Two professors of conservative evangelical Dallas Theological Seminary published books in 1989 challenging MacArthur's "lordship salvation" view. They were notable dispensationalist theologian Charles C. Ryrie, who wrote *So Great Salvation* (Chicago: Moody Press), and Zane Hodges, who wrote *Absolutely Free: A Biblical Reply to Lordship Salvation* (Dallas, TX: Redencion Viva). Both authors affirmed that discipleship to Jesus Christ as Lord is a good thing toward which all Christians should strive, but they both also denied that eternal salvation depends on it, as that would make salvation a matter of good works in addition to faith. Lordship salvation, then, undermines the gospel recovered by the Protestant Reformers, that salvation is by grace alone through faith alone, and reintroduces salvation by faith plus works of love—the Catholic view at the time of the Reformation. Ryrie and

Hodges distinguished strongly between justification and *sanctification* and denied that the former is in any way dependent on the latter. They identified lordship of Christ as sanctification rather than justification and urged that all Christians move on from justification, which is dependent solely on faith in Christ (which includes repentance of sin), to sanctification (which is primarily a matter of obedience to the way of Jesus Christ). They accused the advocates of lordship salvation of confusing justification and sanctification, thereby voiding the Christian life of assurance, and injecting human achievement into salvation so that it is no longer a free gift. Ryrie and Hodges and others who reject lordship salvation sadly admit that the phenomenon of "carnal (i.e., unspiritual) Christians" is real and point out that in the New Testament the apostle Paul mentions it several times. These are persons who are saved by faith but have not brought their lives into conformity with the lordship of Christ.

The lordship salvation controversy takes place primarily among conservative evangelicals and fundamentalists. They have taken sides over the matter, and one view or the other has become a litmus test for employment at certain conservative evangelical institutions. Charges of heresy have been flung by both sides against the other; some evangelicals have argued that only one side is compatible with authentic evangelical faith and *theology*. Some evangelical theologians have attempted to bridge the gap between the two camps by suggesting that the core truths of both can and must be affirmed; genuine saving faith always leads to discipleship of Christ and submission to his lordship, but salvation itself is not dependent on that. Of course, this is closer to the lordship salvation side of the controversy, and few, if any, of its opponents will accept that way of stating the solution. When pressed on the question "What about those who do not accept Christ's lordship?" the middle way inevitably falls to the side of lordship salvation: they were never really saved in the first place or (in the case of Wesleyan and many Arminian evangelicals) they fall from grace into apostasy. Although the controversy over lordship salvation died down somewhat in the 1990s, it is still dividing conservative evangelicals from each other in the early part of the twenty-first century.

Kenneth L. Gentry Jr., *Lord of the Saved: Getting to the Heart of the Lordship Debate* (Philadelphia: Presbyterian & Reformed Publishing Co., 1993).

Sanctification: Entire Sanctification/Progressive Sanctification

Evangelicals agree that *regeneration* and *justification* (inward renewal by the *Holy Spirit, forgiveness*, and imputed righteousness) are instantaneous; they are gifts of God received all at once upon *repentance* and *faith. Conversion* to *Jesus Christ* may be a process, but it is a process with a definite turning point within it. At some moment in a Christian's life he or she confessed and repented of *sin*, trusted in Christ alone for *salvation*, and was born again. This is the common evangelical witness concerning salvation. Even those evangelicals who practice infant *baptism* believe that the baptized infant must grow up to embrace the *grace* of baptism by confession, repentance, and expression of heartfelt faith. Evangelicals do not agree about the next step in the order of salvation: *sanctification*. Sanctification refers to *holiness* in Christlikeness. It means being set apart for righteousness and for service to Christ and his *church*. All evangelicals view it as a reality that grows out of regeneration—the completion of the inward work of the Holy Spirit renovating the heart and mind of the sinner who repents and trusts in Jesus Christ. But some evangelicals proclaim an *experience* of Christian perfection in which sanctification becomes complete. Other evangelicals vehemently

reject such an experience as an illusion and affirm a gradual sanctification throughout the Christian life after conversion to Christ. For them, Christian perfection is *eschatological*—it arrives only after death when the believer is with Christ in paradise (*heaven*). Some of these evangelicals would even emphasize the *resurrection* as the moment of perfection. This is not a heated debate between evangelical theologians. They have by and large simply agreed to disagree about the matter, but that has not always been the case. And even in the twenty-first century, 250 years after the controversy first erupted in Great Britain during the ministry of John Wesley, the unresolved issue causes division between evangelical institutions. Some require belief in entire sanctification; others require its denial. Some are silent about the issue but would find it difficult to accept a leader who believes in entire sanctification.

Most evangelicals who believe in entire sanctification belong to denominations or churches in the Wesleyan heritage; some are not Wesleyan but have been touched by the *Keswick movement*. As different as they are, both movements affirm the possibility of moral and spiritual perfection in the normal Christian life (as distinct from "sainthood"). Wesleyans (including all in the *Holiness movement* and some Pentecostals) believe that John Wesley recovered a lost Christian truth in his book *A Plain Account of Christian Perfection* (1766). According to the founder of Methodism, every genuine Christian may experience an instantaneous cleansing from sin such that he or she is "perfected in love" and no longer sins intentionally. Wesley rejected "absolute perfection" in any creature and reserved that for God alone; only God is metaphysically perfect and immune to temptation, weakness, and error. The perfected believer is liberated only from conscious, willful sinning, which is the only sinning that makes a person guilty in God's sight. Wesley believed that even an entirely sanctified

Christian would make mistakes out of ignorance and need further progress by God's grace in order to overcome sins of omission and errors of ignorance. The essence of Christian perfection for Wesley is a heart of love for God and all people, a change of motives and intentions that results in a change of behavior. The sinful nature that causes one to give in to temptation continuously or frequently is eradicated by the Holy Spirit; this is a work of God's grace brought about by faith. It cannot be earned or forced.

Christians in the Holiness tradition make this doctrine and experience their distinctive mark. It is their hallmark among evangelicals. They often "tarry" in prayer for this "blessing" of entire sanctification. Sometimes it is accompanied by great emotion. Some of them equate it with the *baptism of the Holy Spirit*. Some non-Wesleyan evangelicals sometimes also believe in a kind of Christian perfection without instantaneous eradication of the inherited sinful nature (depravity). Most of them have been influenced by the Keswick movement, which began in England in the late nineteenth century and had its greatest affect in North America in the early twentieth century. It taught that each Christian is able to consecrate himself or herself entirely to God and God's cause through self surrender by identifying with Christ in his crucifixion. It is an almost mystical experience of dying to self daily. In this process, which involves *prayer, Bible* study, and meditation, the Christian may reach a plateau of perfection where the "flesh" (fallen, sinful nature) dies, but this is likely to involve a process of daily renewal of the death to self and consecration to Christ. The result is that the sanctified person enters into a "higher Christian life" of enthusiastic service to God and others and joyfully rises above temptation and the constant war between the self and the world, the flesh, and the *devil*.

The majority of evangelicals reject both versions of Christian perfection, in favor of the Reformed vision of sanctification as a gradual process consummated only after bodily death. According to this view of sanctification, moral perfection—including perfect love for God and others—is unavailable in this life. They base this belief on passages of Scripture such as Romans 7, where the apostle Paul describes his own Christian existence as paradigmatic for all believers short of death and resurrection. The apostle confesses that he does what he does not want to do and does not do what he wants to do. Whereas believers in entire sanctification point to Jesus' command in the Sermon on the Mount, "Be perfect therefore, as your heavenly Father is perfect" (Matt. 5:48), the majority of evangelicals point to New Testament passages that testify that all sin and stand in need of repentance. The call to perfection, then, is a call to live toward an impossible ideal. Nevertheless, non-Wesleyan evangelicals argue, there can and should be real progress in holiness in this life before death and resurrection. While Romans 7 describes the normal Christian struggle between the "flesh" and "spirit," Romans 8 describes the normal Christian increase in "walking according to the Spirit" and gradual leaving behind of the deeds of the flesh. It also indicates that total liberation from sin comes only in the eschaton (fulfillment of God's plan for history). This was the vision of sanctification held by John Calvin and possibly Martin Luther. (There is some debate about how much progress, if any, Luther believed in.) Even the Radical Reformers (Anabaptists) rejected perfection in this life in favor of gradual sanctification. Most evangelicals agree with the Reformers that the normal Christian life is always marked by being *simul justus et peccator* —simultaneously righteous and a sinner. Even the most sanctified Christian is always in need of forgiveness by the mercy and grace of Christ.

For the most part, evangelicals on both sides of this debate accept one another as equally evangelical. It is now a relatively friendly controversy. However, Wesleyan denominations and institutions of higher education require leaders and professors to believe in and teach Christian perfection according to Wesley's version of sanctification. Nazarenes, Wesleyans, Free Methodists, and other Holiness evangelicals, as well as many Pentecostals in primarily Southern denominations such as the Church of God (Cleveland, Tennessee), hold this as an essential article of belief. The Wesleyan Theological Society is a large and influential evangelical organization of Wesleyan scholars who, for the most part, affirm entire sanctification with varying degrees of conviction and with different qualifications. Most Reformed evangelical denominations and institutions of higher education would be very uncomfortable with any leader or teacher who espoused entire sanctification. Some transdenominational evangelical organizations and institutions allow persons convinced of the truth of entire sanctification as complete consecration to hold leadership positions and teach theology.

Most of the controversy surrounding this theological issue relates to a relatively new movement among evangelicals known as Moral Government Theology. There is no formal organization of all evangelicals who believe in this theology of spirituality, but those who embrace it network with each other via the internet and by means of conferences. Moral Government Theology harks back to the perfectionism of nineteenth-century evangelist and theologian *Charles G. Finney*, who denied inherited total depravity and moral inability and taught that each regenerate person has the ability from God to exercise his or her will toward righteousness and away from sin such that all willful sinning could cease. Finney's view came to be known as Oberlin perfectionism, because he was professor of theology and president of Oberlin College in Ohio. Finney's perfectionism was not identical with Wesley's or that of the Wesleyan Holiness movement. It did not

emphasize instantaneous supernatural eradication of the sinful nature leading to immediate entire sanctification. Rather, somewhat like the later Keswick movement, Oberlin perfectionism viewed sanctification as a process that could arrive at completion and emphasized the cooperation of the human will with God's sanctifying grace. Late twentieth-century and early twenty-first-century evangelical Moral Government Theology agrees with Oberlin perfectionism. Its adherents reject the strong Augustinian doctrine of original sin as inherited depravity and promote the power of the regenerate human will to refuse sin and practice only righteousness.

Evangelical critics of Oberlin perfectionism and Moral Government Theology accuse them of being overly optimistic about human potential and of neglecting the necessity of God's grace once a person is regenerate. That is, according to especially Reformed evangelical critics, they fall into a kind of semi-Pelagian heresy by inflating human initiative and willpower in the achievement of righteousness. Many Wesleyan-Holiness evangelicals and Reformed evangelicals agree that Moral Government Theology falls short of Christian orthodoxy because of its emphasis on the power of the will to attain righteousness and even perfection. And yet Moral Government Theology advocates consider themselves evangelicals.

Donald L. Alexander, ed., *Christian Spirituality: Five Views of Sanctification* (Downers Grove, IL: InterVarsity Press, 1989); Melvin Dieter, ed., *Five Views on Sanctification* (Grand Rapids: Zondervan, 1996).

Scripture: Inerrancy/Infallibility

A perennial issue dividing evangelicals theologically is the problem of Scripture's accuracy with regard to matters unrelated to *salvation*. In other words, evangelicals cannot agree completely about the degree of technical precision of accuracy in the *Bible* about historical and cosmological facts. Is every number given in Scripture accurate by modern standards of accuracy? Is every biblical description of the universe scientifically correct? Critics have long noted discrepancies between the Bible's own accounts of the same events. Do these constitute errors? Critics have also cataloged contradictions between modern scientific descriptions of nature and the cosmos and Scripture's portrayals of the universe and its workings. How are these to be accounted for? If they do exist, do they undermine the Bible's *authority*? Does the Bible's authority depend on factual inerrancy in matters that have nothing directly to do with God or salvation?

Evangelicals have always been "people of the book"; they are committed to the *inspiration* and authority of the Bible. They have consensus about the Bible's *supernatural* origin and the fact that it is uniquely God's Word in written form. They do not always agree about the precise nature of its inspiration or authority, but no evangelical theologian denies them. Some, however, have questioned the Bible's inerrancy in matters of history and cosmology. They prefer to speak of Scripture as infallible rather than inerrant. To them, *infallible* well describes the Bible's power to communicate *God's* message, which is the *gospel*; Scripture does not fail in that task. Inerrancy, however, implies a degree of accuracy not found in Scripture. Proponents of *infallibility* see no need to insist that the Bible achieves modern standards of accuracy in numbers, chronologies, cosmology, and quotations. But, other evangelicals argue, if the Bible contains any errors, it cannot be trusted, and to attribute error to Scripture is to attribute error to God, who is its ultimate author.

The debate over the Bible's inerrancy has been labeled *The Battle for the Bible*, the title of evangelical theologian Harold Lindsell's jeremiad of 1976, which decried a perceived defection from biblical authority among evangelicals who questioned Scripture's strict inerrancy in all matters. Entire evangelical institutions and denominations have been rocked by this controversy, and sometimes divisions have developed. As of the turn of the millennium, no consensus had been reached; evangelicals remain split over this issue. Generally speaking, three views of biblical accuracy tend to dominate the discussion: strict, detailed inerrancy, qualified inerrancy, and infallibility without inerrancy. Not all evangelical scholars who hold these views use these terms, but there is no settled nomenclature for this debate. These are descriptive labels for widely held and promoted views of the Bible's accuracy.

Strict, detailed inerrancy is the view of the Bible's accuracy generally assumed and defended by fundamentalists. Some very conservative evangelicals agree with fundamentalists that the Bible is wholly and precisely accurate in every assertion or statement of fact. (No evangelical claims that poetry or parables are inerrant, and all allow for figures of speech in Scripture.) The great nineteenth-century conservative Princeton theologian Charles Hodge argued that all the Bible's statements are fully reliable and that the alleged discrepancies within Scripture and between it and extrabiblical knowledge of facts are trivial and should not be taken very seriously; they would almost certainly be cleared up with further knowledge. In view of the Bible's overwhelming accuracy and authority, Hodge suggested, Christians should simply suspend judgment when the Bible seems to contain inaccuracies. Hodge's successor **Benjamin Warfield** went further in defending biblical accuracy and argued that the Bible's inspiration requires detailed, comprehensive inerrancy and that its authority depends on it. He allowed that there are apparent errors in Scripture, but appealed to what he believed to be the Bible's overwhelming record of accuracy and to the fact that human judgment of errors is fallible to justify overlooking them. Both Hodge and

Warfield were attempting to protect the Bible from the new higher criticism and from the skepticism that arose with it in the nineteenth century. They appealed to a deductive process of reasoning to defend the Bible's complete inerrancy even in matters of history and cosmology: God is the author of Scripture (through the process called inspiration); God does not lie or deceive; Scripture is inerrant. When examining the actual phenomena of Scripture, they found little disturbing evidence of actual error; when they could not explain an apparent error away, they simply appealed to ignorance of the wider context of facts that would, if known, explain the contradiction or discrepancy.

Twentieth-century evangelicals who defend strict, detailed inerrancy follow much the same line of reasoning as Hodge, and especially Warfield. Harold Lindsell, a faculty member of Fuller Theological Seminary who became editor of *Christianity Today*, in 1976 published *The Battle for the Bible* (Grand Rapids: Zondervan), which fell like a bombshell on the evangelical movement in North America. In it he argued that any view other than strict, detailed inerrancy undermines the Bible as God's authoritative Word and is inconsistent with evangelical faith. He named evangelical organizations and institutions that he believed were in the process of recanting the full faith in the Bible's inerrancy. Lindsell argued that the rooster in the stories of Peter's denial of Christ must have crowed six times, because that is the only way fully to harmonize the Gospels' accounts. He criticized evangelical scholars who averred that minor discrepancies in the Bible do not constitute errors and do not undermine its authority. He appealed to the original autographs and copyist error to explain the discrepancy of one thousand deaths between accounts of the same incident in 1 Corinthians 10:8 and Numbers 25:9.

One catalyst for Lindsell's vehement defense of complete, unqualified inerrancy was the 1973 publication of *Scrip-ture, Tradition, and Infallibility* (Grand Rapids: Wm. B. Eerdmans) by evangelical scholar Dewey M. Beegle. Beegle argued that the Bible manifestly contains factual errors in matters not related to salvation and cataloged them in great detail. He also argued, however, that belief in the divine inspiration and authority of Scripture does not depend on strict inerrancy. Another catalyst for Lindsell's attack on every evangelical view other than strict inerrancy was Fuller Theological Seminary's defection from the ranks of the inerrantist institutions. Lindsell and some other founding faculty members were dismayed by it, but Lindsell went the furthest in claiming that belief in strict, detailed and comprehensive inerrancy of the Bible is the hallmark of authentic evangelical faith.

Lindsell's book stirred up a hornet's nest of conflict and controversy among evangelicals. Throughout the late 1970s and 1980s many evangelical organizations and institutions purged their faculties and ranks of people who did not subscribe to Lindsell's view. Some evangelicals perceived an overreaction in this and called for a *qualified inerrancy*, a more subtle and nuanced account of biblical accuracy that would still be called "inerrancy" but would not fall into obscurantism by ignoring the facts of Scripture or enthrone inerrancy as the sine qua non of true evangelical faith. The "dean of evangelical theologians," *Carl F. H. Henry*, presented such a qualified version of biblical inerrancy in his magisterial, multivolume work *God, Revelation, and Authority* (Waco, TX: Word, 1976–84). He argued against Lindsell's wooden approach to the phenomena of Scripture, which required forced harmonizations of biblical accounts of identical incidents. He also denied Lindsell's assertion that inerrancy–especially strict, technical inerrancy–constitutes the essence of Evangelicalism. Nevertheless, Henry and other conservative evangelicals were also concerned to counter the denials of inerrancy offered by some faculty members of Fuller Seminary, by

Dewey Beegle, and by other progressive evangelicals.

In 1978 a group of evangelical scholars, including Henry, met in Chicago to promulgate a unifying evangelical statement on biblical inerrancy called "The Chicago Statement on Biblical Inerrancy." The group represented members of a newly formed organization known as the International Congress on Biblical Inerrancy, which included many of Evangelicalism's noted conservative theologians and biblical scholars. The statement affirmed biblical inerrancy and warned against its denial. Among other things it affirmed that "being wholly and verbally God-given, Scripture is without error or fault in all its teaching, no less in what it states about God's acts in creation, about the events of world history, and about its own literary origins under God, than in its witness to God's saving grace in individual lives." However, the statement went on to qualify inerrancy in ways that seemed to critics to kill it with the death of a thousand qualifications. For example, contrary to some advocates of strict, technical, detailed inerrancy, the statement says,

We deny that it is proper to evaluate Scripture according to standards of truth and error that are alien to its usage or purpose. We further deny that inerrancy is negated by Biblical phenomena such as a lack of modern technical precision, irregularities of grammar or spelling, observational descriptions of nature, the reporting of falsehoods, the use of hyperbole and round numbers, the topical arrangement of material, variant selections of material in parallel accounts, or the use of free citations.

No doubt many of the evangelicals harshly criticized by Lindsell found good reason to be surprised, if not offended, by the fact that Lindsell himself signed this statement after criticizing them for arguing for such qualifications. In The Battle for the Bible Lindsell seemed to find great fault with evangelical scholars who qualifed inerrancy (often leading them also to discard the term inerrancy in favor of infallibility) in just such ways.

Many defenders of biblical inerrancy jumped into the fray over the concept in the late 1970s and 1980s with their own definitions of the term and their own arguments about what is and is not compatible with it. The controversy resulted in unfortunate divisions among evangelicals, with faculty members of institutions of higher education and administrators and employees of organizations being subjected to inquisitions about their precise views on inerrancy. Many were fired or forced to resign, largely because they would not sign newly crafted statements of belief in inerrancy. Many evangelical organizations that had never required confession of biblical inerrancy adopted such requirements; others resisted inerrancy fever and allowed diversity of opinion about the matter.

The third common view of biblical accuracy among evangelicals is infallibility without inerrancy. More often than not, adherents of this view pay lip service to inerrancy (highly qualified) while expressing strong preference for infallibility or some other equivalent term. A few evangelicals simply deny that the Bible is without any errors at all. Donald G. Bloesch wrote that "Scriptural inerrancy can be affirmed if it means the conformity of what is written to the dictates of the Spirit regarding the will and purpose of God. But it cannot be held if it is taken to mean the conformity of everything that is written in Scripture to the facts of world history and science" (Holy Scripture: Revelation, Inspiration, and Interpretation [Downers Grove, IL: InterVarsity Press, 1994], 107). He expressed preference for the term infallibility because it highlights the power and function of Scripture as God's Word in union with the Holy Spirit; it indicates that the Bible is incapable of deceiving anyone, even if it is not flawless.

Evangelical scholars Jack Rogers and Donald K. McKim collaborated in a historical investigation of the concept of biblical authority and accuracy in 1979 and concluded in *The Authority and Interpretation of the Bible: An Historical Approach* (San Francisco: Harper & Row, 1979; repr. with a new epilogue, Eugene, OR: Wipf & Stock, 1999) that strict notions of biblical inerrancy, such as the ones promoted as the essence of evangelical faith by Lindsell, and even qualified ones, such as expressed by the Chicago Statement, arose more out of Protestant scholasticism than out of the Reformation itself. They demonstrated that evangelical Protestantism stemming from the Protestant Reformation historically included believers in inerrancy and deniers of inerrancy such as Scottish Presbyterian theologian James Orr. According to evangelicals who deny inerrancy, acknowledgment of minor errors in Scripture does nothing to undermine its power and authority as God's Word, and the Protestant faith does not hang on the absolute accuracy of every assertion of Scripture and never did. In fact, blind insistence on inerrancy—even highly nuanced and qualified as in the Chicago Statement— seems to them to undermine Christianity's credible witness in a world that easily discovers minor flaws and discrepancies in the Bible. Furthermore, to them, inerrancy has become little more than a shibboleth designed to detect who is "in" and who is "out" of the true evangelical camp; it is a litmus test of evangelical loyalty. They reach back to the Reformers themselves to retrieve a broader concept of the Bible's authority as the book of the Holy Spirit, whose authority does not rest on delivering a flawless performance in statistics but on communicating God's will to sinful human beings and transforming their lives with the gospel message.

Donald K. McKim, *What Christians Believe about the Bible* (Nashville: Thomas Nelson, 1985); Jack Rogers, ed., *Biblical Authority* (Waco, TX: Word Books, 1977); Ron Youngblood, ed., *Evangelicals and Inerrancy* (Nashville: Thomas Nelson, 1984).

Separatism   *see* **Ecumenism**

Theism: Open Theism/Classical Theism   Evangelical theologians have not always agreed about the details of the doctrine of *God*, but seldom have they fallen into acrimonious debate and attempts at exclusion such as surrounds the so-called open theism controversy, which takes place almost exclusively among evangelicals. Evangelical theology is generally conservative; it seeks to preserve the best of the Great Tradition of Christian belief and thought, while elevating *Scripture* above tradition. Evangelical theologians strive to respect the consensus of the early church fathers and the Protestant Reformers of the sixteenth century, but they reserve the right to correct past beliefs and doctrinal formulations as needed in the light of divinely inspired Scripture. Rarely have they proposed any significant revisions in the doctrine of God as it has been handed down by Protestant orthodox thinkers. The consensus of evangelicals throughout the twentieth century was that classical Christian theism is substantially biblical, even though some evangelicals questioned attributes such as divine simplicity and impassibility, because they seemed speculative and not clearly taught in Scripture. On the other hand, each evangelical systematic theologian portrayed classical theism differently; each put his or her own "spin" on it. God's eternity was sometimes represented as timelessness (simultaneity with all temporal moments) and sometimes as everlastingness (duration throughout time without beginning or end). Calvinists interpreted God's love differently from Arminians, and some evangelicals simply rejected the idea that God is incapable of suffering (impassibility). Nevertheless, in spite of divergences over secondary matters, nearly all evangelical scholars in both the nineteenth and twentieth centuries believed and taught that God's omniscience includes infallible and exhaustive knowledge of the past, present, and future.

In 1986 Canadian evangelical theologian *Clark Pinnock* published a chapter entitled "God Limits His Knowledge" in *Predestination and Free Will* (Downers Grove, IL: InterVarsity Press), edited by brothers David and Randall Basinger. There Pinnock argued from a traditional Arminian viewpoint regarding human *free will* (i.e., that human beings are given the gift of free will that is not compatible with divine determination) to a conclusion seldom if ever reached by earlier Arminians—that God limits himself in relation to free human persons, such that even God does not know with absolute certainty what they will do with their free will until it is determined. Pinnock pointed out a pattern of evidence leading to this surprising (and to some shocking) conclusion. Scripture includes narratives in which God is said to change his mind in response to fervent *prayers*. Responsibility for decisions and choices is an illusion unless persons have significant freedom, and there can be no significant freedom if anyone—including God—knows with absolute certainty what a person is going to do before he or she decides. To be free with regard to any decision is to be able to decide and act otherwise; exhaustive and infallible divine foreknowledge may not cause a person to decide and act, but it renders a person's decisions and actions not truly free, because they could not be otherwise than they are foreknown to be. Pinnock portrayed God's relationship with the world, especially with free *humanity*, as a dance: God leads, but human beings play their parts. God's will and ways are flexible, and God responds to human beings. God is omniresourceful as well as omnipotent; while he can be surprised, he cannot be thwarted.

Pinnock's 1986 essay caused some surprise and consternation among conservative evangelicals; the author had once been a staunch Calvinist and defender of classical Christian theism. Real controversy, however, broke out after the 1994 publication of *The Open-ness of God: A Biblical Challenge to the Traditional Understanding of God* (Downers Grove, IL: InterVarsity Press), by Clark Pinnock, Richard Rice, John Sanders, William Hasker, and David Basinger. The authors agreed with Pinnock's earlier essay and defended it in light of church history (as corrupted by Greek philosophy), contemporary logical analysis (divine foreknowledge is incompatible with freedom and responsibility), ordinary Christian piety, and devotional practices (Christians pray as if prayer changes the mind of God), and systematic *theology* (divine foreknowledge is inconsistent with other beliefs such as the fall of Adam and Eve). The five authors sowed and reaped a whirlwind of controversy as evangelical defenders of classical theism (mostly Calvinists) argued against their new proposal and sometimes accused it of being heretical. Some reviewers of the volume called for caution and open-minded dialogue, while others heatedly hurled invectives against the new proposal.

In 1998 John Sanders, a conservative evangelical who adopted open theism for biblical reasons, published a massive study and defense of the "openness of God" (as open theism is sometimes called) entitled *The God Who Risks: A Theology of Providence* (Downers Grove, IL: InterVarsity Press). Sanders drew heavily on biblical narrative, often interpreting Old Testament passages literally, to argue that God takes risks in history and that risk taking is incompatible with absolute foreknowledge. According to Sanders (and most of the other open theists), God voluntarily condescended to enter into time and history with *creation* and took a genuine risk when he placed Adam and Eve with finite freedom in the garden of Eden. He could predict the outcome, but he could not foreknow it with absolute certainty. God's entire relationship with the world is a calculated risk, but God's plan and purpose for it will be accomplished, because God is omnipotent. The open theists never qualified God's power to intervene in nature and history; they redefined God's sovereignty as his ability to achieve his ends without exhaustive, detailed, and infallible foreknowledge of every decision yet to be made by human persons.

Sanders based much of his argument on the theme of divine relationality, drawn from biblical narratives in which God is affected by and responds to humanity. Genuine relationship, Sanders averred, is incompatible with some of the traditional attributes of classical theism, especially as that was developed by the medieval scholastic theologians and handed down by Protestant orthodoxy to modern evangelical thought. For example, God's immutability must not be understood as absolute unchangingness but as faithfulness; God's omniscience should be understood as God's perfect knowledge of the past and present and knowledge of the future as a realm of possibilities. Of course, Sanders also posited God's absolute knowledge of the future insofar as God decrees what it will be, but he denied that every detail of the future is already exhaustively and infallibly known by God.

An influential and highly controversial evangelical advocate of open theism is Gregory Boyd, whose book of popular apologetics *Letters from a Skeptic* (Wheaton, IL: Victor Books, 1994) sparked an especially divisive controversy within his own Baptist denomination. There he suggested that qualification of God's foreknowledge would help solve the thorny problem of *evil*; for example, if God foreknew the Holocaust with certainty, he could and should have prevented it. Boyd, a pastor and college professor, applied open theism to "spiritual warfare"—the belief in and practice of defeat of evil powers and principalities through prayer and social action. In 2000 he published a popular defense of open theism with the title *God of the Possible* (Grand Rapids: Baker), answering its evangelical critics who accused it, among other things, of presenting God as pathetic and helpless.

Boyd attempted to show that the God of open theism is more admirable and majestic than the God of traditional, classical theism, because he responds resourcefully to human freedom rather than setting it aside by foreknowing free acts thereby settling them. There and in his earlier *God at War: The Bible and Spiritual Conflict* (Downers Grove, IL: InterVarsity Press, 1997) Boyd showed how open theism supports the Christian practice of praying and acting against *Satan* and all evil. If God already knows with absolute certainty precisely what is going to happen in the future, then spiritual warfare loses it meaning and urgency. It cannot make a difference. In 2001 Clark Pinnock published *Most Moved Mover: A Theology of God's Openness* (Grand Rapids: Baker Books), answering his critics. There he especially distanced open theism from process theology—a form of liberal theology that portrays God as evolving with the universe—without attributing classical omniscience to God.

No controversy within evangelical theology in the second half of the twentieth century has been as caustic and divisive as the one over open theism. Even the debates over inerrancy in the 1970s and 1980s fell short of the level of vitriolic polemics displayed by some of open theism's evangelical critics. One major critique of open theism accused it of diminishing God's glory (*The Lesser Glory of God*); another claimed it has *No Place for Sovereignty*. One well-known evangelical apologist and theologian publicly denounced Clark Pinnock (and by extension all open theists) as not a Christian and accused his theology of being more pagan than Christian. One critic claimed that the God of open theism is a pathetic, hand-wringing God who is incapable of assuring anyone's *salvation*. Most of these and other harsh criticisms were raised against open theism by evangelical proponents of classical Calvinism. Few Arminian theologians joined in the fray, and some defended open theism as within the bounds of evangelical orthodoxy. Several evangelical denominations and organizations wrestled with the issue of open theism, and some passed resolutions and doctrinal statements against it. The Southern Baptist Convention effectively ruled it out in its 2000 revision of the Baptist Faith and Message. In 2001 the *Evangelical Theological Society* passed a resolution declaring that the Bible clearly teaches God's exhaustive foreknowledge. The ETS stopped short of expelling open theists, however, much to the chagrin of some of its charter members.

The open theism controversy is still alive at the time of this writing, so it is difficult to tell what its overall impact on evangelical theology will be. Many evangelical theologians have noticed that innovation and creativity, such as that displayed by the open theists, is dangerous; it invites strong criticism and even condemnation from powerful defenders of a perceived "received evangelical tradition." Some evangelical theologians who are not open theists are rising up to defend it in the name of openness and freedom; they fear that an implicit evangelical magisterium is gaining power to marginalize new ideas and creative thinkers within the evangelical community. Many other evangelical theologians are convinced that open theism is dangerous to the health and well-being of the Christian community and that it will seduce impressionable young minds into acceptance of a faulty notion of God that does not honor or glorify his majesty and power. The open theism controversy has had both positive and negative impact on Evangelicalism: positively, it has forced evangelicals to reconsider the grounds and bases for traditional beliefs about God; negatively, it has divided the evangelical community between those who are open to new ways of thinking about God in the light of God's self-revelation in *Jesus Christ* and the biblical narrative and those who are closed to such constructive theological endeavor.

James K. Beilby and Paul R. Eddy, eds., *Divine Foreknowledge: Four Views* (Downers Grove, IL: InterVarsity Press, 2001); John B. Cobb and Clark H. Pinnock, eds., *Searching for an Adequate God: A Dialogue between Process and Free Will Theism* (Grand Rapids: Wm. B. Eerdmans, 2000).